GEORGE BERKELEY

George Berkeley

A PHILOSOPHICAL LIFE

Tom Jones

PRINCETON UNIVERSITY PRESS
PRINCETON & OXFORD

Published by Princeton University Press
41 William Street, Princeton, New Jersey 08540
6 Oxford Street, Woodstock, Oxfordshire OX20 1TR

press.princeton.edu

Library of Congress Cataloging-in-Publication Data

Names: Jones, Tom, 1975– author.
Title: George Berkeley : a philosophical life / Tom Jones.
Description: Princeton : Princeton University Press, [2021] | Includes bibliographical references and index.
Identifiers: LCCN 2020040051 (print) | LCCN 2020040052 (ebook) | ISBN 9780691159805 (hardback) | ISBN 9780691217482 (ebook)
Subjects: LCSH: Berkeley, George, 1685–1753. | Christian philosophers—Ireland—Biography. | Church of Ireland—Bishops—Biography.
Classification: LCC B1347 .J66 2021 (print) | LCC B1347 (ebook) | DDC 192 [B]—dc23
LC record available at https://lccn.loc.gov/2020040051
LC ebook record available at https://lccn.loc.gov/2020040052

British Library Cataloging-in-Publication Data is available

Editorial: Ben Tate and Josh Drake
Production Editorial: Mark Bellis
Jacket Design: Pamela Schnitter
Production: Danielle Amatucci
Publicity: Jodi Price and Amy Stewart
Copyeditor: Cynthia Buck

Jacket Credit: John Smibert (1688–1751), *The Bermuda Group (Dean Berkeley and His Entourage)*, 1728, reworked 1739. Oil on canvas, 69 1/2 x 93 in. Gift of Isaac Lothrop. Photo: Yale University Art Gallery.

This book has been composed in Miller

Printed on acid-free paper. ∞

Printed in the United States of America

10 9 8 7 6 5 4 3 2 1

'[T]is plain, that we cannot know the Existence of other Spirits, otherwise than by their Operations, or the Ideas by them excited in us. [. . .] [T]he Knowledge I have of other Spirits is not immediate, as is the Knowledge of my Ideas, but depending on the Intervention of Ideas, by me refer'd to Agents or Spirits distinct from my self, as Effects or concomitant Signs. [. . .] GOD, is known as certainly and immediately as any other Mind or Spirit whatsoever, distinct from our selves. [. . .] A Human Spirit or Person is not perceiv'd by Sense, as not being an Idea; when therefore we see the Colour, Size, Figure, and Motions of a Man, we perceive only certain Sensations or Ideas excited in our own Minds: And these, being exhibited to our view in sundry, distinct Collections serve to mark out unto us the Existence of Finite, and Created Spirits like our selves. Hence 'tis plain, we do not see a Man, if by Man is meant that which Lives, Moves, Perceives, and Thinks as we do: But only such a certain Collection of Ideas, as directs us to think there is a distinct Principle of Thought and Motion, like to our selves, accompanying and represented by it. And after the same manner we see GOD[.]

—PRINCIPLES OF HUMAN KNOWLEDGE, §§145, 147–48

CONTENTS

ACKNOWLEDGEMENTS

WORKING WITH BEN Tate and his colleagues Josh Drake and Mark Bellis at Princeton University Press has been a great privilege. I would like to thank Ben in particular for his sustained engagement with every aspect of this book. I am very grateful to Cynthia Buck and Tom Broughton-Willet for their excellent work in copyediting and indexing the book. I would also like to recognise the contribution made by colleagues responsible for marketing and production work. I thank the anonymous readers for the Press for their generous commentary on my typescript and the opportunity to improve the book in the light of their suggestions.

Essential archival work for this book was funded by the Carnegie Trust for the Universities of Scotland, who supported a month of research in London and Dublin in the summer of 2009; the Leverhulme Trust, who awarded me a Research Fellowship for the academic year 2014–2015 to continue archival work in London and Dublin and draft early chapters of the book; and the Huntington Library, who awarded me an Andrew Mellon Foundation Fellowship to work with the library's resources in the summer of 2017. I am also grateful to the Royal Society of Edinburgh for supporting a series of research workshops on 'The Philosophical Life' which I coordinated with my colleague James Harris from May 2016 to February 2017.

The research for this book would have been impossible without the assistance of colleagues in numerous libraries and archives. I would like to thank the staff of the Weston Library at the Bodleian Library; the British Library, particularly in the Rare Books and Music and Manuscript Reading Rooms; the Cambridge University Library Munby Rare Books Reading Room; the Huntington Library Ahmanson Reading Room; the Lambeth Palace Library; the National Archives; the National Library of Scotland, particularly in the Special Collections Reading Room; the Representative Church Body of the Church of Ireland Library; Natasha Serne at the

Library of the Royal Dublin Society; St Andrews University Library, particularly in the Special Collections Napier Reading Room; and the Manuscripts and Archives Department at the Library of Trinity College Dublin. Anne Marie Menta at the Beinecke Rare Book and Manuscript Library of Yale University was very helpful in providing reproductions of correspondence between Anne Berkeley, George Berkeley Jr, and Samuel Johnson and William Samuel Johnson.

In the summer of 2017, I had the pleasure of working with Björn Lambrenos as part of the University of St Andrews Undergraduate Research Assistantship scheme. Björn assisted me with bibliographical research into Berkeley's Bermuda project and also the reception of Berkeley in nineteenth-century America—an aspect of Berkeley's afterlife that could not ultimately be addressed in this book. Antares Wells, the picture researcher for this book, made light work of a daunting task. I thank them both for their contributions.

I first broached the possibility of writing a biography of Berkeley at a meeting of the International George Berkeley Society in Tartu, Estonia, in September 2005. That meeting was organised by Bertil Belfrage and Roomet Jakapi, and it also introduced me to a community of Berkeley scholars who have played a significant role in shaping my understanding of my subject and encouraging me to persist with it. They include Timo Airaksinen, Margaret Atherton, Talia Mae Bettcher, Wolfgang Breidert, Richard Brook, Geneviève Brykman, Stephen H. Daniel, Marc Hight, Jorgen Huggler, Laurent Jaffro, Charles McCracken, Ville Paukonen, and Tom Stoneham. I also had the privilege of speaking to meetings of the Society in Karlsrühe in 2009 and Helsinki in 2010, and I thank Bertil, Wolfgang, and Ville for those opportunities. In February 2017, Richard Whatmore and Rory Cox invited me to speak at the Institute of Intellectual History at the University of St Andrews, and Phil Connell invited me to do so at the Eighteenth-Century and Romantic Research Seminar at the Faculty of English, University of Cambridge, in February 2019. Pierre Carboni and Elisabeth Pinto-Mathieu invited me to speak at their conference, 'Poverty: Alienation or Emancipation?' in Angers in November 2017. Jon Blechl and Tom Stoneham invited me to give a public lecture at the opening of their conference on 'Berkeleian Minds' in York in April 2019. Jon and Tom had also kindly allowed me to present to them a 'highlights package' from my research towards this biography in Tom's office in York in December 2016. I thank all the organisers and attendees of these events for the opportunities and the stimulation they provided. Bertil Belfrage and Richard Brook invited me to contribute a chapter on Berkeley's life to *The Bloomsbury Companion to Berkeley*. I am grateful for that opportunity and for the hospitality of Bertil and Birgit Belfrage as Bertil worked with me on the chapter on a visit to their home in Bodafors in February 2013.

I am very grateful to the following people who have read and commented on parts of this book in draft and thereby helped me to improve it: Natalie Adamson, Manuel Fasko, James Harris, Marc Hight, Laurent Jaffro, Joseph Jones, Clare Moriarty, Tom Stoneham, and Marta Szymańska-Lewoszewska.

James Harris has been a great friend and colleague throughout the writing of this book and also provided a model for intellectual biography of a philosopher in his study of Hume. Together with James, Mikko Tolonen and Christian Maurer (and their wonderful families) shared ideas and kept my spirits up in Edinburgh and elsewhere. Patrick Kelly kindly discussed the intricacies of Berkeley's family network with me. Abram Kaplan patiently explained first and last ratios to me over lunch at the Huntington Library. Many other friends and colleagues have helped to ease this book along in a wide variety of ways, sometimes without knowing it, and thanks are therefore due to Gavin Alexander; Matthew Augustine; Laura Berchielli; David Berman; Rowan Boyson; Andrea Brady; Peter Brennan; Vincent Brocvielle; Colin Burrow; Emily Butterworth; Pierre Carboni; Leo Catana; Tom and Laurie Clark; Sara Crangle; Robert Crawford; Beth Crosland; Alex Davis; Pete de Bolla; Ken Dingwall; Alex Douglas; Luke Gartlan; Brigid, Paul, and Hannah Hains; Katherine Hawley; Jon Hesk; Lorna Hutson; Ewan Jones; Trenholme Junghans; Sam Ladkin; Susan Laxton; Susan Manly; Peter Manson; Donald McEwan; Jim Mooney; Jeffrey Murer; Katie Muth; Michelle O'Malley; Stephanie O'Rourke; Tony Paraskeva; Malcolm Phillips; Gill Plain; Robin Purves; Wesley Rennison; François Reynaert; Luke Roberts; Nick Roe; Corinna Russell; Gurch Sanghera; Jane Stabler; Keston Sutherland; Emma Sutton; Barbara Taylor; Eve Thompson; Chris Tilmouth; Kim Timby; Chris Townsend; Jacques-Arthur Weil; and Courtney Weiss

Smith. My family, Margaret, Dan, Joe, Jack, and Finn Jones and Ben, Tania, Lila, and Lottie Silva-Jones, have been a terrific support. Reynold Jones has watched progress on the book from afar and offered encouragement. Natalie Adamson has offered love and support over nearly twenty years and shared her family, Glennis, Libby, Harri, Emily, Christian, and Oskar, with me. Collectively, my colleagues in the School of English at the University of St Andrews have provided a generous and mutually supportive environment in which to work. Two other groups of people provided me with a strong sense of collective endeavour in the years when I was writing this book: Shihan Paul Dempsey and all the instructors and students at Dempsey's Karate Club and the Karate Union of Scotland North; my colleagues in UCU St Andrews, at UCU Scotland, and across the whole of the UK organisation. My thanks go to them for their community.

Abbreviations

Works by Berkeley published in his lifetime are cited from early editions—often a second or third edition incorporating early authorial revisions—as detailed here. When works are cited in later revised editions, an indication is made in the relevant footnote. Berkeley's habit of numbering his works by paragraph or other unit (entry, query) facilitates reference to the works across the editions published during and after his lifetime. Where a work is numbered by Berkeley, I cite it by reference to that number. Also cited by entry number are what I call *Notebooks*: the series of philosophical remarks recorded in a pair of notebooks that were first published in the nineteenth century have been referred to as both *Philosophical Commentaries* and *Notebooks*. Where a work published in Berkeley's lifetime is not numbered by section, I give a page reference to the relevant early edition, and a supplementary reference to the relevant volume and page of Luce and Jessop's edition of 1949–1957. Works not published in Berkeley's lifetime, such as the majority of his sermons and his journals from travels in Italy, are cited by reference to volume and page number in the Luce and Jessop edition. Occasionally I also refer to the manuscripts of unpublished works such as sermons and journals. These citations are made obvious in the main text and footnotes. The 'Manuscript Introduction' to *Principles of Human Knowledge* is cited with reference to Bertil Belfrage's edition. Abbreviated forms of titles of works are used in the main text and footnotes and refer to the editions listed here. Abbreviated titles and publication details of other frequently cited material, such as Berkeley's correspondence and A. A. Luce's 1949 biography, are also provided.

Advice to the Tories	*Advice to the Tories Who Have Taken the Oaths* (London: printed by R. Baldwin and sold by R. Burleigh, 1715)

Alciphron	*Alciphron; Or, The Minute Philosopher,* 2nd ed., 2 vols. (London: J. Tonson, 1732)
Alciphron *(1752 text)*	*Alciphron; Or, The Minute Philosopher,* 3rd ed. (London: J. and R. Tonson and S. Draper, 1752)
Analyst	*The Analyst; Or, A Discourse Addressed to an Infidel Mathematician* (London: J. Tonson, 1734)
Anniversary *Sermon*	*A Sermon Preached before the Incorporated Society for the Propagation of the Gospel in Foreign Parts [...] On Friday the 18th of February, 1731. Being the Day of their Anniversary Meeting* (London: J. Downing, 1732)
Defence of *Free-Thinking* *in Mathematics*	*A Defence of Free-Thinking in Mathematics* (London: J. Tonson, 1735)
Discourse	*A Discourse Addressed to Magistrates and Men in Authority,* 2nd ed. (Dublin: George Faulkner, 1738)
New Theory *of Vision*	*An Essay towards a New Theory of Vision,* 2nd ed. (Dublin: Aaron Rhames for Jeremy Pepyat, 1709)
New Theory of *Vision (1732 text)*	*An Essay towards a New Theory of Vision,* in *Alciphron,* vol. 2
Essay	*An Essay towards Preventing the Ruine of Great Britain* (London: J. Roberts, 1721)
Guardian	*The Guardian,* 2 vols. (London: J. Tonson, 1714)
Ladies Library	*The Ladies Library, Written by a Lady, Published by Mr Steele,* 3 vols. (London: J.T., 1714)

Manuscript Introduction	*George Berkeley's Manuscript Introduction: An Editio Diplomatica,* edited and introduction by Bertil Belfrage (Oxford: Doxa, 1987)
Maxims	*Maxims Concerning Patriotism* (Dublin: [n.p.], 1750)
Miscellany	*A Miscellany, Containing Several Tracts on Various Subjects* (London: J. and R. Tonson and S. Draper, 1752)
De Motu	*De Motu; Sive, De Motus Principio & Natura, Et De Causa Communicationis Motuum* (London: Jacob Tonson, 1721) with translations taken from LJ
Passive Obedience	*Passive Obedience, Or, The Christian Doctrine of Not Resisting the Supreme Power, Proved and Vindicated upon the Principles of the Law of Nature,* 3rd ed. (London: H. Clements, 1713)
Proposal	*A Proposal for the Better Supplying of Churches in our Foreign Plantations, and for Converting the Savage Americans to Christianity, By a College to be Erected in the Summer Islands, Otherwise Called the Isles of Bermuda* (London: printed by H. Woodfall and sold by J. Roberts, 1725)
Querist	(followed by volume and page number, then query number) *The Querist,* 3 vols. (London: J. Roberts, 1736–1737)
Querist (1750 text)	*The Querist,* 2nd ed. (Dublin: George Faulkner, 1750)

Siris	*Siris: A Chain of Philosophical Reflexions and Inquiries Concerning the Virtues of TarWater and Divers Other Subjects Connected Together and Arising One from Another*, 2nd ed. (Dublin: Margt. Rhames for R. Gunne, 1744)
Theory of Vision Vindicated	*The Theory of Vision, or Visual Language [. . .] Vindicated and Explained* (London: Jacob Tonson, 1733)
Three Dialogues	*Three Dialogues between Hylas and Philonous* (London: G. James for Henry Clements, 1713)
Principles of Human Knowledge	*A Treatise Concerning the Principles of Human Knowledge* (Dublin: Aaron Rhames for Jeremy Pepyat, 1710) paragraphs of the introduction numbered separately
Principles of Human Knowledge (1734 text) and ***Three Dialogues (1734 text)***	*A Treatise Concerning the Principles of Human Knowledge [. . .] To Which Are Added Three Dialogues between Hylas and Philonous* (London: Jacob Tonson, 1734)
Word to the Wise	*A Word to the Wise: Or, An Exhortation to the Roman Catholic Clergy of Ireland. By a Member of the Established Church* (Dublin: George Faulkner, 1749)
LJ	(followed by volume and page number) *The Works of George Berkeley*, edited by A. A. Luce and T. E. Jessop, 9 vols. (London: Thomas Nelson, 1948–1957)
Letter	(followed by number, author and addressee, date, and page number) *The Correspondence of George Berkeley*, edited by Marc A. Hight (Cambridge: Cambridge University Press, 2012)

Berkeley and Percival	*Berkeley and Percival: The Correspondence of George Berkeley Afterwards Bishop of Cloyne and Sir John Percival Afterwards Earl of Egmont*, edited by Benjamin Rand (Cambridge: Cambridge University Press, 1914)
Essay	John Locke, *An Essay Concerning Human Understanding*, edited by P. H. Nidditch (Oxford: Clarendon Press, 1975)
Christianity Not Mysterious	John Toland, *Christianity Not Mysterious: Text, Associated Works, and Critical Essays*, edited by Philip McGuiness, Alan Harrison, and Richard Kearney (Dublin: Lilliput Press, 1997)
Luce	A. A. Luce, *The Life of George Berkeley Bishop of Cloyne*, introduction by David Berman (London: Thomas Nelson, 1949; London: Routledge/Thoemmes Press, 1992)

Dating

In the first half of the eighteenth century two dating systems were in use in Great Britain and Ireland. The 'old style' began the new year on 25 March, the 'new style' on 1 January. When giving dates between 1 January and 25 March, therefore, I give both years, separated by a slash.

GEORGE BERKELEY

CHAPTER ONE

Introduction

WHAT DO WE KNOW ABOUT George Berkeley? We know that he was born in 1685 in or near Kilkenny, Ireland, and died in 1753 in Oxford, England; that he studied and taught at Trinity College Dublin (TCD) from 1700; that he spent the best part of a decade between 1722 and 1732 fundraising for and attempting to establish a college in Bermuda; that he was made bishop of Cloyne in the south of Ireland in 1734. But primarily, perhaps, we know that he was the most significant proponent of the philosophical doctrine of immaterialism, the doctrine according to which there is no material substance supporting the sensible qualities we experience as perceptions or ideas.

Immaterialism is a striking doctrine, and Berkeley seems to have appreciated that it could easily be taken as a form of wild and radical scepticism. In 1713, he published a set of three dialogues between Hylas, who begins as a materialist, and Philonous, an immaterialist, to expand on and popularise the doctrine. Hylas, when he accepts Philonous's arguments for immaterialism, believes he has adopted a scepticism that makes knowledge of things as they are in themselves impossible: 'You may indeed know that Fire appears hot, and Water fluid: But this is no more than knowing, what Sensations are produced in our own Mind, upon the Application of Fire and Water to your Organs of Sense. Their internal Constitution, their true and real Nature, you are utterly in the dark as to *that*.'[1] Hylas hasn't yet grasped that Philonous, and Berkeley behind him, are identifying

---

1. *Three Dialogues*, p. 103 (LJ, II.227).

sensations and real natures. Some of Berkeley's near-contemporaries took the doctrine more generally to be 'the most outrageous whimsy that ever entered in the head of any ancient or modern madman', and felt that in arguing for 'the impossibility of the real or actual existence of matter', Berkeley was taking away 'the boundaries of truth and falshood; expos[ing] reason to all the outrage of unbounded Scepticism; and even, in his own opinion, mak[ing] mathematical demonstration, doubtful'.[2] Whilst immaterialism may now have few adherents—and those few proposing something very different from Berkeley—the arguments he used to defend his position are still the subject of philosophical debate. John Campbell and Quassim Cassam, for example, have produced a dialogical book on what they call 'Berkeley's puzzle', which 'is this: to describe the explanatory role of sensory experience without being driven to the conclusion that all we can have knowledge of is experiences'.[3]

''Tis Plain, We Do Not See a Man'

This book gives an account of (and modestly extends) what we know about Berkeley. It offers details of the documented aspects of Berkeley's life, such as the nature of his early schooling, his relationships with women, his work towards establishing a university in Bermuda, his purchase of enslaved people whilst in America. Berkeley was a thinker and writer throughout his life, and his writings are another different but still more important form of documentary evidence about that life. I survey Berkeley's entire career as a thinker and writer, attempting to show how his concerns intersect with those of other thinkers and of the intellectual, social, and political movements of his age as well as previous ages. The line between the two kinds of documentation that support this study is not perfectly clear. We have some knowledge of Berkeley's biographical experience of education through one kind of documentation—the statutes of the school he attended, the assessment procedures for fellowships at TCD when he was submitted to them, records of

---

2. Warburton, ed., *The Works of Alexander Pope*, IV.319–20, Warburton's note to 'Epilogue to the Satires: Dialogue II'.

3. Campbell and Cassam, *Berkeley's Puzzle*, p. 18. For an example of an immaterialism far from Berkeley's, see Harman, *Immaterialism*.

disciplinary issues in college when he was the junior dean, records of the charity for the schooling of Catholic Irish in Cloyne when he was bishop, his choices in educating his own children at home, and so on. That knowledge is difficult to separate from Berkeley's extensive but diffuse writing on education, at its most concentrated in *Alciphron* and *The Querist*, but a perennial concern. The same can be said of his political allegiance, family life, taste, and various other important topics. No attempt has been made for over a hundred years to bring these two kinds of documentation of Berkeley's life together across the full length of his career, as A. A. Luce's biography, dating from 1949 and still the most recent book-length treatment, declines to integrate biographical and philosophical discussion.[4] Berkeley's documented life and participation in various institutions and practices, such as those of the exclusive educational institutions of a Protestant elite, is inseparable from his treatment of major philosophical and social issues.

Any biography might be taken as the answer to a slightly different and more abstract question about its subject from the one just posed—what *can* we know about George Berkeley? To a great extent this question will be answered by what we admit as documentation of a life and by how willing we are to engage in interpretation and speculation about the meaning of documents. But there is a further question concerning what can be said about a life as a whole. Can we attribute character to Berkeley, given that all we have of him is a set of documents, even if some such documents explicitly discuss his character (such as the remarkable letters written by Anne, Berkeley's wife, to their son George Jr after Berkeley's death)? People have not been afraid to characterise Berkeley—as pious and practical, for example, or as more than normally given to dissimulation and deceit.[5] But we may have misgivings about such characterisations, even based on relatively ample documentary evidence. There are always things about people that we do not know, things that have eluded documentation, or which could not

4. Luce, preface, pp. v–vi: 'Any comment that I make here on Berkeley's thought is incidental and strictly subordinate to the biographical interest, and is entirely free from technical discussion'.

5. See Luce, passim; Berman, *George Berkeley*, passim; and Berman, 'Berkeley's Life and Works', p. 24.

be documented (at least not in any straightforward way). The question of what we can know about another person should occur to the writer and reader of a biography, as we worry about the judgements we are inevitably forming of the subject and the basis on which they are founded. In Berkeley's case there is a further complexity: the question of what we can know about other people is bound up philosophically with what we most commonly do know of him—his propounding the doctrine of immaterialism.

What does immaterialism have to do with the question of what we can know about other people? My purpose in addressing this question at the beginning of this book is twofold. First, by offering a brief survey of the immaterialist writings for which Berkeley is best known I want to introduce those unfamiliar with his thought to some of its central topics, and to indicate to those already familiar with his thought something of my own approach to immaterialism. My discussion does not aim to achieve the standard of a technical, professional, philosophical interpretation of Berkeley's immaterialism, nor to offer a summary of philosophical commentary on particular questions or passages. Rather, I aim to broach some of the topics that will be particularly relevant to other parts of this biographical study. I refer in the notes to some selections from the substantial technical commentary on Berkeley's metaphysics, not with the aim of arriving at an interpretive consensus, but to point readers to examples of more philosophical commentary where a variety of approaches to the topic in question can be found. Second, I want to suggest that a consideration of the central topics in Berkeley's immaterialism offers a justification of a biographical approach to his philosophical career—but one that might first require us to rethink our ideas of what people are and how they know one another.

For a student in the early eighteenth century, the most canonical modern philosophy was dualist. Holding that there are two substances in the universe, mind (or spirit) and body, Descartes and his followers upheld a strong distinction between the two—between substance that is thinking and unextended and substance that is unthinking and extended. John Locke identified the two kinds of being known to man as cogitative and incogitative beings.[6] Locke

6. *Essay*, IV.x.9, pp. 622–23.

is clear that spirit is metaphysically prior to matter and should precede it in any course of study:

> [U]nder what Title soever the consideration of *Spirits* comes, I think it ought to go before the study of Matter, and Body, not as a Science that can be methodized into a System, and treated of upon Principles of Knowledge; but as an enlargement of our Minds towards a truer and fuller comprehension of the intellectual World, to which we are led both by Reason and Revelation. [. . .] Matter being a thing, that all our Senses are constantly conversant with, it is so apt to possess the Mind, and exclude all other Beings, but Matter, that prejudice, grounded on such Principles, often leaves no room for the admittance of Spirits, or the allowing any such things as *immaterial Beings in rerum natura*: when yet it is evident, that by mere Matter and Motion, non of the great Phænomena of Nature can be resolved, to instance but in that common one of Gravity, which I think impossible to be explained by any natural Operation of Matter, or any other Law of Motion, but the positive Will of a Superiour Being, so ordering it.[7]

Philosophical understanding of the world, in this type of dualism, is understanding how spirits, principally God but also lower orders of spirits, work upon matter to produce the regular phenomena made evident to us by our senses—from the movement of the planets to the movement of human bodies.

Berkeley is not a dualist of this kind: he believes that 'there is not any other Substance than *Spirit* or that which perceives'.[8] His

---

7. Locke, *Some Thoughts Concerning Education*, pp. 245–46.

8. *Principles of Human Knowledge*, §7. Winkler, *Berkeley: An Interpretation*, p. 309, has provided a persuasive reconstruction of Berkeley's reasons for thinking of spirit as a substance: 'A Berkeleyan idea is not an act of awareness but an object of awareness, and if an object of awareness must be perceived, there must be something that perceives it. Now if there *must* be something by which it is perceived then the perceiver has *something* of the character of a substance, because it is something on which the idea depends for its existence. For all I have said so far, though, a "perceiver" might be nothing more than one pole or aspect of an indivisible thing: an unowned episode of awareness, one of whose aspects is an object, and one of whose aspects is an act. But according to Berkeley I know that *I* perceive, and I know that I perceive an "endless variety" of ideas that succeed one another in time, upon which I exercise "diverse operations", among them willing, imagining, and perceiving (*Principles* 2). I am therefore a persisting thing capable of various acts or operations. I am not a fleeting or momentary thing, but something that resembles what substances are widely held to be'.

rejection of this kind of dualism might lead to comparison with attitudes considered dangerously heterodox, such as Benedict de Spinoza's assertion that there is only one substance in the universe, God.[9] Berkeley makes efforts to distance himself from the 'wild Imaginations' of Spinoza, who is listed next to Hobbes as a believer that matter might exist without mind.[10] Berkeley's assertion of one spiritual substance has much in common with dualism. It is evident from the full range of Berkeley's writing that he shares the belief, expressed by Locke, in a superior intelligence producing lawlike regularity in the world perceived by the senses. But the regular productions of that organising intelligence are not, for Berkeley, bodies or matter, but ideas—understood as what our senses report to us, or images we are able to call up in our minds.[11]

The evidence of the senses might be taken as a report of what is out there in the world: it is an internal impression of an external reality. This attitude is central to the scientific culture of the late seventeenth and early eighteenth centuries, in which the scientist or natural philosopher attended closely to her own sensory experience in order to learn more about the regular behaviour of the external, material world. But Berkeley suggests that it is this attitude, and not his immaterialism, that opens the door to scepticism:

> [W]e have been led into very dangerous Errors, by supposing a two-fold Existence of the Objects of Sense, the one *Intelligible*, or in the Mind, the other *Real* and without the Mind: Whereby Unthinking Things are thought, to have a natural Subsistence of their own, distinct from being perceiv'd by Spirits. This which, if I mistake not, hath been shewn to be a most groundless and absurd Notion, is the very Root of *Scepticism*; for so long as Men thought that Real Things subsisted without the Mind, and that their Knowledge was only so far forth *Real* as it was conformable to *real Things*, it follows, they cou'd not be certain, that they had any real Knowledge at all. For how can it be known,

---

9. Spinoza, *Ethics*, part I, proposition XIV, corollary I, p. 86.

10. *Three Dialogues*, p. 76 (LJ, II.213); see also *Notebooks*, §§826–27.

11. Hight, *Idea and Ontology*, pp. 8, 35, and in the chapters dedicated to Berkeley, argues that Berkeley conceived of ideas as quasi-substances, ontologically dependent on minds but not modes of them.

that the Things which are Perceiv'd, are conformable to those which are not Perceiv'd, or Exist without the Mind?[12]

Berkeley's solution to the sceptical abyss over which one has to leap from idea to external object is to identify them: the object is the idea. As we can never have any report of objects other than our sensory impressions, we have no basis on which to posit their separate existence. When we perceive regular and lawlike behaviour, we are perceiving the 'Ideas imprinted on the Senses by the Author of Nature [. . .] called *real things*'; 'those excited in the Imagination being less Regular, Vivid and Constant, are more properly termed *Ideas*, or *Images of Things*, which they copy and represent'.[13] Ideas take the place of real things in Berkeley's immaterialism, and they are imprinted on the senses by God, not by a material substratum that underlies or provokes sensory response.

It might seem that Berkeley has simply established a mind-idea dualism to replace a mind-body dualism.[14] But his statement that there is only one substance, spirit, should be recalled. Ideas are not a substance. Both spirits and ideas might be called things, but that common name should not be allowed to conceal their radical difference: '*Thing* or *Being* is the most general Name of all, it comprehends under it two Kinds entirely distinct and heterogeneous, and which have nothing common but the Name, *viz. Spirits* and *Ideas*. The former are *Active, Indivisible, Incorruptible Substances*: The latter are *Inert, Fleeting, Perishable Passions*, or *Dependent Beings*, which subsist not by themselves, but are supported by, or Exist in Minds or Spiritual Substances'.[15] Spirits and ideas can be distinguished by their activity or passivity. Ideas are passive: 'the very Being of an Idea implies Passiveness and Inertness in it, insomuch that it is impossible for an Idea to do any thing, or, strictly speaking, to be the Cause of any thing'.[16] Berkeley's goal in asserting this heterogeneity is to reserve causality for spirits in a more complete

---

12. *Principles of Human Knowledge*, §86.

13. Ibid., §33; see also §§30–31.

14. Indeed, McCracken, 'Berkeley's Notion of Spirit', 597–602, suggests that Berkeley goes from being a spirit monist (with activity and passivity the main distinction within spirits) to being a mind-idea dualist.

15. *Principles of Human Knowledge*, §89.

16. Ibid., §25.

way than does Locke. As ideas are passive, and what we tend to call real things are ideas, there is no active or causal power in things whatsoever. All causes are spiritual.

In his philosophical notebooks, Berkeley says, 'Nothing properly but persons i.e. conscious things do exist, all other things are not so much existences as manners of ye existence of persons'.[17] When a spirit has ideas, that spirit is being in a certain way or manner. This is not to say that ideas are in minds in such a way that minds share the qualities of the perceived ideas—being extended or red, for example.[18] Ideas are not modes of being of the mind in that sense. Persons perceive or produce ideas, they understand or they will: 'A Spirit is one Simple, Undivided, active Being: as it perceives Ideas, it is called the *Understanding*, and as it produces or otherwise operates about them, it is called the *Will*'.[19] This division of the undivided being answers a division in our experience of ideas. There are those that we produce ourselves, and those that seem to be produced for us: 'whatever Power I may have over my own Thoughts, I find the Ideas actually perceiv'd by Sense have not a like Dependence on my Will. When in broad Day-light I open my Eyes, 'tis not in my Power to chuse whether I shall See or no'.[20] Those ideas we do not produce by an act of will we perceive or understand.[21] The distinction is not absolute. The philosophical notebooks are ambivalent on the question of whether the will and the understanding are distinct, but Berkeley does say, 'The Understanding taken for a faculty is not really distinct from ye Will', and

17. *Notebooks*, §24.

18. See *Principles of Human Knowledge*, §49.

19. Ibid., §27. For this characteristic sense of the self as active, see Jaffro, 'Le Cogito de Berkeley', p. 97.

20. *Principles of Human Knowledge*, §29.

21. Commentators offer a variety of views on how active the mind is in perceiving and how distinct the mind and its objects are. Migely, 'Berkeley's Actively Passive Mind', p. 157, argues that mind is only passive in determining the content of perceptions it does not will, but active in everything else, from confirming and assenting to those perceptions, to operating about them to create mediate objects of perception. She holds that the will and the understanding, the mind and its ideas, are ontologically distinct but existentially inseparable (pp. 161–65). Daniel, 'Berkeley's Doctrine of Mind', p. 31, suggests that Berkeley wants to distinguish ideas from acts of mind, even though neither 'is intelligible in abstraction from the other'. Ott, 'Descartes and Berkeley on Mind', p. 447, says the mind is passive in perceiving, but active in distinguishing and differentiating ideas within perception.

that 'Understanding is in some sort an Action'.[22] 'Understanding' is Berkeley's word for the relatively passive state spirit finds itself in when perceiving. When producing or operating about ideas in any other way, the spirit adopts its characteristic activity of willing.[23] In producing our own ideas, our spirit is willing, and it is behaving in a certain manner; in perceiving ideas produced by another spirit, our spirit is operating about those ideas, still active in attending to and interpreting them.

Berkeley's philosophical predecessors recognise the mind's activity in relating and judging ideas. Malebranche, a philosopher Berkeley read closely, says that any judgement about ideas is an act of will.[24] Locke describes relation as 'When the Mind so considers one thing, that it does, as it were, bring it to, and set it by another, and carry its view from one to t'other'.[25] Berkeley agrees. All relations, he tells us, include an act of the mind. Relations themselves are not ideas, but they are nonetheless added to the list of things we can know: 'Ideas, Spirits and Relations are all in their respective kinds, the Object of humane Knowledge and Subject of Discourse'.[26] Relations and spirits are alike inasmuch as they are proper objects of knowledge and subjects of discourse, but they are not ideas. We have a 'notion' of relations just as we have a knowledge of our own existence as spirits 'by inward Feeling or Reflexion, and that of other Spirits by Reason'.[27] We do not have ideas of spirits as 'the Words *Will, Soul, Spirit*, do not stand for different Ideas, or in truth, for any Idea at all, but for Something which is very different from Ideas, and which being an Agent cannot be like unto, or represented by, any Idea whatsoever'.[28] As he revised the

---

22. *Notebooks*, §614a and §821; for firmer distinctions, see §708 and §816.

23. Bettcher, *Berkeley's Philosophy of Spirit*, p. 80, notes that agents are normally willing, but that they can experience ideas passively and affect (pleasure and pain) is the mark of their being so experienced. Roberts, *A Metaphysics for the Mob*, pp. 93, 94, argues that Berkeley conceives of spirits as wills, and notes that, 'for Berkeley, thought is one of the modes of volition'.

24. Malebranche, *The Search after Truth*, pp. 8–9, and editors' introduction, p. xii. Malebranche, Elucidation II, p. 560, also states that the soul is one, its different faculties being merely different forms of the soul's operation.

25. *Essay*, II.xxv.1, p. 319.

26. *Principles of Human Knowledge* (1734 text), §§142, 89.

27. Ibid. (1734 text), §89.

28. Ibid. (1734 text), §27.

texts of the *Principles of Human Knowledge* and *Three Dialogues* for republication in 1734, Berkeley more consistently applied the word 'notion' to the type of knowledge we have of spirits and relations. Notions are the medium of knowledge of relations and other spirits. Relating to operations of the mind, they are themselves operations of the mind.[29] We infer spirits with greater powers than ourselves on the basis of the ideas we find we have and are not responsible for. Those caused by God have 'a Steddiness, Order and Coherence, and are not excited at Random, as those which are effects of Human Wills often are, but in a regular Train or Series, the admirable Connexion whereof sufficiently testifies the Wisdom and Benevolence of its Author'.[30] Our knowledge of spirits is an inference of an agent capable of producing the series of ideas we do not ourselves produce.

The ideas that we perceive and attribute to the agency of other spirits operate as signs. We know of the existence of other people in this manner, and even more certainly we know of God:

> I perceive several Motions, Changes, and Combinations of Ideas, that inform me there are certain particular Agents like my self, which accompany them, and concur in their Production [. . .] the Knowledge I have of other Spirits is not immediate [. . .] but depending on the Intervention of Ideas, by me refer'd to Agents or Spirits distinct from my self, as Effects or concomitant Signs.[31]

The admirable regularity of the phenomenal world means 'that GOD, is known as certainly and immediately as any other Mind or Spirit whatsoever, distinct from our selves'. This is a God '*who*

---

29. Lee, 'What Berkeley's Notions Are', pp. 31–32; Flage, 'Relative Ideas and Notions', p. 243, distinguishes the knowledge by description that one can have of notions from the direct knowledge of a positive idea. Here and in *Berkeley's Doctrine of Notions*, p. 5, Flage agrees with Lee (p. 33) that having notions is closely connected to knowing the meaning of words. Atherton, 'The Coherence of Berkeley's Theory of Mind', p. 396, contests the reading of 'notion' as a solution to a problem about spirit.

30. *Principles of Human Knowledge*, §30.

31. Ibid., §145. It should be noted that by parity of reason we might just as well infer matter as the cause of ideas—the only difference in the process of establishing the existence of other spirits and of matter is in the type of intuitive knowledge on which we are reliant. In the case of spirits, it is intuitive knowledge of our own existence as agents; in the case of matter it is that the report of the senses corresponds to an external world. Berkeley must prioritise, like Descartes, the intuitive knowledge of the existence of the self.

works all in all, and *by whom all things consist*.'[32] God is known by signs, is the agent of everything, and is the source of all being. What people perceive is no accidentally produced train of ideas that enables a merely episodic or partial or haphazard set of inferences about the will of another spirit. The train of ideas is organised and reliable, intended by God to be an ongoing, legible set of instructions to people.

The regular and admirable series of connected ideas that God produces gives us 'a sort of Foresight, which enables us to regulate our Actions for the benefit of Life'.[33] Showing that God uses signs to instruct us in how to live is the burden of Berkeley's essay on vision and visual ideas, here quoted as it was republished with his philosophical dialogue *Alciphron* in 1732:

> Upon the whole, I think we may fairly conclude, that the proper Objects of Vision constitute an Universal Language of the Author of Nature, whereby we are instructed how to regulate our Actions, in order to attain those things, that are necessary to the Preservation and Well-being of our Bodies, as also to avoid whatever may be hurtful and destructive of them. It is by this Information that we are principally guided in all the Transactions and Concerns of Life.[34]

We can think of our ideas as signs, and those signs, as we have just seen, provide guidance for current and future conduct. Berkeley gave consideration to the possibility that this instructive function of language—producing attitudes or dispositions in the people addressed, and not raising ideas in the mind—is the primary function of language. He is clear: '[T]he communicating of Ideas marked by Words is not the chief and only end of Language, as is commonly suppos'd. There are other Ends, as the raising of some Passion, the exciting to, or deterring from an Action, the putting the Mind in some particular Disposition; to which the former is in many Cases barely subservient, and sometimes entirely omitted'.[35] People do not engage in speech to no end, or no end other than raising ideas; they often have the ulterior motive of altering the

---

32. *Principles of Human Knowledge*, §147.
33. Ibid., §31.
34. *New Theory of Vision* (1732 text), §147.
35. *Principles of Human Knowledge*, introduction, §20.

conduct of the people they address. Speakers use signs to bring about changes in conduct, and that goes for God as much as for people. Berkeley suggests that when we are speaking, really speaking, it ought to be with some good in mind. That is the attitude expressed by Euphranor, one of the characters of *Alciphron*, when he says that 'the true End of Speech, Reason, Science, Faith, Assent, in all its different Degrees, is not meerly, or principally, or always the imparting or acquiring of Ideas, but rather something of an active, operative Nature, tending to a conceived Good'.[36] Spirits use signs to talk to us in order to effect dispositional change conceived of in relation to a particular good. The phenomenal world is an example of such a discourse. In this sense, then, we might only really be said to understand the signs the phenomenal world presents us with when we heed them, when we take them as encouragements to change our behaviour, to change our practice.

Here it is perhaps appropriate to return to the question of documentary biography and the biographical approach to a philosopher's career. If we want to know what we can about George Berkeley, we should scrutinise as closely as possible all the changes of ideas he causes in us, chiefly through those surviving documents relating to his life, including his own writings. We should not confuse those ideas for the person, but take them as signs of the existence of a person like us, someone who produces changes in our ideas analogous to those that we know we can ourselves produce. We should attend to what Berkeley was trying to communicate to us, what kinds of changes in the practice of other people he hoped to bring about, and what conceived good or goods his communications actively and operatively tended towards. As we do not know other spirits directly but by analogy with the intuitive knowledge we have of ourselves, other people are always works of interpretation, conjectures about the meanings of signs based on analogies from our previous experience. This book endeavours to arrive at an interpretation of the attitudes of the spirit communicated by Berkeley's writings and what can be known of his actions. It is not perhaps surprising that a biographer would have an interest in the attitudinal disposition of the subject of the biography. But it

36. *Alciphron*, VII.17.

is perhaps surprising that Berkeley's immaterialism, his insistence that there is only one substance—spirit—and that ideas are merely passive effects of spirits who exist in willing some conceived and quite possibly indistinct good, lends its support to a biographical approach to his philosophy.

Berkeley's immaterialism, then, in some sense justifies a biographical approach to the philosopher. In the preceding discussion, I was also hoping to indicate an interest—to be pursued throughout this book—in the practical and dispositional component of Berkeley's frequent recurrence to language as an explanatory tool. As John Russell Roberts has pointed out, 'There is nothing mere about practical matters for a Christian philosopher'.[37] An interest in language and practice spans Berkeley's career. In the *Essay towards a New Theory of Vision* of 1709, visual ideas are a language that is used to direct our behaviour. In *The Querist* of 1735-1737, money might be understood as a language that can be used to improve the desires and practice of a population. In *Siris* of 1744, the laws of nature are an instructive discourse, improving the spirits of the philosophically inclined. When Berkeley employs the language analogy, he does so with the active, operative tendency towards a conceived good in mind—and not just the use of a various set of arbitrary signs.

The other aim of this introductory chapter is to expand on another tendency in Berkeley's thought that has not previously been elaborated and which I believe to be useful in uncovering the coherence of his diverse writings and activities. This is the tendency to present thinking and acting as participating in (or of) the divinity. Participation in the divinity is what happens, I suggest, when a finite spirit understands and conforms in practice to the will of the infinite spirit. This is how Crito presents the effects of conscience in *Alciphron*: conscience exists to 'ennoble Man, and raise him to an Imitation and Participation of the Divinity'.[38] It could also be parsed as loving God, or becoming more fully of God. Elaborating on this tendency in Berkeley's thought requires citing a broader range of his texts.

---

37. Roberts, *A Metaphysics for the Mob*, p. 68.
38. *Alciphron*, V.28.

'Participation of the Divinity'

In an unpublished notebook Berkeley indicates that his philosophical project is 'directed to practise and morality, as appears first from
making manifest the nearness and omnipresence of God'.[39] Promoting a 'pious Sense of the Presence of GOD' was one of his chief
aims in writing the *Principles of Human Knowledge*.[40] Twenty-four
years later, Berkeley had the same aims in the *Theory of Vision Vindicated*, where he noted that, in that age of freethinking, 'the Notion
of a watchful, active, intelligent, free Spirit, with whom we have to
do, and in whom we live, and move, and have our Being, is not the
most prevailing in the Books and Conversation even of those who
are called Deists'. Therefore, he concludes, 'I cannot employ myself
more usefully than in contributing to awaken and possess men with
a thorough sense of the Deity inspecting, concurring, and interesting itself in human actions and affairs'.[41] God is a spirit present to
us like other spirits, with whose will ours has to do, and whose concurrence is required for human actions to be brought about. This
spirit takes an interest in us, rather than being detached or indifferent. As Berkeley made clear in the *New Theory of Vision* and the
Principles of Human Knowledge, all our knowledge of the world,
both of its phenomena and of the regularities that underlie those
phenomena, is instruction, another person telling us what to do
for our own good.[42] Becoming scientists or natural philosophers,
we are being discoursed by God about what is best for us. The language of the author of nature tends towards a conceived good—it is
active and operative. Berkeley holds true to this conception of the
phenomenal world and its regularities as an instructive discourse
delivered by a personalised divinity to the later stages of his philosophical career, as *Siris*, the last of his major works, demonstrates.

The personal, present, active, discoursing God of Berkeley's
philosophical world, early and late, is not a concept or belief that
many of his recent students have shared (I do not share it), and yet
the presence of this God is so essential to Berkeley's philosophical,

39. BL Add MS 39304, f. 4r.
40. *Principles of Human Knowledge*, §156.
41. *Theory of Vision Vindicated*, §§2, 8.
42. *New Theory of Vision*, §147; *Principles of Human Knowledge*, §§107, 109.

and indeed personal, enterprise that it must be admitted if we are accurately to infer anything about the person or spirit 'Berkeley' behind the various concomitant signs which the documents associated with his life provide us.[43] Perhaps not everyone feels that Berkeley's God is an embarrassment, but both those who do and those who don't, I think, have tended to see the specific, even idiosyncratic, attributes of Berkeley's God as of relevance only to Berkeley's metaphysics and philosophical theology. This book will indeed consider what it means, from metaphysical and theological points of view, for Berkeley to believe that good human life is full participation in the divinity.[44] But another way of thinking about participating in the divinity will also be important, and that is to think of participating in the divinity not as a matter of acquiring ideas only, but of acquiring moral, social, and institutional commitments, and indeed privileges. Berkeley's metaphysics, theology, and social philosophy of morally committed and politically privileged Anglicanism equally draw on his concept of the end of human life as participation in the divinity.

God is 'to be considered as related to us', Berkeley says in the notes on moral philosophy contained in one of his notebooks and possibly dating from the last years of his life.[45] A relationship with God is a personal relationship, inasmuch as spirit and person are synonymous: identity of the person consists in identity of the will, as Berkeley says, and spirits are, as I have just suggested, fundamentally willing substance.[46] Personal relationships with God should be loving. Love of God is the first principle of religion, Berkeley said in a sermon preached in Newport, Rhode Island, in August 1730. That love should be shown in various ways, like the love we show to

43. Atherton, 'Berkeley without God', explores the possibility that a distinctively Berkeleian world requires only languagelike regularity and not necessarily a God.

44. Herdt, 'Affective Perfectionism', p. 44, describes the concept of participation of the divinity in the Cambridge Platonists—at least one of whose works, Cudworth's *True Intellectual System of the Universe*, Berkeley knew intimately—in terms that could be related to Berkeley: 'The language of "participation" in God is another reminder that friendship with God is unique, that human beings are not in an ontological sense independent of God. [. . .] [F]or the Cambridge Platonists, participation in God's mind is first and foremost a participation in the love of God, not in abstract rules of practical reasoning'.

45. Belfrage, 'Notes by Berkeley on Moral Philosophy', p. 7.

46. *Notebooks*, §194a.

human persons for a variety of comparable reasons. One of these kinds of love involves endeavouring to do the will of another, better person: 'Love of gratitude & respect to Benefactors and Superiors. [. . .] We shew love to superiors & benefactors by consulting their honour i.e. by performing their will, & endeavouring that others perform it'.[47] Love of God should produce conformity of our wills to God's, or obedience, and it ought to include the endeavour to make other people also conform.[48] As Stephen R. L. Clark says, 'That virtue lies in conformity and obedience is a thought to which we have grown unaccustomed', but it is clearly Berkeley's view.[49] On Whitsunday 1751, Berkeley preached in Cloyne and asserted again that 'religion is nothing else but the conforming our faith and practice to the will of god'.[50] The manuscript of this sermon asks, 'What else is the design and aim of vertue or religion, but the making our several distinct wills coincident with, and subordinate to, the one supreme will of God?'[51] In the roughly contemporary notes on moral philosophy, conformity to, subordination to, or coincidence with the will of God is said to be happiness and virtue.[52] Thirty-five years previously, Berkeley had identified charity as that to which our own and others' wills should be conformed: 'mutual Charity is what we are principally enjoyn'd to practice' by God.[53] As will be shown in discussions of Berkeley's attitude to trade in the 1710s as a form of mutual, charitable interest and of his activity in establishing institutions for the poor (hospitals, weaving schools, schools), practically whilst bishop of Cloyne and theoretically as "the Querist", charity is a love of others that takes an interest in their practice and

47. LJ, VII.71.

48. One might here contrast Berkeley's intuition that we should love our superiors with the views of Jacques Abbadie, *The Art of Knowing One-Self*, pp. 211–12: 'Man naturally hates God, because he hates the Dependance which submits him to his Dominion, and the Law which restrains his Desires. This Abhorrence of the Deity lies hid in the bottom of Man's Heart, or Infirmity and Fear many times conceal it from the Eyes of Reason: This inward Aversion perceives a secret Pleasure at any thing that dares and affronts GOD; Men love those slights of Wit which scandalize the *Divinity*'. Abbadie's view of human depravity in this respect might offer an insight into the psychology of freethinking.

49. Clark, 'God-Appointed Berkeley and the General Good', p. 245.

50. LJ, VII.136.

51. BL Add MS 39306, f. 212r.

52. Belfrage, 'Notes by Berkeley on Moral Philosophy', pp. 6–7.

53. LJ, VII.27–28, sermon 'On Charity', spring 1714.

attempts to bring it into line with a conceived good: charity can be an obligation to attempt to change others' conduct. Charity is the form that love of God takes when God's superiority is recognised and the duty to obey acknowledged.[54]

Berkeley's obedience extends beyond the charitable to the disciplinary: the obligation to attempt to make others' conduct conform to the will of God might require the threat and execution of punishments. His unwavering commitment to the obligation to obey temporal and spiritual authorities is connected to a reverence and love for superiors. These aspects of his thinking will become evident in discussions of *Passive Obedience* (1712) and the *Discourse Addressed to Magistrates* (1738), as well as of Berkeley's insistence on the binding nature of oaths in his *Advice to the Tories* (1715) and elsewhere. People are obliged to obey their superiors out of love for the benefits those superiors bring—chiefly the benefit of protection. If the sovereign's law protects us, we should love, reverence, and obey that sovereign. Likewise, wives should obey husbands, as is suggested by an insertion Berkeley makes into one of the texts he excerpts for *The Ladies Library* (1713). And the philosophical elite of educationalists and the clerisy should be obeyed on account of their superiority.[55]

As well as the metaphysically challenging notion that God's concurrence is required for individual human wills to bring about any phenomenal effect—even the tangible and visible ideas of moving our own bodies, for example—there is this other more broadly social sense of what it is for people to participate in the will of God: entering into a hierarchical network of obligations, dependencies, responsibilities. Berkeley shares both of these interests with Saint Paul, probably the most significant apostolic example for him. Insisting on the participation of the human in the divine will, Saint Paul says that God works in people to will and do his good pleasure

54. Holtzman, 'Berkeley's Two Panaceas', pp. 479–80, captures this same relationship between charity, education, and conformity to God's will in Berkeley's thought. Similar attitudes to Berkeley's can be found in other writers; for example, Henry More, *Theological Works*, p. 263, calls charity, or love of God and man, 'the highest Participation of Divinity that humane Nature is capable of on this side that mysterious Conjunction of the Humanity of Christ with the Godhead'.

55. See again the *Discourse Addressed to Magistrates*, p. 18 (LJ, VI.209) and the attitudes set out in *The Querist* I.22, §192.

(Philippians 2:13) and that the faithful are labourers together with God (1 Corinthians 3:9). He also insists that the submission of wives to husbands should be like the submission of the faithful to the Church, that children should submit to parents and servants to masters (Ephesians 5:22–33, 6:1–6), and that apostles should teach submission to principalities and magistrates (Titus 3:1). Union with God and a life of institutional submission and obedience go together. The two belong together in the interpretation of Berkeley's life and work offered in this book. It is therefore an interpretation that challenges views of Berkeley, such as Michael Brown's in his recent history of *The Irish Enlightenment*, that he 'accepted the central Enlightenment premise that the human being was the basic unit of analysis'. Brown argues that 'Berkeley's intellectual endeavour was directed to defending the faith from within the Enlightenment's terrain'. Berkeley's defence of the faith is unquestionable, but aligning him with an Enlightenment that displaces God from the centre of the known universe glosses over a significant aspect of Berkeley's thought that is at once highly traditional and deeply idiosyncratic: his arguments for the nature of the relationship between finite and infinite spirits, and the scientific, moral, social, and religious consequences of those arguments.[56]

Participating in God is not something that all people or finite spirits achieve equally. There are degrees of participation. As Berkeley put it in an undated set of notes for a sermon at Newport, 'Some sort of union with the Godhead in prophets, apostles, all true Christians, all men. but with men, Xtians, inspired persons, Xt in different degrees'.[57] There is a hierarchy of participation in the divinity.[58] Berkeley states the belief clearly in a sermon on religious zeal delivered during the period 1709 to 1712: 'As we are Christians we are members of a Society which entitles us to certain rights and privileges above the rest of mankind. [?] But then we must remember those advantages are conveyed unto us in a regular dispensation by the hands of a Hierarchy constituted by the Apostles, and

---

56. Brown, *The Irish Enlightenment*, pp. 92–93.

57. LJ, VII.61.

58. For a description of Berkeley's mental universe as hierarchical, see Charles, 'Berkeley polémiste', p. 414.

from them continued down to us in a perpetual succession'.[59] Not only is this hierarchy metaphysical, but it will have consequences for the privileges into which certain people are admitted. Berkeley's 'Address on Confirmation' identifies a twofold meaning of the kingdom of Christ into which the confirmed are entering:

> [T]he whole world or universe may be said to compose the kingdom of Christ. But secondly, besides this large and general sense, the Kingdom of Christ is also taken in a more narrow sense as it signifies his church. The Christian church, I say, is in a peculiar sense his kingdom being a Society of persons, not only subject to his power, but also conforming themselves to his will, living according to his precepts, and thereby entitled to the promises of his gospel.[60]

The Church is a social organisation founded on subjection and obedience to the will of a sovereign. The members of that society must endeavour to conform to the will of the sovereign in practice. Doing so gives them an entitlement not just to protection but to reward. Berkeley here specifies the promises of the gospel. But membership in the Church confers temporal privileges also, and Berkeley worked throughout his life to guard those privileges against the incursions of freethinkers, whom Berkeley feared as an internal enemy, and of worldly minded politicians. He understood Anglican Protestantism to be in competition with Catholicism and dissent.[61] Even if, in his more ecumenical attitudes in later life, Berkeley would consider extending some of the practical, temporal privileges of membership of his church to others (primarily Irish Catholics), those privileges were only ever to be shared in part, and

---

59. LJ, VII.20. The question mark indicates illegible material in the MS.

60. LJ, VII.169.

61. Hill, 'Freethinking and Libertinism, pp. 58–59, suggests that 'so widespread was the radical idea that religion had been invented to keep the lower orders in place that defenders of Christianity took it over' by presenting the capacity of a future state of rewards and punishments to maintain social subordination as a good thing. In considering confession as a central aspect of Berkeley's thought and practice, I take a different view from Brown, *The Irish Enlightenment*, p. 20, who says of Toland, Berkeley, and Arthur O'Leary that '[f]or none of these writers was confession a determining facet of their intellectual ambition, but a strategic and specific problem encountered when applying Enlightenment methods to the context of eighteenth-century Ireland'.

only ever as part of the project of winning others not just to the Church but to the Protestant church.

To participate in the divinity is to be a member of a hierarchical society that confers privileges in both this world and the next. That society has practical, embodied forms in the Church and its established institutions, and also in the institutions of educational establishments—schools, colleges, libraries, learned societies—as documented in charters and rules. Berkeley's participation in the divinity through such social institutions forms a major part of this study. His major philosophical works testify to a belief in an infinite mind creating lawlike regularities in the succession of ideas in finite spirits, instructing them in how to behave for their own good, and demanding love and respect. So too do Berkeley's works of moral, social, and religious philosophy and his actions in shaping the institutions of social and religious life testify to his conception of the infinite spirit. The inequalities produced by his enactment of his beliefs are also a concern of this study: whilst the people subordinated to Berkeley's privilege (Irish Catholics, women, enslaved people) have not displaced him from the centre of this narrative, I hope at least to do more to recognise the consequences of Berkeley's practice for the lives of other people.

A passage that Berkeley excerpted from Isaac Barrow when compiling the anthology *The Ladies Library* in 1713 suggests what it meant to be admitted into the society of the Church on the occasion of confirmation, when one first takes the sacrament. In this ritual, confirmands commit themselves to an organised society through communion with Christ, and also with other communicants, when they sacramentally partake of his body:

> The *Sacrament* of the *Lords Supper* declares that Union, which good Christians partaking of it, have with Christ; their Mystical Insertion into Him by a close Dependence upon him for Spiritual Life, Mercy, Grace, and Salvation; a constant adherence to him by Faith and Obedience; a near Conformity to him in Mind and Affection; an inseparable Conjunction with him by the strictest Bonds of Fidelity, and by the most endearing Relations. [. . .] We in the outward Action partake of the *Symbols* representing our Saviour's Body and Blood: We in the Spiritual Intentions *communicate* of his very Person, being according to the Manner insinuated, intimately united to him.

By this *Sacrament* consequently is Signify'd and Seal'd that *Union* which is among our Saviour's true Disciples *communicating* therein; their being together united in consent of Mind and Unity of Faith, in mutual Good Will and Affection, in Hope and Tendency to the same blessed End; in Spiritual Brotherhood and Society, especially upon Account of their *Communion* with Christ, which most closely ties them to one another. They partaking of this individual Food, become translated as it were with one Body and Substance; *Seeing*, says St. *Paul, we being many are one Bread and one Body, or all of us do partake of one Bread.*[62]

What Barrow says of communion is very close to what Berkeley says of unity in the divine intellect in *Siris*. All properties of mind in lower orders of being are derived from the infinite mind, and the true student of nature looks up from study of the physical world to see that 'the mind contains all, and acts all, and is to all created beings the source of unity and identity, harmony and order, existence and stability'.[63] Communion with God is being in God; being in God is the only nonmetaphorical way in which one thing can be in another, as it is the participation of finite spirits in the infinite spirit.[64] Sharing in the nature of God is a social commitment in Barrow, and will appear to be so in Berkeley's practice.

It is not trivial that those who take communion become communicants. Berkeley's theory of communication—God and other spirits continually and actively discoursing with one another through signs and with some conceived good in view—is a theory of communion, of bringing wills into conformity with one another in the process of forming a religious brotherhood or society obedient to God. Participation in the divinity understood in the sense I have

---

62. *Ladies Library*, III.360, excerpting Barrow, 'The Eucharist', in *A Brief Exposition of the Lord's Prayer and the Decalogue*, pp. 238–67, closing with a citation of 1 Corinthians 10:17.

63. *Siris*, §295.

64. The point I am making here is more or less the same as Roberts's when he says in *A Metaphysics for the Mob*, pp. 74–75: 'Our basic epistemological relation to reality must be conceived of as a relation to another mind [. . .] our basic epistemological link to reality is *attitudinal* in nature'. Malebranche, *The Search after Truth*, p. 230, suggests that minds are in God as extension is in space.

just specified is the consistent aim of Berkeley's diverse activities and his ambition to do good as a philosopher and churchman.

Itinerary

The following chapters are an attempt to interpret the documentary remains of Berkeley's life so as to give a characterisation of his thought and to show that his practice also testifies to some of the same overriding concerns—the omnipresence of God, the communication of spirits' intentions for one another through more or less regular and predictable signs, and the mutual dependence of the creation in a system of obligations and responsibilities, with all ultimately depending on God. Some chapters offer chronologically organised accounts of epochs in Berkeley's life, often ending with a change of residence; publications are placed in the context of the philosophical discourses in which they participate, and also of the personal relationships and institutional and political frameworks that sustained Berkeley.

Chapter 2 considers Berkeley's early life in Protestant educational institutions in a period when the effects of the civil wars and the War of the Two Kings were still keenly felt. It reconstructs the syllabus he worked from and the examinations he passed to become a fellow and also relates his early sermons and other writings to the scientific culture of Trinity College. The chapter culminates in an account of the *New Theory of Vision* as an exploration of laws of nature. Chapter 4 places Berkeley's book on moral law as it relates to political obligation in a variety of contexts: his recommendation to John Percival and discussion of the political writings of William Higden; student politics and discipline at TCD; and his frequent insistence on loyalty and the obligations of the clergy to encourage it. It concludes that, whatever the failings of Berkeley's rhetorical strategy, he cannot be considered other than a loyalist to Queen Anne and the Hanoverian succession. Berkeley's personal connection with Tories associated with Jacobitism is evident, however, in the connections he forged in the 1710s, one of the subjects explored in chapter 6. As well as meeting Matthew Prior and the Earl of Peterborough, Berkeley was friendly with the Whigs Richard Steele and Joseph Addison. This period (1713–1716) is one in which Berkeley attempted to use new and different publication media (dialogues, the essay, an anthology) to promote his ideas and then travelled to Italy by accepting an appointment in public life. This visit to Italy, particularly the time Berkeley spent in the trading colony of Livorno, was the occasion of his early engagement with missionary Anglicanism in a commercial world order, as shown in the sermons he preached there.

In a different role, as tutor to St George Ashe Jr, Berkeley returned to Italy as one of a party that completed one of the longest tours of the country of the early eighteenth century, described in chapter 8. Taking in the full length of the peninsula, Berkeley reflected in his notebooks of this period on the relationship between architecture, custom, and modes of political organisation, and he considered the role of artworks in an economy, including the tourist and educational economies. He expressed fairly typical Protestant attitudes to what he regarded as Catholic superstition. There is little trace of the thinking that lay behind the essay on motion that Berkeley composed at this time or Part II of his *Principles of Human Knowledge*, said to have been lost on the road. But his *Essay towards Preventing the Ruine of Great Britain* begins to express his concerns about the corrupting effects of a consumption-based economy. Chapter 10 places Berkeley's scheme of founding St Paul's College, Bermuda, a university for colonists and Native Americans taken from mainland America, in the context of the major existing institutions for colonial and Native education, particularly the College of William and Mary.[65] Though previously often presented as whimsical, I suggest that Berkeley's plans were quite typical of missionary Anglican educational work. The chapter closes by noting the practical difficulty of retiring from a globalised commercial world to an institution of polite learning, given the dependency of such institutions on income from that world, and traces the afterlives of Berkeley's scheme in the island of St Kitts and the colony of Georgia.

From 1713 to 1731, Berkeley travelled widely; then, from 1734 to 1752, he rarely left Cloyne, of which he was made bishop in 1734.

---

65. I use the term 'Native American' rather than 'indigenous American' or 'American Indian' throughout this book without thereby wishing to express a view on the politics of the terminology and in the hope of achieving a respectful neutrality of reference.

Chapters 13 and 15 focus on groups of activities and associated texts from this long period in which Berkeley for the first time in his adult life lived in a majority-Catholic area of Ireland. Chapter 13 considers Berkeley's schemes for converting the Catholic population, persuading them of their loyalty to the House of Hanover in the case of a Jacobite invasion, and training a militia for those same circumstances. Its focus, however, is on the threat to the established church from irreligious statesmen seeking to abolish the Tests (the acts of Parliament that made being a communicant in the Church of England a condition of holding public office) and various groups, from pragmatic politicians to diabolical freethinkers, challenging the political authority of the Church. Berkeley is shown to be a defender of the civil authority of the religious orders and the right to police conscience. Chapter 15 focuses on the therapeutic role Berkeley cultivated as a philosopher and churchman to regulate not only the national economy and the spirit or momentum of the country through his socioeconomic text *The Querist* but also the bodies and minds of individuals through his recommendations for drinking tar-water and the philosophical reflections that make up most of his last major work, *Siris*. Berkeley's mode of writing in *Siris* is rather different to many of his previous works. Besides citing more authorities and deploying a far larger vocabulary, his analysis of the physical world seems very different—he makes aether the first register of spiritual causes in the phenomenal world. Nonetheless, this late text is shown to demonstrate Berkeley's persistent concern with the expressive and communicative nature of the phenomenal world and of the dependence of finite minds on the infinite mind. Berkeley's interest in systematic but not perfectly predictable phenomena, such as the weather, is related to his belief in a free and even idiosyncratic deity.

These are the principal chronological chapters of the book, and a reader wishing to progress through the narrative of Berkeley's life could focus on them. Other chapters of this study focus more exclusively on a work or set of works that are highly characteristic of a particular moment in Berkeley's career and offer an account of the pressures to which Berkeley was responding in composing them. So, in chapter 3, the key features of what Berkeley calls his 'new doctrine' are set out and a reconstruction offered of some elements of the later stages of the formulation of that doctrine, based on Berkeley's philosophical notebooks and the *Manuscript Introduction* to the *Principles of Human Knowledge*. This new doctrine is presented as a response to the philosophical challenge of a dualist conception of the world that seemed to Berkeley to open up a gap between things as they are in themselves and things as we perceive them that had been exploited by sceptics and free-thinkers. It was also a response to some old and some new conceptions of the philosopher as moral-religious guide, as scientist, and as iconoclast. I present what remains for many the counterintuitive central claim of immaterialism as a success from the point of view of the internal consistency of Berkeley's thought, and yet as a (strangely unanticipated) failure from the programmatic and rhetorical point of view of stemming a rising tide of atheism and scepticism.

Chapter 11, focusing on *Alciphron*, considers Berkeley's major work of Christian apology, which came at roughly the midpoint of his career as a writer and churchman. The dialogues present, in the opposition of freethinkers and right-thinkers, the antagonistic habits of thinking and practices of living on which Berkeley had already been writing occasionally for twenty years. The freethinkers were lazy sceptics, quick to doubt biblical chronology and providential history on evidence they did not subject to the same degree of critical scrutiny as scripture. They were badly cultivated humans, to use the dominant agricultural metaphor of the book, and closely aligned with calculating office workers. They are cast into the shade by the arguments of Crito and, most of all, Euphranor, the genteel farmer of elevated and enlarged views. As well as recapitulating arguments for conceiving of vision as a language, the text points forward to Berkeley's concerns of the 1730s onwards—the health of individuals and social groups, the reasonableness of accepting local prejudices when guided by superiors, and the meaning of patriotism and how to practise it. Immediately following this chapter, I survey Berkeley's thinking about language and speech and suggest that throughout his career Berkeley remained interested in their use in motivating and encouraging other agents to adopt attitudes and engage in practices, whether or not the terms employed in a discourse signify ideas, or something else, or nothing at all.

Still other chapters reconstruct aspects of Berkeley's practice that have been little studied or understood from a perspective that stretches across his life, and they draw variously on philosophical writings, miscellaneous published writings, correspondence and manuscripts by Berkeley and others, and testimony about Berkeley. Chapter 5 suggests that Berkeley might be understood as a philosopher of education who worked through formal and informal institutions to shape people, especially the nobility and the clergy, for their public responsibilities. The chapter relates Berkeley's educational projects to works by Fénelon, Mary Astell, and John Locke. Chapter 7 gathers reflections from Berkeley's time in Italy, America, and Cloyne to assess his attitude to Roman Catholics, Native Americans, and enslaved people. He criticised Catholic superstition and ritual for their defiance of the evident regularity of phenomena and the instruction it offers to produce health. I suggest that Berkeley, when planning his Bermuda project, made no obvious effort to engage with the existing body of literature that described the cultural life of Native Americans, and that he made similarly little effort to learn about that culture when he engaged with Native Americans whilst in Rhode Island. Drawing on research by Travis Glasson, I note that Berkeley's time in Rhode Island also likely served to entrench the institution of slavery, and that his vision of the public good happily encompassed temporary servitude and forced labour, which he presented as continuous with slavery (rather than more sharply distinguished from it, as in Locke or Pufendorf).

Berkeley would have spent a great deal of time more or less exclusively in the company of his wife Anne Forster/Berkeley whilst in Rhode Island. In chapter 9, I offer a thorough revision of previous accounts of Anne by studying character sketches written by her and preserved in the Berkeley Papers, as well as translations of Fénelon that, I propose, she produced. I also offer a detailed sketch of Anne Donnellan, to whom Berkeley earlier proposed, and consider the evaluations that both Annes made of Berkeley's character: though they describe him as disputatious, destructive, and slightly disappointing, both remember him with loyalty. Chapter 14, the final thematic chapter, concerns Berkeley's daily habits: his early rising; his presentation in *Three Dialogues*, *Alciphron*, and elsewhere of the philosophical benefits of early rising; his attitudes to eating and drinking; and his reported failure to manage his own appetites. The chapter explores the discipline of Berkeley's daily practice, relating it to the social discipline he was unafraid to evoke. The book closes with chapter 15's study of the relationships between Berkeley's widow and children with Catherine Talbot—the writer, intellectual, and daughter of Berkeley's deceased friend Charles Talbot—and with a conclusion that insists on the provisional nature of my interpretation of Berkeley's personality.

CHAPTER TWO

Birth to the New Doctrine

AFTER SKETCHING THE DETAILS of Berkeley's birth, family context, and early years, this chapter offers an account of his education that draws extensively on the charters and statutes of the educational institutions he attended. I reconstruct the syllabuses and timetables of Kilkenny College and Trinity College Dublin, noting that the statutes and charters of these institutions sought to create specific forms of society, forms of society that emphasised hierarchy and loyalty. At TCD, Berkeley participated in an extracurricular culture of natural historical investigation and discussion. His interest in natural history, astronomy, and mathematical investigation of the forces generating the earth's atmosphere is seen in his earliest writings. Berkeley was also considering questions of theology and morality from a scientific or philosophical perspective in his earliest sermons. The chapter concludes with a discussion of Berkeley's *New Theory of Vision*, in which the study of natural and psychological laws of vision borders on questions of the moral organisation of the world and God's providence in managing the various perceptible phenomena that humans experience.

Birth, Family, and Education

Little is known with any certainty about the first ten years of Berkeley's life or his family. Joseph Stock, author of the first significant biography, gives his birth date as 12 March 1684/85.[1] His father was William Berkeley. Eliza Frinsham/Berkeley, who married Berkeley's son (also George), produced a voluminous preface to posthumously published poems of her own son, George Monck Berkeley, that relates much family tradition. She says that William Berkeley was the collector of customs at an unspecified Irish port. Eliza also calls this 'a more respectable post than in England, noblemen's sons often accepting it'.[2] Luce speculates that William Berkeley combined genteel farming with this post and notes that he is described as 'vexill. equestris' and 'ducis militum' (each phrase suggesting a role in a militia) in the entries in the Trinity College register for two younger sons, Robert and Thomas.[3] Anne, Berkeley's wife from 1728, seems to concur in this estimation of William Berkeley's gentility, as in her interleaved and annotated copy of Stock's biography of her deceased husband she inserts 'Esq' after William's name and notes that he was 'formerly of Salt in Staffordshire'.[4] In the parish records in which Salt was to be found, however, held in the Lichfield Record Office for St Mary, Stafford, there is no record of baptism, marriage, or funeral for a Berkeley for the period 1559 to 1671.[5] Whilst a bill of 10 October 1747 that Berkeley asked his friend Tom Prior to enter to test the legitimacy of the will of a cousin specifies Staffordshire as the county of Berkeley's grandfather's residence, a gap is left in the document where one might expect a town to be named.[6]

The geographical origin of the Berkeley family may have a political relevance. Charles I had retreated to Staffordshire after defeat at the battle of Worcester in 1651, and the county had Jacobite

---

1. Stock, *An Account of the Life of George Berkeley*, p. 2.

2. Eliza Berkeley, preface to Berkeley, *Poems*, p. ccclxxii (n).

3. Luce, p. 22.

4. TCD MS 5936, Stock, *An Account of the Life of George Berkeley*, opposite p. 1.

5. My thanks to Anita Caithness of the Lichfield Record Office for this information.

6. See letters 347, 349, 354; and National Archives, C 11/1091/9. The same is true of a further bill dated 27 January 1748 (National Archives, C 11/1093/9).

associations in the eighteenth century.[7] Eliza relates that William Berkeley, the grandfather, 'expended a large fortune in the service of King Charles the First, and in remitting money to King Charles the Second and his brothers'. The only return on this investment was, apparently, a collectorship like that his son would go on to hold. 'This occasioned the old gentleman's leaving his *malediction* on any descendent of his, who should ever, in *any way*, assist *any* Monarch'.[8] Berkeley's recent ancestors, then, may have been Stuart loyalists, even if of a disgruntled kind. Berkeley's own relation to the dynastic politics of his time is discussed frequently in this book.

No correspondence between Berkeley and his parents is known, nor with his five brothers. The document of 1747 just cited provides places of residence for Berkeley's surviving siblings: Rowland in Thomastown; William in Belturbet, County Cavan, but living in the City of London; Ralph, also in Thomastown; and Robert, who was rector of Middleton, in Berkeley's diocese of Cloyne. Very little is known of Rowland or Ralph Berkeley. There is little mention of William in Berkeley's correspondence, but he is identified as a coronet, and Eliza Berkeley notes that he served as a military officer in Fife, Scotland, during the Jacobite conflict of 1745. His profession may therefore bear upon Berkeley's thinking about military matters at the same period. A George Berkeley whose place of birth is given as Cloyne entered TCD on 25 April 1752. Luce says that George arrived from Belturbet School, though the entrance book says only that he was educated by Dr Irwin.[9] Luce suggests that this was the same George Berkeley to whom a Plato was presented by George Berkeley, Bishop of Cloyne, 21 November 1751, and notes that the book is now in the TCD library. If Irwin taught at Belturbet, this could then be William Berkeley's son, George's nephew. It is likely the same George Berkeley, identified as our George Berkeley's nephew, who joined the Berkeley family and other guests in a visit to John Percival's Lohort estate in 1750.[10] Robert worked

7. Staffordshire was home to one of the first Jacobite clubs, founded in 1699. See Monod, 'Jacobitism and Country Principles', p. 306; see also Monod, 'Voyage out of Staffordshire'.

8. Eliza Berkeley, preface to Berkeley, *Poems*, p. ccclxxii (n).

9. Luce, p. 28; TCD MUN V 23/3, p. 199.

10. BL MS Add 47006, ff. 76–77, William Cooley to Percival, 4 September 1750. The letter is reprinted by Luce, pp. 212–13.

alongside George in Cloyne, as a rector and in various administrative positions. It seems likely that Robert and George shared views on ecclesiastical organisation and management. Another brother, Thomas, is known only for being condemned to death for bigamy in 1726. It seems likely that the sentence was not carried out, partly thanks to the intervention of friends of Berkeley. Though little can be said about Berkeley's brothers, they nonetheless make points of reference for him over the course of his career.

One other connection that may have been inherited through his grandparents was to Archbishop James Ussher (1581–1656), one of the first scholars to enter Trinity College Dublin, later a fellow, and author of one of the most influential works of ancient chronology, in which he dated the creation of the world to 23 October, 4004 BC.[11] Eliza Berkeley reports her son's sense of lineage from Archbishop Ussher and claims that George Berkeley was his 'nephew'.[12] Attempts to confirm this connection have not yet been successful.[13] If the connection is actual, it may have had some influence

11. Ford, 'Ussher, James (1581–1656)'.

12. Eliza Berkeley, preface to Berkeley, *Poems*, p. ccclxxiii and note.

13. Luce interprets the connection as follows: John Stearne, a senior fellow at Trinity, was Ussher's great-nephew, and brother to a Margaret who married a Dublin brewer (Francis Sotherne) and bore Elisabeth, who may later have married a William Berkeley (Luce, p. 23). Elizabeth Southerne (as the name is spelt in the church record), daughter of Francis and an otherwise unnamed Mrs Southerne, was baptised on 27 March 1655; see *Parish Register: Baptisms*, p. 34, record DU-CI-BA-150695, http://churchrecords.irishgenealogy.ie/churchrecords/details/d233f60150694 (accessed 11 March 2015). This Elizabeth is unlikely to have been George Berkeley's mother, as Luce speculates. Elizabeth Southerne may have borne children in the 1680s, but Luce records Thomas's year of birth as 1704. Moreover, if, as Luce seems to conjecture, an Elizabeth Berkeley, 'wife of Will. Berkeley, merchant' whose burial is recorded in the same parish register on 24 October 1694, is the same Elizabeth who was Berkeley's mother, she is even less likely to have borne Thomas Berkeley, and her early death conflicts with the report of Eliza Frinsham/Berkeley, who says (and Luce reproduces her comment) that Berkeley's parents lived to see six sons bred up gentlemen and died in the same week, aged around ninety; see *Parish Register: Burials*, p. 410, record DU-CI-BU-186657, http://churchrecords.irishgenealogy.ie/churchrecords/details/d5d08f0417708 (accessed 11 March 2015); Eliza Berkeley, preface to Berkeley, *Poems*, pp. ccclxxii, ccclxxiii (n), ccccxcviii; Luce, p. 22. Patrick Kelly, in personal correspondence, has suggested that a second John Stearne, who was bishop of Clogher to his death in 1745, was the brother of Berkeley's grandmother, but he has also noted that the absence of any mention of a family connection between the two men when both were serving as bishops mitigates against the possibility. 'The Life of Thomas Southerne', in Jordan and Love, eds., *The Works of Thomas Southerne*, I.xi, suggests that Elizabeth Southerne lived only two

on one important relationship for Berkeley. Anne Donnellan, to whom Berkeley proposed (at an unknown date), was the daughter of Nehemiah and Martha Donnellan, and Martha had been born an Ussher. The social connection was probably made through the Percivals.[14] The possibility that they were both descended from the same renowned family may have encouraged their intimacy.

Where the Berkeleys were living at the time of George's birth and during his early life is not known with certainty. Stock identifies William Berkeley Sr as from Thomastown, as does the bill entered on 19 October 1747 and mentioned earlier. (Thomastown is a few miles southeast of Kilkenny city.) Stock says that Berkeley was born at 'Kilcrin near Thomastown'. (Kilcrin is just to the west of Kilkenny city.) There is no obvious way to adjudicate between these statements.[15]

It is certain that Berkeley attended Kilkenny College. The register reads 'George Berkley, Gent: Aged 11 years Entered the second Class, July 17: 1696'.[16] Keeping such a register was one of the duties assigned to the master of Kilkenny College in its revised statutes, which date from 18 March 1684/85, six days after Berkeley's birth.[17] After the refoundation of the school around 1667, the duke of Ormond, the school's patron, asked Edward Hinton to replace the Rev Dr Henry Ryder as master. Hinton had previously worked at a school in Witney, Oxfordshire, and it has been suggested that

years. I thank Patrick Kelly for pointing me to this source. Kelly also notes that if Elizabeth Southerne was Berkeley's mother, Thomas Southerne would have been his uncle, and it would therefore be strange that no mention was made of this relationship when Thomas Southerne was close to Swift and his circle in London in the 1710s and Dublin in the 1730s, both scenes on which Berkeley could have been present (see *Works of Southerne*, I.xxxiii).

14. See March, 'Anne Donnellan'.

15. Luce attempts to adjudicate between this assertion, the fact that Berkeley's geographical origin is given as 'Kilkenny' in the Trinity College register, and the claim made in a topographical survey of 1802 that Dysart Castle was the birthplace of Berkeley (Tighe, *Statistical Observations Relative to the County of Kilkenny*, p. 638). He suggests that Kilcrene was Berkeley's birthplace, but that he was brought up at Dysart. Recent excavations provide evidence of there having been a late-seventeenth-century dwelling on the site, and reports on those excavations refer to that dwelling as the 'Berkeley house' (Murtagh and Hall, '1989:061—"Dysart", Dysart, Kilkenny'). But there is no obvious reason to accept Stock's Kilcrin over Dysart, nor indeed any strong reason to accept either.

16. TCD MS 2019, f. 4v.

17. TCD MS MUN-P-1-518a.

its statutes, dating from 1663, guided Ormond in drafting those for Kilkenny.[18] If the statutes were adhered to up to and including the time of Berkeley's days at Kilkenny College, some picture of his time there can be sketched.

Edward Hinton was named as master in the 18 March 1684/85 statutes. There were educational and politico-religious qualifications for his role:

> [T]here shall forever be a Master constantly resident and attending the Duties of the said Schoole who shall at least bee a Master of Arts either here in Ireland or of one of the Universities of England, a person of good life and reputation, well skilled in humanity and Grammar learning, Loyall and Orthodox, who shall take the Oathes of Allgeance [*sic*] and supremacy and Conforme to the doctrine & discipline of the Church of Ireland as it is now established by law[.]

An usher, who was to hold at least a bachelor of arts degree and have good manners, was to be appointed to assist the master. The qualifications of appointees were to be assessed by 'Visitors to the School', specified as Thomas Otway, bishop of Ossory (died 1693); Narcissus Marsh, bishop of Leighlin and Ferns (and archbishop of Dublin by 1694); and Robert Huntington, provost of Trinity College Dublin, who moved to Essex in 1692. These visitors would also inspect the school once a year: between eight and twelve o'clock on the designated morning, they would have the statutes read; examine the pupils; and enquire after the performance of the master and usher, the methods of instruction used, and what would now be called the ethos ('the Methods Usages and Customes') of the school. They would also inspect the buildings, land, and trees attached to the school. The visitors were to advise the master of any changes required, and the master might ultimately be removed from his post by the governor if they were not acted on. Though all of the visitors named in the statutes had died or moved to other posts by the time Berkeley attended the school, he may have been present at these official visits, with their palpable connection to the ecclesiastical and academic hierarchies of Protestant Ireland.

18. Welch, 'Edward Hinton'.

To be admitted to Kilkenny College, Berkeley should 'have first read [his] Accidence & [be] fitt to Enter upon Grammar Learning'. That is, he should have had a basic understanding of the parts of speech in Latin and have been in a position to move on to more advanced syntactic study of Latin literary texts.[19] As Berkeley entered the second class, it is possible he was a little further on with his studies. The master was appointed 'to Instruct the Scholars in Religion and Learning in the Latine Greek and Hebrew Languages as also in oratory and Poetry according to the best method'. Oratory and poetry were not prescribed by the charter for Witney School, suggesting the desire for a broad curriculum at Kilkenny.[20] The entrance book for Trinity records that Berkeley had been taught by Hinton himself. Hinton had a particular reputation as a teacher of Greek: Dryden admired the skills of another student of Hinton, the dramatist William Congreve.[21] (The teaching of Greek was also one of Berkeley's lifelong interests: he established a Greek medal to be awarded at Trinity in 1734 and made provision for it to be awarded in perpetuity in 1752.)[22] After four years at Kilkenny, Berkeley's Latin and Greek would have been good, and there is no reason to assume he did not have some Hebrew as well, given its mention in the statutes, and the fact that Huntington, the visitor and provost of Trinity, had studied Hebrew and Arabic under Edward Pococke at Oxford, worked as a chaplain at Aleppo, learnt Arabic and Turkish, and collected manuscripts in the ancient Middle Eastern languages for himself, Narcissus Marsh, and others.[23]

Hard work on the part of teacher and pupil were required if the latter was to leave the school with Latin, Greek, and Hebrew. An earlier pupil, and later a friend of Berkeley's, Jonathan Swift, wrote to his friend Charles Ford, saying that he 'formerly used to envy my own Happiness—when I was a Schoolboy, the delicious Holidays, the Saterday afternoon, and the charming Custards in a blind Alley; I never considerd the Confinement ten hours a day, to nouns & Verbs,

19. For this definition of 'accidence', see Brinsley, *The Posing of the Parts*, p. 1. Welch, 'A History of Kilkenny College', p. 116, takes the statute to refer to English accidence.

20. Welch, 'A History of Kilkenny College', p. 130.

21. Welch, 'Edward Hinton'.

22. Luce, p. 42.

23. Hamilton, 'Huntington, Robert '.

the Terror of the Rod, the bloddy Noses, and broken Shins'[.][24]
The programme of study was intense. School could 'breake up [. . .]
Eight dayes before Christmas and [. . .] three dayes before Easter
and Whitsuntide'. In session, pupils were to be present from 6:00 to
11:00 a.m., March to September; from 7:00 a.m. (or as soon as the
gates of Kilkenny city opened) to 11:00 a.m., September to March;
and from 1:00 to 5:00 p.m. all year, 'the afternoons of Thursdayes
and Saturdayes excepted, which shall bee alwaise allowed for Recreation'. These afternoons could have been spent on Pigeon House
Meadow, the field adjoining the schoolhouse, which the master was
told to make available to the scholars for that purpose. From September to March, the scholars would stay an extra hour on Saturday
mornings to learn the Catechism; from March to September, they
were required to attend on Sunday mornings for that purpose, and
afterwards to accompany the master and usher to church. There
seems to have been an extraordinary provision for additional holidays: 'the Master shall grant no Playday ~ except to such as shall pay
[?downe] [?tenn] shillings into the Masters hands to bee by him
im·ediatly disposd of to the most indigent and deserving Lads of
his School'. Play is paid for by charity. The statutes also testify to the
presence of punishment. Discipline for unruly behaviour (including
shutting out the instructors or damaging school property) was the
subject of 'Exemplary Punishment', followed by expulsion for persistent offenders.

If anyone offered to pay for the board of 'ingenious and orderly
Lads', the statutes demanded that they be taught for free, as would
be anyone selected by Ormond or another benefactor as one of the
'Ormond Schollars' (who might also proceed to Trinity, if fit to do
so). The children of the duke's servants were also to be educated
free. The master was allowed to charge 'according to the Rates
and Usages of the most [?remarquable] Schoole in Dublin both
for Entrance and Schooling', but children with parents who inhabited Kilkenny city or one of its 'liberties' when the child was born
would be given half-price rates. The liberties of Kilkenny included
six parishes (St John's, St Mary's, St Canice, St Patrick's, St Maul's,

24. Swift to Charles Ford, 12 November 1708, in Wooley, ed., *The Correspondence of
Jonathan Swift*, I(1999).217, cited in Welch, 'A History of Kilkenny College', p. 86.

and Dunmore), but given uncertainty over the Berkeley family's residence in 1684/85, it is speculation under which rate Berkeley may have studied. Hinton was to receive £140 annually as salary for his post.

Being a student at Kilkenny initiated Berkeley into a life of study and piety that he reproduced in various ways throughout his own diverse career as an educator—at Trinity, in print, and as a churchman, private tutor, husband and father, administrator, and projector. He was inured to long hours of work devoted to linguistic and literary study. He may have been in the presence of visitors from Trinity College and the church hierarchy and would have become familiar with the established means of progression from Kilkenny to Trinity. He studied most of the year, six or seven days a week, with outdoor recreation on two afternoons.

A different document, setting out the 'Rules to be observed by ye the professors of my College in Kilkenny' (with some text scored through and mostly illegible mentions of Lord Bishop Ossory), has been identified as describing rules for a Catholic college founded by James II in 1690 at the request of William Daton, who was running a Catholic educational institution in Kilkenny, and James Phelan, Catholic bishop of Ossory when Hinton (and his employer Ormond) had left Ireland and vacated the school buildings.[25] The charter for this foundation exists and has been confirmed as enacted.[26] Some of the rules are noted here for comparative purposes. The rules for professors give precise instructions on the means of inculcating the scholars in piety:

> The teachers of Colledges are to know yt piety is ye cheif thing they ought to teach, & all other things yt are taught, are nothing but means to attaine yt end; & therefore piety is to be taught by word & example, in all occasion in generall & particularly in ye following exercises.
>
> 1. the teachers are to get up a half an hour ^at least before ye boarders & spend at least a half an hour in mentall prayer togeather in ye roome where ye boarders come to ye vocall prayer & to remain there untill ye boarders come yt they may see so good an example to imitat; this

25. TCD MS 2016.

26. See Leonard, 'Kilkenny's Short-Lived University'; Connolly, 'The Royal College at Kilkenny, 1690'.

being very easy & beneficiall, no one ought to forgoe it or be cold or negligent to appeare togeather w.th ye rest, if he were not very sick; & to be notably remisse at yt exercise, is a fault whereof ye ordinary is to be informed; when ye boarders come those yt have not ye breviary to say ought to say ye prayers w.th ye scholars & give them good example by often going to confession & comunion. ye mentall prayer may ^be omitted ye playdays & made an hour later ye holy days & Sundays.

Professors were to move to classes at the same time, as a group, to be courteous but distant, avoiding any passion or lightness. They must 'nev^r make ye Scholars their camarades, by familiarity yt denotes equality & makes fellows as laughing chatting playing togeather & such other familiaritys, wherein ye Scholars may discover any weaknesse in ye master, or diminish his ^{their} esteeme for him, no man being fitter to teache & persuade then he who is well possess'd of his auditors esteeme'. They were always to be diligent, never excuse themselves from teaching duties on account of study commitments, never leave the scholars idle ('if scholars be neglected but one hour a day, it will give them an occasion of idleness & takeing of liberty'); they were to be collegial and supportive, but also to regard it as their duty to report on and admonish privately any omission that might damage the aims of the school: 'every ^one ought to be watchfull on all occasions of ye scholars, servants household affaires &c. & when they see any thing amisse or that may be reformed to give notice thereof to him whose charge it is to looke after it, w.th remonstrances of ye utility'. Piety was at the centre of this educational mission.

The conflicts of the late 1680s that led to Hinton abandoning the school also left their mark on Trinity College, which was used as a barracks and prison by the Jacobite army in September 1689.[27] George Browne, provost just before Berkeley's time at Trinity, is said to have died in 1699 of an injury sustained in 1698 when attempting to admonish disorderly students, who proceeded to riot.[28] Berkeley entered Trinity College as a pensioner on 21 March 1699/1700, his tutor being Joseph Hall.[29] It was not a very large establishment:

27. McDowell and Webb, *Trinity College Dublin 1592–1952*, p. 29.
28. Luce, *Trinity College Dublin*, p. 37.
29. See TCD MUN V 23/1, digitised by TCD Library Imaging Services, p. 222.

'In 1700 the academic staff consisted of nineteen persons—the Provost, seventeen Fellows and the Regius Professor of Physic. The Professorships of Divinity and of Civil and Canon Law, as well as the Donegall lectureship in Mathematics, were also in existence at this time, but these three posts were always held by Fellows'.[30] But the college was integrally involved in the elite intellectual culture of Dublin, and Berkeley's personal and intellectual connections to key staff members, including several provosts past and present, signal the nature of his participation in that culture. The provost when Berkeley arrived was Peter Browne, who had already written his *Letter in Answer to a Book Entitled, Christianity Not Mysterious* (1697), a response to the work of John Toland. It was supposedly on account of this book that Browne was recommended for the role of provost by Narcissus Marsh, who, as well as being a visitor at Kilkenny College, had been provost at Trinity himself, from 1679 to 1683. Marsh had been succeeded by Huntington, also a visitor at Kilkenny, and Huntington was succeeded by St George Ashe, with whom Berkeley became closely connected.[31]

TCD must have been a still more formative institution for Berkeley than Kilkenny College. The historians of the college note the lack of clear evidence concerning the curriculum in the late seventeenth century, but suggest that, whilst the statutes drafted by Archbishop Laud would still formally have been in place, it was most likely that recent tendencies in scholarship would have been reflected in the college's syllabus, particularly under St George Ashe, the man who would ordain Berkeley in 1710 and with whose son Berkeley toured Italy in the late 1710s.[32] Locke's *Essay* was introduced by Ashe in 1692. William Molyneux wrote to Locke on 20 December 1692 that 'I was the First that recommended and lent to the Reverend Provost of Our University Dr Ashe, a most Learned and Ingenious Man, Your Essay, with which he was so wonderfully pleased and satisfyd, that he has Orderd it to be read by the Batchelors in the Colledge, and strictly examines them in their Progress therein'.[33] McDowell and Webb paraphrase a 1703 letter from a student at Trinity who

30. McDowell and Webb, *Trinity College Dublin 1592–1952*, p. 41.

31. See Trinity College Dublin, "Former Provosts," https://www.tcd.ie/provost/history/former-provosts/ (accessed 14 July 2019).

32. McDowell and Webb, *Trinity College Dublin 1592–1952*, p. 31.

33. Locke, *The Correspondence of John Locke*, pp. 601–2.

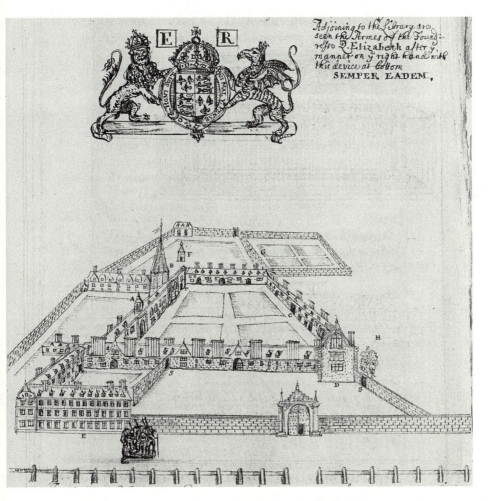

FIGURE 2.1. Thomas Dineley, 'Drawing of Trinity College', prior to 1682,
courtesy of the National Library of Ireland

reported that 'philosophical teaching consists of a farrago of con-
flicting hypotheses from Aristotle, Descartes, Colbert, Epicurus,
Gassendi, Malebranche and Locke. Plato, he asserts, was made
little of, and Bacon and Boyle ignored'.[34] Berkeley's early works
refer to Gassendi, Descartes, Locke, and Malebranche.

34. McDowell and Webb, *Trinity College Dublin 1592-1952*, p. 32. The letter is by John
Shadwell, Bodleian Library, MS Rawl[inson] D.842, f. 35, copied as TCD MS 7971/misc.
aut. 271. Luce, *Trinity College Dublin*, p. 39, mentions the letter.

McDowell and Webb state that the earliest date for which a more or less complete syllabus is available is 1736. I reproduce their efficient summary of the manuscript source:

> In Classics the four years' reading covers a full and varied course: the Aeneid and Georgics, Horace, Juvenal, Terence, all Livy, Tacitus, Suetonius, Sallust, Caesar, some Cicero or Pliny, Velleius and Justin; the Iliad and Odyssey, three plays of Sophocles, Lucian, Demosthenes, Longinus on the Sublime, some Xenophon and Theocritus and one or two other authors. [. . .] In 1736 the undergraduate course in Science was clearly still modelled on the course prescribed by Laud a century before. Logic was studied in the first two years, natural science in the third and ethics in the fourth. But the textbooks had been changed, and Aristotle, though his influence still lingered, was no longer studied directly.
>
> Three separate works on logic are prescribed. The Junior Freshman year was devoted entirely to the *Institutiones logicae* of Burgersdicius; the Senior Freshmen studied Le Clerc's *Logica, sive ars ratiocinandi* and extracts from the *Logica* of Smiglecius. [. . .] Burgersdicius and Smiglecius were the two most distinguished of the *Systematici*, the logicians of the early seventeenth century, who, though they usually considered themselves to be Aristotelian and anti-Ramist, had been to some extent influenced by both sides in the Ramist controversy. Burgersdicius (or Burgersdijk) was a professor at Leyden, who published his treatise there in 1626; it was reprinted at Cambridge in 1637 and several times later. Smiglecius (Śmiglecki), a Polish Jesuit, published his *Logica* in 1618. The two books are essentially similar in their aims and methods, though that by Smiglecius is the more detailed and discursive; and both contain, as well as what we understand by logic today, a good deal of grammar and metaphysics. [. . .] Lockian logic was, however, represented in the course which we are considering by Le Clerc, a French Protestant theologian and polymath who settled in Amsterdam and there made friends with Locke during his period of exile. His *Logic* and his *Physics* [. . .] had been published in English editions in 1692 and 1700 respectively, and both were well known at Cambridge.
>
> The prescribed books for the natural science of the Junior Sophister year were Wells's *Astronomy*, the *Universal geography* of Varenius, part of the *Physics* of Le Clerc, and Colbert's *General physics*. [. . .]

Geometry was not introduced into the undergraduate course until about 1760, and algebra not until 1808. [. . .] the schools, in Ireland as in England, taught little but classics. [. . .] The Science of the final year consisted of ethics and metaphysics; and once more four books are prescribed, one for each term. They are the *Ethics* of Eustachius, selections from the *Metaphysics* of Baronius, Sanderson's *Prelections* and "the small Puffendorf" [said to be *Whole Duty of Man*].[35]

Wells's *Astronomy* (1712) is the only book on this syllabus that was not published before Berkeley entered as a student.[36] McDowell and Webb omit Hesiod, Anacreon, Pythagoras, and Epictetus (with the Table of Cebes) from the list of humanities texts studied.[37] Their listing of the science course is complete.

Some evidence suggests that the syllabus was quite stable in the period from the late seventeenth century to the second quarter of the eighteenth century. Josias Haydock, a student who moved from Kilkenny to Trinity in 1677, twenty-three years before Berkeley, kept a commonplace book in which he recorded the college statutes, some of his course in comparative Greek and Latin syntax, and an outline of Roman history.[38] The commonplace book also includes a 'Catalogus Librorum'. Haydock's list includes three works by Descartes, the *Principles of Philosophy, On Man,* and *Meditations*; Śmiglecki and Burgersdijk; and works on logic by Heerebord, Zabarella, and Didacus.[39] If Haydock was reading Descartes, Burgersdijk, and Śmiglecki in the late 1670s, Descartes is mentioned by

35. McDowell and Webb, *Trinity College Dublin 1592–1952*, pp. 45–48.

36. I have not, however, been able to identify a text corresponding to Colbert's *General Physics*. Perhaps the similarities with the Cambridge syllabus as described by Daniel Waterland in 1706 are not deeply surprising. Students there also used Burgersdicius in the first year, had Locke's *Essay* in the second year, some Pufendorf in the third year, and Baronius's *Metaphysics* in the fourth year. There are several texts in mathematics, physics, astronomy, and optics. See Hans, *New Trends in Education in the Eighteenth Century*, p. 51.

37. TCD MS MUN V 27, f. 1r–v. The volume also contains a 'list of Questions to be disputed upon in Hall', all introduced with '*an*' (whether), and including the following Berkeleian topics: 'ideae nostrae sunt similes objectis a quibus [?]excitantur' (f. 2v), 'materia sit divisibilis in infinitum' (f. 3r).

38. TCD MS 2642, beginning ff. 112r and 152r, respectively.

39. TCD MS 2642, ff. 104r–109r; 104r; 104v, 105r; 105r, 107v.

Shadwell in 1703, and the two logicians were set reading in what is likely to be a syllabus from the 1730s, it is probable that all three authors were part of the syllabus in Berkeley's time as a student, which fell in the middle of that date range.

In 1692, William Molyneux also hinted that requirement by statute to teach the older philosophy was still felt to be in force, even though the impetus to introduce new texts, particularly in logic, was active:

> [A] verbose Philosophy [i.e., scholasticism] is that, which for many Generations prevail'd in the World: This it is, which is injoyn'd to be read and studied in our Colleges and Academies, by the Statutes and Charters thereof; which in this Particular, to the apparent Hindrance of the Advancement of real and useful Knowledge, do yet remain unaltered in our Universities: wherein the first years of young Students may be imploy'd with much more Advantage by prosecuting other Methods. [. . .] *Logick* has put on a Countenance clearly different from what it appeared in formerly: How unlike is its shape in the *Ars Cogitandi* [of Le Clerc], *Recherches de la Verite* [of Malebranche], &c. from what it appears in *Smigletius*, and the Commentators on *Aristotle*? But to none do we owe for a greater Advancement in this Part of Philosophy, than to the incomparable Mr. *Locke*[.]⁴⁰

There is regret here that statute forbade, or at least slowed, the abandonment of the old philosophy in favour of the new, as well as further evidence of Śmiglecki's place on the TCD syllabus in the 1690s and the esteem accorded Le Clerc, Malebranche, and Locke.

According to the college statutes, the syllabus was delivered by lecture, followed by examination, with the purpose of examination being that 'by way of Questions and Answers [the lecturer] clearly explain, repeat, and often inculcate, the same Thing, nor shall he be satisfied, 'till the Scholar in some Measure perceives and understands the thing proposed'.⁴¹ In addition to being taken through the prescribed course by lecture and examination, scholars would dispute three times a week, provide a Latin comment on the lectures, and compose on a theme or make a Latin version of an English text

---

40. Molyneux, *Dioptrica Nova*, sig. A2r–v.
41. Bolton, *A Translation of the Charter and Statutes*, p. 68.

every week. Students were to be instructed in Greek, and senior students also in Hebrew, for three hours a week in each language. There were regular disputations and declamations by different levels of students, by bachelors on a subject in mathematics, metaphysics, or physics, by masters on divinity. Prayers were scheduled three times a day (6:00 a.m., 10:00 a.m., and 4:00 p.m.), along with sermons after prayers on Sunday and Catechism for half an hour on Saturday afternoons. Though the four-term academic year allowed for a recess or vacation from 9 July to 1 October, it was suggested that students in the earlier stages of their career should be disputing frequently during this period in order to be better prepared for the class in logic.[42]

The statutes at Trinity emphasised still more than those of Kilkenny the need for politically and religiously loyal officeholders. They might do so in part because they also advertised more strongly than Kilkenny the fact that the College was itself a society, and as such ought to embody social order. The statutes make clear that hierarchy was the basis of order. The original Elizabethan statutes of the college were being revised 'forasmuch as to the Preservation of any Society, good Laws are in the first Place necessary for the pious and happy Government of the same'.[43] Description of the provost's role was an opportunity to point to the necessity of a sovereign individual: 'The Nature of a Body Politic requires, that in the first Place a fit head be appointed, by whom the rest of the Members may be directed to the common Good of the whole Body[.] [. . .] Forasmuch as in every well-constituted Society a parity of Members is principally to be avoided, as tending to Anarchy and universal Confusion, therefore we appoint the Provost head of this Society'.[44] Fellows were to be more or less senior according to the 'Order and Priority of their Degree'. Juniors would give place to seniors in conversation. The more senior of the junior fellows

42. Ibid., pp. 69–78.

43. Ibid., p. 25.

44. Ibid., pp. 27, 31. *Ladies Library*, III.211, excerpting John Scott, *The Christian Life*, also asserts the evident value of social hierarchy: 'As we are *rational Creatures* related to one another, we are oblig'd modestly to submit to our *Superiors*, and chearuflly to condescend to our *Inferiors*, in those respective *Societies* of which we are *Members*. It being necessary to the Order and End of all *Societies*, that their Members shou'd be distinguished into *superior* and *inferior* Ranks and Stations'.

would receive preference when it came to promotion.[45] Practical deference would be shown to the head of the institution: 'all shall rise up to the Provost, whenever he comes into any Place of assembling, nor shall they pass by him any where without bending their Body'.[46] This last custom seems to have remained in place for seventy years, if not more, as John Shadwell, in the letter describing the syllabus mentioned earlier, also 'remarks on the respect shown to the Provost. If the Provost was present in any meeting (*curia*) every one under the degree of doctor, except noblemen and noblemen's sons, was bare-headed: when he entered the chapel or the examination hall, all rose to their feet'.[47]

However, as was also seen at Kilkenny, the emphasis on hierarchy was combined with an impulse to distribute the goods of education. In the choice of scholars for financial support, those from areas where the college held land (emphasising the socioeconomic connection between the college and the commonwealth) and from amongst them those who were least wealthy were to be given preference, and their tutors were to charge them less than other students. Whereas most scholars would receive ten shillings a year, 'the Native Scholars, (who shall be always chosen out of the poorest, if they be deserving) shall be allowed three Pounds Sterling', when the provost's salary was £100.[48] Berkeley is listed as a scholar on 1 June 1702, receiving a £3 grant.[49] With the statutes being read publicly every term, Berkeley would have been closely familiar with them, and the principles of strict academic and social hierarchy combined with a sense of socioeconomic integration and mutual obligation are not distant from those he would give life to in his own educational and other projects.

The statutes required students to have the written permission of their tutor for any trip to Dublin city and listed punishments for those making unauthorised visits and for student recreations such as visiting taverns.[50] The minute books of board meetings con-

45. Bolton, *A Translation of the Charter and Statutes*, p. 39.
46. Ibid., p. 55.
47. McNeill, 'Rawlinson Manuscripts (Class D)', p. 74.
48. Bolton, *A Translation of the Charter and Statutes*, pp. 34, 52; p. 93.
49. TCD MUN V-5-2, f. 196r (p. 385).
50. Bolton, *A Translation of the Charter and Statutes*, pp. 55-56.

tain many notes of students punished for drinking, fighting, and rioting.[51] Berkeley's life in the college, however, was likely to have been fairly quiet. In 1712, after five years as a fellow, he referred to his existence as that of 'a sort of monk or recluse in a college'.[52] One of the roles Berkeley took on as a fellow was librarian, from 20 November 1709 for a year. The seventeenth-century statutes say that this role should be assumed by a junior fellow or scholar 'who is careful, who generally keeps at home, is given to Study, and a lover of Books'.[53] Berkeley would have needed to be studious in order to succeed in the fellowship examination for the post.[54] After it became available on 24 September 1706—when 'Mr. William Mullart was nominated to the college living of Clinish, and vacated his fellowship'—Berkeley was awarded the post on 9 June 1707.[55] The election process followed a four-day examination close in form to that for choosing scholars, and as with scholars, financial background and moral character could be taken into account:

> [T]he Scholars of the College shall always have the preference, and in like Manner the Poorer shall be preferred to the richer, the more Learned to the less Learned, the more Virtuous to the less Virtuous, provided they be equal in other Respects. [. . .] The four Days preceding that of the Election, from Eight of the Clock in the Forenoon to Ten, and from Two in the Afternoon to Four, all the Electors shall carefully examine what Progress the several Candidates, whether they be Batchelors or Masters, have made in Learning. On the first Day in Logic and Mathematicks: on the second, in Philosophy, both Natural and Moral; on the third in the Knowledge of Languages, in History, and the Poets, and all Kind of Humanity; on the fourth, in Writing on a Theme, and composing Verses.[56]

Stock says that Berkeley was admitted as a fellow for having 'sustained with honour the very trying examination, which the

---

51. See TCD MUN V-5-2, f. 184v (p. 362) and f. 188r (p. 369), for example.

52. Letter 34, Berkeley to Percival, 17 May 1712, p. 72.

53. Bolton, *A Translation of the Charter and Statutes*, p. 89.

54. TCD MUN V-5-2, f. 209r (p. 411).

55. Luce, p. 37.

56. Bolton, *A Translation of the Charter and Statutes*, pp. 37–38.

candidates for that preferment are by the statutes required to undergo'.[57] As a fellow himself, Stock's use of the present tense suggests that the fellowship examination as set out in the statutes was a live tradition into the 1760s. The topics on which Berkeley is known to have been exercising himself in the years leading up to this fellowship examination were mathematics and natural philosophy, two subjects that received greater emphasis in the final years of the curriculum and may have been regarded as more advanced knowledge. Or it may be that Berkeley's career to date had provided him with such solid foundations in humanity that he felt secure in those subjects.

Intellectual culture at the college was closely interwoven with the broader civic expression of scientific and philosophical curiosity exemplified in the activities of the Dublin Philosophical Society. William Molyneux, who had already published a translation of Descartes's *Meditations* and would later write an important treatise in optics, is credited with forming this group in 1683. He had previously been meeting with Narcissus Marsh to work on an Irish contribution to an atlas of natural history; he then sought out St George Ashe as a participant and initiated informal meetings in a coffeehouse in October 1682. In 1683, Provost Huntington invited the group to meet in his rooms at Trinity.[58] William King was also a member. The Dublin Philosophical Society was in close correspondence with the Royal Society in London and the Oxford Philosophical Society, Marsh and Huntington having previously been fellows in Oxford colleges.[59] The Society was in abeyance between the death of Molyneux in 1698 and its refoundation by his son Samuel in 1707.[60] Its activities must, however, have shaped the ways in which scientific and philosophical debate was conducted, and the sense of what such debate was for. Berkeley was in close personal contact with these people who were expressing a new vision for the sciences based on a rejection of canting scholastic philosophy, and they explicitly recognised the Royal Society as a model. Ashe wrote

57. Stock, *An Account of the Life of George Berkeley*, p. 2.

58. Hoppen, 'The Papers of the Dublin Philosophical Society: Introductory Material and Index', pp. 166–67.

59. Ibid., pp. 175–76.

60. Hoppen, *Common Scientist*, pp. 185–86, 195–97.

a speech on the occasion of Lord Clarendon recommending the Dublin Philosophical Society, in which he reflected on the encouragement given to learning by Charles II and James II:

> Captive truth was rescued from its former bondage, & clouded knowledge began to shine more bright; when instead of words and empty speculations were introduc'd things and Experiments, and the beautifull bosome of nature was exposed to view, where we might enter into its Guarden, tast of its fruits, satisfy our selves with its plenty, instead of Idle talking and wandering under its fruitless shadows; Then Philosophy was admitted into our palaces and our Courts, began to ke^e^p the best Company, to refine its fashion and appearance, and to become the Employment of the rich and of the great.

The old philosophers thought it 'the gravest piece of Science to contemn the use of Man-kind', whereas Ashe's emphasis was very much on the 'useful' aspects of the Society's investigations.[61] This new learning would be both polite and useful, appealing to the rich and great, but not despising practical life.

The minutes of the meetings of the Society combine reports on subjects of pure scientific interest with more practically oriented concerns and speculative experiments. On 7 July 1684, Ashe and Molyneux reported on a solar eclipse they had observed together and estimated the portion of the sun that was covered; at the 21 July 1684 meeting, there were reports on the dyeing properties of the mineral residues of certain waters when mixed with oak leaves, and the Society resolved to conduct experiments related to dyeing; on 16 June 1684, a 'Letter from Mr Musgrave was read, which containd the result of some experiments he had Made by injecting Water into the Thorax of a Dog, which recovered perfectly without any applycation or Medicine'.[62] The new philosophy practised by the Dublin Philosophical Society was astronomical, industrial, and physiological, and it sometimes included experiments that must have been motivated by questions and pursued by methods it is not now easy to supply.

---

61. TCD MS 888/1, ff. 32–33.
62. Ibid., ff. 98–100, contain the minutes for meetings from 16 June to 4 August 1684.

Berkeley's notebooks record some rules for what seem to have been two different discussion societies with which he was involved just after concluding his bachelor's studies in the spring of 1704.[63] The more extensive set is preceded in the notebook by a memorandum that 'the following Statutes were agreed to & sign'd by the society consisting of eight persons, Jan: 10. A.D. 1705'. Of these eight persons, four would have been officeholders (the 'President, Treasurer, Secretary and Keeper of the Rarities'), and the society was planning on admitting no new members until 9 July 1706. Discourse was to be managed in a very orderly fashion, with everyone speaking through the president: turns in speech began with the president and then moved to his right until everyone had had a chance to speak; then the floor opened. No reflections were to be made 'on the person or opinion of any member whatsoever'. The president chose three people to read each paper submitted by members and write a report on it (a form of peer review). There were fines for late arrival at meetings and early departure. Following the formal discussion, 'the members may propose to the assembly their inventions, new thought or observation in any of the Sciences'. That this society worked with physical specimens is suggested by the office of the keeper of the rarities. The keeper was to 'attend at the Musaeum from 2 to 4 on Friday or the person whom he shall depute'.[64] It may be worth noting that Berkeley's letter to Hans Sloane of 11 June 1706—in which he discusses the influence of heavenly bodies on the tides—is signed 'e Musaeo in Trin. Coll. Dub.'[65] Perhaps Berkeley was the keeper of the rarities, and was writing from his office?[66]

The second and later set of notes for a society were more succinct:

> December the Seventh in the year one thousand seven hundred and six. Agreed
>
>> That we the under-written persons do meet on every Thursday at five of the clock in the evening.

63. Luce, p. 32.
64. BL Add MS 39305, ff. 96v, 97r, 99r, 101r, 98r.
65. Letter 2, p. 13.
66. Luce, p. 35, suggests that Berkeley was secretary, on the basis that he possessed the notebook containing the rules.

That the business of our meeting be to discourse on some part of
the new Philosophy.

That the Junior begins the conference, the second Junior speak
next & so on.

That at the close of every Conference, we appoint a subject for the
following.[67]

It may be that Berkeley's text on Dunmore cave—a description of
a cave network and its mineral deposits that lay around ten miles
north of Kilkenny, and the earliest sustained piece of writing attrib-
utable to him—was read to the Society: the notes appear in the
same manuscript volume as one draft of the description of the cave.

Earliest Writings

The description of Dunmore cave suggests that Berkeley shared
the interest of the early members of the Dublin Philosophical Society in the topography and historical geography of Ireland. Written
in the form of an address to an illustrious assembly and dated 10
January 1705/6, it is based on Berkeley's recall of a visit he made
six years previously and incorporates elements from other verbal
reports he had heard. The account is mostly geological, reporting
on 'small round pipes as thick as a goose-quil' hanging from the
roof, water dropping from which caused petrifactions on the floor
of the cave, an 'obelisque of a duskish, gray colour', a 'channeled
pillar' containing a cavity called the 'alabastre chair', 'a great white
congelation set against the side of the cave which resembles a pulpit with a canopy over it', and a spring that 'is all over spread with
dead men's bones'. '[W]hat brought these bones hither' there was
not 'the least glimmering of tradition that ever I could hear of to
inform us', though Berkeley speculates on the place being used as
a catacomb by earlier Irish inhabitants, who may have placed bodies deep in the interior in the belief that 'their deceased friends
might enjoy a more undisturbed security in the innermost chambers of this melancholy vault'.[68] Most of the human remains in the

---

67. BL Add MS 39305, f. 103r.

68. One manuscript of the account identifies Berkeley's father as the person from
whom Berkeley had heard the story that a carnivorous monster was responsible for the

cave have now been dated to the ninth and tenth centuries, and Viking remains have also been discovered, though it is not clear whether the site was a Viking burial ground, the site of a massacre, or both.[69] Berkeley offers geological explanations for the properties of the atmosphere and the widely differing temperatures experienced in the cave by different visitors. In references to Descartes, Woodward, and Pierre Perault, the essay develops the geographical knowledge that Berkeley may have gained by reading Varenius as part of the syllabus at Trinity.[70]

The same manuscript volume that contains one draft of Berkeley's text also contains a journal of a tour of Ireland that began 8 November 1709 and included a trip to Dunmore cave. The language of this writer echoes Berkeley's quite closely. The stalactites are described as 'long thin pipes of a whitish Stone of y.ᵉ biggness of a Goose Quill some longer some shorter generally of 4 or 5 Inches long'. As in Berkeley's party, a gun was discharged, and its report was of a remarkable duration; the presence of rabbits in the cave and their striking capacity to see in the dark was also noticed by both parties.[71] These similarities could suggest that both Berkeley's party and the later party of tourists were shown the caves by the same guide, or a guide with a comparable script, who pointed out the same features and either made the same experiments or suggested making them. Berkeley's observations, that is, might have a traditionary element, which can also be observed in his journals of later travels in Italy.

Berkeley's description of Dunmore cave was sent by Thomas Molyneux to Hans Sloane, delivered by William Jackson. Molyneux says that it was 'communicated to me by the young gentleman that

---

human remains, but the word that identifies him has been scored through. Luce speculates that Berkeley was attempting to remove any association of his father's name with the violence of the wars of the three kingdoms in the mid-seventeenth century: 'The bones were the remains of those who were massacred at the cave in the rebellion of 1641, or at any rate that explanation was commonly given' (p. 25). There seem to be no grounds for believing that Berkeley associated the remains with the wars of the seventeenth century.

69. Dowd, Lynch and McCarthy, 'Recent Archaeological Discoveries in Dunmore Cave'.

70. Letter 1, pp. 3–10; Varenius, *Cosmography and Geography in Two Parts*, p. 139, for example, suggests that '*earthy, stony*, and *saline particles*' contained in water were the cause of its petrifying capacity.

71. TCD MS 888/2, ff. 169r, 170r.

drew it up. I never was there myself, but am persuaded the account is faithful, and as far as the observations in it goes may be relied on. If you think it deserves a place in the *Philosophical transactions*, you may insert it. 'Twas writ by one, Mr George Barkley'.[72] Berkeley's next known writing is a letter directly addressed to Hans Sloane, again as a submission to the *Philosophical Transactions*, this time on a subject that would remain of great interest to Berkeley throughout his life: the science of the forces acting on the world's waters and atmosphere.[73] Berkeley takes issue with some of the premises of a short treatise by Richard Mead.[74] Mead argues that the responsiveness of the earth's atmosphere, as well as its waters, to the position of other planets produces different effects at different times partly on account of the earth being an oblate spheroid (flattened at the top and bottom). Berkeley says that he has been informed that the earth is a prolate spheroid by Jean Chardellou, a French astronomer who was visiting Dublin in June 1704, as his correspondence with Flamsteed demonstrates.[75] It seems likely that Berkeley discussed Chardellou's work with him in person during that visit.[76]

Berkeley claims to have calculated only a minimal difference in the forces exerted by the moon upon the earth's waters and air under the two different hypotheses of the earth being perfectly spheroid or oblately spheroid. He sees no need for more explanation than Newton offered when he demonstrated the lesser force of the sun and moon on the earth's waters as they move from the equator to the poles, forces that also operate upon the atmosphere.[77] One of Mead's interests in the book is demonstrating that

72. Hoppen, *Papers of the Dublin Philosophical Society*, II.721, no. 416, Thomas Molyneux to Hans Sloane, 10 May 1706.

73. The British Library catalogue entry for Sloane MS 4040, f. 176, gives the letter to George Browne, a former provost of Trinity College, but as noted earlier, Browne died in 1699. E. St John Brooks attributed the letter to Berkeley and noted its similarity to a section of Berkeley's *Miscellanea Mathematica*, 'De aestu aeris' (LJ, IV.209–12); see TCD MS 2167/misc. box 17, item 10.

74. Mead, *Of the Power and Influence of the Sun and Moon*. The original Latin text was published in 1704.

75. Flamsteed, *The Correspondence of John Flamsteed*, Chardellou to Flamsteed, 13 June 1704, letter 943, pp. 80–81.

76. Letter 2, Berkeley to Sloane, 11 June 1706, p. 14.

77. Ibid., pp. 14–15; Newton, *The Principia*, book III, proposition 24, pp. 835–39.

God's general laws produce greater human goods than the suffering they also seem to cause: 'The Evils that fall on poor Mortals from these Causes does not lessen the Praise that is due to the great Creator, who has given these Laws of Motion to the Air; for he has excellently provided for all Animals, tho' this very Care by accident may sometimes be detrimental to some few in particular'.[78] Though Berkeley's letter has a technical focus, these commonly considered mathematical and geodesic problems touch upon the nature of God and of God's intentions in making the world as it is.

The letter to Sloane is incorporated into Berkeley's first publication, two Latin mathematical texts, 'Arithmetic Demonstrated without Euclid or Algebra' and 'Mathematical Miscellanies', dedicated respectively to two of Berkeley's students, William Palliser, the only son of the archbishop of Cashel, and Samuel Molyneux. They appear under one title page, published by A. and J. Churchill in London and Samuel Pepyat in Dublin. The first treatise is in two parts and deals with the number system, addition, subtraction, multiplication, division, squares, cubes, and their roots in the first part. The second part turns to fractions, proportional series, alligation, and logarithms. The second treatise runs through the topics of its long title: 'Some Thoughts Concerning Surd Roots, the Atmospheric Tide, and Equilateral Cone and Cylinder Circumscribed about the Same Sphere, on the Algebraic Game, and Some Persuasives to the Study of Mathematics, Especially Algebra'. These treatises may shed some light on the mathematical texts that students and tutors were using at Trinity in the 1700s. Reference is made to the work of André Tacquet, perhaps his *Arithmeticœ theoria et praxis* (1682), as well as to John Wallis's *Mathesis Universalis* (1657), John Caswell's *A Brief (but full) Account of the Doctrine of Trigonometry, Both Plain and Spherical* (1685), and Claude-François Milliet Dechales's *The Elements of Euclid, Explained* (translated in 1685).

The final section of the second treatise presents rules for an algebraic game in which a board Berkeley has designed is to be used to generate equations that the players must solve to score points. Berkeley stops short of suggesting stakes for the game, but does say

---

78. Mead, *Of the Power and Influence of the Sun and Moon*, pp. 25–26.

that students '[may] make a little money' in playing it.[79] The game has a philosophical heritage. Berkeley says that, taking 'the advice of that profound thinker, John Locke, on a similar occasion', he invented the game because he was confounded that students would spend half a day in the trifling activity of playing chess.[80] This occasion may be the moment in his educational treatise at which Locke advises that 'the chief Art is, to make all that they have to do, Sport and Play too'.[81] Berkeley notes that Malebranche, in book 6 of *The Search after Truth*, recommended algebra as a means of sharpening the mind so that it becomes aware of a broader range of evident truths.[82] In designing a game with stakes to lure students from trifling to improving pastimes, Berkeley may be imitating the pragmatic strategy of Pascal, who, in his trope of the wager, used the language of gaming to make belief in God attractive. Berkeley quotes Horace as he describes the purpose of his game ('omne tulit punctum qui miscuit utile dulci' [he has won every vote who has blended profit and pleasure]).[83] He is practising an educational art that attempts to make what is useful to his students a pleasure.

The utility of mathematics is important to Berkeley. Enumerating the uses to which algebraic facility might be put would require, he says, a review of all the arts and sciences, and their contribution to 'advancing civil and military affairs'. He also notes that 'there are algebraic theorems on the certainty of human evidences and traditions' in number 257 of the *Philosophical Transactions of the Royal Society of London*.[84] The essay to which Berkeley is referring is 'A Calculation of the Credibility of Human Testimony', attributed to George Hooper.[85] Hooper's essay was an early response to a widely discussed essay by John Craig/e, *Theologiae Christianae principia mathematica*, which (with its Newtonian title) 'produced a "theorem" to calculate the rate of decay in different testimonial

79. Sampson, ed., *The Works of George Berkeley*, I.56. This edition includes the English translation of these publications by G. N. Wright.

80. Ibid., I.51.

81. Locke, *Some Thoughts Concerning Education*, §63, p. 120.

82. Sampson, ed., *The Works of George Berkeley*, I.57–58.

83. Horace, *Ars poetica* 343, in *Satires, Epistles, Ars Poetica*, pp. 478–79.

84. Sampson, ed., *The Works of George Berkeley*, I.57.

85. Hooper, 'A Calculation of the Credibility of Human Testimony'. For the attribution, see Perinetti, 'Philosophical Reflection on History', p. 1136n23.

scenarios (single successive chains, concurrent chains, oral or writ-ten chains), and this revealed that any history is doomed to be buried in disbelief'.[86] Hooper's response quantifies relative moral certainty by making a my certainty of the truth of a person's testi-mony, and c what is lacking to make that certainty absolute. Thus, $a \div (a + c)$ is my share of certainty in a particular testimony. Hooper realises this fraction by reference to an interest rate: a is 100 (for £100) and c is 6 (for 6 percent interest per annum). Belief is then a matter of potential yield from investment: if I was informed by testimony that I had £1,200, calculating my share of certainty in that testimony as a negative interest rate (the fraction of my certainty against absolute certainty) will inform me whether it is likely or unlikely that I actually have that money; or, put another way, whether it is worth believing the testimony.[87] More impor-tantly, perhaps, Hooper argues that concurrent testimony mas-sively increases the likelihood of its truth. The tendency of Hooper's quantification of moral certainty is, of course, to show how good the odds on the truth of revelation are, particularly miracles. Berkeley is interested in this use of algebra in calculating moral certainty. These early mathematical treatises, then, have an ulterior intention of producing practically minded graduates who will use their math-ematical rigour to improve civil and military life and demonstrate the certainty of Christian revelation.

In November 1707, Berkeley read a paper, 'Of Infinites', to the Philosophical Society that shows his mathematical interests turn-ing to abstract concepts that are impossible to quantify.[88] The paper refuses to grant an idea that Berkeley feels is unnecessary or incon-ceivable, in this case infinity. Berkeley believes that Locke is accurate

86. Perinetti, 'Philosophical Reflection on History', p. 1115. Perinetti continues: 'Although unanimously rejected or criticised, the argument was nevertheless discussed by a host of serious philosophers and mathematicians: Bayle, Bernouilli, Samuel Clarke, Hume, and Reid. [. . .] A first answer to Craig by George Hooper pointed out that probability increases with concurrent chains of testimony. Hooper provided a different mathematical treatment of the problem, based on the quantification of the expectation yielded by single witnesses, and arrived at the opposite conclusion that, with multiple and independent chains of testimony attesting a historical fact, the probability of the report increases with the number of testimonies' (ibid.).

87. Hooper, 'A Calculation of the Credibility of Human Testimony', pp. 360–61.

88. Hoppen, *Papers of the Dublin Philosophical Society*, II.214, no. 447.

in his description of the contents of our minds when we attribute infinite value to any quantity. Locke says that our minds can very easily add to any particular quantity they conceive, and so have an idea of an infinitely increasing quantity, but that we cannot have a completed idea of infinite quantities. He gives space as an example:

> [W]e are carefully to distinguish between the *Idea* of the Infinity of Space, and the *Idea* of a Space infinite: The first is nothing but a supposed endless Progression of the Mind, over what repeated *Ideas* of Space it pleases; but to have actually in the Mind the *Idea* of a Space infinite, is to suppose the Mind already passed over, and actually to have a view of all those repeated *Ideas* of Space, which an endless repetition can never totally represent to it, which carries in it a plain contradiction.

Though mathematicians may now have some idea of infinity that is positive, rather than merely negative or additive, 'this hinders not, but that they themselves, as well as all other Men, got the first *Ideas*, which they had of Infinity, from Sensation and Reflection'.[89] As it is plain to Berkeley that 'we ought to use no sign without an idea answering it', we ought not to talk of infinite quantities. (His views would change significantly on this point, as the next chapter shows.) The paper applies this thought to infinite quantities as used in recent mathematics, particularly infinite divisibility, attacking several prominent writers. Nieuwentijt should not say that whilst the first order of infinites used in calculating fluxions (the forces that cause changes in motion, and in which Berkeley takes an interest later in his career) has a value, the second order (the square or root of an infinite) has none: either both have value or neither does. Berkeley prefers the latter option. Leibniz should not say that infinitely small quantities can be added to otherwise equal quantities without altering the equality of those two quantities.[90] Raphson should not say that there are geometrical figures with infinite properties, such as sides.[91]

---

89. *Essay*, II.xvii.7, pp. 213–14; II.xvii.22, p. 223.

90. Vermeulen, 'Berkeley and Nieuwentijt on Infinitesimals', sets out some similarities between the two thinkers, as well as noting Berkeley's main objection. Vermeulen thinks that Berkeley may have taken his account of Nieuwentijt from a text by Leibniz.

91. LJ, IV.236–38.

The paper manifests a view that endures in Berkeley's immaterialist writings: bodies are not infinitely divisible. Lines are made of points. When one divides a line to the final degree, one has a point, not a line. Points are necessarily indivisible. Geometry, that is, concerns real figures made of real things. Berkeley is rejecting the hypotheses of mathematicians like John Ward, who supposed that 'every *Line* is supposed to consist or be composed of, an *Infinite Series* of Equidistant *Points*' and that surfaces 'consist of an *Infinite Series* of *Lines*'.[92] Berkeley would think there is a limit to the division of the sheets of paper because they are real sheets and not merely hypotheses. The 'arithmetick of infinites' is then one of those areas in which, as Berkeley would put it in the *Principles of Human Knowledge*, theoretical number terms, 'abstracted [. . .] from all Use and Practice, as well as from the particular things number'd, can be supposed to have nothing at all for their Object. Hence we may see, how intirely the Science of Numbers is subordinate to Practice, and how jejune and trifling it becomes, when consider'd as a matter of meer Speculation'.[93] When infinitesimal quantities themselves become the object of speculation, error follows.

Two years later, when asked by Molyneux what a geometer might be thinking of when making demonstrations based on lines, Berkeley asserted that 'we do not make any discovery by contemplating the ideas of the lines whose properties are investigated'. Rather, it is by 'regard to the equation' expressing the nature of the geometrical figure, and not by the idea of the figure, that solutions are reached.[94] The geometer is occupied by the language of mathematics, not some supposed but actually nonexistent abstract referent of that language, the idea of a line in the abstract, a line that might be infinitely long. Between 1707 and 1709, Berkeley came to see that there are some kinds of thinking in which it is beneficial to work with signs that do not refer to ideas. (More space will be dedicated to this development in Berkeley's thought in chapter 3.)

92. Ward, *The Young Mathematician's Guide*, pp. 395–96.
93. *Principles of Human Knowledge*, §120.
94. Letter 10, 19 December 1709, p. 31.

The possible reaction of other members of the Philosophical Society to Berkeley's paper has been presented as a moment of considerable importance to his intellectual development. William King and Peter Browne were probably both present at the meeting to which Berkeley read his paper.[95] They both believed it possible to talk meaningfully of infinite qualities and to use terms to which no idea corresponds: if we say that it is meaningless to talk of God's being infinitely wise because we have no idea of infinity, we do so at considerable cost to the grounds for piety and religious awe.[96] David Berman imagines that King and Browne took Berkeley to task in the discussion of his paper for approaching dangerously close to the position of John Toland, whose *Christianity Not Mysterious* attacked the self-interest of a priesthood that made the laity depend on them for administering rites relating to religious mysteries supposedly beyond reason. Nothing, said Toland, is beyond reason.[97] But it is a little difficult to make the leap from Berkeley's paper to this theological context in which the meaningfulness of religious mysteries and the attributes of God are suddenly at stake.

First, Berkeley says only that one sense of infinity is meaningless (that is, corresponds to no idea)—that of completed infinity. He is happy to let the sense of unceasing addition to quantities be a meaningful idea of infinity. Second, Toland himself is perfectly happy that the terms 'eternity' and 'infinity' are meaningful in their own ways. We have notions of them even if we cannot imagine them:

> *Eternity* [. . .] is no more above Reason, *because it cannot be imagin'd*, than a Circle, *because it may*; for in both Cases *Reason* performs its Part according to the different Natures of the Objects, whereof the one is essentially imaginable, the other not.
>
> Now it appears that the pretended *Mysteriousness* of *Eternity* do's not consist in the want of an adequate Notion, which is all that we consider in it at present. The Difficulties rais'd from its Duration, as, that *Succession seems to make it finite*, and that *all things must exist together if it be instantaneous*, I despair not of solving very easily; and

95. Berman, *George Berkeley*, p. 14, citing Hoppen, *Common Scientist*, pp. 192–93.
96. Berman, *George Berkeley*, pp. 14–15.
97. *Christianity Not Mysterious*, pp. 10, 17, 48, 55–56.

rendring *Infinity* also (which is inseparable from it, or rather a different Consideration of the same thing) as little *mysterious* as that *three
and two make five*.[98]

Either Berkeley approaches Toland and allows for an idea of infinity that is not imaginable (at least not as a completed quantity) but
is nonetheless meaningful, or he departs from Toland in saying
that infinity is not comprehensible as a completed quantity, even
if it may be conceived as continual extension. Neither scenario
lends itself particularly well to the conjectured altercation between
Browne, King, and Berkeley, which Berman makes a contributing
factor to Berkeley's semantic revolution (the realisation that signification of a clear and distinct idea is not the only criterion for
meaningfulness in the use of words), and also to Berkeley's later
altercation with King over the former's ordination.[99] A closer parallel to Berkeley from this passage from Toland may be Berkeley's
insistence that we have no idea of other spirits, though we may have
a notion of them—an assertion of vital importance (as I tried to
show in chapter 1 and will pick up again in the following chapter when considering Berkeley's refinement of his use of the term
'notion' as he revises his early immaterialist texts).

It is possible that Berkeley was responding to another of the
freethinking writers who would remain his targets for decades:
Anthony Collins. Collins, in a short treatise published the same
year Berkeley delivered 'Of Infinites', argues, like Toland, that being
above or contrary to reason are in fact the same thing. He is happy
to admit that there may be many things people do not understand,
and that God may understand and reason about those things, but
that this does not make them any less contrary to human reason.
Collins points to 'some mathematical and physical Instances [. . .]
where it is pretended that Men assent upon no less evidence than
Demonstration; and yet the Propositions assented to do seem to us
to involve or imply Contradictions'.[100] The contradictions to which
he points are asymptotic lines (lines that are curved yet have neither positive nor negative curvature) and the infinite divisibility

98. Ibid., p. 61.
99. Berman, *George Berkeley*, pp. 16–17.
100. Collins, *An Essay Concerning the Use of Reason in Propositions*, pp. 41–42.

of matter. Berkeley, then, shared ground with Collins in 1707. The ends to which this critique of abstraction are put by Collins and Berkeley are very different, however, as later chapters of this book will show. Identifying propositions that imply a contradiction or an absurdity around the notions of infinity is the argumentative move that Berkeley would also make when he wrote *The Analyst* in 1734, for example, with the explicit aim of countering an 'infidel mathematician', as he said in the subtitle of that work.

Berkeley's verbal performance at the Dublin Philosophical Society meeting at which he delivered 'Of Infinites' was significant for bringing him into the most prominent circles of patronage. One of the reasons Berkeley gives for dedicating his book, the *Principles of Human Knowledge*, to the Earl of Pembroke is 'his approving my harangue'.[101] (John Locke had also dedicated his *Essay* to Pembroke.) Pembroke was president of the Dublin Philosophical Society at the time.[102] At meetings of such societies one performs verbally and intellectually; one is noticed by the great; and, with suitable shows of deference and obligation, one is patronised and allowed to claim forms of intellectual and social protection.

In the years between 'Of Infinites' and 1709, the year of Berkeley's next publication, the *New Theory of Vision*, and of his first surviving private correspondence, Berkeley was working in his philosophical notebook on the *Manuscript Introduction* to the *Principles* and on sermons. These texts bring Berkeley's moral, mathematical, and optical concerns together. (I consider the notebooks, the *Manuscript Introduction*, and the two works that follow from them, the *Principles of Human Knowledge* and *Three Dialogues*, in the next chapter.) Luce suggests that Berkeley's first surviving sermon, on immortality, was one of the discourses that fellows at Trinity not yet ordained were obliged by statute to deliver on Sunday afternoons: it is dated Sunday evening, 11 January 1707/8, and was delivered in the college chapel.[103] Luce also notes that the sermon draws loosely on Pascal's wager, and that Berkeley cites Pascal in §21 of *Passive Obedience*. Berkeley may have been making some use of Pascal and

101. *Notebooks*, §396.

102. See Hoppen's notes to the paper in *Papers of the Dublin Philosophical Society*, II.793, no. 447.

103. Luce, pp. 42–43; Bolton, *A Translation of the Charter and Statutes*, p. 73.

the trope of the wager at this time. He takes issue with Pascal's assertion that 'A Tree is no more sensible of Misery than of Felicity' when he notes the 'Strange impotence of men. Man without God. Wretcheder than a stone or tree, he having only the power to be miserable by his unperformed wills, these having no power at all'.[104] I said earlier that the algebraic game, and the ways in which Berkeley attempts to lure students to it, may have borrowed from Pascal's rhetorical and pragmatic strategy of talking to people in the terms with which they are most familiar. The trope of the wager might be one way in which Berkeley puts into practice a rhetorical strategy he recorded in a notebook:

> He that wou'd win another over to his opinion must seem to harmonize with him at first and humour him in his own way of talking.
>
> From my Childhood I had an unaccountable turn of thought that way.[105]

The trope of the wager is also an example of the attempt to establish moral certainty by means of calculation, and so it may be related to the suggestion that 'Morality may be Demonstrated as mixt Mathematics'.[106]

In this first sermon, Berkeley asks why so few people follow the path of virtue after God's revelation and the incarnation of Christ. 'Rational desires', after all, 'are vigorous in proportion to the goodness &, if I may so speak attainableness of their objects. [. . .] [A]n object with half the goodness & double the certainty, & another wth half ye certainty & double ye goodness are equally desired. & universally those lots are alike esteem'd wherein the prizes are reciprocally as the chances'. As eternal life is an inconceivably great good,

> by ye foregoing rule the hazard tho never so small & uncertain, of a good so ineffably so inconceivably great, ought to be more valu'd & sought after than the greatest assurance we can have of any sublunary good since in wt proportion this good is more certain than that, in as great, nay in a much greater proportion that good is more excellent than this. [. . .] [W]n life & immortality are at stake we should play

104. *Notebooks*, §107 Pascal, *Thoughts on Religion and Other Subjects*, p. 193.
105. BL Add MS 39304, f. 4r.
106. *Notebooks*, §755.

our part with fear & trembling tho 'twere an hundred to one but we are cheated in the end.[107]

By a rule of returns on that in which we certainly believe (and on which belief we act), we ought to follow the true path. But, Berkeley recognises, people evidently do not. We are irrational. Berkeley says this is the case because we have no clear idea of heavenly goods, which we imagine to be at a great distance.[108] But it is clear that we can talk meaningfully about heavenly goods—as Berkeley and others constantly do—without a clear idea of them (for the variety of reasons Berkeley would later set out in the introduction to the *Principles of Human Knowledge*). We ought also to bear in mind that identifying objects by means of vision is largely a matter of interpretation or suggestion, rather than simple evidence or inference: 'is an object in reality little because it appears so at a distance?' he asks.[109] We need to overcome our tendency to dismiss those goods of which we do not have clear ideas, and those goods which appear small but are actually great and distant, in order to benefit from God's revelation and the natural appetitive-computational faculties with which God has endowed people—the physiological and psychological natural laws by which God delimits the human.

There are some disjointed notes in one of Berkeley's notebooks that Luce takes to be connected to this sermon on immortality. Luce does not say so, but his reason is probably that Berkeley jots down 'object at a distance' in these notes, recalling the heavenly goods that are objects at a distance. Berkeley goes on to ask (or imply a known but unstated answer to the question) 'why we see not the joys of blessed spirits'?[110] Why do we not see what the blessed spirits enjoy, or see that they are enjoying it? Why do we not have a clear visual idea of the pleasures of heaven? Berkeley's sermon offers some answer to these questions.

In the close dialogue with Locke he kept up in the same notebook, Berkeley was considering similar questions about the

107. LJ, VII.11–13.

108. On this point and in relation to this text, see Bettcher, *Berkeley's Philosophy of Spirit*, p. 18.

109. LJ, VII.14.

110. BL Add MS 39305, f. 165v.

perceptibility of objects other than things. In some remarks that are not included in most standard editions of the *Notebooks*, Berkeley asks 'why powers mediately perceivable thought such, immediately perceivable not', and refers to 'b.2.c.8 S19'.[111] In that section of the *Essay*, Locke notes that people tend to think colour is in an object, even though what they see is the light determining the colouration of that object. (His example is the red and white in porphyry.) Particles giving a certain texture to the stone are always there; its colour is only there in the light. How does Berkeley's comment relate to this section? Perhaps he is thinking of light as a power. It is mediately perceptible because it produces colour. Because its action is perceptible when mediated, we take it for a power. Berkeley writes in the same set of notes that 'Power is not perceive'd by sense', an expression of the view that will or agency is not a perceptible idea, but the chief characteristic of spirits.[112] One can see in such patterns of commentary and response to Locke the germinal role of certain passages of the *Essay* in generating Berkeley's new doctrine of immaterialism, the subject of the following chapter.

The sermon may be compared with the work of William King and provides another explanation for the antagonism between King and Berkeley. King's major philosophical work, *De origine mali* (1702), seeks to defend freedom of will from philosophers who believe that will is determined necessarily by the properties of objects presented to the understanding, with the only choice being whether to allow the body to accede in the determinations of the will. King suggests that humans have a power of election that makes the things chosen by their will good.[113] This power enables people to experience goods even when 'such things must be endured as are quite contrary to the Appetites'.[114] At least some readers of King's text understand him here to be referring to the choice of something that is immediately unappealing, but which

111. BL Add MS 39305, f. 102r; transcribed in a section Luce calls '*Disputatio* on Locke's *Essay* ('The Queries')', in Berkeley, *Philosophical Commentaries*, p. 472.

112. BL Add MS 39305, f. 102v and Berkeley, *Philosophical Commentaries*, p. 473.

113. Greenberg, 'Leibniz on King', p. 213, notes King's project of limiting the determining power of pleasure and pain.

114. King, *Essay on the Origin of Evil*, pp. 152–54, 179. For an outline of King's argument and its place in his career and in European intellectual life, see Richardson, 'William King—European Man of Letters'.

is ultimately better, such as taking a painful remedy, the example given by the translator of the English edition published in 1731, Edmund Law, in a note. King himself seems to suggest that election is a matter of rank-ordering goods. He describes a net gain in pleasure of +4 arising from −2 in pain borne with +6 patience and decorum.[115] These calculations, however, require that patience and decorum are themselves goods, prior to their being chosen, and not things that become good by being chosen. They are higher goods, and therefore subject to precisely the kind of calculation King here employs, and which Berkeley employed when considering quantities and certainties of particular goods. Berkeley, that is, may not follow King on the power of election to create goods over and above their goodness for particular predetermined human ends.

Elections should be free. King says 'daily Experience teaches' that 'we can, by the force of Election, conquer not only the Appetites and Senses, but the Understanding too'.[116] His example here is an atheist who happily undergoes torture in defence of his atheism. But this is clearly supposed to be a bad choice.[117] The 'good' the atheist elects is not one that Berkeley or King would find publicly defensible. King himself constrains the freedom of elections to create goods. Only creatures who can elect goods can be happy, because they can conform their will to the nature of things, that is, to the will of God.[118] So, to be happy, we have to elect true goods, those that conform with God's will. This limitation seems to place goodness back in objects, the nature of things, rather than in election. If a person who elects a good that is against the nature of things experiences the satisfaction of the power of election, and therefore the highest good, that seems to make human goods independent of God's will; if the power of election to be satisfied is dependent on the nature of things, it is not absolutely free. Berkeley's more direct insistence on rational moral calculus in his sermon may be a reaction to and distinction from King's treatment of the problem of

---

115. King, *Essay on the Origin of Evil*, p. 218.

116. Ibid., pp. 204–5.

117. Pearce, 'William King on Free Will', p. 2, parses King's/Law's 'elections' as 'attitudes of valuing adopted by agents'. He does not engage, however, with the rather counterintuitive examples King uses of things made good by election.

118. King, *Essay on the Origin of Evil*, p. 217.

free will. How wills are directed, and under what forms of guidance, is an issue to which Berkeley returned in the 1730s. It is a topic he considered in relation to unspecified goods, as the next chapter shows: the *Manuscript Introduction* to the *Principles of Human Knowledge* uses the example of children modifying their behaviour on the guidance of an adult, with the promise of an unspecified good.[119] That choice takes place in the context of guidance from an appropriate superior authority is one feature of Berkeley's moral thought that distinguishes it from King's. The guidance of a superior intellect, working through the laws of pleasure and pain, rather than election, will form the basis of Berkeley's account of appropriate human action.

Many of the interests of Berkeley's earliest published and unpublished writings are developed in the *Notebooks*, and infinites are no exception. Berkeley is a contrarian on this subject, opposing all comers. John Keill, probably in his *Introductio ad veram physicam* (1705), is said to have made a whole equal to a part.[120] There is a 'Mem. to remark Cheyne & his Doctrine of infinites', perhaps to object to Cheyne's acceptance of the infinite divisibility of matter, stated in response to the fact that the sun does not seem to diminish in size, despite giving off wave after wave of light.[121] Newton's fluxions are said to be needless.[122] And Cavallerius/Cavalieri, who worked in the geometry of indivisibles, is someone who could be improved upon on the subject.[123] Berkeley's opposition to the theory of infinites unites his mathematics and his optics in *Notebooks*, and is one means by which he develops the core of the *New Theory of Vision*. His theory of vision is built on visible minima, just as his geometry is built on extended minima. Just as he was opposed to Leibniz's mathematical use of infinitely small quantities, so he is opposed to the idea of the conjunction of invisible things producing

119. See *Manuscript Introduction*, f. 23r.

120. *Notebooks*, §322.

121. Ibid., §459; Cheyne, *Philosophical Principles*, p. 98, states that 'this can surprise no Body, who considers that Matter is infinitely divisible; for it is possible to assign in Number, a Quantity, whereof a Body as big as the *Sun* may constantly, for any finite Number of Years emit *Oceans*, and yet the Sum of 'em all, may not be greater than a cubical Inch, or even a Grain of Sand'. Berkeley echoes this text closely at *Notebooks*, §617 (see also chapter 3).

122. *Notebooks*, §333.

123. Ibid., §346; *Histoire de l'académie royale des sciences*, p. 2.

visible things: '[T]wo invisible things say you put together become visible therefore that m.v. [minimum visibile] contains or is made up of Invisibles. [. . .] It remains for you to prove that I came by the present idea because there were 2 invisibles added together. I say the invisibles are nothings, cannot exist, include a contradiction'.[124] Visible minima are the basic units of the visual world.

The theory of visible minima prompts some interesting conjectures in *Notebooks*. One concerns physical contact, a phenomenon Berkeley does not regard as self-evident, 'for that if my optiques were improv'd I should see intervalls & other bodies betwixt those wch now seem to touch'.[125] If this scenario were infinitely regressive, with the improvement of my 'optiques', I would see that the minute particles (of grit or dirt or dust) and air that actually sit between, say, the book and the table on which it appears, to someone with less improved optiques, to rest do not in fact touch one another, but are separated by intervals and other smaller bodies. But for a person committed to visual minima, there must be a point at which such improvement ceases and one minimum rests on another.

Douglas Jesseph has pointed to a different difficulty for the theory of adjacent minima:

> Consider the problem of how to compose a line out of minima. The minima that compose the line must, it seems, be in immediate contact with one another, because otherwise an unbroken line must contain gaps. Then a single minimum in the interior of the line has at least two distinguishable parts: that part in contact with the adjacent minimum on either side. The indivisibility of minima, however, guarantees that they can have no parts. Hence, if the minima touch at all, they must coincide completely, and it is impossible that there can be a line consisting of more than one minimal part.[126]

The theory of visible minima seems to pose this insoluble dilemma. Further, if, as Berkeley holds consistently, number 'is nothing fix'd, and settled, really existing in things themselves. It is entirely the Creature of the Mind', should he really be so committed to minima

124. *Notebooks*, §464.
125. Ibid., §632.
126. Jesseph, 'Berkeley's Philosophy of Mathematics', p. 281.

that are units the mind does not determine?[127] If there are minima, there is natural, non-mind-dependent unity and number is in the world, not just in the mind. It was not until the publication of *Siris* in 1744 that Berkeley provided a justification for his commitment to unity, even whilst maintaining that number is mind-dependent. That justification rests on the essential unity of divinity and the unity of other minds as derived from and participating in God. Berkeley in that later text is clear that unity is not a quality of perceptible objects but of the mind.[128]

An Essay towards a New Theory of Vision

The question of whether the visual field always contains the same number of minima, or whether it may be expanded or contracted (by focus or by the nature of the optic instrument itself) so as to contain more or fewer minima, is raised by this passage about refined optiques. It is a question treated at several points in the *New Theory of Vision*, to a discussion of which I now turn, concentrating in the first instance on visible minima and the language analogy. (Though I concur with those who, like Kenneth Pearce, argue that Berkeley does not think vision is merely analogous to language, but that it is a language, I shall continue to refer to the language analogy. I do so because Berkeley's assertion that vision is a language challenges what I take to be some commonly held core features of concepts of a linguistic sign and a natural language. That is, vision is a language not just analogically, but only if we are prepared to revise some views we might hold of what a language is.)[129] This is the first of Berkeley's major publications (1709), and its concepts and arguments were very likely developing at the same time as those of his new doctrine of immaterialism, which are more thoroughly witnessed by his *Notebooks*.

Does the visual field contain the same number of minima no matter what the focus of the optic instrument/eye, and no matter

127. *New Theory of Vision*, §109.

128. *Siris*, §§355–56.

129. Pearce, *Language and the Structure of Berkeley's World*, pp. 173–82. See also Stoneham, 'Response to Atherton', pp. 219–21. I thank one of the anonymous readers at the Press for these references and for encouraging me to be more precise on the language analogy.

how refined the optic instrument/eye? One (at least partial) answer to this question is given in the main text: '[T]he *Minimum Visibile* is exactly equal in all Beings whatsoever, that are endow'd with the Visive Faculty. No exquisite Formation of the Eye, no peculiar Sharpness of Sight, can make it less in one Creature than in another. For it not being distinguishable into Parts, nor in any wise consisting of them, it must necessarily be the same to all'. More directly: 'Of these Visible Points we see at all times an equal Number'.[130] The minimum visibile is the same in all creatures, with all kinds of eyes, with all kinds of variation within kinds. (And it is not necessarily very small: Berkeley describes the moon as 'a round, luminous Plain, of around Thirty visible Points in Diameter'.[131]) But Berkeley refines his answer in the appendix attached to the second 1709 edition of the text:

> Against what is said in *Sect*. LXXX, it is objected, that the same thing which is so small, as scarce to be discern'd by a Man, may appear like a Mountain to some small Insect; from which it follows, that the *Minimum Visibile* is not equal in respect of all Creatures. I Answer, If this Objection be sounded to the Bottom it will be found to mean no more, than that the same Particle of Matter, which is mark'd to a Man by one *Minimum Visibile*, exhibits to an Insect a great Number of *Minima Visibilia*. But this does not prove, that one *Minimum Visibile* of the Insect is not equal to one *Minimum Visibile* of the Man.[132]

The visual field, then, is like a pixelated screen, with each pixel corresponding to different quantities of matter in the world in proportion as the optics of the perceiving creature are more broadly or narrowly calibrated. (I return to the talk of matter and its relevance to Berkeley's immaterialism shortly.)

In *Notebooks*, Berkeley reflected, 'It seems not improbable that the most comprehensive & sublime Intellects see more M.V.s at once i.e. that their Visual spheres are the largest'.[133] These higher beings must have screens made up of more pixels. (Berkeley will often make reference to expanded or enlarged views when he discusses

---

130. *New Theory of Vision*, §§80, 82.
131. Ibid., §44.
132. Ibid., appendix, p. 196.
133. *Notebooks*, §749.

matters of morality and religion.) They cannot have smaller or finer pixels in a screen of the same size, if there is to be consistency between *Notebooks* and the *New Theory of Vision*. In the published work, Berkeley returns to the topic and notes an imperfection in human vision: 'In respect of the Extent or Number of visible Points that are at once perceivable by it, which is narrow and limited to a certain Degree', he suggests that there may be a corresponding perfection in higher orders of being, '[t]hat of comprehending in one View, a greater number of Visible Points'.[134] Whilst the minimum remains the same for all creatures, the size of the field of vision may be different. Berkeley's claim strains against some intuitions about visual fields. Although any visual field is the entire visual field for the seeing creature that has it, Berkeley is asking us to conceive that there may be larger or smaller visual fields for more or less elevated creatures. We are asked to conceive of 'everything visible' being larger or smaller for different kinds of being, suggesting that we must form a concept of what we cannot ever see—the outside edge of our visual field. One might expect Berkeley, who would oppose the idea of absolute motion in the *Principles of Human Knowledge* and *De Motu*, also to be against an absolute visual field, which is implied by this suggestion that different creatures have lesser or greater visual fields.[135] The difficulty of imagining larger or smaller fields of vision in which the smallest thing visible is the same size, no matter how close the focus of the optical instrument doing the viewing, is great. It is also one of the few difficulties of the *New Theory of Vision* that is not in any way resolved by what is perhaps the most prominent feature of that text: Berkeley's suggestion that vision is a language.

The analogy Berkeley develops between vision and language is his solution to questions that earlier geometrical approaches to optics had attempted to answer by reference to the angles of convergence of rays of light striking the eye: how do people see distance and size? Berkeley is considered revolutionary in his work on vision for the commonsensical assertion that as we do not see the angles of convergence of rays of light upon the eye, such information is not

134. *New Theory of Vision*, §§83–84.
135. *Principles of Human Knowledge*, §§112–14; *De Motu*, §53.

part of the human visual world and has no impact on judgements of size or distance.[136] In an addition to the text when it was republished in 1732, Berkeley directly states his restricted sense of what we see, or the immediate objects of vision: 'what we immediately and properly see are only Lights and Colours in sundry Situations and Shades, and Degrees of Faintness and Clearness, Confusion and Distinctness'.[137] We do not even see flat surfaces: 'What we strictly see are not Solids, nor yet Plains variously coloured; they are only Diversity of Colours'.[138] Berkeley's emphasis is on the psychology and phenomenology of vision, on how we get from lights and colours to a world of spatially oriented objects.

Berkeley is conscious of his departure from the many treatises of the seventeenth century which he cites in the course of the *New Theory of Vision*, such as Descartes's *Optics*. In developing the language analogy, however, Berkeley may also have been taking Descartes as a point of departure. For although Descartes bases his work on the geometry of rays of light, he notes that images and their source may be heterogeneous. Descartes maintains that the signs that call to mind other objects need not resemble those objects, and he applies this thought to the relationship between images received by sense organs:

> We should [. . .] recall that our mind can be stimulated by many things other than images—by signs and words, for example, which in no way resemble the things they signify. And if, in order to depart as little as possible from accepted views, we prefer to maintain that the objects which we perceive by our senses really send images of themselves to the inside of our brain, we must at least observe that in no case does an image have to resemble the object it represents in all respects, for otherwise there would be no distinction between the object and its image. It is enough that the image resembles its object in a few respects.[139]

Images may be like objects, but they are not the same as objects, and they may be treated as signs of the objects. These are ideas that Berkeley will develop in the *New Theory of Vision*. But his language

---

136. Copenhaver, 'Perception and the Language of Nature', pp. 108–9.

137. *New Theory of Vision* (1732 text), §77.

138. *New Theory of Vision*, §158.

139. Descartes, *Philosophical Writings*, I.165.

analogy is not focused solely on language as a system of arbitrary correspondences between signs and referents. Berkeley's language analogy also embraces the fact that languages have speakers, that languages are used to tell people things, and that the telling itself often has one or more ulterior purposes, such as putting people in different relations to things or to each other. These pragmatic considerations are still more important to Berkeley's theory of vision than the systematic or codal aspects of the language analogy and explain his concern for the visibility of passions: it is good that people can understand the language of vision sufficiently well to navigate the goods and ills of their environment, but it is even better that this language can be understood as communicating the attitudes of the infinite being whose creation that environment is.

The language analogy is proposed as a better means of explaining how distance is seen than the geometric model. Berkeley points to a commonly noted phenomenon—the appearance the moon gives of being much larger on the horizon than in the meridian. The apparent difference in size is not explicable by means of the geometric model (by the angle of convergence of rays of light entering the eye), and Berkeley cites authors of the geometric school who resort to dubious measures to solve the problem (claiming that there being objects between the eye and the moon enables the viewer to judge magnitude by means of distance).[140] One of Berkeley's antagonists here is John Wallis, yet Wallis's writing on this subject might have provided Berkeley with a prompt as well as a problem: Wallis states that, 'according to the different Posture in the Eyes, requisite to a clear Vision by both, we estimate the Distance of the Object from us'.[141] Berkeley agrees that distance is seen by turning the eyes inwards or outwards, but this is a proprioceptive idea, and therefore an idea of touch rather than vision. It is also connected by association with confused vision (objects appearing out of focus).[142] That connection is contingent rather than necessary, like that between shame and a red colour in the cheeks.[143]

---

140. *New Theory of Vision*, §75.

141. Wallis, 'The Sentiments of the Reverend and Learned Dr. John Wallis', p. 327.

142. *New Theory of Vision*, §§16–17, 23.

143. Whether Berkeley's theory of confused vision being caused by 'Rays proceeding from each distinct Point of the Object [. . .] not [being] accurately recollected in one

These proprioceptive and visual ideas are associated in experience with other ideas, primarily those of touch, to produce visual knowledge of distance:

> Having of a long time, experienced certain *Ideas*, perceivable by Touch, as Distance, Tangible Figure, and Solidity to have been connected with certain *Ideas* of Sight, I do upon perceiving these *Ideas* of Sight, forthwith conclude what Tangible *Ideas* are, by the wonted, ordinary course of Nature like to follow. [. . .] I believe whoever will look narrowly into his own Thoughts, and examin what he means by saying, he sees this, or that thing at a Distance, will agree with me that, what he sees only suggests to his Understanding, that after having pass'd a certain Distance, to be measur'd by the Motion of his Body, which is perceivable by Touch, he shall come to perceive such, and such Tangible *Ideas* which have been usually connected with such and such Visible *Ideas*.[144]

That ideas of vision and touch are heterogeneous and require customary association to connect them is what makes the language analogy necessary for Berkeley's theory of vision. Customary association of visual and tactile ideas allows people to see distance and size.[145]

The heterogeneity of ideas of the different senses is upheld strictly by Berkeley. Both sensory realms are made up of points, but those points are not of the same stuff—they cannot be added to one another to make a total. Trying to add a visible line to a tangible line, Berkeley says, is like trying to add a surface to a volume. Likewise, no tangible thing can be said to be any number of visual points away from anything, or vice versa. The heterogeneity thesis helps to loosen the conceptual grip of the theory of abstract ideas,

---

corresponding Point on the *Retina*' (*New Theory of Vision*, §35) can be squared with his commitment to visual minima is another matter. That commitment means that we see points neither in the object nor on the retina but in our visual field, and these points cannot be greater or smaller, and so cannot, presumably, be more or less confused.

144. *New Theory of Vision*, §45.

145. Not everyone allows Berkeley the point that distance is only known visually by correlation with tactile ideas. Brook, 'Berkeley's Theory of Vision', denies that distance is read into vision from touch, as there is no means of making the visual signs of distance opaque (of seeing back to the immediate objects of vision that we mediate as objects at a distance). Copenhaver, 'Perception and the Language of Nature', p. 116, emphasises that seeing distance is no less a form of seeing for its being mediate rather than immediate.

one of Berkeley's targets in the *Principles of Human Knowledge*. People are deluding themselves when they imagine an extension that is both tangible and visible, of which they have an idea other than ideas of certain tangible or visible properties.[146]

Berkeley's application of the heterogeneity thesis in the *New Theory of Vision* privileges touch over sight and so is an implicit departure from that tradition which identifies sight as 'the noblest and most comprehensive of the senses'.[147] Our vision points us to tangible phenomena, because it is those that cause us pleasure and pain:

> We regard the Objects that environ us, in proportion as they are adapted to benefit, or injure our own Bodies and thereby, produce in our Minds the Sensations of Pleasure, or Pain. Now Bodies operating on our Organs, by an immediate Application: And the Hurt or Advantage arising there-from, depending altogether on the Tangible, and not at all on the Visible, Qualities of any Object. This is a plain Reason, why those shou'd be regarded by us much more than these: And for this End, chiefly, the *Visive sense* seems to have been bestowed on Animals, *viz.* that by the Perception of Visible *Ideas* (which in themselves are not capable of affecting, or any wise altering the Frame of their Bodies) they may be able to foresee (from the Experience they have had, what Tangible *Ideas* are connected with such, and such Visible *Ideas*) the Damage or Benefit which is like to ensue, upon the Application of their own Bodies to this, or that Body which is at a Distance.[148]

Touch is the sense that determines our pleasure and pain, it is the sense that is referred to by visual ideas when they are regarded as signs.

At this point in his career, tactile ideas were said to inhere in extended things outside the body, a position Berkeley would later attack. In the *New Theory of Vision*, Berkeley says that 'all Visible Things are equally in the Mind, and take up no part of the External Space: And, consequently are Equidistant from any Tangible Thing

---

146. *New Theory of Vision*, §§131, 112, 122–23.

147. Descartes, 'Optics', in *Philosophical Writings* I.152.

148. *New Theory of Vision*, §59. Compare *Ladies Library*, I.227: 'The Ant has Eyes, and turns away, if it meets with such Objects as may be hurtful to it'. The passage from which this citation is taken has not been attributed; it may therefore be Berkeley's own.

which exists without the Mind'. In the passage from the appendix just quoted, Berkeley also talks about different visible ideas marking 'the same Particle of Matter', as if matter both exists beyond sensible ideas of it and is the same thing for different perceivers of it—neither of which are views Berkeley tolerates in *Principles of Human Knowledge*.[149] The Berkeley of just a year or so later would argue that ideas of touch are every bit as much in the mind as ideas of vision, and that their distance from one another is no more basic than the distance of visual ideas from one another.[150] But at the moment of the *New Theory of Vision*, either for developmental or rhetorical reasons, the objects that provoke ideas of touch are outside the mind.

Berkeley sets his readers the imaginative challenge of conceiving the relationship between visual signs and their tactile referents as entirely arbitrary, customary, and contingent: 'there is no necessary Connexion, between Visible, and Tangible *Ideas* suggested by them'. It could perfectly well have been the case that entirely different visual cues suggested distance or size. We are well enough aware of the arbitrariness of such connections in human natural languages, and Berkeley encourages us to think of the language of vision in the same way: 'the manner wherein [visual signs] signify, and mark out unto us the Objects which are at a distance, is the same with that of Languages and Signs of Human Appointment; which do not suggest the things signify'd, by any Likeness or Identity of Nature, but only by an Habitual Connexion, that Experience has made us to observe between 'em'. Even though 'this Language of Nature does not vary, in different Ages or Nations', we should not forget that it is arbitrary.[151]

Berkeley's treatment of vertical orientation in the visual field attests to the arbitrariness of the connection between visual and tactile ideas. He may be developing William Molyneux's insight, with regard to the inversion of retinal images, that such orientation is relational: '*Erect* and *Inverted* are only Terms of *Relation* to *Up* and *Down*, or *Farther from* and *Nigher to* the Centre of the Earth,

149. *New Theory of Vision*, §111 and appendix, p. 196.
150. See, for example, *Principles of Human Knowledge*, §§3–4, 10.
151. *New Theory of Vision*, §§45, 147, 140.

in parts of the same thing'.[152] Berkeley imagines a blind person understanding the terms of orientation 'high' and 'low' by experiencing through touch the relative distance from the earth of the parts of the human figure. If this person had his sight restored, Berkeley says, the information provided by sight would not include orientation higher and lower. This person, that is, would not see an inverted image of a human figure. He would merely see colours more or less clear and confused, faint and vigorous. The orientation of the eye itself (that is, which part of it is closer to the earth) is irrelevant to bringing high and low into the visual world of this person. What happens is that proprioceptive ideas of touch are seen to alter the visual scene in a regular way:

> [W]hen upon turning his Head or Eyes, up and down, to the right and left, he shall observe the Visible Objects to change, and shall also attain to know, that they are call'd by the same Names, and Connected with the Objects perceiv'd by Touch; then, indeed, he will come to speak of them, and their Situation, in the same Terms that he has been us'd to apply to Tangible Things. And those that he perceives by turning up his Eyes, he will call *Upper*, and those that by turning down his Eyes, he will call *Lower*. [. . .] [T]o the immediate Objects of Sight, consider'd in themselves, he'd not attribute the Terms *High* and *Low*.[153]

These two sensory realms do not share, in advance of experiences that allow people to associate ideas of one realm with those of another, basic qualities such as orientation.[154] There is 'no necessary connexion' between visible and tangible extension, Berkeley says, suggesting that we could experience precisely the same visual world, but that everything we see might be smaller than the smallest thing we could touch—in which case there would be a radically different relationship between vision and touch than now holds, even though the objects of vision would be the same.[155]

152. Molyneux, *Dioptrica Nova*, p. 105. Lindberg, *Theories of Vision from Al-Kindi to Kepler*, pp. 202–5, notes the reliance in Al Hazen and Kepler on a concept of visual spirit to manage the transition from (inverted) retinal image to visual experience.

153. *New Theory of Vision*, §§97–98.

154. Grush, 'Berkeley and the Spatiality of Vision', pp. 420–21, 425, 430, suggests that the visual and tactile spheres naturally correspond, and that Berkeley is wrong to take the possibility of those spheres being discalibrated for their being uncalibrated.

155. *New Theory of Vision*, §62.

This is a radically contingent connection between the sensory realms, and there are signs that Berkeley himself wavers from it. The microscope, he says, 'brings us, as it were, into a new World', but 'whereas the Objects perceived by the Eye alone have a certain Connexion with *Tangible* Objects, whereby we are taught to Foresee what will ensue, upon the Approach or Application of distant Objects to the Parts of our own Body, which much conduceth to it's Preservation; there is not the like Connexion between things *Tangible* and those Visible Objects, that are perceiv'd by help of a fine *Microscope*'.[156] Surely in a relationship of radical contingency between the visual and tactile realms creatures with this microscopic vision (where a great many more visible points correspond to the same tangible extension) would simply make a different set of linguistic correspondences between touch and vision? But Berkeley naturalises the specific calibration of the visible and tangible for humans as they are: God has made the proper connection between visible and tangible ideas for the preservation of the human creature. The correspondences are arbitrary but happen to be the best.

Another form of naturalised connection between the visible and tangible realms is suggested when Berkeley admits that 'the Visible Square is fitter than the Visible Circle to represent the Tangible Square'. This 'is not because it's liker, or more of a Species with it. But, because the Visible Square contains in it several distinct Parts, whereby to mark the several distinct, corresponding Parts of a Tangible Square'. So the two realms share basic dispositions to be experienced as having parts, as having number—dispositions quite like that of orientation that Berkeley otherwise strips from the immediate visual field. Such a correspondence, Berkeley says, is still to be considered arbitrary: God was under no necessity to make visual part and tactile part correspond in the way that they do. But once that decision was made, it is no longer arbitrary that a four-parted visible idea corresponds better than a one-parted visible idea to a four-parted tactile idea.[157] That is, Berkeley conceives of the visual language as a set of systematic rather than atomic correspondences between the two realms.

156. Ibid., §85.
157. Ibid., §§142–43.

The systematic nature of correspondences between sensory realms makes it appropriate to think of them as linguistic. So too does context-sensitivity: if signs are arbitrary but participate in a system, they can have different values in different contexts. Berkeley says this is the case with faintness:

> Faintness, as well as all other *Ideas* or Perceptions, which suggest Magnitude or Distance, does it in the same way, that Words suggest the Notions to which they are annexed. Now, it is known, a Word pronounced with certain Circumstances, or in a certain Context with other Words, hath not always the same Import and Signification that it hath when pronounced in some other Circumstances, or different Context of Words.[158]

The context, the co-presence of other signs, is a determining factor in the meaning of a sign. So too are the circumstances of its use. I believe that Berkeley is here referring to extra-codal circumstances that are not internal to the sign system but which, being determined by the makers and users of that sign system, are relevant to its purport in a different manner, and possibly to an even greater extent.

God uses vision as a language to communicate to people (and presumably other creatures also) facts about distant objects of touch, so that people can seek or shun appropriate objects. Sharing this language with God is one way in which people purposefully inhabit and negotiate their environment.[159] Having ideas of vision is vital to having foreknowledge or understanding about ideas of touch. But having ideas of touch is vital to understanding what God intends humans to do—how they should orient themselves in the world. Ideas of touch are not an ultimate referent. They are a medium for something else. That something is the will of God, the ultimate cause of all things in Berkeley's philosophy—as indeed in much other Christian philosophy. Willing is an (or the) activity of spirit that has the effect of producing ideas in others. We become practised interpreters of the acts of will or the dispositions of spirit behind various kinds of ideas.

---

158. Ibid., §73.
159. See Grush, 'Berkeley and the Spatiality of Vision', pp. 441–42.

Berkeley persistently compares seeing magnitude and distance to seeing passions in the countenance of another person. In the *Notebooks*: 'I saw gladness in his looks, I saw shame in his face so I see figure. or Distance'. In the *New Theory of Vision*:

> [T]he Passions which are in the Mind of another, are of themselves, to me invisible. I may nevertheless perceive them by Sight, tho' not immediately yet, by means of the Colours they produce in the Countenance. We do often see Shame or Fear in the Looks of a Man, by perceiving the Changes of his Countenance to Red or Pale.
>
> As we see Distance, so we see Magnitude. And we see both, in the same way that we see Shame or Anger, in the Looks of a Man. Those Passions are themselves Invisible, they are nevertheless let in by the Eye along with Colours, and alterations of Countenance, which are the immediate Object of *Vision*: And which signifie them for no other Reason, than barely because they have been observ'd to accompany them. Without which Experience, we shou'd no more have taken Blushing for a Sign of Shame, than Gladness.[160]

The dispositions of spirits, active or passive, can be read from ideas perceived by the various senses, even if those dispositions are not themselves ideas. God is never passive in having ideas, but always active. All the ideas we perceive must be taken as actions of God, the perceptible effects of his active spirit willing us to do this or that. These acts of will are evident to us as laws of nature (such as those of human physiology and psychology) that make the consequences of our own acts of will dependable, the signs of others' states of mind legible. Orientation in the environment is determined by pleasurable or painful ideas of touch, of which we are given foreknowledge by ideas of sight. These ideas of sight, however, thereby become the occasion of pleasure themselves.[161] We become conscious of how well the language of vision produces the ends for which God has devised it and find that realisation pleasurable: 'the vast Extent, Number, and Variety of Objects that are, at once, with so much Ease, and Quickness, and Pleasure, suggested

---

160. *Notebooks*, §231; *New Theory of Vision*, §§9, 65.
161. For a discussion of aesthetic pleasure in Berkeley's work, see Jones, 'George Berkeley and the Value of the Arts'.

by [the language of vision]: All these afford Subject for much and pleasing Speculation; and may, if any thing, give us some Glimmering, Analogous, Prænotion of Things, that are placed beyond the certain Discovery, and Comprehension of our present State'.[162] This second-order pleasure from reflecting on the language of vision even gives us a glimpse of the pleasures of higher orders of creature. Reflecting on the nature of visual language, understanding the laws of nature—the reliable connections between the phenomena of different senses—in short, being a philosopher, is one way in which humans can start to see some of the joys of the blessed spirits, the invisibility of which Berkeley queried in that unpublished remark in his notebooks.

162. *New Theory of Vision*, §148; Astell, *A Serious Proposal to the Ladies*, pp. 75–76, says that the pleasure of union with God 'is only intelligible to those who have tried and felt it, which we can no more describe to the dark and sensual part of Mankind, than we can the beauty of Colours and harmony of Sounds to the Blind and Deaf'. Berkeley may adapt Astell's analogy between union with God and sensory perception to make his analogy between the language of the visible world and the joys of the afterlife. Berkeley excerpted this text in *Ladies Library*.

CHAPTER THREE

Immaterialism

HOW AND WHEN BERKELEY came to formulate the doctrine for
which he is best known, the doctrine of immaterialism, is not
easy to determine. It is expressed fully in the *Principles of Human
Knowledge*, published in 1710, but many of its elements were
already stable in the *Notebooks*, the two sets of notes in which
Berkeley recorded brief and only occasionally thematically sustained philosophical remarks. These notebooks have different dates
of composition. Notebook B, the earlier of the two, containing the
first 399 notes, was used for a number of other purposes: it holds
versions of Berkeley's paper on Dunmore cave and equations relating to the algebraic game described in *Miscellanea Mathematica*.
These are likely to date from early 1706 and early 1705, respectively.[1] It is not known when the notes constituting the *Notebooks* were
begun or ended. Later entries in notebook A mention a correspondence between Locke and Limborch that was published in May–
June 1708 and so cannot have been composed before then.[2] On the
evidence of a clear and significant change in view between entries
§696 and §750 of notebook A (on the question of whether all words
signify ideas) and the fact that the *Manuscript Introduction* shares
the later view, it has been suggested that the *Manuscript Introduction* was written at some point between the composition of those
two entries. As Berkeley recorded in the margins of the manuscript

1. Belfrage, 'Dating Berkeley's Notebook B'.
2. *Notebooks*, §§709, 743.

the dates during the last two months of 1708 on which he made revisions to the text of the *Manuscript Introduction*, the first draft must have been composed earlier. Bertil Belfrage therefore concludes that the *Manuscript Introduction* was written and revised in the summer of 1708.[3]

Considering that the *Manuscript Introduction* likely dates from a moment within the span of the *Notebooks* and is so clearly preparatory work for the *Principles of Human Knowledge*, and that *Three Dialogues* is so clearly a recasting and development of the ideas and attitudes central to the *Principles of Human Knowledge*, I work in this chapter with all of these texts in order to give a sense of what was fixed and what was fluid in Berkeley's immaterialism in this period of around five years. My discussion will confirm what many scholars have already noted: that this suite of writings serves a social and religious programme.[4] I suggest that the idiosyncratic solution Berkeley proposes to the problems he is confronting is a good reconciliation of the competing conceptions of philosophy and its purpose at his time, but that it was not necessarily a solution well suited to achieving his social and religious ends. It was more of an esoteric than exoteric solution. It achieved a strategic negotiation of the competing institutional and social roles exerting an influence on the practice of philosophy, but it did not prove to be a strategic selection of the means of discursive intervention most likely to bring about the proposed social objectives of the philosophy of Berkeley's heroic period.

One way of illustrating the disjunction between Berkeley's new doctrine and his historical moment is to think of immaterialism as a defence of one of Berkeley's favourite biblical texts, Saint Paul's assertion that people live and move and have their being in God (Acts 17:28), but in the language and by the standards of contemporary (post-Lockean) philosophical discourse. The text of Paul is cited very often, of course, and the truth it is supposed to capture is treated in quite different ways by different kinds of writers. The truth of this text might be a kind of knowledge gained by faith, as with other Christian mysteries, just as certain as the knowledge of

---

3. *Manuscript Introduction*, introduction, pp. 20–23, 51–57.
4. See, for example, Charles, 'Introduction', p. 1.

the senses. This is the context in which Robert Dixon cites the text from Paul: 'I Am, hath sent me, to you that are. And because I am, is, therefore we are, are by him, and are, from him, and in him, in whom we live and move and have our being, and from whom through Jesus Christ, we hope for an everlasting well being'.[5] Another writer, having cited Paul and argued that God is an immanent cause, not a transient one, describes this theological intuition as 'Common *Metaphysicks*, which tell us, that all Beings are either First, or second Beings; and that Second Beings are *Participations* of the First'.[6] The claim that God 'concurs with our motion', in the context of an argument that nothing subsists without God's power, is supported by reference to the historical fact that 'the Heathen in all their streights fly to their Altars, and fill their Temples with cries and sacrifices'.[7] The behaviour of non-Christian peoples can demonstrate the universality of the intuition that human action depends on God.

Writers with whom Berkeley was compared, to his distaste, also cite the text. John Norris, just before citing the text, proposes a natural union between God and the soul: 'she dwells and subsists in *God*, who is the Place of Spirits, as Space is of Bodies'.[8] Malebranche similarly proposes that minds are in God as extension is in space, and he goes on to cite Paul.[9] In a different text, again citing Saint Paul, Norris says that he will not explain, though he could, 'how Man depends upon God, both as to the motions of his Body, and as to the thoughts of his Mind [. . .] fearing lest this should engage me too far in School-niceties and Philosophical Notions, such as would rather amuse than instruct the ordinary Reader, (there being hardly in all Philosophy, a more nice Point than that of the *Divine Concourse*)'.[10] Malebranche offers just the kind of nice philosophical justification that Norris declines to provide, and one general characteristic shared by Berkeley and Malebranche, however far apart some of their philosophical assumptions were, is that

5. Dixon, *Short Essay of Modern Divinity*, p. 33.

6. Burthogge, *Essay on Reason and the Nature of Spirits*, p. 256.

7. Charnock, *A Treatise of Providence*, p. 22.

8. Norris, *Practical Discourses*, p. 167.

9. Malebranche, *The Search after Truth*, p. 230.

10. Norris, *Practical Treatise Concerning Humility*, p. 82.

they offer a modern philosophical defence of the truth of a scriptural text that was often defended on grounds of faith, intuition, or anthropology. Locke treats the text very differently. Towards the end of his demonstration that people have distinct ideas of space and body, Locke seems to assume that Solomon's expression 'The heaven, and the heaven of heavens, cannot contain thee' and the text from Paul are not 'to be understood in a literal sence'.[11] Defending the truth of this scriptural text in a nonmetaphorical sense, and doing so in the language of modern philosophy, is one way of understanding the project of Berkeley's new doctrine and seeing its disjunction with some major philosophical currents of his time.

I preface my discussion of the doctrine of immaterialism with some remarks on the social and intellectual context evoked by the *Notebooks*, which provide significant details of Berkeley's personal friendships and reading. Daniel Dering, who would later marry Mary Parker, sister of Catherine, who would herself marry John Percival, provided anecdotes in conversation that gripped Berkeley. Dering asked a 'Question [. . .] touching the thief & paradise', presumably referring to the story in Luke 23:43 in which Jesus tells one of the thieves with whom he is being crucified that he will be with him in paradise today. The question is, perhaps, whether any time passes between the moment of death and the attainment of paradise, as time is nothing but the succession of ideas in the mind, and the interval between death and resurrection is without ideas: 'No broken Intervals of Death or Annihilation. Those Intervals are nothing. Each Person's time being measured to him by his own Ideas'. The second mention of Dering, in which Berkeley makes a memorandum of the 'story of Mr Deering's Aunt', is less easy to gloss.[12] But Dering is a discussant of Berkeley's emerging immaterialism and provides narrative challenges to or confirmations of its cruxes.

The 'Doctrine about relative Good', 'that if the Happyness of my Acquaintance encreases & mine not proportionably, mine much [*sic*] decrease', was 'discuss'd with French, Madden etc'.[13] One French was Matthew French, a fellow at TCD (who was charged

---

11. *Essay*, II.xiii.26, p. 179.
12. *Notebooks*, §§127, 590, 201.
13. Ibid., §569.

with preparing an account of the case of Forbes, a Jacobite student; see chapter 4), and another French was a student in the year above Berkeley. One of these two Frenches is also greeted in a letter from Berkeley to Prior, sent from Livorno, 26 February 1713/14.[14] Samuel Madden, who acquired the nickname "Premium Madden" for the generous prizes he donated for performances in the useful arts through the (Royal) Dublin Society in the 1730s, was still discussing social philosophy with Berkeley in that decade. Berkeley tells Prior that Madden was the editor of all three parts of *The Querist*.[15] Madden had joined TCD the year after Berkeley, on 28 February 1700/1701.[16] Berkeley's philosophy is being tested with and by a group of intimates at TCD, intimates who would share—or perhaps already did—Berkeley's social and political concerns and responsibilities.

The *Notebooks* also provide evidence of Berkeley's wide reading in logic, metaphysics, optics, and mathematics. The presence of Newton, Leibniz, Cheyne, Cavallerius, Wallis, and Raphson in *Notebooks* and/or 'Of Infinites' was noted in the previous chapter.[17] Further mathematical, geometrical, and astronomical authors also present in *Notebooks* are Charles Hayes, author of a 1704 treatise on fluxions; Isaac Barrow, Copernicus, and Euclid; Ignace Gaston Pardie's 1705 book on trigonometry; and Edmund Halley. In optics, Molyneux and Cartesians appear.[18] In the broad and related fields of logic, epistemology, and metaphysics, Berkeley knew Locke and Le Clerc through his instruction at TCD. Other readings to which the *Notebooks* bear witness include Malebranche, Michelangelo Fardella's *Universae Philosophiae Systema*, Aristotle, Henry More, Descartes, Hobbes, Spinoza, J.S. (John Sergeant, whose *Solid Philosophy Asserted* of 1697 distinguished between notions implanted in the mind by God and mere phantasms produced by things and perceived by the senses), and a book by Gerard De Vries referred to

14. Letter 63, p. 115.

15. Letter 263, Berkeley to Prior, 5 March 1735/36, p. 398.

16. Richey, 'Madden, Samuel Molyneux'.

17. *Notebooks*, §§30 (Newton), 333 (Leibniz), 367 (Cheyne), 346 (Cavallerius), 482 (Wallis), and 298 (Raphson).

18. Ibid., §§308 (Hayes), 75 (Barrow), 404 (Copernicus), 425 (Euclid), 432 (Pardie), 448 (Halley), 32 (Molyneux), and 281 (Cartesians).

in abbreviated form as 'de id.', his *Diatribe de ideis rerum innatis*, which suggests that mind is known by means other than those of sensory perception. There is an A.B., identified as William King (A.B. for Arch Bishop), who writes on *potentia* in his *De origine mali*.[19] Berkeley was also reading works in the history of human knowledge by Francis Bacon, Pierre Bayle, and Thomas Sprat. The presence of Joseph Justus Scaliger and Marsilio Ficino demonstrates his acquaintance with canonical early modern polymathic writers.[20] The *Notebooks* testify to Berkeley's general learning in modern philosophical science.

By no means all of the writers who shaped the thinking of the *Notebooks* are named. Smiglecius (Śmiglecki), whose *Logica* featured along with Burgersdijk's in the TCD syllabus, may have been the prompt for Berkeley's shift in the orientation of his new doctrine with respect to the scholastic distinction between *ens rationis* (a being of reason) and *ens reale* (a real being). Berkeley first makes an 'N.B. according to my Doctrine all things are entia rationis i.e. solum habent esse in Intellectu' (beings of reason, i.e., they only have a being in the intellect). The first question of the first disputation of Smiglecius's book is 'Quid sit Ens rationis?' (What is a being of reason?). The mode of being of real and intellectual things is distinguished: 'nomine entis rationis intelligimus, quod cùm non sit ens reale, in solo intellectu existit' (by the name 'a being of reason' we understand that which as it is not a real being, exists solely in the intellect).[21] Berkeley answers his own assertion in a facing-page note: 'according to my Doctrine all are not entia rationis the distinction between ens rationis & ens reale is kept up by it as well as any other Doctrine'. Another remark presents 'Entia

19. Ibid., §§230 (Malebranche), 79 (Fardella), 41 (Aristotle), 298 (More), 784 (Descartes), 796 (Hobbes), 824 (Spinoza), 840 (Sergeant), 887 (De Vries), and 142 (King). McCracken, 'Stages on a Cartesian Road to Immaterialism', p. 30, 40, contends that Berkeley knew Fardella's text through Bayle and also notes its participation in a route to immaterialism. For John Sergeant, see Sergeant, *Solid Philosophy Asserted*, p. 15. For De Vries, see Bracken, *George Berkeley*, p. 124. For King, see Berkeley, *Philosophical Commentaries Generally Called the Commonplace Book*, p. 351.

20. *Notebooks*, §§564 (Bacon), 358 (Bayle), 506 (Sprat), 370 (Scaliger), and 390 (Ficino).

21. Śmiglecki, *Logica Martini Smiglecii*, p. 2. I thank my colleague Alex Douglas for his advice on translating the Latin terminology.

realia & Entia rationis' as 'a foolish distinction of the Schoolmen', only to be answered in another facing-page note: 'there not so foolish neither'.[22] Whether and how a distinction between rational and real beings should be maintained is a matter Berkeley wrestles with, and one which he may develop from Smiglecius. As will already be evident, Berkeley carried on a dialogue with himself over the course of the notebooks, sometimes challenging or revising his views on a facing page. He also employed a system of marks next to almost every entry. Some of these are letters abbreviating a certain philosophical topic and follow a key that is included in the notebooks themselves: M for matter, P for primary and secondary qualities, for example. There are also + and x marks, the meaning of which is uncertain. I will mention these marks only when I suspect they have a particular relevance to the point I am discussing.

The New Doctrine

The kind of philosophical insight that leaves things as they are can nonetheless give the person who experiences it a sense of deep comprehension that might also distinguish her or him from others who go about in what is undeniably the same world, but without the same understanding of its organisation.[23] The self-consciousness with which Berkeley remarks on the development of his thinking suggests he had an experience of this kind in arriving at his immaterialism. In an isolated notebook entry, he remarks, 'My speculations have the same effect as visiting forein countries, in the end I return where I was before, set my head at <u>ease</u> and enjoy my self with more satisfaction'.[24] Having travelled far to return to the same place, Berkeley has therefore a deeper knowledge of what is there, and a greater relish for it, than those around him. The second half of the first decade of the eighteenth century saw Berkeley attempting to formulate, systematise, and communicate what he would come to call a doctrine. It is not possible to say how and when Berkeley

22. *Notebooks*, §§474 and a, 546 and a.

23. See Wittgenstein's remark, 'Philosophy [. . .] leaves everything as it is', in *Philosophical Investigations*, p. 49e, §124.

24. BL Add MS 39304, f. 4r. I thank Joseph Jones for prompting me to consider how Berkeley felt about his new doctrine.

arrived at many of the specific features of the new doctrine. The most strongly marked developments—Berkeley's acceptance of the possibility of talk about infinity and rejection of the necessity of words signifying ideas in order to be meaningful—have already been noted by historians of philosophy, and I echo them in this and the previous chapter.[25] But it is not possible to say, on the basis of sources currently known, if or when Berkeley had the insight that there is no substance or matter underlying and provoking sense perceptions, or when he came to attribute such perceptions directly to the lawlike regularities instituted by a caring God. Rather than attempt to identify such a point in time, or consider how Berkeley might have adapted specific sources with which he was working, I focus on indicating the character of the position Berkeley developed at this point in his career, and how it might relate to his philosophical and practical needs.

In the suite of texts that formulate and propagate immaterialism, Berkeley is presenting a doctrine. He talks of 'my doctrine' in the *Notebooks*.[26] A doctrine might well be a systematic theory. But it is also the body of knowledge that is taught in any particular discipline. Berkeley's doctrine has a specific aim, that of enquiring into 'the Grounds of *Scepticism, Atheism*, and *Irreligion*', as the title page to the *Principles of Human Knowledge* puts it. The 'very Root of *Scepticism*' that Berkeley is enquiring into—and digging out—is that 'Men thought that Real Things subsisted without the Mind, and that their Knowlege was only so far forth *Real* as it was conformable to *real Things*', a view that makes all knowledge uncertain. 'For how can it be known, that the Things which are Perceiv'd, are conformable to those which are not Perceiv'd, or Exist without the Mind?' Ridding the learned world of the concept of material substance dispels 'so many Sceptical and Impious Notions, such an incredible number of Disputes and puzzling Questions', that 'all Friends to Knowlege, Peace, and Religion' have a reason to wish Berkeley's arguments for immaterialism true. The goal of the book is to 'inspire [. . .] a pious Sense of the Presence of GOD'.[27] The

---

25. See Berman, *George Berkeley*, pp. 16–17.
26. *Notebooks*, §194.
27. *Principles of Human Knowledge*, §§86, 96, 156.

principles, expanded on in *Three Dialogues*, will leave '*Atheism* and *Scepticism* [. . .] utterly destroyed', and Berkeley aims 'to convince *Sceptics* and *Infidels* by Reason'.[28] This type of ambition for a work of philosophy was not uncommon in the Dublin and TCD of Berkeley's time. William King had explained to Peter Browne why he took up the topic of free will in his treatise on the origin of evil, *De origine mali*, which was published in 1702: ''Tis a nice and metaphysical subject, I confess, but of great moment and most necessary to be duly understood at a time when Epicurism, Deism, and the denial of revealed religion are so much in vogue'.[29] Berkeley shares the sense that a religious philosophy defending revealed religion is urgently needed.

Berkeley claims a practical advantage for his doctrine in its elegance and efficiency. The *Principles* Berkeley expounds 'abridge the labour of Study, and make Human Sciences far more Clear, Compendious, and Attainable than they were before'.[30] Philonous, the immaterialist in *Three Dialogues*, lists the 'great Advantages [. . .] both in regard to Religion and Humane Learning' that flow from immaterialism: belief in God and the immortality of the soul; evaporation of all the problems associated with matter and physical causation, as too the problem of how spirit and matter operate on one another; and an end to the 'Frenzy of the ancient and modern *Sceptics*'.[31] If there is a little uncertainty in *Notebooks* about the details of the doctrine and how best to express it rhetorically, the practical and socioreligious orientation of the enterprise is evident in the published work: banish the concept of matter from the physical and mathematical sciences, and with it atheism and scepticism, and reap the rewards in morality and theology as people make their moral decisions in the knowledge that God is immediately present to humans and active in producing the phenomenal world.

The *Notebooks, Manuscript Introduction, Principles of Human Knowledge,* and *Three Dialogues* present a core of immaterialist tenets. That spirit is the only substance of the world and the only causal power, ideas are a manner of being of spirit, and ideas

28. *Three Dialogues*, preface, sig. A5.
29. TCD MS 750/2/2/56, 2 February 1700, cited in Greenberg, 'Leibniz on King', p. 206.
30. *Principles of Human Knowledge*, §134.
31. *Three Dialogues*, pp. 155, 157 (LJ II.257–58).

are signs rather than causes and often mediate the communication of spirits with one another—these aspects of immaterialism
have already been discussed in chapter 1. I now itemise some of the
other consistent elements of Berkeley's doctrine, beginning with
his critique of abstraction. This critique, which often takes up topics written about by Locke, is broad and comprehends alternative
accounts of the phenomenology of perception, the mechanics of
natural languages, and ontology in general.[32]

Newton's work on the refraction of light provides the starting
point for the development of a view of colour perception as gradual
and particular: 'We have not pure, simple ideas of blue, red or any
other colour (except perhaps black) because all bodies reflect het-
erogeneal light'.[33] An idea of blue can never be simple because it
will always be a shade of blue. We cannot experience a blue that
is not a shade of blue. Likewise, 'we have not an idea of Colour
without extension. we cannot imagine Colour without extension'.
Any blue we imagine must be extended. This report on the nature
of human imaginative capacity is a challenge to the commonplace
view that '[t]he word Blue stands for a Colour without any extension or abstract from extension'. Given that we can meaningfully
say 'blue' without there being a simple idea of the colour blue, without extension or any other property, Berkeley is led to ask: 'How
can all words be said to stand for ideas?' (I will pick up on the relationship of words and ideas later.) Berkeley thinks that because
'blue' is meaningful, and because correspondence to an idea is traditionally the criterion for meaningful use of a word, people have
assumed there must be an abstract idea 'blue'. But he thinks that
'very evil consequences in all the Sciences' flow from this 'Doctrine
of Abstraction' that is 'Entirely owing to Language'.[34]

Berkeley's new doctrine will extirpate abstraction, with challenging consequences for the very definition of what it is to be human: 'If

32. For one sustained account of abstraction in Berkeley, see Pappas, *Berkeley's
Thought*.

33. *Notebooks*, §151. Berkeley is picking up on Newton's experiments in *Opticks*, in
which white light is said to be heterogenous because it contains all the other colours of the
spectrum, which can be refracted from it at their individual frequencies. See, for example,
Newton, *Opticks*, p. 141: 'the commix'd Impressions of all the Colours do stir up and beget
a Sensation of white, that is, that Whiteness is compounded of all the Colours'.

34. *Notebooks*, §§494, 564.

you take away abstraction, how do men differ from Beasts. I answer by shape. By Language rather by Degrees of more & less'.[35] The human-animal distinction may be weaker in a world without abstraction, but it is still language that will mark it. The theme continues in *Principles of Human Knowledge*. Citing Locke's suggestion that animals are bound in their reasoning by sensory particulars, having no capacity for abstraction, as is evident in their lack of language, Berkeley again attacks the idea that language capacity is evidence of abstraction. He fears that 'a great many of those that pass for Men' must be counted animals if abstraction is the distinguishing mark of the human.[36] The *Manuscript Introduction*, too, doubts the basis of Locke's distinction and proposes an alternative manner in which words signify generally: 'a Word becomes general by being [the] made the Sign, not of a General Idea but of many particular Ideas'.[37] This formulation obviates the difficulty of abstract general ideas that they must include a certain property, but cannot complete it with any determinate value. Berkeley's preferred examples of this problem are the abstract triangle, which cannot be equilateral, isosceles, or any other kind of triangle, and a man who has colour but is neither black nor white, nor any other particular colour. In the 1734 edition of *Principles of Human Knowledge*, Berkeley qualifies somewhat: people might be capable of abstraction if they have an idea of a triangle without particularly attending to the specific relation between its sides, but they cannot have an idea of a triangle that is both isosceles and equilateral.[38]

The critique of abstraction is designed to put in doubt the abstract ideas of existence and of matter. Berkeley thinks it 'an Opinion strangely prevailing amongst Men' that things like mountains 'have an Existence Natural or Real, distinct from their being perceiv'd by the Understanding'. The supposed error is one of abstraction: 'For can there be a nicer Strain of Abstraction then to distinguish the Existence of sensible Objects from their being Perceiv'd'? To imagine existence we must have imagined some other properties, and we have therefore imagined a particular thing

35. Ibid., §594.

36. *Essay*, II.xi.10–11, pp. 159–60; *Principles of Human Knowledge*, introduction, §11.

37. *Manuscript Introduction*, ff. 8–9r.

38. *Principles of Human Knowledge*, §§9, 17; *Principles of Human Knowledge* (1734 text), §16.

or a set of particular things. Berkeley is not trying to do away with objects like mountains, but rather the 'Matter or Corporeal Substance' that is taken to be the external, unthinking, and unperceived cause of the ideas we have of them.[39] Existence and matter are paradigmatic abstractions in that they are not properties: they are not perceived in any particular ideas, as extension or colour might be. Matter is that in which real things, beyond their being perceived, are said to have their existence. Matter and existence, then, are the abstractions most in need of abolition in order to close the sceptical gap between things as they seem and things as they are.

Berkeley's campaign against abstraction has consequences for the distinction between primary and secondary qualities, as expressed, for example, by Locke, who identifies qualities as powers in objects to cause ideas in perceivers.[40] Primary qualities are inseparable from bodies. Secondary qualities are the powers of primary qualities to cause, for example, ideas of colour. When Hylas is obliged to admit to Philonous that colour is mind-dependent, he holds to the non-mind-dependence of primary qualities—'Extension, Figure, Solidity, Gravity, Motion, and Rest'.[41] In the *Principles of Human Knowledge*, this move is presented as characteristic of materialists, who 'will have our Ideas of the Primary Qualities to be Patterns or Images of things which exist without the Mind, in an unthinking Substance which they call *Matter*'. These materialists think that 'the different Size, Texture, Motion, &c. of the minute Particles of Matter' constitute the primary qualities of objects. Berkeley counters that it is not possible to form an idea of these primary qualities without specific secondary qualities attached to them; he concludes, 'Where therefore the other sensible Qualities are, there must these be also, *i.e.* in the Mind and nowhere else'.[42]

39. *Principles of Human Knowledge*, §§4–5, 35.

40. *Essay*, II.viii.8–10, pp. 134–35.

41. *Three Dialogues*, p. 32 (LJ, II.187).

42. *Principles of Human Knowledge*, §§9–10. Rorty, 'A World without Substances or Essences', p. 55, has described this Berkeleian response to Locke on primary and secondary qualities as the first pragmatic, anti-essentialist move. Winkler, *Berkeley: An Interpretation*, pp. 256, 262, 274–75, on the other hand, suggests that Berkeley distinguishes between primary and secondary qualities as types of sign, the primary being more helpful in avoiding pain and the secondary better for the construction of more complex predictive hypotheses.

Ideas are comprehensively subordinated to spirits in immaterialism: they have no existence without being perceived by a mind. Spirit is that wherein ideas 'Exist, or, which is the same thing, whereby they are Perceiv'd; for the Existence of an Idea consists in being Perceiv'd'. For unthinking things, 'Their *Esse* is *Percipi*, nor is it possible they shou'd have any Existence, out of the Minds or thinking Things which perceive them'.[43] It took Berkeley some time to arrive at this formulation, his earlier phraseology retaining an emphasis on the power to produce effects, as was seen in Locke's definition of a quality. All 'things by us conceivable are 1st thoughts 2^{d}ly powers to receive thoughts, 3^{d}ly powers to cause thoughts neither of all wch can possibly exist in an inert, senseless thing'. Bodies are said to exist 'whether we think of 'em or no, they being taken in a twofold sense. Collections of thoughts & collections of powers to cause those thoughts'. Bodies are 'combinations of thoughts & combinations of powers to raise thoughts'. These remarks are found in notebook B. Notebook A seems to abandon the conception of bodies as collections of thoughts and powers to cause them. 'Existence is percipi or percipere' (to be perceived or to perceive), Berkeley says in the fourth entry in that notebook, adding in a later facing-page remark, 'or velle i:e. agere' (to will or to act).[44] Spirits perceive and ideas are perceived, and in that way they exist. The afterthought that spirits may also exist in willing or doing, and not only in the act of perceiving, relates to a topic that was much more fluid in this period of Berkeley's thinking: whether the existence of mind depends upon the existence of perceived ideas. I now turn to this topic and other such fluid elements of the early immaterialist doctrine.

Adjustments

The dependence of mind on its ideas is a topic on which Berkeley adopts opposing views at different points in the composition of notebook A, as is evident in this remark and the facing-page comment later made upon it:

---

43. *Principles of Human Knowledge*, §§2–3.
44. *Notebooks*, §§228, 282, 293, 429 and a.

Qu: how is the soul distinguish'd from it's ideas? certainly if there were no sensible ideas there could be no soul, no perception, remembrance, love, fear etc. no faculty could be exerted.

The soul is the will properly speaking & as it is distinct from Ideas.

For the earlier Berkeley, for there to be an operative force such as spirit, there needs to be something for it to operate on. He therefore suggests that minds have an intuitive knowledge of the existence of ideas before they have an intuitive knowledge of themselves, 'in that we must have Ideas or else we cannot think'. The beginnings of a change to this view can be seen in the distinction Berkeley makes between different faculties that might constitute the mind. 'The Understanding seemeth not to differ from its perceptions or Ideas', but what about 'the Will and passions'?[45] Can those faculties of the soul that incline spirits to seek or shun things also be identified with the ideas that are their objects? They cannot be wholly identified with ideas, as they contain an attitudinal or affective surplus. If an idea we experience makes us suffer—the idea of intense heat, for example—we are aware of a passive phase in our otherwise active being as spirits, something the idea makes us feel.[46] Attitude or affect seems to be the basis for Berkeley's growing sense of the separation of mind and idea. Later in notebook A, Berkeley is 'certain that our Ideas are distinct from the Mind i.e. the Will, the Spirit'. Twenty-six years later, in the 1734 text of *Three Dialogues*, the self, exemplified in a list of faculties, is said to be altogether distinct from ideas: 'PHILONOUS. [. . .] I my self am not my Ideas, but somewhat else, a thinking active Principle that perceives, knows, wills, and operates about Ideas'.[47] To arrive at this position Berkeley also had to work through the question whether the faculties, particularly the will and understanding, are themselves distinct. I now turn to these internal distinctions.

Berkeley was in dialogue with himself across the period of composing and making facing-page annotations to notebook A:

the Understanding not distinct from particular perceptions or Ideas.

45. Ibid., §§478 and a, 547 (see also 563), 587.
46. Bettcher, *Berkeley's Philosophy of Spirit*, pp. 75–76, 80.
47. *Notebooks*, §847; *Three Dialogues* (1734 text), p. 297 (LJ, II.233).

The Understanding taken for a faculty is not really distinct from yᵉ Will.

The Will not distinct from Particular volitions.

This alter'd hereafter.

The distinction between understanding and ideas is corrected by a refusal entirely to distinguish between understanding and will. Berkeley makes definite steps away from the belief that spirits have a faculty that enables them to perceive ideas without willing anything at all and that the will and understanding are 'distinct beings'.[48] As the notebook proceeds, understanding is taken to be more active. 'Understanding is in some sort an Action'. 'Will & understanding Volitions & ideas cannot be severed [. . .] either cannot possibly be without the other'. Existence is willing: 'While I exist or have any Idea I am eternally, constantly willing, my acquiescing in the present State is willing'.[49] Spirit, as noted in chapter 1, is characteristically active and volitional. Berkeley's public formulation is that a 'Spirit is one Simple, Undivided, active Being, as it perceives Ideas, it is called the *Understanding*, and as it produces or otherwise operates about them, it is called the *Will*', and no ideas can be formed of it, he maintains, because ideas are 'Passive and Inert'.[50] The *Notebooks* show Berkeley moving towards the conception of spirit as a simple, undivided, active being.

In their later stages, the *Notebooks* engage frequently in notes and memoranda concerned with the verbal and rhetorical presentation of Berkeley's doctrine, such as we have just seen. Berkeley is attempting to transform a philosophical vocabulary from within. But he has an additional difficulty that is very specific to his doctrine, one that was mentioned at the opening of this chapter: he does not believe the mind has a capacity to form abstract ideas, but does think the belief in that capacity has created grave dangers for natural, human, and divine science; he does believe that words such as 'blue' or 'extension' can be used meaningfully, but

48. *Notebooks*, §§614–65 and a, 645, 708.

49. Ibid., §§821, 841, 791; see also Roberts, *A Metaphysics for the Mob*, p. 104: 'The identification of the mind with the will leads Berkeley to undertake one of the boldest maneuvers in the history of the philosophy of mind: the elimination of the understanding'.

50. *Principles of Human Knowledge*, §27.

not, as those who preceded him, because they signify abstract general ideas. That words can be used meaningfully without signifying ideas is another integral element of Berkeley's doctrine towards which the *Notebooks* show him travelling.[51]

The later stages of notebook B and the early stages of notebook A are clear.

> Language & knowledge are all about ideas, words stand for nothing else.
>> Axiom. No word to be used without an idea.
>> No word to be used without an idea.[52]

Around seventy entries later, however, Berkeley is asking how all words can stand for ideas if we can meaningfully use the word 'blue' to signify a colour without extension. As we have already seen, general terms such as 'blue' are one difficulty for restricting the signification of words to ideas. Berkeley notices others as well:

> Some words there are wch do not stand for Ideas v.g. particles Will etc particles stand for volitions & their concomitant Ideas.[53]

There are words that stand for something other than ideas, such as 'will', which signifies the activity of spirit, and there are particles (by which Berkeley means conjunctions, prepositions, and so on, following Locke) that express relations between ideas, or the active operations of a spirit in ordering ideas according to what seems good.[54] Locke, no less than Berkeley, presents relation as an act of mind: 'When the Mind so considers one thing, that it does, as it were, bring it to, and set it by another, and carry its view from one to t'other:

---

51. I follow Losonsky, 'Locke on Meaning and Signification', p. 130, in thinking that a pre-theoretical, minimal concept of meaning operates in Locke (and in Berkeley too), and that meaning is 'whatever makes language intelligible to us as well as others'. Losonsky is arguing against Ashworth, 'Do Words Signify Ideas or Things?', who distinguishes between words having meanings and the use of words to reveal or express certain ideas. I thank one of the anonymous readers for the Press for pointing me to these sources.

52. *Notebooks*, §§312, 356, 422.

53. Ibid., §§494, 661 and a.

54. *Essay*, II.vii, pp. 471–73. Lee, 'What Berkeley's Notions Are', pp. 28–29, takes the same view and refers to *Essay*, III.vii.1 and 4, for confirmation that particles are prepositions and conjunctions that indicate an act of mind.

This is, as the Words import, *Relation* and *Respect*.[55] In the revised edition of *Principles of Human Knowledge* Berkeley published in 1734, he emphasises the activity of mind in relating: 'all Relations including an Act of the Mind, we cannot so properly be said to have an Idea, but rather a Notion of the Relations or Habitudes between Things'. If this mental distinction is preserved, Berkeley will not fight over the terms used: 'if in the modern way the Word *Idea* is extended to Spirits, and Relations and Acts; this is after all an Affair of verbal Concern'.[56] Looking back a quarter of a century later, Berkeley has not effected the change in philosophical vocabulary he might have hoped for, by preventing 'idea' being applied to spirits and their operations, but is still encouraging the mental hygiene that distinguishes between active spirits and passive ideas.

The *Manuscript Introduction* and *Principles of Human Knowledge* state the case at greater length for meaningful uses of words that do not signify ideas. As this subject is discussed in chapter 12, I shall mention only some features of Berkeley's arguments here. Something like the Lockean scheme according to which words are means of externalising our internal ideas or conceptions persists in *Principles of Human Knowledge*: 'it is agreed on all hands, that the proper Use of Words, is the marking our Conceptions, or Things only as they are Known and Perceiv'd by us'. This is a commitment that survives beyond the carefully justified assertion that 'the communicating of Ideas marked by Words is not the chief and only end of Language, as is commonly suppos'd', and that 'other Ends, as the raising of some Passion, the exciting to, or deterring from an Action, the putting the Mind in some particular Disposition', may mean that ideas are 'intirely omitted'.[57] '[O]ur Conceptions' or 'Things [. . .] as they are Known and Perceiv'd by us' are not limited to ideas, but may, as we have seen, encompass objects of knowledge of which we have no idea, such as spirits and relations. 'Conception' does the work that Berkeley, in 1710, was unhappy should be done by 'idea', the work of signifying relations and spirits. The 1734 text clarifies:

---

55. *Essay*, II.xxv.1, p. 319.
56. *Principles of Human Knowledge* (1734 text), §142.
57. Ibid., §83 and introduction, §20.

To me it seems that ideas, spirits and relations are all in their respective kinds, the object of human knowledge and subject of discourse: and that the term *idea* would be improperly extended to signify everything we know or have any notion of.[58]

Knowledge and discourse can be about things other than ideas; ideas are not always required for a use of language to achieve its ends. These are significant departures from the Lockean conception of language and from the philosophical vocabulary that goes along with it.

Reading the introduction to *Principles of Human Knowledge* next to the *Manuscript Introduction* is productive here. The *Manuscript Introduction* is a little fuller in its account of the uses of language other than signifying discrete ideas. Words may signify more than one idea, work as letters do in algebra (i.e., they may be manipulated without continual consciousness of their signification), or signify no ideas at all. Propositions involving abstract ideas (such as the categories of 'human' or 'animal') produce tautologies or contradictions, but not ideas: Berkeley does not believe that 'George Berkeley is a human' is a proposition that signifies ideas in the mind. When (or indeed if) we formulate such propositions— Berkeley's example is about a dog called Melampus—we are saying that one thing has a right to be addressed by an alternative description: 'That the particular [creature] thing I call Melampus has a right to be called by the name Animal'.[59] This is not a matter of the formation of propositions that are meaningful because they relate to an underlying nexus of ideas in relation to one another, but of the right to be called one thing or another.[60]

The use of 'good' concerns Berkeley in the *Manuscript Introduction* just as it does in *Principles of Human Knowledge*, and he has already arrived at the conclusion that references to goods of which we can have no idea (principally the goods of the next life) can meaningfully be made when the 'design' of the speaker is to

---

58. Ibid. (1734 text), §89.

59. *Manuscript Introduction*, ff. 19–21, f. 21r.

60. One might take this as a hint that Berkeley thinks language is more likely to provide profitable redescriptions than access to the truth, as does Rorty, 'A World without Substances or Essences', p. 64.

make her addressees 'chearfull and fervent in their Duty'.[61] The *Manuscript Introduction* is fuller, however, on what is achieved by the promise of a *'Good thing'* of which we have no idea, and how this happens.[62] In this account, the important element, which is elided in *Principles of Human Knowledge*, is the image of children accepting parental discipline and later being able to rationalise their obedience to the honest person who promises them an as yet unknown good:

> Upon mentions of ^a Reward to a Man for his pains and performance in any occupation whatsoever, it seems to me that [?]diverse things do ordinarily ensue. For there may be excited in his Understanding an Idea of the particular good thing to him proposed for a Reward. There may also ensue thereupon an Alacrity and Steddiness in fulfilling those Conditions on which it is to be obtain'd, together with a zealous desire of serving and pleasing the Person in whose Power it is to bestow that good Thing. All these things, I say, may and often do follow upon the pronunciation of those words that declare the Recompence. Now I do not see any reason why the latter may not happen without the former. What is it that Hinders why a Man may not be stirr'd up to diligence and zeal in his Duty, by being told he shall have a good Thing for his Reward, tho' at the same time there be excited in his Mind no other Idea than those of Sounds or Characters? When he was a Child he had frequently heard those Words used to him to create in him an obedience to the Commands of those that Spoke them. And as he grew up he has found by experience that upon the mentioning of those Words by an honest Man it has been his Interest to have doubled his zeal and Activity for the service of that Person.[63]

This register of vocabulary, one in which human understanding of what is good is compared to the induction of the child into the world of adult preferences and ultimately, though in the *Manuscript Introduction* only implicitly, the induction of humans into a providentially governed order, is not frequent in Berkeley's writings. He may have encountered it in a text of 1705 that he excerpted

---

61. *Manuscript Introduction*, f. 23r.
62. *Principles of Human Knowledge*, introduction, §20.
63. *Manuscript Introduction*, f. 23r.

for the anthology he published in 1713, *The Ladies Library*. There it is noted that 'tho' the *Children* see nothing but *Pleasure* in what they propose, yet the *Parent* stands higher, and sees there is also *Sin*, or *Danger* near it, and how it will Operate at a distance, and what Fruits it will produce'. Children should learn from parents' guiding their choices 'that the commanding them Things for the present uneasie, and forbidding them Things for the present sweet and desirable, may be full as reasonable to be comply'd withal'. 'There is all the Reason in the World, that while *Children* want Understanding to direct their Choice and Will, they should have no other Will but that of their *Parents*, and therefore should obey while they do not understand'.[64] Children should conform their wills to a parent, who is superior, sees further, and understands consequences. (Berkeley would use similar arguments for instilling correct prejudices in *A Discourse Addressed to Magistrates and Men in Authority* [1738].)

The same language is put to use again in his dialogue *Alciphron* (1732), in which it is taken for granted, by both the freethinking and the right-thinking speakers, that 'the Conduct of a Parent [must] seem very unaccountable to a Child, when its Inclinations are thwarted, when it is put to learn the Letters, when it is obliged to swallow bitter Physic, to part with what it likes, and to suffer, and do, and see many things done contrary to its own Judgment, however reasonable or agreeable to that of others', but that the parent is nonetheless self-evidently better and wiser than the child.[65] It is not just that uses of 'good' may help us to act with a view to the goods of the next world that should ultimately determine our actions, even without our having ideas of them, but that a personal, subordinate, loving, and familial relationship with God, a relationship of servitude, is the means by which we can develop the attitudes of obedience necessary to orient our actions towards as yet unknown goods.[66]

---

64. *Ladies Library*, II.14 and 9, excerpting Fleetwood, *Relative Duties of Parents and Children*.

65. *Alciphron*, VI.17.

66. Williford, 'Berkeley's Theory of Operative Language', notes the importance of this example in the *Manuscript Introduction* to Berkeley's theory of meaning, but he does not emphasise the role of paternal authority in creating the conditions for taking terms on

In the *New Theory of Vision*, it was the structure of the visible world and its relationship to the tangible that was given as the source of 'some Glimmering, Analogous Prænotion of Things, that are placed beyond the certain Discovery, and Comprehension of our present State'.[67] In *Manuscript Introduction*, we need to attend to the actual goods that follow on from a superior's or a parent's promise of as yet unknown goods. We need to develop a reading of the phenomenal world not based on experience alone, but on the instruction and advice of other spirits to whom we attribute a superior sense. Authority and experience go together. Berkeley's empiricism, if that term can be applied to him, is tempered by a quiet commitment to the authority of those who know better that is evident in the *Manuscript Introduction* and resurfaces at many points in his career when he considers social obligations and responsibilities. It is interesting to note that the corresponding paragraph of the *Principles of Human Knowledge* also treats uses of language that ask us to accept the claims made by authority, but from a critical point of view: 'when a Schoolman tells me *Aristotle hath said it*, all I conceive he means by it, is to dispose me to embrace his Opinion with the Deference and Submission which Custom has annex'd to that Name'.[68] Given the anti-scholastic tenor of the *Principles of Human Knowledge*, this is not a claim to authority that sympathetic readers will be inclined to accept. *Principles of Human Knowledge* elides the picture of the appropriate acceptance of authority—in the image of the personal, familial relationship—that fills out the linguistic theory of *Manuscript Introduction*, preferring to emphasise the anti-scholastic, introspective activity of the modern philosopher.

Philosophical Personae

Berkeley passes from this discussion of words that do not necessarily refer to ideas—the theory of language variously called emotive or noncognitive or operative by different historians of philosophy and one of the most characteristic and modern-feeling elements of

---

trust. Brykman, 'La Sémantique dans le Dialogue VII', pp. 411–12, compares these passages from the *Manuscript Introduction* and *Alciphron*.

67. *New Theory of Vision*, §148.

68. *Principles of Human Knowledge*, introduction, §20.

his doctrine[69]—to the claim that he will *therefore* take ideas 'bare and naked into my View, keeping out of my Thoughts, so far as I am able, those Names which long and constant Use hath so strictly united with them'.[70] This is quite a shift, from a sociable world of disposition and persuasion to an introverted world. The shift is still more apparent in the *Manuscript Introduction*, which has, proportionately, given more room to the linguistic aspect of the new doctrine and also to the socialised aspect mentioned earlier.[71] This is a matter of philosophical persona. Berkeley is shifting from the persona of the philosopher as guide and instructor to the persona of the philosopher as iconoclast and introvert who disregards custom, looks hard into his own mind, and dispassionately reports the truth.

The study of philosophical personae as they emerge historically has been proposed as an alternative to a history of philosophy that presents philosophy as a coherent enterprise, continually unfolding in the reflection of reason upon itself. To study philosophical personae is to study a range of practices (experimental, linguistic, and spiritual, for example) loosely held together by a privileged type of person, often operating in a particular institutional context. It is to recognise that induction into philosophy must be achieved by certain means, implying a certain philosophical pedagogy, rather than reason calling out singly and purely to the individual and yet transcendent human subject.[72] In a study of the history of early modern philosophy through its personae, conflicts between types of personae and their respective practices are understood in cultural-political terms as border disputes 'between the scholastic logician and the humanist rhetorician, the Aristotelian physicist and the Galilean astronomer, the philosopher and the jurist, the arts professor and the metaphysician, the court Neoplatonist and the university Aristotelian, and the philosopher and the theologian'.[73]

---

69. Belfrage, 'Editor's Commentary', pp. 46–50; David Berman, *George Berkeley*, pp. 11–20; Williford, 'Berkeley's Theory of Operative Language'.

70. *Principles of Human Knowledge*, introduction, §21.

71. See *Manuscript Introduction*, f. 27r.

72. Hunter, 'The History of Philosophy and the Persona of the Philosopher', pp. 575, 583–84.

73. Condren, Gaukroger, and Hunter, 'Introduction', p. 8.

Berkeley's early philosophical writing presents some shifts of doctrine, as we have just seen. It also presents some shifts between philosophical personae and in how people are called to philosophy and then act as philosophers. Berkeley is trying out different personae at different moments in these writings, and the attitudes he performs and the roles for philosophy in social, moral, and religious life they imply are expressive of broader tensions within the concepts of philosophy and the philosopher that were being formulated in his historical moment.[74]

At times Berkeley adopts an anti-scholastic persona. We have just seen the implicit distrust of the invocation of the name of Aristotle by schoolmen seeking an authority on which to found their claims, followed by Berkeley's claim that he will consider his own ideas bare and naked as the best way to arrive at truth. Locke is just one strong precedent for such a combination of attitudes: '*Aristotle* was certainly a knowing Man, but no body ever thought him so, because he blindly embraced, and confidently vented the Opinions of another', he says. Those 'bred up in the Peripatetick Philosophy' wrongly 'think the Ten Names, under which are ranked the Ten Predicaments, to be exactly conformable to the Nature of Things'. People 'may find an infinite number of Propositions, Reasonings, and Conclusions, in Books of Metaphysicks, School-Divinity and some sort of natural Philosophy' that join together undoubted statements about things such as the soul 'without knowing at all what the Soul really is', neither expressing nor gaining any knowledge.[75] Following Locke, Berkeley has already adopted a style of philosophising that calls for the abolition of scholastic vocabulary in favour of the close inspection of one's own ideas and notions.[76]

---

74. For a sketch of the range of practices and habits of thought encapsulated in 'philosophy' and the 'philosophical', see Harris, 'Introduction'.

75. *Essay*, I.iv.23, p. 101; III.x.14, p. 497; IV.viii.9, p. 615.

76. It ought to be noted, however, that an Aristotelian logic more oriented towards experience and experiment was transmitted from Padua, where Zabarella was working, to Britain and Ireland from the seventeenth century. This transmission was effected partly through textbooks that Berkeley studied in Dublin, such as those of Burgersdijk and Śmiglecki. This experiential and experimental Aristotelianism may have made a more positive contribution to British and Irish empirical philosophy. See Sgarbi, *The Aristotelian Tradition*, pp. 53–77, 233. Luce, *Berkeley and Malebranche*, p. 53, suggests that Berkeley would have read Bayle's entry on Zabarella closely. Sgarbi, *The Aristotelian Tradition*,

To adopt this persona was to announce oneself as unafraid to challenge the terminology and procedure of philosophical logic as it was still being taught at university. Swaths of scholastic vocabulary could be cut off in favour of the study of one's own notions. As Berkeley has it, 'Anima Mundi. Substantial fforms. Omniscient radical Heat. Plastic vertue. Hylarchic principle. All these vanish'.[77] As it turns out, this list of arcane terms from the sects of philosophy is borrowed from George Cheyne:

> That there is no such thing as an *Universal Soul* animating this vast System according to *Plato*, nor any *Substantial Forms* according to *Aristotle*, nor any Omniscient *Radical Heat* according to *Hippocrates*, nor any *Plastick Virtue* according to *Scaliger*, nor any *Hylarchic Principle* according to *Henry More*, is evident[.]

Such terms, Cheyne says, mask their authors' ignorance, take power from God, assume powers beyond those ascribed to them, and attempt to explain phenomena much better accounted for by the materialist philosophy. Cheyne's abolition of this vocabulary serves a purpose directly opposed to Berkeley's: the use of the materialist hypothesis to argue for the existence and causal priority of God. 'The *Existence* of *Matter*, is a plain *Demonstration* of the *Existence of a Deity*'. Matter is 'destitute of all *active* Qualities whatsoever', so cannot have caused itself to exist. '[T]his *Universe* was not form'd by the same Laws it now is govern'd [*sic*], and which it's several Parts in their Actions do now obey; and therefore of necessity there must have been some Power superior to, and distinct from, that of Matter, which form'd this *System* at first, and prescrib'd Laws for it's Parts afterwards to observe'.[78] Berkeley adopts the persona of the anti-scholastic philosopher, purging pseudo-philosophical vocabulary to clear room for a new hypothesis, only to include 'matter' in the bonfire of the concepts such philosophers have set.

---

pp. 217, 223–27, also aligns Richard Burthogge and Narcissus Marsh with Zabarella. Fraser, in *The Works of George Berkeley, D.D.*, IV.44, suggests that Burthogge anticipates some of Berkeley's views. Marsh's presence in Dublin was no doubt still felt when Berkeley was considering his new doctrine.

77. *Notebooks*, §617.

78. Cheyne, *Philosophical Principles*, I.3–4, II.79–81.

But not everything about the early immaterialist writings points away from scholasticism and towards modernism. Recalling the *Manuscript Introduction* and its willingness to grant authority some role in determining the ends we pursue and the reasons for which we pursue them, Berkeley might not appear altogether to throw off the veneration for Aristotelian authority that marks the schools. Berkeley was himself a teacher in one of those schools as he composed *Notebooks* and the other works of this early period, and he had only a year previously completed the arduous series of examinations and disputations required to become a fellow at TCD. It has been remarked that philosophical textbooks, such as Burgersdijk's, were composed for juniors, and that the junior party in acquiring disciplinary knowledge must believe the master, with Aristotle's *De sophisticis elenchis*, 1.2, cited as authority for the view. 'The persona of the philosophical pupil was therefore submissive, deferential, and necessarily credulous', as Richard Serjeantson puts it. It would be for 'modernists' such as Francis Bacon, whose *Advancement of Learning* Serjeantson cites, to set a limit to such subordination: 'Disciples doe owe vnto Maisters onely a temporarie beleefe, and a suspension of their owne iudgement, till they be fully instructed, and not an absolute resignation, or perpetuall captiuitie'.[79] Deference to the authority of the master is an induction into a particular practice of philosophy, one that, centred in Aristotelian metaphysics, sees the human as a combination of the intellectual substance of the divinity and the corporeal substance of the animals, and philosophy as the means of becoming more consubstantial with the divine.[80] Berkeley's interest in participation in the divinity through conformation of the human to the divine will is perfectly in tune with such a conception of philosophical education and induction, one that has been presented as scholastic and Aristotelian.

A similar ambivalence in the persona Berkeley adopts is evident if one considers a bifurcation between the theological and scientific impulses in the philosophy of Berkeley's time.[81] One might present

79. Serjeantson, 'Becoming a Philosopher', p. 11.

80. Hunter, 'The History of Philosophy and the Persona of the Philosopher', pp. 585–86.

81. This is the way in which Berkeley's place in the history of philosophy is presented by Schneiders, 'Concepts of Philosophy', pp. 26–33.

this as the question of how long a consideration of God's will can be deferred in the study of the laws of nature. The two societies for which Berkeley recorded rules were to discuss topics 'in any of the Sciences' and in the 'new Philosophy'.[82] The Dublin Philosophical Society, to which Berkeley presented his paper 'Of Infinites', would, according to St George Ashe, introduce 'things and Experiments' in the place of 'words and empty speculations'.[83] Berkeley himself was interested in algebraic demonstrations of 'the certainty of human evidences and traditions' and in the mathematical demonstration of morality.[84] He was to that degree at least engaged in the broad project of applying Newtonian principles to the human and divine sciences. Neither of his two earliest surviving letters—efforts in natural history and the calculation of the effects of gravity on the atmosphere—make any reference to God. When Berkeley stated his distinctive doctrine that the visible world is the language of nature in *New Theory of Vision*, published in 1709, he revised his text to mention the author of the language of nature only in the edition of 1732.[85] God is not as emphatically present in these earliest writings for publication.

At this same time (1707/8), however, Berkeley was delivering a discourse in the college chapel on the infinite goods of heaven, noting that the being of God is the first great principle of morality and that without God humans would be '[w]retcheder than a stone or tree'.[86] Isolated remarks in a notebook refer to 'all the sciences' as 'false for the most part' and made up of 'useless labour'; Berkeley's own speculations are 'directed to practise and morality, as appears first from making manifest the nearness and omnipresence of God'.[87] As he sets about notebook A, Berkeley imagines 'a mighty sect of Men will oppose me'. He expects the support of 'Moralists, Divines, Politicians, in a word all but Mathematicians & Natural Philosophers (I mean only the Hypothetical Gentlemen).

---

82. BL Add MS 39305, ff. 101r, 103r.

83. TCD MS 888/1, f. 32v.

84. *Miscellanea Mathematica*, in Sampson, ed., *The Works of George Berkeley*, I.57; *Notebooks*, §755.

85. *New Theory of Vision* and *New Theory of Vision* (1732 text), §§147, 152.

86. LJ VII.9–15; *Notebooks*, §§508, 107.

87. BL Add MS 39304, f. 4r.

Experimental Philosophers have nothing whereat to be offended in me'.[88] Berkeley's aim in the *Principles of Human Knowledge* is to 'inspire my readers with a pious sense of the presence of God', as 'the Consideration of GOD, and our *Duty*', he claims, 'deserves the first place in our Studies'.[89] The text clearly instructs philosophers to consider God as the cause of the phenomena of nature and reminds them that when they discover 'the general Laws of Nature', they are not uncovering 'immutable Habitudes, or Relations between Things themselves, but only [. . .] GOD's Goodness and Kindness to Men, in the Administration of the World'. Berkeley acknowledges that generalising from observations enables us to predict very distant events, but discourages his readers from proceeding from observed regularity to the statement of universal principles.[90] The published text of the *Principles of Human Knowledge* omits an example of one such predicted event that is given in a manuscript draft, that the earth, 'in after ages when the motion of that planet round the sun shall be quite stopt [. . .] shall fall into the Sun'.[91] This prediction, perhaps, does not tend sufficiently to reinforce the impression of God's goodness and kindness to men in the administration of the world. The aim of natural philosophy is not to reduce phenomena to general rules, but to provide a recreation for the mind and make nature serve God's glory and 'the Sustentation and Comfort of our Selves and Fellow-Creatures'.[92] Perceptible regularity in nature is the immediate product of God's will, not of an arm's-length creation whose laws God once established. Seeing God as present in this way is taking an extended or enlarged view. Advice to 'enlarge our View' would continue to form part of Berkeley's theological, educational, and moral programme for the rest of his career.[93] Berkeley the natural scientist and Berkeley the theologian are engaging in slightly different styles of being a philosopher.

88. *Notebooks*, §406.

89. *Principles of Human Knowledge*, §156.

90. *Principles of Human Knowledge*, §§107, 105–6.

91. BL Add MS 39304, f. 40r.

92. *Principles of Human Knowledge*, §109. Compare Malebranche, *The Search after Truth*, p. 292: 'God has formed the universe that minds might study it, and that through this study they might be led to the knowledge and worship of its Author'.

93. *Principles of Human Knowledge*, §153.

In slightly more general terms, a performative and rhetorical struggle is evident between the upstart and the conformist in the notes of Berkeley's early period. Berkeley presents himself as a seeker after truth, impartial in his view, indifferent to the consequences of expressing it:

> I am young, I am an upstart, I am a pretender, I am vain, very well. I shall Endeavour patiently to bear up under the most lessening, vilifying appellations the pride & rage of man can devise. But one thing, I know, I am not guilty of. I do not pin my faith on the sleeve of any great man. I act not out of prejudice & prepossession. I do not adhere to any opinion because it is an old one, a receiv'd one, a fashionable one, or one that I have spent much time in the study and cultivation of.[94]

By the time of publication, Berkeley knows, he will be presenting 'some passages that, taken by themselves, are very liable (nor could it be remedied) to gross misinterpretation, and to be charged with most absurd consequences'. Still, he will be courageous in presenting demonstrable truths:

> As for the Characters of Novelty and Singularity, which some of the following Notions may seem to bear, 'tis, I hope, needless to make any Apology on that account. He must surely be either very weak, or very little acquainted with the Sciences, who shall reject a Truth, that is capable of Demonstration, for no other Reason but because it's newly known and contrary to the Prejudices of Mankind.[95]

Principles of Human Knowledge asserts the simple strength of mind required to follow the truth where it leads.

But the expression of truths to which the philosopher is naturally committed is hardly unpremeditated, and Berkeley's notes show that he is highly aware of his own rhetorical tendencies and of the need to control them in order to present his work in the most acceptable form. For example, he makes an 'N.B. to rein in y^r Satyrical nature'. The kind of satire Berkeley is thinking of might be seen in the series of entries in which he claims that 'we Irish' are not sophisticated enough to comprehend entities such as a

---

94. *Notebooks*, §465.
95. *Principles of Human Knowledge*, preface, sig. A5r.

mathematical point that is 'not altogether nothing nor is it down-right something', entities that are the fictions of self-deluding phi-losophers.[96] Such satirical philosophic wit might align Berkeley with the rhetorical practice of Hobbes or other equally undesirable antecedents.[97] Reining in satirical tendencies is not the only rhe-torical craft Berkeley practises, as the series of instructions to him-self he sets out in *Notebooks* demonstrate ('Mem: Carefully to omit Defining of Person, or making much mention of it', for example).[98] Berkeley is planning a rhetorical strategy that will extend over the *Principles of Human Knowledge* as we have it as well as the pro-jected second (and third) books, which were never published. His purpose is conservative—to leave things as they are:

> Say you, at this rate all's nothing but Idea meer phantasm. I answer every thing as real as ever. I hope to call a thing Idea makes it not the less real. truly I should perhaps have stuck to ye word thing and not mention'd the Word Idea were it not for a Reason & I think a good one too wch I shall give in ye Second Book.

As Berkeley put it slightly earlier in the notebook: 'the horse is in the stable, the Books are in the study as before'.[99] To what is Berke-ley a pretender if his new doctrine leaves things just as they are? Which is the rhetorical gesture, that which upsets existing ideas or that which conserves them?

The disjunctive attitudes that Berkeley's early immaterialist writings exhibit might characterise British and Irish philosophy of the period, even post-Reformation European philosophy more generally. The editors of *The Cambridge History of Seventeenth-Century Philosophy*, for example, identify the common theme of their contributors as the conflict between the Aristotelian-scholastic philosophy that was dominant at the start of the century and the corpuscularian philosophy—descended from ancient atom-ism and the progenitor of modern physics—that was making such

96. *Notebooks*, §§634, 394.

97. Lund, *Ridicule, Religion, and the Politics of Wit*, p. 31, presents Hobbes as the first master of Augustan wit, having perfected the 'bite', in which the reader does not know whether to take the author in jest or earnest.

98. *Notebooks*, §713; see also §848.

99. *Notebooks*, §§807, 429.

an impact towards its end.[100] The picture of the philosopher this culture produces can be introspective and solitary, and when philosophers themselves depict the fundamental scene of philosophy, it is often one in which all other people are banished. Descartes's *Meditations* provide an instance too well known to require citing. Berkeley's *Manuscript Introduction* provides another:

> Let us conceive a Solitary Man, °one born and bred in such a place of the World, and in such Circumstances, as he shall never have had Occasion to make use of Universal signs for his Ideas. That Man shall have a constant train of Particular Ideas passing in his Mind. Whatever he sees, hears, imagines, or any wise conceives is on all hands, even by the Patrons of ^Aabstract Ideas, granted to be particular. Let us withall suppose him under no Necessity of labouring to secure him^self from Hunger and Cold: Bbut at full Ease, naturally of good Facultys [but] and Contemplative. Such a one I should take to be nearer the Discovery of certain Great and Excellent Truths yet unknow, than he that has had the Education of the Schools, ~~has been instructed in the Ancient and Modern Philosophy,~~ and by much reading and Conversation has [furnish'd his Head] attain'd to the Knowledge of Those Arts and Sciences, that make ~~such~~ ^So great a Noise in ^the Learned World. It is true, the Knowledge of Our Solitary Philosopher is not like to be so very wide and extended, it being confin'd to those few Particulars that come within his own observation. But then, if he is like to have less Knowlege, he is [~~withall~~] also withall like to have fewer Mistakes than Other Men.[101]

The untroubled, solitary intellect models access to truth. The revisions to this text show Berkeley questioning how much of the social world of learning must be rejected to come to such truths— is it only the prior philosophy that is rightly called scholastic, or all ancient and modern philosophy? Is it only those branches of knowledge that are currently fashionable (make noise in the world), or also those that are deemed significant by the educated elite (the learned world)? As he wrote this, Berkeley was, of course, also participating in the formal and informal institutional life of

---

100. Ayers and Garber, 'Introduction', I.1–6 (pp. 2–3).
101. *Manuscript Introduction*, ff. 27r–28r.

philosophy. He was teaching in a college, having passed its highly scholastic fellowship examination; he had dedicated a work of mathematics to two of his students; in his notebooks, he names friends with whom he has discussed particular topics and the future patron he impressed with a harangue (Pembroke); he had belonged to at least two societies that met to discuss the sciences and the new philosophy; and he prepared papers to present to those societies and for publication in the journal of record for such enterprises, the *Philosophical Transactions of the Royal Society*. Berkeley, and other philosophers of his moment, modelled the philosopher as asocial, and yet they philosophised within specifically constructed and intensely social worlds.

Berkeley's model for the philosopher became increasingly socialised over this early period. When he reworked and developed *Principles of Human Knowledge*, he did so in the form of a dialogue: an extended social interaction between two people provides the dramatic context for Hylas coming to see the truth of Philonous's views. The setting of *Three Dialogues*, indeed, offers a strikingly different scene for philosophising than the solitary philosopher of the *Manuscript Introduction*. The dialogue takes place in college grounds, and the ringing of the bell for prayers interrupts its first part. Philonous is happy to return to the conversation: he is sociable and conceives of argument as a social duty. A person of taste, he enjoys the beauty of the creation. He is pious and recommends immaterialism as an aid to piety.[102] *Three Dialogues* presents a way to truth that is sociable and that calls for specific forms of words suited to particular interlocutors in particular times and places. The religious, collegiate man of taste is the persona to deliver such truths. This is a persona to which Berkeley would adhere closely in his later life, as the following chapters will demonstrate.

One could continue to multiply the subterranean attitudinal tensions in Berkeley's early writings. He is in some ways a philosopher of the reformed church, proudly Protestant, unafraid to challenge authority. But there is also a countervailing tendency to feel

102. *Three Dialogues*, p. 66 (LJ, II.207); pp. 71–73 (LJ, II.210–11); pp. 155–58 (LJ, II.257–58).

a real and present social threat from confessional difference and to recognise legitimate authority as the means of preserving order. (The following chapter will show the degree to which Irish political and religious thought registered the events of 1688–1689 as the collapse of the social order.)[103] Besides the allowance for meaningful uses of terms accepted on authority in the *Manuscript Introduction*, Berkeley presents quite an authoritarian God: the laws of nature in *Principles of Human Knowledge* derive directly from the authority of God, untempered by a semi-autonomous conception of nature, subject to change at God's discretion, and devised for the good of the whole creation, even should, as Pope would later put it, some partial ills be involved in producing universal good.[104]

Again, Berkeley is a philosopher of the way of ideas, building arguments from the phenomena of sensory experience and introspection, scrupulously avoiding the errors derived from the customary use of words and language. And yet he presents one of the most developed accounts of the legitimate functioning of language without referring to ideas, an account that recognises the goods in conduct and outcome that can be produced by the honest and responsible deployment of this function of language. And again, he is an anti-abstractionist and yet argues that 'Ideas or Things by me perceived, either themselves or their Archetypes exist independently of my Mind[.] [. . .] They must therefore exist in some other Mind, whose Will it is they should be exhibited to me'.[105] World history is the gradual revelation, by decree, to finite minds of ideas eternally present to the divine mind:

> All Objects are eternally known by God [. . .] when Things, before unperceptible to Creatures, are, by a Decree of God, made perceptible

103. For the ways in which reform, the new science, and the cultivation of philosophical virtues are related, see Harrison, 'The Natural Philosopher and the Virtues'.

104. *Manuscript Introduction*, ff. 23–24r; *Principles of Human Knowledge*, §§30–31, 107–9, 151.

105. *Three Dialogues*, pp. 78–79 (LJ, II.214–15). Wenz, 'Berkeley's Christian Neo-Platonism', argues that Berkeley is consistently both an empiricist and a Christian neo-Platonist across his career. Brown, 'Leibniz and Berkeley', is more aware of the tensions between the early modernist Berkeley and a later Platonic Berkeley, though he notes that they can be reconciled by making mind a unified and the only causal substance (pp. 250–51).

to them; then are they said to begin a relative Existence, with respect to created Minds. Upon reading, therefore, the *Mosaic* Account of the Creation, I understand, that the several Parts of the World became gradually perceivable to finite Spirits, endowed with proper Faculties[.][106]

This is the anti-abstractionism of a philosopher who was recommending Plato to Percival in 1709 and celebrating Socrates, whose 'whole employment was the turning men aside from vice, impertinence, and trifling speculations to the study of solid wisdom, temperance, justice, and piety, which is the true business of a philosopher'.[107] In 1744, Berkeley was still striving to reconcile Platonism with accounts of the trinity and his own concept of spirit in *Siris*.

Berkeley, then, cultivated more than one style of philosophical persona. The different personae suggest that he shifted between different conceptions of his philosophical orientation, or, perhaps better, of the orientation of philosophy at his moment in the history of that family of practices. At times he was an upstart, satirical, defiant, and solitary as he overturned prevalent doctrines through unabashed commitment to the truth. But all this defiance would be for a doctrine that was conceived of as friendly to the moralists, divines, and politicians, one that argued for the legitimacy of authority and the personal choice of God in framing laws of nature. It was a doctrine developed in the schools, partly for the schools, in collaboration with friends and with other members of philosophical societies. This 'most extravagant Opinion that ever entered into the Mind of Man, *viz.* That there is no such Thing as *material Substance* in the World', was a doctrine that sought to leave everything where it was.[108] There is at least one account of Berkeley, Ann Donnellan's, that presents him as unafraid of being thought original (in that slightly pejorative eighteenth-century sense) and as enjoying argument, which he took to be a foundation of human sociability (see chapter 9). Did Berkeley's new doctrine of immaterialism appeal to him perhaps in part because of its originality, the likelihood of its provoking opposition, and its wilful rejection

106. *Three Dialogues*, p. 145 (LJ, II.252).

107. Letters 6 and 11, Berkeley to Percival, 21 October 1709, p. 24, and 27 December 1709, p. 32, where Berkeley recommends the *Crito* and *Phaedo*; citation from p. 32.

108. *Three Dialogues*, p. 3 (LJ, II.172).

of a powerful hypothesis in the physical sciences and metaphysics, that of a material world? Or did his character simply make him unafraid of the consequences of adopting the solution to the problems of materialism—particularly the chasm it opens up between things as they are and things as they seem—when once it occurred to him? It is in any case an important feature of this new doctrine that it allows Berkeley to exercise all the personae he has a desire to inhabit—to upset, overthrow, strike out alone; to preserve, revere, obey; to socialise and be socialised.

Without expressing an evaluative judgement of the doctrine in itself, one can note its historical reception in a modest number of concentric circles.[109] The doctrine was broached amongst intimates, such as those mentioned in *Notebooks*—French, Madden, Dering—and friends and patrons such as Percival. Berkeley told Molyneux that he had 'communicated my design & papers to' Dr Elwood, whom he found to be 'a man of very good sense'.[110] Presumably this good sense was evident in Elwood's response to some combination of the working and draft materials for *Principles of Human Knowledge*. Percival himself was noncommittal. Noting that he may not be able to understand *Principles of Human Knowledge* thoroughly 'for want of having studied philosophy more', he reports the scorn of some of his acquaintance with whom he has shared the outline of the doctrine:

A physician of my acquaintance undertook to describe your person, and argued you must needs be mad, and that you ought to take remedies. A Bishop pities you that a desire and vanity of starting something new should put you on such an undertaking, and when I justified you in that part of your character, and added the other deserving qualities you have, he said he could not tell what to think of you. Another told me an ingenious man ought not to be discouraged from exercising his wit, and said Erasmus was not the worse thought of for writing in praise of folly, but that you are not gone so far as a gentleman in town who asserts not only that there is no such thing as matter but that we have no being at all.

109. For the fullest account of this material, see Bracken, *The Early Reception of Berkeley's Immaterialism*.

110. Letter 9, Berkeley to Molyneux, 8 December 1709, p. 30.

Even those who had read *Principles of Human Knowledge* and admired its argument and perspicuity placed Berkeley with Malebranche and Norris, whose 'labours' are 'of little use to mankind for their abstruseness'. Samuel Clarke refused to be drawn into a correspondence. The dedicatee, Pembroke, thought Berkeley 'ingenious' and 'to be encouraged, but [. . .] he could not be convinced of the non-existence of matter'.[111]

Three Dialogues was clearly designed to meet some of these criticisms of *Principles of Human Knowledge*, as it is far more explicit in distancing Berkeley from Malebranche, for example.[112] When Berkeley travelled to London in 1713, even before *Three Dialogues* had been published, there were reports that 'your opinion has gained ground among the learned' and had made a convert of Joseph Addison, at least according to Percival. Berkeley called John Arbuthnot 'the first proselyte I have made by the Treatise I came over to print'.[113] Percival himself, once he read *Three Dialogues* through, was 'much more of your opinion than I was before. The least I can say is, that your notion is as probable as that you argue against'. But the same letter notes Swift's view that Arbuthnot hadn't been converted after all. Berkeley, however, will fight for his convert: 'As to what you write of Dr. Arbuthnot's not being of my opinion, it is true there has been some difference between us concerning some notions relating to the necessity of the laws of nature, but this does not touch the main point of the non-existence of what philosophers call material substance, against which he has acknowledged he can object nothing'.[114] A decade later, Swift wrote that Berkeley was 'the Founder of a Sect called the Immaterialists', and that 'Doctʳ Smalridge and many other eminent Persons were his Proselytes'.[115] The early reviews of *Principles of Human Knowledge* in the *Journal des Sçavans* and *Mémoires de Trévoux* and of

111. Letter 17, Percival to Berkeley, 26 August 1710, p. 42; letter 20, Percival to Berkeley, 30 October 1710, p. 48; letter 23, Percival to Berkeley, 28 December 1710, p. 52.

112. See McCracken and Tipton, *Berkeley's Principles and Dialogues*, p. 170.

113. Letter 47, Percival to Berkeley, 14 May 1713, p. 94; letter 43, Berkeley to Percival, 16 April 1713, p. 88.

114. Letter 50, Percival to Berkeley, 18 July 1713, p. 98; letter 52, Berkeley to Percival, 7 August 1713, p. 100.

115. Wooley, ed., *The Correspondence of Jonathan Swift*, II.518; letter 622, Swift to Lord Carteret, 4 September 1724.

Three Dialogues in *Mémoires de Trévoux, Journal littéraire,* and *Memoirs of Literature* collectively did little justice to the arguments of the books and tended to assimilate Berkeley with, and then criticise him alongside, Malebranche.[116]

The public expression of immaterialism was not a success of the type we might imagine Berkeley anticipated, one in which moralists, politicians, divines, and true experimental philosophers rallied around him in grateful support when they realised that he had provided them with the defences against the encroachments of materialists (who opened the door for sceptics and atheists) which they required (even if they did not yet know it) in order to prevent social disorder and promote eternal truths. The doctrine was too new, required too much courageous adherence to truth, and made God immediately present in the regular phenomena of nature accessed by the senses in ways that were unanticipated and whose consequences were equally difficult to anticipate. If *Principles of Human Knowledge* did not offer this audience enough to make them vocal in its support, it stood little chance with those ingenuous materialists who might have come to it in the expectation of another treatise working from the succession of their ideas to the regularity of the material world, like Cheyne's. It was just as unlikely to garner support from those disingenuous materialists whose design was to loosen the grip of religious and political authority on the conduct of humans by opening up the sceptical gap between things as they are and things as they seem. Berkeley's new doctrine of immaterialism was good for him in his immediate context: it enabled him to reconcile, after a manner, the competing conceptions of philosophy and the philosopher to which he was attracted, and with which the northwestern European philosophy of his time was also struggling. For Berkeley himself and for the inner circle of intimates with whom the doctrine was developed, immaterialism worked. But it worked less well in the controversial, polemical setting in which Berkeley imagined it performing its main role, that of challenging scepticism and atheism while establishing the grounds for peace and social order in a sense of the presence of God and the

116. See McCracken and Tipton, *Berkeley's Principles and Dialogues,* pp. 173–90, for texts of most of these reviews and commentary.

subordination to authority properly required. The lack of success on these counts may be one of the reasons Berkeley turned, in the period contemporary with the publication of *Three Dialogues* in 1713, to alternative means of pursuing his chief aim of inspiring a pious sense of the presence of God: political discourse and practice, journalism, anthology-making, and preaching.

There are no strong reasons to think that Berkeley departed from the core of his immaterialism, nor that he sought further to elaborate it. After 1713, Berkeley published no new text for which immaterialism is a central concern. Some of his later publications use language that is not strictly compatible with immaterialism. His *De Motu* (1721) employs a dualistic framework of minds or spirits moving bodies, and *Siris* (1744) places air, aether, fire, or light somewhere between spiritual causes and effects in the phenomenal world. But neither of these cases indicates a serious revision of Berkeley's immaterialism, and his language is explained by the probable audience and type of text Berkeley was composing. Berkeley republished his two major immaterialist works in the years following his major ecclesiastical appointments. In 1724, he was made dean of Derry, and in January 1725 a second edition of *Three Dialogues*, identified by T. E. Jessop as the sheets of the first edition with a new title page, was published. The second edition coincided with the launch of Berkeley's scheme for St Paul's College in Bermuda, the proposal for which was first published late in 1724 or early in 1725. The new edition may be an example of a publisher attempting to capitalise on the visibility of an author on account of his preferment and eye-catching project, or Berkeley himself may have pushed for the new edition in order to promote his project, give an example of the type of polite and improving dialogue that could take place in a college, or simply promulgate his immaterialism.

Principles of Human Knowledge and *Three Dialogues* were published once again in 1734, just after Berkeley's appointment to the diocese of Cloyne in January of that year. As with the new edition of *Three Dialogues*, there is no correspondence from Berkeley relating to these publications. They could have been conceived as part of his campaign for a bishopric and initiated before he was certain of Cloyne. They may have been brought to the press after Berkeley's appointment. The prefaces were removed from both treatises. Revisions to the text of *Principles of Human Knowledge* include: sentences added to introduction, §16, to acknowledge that there is a certain power of abstraction that consists in not attending to any particular feature; a sentence added to §27 to indicate that we have notions of 'spirit' in that we understand the meaning of the word; a sentence on fire removed from §41; a parenthetical phrase on matter and unknown occasions removed from §71; a gloss of ideas as passions removed from §89; a passage on impressed forces and motion in absolute space cut from §115; and revisions to §§138–42 to clarify that one can have a notion but not an idea of a spirit or relation. In *Three Dialogues*, an elaboration of the impossibility of extension existing unperceived was added; several sentences elaborating distinctions between Berkeley's position and that of Malebranche were added; four turns in the dialogue were added in which Philonous defends his position from the parity of reasoning argument (that the existence of matter might be inferred just as the existence of spirits can be inferred) by repeating that the concept 'matter' is internally inconsistent; and a phrase repeating a (scholastic-sounding) 'old known axiom' was removed.[117] Whilst these revisions could easily have been accomplished in a single read-through, the additions to *Three Dialogues*, particularly those relating to Malebranche and the parity of reasoning allegation, demonstrate a continuing engagement with the demonstration of immaterialism and its distinction from other schools of thought. Immaterialism remained at least to this degree a living doctrine.

Despite not achieving the type of public success he desired, Berkeley publicly maintained his immaterialism. Speculations about Berkeley's character or disposition might draw on this fact. He showed in pursuit of his Bermuda project that he could be dogged in the face of opposition and exercise himself extremely in order to accomplish a project that seemed at least to some rather impossible. Berkeley may even have been attracted to such ideas or projects and the opportunity they offered for the exercise of his intellectual, rhetorical, and personal talents. He may simply have

117. As revisions to the text are being discussed, I provide references only to LJ, II.190, 214, 232–34, 236.

been a dispassionate enough metaphysician simply not to have been convinced by any of the arguments against his doctrine, regardless of its seeming novelty, whimsicality, or difficulty of demonstration. His commitment to immaterialism also gained strength from his religious commitment. Without reference to mystery or faith or the authority of scripture, Berkeley had undertaken, in a way unlike anyone before him or any of his contemporaries, and according to the standards of advanced professional science and philosophy of the time, to demonstrate that we live and move and have our being in God.

CHAPTER FOUR

Passive Obedience and Early Politics

THIS CHAPTER CHARACTERISES Berkeley's political position in the years 1709 to 1713 and uses that characterisation to ground an interpretation of his early contribution to political theory, *Passive Obedience*. I consider Berkeley's institutional role at TCD, his correspondence with Percival on political matters, his relationship to Archbishop William King, and the problems that *Passive Obedience* presents, in terms of both its argument and its effect on Berkeley's career. It appears from Berkeley's correspondence and friendships that he was a Tory who respected the Revolution of 1689 and was loyal to the Hanoverian succession in the era of its establishment. Theoretically, he recognised that the legitimacy of government is established, rather than being an a priori fact. He also described the obligation to obey legitimate governments as absolute, even as he acknowledged the complexity of the circumstances that can from time to time conspire to question the legitimacy of a sovereign. Like the texts of Berkeley's new doctrine of immaterialism, *Passive Obedience*, in adopting some of the language of more radical Tories and Jacobites, is an instance of a rhetoric that seemed strategically appropriate to Berkeley nonetheless failing to have its intended effect on his audience, as evidenced by Berkeley's difficulties in defending himself from the accusation of disaffection to the government at various stages in his career.

Early Politics

As has been seen already (in chapter 2), Trinity College Dublin's statutes demanded loyalty of its fellowship. That fellowship had to deal with Jacobite student unrest in the period 1708 to 1711. (Jacobites believed that the house of Stuart remained the legitimate monarchic dynasty after 1689.) In 1708, a student called Forbes gave a Latin speech at a master's supper comparing William III to a notorious highwayman. The student was expelled by Provost Peter Browne. St George Ashe (to whose son Berkeley would later act as tutor), William King, and Browne all spoke in favour of William III and prepared a declaration of loyalty to Anne. In August 1710, students removed the baton from the hand of the statue of William III on College Green at TCD and were expelled. In June 1711, a student called Whitway was expelled by Ashe, after investigation by William King, for speaking against the memory of William III.[1] Berkeley, who was a fellow at this time, was given additional appointments relating to student discipline: on 20 November 1710, he was made junior dean, and on 20 November 1711 he was appointed junior proctor and junior dean for a further year.[2] As Ian Campbell Ross puts it, 'Berkeley was not only seen by the College authorities as a reliable enforcer of student discipline in the immediate aftermath of the trouble caused by the defacing of the statue of William III but was confirmed in his post a year later, shortly after the Whitway incident'.[3] Ross's speculation that *Passive Obedience* was intended as part of Berkeley's educational and disciplinary mission, and that he could not have been in a position to deliver it had he been a Jacobite, is very reasonable on these grounds.

1. Breuninger, *Recovering Bishop Berkeley*, p. 25; Ross, 'Was Berkeley a Jacobite?', p. 23. Such episodes continued after the publication of *Passive Obedience*. Matthew French, a fellow, in a document that includes an account of the Forbes case he was asked to draw up, records that on 8 February 1713/4, 'Theodore Baxter was expelled for drinking [. . .] to ye Pretender, & confusion to ye H of Hanover'; see TCD MS 2215, f. 3r.

2. TCD MUN V-5-2, f. 220v (p. 434) and f. 223r (p. 439). Luce, p. 46, notes that Berkeley was given £12 by the vice-provost and fellows 'for his care in discharging the office of junior dean' and calls this a sign of Berkeley's considerable success. The minute book notes on 12 June 1699 that 'it hath been usuall to give ye junior Dean some consideration besides his salary' (f. 180r [p. 353]), and the same sum was awarded to the two junior deans preceding Berkeley (f. 214r [p. 421] and f. 220v [p. 434]).

3. Ross, 'Was Berkeley a Jacobite?', p. 24.

Institutionally, then, Berkeley was obliged to be loyal. His correspondence provides another kind of evidence for his attitudes to political obligation. On 21 October 1709, Berkeley wrote to Percival giving his response to a suggestion from his correspondent that he read William Higden's *A View of the English Constitution*. Higden spent twenty years as a non-juror, someone who would not take the oath of allegiance to William III, and this text explains his change of view on the basis that the constitution recognised the legitimacy of kings for the time being, or kings *de facto*.[4] Berkeley tells Percival that the book is 'written with great solidity', and he reflects that the practice of swearing allegiance to a king *de facto* is 'agreeable to reason' from 'the very nature and design of government'. Berkeley seems supportive of the 1689 settlement in this letter. He disapproves of Higden being 'against all resistance whatsoever to the king *de facto*', which suggests that Higden did not 'favour the late Revolution'. Berkeley's disapproval suggests that he himself did favour it, presumably as an occasion on which the sovereign appeared either unhinged or to have invaded the supreme power by craft or violence (the conditions Berkeley placed on supreme authority in *Passive Obedience*, as we shall see later). Berkeley is, indeed, sceptical concerning the entire *de jure–de facto* distinction: 'when I consider what the difference is between a king *de jure* and a king *de facto*, I cannot easily find it'.[5] If there are grounds to recognise the legitimacy of the king *de facto*, one has effectively recognised *de jure* legitimacy.

The letter also recommends Locke's *Treatise of Government* as a guide on the subject into which Percival is looking, 'the bounds of their power who rule', and in comparing Cromwell the usurper and William the Conqueror, root of the royal line, Berkeley casts doubt on legitimacy by heredity: what is a conqueror but a usurper, he asks? '[A]fter all, we are forced to place the right of kings in the consent and acquiescence of the people', and if 'Cromwell had taken the title of king, and got it confirmed to his posterity in a free Parliament, and they remained in possession of it, and the laws ran in their usual channel down to this time, it should seem to be

4. Higden, *A View of the English Constitution*, 'To the Reader', sigs. A2r–A3r.
5. Letter 6, pp. 22–24.

FIGURE 4.1. John Smith, 'Sir John Percivale Bart of Burton in County of Cork in Ireland', 1704, courtesy of the National Library of Ireland

wickedness in anyone to attempt to disturb the public peace, by introducing the family of the Stewarts'.[6] This controversial statement recognises that legitimacy can be instituted, and that once instituted it must be respected. Consent and acquiescence of the people seems to be the source of legitimacy. There may be certain signs of this legitimacy, such as confirmation of a title by a free parliament and the continuation of laws in their course, but these are no more absolute requirements than is hereditary right. The fact that government is functioning and producing the unarguable social good of simply not being anarchy is its own form of legitimacy. Though the example is unsettling, Berkeley is presenting a case for the legitimacy of a new sovereign that is clearly applicable, and less controversially so, to the case of William III.

There are further connections between Higden's book, the views Berkeley expresses in this letter to Percival, and the views that will be communicated in *Passive Obedience*. Higden invokes the capacity of a king to protect the people as a source of his legitimacy, and the loss of that capacity as grounds for changing allegiance: 'the several Nations of the World, have *agreed* in this: That after they have done what they can to preserve their *Prince*, they are at Liberty to *preserve themselves*, under a new Government, when the Prince can neither defend himself, them, nor his Government over them'.[7] Berkeley, reflecting on why non-juring should be only a very recent historical phenomenon, invokes the same principle: 'men having felt not long before [that is, during the civil wars] the great mischief there was in forsaking the king, they now [in the reign of James II] (as is usual to go from one extreme to another) thought they could not adhere too closely to his person, even when he was divested of all government, and utterly unable to protect them'.[8] It was reasonable to abandon James II once his power to protect

6. Letter 6, pp. 23–24.

7. Higden, *A View of the English Constitution*, p. 112. Higgins, 'Jonathan Swift's Political Confession', pp. 13–14, aligns Swift with Higden: 'His view expressed in the *Sentiments* of 1708 and elsewhere that sovereignty was absolute but that in the English constitution it was placed in the legislature of monarch in parliament aligns him with the reconstructed Tory positions advanced in the first decade of the eighteenth century by Humphrey Mackworth, Ofspring Blackall, and William Higden, and by Henry Sacheverell's Tory defence team at his trial'.

8. Letter 6, p. 23. See also letter 37, Berkeley to an Englishman, c. 1712, pp. 75–78, esp.

himself, his people, and his government had been lost. Nonetheless, Berkeley recognises that recent history has its effect on the behaviour of political subjects, who in this case overcorrected for the abandonment of the king during the earlier revolution.

Higden comes to the view that submission is preferable to the anarchy that would follow if people decided to rebel because magistrates were thought not to be serving the public good. Such rebellion would 'destroy the very Notion of' government. 'For by making as they do any of the Subjects, as much Judges of the *publick Good* as those, who are invested with the Authority of the Government; and by giving them a Liberty, to overturn both the Laws, and Lawmakers, when they do not pursue what they think to be, the publick Good: They leave no *Authority* in the *Laws*', reducing law to counsel and confusing governors and governed.[9] Berkeley adopts a similar view when objecting to Grotius's and Pufendorf's argument that a sovereign offering fatal violence to subjects dissolves the obligation of people to the sovereign.[10] Berkeley suggests that people who make this argument simply do not understand that dissolution of that obligation is the admission of anarchy:

> [I]it is evident, that a Man had better be exposed to the absolute irresistible Decrees, even of one single Person, whose own and Posterities true Interest it is to preserve him in Peace and Plenty, and protect him from the Injuries of all Mankind beside, than remain an open Prey to the Rage and Avarice of every wicked Man upon Earth, who either exceeds him in Strength, or takes him at an Advantage.[11]

Berkeley and Higden assert general good to be the purpose of government, but deny that this view legitimises rebellion, as lawlessness will always be worse than tyranny. A sovereign, however, must

---

p. 78, for the view that contracts (international alliances) are dissolved under certain circumstances, as when one party fails to maintain its side of the bargain.

9. Higden, *A View of the English Constitution*, p. 100.

10. It is not clear that this is an accurate report. See Pufendorf, *The Whole Duty of Man* and *Two Discourses and a Commentary*, p. 209: 'There is also a peculiar *Veneration* to be paid to the supreme Government under which we live[.] [. . .] Wherefore, when a Prince proceeds to offer the most heinous Injuries imaginable to his People, let them rather undergo it, or every one seek his Safety by Flight, than draw their Swords upon the Father of their Country'.

11. *Passive Obedience*, §51.

be able to protect the people.[12] Berkeley may well be drawing on a tradition of Irish responses to James's abdication in 1688 that see it as the collapse of all government in the nation, thereby releasing the people from their obligations and also providing a practical demonstration of the dangers of anarchy.[13] This is an argument based not on James's abandonment of public good as the organising principle of his rule, but on the collapse of government altogether.

The commitments to the Revolution settlement in this 1709 letter to Percival do not prevent Berkeley from being sympathetic to Henry Sacheverell, the Oxford academic and preacher whose sermons against the toleration of dissent and refusal to celebrate the Revolution settlement led to his being impeached by the House of Lords and tried in early 1710.[14] It has been noted that Sacheverell's name was rarely invoked by Irish Tory parliamentarians, both because the accusation of disloyalty that could be made as a result of questioning the Revolution settlement was a greater risk in Ireland than in England, and because Ireland adopted other figures to fulfil a comparable role of symbolising emotional Toryism.[15] Writing to Percival on 1 March 1710, Berkeley closes by reporting, 'The other night Archdeacon Percival, Dan. Dering and myself were drinking your and Dr. Sachervell's healths at your brother's'. Though this private toast seems to have been freely undertaken and reported, six months later Berkeley was worried about the reputation he might acquire after being coerced into drinking to Sacheverell's health in a coffeehouse by a drunkard. The episode prompted Berkeley to reflect that Sacheverell was not so much to be admired for his sermons as for 'the events which his preaching may have brought about; for (if I may judge of such things) it seems to me the Government had been much too long in the hands of a party'.[16] Sacheverell made

12. These are not particularly remarkable views. See Parkin, 'Probability, Punishments, and Property', p. 84: 'Cumberland makes it plain that there is no right of resistance, because to resist the sovereign is to attack the basis of ordered society and to violate natural law. God provides the only punishment for errant sovereigns and the only legitimate recourse for suffering subjects is passive obedience'.

13. Eccleshall, 'Anglican Political Thought', pp. 50–51.

14. Speck, 'Sacheverell, Henry'.

15. Hayton, 'Irish Tories and Victims of Whig Persecution', pp. 83 and passim. The figures were Francis Higgins and Constantine Phipps.

16. Letter 12, p. 36; letter 18, Berkeley to Percival, 6 September 1710, pp. 45–46.

it possible to displace the previous ministry, largely on account of popular support after his prosecution. In doing so, he had brought down a ministry that was becoming corrupt.

Percival's response to Berkeley's earlier letter made it clear that this embodiment of party as self-interest set more extreme ideological claims to work in the business of moulding popular opinion and securing electoral success:

> It must needs grieve to the heart all good men who love their country and have nothing to get by changes at court to see the divisions now amongst us. For my share I look upon the differences between Whig and Tory to proceed only from a desire of the one to keep in and the other to get into employment. This their ambition, avarice, and personal pique being but ill inducement for to obtain followers, one party pretends we are in danger of anarchy or presbytery, and the other of tyranny and popery, all which is only to beguile the multitude and support their interests. I cannot think that the Whigs (on one hand) who are most of them of the Church of England and have good fortunes and know the excellency of our constitution can have in view the destruction of it, though they enforce their party by the junction of dissenters and commonwealth men; nor can I on the other hand believe that the Torys are not entirely satisfied with a limited monarchy and the succession as established by law, for the bulk of them are true professors of the Church of England, and very distant from popery, though Papists and Jacobites [?enroll] under that name. The mighty feuds do therefore rise in my opinion from desire of places[.][17]

Such a view of Whigs as 'link'd to a certain Set of *Persons*, [rather] than any certain Set of *Principles*', and as therefore corrupt, was shared by Swift, writing anonymously as the *Examiner*, though Percival presents this as a problem that besets both parties.[18] Berkeley's toast to Sacheverell might partly have extended from principled

---

17. Letter 14, Percival to Berkeley, 20 April 1710, pp. 38–39.

18. *Examiner* 44, 31 May 1711, in Ellis, ed., *Swift vs. Mainwaring*, p. 455; see also introduction, xxvii. Berkeley suggests that the *Examiner* was still held to be a Tory paper, but that its appeal was not limited: 'The other day dining at a tavern with two or three Irish clergymen, I found it a very difficult matter to persuade them you were no Whig: I venture however to send you the enclosed *Examiners*, as well knowing that you are no enemy to wit and humour, though in a Tory'. Berkeley refers to himself and Percival as 'we moderate sort of men' (letter 38, Berkeley to Percival, 26 January 1713, p. 80).

Toryism, as it were, but also from the perception of his disruption of a corrupt (Whig) place system. Berkeley on other occasions interpreted accusations of pseudo-Jacobite allegiance as Whig machinations: he thought the accusation that an old Kilkenny schoolmate named Langton had been 'preaching passive obedience' a 'mighty undertaking' on the part of the Whigs to oust Tory preachers.[19] Berkeley sees, with Percival, that ideological claims can be used to place people in or remove them from positions, but he is more inclined than Percival to see the Whig manipulation of ideology in this light.

At the period of the delivery and publication of the discourses that make up *Passive Obedience*, then, Berkeley was a Tory who had expressed support for Sacheverell, but not a Tory who questioned the settlement of 1689. He considered the question of the limits of subjects' obligations to monarchs, including the view that such obligations endured only as long as the sovereign was able to offer protection. He recognised the emergence over time of legitimacy in regimes that appear to have the consent of the people governed by them and which, importantly, produce social order. Against this background, we might be primed to agree with assessments such as that of Robert Eccleshall, who finds that '*Passive Obedience* was a characteristic expression of Irish Toryism, and there is not a shred of evidence that Berkeley was a Jacobite in 1712'.[20] Yet, no matter how clear of Jacobitism his institutional life and private correspondence might demonstrate him to be, Berkeley was entering with his discourses into a field in which the natural ambivalence of political language made him likely to be interpreted, whether ingenuously or with the hope of discrediting a Tory, as desiring the restoration of the Stuart line.[21] Berkeley himself recognises that

19. Letter 22, Berkeley to Percival, 20 December 1710, p. 50. McBride, *Eighteenth-Century Ireland*, p. 41, reports that 'the Whig garrison at Limerick subjected the local bishop to several nights of harassment' during the Sacheverell trial.

20. Eccleshall, 'Anglican Political Thought', p. 56. One should also bear in mind the assessment of Connolly, 'Reformers and Highflyers', p. 158, that the association of high Anglicanism and Jacobitism in the 1710s 'was given even greater credibility by the remarkable revival that had by this time taken place in traditional Anglican political doctrine'.

21. For a characterisation of this kind of ambiguity in political discourse, see Pocock, *Virtue, Commerce, History*, pp. 8–9: '[P]olitical language is by its nature ambivalent; it consists in the utterance of what have been called "essentially contested concepts" and

the scope of terms in political discourse enables factional dispute: 'We read in History there was a time when fears & jealousies, Privileges of Parliament, Malignant Party & such like expressions of too unlimited & doubtfull a meaning were words of much sway. Also the Words Church, Whig, Tory etc. contribute very much to faction & Dispute'.[22] Berkeley understands that the interpretive scope of terms facilitates faction by allowing others to manipulate a pronouncement and make exaggerated claims on its basis. His choice of rhetorical strategy in entitling and composing his text is, then, surprising.

Passive Obedience

Passive Obedience was 'Publish'd' 'This Day', according to the 15–22 May 1712 issue of *The Examiner*. The text was based on three discourses delivered in the chapel of TCD 'not many Months since'.[23] In his major published writings up to this point, the *New Theory of Vision* and *Principles of Human Knowledge*, Berkeley had discussed laws of nature as producing dependable, regular appearances from which people could make predictions about goods and ills that might follow from observed events or their own actions. Berkeley often used an analogy with language to characterise these laws and also attributed them to the agency of a benevolent and active divinity. *Passive Obedience* is an argument for the absolute duty to observe moral laws of nature, laws that can be identified by reason and that take the form of prohibitions. They include a prohibition against rebellion. This main claim of the text can of course be taken in at least two ways in the climate of political controversy that prevailed in Berkeley's time: to say that one has an absolute duty not to rebel against the sovereign could be taken to mean that one should not rebel against the Williamite regime and its successors, or that one should not have rebelled against James II. It may be that

---

propositions, and in the simultaneous employment of languages favoring the utterance of diverse and contrary propositions. But it further follows—what is nearly but not quite the same thing—that any text or simple utterance in a sophisticated political discourse is by its nature polyvalent'.

22. *Notebooks*, §609.

23. *Passive Obedience*, 'To the Reader', sig. A2v.

Berkeley's discourses were immediately subject to criticism based on this ambiguity. They were published to dispel rumours about them that had circulated since their delivery, including rumours that they might represent disaffection with the government.[24] Their use of the language of passive obedience has been considered an attempt to harmonise with TCD students of Jacobitical inclinations, a part of Berkeley's strategy to get them to change their views without having to change their language. It has also been suggested that this strategy betrayed Berkeley's naïveté in thinking the discourses would be recognised as transparently loyal to the Revolution and the succession when published.[25] By proposing an absolute negative moral duty not to rebel, and yet noting certain sets of circumstances in which a sovereign no longer commands obligation, Berkeley was almost certain to open the door to accusations of political disaffection, given what has been noted of the ambivalence of political language. The following account focuses on how this particular problem, of the absolute obligation to which there are exceptions, emerges over the course of the text in order to re-create some of the interpretive ambiguity that surrounded *Passive Obedience*.

If the beautiful array of objects of vision, so quickly comprehended and so instructive, gives us 'some Glimmering, Analogous Prænotion' of the greater knowledge higher beings might have of their world, the world of human moral and political reflection can also cultivate higher and more refined perspectives. Arriving at a true estimate of universal moral rules requires people to see things from a greater distance, to alienate their current, interested perspective and adopt one of greater detachment. Berkeley compares moral to natural laws in *Passive Obedience*. The laws of nature such as gravity are constant and do not vary for particular individuals, even if their doing so might save a good life:

> [W]ithout such a Steddiness in Nature, we shou'd soon, instead of this beautiful Frame, see nothing but a disorderly, and confused Chaos: So if once it become current, that the Moral Actions of Men are not to be guided by certain definite inviolable Rules, there will be no longer

24. Ibid.
25. Ross, 'Was Berkeley a Jacobite?', pp. 21, 29.

found that Beauty, Order, and Agreement, in the System of Rational Beings, or Moral World, which will then be all cover'd over with Darkness and Violence. It is true, he who stands close to a Palace can hardly make a right Judgment of the Architecture and Symmetry of its several Parts, the nearer ever appearing disproportionably great. And if we have a mind to take a fair Prospect of the Order and general Wellbeing, which the inflexible Laws of Nature and Morality derive on the World, we must, if I may so say, go out of it, and imagine our selves to be distant Spectators of all that is transacted and contained in it; otherwise we are sure to be deceived, by the too near View of the little present Interests of our Selves, our Friends, or our Country. [. . .] [H]owever Men may differ, as to what were most proper and beneficial to the Publick to be done or omitted on particular Occasions, when they have for the most part narrow and interested Views; yet in general Conclusions, drawn from an equal and enlarged View of Things, it is not possible there should be so great, if any, Disagreement at all amongst Candid, Rational Enquirers after Truth.[26]

The human subject of *Passive Obedience* is, as in the *New Theory of Vision*, constantly determining goods and evils in the environment on the basis of pleasure and pain, it being 'the whole business of our Lives, to endeavour, by a proper application of our Faculties, to procure the one and avoid the other'.[27] Likewise in the *Notebooks*, Berkeley asserts that '[n]o agent can be conceiv'd indifferent as to pain or pleasure', that profit, pleasure, and interest are central to any true conception of morality, and that, though sensual pleasures may be ranked, 'Sensual Pleasure is the Summum Bonum. This the Great Principle of Morality'.[28] Just as Berkeley's sermon on immortality pointed out the moral calculation we ought to make when faced with distant but infinite goods (or ills), so he asks in *Passive Obedience* 'who sees not that every reasonable Man ought so to frame his Actions, as that they may most effectually contribute to promote his Eternal Interest?'[29] Curiously, however, the rationality of the calculations of agents in *Passive Obedience* is imagined as

26. *Passive Obedience*, §§28–29.
27. Ibid., §5.
28. *Notebooks*, §§143, 541–42, 773, 769.
29. *Passive Obedience*, §6.

prevailing, whereas the earlier sermon remarks the prevalence of irrationality.

The main argumentative burden of *Passive Obedience* is to establish that there is an absolute negative moral law not to rebel against the current sovereign power. Moral laws are also laws of nature, and nature, Berkeley says, 'is nothing else but a series of free Actions produced by the best and wisest Agent'. Berkeley notes that 'we ought to distinguish between a Two-fold Signification of the Terms *Law of Nature*; which Words do either denote a Rule or Precept for the Direction of the voluntary Actions of reasonable Agents, and in that Sense they imply a Duty; or else they are used to signify any general Rule, which we observe to obtain in the Works of Nature, independent of the Wills of Men; in which Sense no Duty is implied'.[30] The '*Laws of Nature*' are 'Rules or establish'd Methods, wherein the Mind we depend on [i.e., God] excites in us the Ideas of Sense', and we 'learn by Experience' which ideas are produced by the wills of finite spirits, which by the will of the infinite spirit.[31] But there are laws of nature that include human will. As Stephen Darwall has put it, 'God also wills that *we act* in certain ways. This is a will he can only have for *agents*, for active minds'.[32] *Passive Obedience* demonstrates that God shows people, who are constantly and rationally calculating their own greatest good, the means to achieve that good, and that the means is a set of absolute negative moral precepts, such as one forbidding rebellion.

Berkeley may have been predisposed to imagine that laws relating to the will are general rather than particular, as that other category of laws of nature, those that do not involve human will, seem to be general rather than particular.[33] We pursue isolated goods, and in doing so realise that the physical world is governed by stable laws that enable us to make predictions about what will bring us pleasure. We realise that there is an infinite being establishing these laws (by the processes described in chapter 1) and that this being therefore desires our good. Knowing that the laws of physical nature are general (they do not just apply to me), it must be

30. Ibid., §§14, 33.
31. *Principles of Human Knowledge*, §30.
32. Darwall, 'Berkeley's Moral and Political Philosophy', p. 325.
33. Ibid., p. 331.

the case that God desires the good of all people, not just me. Any form of behaviour that would necessarily produce common goods if practised by all people is to be 'look'd upon as enjoined by the Will of God'.[34] Realisations of this sort are not occasional—they do not relate to one occasion only but are general laws of nature.

Such laws are on the whole negative rather than positive. It is too difficult to frame positive moral laws because

> very often, either through the Difficulty or Number of Moral Actions, or their Inconsistence with each other, it is not possible for one Man to perform several of them at the same time; whereas it is plainly consistent and possible, that any Man shou'd, at the same time, abstain from all manner of positive Actions whatsoever [. . .] the Positive Laws themselves, at least the Exercise of them admits of Suspension, Limitation, and Diversity of Degrees.[35]

Here, however, Berkeley produces a tension with his earlier thinking, this time on the will. The *Notebooks* suggest that there is no state of volitional inertia for any agent at any time: 'While I exist or have any Idea I am eternally, constantly willing, my acquiescing in the present State is willing'.[36] Spirits are agents, and they are characteristically active; even their understanding or perception of ideas is a type of action. So there is no such thing, in *Notebooks*, as a spirit that is not acting. Yet it is central to the political and moral claims of *Passive Obedience* that an agent may 'abstain from all manner of positive Actions whatsoever'.

Even though we arrive at our knowledge of the universal negative moral precepts by pursuing our own pleasure and rationally reflecting on how we were able to achieve such pleasures as we have, the public good produced by any particular action is not to be taken as the justification for that action. General or public good is an important step in our being able to identify moral laws, but it is not the public good that should immediately direct our actions:

> [N]othing is a *Law* merely because it conduceth to the Publick Good, but because it is decreed by the Will of God, which alone can give the

34. *Passive Obedience*, §§7, 11.
35. Ibid., §26.
36. *Notebooks*, §791.

Sanction of a *Law of Nature* to any Precept[.] [. . .] In framing the
general Laws of Nature, it is granted, we must be entirely guided by the
Publick Good of Mankind, but not in the ordinary Moral Actions of our
Lives. [. . .] The Rule is framed with respect to the Good of Mankind;
but our Practice must be always shaped immediately by the Rule.

The proof that Berkeley provides for universal negative moral precepts not requiring direct reference to public good to make them
binding is his own refusal to believe that anyone would attempt to
justify adultery or perjury on the basis of their producing public
good.[37]

Unfortunately for Berkeley's claims that all rational beings
would soon settle on the same set of universal negative moral precepts, he encounters—apparently between the first publication of
Passive Obedience and its third edition in 1713, when he adds a footnote referring to it—an argument justifying murder by reference
to the public good. Berkeley hopes he need do no more than he
already has to make obvious 'the Absurdity and Perniciousness' of
the view.[38] The view is Matthew Tindal's in his *Discourse Concerning Obedience to the Supreme Powers*, where he asks: 'What can be
more unjust than to take away the Life of an innocent Person? Yet if
it be for the Publick Good, 'tis so far from being unjust, that 'tis the
Duty of those who have the publick Administration of Affairs to do
it'.[39] The acceptable example of taking away the life of an innocent
person for the public good is sending soldiers one knows will die
to war. Though this example is complex (one might say one is not
directly taking the innocent life), that there could be a reasonable
alternative view of this sort militates against Berkeley's invocation
of the strength and certainty of moral deductions: 'let any one who
hath the use of Reason take but an impartial Survey of the general frame and circumstances of human Nature, and it will appear
plainly to him, that the constant observation of Truth, for instance,
of Justice, and Chastity, hath a necessary connexion with their universal well-being'.[40] But Tindal, with some reason, does not see that

37. *Passive Obedience*, §§31, 48.
38. Ibid., §48n.
39. Tindal, *Four Discourses*, p. 27.
40. *Passive Obedience*, §15.

it is necessarily connected to universal well-being that the innocent are not sent to their deaths. Berkeley's defence is the deployment of metaphors from vision—if we take the proper view, perspective, or survey, we will see it is so.

Detachment from personal or particular interests should, Berkeley claims, produce a general view of social relations. Berkeley says that we have a choice between imagining that public good is best produced by continual individual reflection on the best course of action or by adhering to universal laws. Like Higden, as we saw earlier, Berkeley prefers universal law to individual calculations of good. After a 'comprehensive Survey' of humanity and the realisation 'that God willeth the Universal Well-being of Mankind should be promoted by the concurrence of each particular Person', it is the case that 'every such practical Proposition, necessarily tending thereto, is to be esteemed a Decree of God, and is consequently a Law to Man'. These laws 'do not derive their Obligation from any Civil Sanction' and are '*Eternal Rules of Reason*, because they necessarily result from the Nature of Things, and may be demonstrated by the infallible deductions of Reason'. These are laws not for any one particular society, but for society in general. Being a subject of law is, Berkeley claims, a general, not a particular, situation: 'what relation is there more extensive and universal than that of Subject and Law?'[41] (This is indeed the fundamental relation for Berkeley, as finite spirits being subject to the law of the infinite spirit is the most extensive relation of all.) Still, human compact (that which begins to make the particular classifications of people in one place and time or another) can express natural law: 'most Moral Precepts do presuppose some voluntary Actions, or Pacts of Men, and are nevertheless esteemed Laws of Nature'.[42] There are, however, laws to which one can apply individual conscience 'because the private Ends they were intended to promote, respect only some particular Persons, as engaged in Relations not founded in the general Nature of Man, who, on various Occasions, and in different Postures of Things, may prosecute their own Designs by different

41. Ibid., §§8, 11, 12, 18.

42. Ibid., §25; compare Pufendorf, *The Whole Duty of Man* and *Two Discourses and a Commentary* pp. 56–57.

Measures, as in Humane Prudence shall seem convenient'.[43] There will, of course, be a degree of argument about what the general and what the individual or historical features of human societies are, and therefore where we are obliged absolutely and where we may act prudentially.

Berkeley offers a defence of the absolute nature of the negative duty not to rebel from a restriction of its object:

> In Morality the eternal Rules of Action have the same immutable, universal Truth with Propositions in Geometry. Neither of them depend on Circumstances or Accidents, being at all Times, and in all Places, without Limitation or Exception true. *Thou shalt not resist the Supreme Civil Power*, is no less constant and unalterable a Rule for modelling the Behaviour of a Subject toward the Government, than *multiply the Height by half the Base*, is for measuring a Triangle. And as it wou'd not be thought to detract from the Universality of this Mathematical Rule, that it did not exactly measure a Field which was not an exact Triangle, so ought it not to be thought an Argument against the Universality of the Rule prescribing Passive Obedience, that it does not reach a Man's Practice in all Cases, where a Government is unhinged, or the Supreme Power disputed. There must be a Triangle, and you must use your Senses to know this, before there is Room for applying your Mathematical Rule. And there must be a Civil Government, and you must know in whose Hands it is lodged, before the moral Precept takes Place.[44]

Berkeley requires that there be a supreme civil power in order for there to be an obligation not to rebel against it. At the same time as Berkeley states that this is the proper object to which we are obliged by the law of nature, he gives examples of occasions when the obligation is not in force: the absolute duty of passive obedience does not always 'reach a man's practice' when the supreme power is 'unhinged' or 'disputed'. These are cases in which it is not clear if there is a government or who its magistrates are.

The character or behaviour of such magistrates is one basis on which one may judge that the circumstances fall beyond the

43. *Passive Obedience*, §18.
44. Ibid., §53 (a section added in the third edition).

scope of the absolute negative duty: 'by Virtue of the Duty of *Non-Resistance*, We are not obliged to Submit the Disposal of our Lives and Fortunes to the Discretion either of Madmen, or of all those who by Craft or Violence invade the Supreme Power'. Berkeley's response to this apparent violation of universality is to say that the object of obedience is limited, but not the occasion:

> In the various Changes and Fluctuations of Government, it is impossible to prevent that Controversies shou'd sometimes arise concerning the Seat of the Supreme Power. And in such Cases Subjects cannot be denied the Liberty of Judging for Themselves, or of taking part with some, and opposing others[.] [. . .] In short, it is acknowledged, that the Precept enjoining Non-Resistance is Limited to particular Objects, but not to particular Occasions.[45]

As Berkeley was drafting this text for publication (presumably working from the notes he had for his discourses delivered in the college chapel), he initially tried a different formulation: suggesting that passive obedience is limited 'in respect of the object but not in respect of the degree'.[46] Having admitted that controversies with respect to legitimacy will arise, and that individuals are at liberty in such cases to decide for themselves where legitimacy resides, Berkeley seems in danger of giving over the universal rule to the type of local, contingent, historical, and prudential deliberation that is characteristic of partial rather than general moral laws of nature.

If there had been any hope that Berkeley's discourse might have unambiguously resolved the vexed matter of obligations to the persons and institutions competing for supreme civil authority in Britain and Ireland in 1712, it is gone with this admission of individual liberty in determining the object of the obligation.[47] A cleric with whom Berkeley was later competing for jobs referred to his writing

45. Ibid., §§52, 54.

46. BL Add MS 39304, ff. 130v–131r. The published text also removes references to being 'legally invested ˄with of the supream power' and to the 'legal right to Government' made in this section of the draft.

47. Breuninger, *Recovering Bishop Berkeley*, p. 31, notes that there are exceptions to the universal rule, but not that this is problematic for Berkeley. Häyry, '*Passive Obedience* and Berkeley's Moral Philosophy', pp. 4–5, 10–11, notes that Berkeley makes specifications of his universal negative duty and thereby softens the rigour of the claim of absolute obligation

on 'the slavish doctrine of passive obedience' as something that had made him popular with Jacobites, and which was of a piece with the association with Jonathan Swift and Lord Peterborough that Berkeley would develop in 1713 (see chapter 8).[48] Berkeley's friends would still in the early 1730s be making reference to his publications and actions in the period immediately following the publication of *Passive Obedience* to try to save him from the charge of disaffection. Even if the accusations about Berkeley's politics were superficial—merely the exploitation of his strategy of using the phrase 'passive obedience' as his title—and based on no familiarity with the arguments of his text, those arguments nonetheless leave some room for the interpretation that the first half of the 1710s was one of those times during which it was reasonable for people to choose their side amongst different individuals or groups competing for recognition as the supreme civil authority. It may not be coincidental that in 1712, following the publication of *Passive Obedience*, Berkeley is more emphatic in his commitment to the Revolution settlement in his private correspondence, reporting that 'two malefactors were publicly pilloried and afterwards burnt alive in Felster's shop for having offered some affront to the memory of King William, which for ever ought to be held (at least by all Protestants of these nations) glorious and immortal as are his actions'.[49]

William King and Other Activities

From Berkeley's published and unpublished writings it is possible to follow some of his interactions with William King, specifically on questions of optics, on theology, and on ecclesiastical discipline. In light of the previous discussion, I suggest that a difference of political approach to recent history also separates the two men. Writing to Percival on 1 March 1710, Berkeley says that the appendix he added to the *New Theory of Vision* was an endeavour 'to answer the objections of the Archbishop of Dublin', William King.[50] In

---

to negative moral precepts, whilst nonetheless choosing to defend the strictest form of the thesis.

48. State Papers Online, SP 63/374, f. 187r.
49. Letter 38, Berkeley to Percival, 18 August 1712, p. 74.
50. Letter 12, p. 35.

that appendix, Berkeley defends himself from the accusation that he has misinterpreted the position of theorists of geometric optics by producing a passage from Descartes; distinguishes his solution to the problem of the horizontal moon from that of Gassendi; and clarifies his thesis of the minimum visibile.[51] In the same letter, Berkeley notes his surprise that not only followers of King but King himself believes that God may only be called wise, benevolent, and so on, in a figurative sense. King thinks people derive their talk of the attributes of God from a sense of which of their human attributes they would require to produce the effects they see God producing, 'but at the same time we cannot but be sensible, that they are of a Nature altogether different from ours, and that we have no direct and proper conception of them'.[52] Berkeley contends, on the contrary, that there is 'no argument that I know of for his [God's] existence, which does not prove him at the same time to be an understanding, wise, and benevolent Being, in the strict, literal, and proper meaning of those words'.[53] Berkeley's immaterialism will only admit of the pious application to which he intends it (and which he reaffirms in this same letter) if people know God to have the same capacity of producing ideas as we finite spirits have, but to an infinite degree. Berkeley and King disagree on what is known of the attributes of God, on the function of the human senses, and on how the former are evident to the latter.

These differences may have disinclined Berkeley from seeking ordination from King, as he should have done. There was, whatever the cause, a serious ecclesiastical rift between them. On 18 April 1710, Berkeley wrote to King expressing his 'great concern and surprise' that he was being prosecuted in King's court for having been ordained by St George Ashe whilst King was absent from Dublin. Berkeley says that he knew another person who had applied to Ashe to be ordained, was ignorant of the extent of King's jurisdiction, and thought Ashe would have let him know if there had been a problem. Berkeley avows that he had not meant to 'lessen or dispute' King's authority, has had the prosecution suspended by

---

51. *New Theory of Vision*, pp. 191–98. On this point, see Berman, *George Berkeley*, p. 19.
52. King, *Divine Predestination and Fore-Knowledge*, p. 7.
53. Letter 12, p. 36.

the dean of St Patrick's (John Stearne, who might have been a relation), and promises not to 'exercise any ecclesiastical function in your diocese' until King has licensed him.[54]

In a letter to Ashe of 27 March 1710, King suggests that Berkeley had put off his ordination for nearly the maximum three years since becoming a fellow at TCD in hopes to avoid being 'discoursed' as King did others before ordination.[55] King acknowledges himself to be a strict ecclesiastical disciplinarian in his time as archbishop of Dublin, as S. J. Connolly has noted:

> Writing to Francis Annesley on 24 March 1713, he admitted that he was not surprised by claims that he was excessively strict:
>
> > . . . on recollection I remember I have degraded four from their orders. I have laid in jail two excommunicated clergymen who died there. I have writs or warrants out against three more. I have discovered six or seven with counterfeit letters of orders and some in good places turned out on that account. I have deprived of their living six or seven and have suspended or otherwise censured about 30. Add to these many that I have rejected from orders, several to whom I have refused benefices or institution for want of qualifications and the many I have chid or reproved, both publicly and privately. (TCD, MS 750/4/1, pp. 133–34)
>
> In addition to measures against unsatisfactory clergy King was particularly insistent on refusing to ordain those who seemed to him unprepared or unsuited for the clerical life, or for whom there was no realistic prospect of employment.[56]

To provide just one other example, King was involved in a ten-year legal battle against the dean and chapter of Christ Church Cathedral over control of the nomination of a rector to St Paul's in Dublin (presumably the same St Paul's that played a part in Berkeley's career, as will be noted in chapter 6).[57] It may have been prudent of Berkeley to wish to avoid King's discoursing if he had reason to

---

54. Letter 13, pp. 37–38.

55. TCD MS 750/11, cited in Berman, *George Berkeley*, p. 18.

56. Connolly, 'King, William (1650–1729)'.

57. Twomey, *Dublin in 1707*, pp. 47–48. See also Connolly, 'Reformers and Highflyers', pp. 153–54, on King as a reformist.

anticipate refusal of ordination on account of their philosophical differences, or simply on account of King's severity.

It may be that political differences between the two men were also a factor in their rift, in which case the episode initiated the series of problems Berkeley had with pursuing his career in the Church on account of his politics, or the politics attributed to him, predating the publication of *Passive Obedience*. The philosophical politics of Berkeley and King were substantially different. *Passive Obedience* is strongly committed to moral law, including basic political obligations, being instituted by God as general and dependable laws of nature. King's defence of the Revolution of 1689 emphasised, on the contrary, providential signs that circumstances were exceptional and therefore that William's regime ought to be accepted.[58] *Passive Obedience* has been understood to distinguish itself from King's position.[59] Berkeley's account suggests that an absolute duty of passive obedience is owed to the legitimate government, but admits that the obligation is dissolved in exceptional circumstances, or when subjects are able to choose between contending parties. King's account suggests that a combination of extrinsic circumstances might be taken as evidence of God's will that exceptional political events have come about. One might say that Berkeley is a qualified rationalist in politics, and King a providentialist. If this difference was evident in Berkeley's political self-presentation before the publication of *Passive Obedience*, it is possible that it informed the dispute between them.

Alongside presenting his political thought, Berkeley worked during the period 1709 to 1713 both publicly and privately to manage the reception of his immaterialism. In response to Samuel Molyneux's suspicions that he opens the door to reasoning and discoursing without the presence of clear and distinct ideas (understood as images) in the mind, Berkeley points to the capacity for reasoning about large numbers or large cities without being able to

58. King, *A Sermon, Preached at St Patrick's Church Dublin*, passim; for the providentialist and exceptionalist tone of the sermon, see p. 21: '[W]e must acknowledge that it is by the *Grace of God* that *William* and *Mary* are now our King and Queen. [. . .] Let us therefore own the whole of our deliverance to be a work of God, and ascribe it intirely to him, without assuming any part of it to our selves'.

59. Breuninger, *Recovering Bishop Berkeley*, p. 29.

picture them in every detail. Geometers do not reason about clear and distinct ideas of figures, but rather think of principles and processes that produce figures. The equation, not the figure, is the object of their reasoning, and that is why it does not matter if lines in geometrical diagrams are perfectly straight.[60] Berkeley congratulates Percival on his marriage, on 20 June 1710, to Catherine Parker, and asks Percival to do something he knows to be a little indecorous: to deliver a copy of *Principles of Human Knowledge* to its dedicatee, the earl of Pembroke. To Catherine Parker's query about the compatibility of immaterialism with the biblical account of creation, Berkeley responds that 'the act of creation consists in God's willing that those things should be perceptible to other spirits, which before were known only to Himself'.[61] Berkeley defends himself from an association with the metaphysics of John Norris and Nicolas Malebranche made by Samuel Clarke and William Whiston. Clarke and Whiston resist Berkeley's attempts to draw them into debate.[62] Having approached Jean Le Clerc (whose *Logic* was taught at TCD) to ask for a review of *Principles of Human Knowledge* in Le Clerc's journal *Bibliothèque choisie*, Berkeley has to defend some of the principles of the *New Theory of Vision*, which had already received a notice. He denies that there is a faculty of the intellect that has ideas without recourse to the imagination, and which conceives motion, for example, separate from any moving thing. And he expands on his assertion that ideas of touch are the object of geometry by saying that his position includes ideas formed by reference to touch.[63]

Berkeley left Ireland at the beginning of 1713 and in the following twenty years travelled extensively—to London and other English cities, to France and Italy (twice), and to the American colonies of Virginia, Rhode Island, and Massachusetts. If his earliest known intellectual interests extended out of the established concerns of

60. Letters 10 and 11, Berkeley to Molyneux, 19 December 1709 and 27 December 1709, pp. 29–31.

61. Letter 15, Berkeley to Percival, 29 June 1710, p. 40; letter 18, Berkeley to Percival, 6 September 1710, p. 45.

62. Letters 20 and 21, Percival to Berkeley, 30 October 1710, and Berkeley to Percival, 27 November 1710, pp. 47–49; letter 23, Percival to Berkeley, 28 December 1710, pp. 51–52.

63. Letter 27, Berkeley to Le Clerc, 28 March 1711, p. 57; letter 32, Berkeley to Le Clerc, 14 July 1711, pp. 65–66.

the Dublin Philosophical Society and the TCD milieu, in historical topography, planetary physics, and mathematics some of his enduring and idiosyncratic tendencies become apparent. Humans are rational agents to whom it should be obvious that God's creation of a rule-governed world is not a neutral fact, but a fact that ought to guide the choices of those agents. Rational humans always calculate to maximise pleasure, but they must learn about their environment and about (higher forms of) pleasure in order to do so in the most human way. Learning of this sort is learning a language, not just a set of correspondences, and also becoming aware of the underlying motivations of the speaker of the language. The world of which humans learn is a world of ideas, ideas caused by humans themselves and by God. For all that the world may appear to have physical being, tangible or visible extension, its real existence is as ideas.

There is only spiritual substance, and relations between ideas, or between spirits and ideas or spirits and spirits, are attitudinal, dispositional, temperamental, affective. These idiosyncrasies present challenges, both to Berkeley and to his readers, challenges so great it is not clear Berkeley manages them all of the time. Though ideas are in minds, he speaks in the *New Theory of Vision* of objects outside of us, and of the minimum visibile and tangible units having more or less natural correspondence with one another. Number and unit are said to be entirely mind-dependent, yet there are objective sensible minima. Although human agents are equipped to make rational choices of the greatest good, they do not. Although one ought to be able to deduce moral laws of nature in a similar way to that in which physical laws are deduced, qualifications of such scope are admitted into the formulation of moral laws that any historical humans would find it very difficult to shape their actions in accordance with them. Berkeley insists on the practical devotional purpose of a philosophical project that is a challenge to the routine conceptualisation of the practical world and a startling redescription of creation. These are the idiosyncratic responses to debates about material substance, the psychology of vision, and the being and attributes of God that characterise Berkeley's early career.

CHAPTER FIVE

Philosopher of Education

ON 28 AUGUST 1708, Berkeley wrote in a notebook 'The Adventure of the Shirt'. David Berman has suggested that the enigmatic note refers to Berkeley's experiment in re-creating the sensations of someone being executed by hanging, an experiment that left him with a rumpled shirt.[1] Beneath the note a citation is found:

> It were to be wish'd that Persons of the greatest title Honour, & fortune would take that care of themselves by Education, Industry, Literature & a love of virtue to surpass all other men in knowledge & all other qualifications necessary for great actions as far as they do in Quality & Titles; That Princes out of them might always choose Persons Men fit for all Employments & high Trusts. Clar: B.7.

At this point in *History of the Rebellion* by Henry Hyde, Earl of Clarendon, the source of the citation, Clarendon is discussing one of the failings of Prince Rupert, the militaristic nephew of Charles I. Rupert has noticed that most people when they speak in counsel have some shortcoming, and he is therefore inclined to undervalue the importance of counsel altogether. This tendency is exacerbated by his not being a British native, and not having an understanding of the advisory role of court. Clarendon points out how important it is to take wide-ranging counsel, both to benefit from the views expressed (which cannot always be anticipated

1. BL MS Add 39305, f. 95r; Berman, *George Berkeley*, p. 204n9. For more on this episode, see chapter 14.

from the verbal behaviour of the counsellor speaking in another context) and to make sure that all the interests feel they are a part of a final decision and course of action. In the excerpt from Clarendon's astute analysis of the psychology of statecraft that Berkeley transcribes, Clarendon wishes that people of high rank had the abilities that lower people have, and for which they are promoted to high office, for the reason that people of high rank have a natural capacity for command. Sadly, sometimes they want the necessary education (and subtlety) to exploit fully their aristocratic superiority.[2]

Berkeley is here transcribing a text on the importance of educating noble youth at the end of his first year as a fellow at TCD (providing the notes are roughly contemporary). Clarendon's text emphasises the role of education in preparing noble youth for employments entrusted to them by the sovereign. The particular context of his discussion was, of course, the management of dissent and rebellion in the state: nobles needed to be educated in order to preserve the monarchic and aristocratic system of government and protect it from popular assault. Clarendon knows that people of all ranks may rise up to high employment, but he has a preference for those of high birth preparing themselves for such roles, as others are predisposed to acknowledge their authority. Whilst Berkeley partly obscures the naturalisation of aristocracy that is central to Clarendon's argument by cutting off his citation before the end of the sentence (it continues 'which would exceedingly advance their Service, when the reputation and respect of the Person carries somewhat with it, that facilitates the business'), Clarendon is also criticising Prince Rupert for his lack of insight. At the outset of his career, then, Berkeley showed an interest in education of the nobility for public service in order to preserve (the old) order against rebellious incursions—the ultimate purpose of literature, industry, and virtue.[3] The inculcation of those qualities in various bodies of people (students, peasants, nobles, the state) was a lifelong concern

2. Hyde, *The History of the Rebellion and Civil Wars in England*, II.298.

3. Rorty, 'The Ruling History of Education', p. 1, naturalises philosophers' interest in elite education: 'Philosophers have always intended to transform the way we see and think, act and interact; they have always taken themselves to be the ultimate educators of mankind. [. . .] Philosophical reflection on education from Plato to Dewey has therefore

for Berkeley, and one that he furthered with every turn in his career. One can see Berkeley's diverse career as a career in education, where education can never be dissociated from its political function, which is to naturalise certain forms of privilege, colonial or otherwise, and specifically the privileges of rank, gender, sect, and cultural-ethnic background that define the power and obligations of a member of the governing elite of a confessional state coping with religious and cultural diversity in different territories.

There was no question for Berkeley that societies are hierarchical, that they have upper and lower parts (see chapter 7 for a discussion of Berkeley's application of this language to the population of Ireland), and educating the upper part of society was a particular concern. Eliza Frinsham/Berkeley reports that 'Bishop Berkeley used to say, "If I had the voice of Stentor, I would become hoarse in calling on all, particularly on persons of high rank, *Take care of the education of your children*"'.[4] The Querist also asks 'whether an uneducated Gentry be not the greatest of national Evils'. (It is worth noting that this question is preceded by another in the same query: 'Whether a general good Taste in a People would not greatly conduce to their thriving?' Education of taste is a nontrivial means of improving the life of a people.)[5] In fighting against this evil, Berkeley adopts the role of educator as heroic preserver of the state, the role that Mentor plays in Fénelon's enormously influential narrative treatise on the education of nobility, *Telemachus*.[6] The upper part of a society needs to be educated, to become wise and reflective, to be able to make good law and regulate the body of society. The lower part needs to be fitted to a life of service and industry. Both parts of society learn self-discipline; the upper part also learns to discipline the lower. Berkeley expresses the view, seen in Fénelon's distinction between male and female education, that the knowledge in which one is instructed ought to be fitted to one's

---

naturally been directed to the education of rulers, to those who are presumed to preserve and transmit—or to redirect and transform—the culture of society, its knowledge and its values'.

4. Eliza Berkeley, preface to Berkeley, *Poems*, p. cccclxxix.

5. *Querist*, I.2, §15.

6. Fénelon, *Telemachus*, introduction, p. xx: 'the true hero is the moral-civic educator' (Mentor).

social position and function: 'La science des femmes, comme celle des hommes, doit se borner à s'instruire par rapport à leurs fonctions' (The knowledge of women, as that of men, should be limited to being instructed in relation to their functions).[7] Education is always for a certain rank and station in life.

Berkeley may, in this respect, echo the impulses of the early and later northern European humanists, Lipsius and Pufendorf in particular, whose educational programmes were practically oriented towards a strong state that encouraged discipline (military and moral-civic) in its people in order to avoid the fatal extremes of religious conflict. And yet, in other respects, Berkeley resists the more egalitarian and bourgeois elements of this programme, maintaining a commitment to personal authority, aristocratic elites, and the ecclesiastical nature of civil government.[8] One can see again two different types of philosophical personality in play. A survey of Berkeley's educational projects throughout his career will enable an assessment of his work as an educationalist: he was not in any strong sense a philosopher of education, but his activity as an educationalist provides a background against which to read his occasional reflections on the role of education. There is no published work of equivalent stature to John Locke's *Some Thoughts Concerning Education*, on the one hand, or Jean-Jacques Rousseau's *Émile, ou de l'éducation*, on the other, but Berkeley's practical orientation

7. Fénelon, 'De l'éducation des filles' (1696 text), in *Œuvres*, I.154.

8. For Lipsius, see Oestreich, *Neostoicism and the Early Modern State*, p. 68: '[T]he modern state emerged, based on order, power, unity, authority, discipline and obedience. It is assuredly due partly to the prestige of Lipsius that the older doctrine of the state, based on monarchy and representation and proclaiming the right to resistance and tyrannicide, so quickly became outdated. [. . .] Although Lipsius regarded monarchy—admittedly of a moderate kind—and personal rule by the prince as the ideal form of government, the general tenor of his teaching is bourgeois. Its principles—strict performance of duty, inspection of conscience, constant work and equality of legal status for all—had little to do with the old world of the European nobility'. For Pufendorf, see Pufendorf, *The Whole Duty of Man* and *Two Discourses and a Commentary*, 'Introduction', pp. xi–xiii: 'Duties [. . .] are incumbent upon a Man with Regard to that *Particular State* wherein he finds himself ordained by Providence to live in the World. What we mean by such *State*, is in general, that *Condition* or *Degree* with all its Relatives, in which Men being placed, they are therefore supposed to be obliged to these or those Performances: And such *State*, whatever it be, has some peculiar Rights and Offices thereunto belonging' (p. 166).

towards education is an equivalent commitment.[9] This chapter proceeds from a survey of Berkeley's educational projects to a comparison of his educational thought with John Locke; Mary Astell, philosopher of education, religion, and society and a correspondent of John Norris; and François de Fénelon, philosophical theologian, archbishop of Cambrai, and tutor to the son of Louis XIV. These three educational theorists are excerpted at length in *The Ladies Library*, and Berkeley's writings and practice resonate with them.

Berkeley's Educational Projects

Educational institutions discipline their members, and Berkeley would have been disciplined into his membership of the Protestant elite at Kilkenny College. His possible involvement in the Charter School movement of the 1730s shows a concern for school education for a different social stratum.[10] The orderliness of the college environment was still more explicitly political in the TCD statutes, with the college community presented as a society in little, with its own laws and an appointed head to lessen the inherent dangers of equality and anarchy.[11] Education as a means of preserving social order and inculcating that order was evident in Berkeley's schooling. The range of Berkeley's extracurricular educational pursuits whilst at TCD was also outlined in chapter 2. Establishing educational societies, reading papers to the Philosophical Society, dedicating publications to students (publications that explicitly address the student body and attempt to reform its behaviour)—these

9. An oft-cited passage from *Some Thoughts Concerning Education* is excerpted at *Ladies Library*, II.270: '[O]f all the Men we meet with, nine Parts of ten are what they are, good or evil, useful or not, by their *Education*. 'Tis that which makes the great Difference in Mankind'.

10. Milne, 'Irish Charter Schools', p. 19, says that Berkeley was a founding member of the Incorporated Society in Dublin for Promoting English Protestant Schools in Ireland. The bishop of Cloyne is listed as a founding member of the society in its *Abstract of the Proceedings*, p. 30. As Milne's narrative of the beginnings of the society draws on correspondence between Henry Newman and Henry Maule, the bishop of Cloyne before Berkeley (p. 14), and as the charter was made public early in 1734, before Berkeley became bishop of Cloyne, it seems very possible to me that Maule rather than Berkeley is the bishop of Cloyne in question. I thank Marta Szymańska-Lewoszewska for bringing Milne's article and the Charter School movement to my attention, and for discussing this point with me.

11. Bolton, *A Translation of the Charter and Statutes*, pp. 25, 27, 31.

means of pursuing education were at once means of integrating oneself into an existing network of loyalties and interests, and also intervening in the social practice of the people who made up that network. Berkeley's formal association with TCD was not altogether extinguished when he resigned his fellowship on 18 May 1724.[12] Indeed, he was considered for the post of vice-chancellor in 1734 and 1741.[13]

Being a university instructor initiated Berkeley's career in preaching, and the pulpit was also an educational opportunity. Christian education through the pulpit could have a broad general aim of showing people that their true interest was in the next life: 'we must learn to wean ourselves from self-interest, or rather learn wherein our true interest consists'. And again: 'Eternal life is the ultimate end of all our views: It is for this, we deny our appetites, subdue our passions and forgo the interests of this present world'.[14] The pulpit was an opportunity to educate and discipline at once. When Berkeley delivered his discourses on passive obedience in the college chapel he was contributing, it has been suggested, to the discipline of the student body (as he was in a different way as junior dean) by adopting some of the students' Jacobitical vocabulary in order to persuade them out of that position. And he responded to Percival's suggestion in the charged political climate of the early 1710s that the clergy did not preach strongly enough against rebellion by stating, 'I think it my duty to disclaim perjury and rebellion on all occasions'.[15] He had indeed preached that 'submission to lawful authority is [. . .] a main part of our duty'.[16] Educational institution, church, and state ran together in Berkeley's thinking of the 1710s. Schools and universities, he says in *The Guardian*, may well be means of leading people from the youthful pleasures of the imagination to the higher pleasures of reason, but they are also 'Nurseries of Men for the Service of the Church and State', and it is

12. TCD MS MUN V-5-2, ff. 266v (p. 530), 267v (p. 532).

13. BL Add MS 20105, ff. 128v–129r, John Baron Wainwright to Caroline Clayton, Viscountess Sundon, 25 May 1734; letter 280, Berkeley to Henry Clarke, 16 April 1741, p. 420. For further discussion, see chapter 13.

14. LJ, VII.33, 'Of Charity', Leghorn, probably spring 1714; LJ, VII.105–6, 'On Eternal Life'.

15. Letter 72, Berkeley to Percival, 9 August 1715, p. 126.

16. LJ VII.25, 'Of Religious Zeal', probably 1709–1712.

alleged that '[i]t was chiefly, if not altogether, upon religious Considerations that Princes, as well as private Persons, have erected Colleges and assigned liberal Endowments to Students and Professors'.[17] When people enlarge their views and shake off the pedantry that leads to materialism and freethinking, they are being educated. This is a religious aim, and one that lies behind the foundation of educational institutions.

The Guardian might not be as celebrated for its statement of purpose as *The Spectator*, in which Mr Spectator aspires to be known as one who 'brought Philosophy out of Closets and Libraries, Schools and Colleges, to dwell in Clubs and Assemblies, at Tea-Tables and in Coffee-Houses'.[18] Nor does the journal state as explicitly as Hume a sense of the essayist functioning as 'a Kind of Resident or Ambassador from the Dominions of Learning to those of Conversation'.[19] But as an essayist in *The Guardian*, in *An Essay towards Preventing the Ruine of Great Britain*, and in other occasional writings, Berkeley was engaged in an educational project of making the specialist knowledge acquired in universities and the Church available to and practically applicable for people who were not salaried members of those institutions. Berkeley's socialising in London in 1713 with Steele and Addison also resulted in his work on *The Ladies Library*, a project in female education that was probably intended to counteract some of the problems identified in the pages of *The Spectator* and *The Guardian*, and which had been trailed in *The Guardian*. Berkeley adopted a conservative position with respect to female education—that it should neither be equal to male education nor fundamentally change the social roles of the genders—characteristic of his attitude to social improvement more generally.[20]

Berkeley's second visit to Italy, as a tourist rather than a chaplain, can be considered from various points of view, as anthropological fieldwork, for example, or preparation for the Bermuda scheme. It was also an educational brief for Berkeley, who was acting as the tutor to George Ashe. The itinerary of cultural visits in Rome and the tour around the southern parts of the country is an

---

17. *Guardian*, I.387–88, no. 62, Friday, 22 May 1713.
18. *The Spectator*, no. 10, Monday, 12 March 1711, in Bond, ed., *The Spectator*, I.44.
19. Hume, *Essays Moral, Political and Literary*, p. 535.
20. Kendrick, 'Berkeley's Bermuda Project and *The Ladies Library*', pp. 245, 247–52.

itinerary designed to instruct a young man, not just preparation for a projected Italian guidebook. Berkeley had his eye on educational practice whilst in Italy, noting in Tarentum on 20 May 1717 that the archbishop's palace was used as a seminary: 'logic Philosophy theology humanity taught in the same / youth secular & ecclesiastic are taught dieted and lodged for 30 ducats per annum each / N:B: These seminary's common'.[21] Perhaps Berkeley felt that the established Protestant church should have been doing more to provide public education? Certainly comparison with the Catholic church's missionary work was one stimulus for Berkeley's missionary educational project to found St Paul's College on Bermuda.

Other fascinations of the project can sometimes distract from the fundamental fact that St Paul's College was to be a university. The college would have involved kidnapping and forcibly transporting Native Americans; one of its aims was to settle the Anglican church in America and possibly establish a bishopric there;[22] and it was a utopian project informed by insufficient knowledge of the island targeted and of the complexities of American colonial life into which Berkeley would have to integrate himself in order to function. But it was a project for a university. The fellowship of nine proposed for the college bears comparison to the sixteen fellows and provost who made up the academic staff of TCD according to the seventeenth-century statutes.[23] Berkeley sought a monopoly over the teaching of the liberal arts on the island.[24] One might expect the curriculum to have mirrored those of TCD and other similar institutions, such as Cambridge, and to include mathematical and physical sciences, natural history and geography, and philosophy, as well as classics. Berkeley may, however, have had broader ambitions, given his inclusion of the practice and perhaps the history and theory of the fine arts in his project, as indicated by the invitation of John Smibert, the painter, to become a fellow and the discussion of an academy of music at the college.[25] In size and

21. LJ, VII.288.

22. For a 1788 note by Eliza Frinsham/Berkeley on the list of subscribers to the Bermuda scheme, see BL MS Add 39311, f. 63.

23. Bolton, *A Translation of the Charter and Statutes*, p. 26.

24. LJ, VII.364–65, in his petition for the college.

25. For the teaching of the visual arts, see Saunders, *John Smibert*, p. 59; for the

breadth of curriculum, St Paul's would have been a considerable establishment.

Berkeley's legacy in America is perhaps seen most clearly in her universities.[26] Whilst still in America, Berkeley donated copies of his own works to Yale, asking Samuel Johnson, the educationalist, churchman, and philosopher he met in America, if they would also accept copies of Hooker and Chillingworth. He directed Johnson to distribute a further parcel of books to individual students, to Yale, or to the school in New Haven.[27] He was able to combine unreturnable subscriptions to the Bermuda project and new donations into a gift of his farm at Whitehall to Yale:

> Some part of the benefactions to the College of Bermuda, which I could
> not return, the benefactors being deceased, joined with the assistance
> of some living friends, has enabled me without any great loss to myself,
> to dispose of my farm in Rhode Island in favour of the college in Con-
> necticut. [...] I shall make it my endeavour to procure a benefaction
> of books for the college library, and am not without hopes of success.

Eight cases of books were duly sent to Mr Williams, rector at Yale, on 31 May 1733.[28] On the same day, Berkeley sent to Harvard 'a box of books containing all the Latin classic authors in quarto being the fairest editions and the best comments for the use of your society'. The rent of Whitehall was used to pay the expenses of students in between their first and second degrees, according to the deed of conveyance. The students at Yale to benefit from the scholarship funded by the disposition of Whitehall were to be chosen by 'public trial', and when Berkeley wrote to Johnson two years later, he was pleased that 'the public examinations appointed in your College have not failed of their design in encouraging the studies of the youth educated therein'. Alongside this design was the hope to 'promote better

academy of music, see BL Add MS 47030 (Egmont Papers), f. 136r, Philip to John Percival, 24 February 1724/5.

26. See Conroy, 'Berkeley and Education in America'.

27. Letter 199, Berkeley to Johnson, 24 March 1730, p. 320; letter 213, Berkeley to Johnson, 7 September 1731, p. 342.

28. Letter 216, Berkeley to Johnson, 25 July 1732, p. 345; letter 223, p. 352; letter 225, Berkeley to Wadsworth, 31 May 1733, p. 354. A reconstructed catalogue of the Yale gift can be found in Keogh, 'Bishop Berkeley's Gift of Books in 1733'.

understanding with the Dissenters, and so by degrees to lessen their dislike to our Communion'.[29] Education served the sectarian ambitions of the Anglican church in America. In 1747, Berkeley made a donation to the Society for the Propagation of the Gospel (SPG) to donate more books to Harvard, this time specifying certain titles:

> Hooker, Chillingworth, the Sermons of Barrow, Tillotson Sharp & Clarke, Scot's Christian life, Pearson on the Creed, Burnet on the 39 Articles, Burnet's history of the Reformation, A.B. Spotswood's history of the church of Scotland, Clarendon's history, Prideaux's connection, Cave's historia literaria eccles: Hammond's annotations, Pool's Synopsis Critic., the Patres Apostolici published by Le Clerc with the dissertations of Pearson etc. in the epistles of S. Ignatius.[30]

The Anglican bent of this selection is clear. (American universities were not the only ones to receive Berkeley's donations. He funded a medal for Greek at TCD that was first awarded on 24 April 1737.[31])

Berkeley gave organisational and strategic advice to American universities as well as books and money. His reflections and experiences during the life of the Bermuda scheme made his advice desirable. Samuel Johnson let Berkeley know of a plan for an Anglican college in New York, the institution that would eventually be founded in 1754 as King's College and become Columbia University in 1784. Berkeley offered his advice:

> I would not advise applying to England for charters or statues (which might cause great trouble expense and delay), but to do the business quietly within themselves.
>
> I believe it may suffice to begin with a president and two fellows. If they can procure but three fit persons, I doubt not the college from the smallest beginnings would soon grow considerable. I should conceive good hopes were you at the head of it.
>
> Let them by all means supply themselves out of the seminarys in New England. For I am apprehensive none can be got in Old England (who are willing to go) worth sending.

29. The deed is reproduced in Luce, pp. 236–38; letter 216, p. 345; letter 253, 11 June 1735, p. 384.

30. Letter 357, Berkeley to Bearcroft, after April 1747, pp. 534–35.

31. TCD MS MUN V 27, f. 7v.

Let the Greek and Latin classics be well taught. Be this the first care as to learning. But the principal care must be good life and morals to which (as well as to study) early hours and temperate meals will much conduce.

If the terms for degrees are the same as in Oxford & Cambridge, this would give credit to the college, and pave the way for admitting their graduates *ad eundem* in the English Universities.

Small premiums in books, or distinctions in habit may prove useful encouragements to the students.

I would advise that the building be regular, plain and cheap, and that each student have a small room (about ten feet square) to himself.

I recommended this nascent seminary to an English bishop to try what might be done there. But by his answer it seems the colony is judged rich enough to educate its own youth.

Colleges from small beginnings grow great by subsequent bequests and benefactions. A small matter will suffice to set one a going. And when this is once well done, there is no doubt it will go on and thrive. The chief concern must be to set out in a good method, and introduce from the very first a good taste into the Society. For this end its principal expense should be in making a handsome provision for the President and Fellows.[32]

In small compass Berkeley offers a vision of all university life, from finance and remuneration to buildings, accommodation, student discipline, ethos, instruction, supply of staff, connections to other institutions of national and colonial life, compatibility with other degree programmes internationally, and the taste cultivated in the society. And he shifts from college to seminary to society as the term to describe this institution: these are the same thing, seen from different angles, depending on whether one is seeing (classical) learning, piety, or social order as the foremost of the inseparable attributes to be produced in graduates.

This advice was passed from Samuel Johnson to Benjamin Franklin, who received it on 9 August 1750 and wrote to thank Johnson both for his letter and for Berkeley's, 'which I will take care of, and beg Leave to keep a little longer'. Franklin was working to support an academy that would eventually become the University

32. Letter 363, Berkeley to Johnson, 23 August 1749, pp. 541–42.

of Pennsylvania, and his *Proposals Relating to the Education of Youth in Pensilvania* had been published in Philadelphia in 1749. His proposals devoted more attention to describing a curriculum in which the study of history and languages would have a pragmatic orientation towards use—persuasion of one's peers, understanding practical justice, the purpose of (free) government, the history of trade—and go along with the study of the elements of drawing, engineering, and mechanics than did Berkeley's succinct pointers. But unsurprisingly, they chime with Berkeley's view of the ethos of an educational institution at certain points, as when Franklin recommends the scholars dine together 'plainly, temperately, and frugally'.[33] Franklin tried to lure Johnson to teach in the Academy of Philadelphia with the offer of £100 (GBP) in salary, noting that the city was supporting the academy to the tune of £200 a year, following Franklin's presentation of a 'Paper on the Academy' to the Common Council on 31 July 1750.[34] (The third reason Franklin argued for funds from the council was that 'a Number of our Natives will hereby be qualified to bear Magistracies, and execute other public Offices of Trust, with Reputation to themselves and Country; there being at present great Want of Persons so qualified in the several Counties of this Province', echoing Berkeley's concern in the transcription from Clarendon that people be sufficiently educated to bear the responsibilities of public life.) Franklin already had £5,000 in subscriptions for his college.

Franklin's educational vision had a kinship with Berkeley's, a kinship that was expressed in the exchange of letters and schemes between these literary and philosophical men who saw education as central to the well-being of the colonies. But there were very significant differences between them. Franklin's project was nonsectarian. It was not part of the attempt to establish episcopacy in America, as was St Paul's College and Johnson's ambition for King's College. Its purpose was to produce governors rather than missionaries.[35] Its

---

33. Franklin, *Proposals Relating to the Education of Youth in Pensilvania*, p. 10.

34. Benjamin Franklin, 'Paper on the Academy', minutes of the Common Council, 31 July 1750, The Papers of Benjamin Franklin, vol. 4, https://franklinpapers.org /framedVolumes.jsp (accessed 14 September 2018).

35. Overhoff, 'Franklin's Philadelphia Academy and Basedow's Dessau Philanthropine', p. 804: 'It was an entirely new kind of Academy as it was an institution designed to train

educational focus was more practical, placing correct and elegant English for political, civil, and economic life above the classical languages, finding more room for the mechanical arts, and focusing world history and chronology on the study of productive social and economic arrangements.[36] Franklin conceived of the college as a motor of economic development, bringing money into Pennsylvania along with students and improving the civic structure of the town through the activities of its graduates.[37]

As the Querist, Berkeley shared Franklin's sense of the contribution that universities could make to economic development, suggesting that a 'Mart of Literature' would be 'an infallible Means of drawing Men and Money into the Kingdom'.[38] But beyond this similarity, Berkeley's educational thinking was by contrast privatised and elite. Perhaps burnt by the non-appearance of his funds for St Paul's, he thought bequests were a better source of funding than government grants. The tone of the institution was to be handed down from the head and fellows to the students, and the salaried staff were to be sufficiently well maintained for their material status to reinforce their

---

not ministers for the dominant sect in the region but political leaders for the province and its capital. The trustees of this new school cherished the notion that learning ought not to be restricted to a single leading religion and that education should be rendered rather practical by focusing on modern languages, contemporary literature and the natural sciences. In particular the varied religious backgrounds of the trustees and faculty distinguished the school from all other American institutions of higher education before the Revolution'.

36. The educational programme of Madden, *Reflections and Resolutions Proper for the Gentlemen of Ireland*, pp. 76–86, may share as much of this commitment to practically oriented schooling as it does with Berkeley's programme for improvement in Ireland.

37. Franklin, 'Paper on the Academy', notes the benefits of the foundation of schools and colleges to the local economy, one of the arguments currently in favour with university senior managements and governments: 'It is thought that a good Academy erected in Philadelphia, a healthy Place, where Provisions are plenty, situated in the Center of the Colonies, may draw Numbers of Students from the Neighboring Provinces, who must spend considerable Sums yearly among us, in Payment for their Lodging, Diet, Apparel &c. which will be an Advantage to our Traders, Artisans, and Owners of Houses and Lands. This Advantage is so considerable, that it has been frequently observed in Europe, that the fixing a good School or college in a little inland Village, has been the Means of making it a great Town in a few Years; And therefore the Magistrates of many Places, have offer'd and given great yearly Salaries, to draw learned Instructors from other Countries to their respective Towns, merely with a View to the Interest of the Inhabitants'.

38. *Querist*, I.22, §187.

moral and intellectual superiority. Berkeley thought of education in politico-theological terms, as a means of training people in the ways of the true church so that they could proselytise, by more or less subtle means, throughout their lives. If people who were not from a background already integrated into the governing elite were to be admitted, it was with the end of their integration into precisely the same governing arrangements and the reproduction of those governing arrangements through the generations. Berkeley's educational theory and practice naturalised the privileges of sect and ethnic, family, and socioeconomic background in order to preserve the naturalised social order that Berkeley had decided it was better to maintain than to challenge, even if it produced significant social ills—and not because those ills were necessary to some other, greater good, but simply because order is always better than disorder.[39] Though Franklin and Berkeley were working towards founding and sustaining comparable educational institutions in colonial America in the middle decades of the eighteenth century, their different emphases suggest two quite different futures for education and for civic life more generally.

I would like to discuss two further educational episodes in Berkeley's career that do not receive much attention elsewhere: the education of his children, and the attractions of Oxford as a place of study. Children of course represent an opportunity for the educationalist. Eliza Frinsham/Berkeley relates that 'Bishop Berkeley, at one time, for several years paid four hundred pound *per annum* to different masters to instruct his children in Music, Painting, Fencing, Riding and French; the Latin and Greek he entrusted to none but himself'.[40] Personal engagement in the perceived core of education—Greek and Latin—was something Berkeley took very seriously. George Berkeley Jr drew a response from his mother by saying something critical about his father (perhaps complaining that he had not been sent to a public school):

[H]ow carefully was your Infancy protected by your dear Fathers skill & Mothers care? You were not for our ease trusted to mercenary

39. See *Passive Obedience*, §51, and discussion of this topic in chapter 4.

40. Eliza Berkeley, preface to Berkeley, *Poems*, p. ccxliv. *Ladies Library*, II.197, 205, excerpting Allestree, *The Ladies Calling* and Masham, *Occasional Thoughts*, suggests that servants are not to be entrusted with the task of educating children.

hands. In Childhood you were instructed by your Father—he though old & sickly performed the constant tedious task himself, & would not trust it to Another care—You were his business & his pleasure—short sighted people see no danger from common vulgar errors of Education. He knew that fundamental Errors were never cured & that the first seasoning of the Cask gives the flavor, & therefore he chose rather to prevent than cure—as much as possible he kept you with himself or else Alone[.][41]

Anne describes George's personal attention to the instruction of his children as a matter of enlarged views and an understanding of the formative role of early education.

Neither the names nor any account of the effects of the masters in riding or fencing have come down to the present. The only evidence of the level of proficiency in French amongst the Berkeley children I know of is that Catherine Talbot, when exchanging journals with Julia Berkeley after George Berkeley's death in 1753, suggested that Julia not write in French, as that would render it too fatiguing a task for her, and the journal itself less accurate. (Julia would have been only fourteen at the time.) Julia had some knowledge of the harpsichord, she painted, and she wanted to learn Italian.[42] Given that Berkeley described the household at Cloyne as 'musically mad' in a letter to Gervais of 6 September 1743, and that much of the correspondence between the two men that survives from the 1740s concerns the acquisition of viols, it is perhaps not surprising that the Berkeley children were musically literate.[43] Musical instruction may have been the responsibility of a Mr DuBois, whose apparent marriage to Dorothea Annesley is the subject of Berkeley's last surviving letters (from 1752). Eliza Frinsham/ Berkeley also records an anecdote about an Italian music master named Pasquilino, who was resident with the family.[44] Improving his English through the use of a dictionary, he once saluted Berkeley

41. BL Add MS 39312, f. 227r.

42. See BL Add MS 46688, ff. 29v, 21v, 39r–v. For more on the friendship between Talbot and Julia Berkeley, see chapter 16. French and Italian were said to be suitable languages for women to acquire; see *Ladies Library*, I.23, excerpting Fénelon, *Education of a Daughter*.

43. Letter 302, p. 454; see also letters 290, 292, 295.

44. Eliza Berkeley, preface to Berkeley, *Poems*, p. ccccxii (n).

with the phrase 'may God pickle your Lordship', 'pickle' being synonymous with 'preserve'.

DuBois's presence at a trip to Percival's Lohort Castle in 1750 is
recorded in a letter from Will Cooley to Percival. He is the family's
'Master of Musick' and in attendance along with some clergymen
and 'Mr Mitchell a painter'.[45] It has been suggested that Lohort,
with its carefully managed and improved physical estate, may
have been partly responsible for spreading the vogue for the pic-
turesque in Ireland.[46] Given that William Berkeley sketched the
castle, its appearance and situation, as matters of aesthetic consideration, may have been part of the attraction of the visit. Mitchell
might have been the second choice as tutor. Berkeley had written
in 1735 to his old friend John Smibert, who had accompanied him
to Rhode Island and remained in Boston to pursue his career as
a painter. The letter, framed as a series of queries such as those
Berkeley was producing for *The Querist*, hints that there would be
a market for Smibert's portraits in Cork and that Smibert should
consider a move to Ireland. Berkeley may well have been thinking

45. See Luce, pp. 212–13. I have not been able to identify this Mitchell with certainty. A
Thomas Mitchell, a master ship builder as well as painter, is known for naval works, some
of which are in the collection of the National Maritime Museum in Greenwich, and for two
paintings with an Irish connection, *A View of the River Boyne with Gentlemen and Horses
by a Statue to William III in the Foreground, the Boyne Obelisk Beyond* (1757), now in the
Ulster Museum, and *Sir John and Lady Freke and a Friend in Ireland* (1757; ex Sothebys,
9 July 1980, lot 36, according to Cust and Adolph, 'Mitchell, Thomas'. These works may be
later oil paintings based on sketches Mitchell made during a 1750 visit to Ireland acting as
tutor to the Berkeley children. Mitchell worked in London in the later eighteenth century.
Another Thomas Mitchell was in correspondence with Anne Berkeley in the later eighteenth century, writing to her from Ballyroan, 4 September 1779 (see BL Add MS 39312,
ff. 14–15). It seems possible that the family of this Thomas Mitchell had a continuing connection with the Berkeleys, as Julia and Henry Berkeley, the two children who experienced
serious mental ill health, were living with a Mrs Mitchell. Eliza Berkeley bequeathed items
in her will to friends as an encouragement to take a charitable interest in Henry and Julia:

> [I]ntreating them all and every one to have the Charity to take care that the poor
> insane Son and Daughter of Bishop Berkeley may not want any attention or com-
> forts that their Melancholy state will admit of and that the care of them may
> never on any Account devolve on the very unworthy George and as he chooses
> to stile himself George Berkeley Mitchell youngest Son of their I believe wor-
> thy present Keeper M.rs Mitchell Widow of Thomas Mitchell under whose
> care they were placed by their own Mother'. TCD MS 3530, f. 23r (p. 20).

This Thomas Mitchell may also have been a painter, of course.

46. Barnard, *Improving Ireland?*, p. 126.

of enlisting Smibert as a tutor for his family.[47] Berkeley was taking the aesthetic education of his children seriously, just as *The Querist* had considered it the duty of the governing elite to establish good taste, so that their health and the health of the state could be maintained and improved.

At the end of his life, Berkeley was able to spend a short time in Oxford, which, almost forty years previously he had called 'the most delightful place that I have ever seen'. Berkeley had been taking care over the selection of a tutor for George Jr, as reflected in Martin Benson's letter to him saying that the bishop of Bristol had recommended the same person Berkeley had been making enquiries about for that role.[48] One source claims that Berkeley had received royal permission to leave Cloyne: '[T]he King declared he should die a Bishop, and gave him liberty to reside where he pleased. He accordingly left Cloyne, and let the Demesne lands for £200 per an., ordering the money to be divided among the poor of Cloyne, Youghal, and Aghada'.[49] Others suggest that a strong desire to be in Oxford and a niceness about abandoning his bishopric led him to consider an unprecedented career move:

> [R]esolv'd to educate his son at Oxford, his paternal tenderness incited him to accompany him, & he intended to have passed three years among Books & scholars; a satisfaction, which his fear of neglecting the sacred charge of Episcopacy, inclined him to have purchased by an exchange of his Bishopric for a Canonry of Christ Church; but the clergy could find no precedent for such resignation.[50]

This private biographical note may have drawn on a note in the *London Evening Post*: 'The Right Rev. Dr. Berkly, Bishop of Cloyne, is so greatly desirous of ending his Days at the University of Oxford, where he has some time since resided, that his Lordship has offered

47. Letter 252, Berkeley to Smibert, 31 May 1735, pp. 383–84. I thank Marta Szymańska-Lewoszewska for this suggestion.

48. Letter 51, Berkeley to Percival, 19 July 1713, p. 99; letter 387, Benson to Berkeley, 18 February 1752, p. 573.

49. Brady, *Clerical and Parochial Records of Cork, Cloyne, and Ross*, III(1864).117.

50. BL Add MS 39311, f. 92v, William Price to George Berkeley Jr, 17 July 1760, apparently in response to George Jr's request for a written character of his father.

as is currently reported, the valuable Bishoprick of Cloyne in Ireland, worth 3000 l. per Ann. for a Canonry of Christ Church, Oxon, not worth 400 l.'[51] If this was indeed Berkeley's intention for his time at Oxford, it was a scheme that might have been maturing for several years. He wrote to Prior on 12 September 1746 saying he was uninterested in any other clerical promotion than perhaps the archbishopric of Dublin, which could have 'tempted me by a greater opportunity of doing good'. But he says nothing else would persuade him away from Cloyne, and 'my Oxford scheme; which, though delayed by the illness of my son, yet I am as intent upon it, and as much resolved as ever'.[52] It seems that Berkeley's friend John Baron Wainwright was soliciting on Berkeley's behalf for the deanship of Christchurch, Oxford, in late 1732.[53] The Oxford scheme may have been twenty years in the making.

Oxford signified intellectual promise, retirement, and all the goods of learning for Berkeley. Five years earlier, he had written to John James, countering his friend's arguments in favour of the Catholic church. We do not have the letter from James to Berkeley, but James must have suggested that the monastic scheme of life had educational and religious advantages. Berkeley recognised the value of a group of people who seclude themselves and give themselves to contemplation and learning: they are the vanguard of 'Divine Philosophy'. But these people should be those with a natural inclination towards reflection, he believed, and need not be committed for life:

> I should like a convent without a vow or perpetual obligation. Doubtless a College or monastery (not a resource for younger brothers, not a nursery for ignorance laziness & superstition) receiving only grown persons of approved piety, learning, and a contemplative turn would be a great means of improving the divine philosophy, and brightening up the face of religion in our church. But I should expect still more success from a number of Gentlemen living independently at Oxford who made

51. No. 3900, October 26–October 28, 1752.

52. Letter 339, p. 508.

53. Clayton, *Memoirs of [Charlotte Clayton,] the Countess of Sundon*, II.181, Wainwright to Clayton, 26 December 1732; BL Add MS 20105, f. 83r.

divine things their study, and proposed to wean themselves from what is called the world.[54]

Oxford could be the scene of an informal monasticism, a dedication to God and learning that was free of the corruptions of institution-alised religious training as Berkeley supposed it was practised in Catholicism. Maybe this was the kind of life Berkeley proposed to himself in Oxford in his late years. Travelling to Oxford together was an intergenerational educational compact between the (male) members of the Berkeley family and one that related to both the education and formation of young (male) adults and the reforma-tion of the church by its advanced philosophical divines.

Locke, Astell, Fénelon

Education was not just a practical concern for Berkeley, but also a matter for philosophy. As in many fields of enquiry, Locke was one of his most important predecessors. *Some Thoughts Concern-ing Education*, harmonising as it does with the epistemological work of Locke's *Essay Concerning Human Understanding*, strongly marked educational theory and practice of the early eighteenth century. Berkeley recommended it to Percival on the birth of Per-cival's first son, as a book that 'abounds with excellent maxims'.[55] Geraint Parry has suggested in a survey of eighteenth-century edu-cational philosophy that Locke's 'educational objective', itself part of the 'process of conscious social reproduction', 'is to prepare the minds of children so that they can examine in a rational manner whether they should grant or withhold assent to the propositions about the world, morality, religion, and politics with which they will be faced in adult life'. Locke's *Thoughts*, like his *Essay*, leave his readers with questions about the universality or diversity of human dispositions and practices, and about the degree to which the understanding can overcome the delusions of the association of ideas and of prejudice and locality. Parry summarises the ques-tions Locke left his successors: 'whether human beings were almost entirely the products of education and whether society had the will

54. Letter 282, Berkeley to John James, 7 June 1741, p. 430.
55. Letter 26, Berkeley to Percival, 6 March 1711, p. 55.

to permit education to initiate a radical reconstruction of the social order'.[56] To what degree are natural appetites and inclinations a true guide? To what extent must we be trained out of them? To what degree can we re-describe the practices into which we train ourselves as natural to us, to our higher selves? These are questions Berkeley picks up from Locke, whilst making it clear that the social order is to remain entirely stable, with no challenge to the sources of power or their expression in ranks and hierarchies in social and religious life. Changes in practice achieved by education are conceived as personal first, and as socially transformative only inasmuch as they will lead to the better, proper, healthy functioning of the existing regime, not to the installation of a new one. The transformation of human practices through education is a matter of cultivating a species to its naturally ordained end, not the discovery of new ends for a species that is characteristically undetermined and free. Berkeley's educational programme aims at reforming practice, but not in any way that could be described as radical or democratic.

There is much in common between Locke's and Berkeley's thinking on education. In what follows I emphasise these connections and also connections to two other educational philosophers important for Berkeley: Astell and Fénelon. Important educational works by these writers are extensively excerpted in the anthology Berkeley prepared in 1713, *The Ladies Library*. As we have already seen, Berkeley emphasises the education of the aristocracy. Locke too thinks that the gentry are most assiduously to be educated, as they will order the other ranks of society.[57] It has been pointed out that Locke's educational programme for the poor did not extend beyond teaching basic manual skills for a trade and imparting 'some sense of religion'; its primary concern was making poor children self-financing—concerns not unlike those of Berkeley in the 1730s and '40s.[58] (Mary Astell, when writing to propose an educational institution to which women could retire, specifies that both students and instructors ought to be people of rank.)[59] The rela-

56. Parry, 'Education', pp. 608, 610, 614.

57. Locke, *Some Thoughts Concerning Education*, p. 80.

58. Gay, 'Locke on the Education of Paupers', p. 191, citing Bourne, *A Life of John Locke*, II.385.

59. Astell, *A Serious Proposal to the Ladies*, p. 103.

tionship between appetite and practice is also comparable, though Locke frames his discourse in the terms of denial, whilst Berkeley prefers to talk of enlarging views.[60] Both philosophers recognise that humans have appetites that are natural to them, that are part of being the type of creature man is. These appetites, however, are to be trained, and that training must also have regard to the kind of creature man is—a rational creature. For Locke, the mind must be 'disposed to consent to nothing but what may be suitable to the Dignity and Excellency of a rational Creature'.[61] Being educated into humanity is not to give in to appetites that draw us to immediate pleasures, but on the contrary to deny those pleasures:

> It seems plain to me, that the Principle of all Vertue and Excellency lies in a power of denying our selves the satisfaction of our own Desires, where Reason does not authorize them. This Power is to be got and improved by Custom, made easy and familiar by an *early* Practice. If therefore I might be heard, I would advise that, contrary to the ordinary way, Children should be used to submit their Desires, and go without their Longings, even *from their very Cradles*. The first thing they should learn to know should be, that they were not to have any thing, because it pleased them, but because it was thought fit for them.[62]

Locke recommends working with the natural appetite for pleasure by introducing a new object of desire (and a new object of aversion): the regard in which other people hold you. '*Esteem* and *Disgrace* are, of all others, the most powerful incentives to the Mind, when once it is brought to relish them'.[63] Educating people is getting them to avoid shame rather than pain, to avoid those things that a (or an imagined) community says are good or bad rather than those things one's most immediate desires say are good or bad. Displacing pleasure with esteem, and pain with shame, is displacing the natural with the social, but also training people into rational

60. See Nurock, 'La Conscience morale selon Berkeley', p. 323, where it is noted that education of the moral sense is presented as education of the sight. See also Taranto, 'Le Travail de la sagesse', p. 270, who notes the role of broad and synoptic views and imagination, as forms of spiritual exercise that enable moral life, citing *The Guardian* 7.

61. Locke, *Some Thoughts Concerning Education*, p. 103.

62. Ibid., pp. 107–8.

63. Ibid., p. 116.

forms of consent to what is truly desirable for the kind of creature they are.[64]

Astell refuses the identification of social coercion with education. Though she holds the belief that humanity is united by a social bond (a species bond), she thinks that generous neglect of others' views is also vital to being educated:

> It was not fit that Creatures capable of and made for Society, shou'd be wholly Independent, or Indifferent to each others Esteem and Commendation; nor was it convenient considering how seldom these are justly distributed, that they shou'd too much regard and depend on them. It was requisite therefore that a desire of our Neighbours Good Opinion shou'd be implanted in our Natures to the end we might be excited to do such things as deserve it, and yet withall a Generous neglect of it, if they unjustly withheld it where it was due.[65]

Astell also prefers the explanation that one arrives at higher pleasures through Epicureanism rather than through the performed social approval or disapproval of actions: the true Christian is really the greatest Epicurean, in love with the greatest pleasures.[66] (Alongside this Epicurean love of God we might place Berkeley's insistence on a 'natural appetite of immortality').[67] Astell, like Berkeley, employs analogies with vision to describe the pleasure of loving God and thinks of the obligation to educate oneself as proportional to one's natural capacity for enlarged or extended views: 'tho Truth is the Object of every Individual Understanding, yet all are not equally enlarg'd nor able to comprehend so much; and they whose Capacities and Circumstances of Living do not fit 'em for it,

---

64. On the different senses of 'nature' that seem to lie under Locke's writings on education, see Bantock, *Studies in the History of Educational Theory*, I(1980).228: 'Lurking in Locke's advice, indeed, are three different views of "nature" all of which are broadly familiar from humanist times: two relate to innate disposition. [. . .] Sometimes he speaks as if such "natural" characteristics (manifest largely in psychological terms) are matters to be encouraged, sometimes he writes as if "nature" is something to be overcome in the course of human education. Finally he seems to indicate that what is achieved as a result of education, nurture, is itself "natural"'.

65. Astell, *A Serious Proposal to the Ladies*, p. 141.

66. Ibid., pp. 86, 221.

67. LJ, VII.73, in an undated sermon at Newport; see also LJ, VII.109, 'On Eternal Life'.

lie not under that obligation of extending their view which Persons of a larger reach and greater leisure do'.[68]

Berkeley's *Guardian* essay describing the purpose of public schools and universities, before turning towards religion, opens by identifying educational institutions as the instrument to fulfil a providential succession of the pleasures from the lower, sensual pleasures to the higher, intellectual pleasures:

> Providence hath with a bountiful Hand prepared Variety of Pleasures for the various Stages of Life. It behoves us not to be wanting to our selves, in forwarding the Intention of Nature, by the culture of our Minds, and a due Preparation of each Faculty for the Enjoyment of those Objects it is capable of being affected with.
>
> As our Parts open and display by gentle degrees, we rise from the Gratifications of Sense to relish those of the Mind. In the Scale of Pleasure the lowest are sensual Delights, which are succeeded by the more enlarged Views and gay Portraitures of a lively Imagination; and these give way to the sublimer Pleasures of Reason, which discover the Causes and Designs, the Frame, Connexion and Symmetry of Things, and fills the Mind with the Contemplation of intellectual Beauty, Order and Truth.[69]

This is not discipline, but the easy succession of pleasures, to which social formations such as educational institutions are midwives rather than police. It sounds a fair distance from Locke, who prescribes the performance of disapproval, practised collectively by family, servants, and tutors, to develop the sense of shame. That which educators want children to do must be the result of 'indispensible practice' and not the declaration of a rule.[70] As we will see, however, Berkeley, like Locke, has a developed interest in education as discipline and coercive practice.

The cleavage of natural and acquired appetites can lead to tensions in Locke's writing and recommendations. He acknowledges that people have temperaments that are very difficult to alter, and that even in adults certain pleasurable activities, such as playing

68. Astell, *A Serious Proposal to the Ladies*, pp. 75–76, 153.

69. *Guardian*, I.387, no. 62, Friday, 22 May [1713]. Holtzman, 'Berkeley's Two Panaceas', pp. 479–80, notes that study of the laws of nature, which are God's volitions, is part of the process of education or conforming one's will to God's.

70. Locke, *Some Thoughts Concerning Education*, pp. 117, 121,

music, are not always pleasurable. The educator must study and work with these tempers, the fixed and the changeable, as 'it is of great moment, and worth our Endeavours, to teach the Mind to get the Mastery over itself; and to be able, upon Choice, to take it self off from the hot pursuit of one Thing, and set it self upon another with Facility and Delight'.[71] Temper is recognised as entirely natural and impossible to extirpate, yet the ability to change pursuit regardless of temper is the ultimate product of education.

Difference of temper or character is approached in a slightly different way by Astell and Berkeley—not as a question of disciplining nature, but of rhetorically harmonising with others so that they come over to a different practice without feeling belittled. Again, Astell emphasises generosity of temper:

> Human Nature is not willing to own its Ignorance; Truth is so very attractive, there's such a natural agreement between our Minds and it, that we care not to be thought so dull as not to be able to find out by our selves such obvious matters. We shou'd therefore be careful that nothing pass from us which upbraids our Neighbours Ignorance, but study to remove't without appearing to take notice of it, and permit 'em to fancy if they please, that we believe them as Wise and Good as we endeavour to make them. By this we gain their Affections which is the hardest part of our Work, excite their Industry and infuse new Life into all Generous Tempers[.][72]

Berkeley's self-proclaimed aptitude for harmonising with others has already been noted in this study. In his sermon on religious zeal, Berkeley recognises again that the strategy of harmonising is required to educate people out of one way of thinking and acting and into the way of thinking and acting we prefer. We can arrive at seeing the necessity of harmonising with others from the hate that antagonists feel for one another:

> It is with difficulty, with violence to our nature, that we restrain our selves from hating those who hate us, and it is against nature, against reason, against experience to seek advice or direction from those we hate. And are not other men of like passions with ourselves? if therefore

71. Ibid., pp. 122, 135, 136.
72. Astell, *A Serious Proposal to the Ladies*, p. 193.

we design they shoud take effect ought we not to insinuate our exhortations and reproofs with a kind and friendly demeanour?[73]

Comprehending that others are like us, even when they are unlike us, is part of Berkeley's rhetorical strategy. It is the beginning of a generosity of temper that can bring others round to our way of seeing things. If we wish, as Astell put it—using a phrase that returns in Berkeley's *Querist*—to excite the industry of others, we need to enter somewhat into their ways of thinking and speaking. (I explore the limits of Berkeley's capacity for this exercise in chapter 7.)

A significant difference between Locke, Astell, and Berkeley is in the status of prejudice in the practice of education. All three thinkers argue that rational pursuit of truth is the only way to arrive at appropriate forms of behaviour.[74] Astell argues that the desire for happiness and for human perfection are the same. Although everyone shares the same object of desire, there is no self-evident way of achieving the object. So people must consult their reason, which is unfortunately 'at first too weak, and afterwards too often too much sophisticated to return a proper Answer, tho it be the most important concern of our Lives'. We should be very critical of our prejudices, because we have a tendency to take them for truths, and then, when they are disproved, to believe there is no truth at all.[75] Berkeley would not remove prejudice altogether, though he makes a similar observation to Astell in the sermon on zeal:

> Even in our riper years we are prejudiced in favor of the opinions entertained by our country, our friends, or those we esteem. But we wou'd do well to consider that other men have imbibed early notions, that they as well as we have a country, friends, and persons whom they esteem. These are pleas which may be made for any opinion, and are consequently good pleas for none.[76]

Alciphron, the freethinker in the philosophical dialogues taking his name as their title, takes diversity of religious belief and practice

---

73. LJ, VII.18.

74. See Carey, *Locke, Shaftesbury, and Hutcheson*, pp. 67–68, for rationality as the means of avoiding moral relativism in Locke.

75. Astell, *A Serious Proposal to the Ladies*, pp. 129, 133,

76. LJ, VII.20.

as the grounds for describing all such belief and practice as mere prejudice. Euphranor responds, as the argument develops, that freethinking can be a prejudice too:

> May not a Minute Philosopher, as well as another Man, be prejudiced in Favour of the Leaders of his Sect? May not an Atheistical Education prejudice towards Atheism? What should hinder a Man's being prejudiced against Religion, as well as for it? Or can you assign any Reason why an Attachment to Pleasure, Interest, Vice, or Vanity, may not be supposed to prejudice Men against Virtue?[77]

There is no way out of this description of others' views as mere prejudice other than the assertion of a final vocabulary (to use Richard Rorty's phrase) about what is desirable, a set of terms that cannot be justified in a noncircular manner. For the characters in *Alciphron* Berkeley argues through, and for Berkeley more generally, that vocabulary is of the cultivation and improvement of the truly human.

The mind, says Crito, adopting a phrase of Euphranor's, 'is like Land, better or worse, as it is improved, and according to the Seeds or Principles sown in it'. Euphranor had earlier said that what is natural to anything is not just what is immediately apparent in it, but that which is developed over the course of time, with the appropriate care and in the best circumstances. Euphranor illustrates his point by talking about an orange tree, whose blossoms are not present from its first appearance and which grows and fruits better or worse in different climates and soils. Why, he asks, 'may we not conclude, by a parity of Reason, that things may be natural to Humane Kind, and yet neither found in all Men, nor invariably the same where they are found?'[78] The final vocabulary of cultivation allows one to maintain a belief in the proper ends of the natural kind of 'human' at the same time as recognising wide differences in the practice of being human. The final vocabulary of culture is that which Euphranor and Crito are arguing is the best, the most reasonable way of talking about humans.

---

77. *Alciphron*, I.5, II.11.
78. *Alciphron*, II.20, I.14.

How land is owned, occupied, and cultivated is itself a practice that favours different kinds of life. Berkeley's preference for the vocabulary of cultivation is also a preference for a certain view of land occupation and ownership. Lysicles, another freethinking character, favours land seizure as a means of challenging the inherited rights of the church. Crito responds by saying that this is equivalent to an attack on all property rights, and he defends the existence of church lands and the payment of tithes: the former are a genuine property right based on land grant, and the latter are merely a diversion of rent to a priest that would otherwise be paid to a landlord. The ultimate argument in favour of this kind of landownership and right is that it is characteristic of the states that are generally recognised as being great: 'all other States, which ever made any Figure in the World for Wisdom and Politeness, have thought Learning deserved Encouragement as well as the Sword: that Grants for religious Uses were as fitting as for Knights Service: and Foundations for propagating Piety, as necessary to the publick Welfare and Defence, as either Civil or Military Establishments'.[79] Sovereign ownership of land which is then granted to nobles or noble institutions (the church and educational institutions) for their rightful use is the form of ownership or consumption underlying Berkeley's ideas of cultivation. A cultivated society gives over some of its land to religious and educational uses. It does so to defend itself and maintain its health.

The vocabulary of cultivation is not always required to support the idea of a human natural kind with proper ends. In the context of the pulpit rather than printed dialogue Berkeley states that there are natural, universal human inclinations:

> That there are appetites and aversions, satisfactions and uneasinesses, inclinations and instincts, originally interwoven in our nature, must be allowed by all impartial and considerate men. [. . .] [W]hich affections, because they are universal not confined to any age or country, and not to be accounted for by custom or education, but alike in all nations and times, are properly said to be natural or innate.[80]

---

79. Ibid., V.31.
80. LJ, VII.130, 'On the Will of God', Whit Sunday 1751.

Berkeley makes the claim for human universality, even though he recognises the important role of prejudice and custom in shaping beliefs and keeping people in beliefs that are not reasonable. His defence of his version of rationality is made on the basis of the deep vocabulary of development according to natural kind, where variety is merely the contingent product of local variations barely complicating an underlying uniformity of nature.[81] Education consists in pointing to flourishing examples of a kind, in being such an example, but at the same time having some consideration for the different circumstances in which one's interlocutor, or student, might have been reared. An interest in practical education is another way of describing what can appear to be an interest in strategy and dissimulation in Berkeley. Recognising that human flourishing may look different in different circumstances, but that it is nonetheless the flourishing of universal attributes, is Berkeley's way of arguing with others: arguing for his Anglican social paternalism, and arguing others into it.

The Querist brings together many of Berkeley's concerns in and for education. Images of cultivation, development, and improvement remain central in that text. As in *Alciphron*, there is little distance between the interest in literal and in metaphorical cultivation. Good husbandry is both an agricultural and a moral practice. It is one that is available to women and that relates to Berkeley's concern for women's education. Berkeley writes with pride of his wife Anne's farming in the famine year 1741: 'She is become a great farmer of late. In these hard times we employ above a hundred men every day in agriculture of one kind or other all which my wife directs. This is a charity which pays it self'.[82] Fénelon gave a rationale from state management for thinking that women should be instructed in and become responsible for the agricultural management of estates: 'La force et le bonheur d'un État consiste non à avoir beaucoup de provinces mal cultivées, mais à tirer de la terre qu'on possède tout ce qu'il faut pour nourrir aisément un peuple nombreux'. (The strength and happiness of a State consists not

---

81. For custom building on inherent potentials of the human spirit, see Girard, 'La Bonne société d'après Berkeley', p. 233.

82. Letter 282, Berkeley to James, 7 June 1741, p. 433.

in having many poorly cultivated provinces, but in drawing from the land one does possess all that is necessary easily to nourish a large population.)[83] Careful estate management improves national strength and combats natural evils. It is an admirable objective in education. It is also an image of or model for education. In both these forms it is a practice open, selectively, to women.

The delegation of responsibilities to certain members of a family is also an image of or model for education. The state is naturalised by being presented as a family. Again, Fénelon may have influenced Berkeley's thinking. The political education of Telemachus revolves around the idea of a king treating a city-state as a family. King Sesotris of Thebes is admirable because he treats his people as his children; Bétique is admirable for its restrained way of life in which heads of families are kings and governors.[84] The political model Fénelon promotes is a highly interventionist paternalistic state gearing all social activity towards the production of virtue through the regulation of consumption and production and the disciplining of bodies; virtue *is* regulation. The independent family unit, self-sufficient and free, with a variety of tasks, powers, and obligations delegated to the various members on account of their natural aptitudes—this is the model for the state that Berkeley invokes when he asks, 'Whether a Nation might not be consider'd as a Family?'[85] Such a way of considering the state, and the family, is a matter of recognising the different forms of education appropriate to the different naturalised ranks and statuses of different people. A string of queries on education builds on the combination of naturalised political status and educationally acquired attributes that were the subject of Berkeley's citation of Clarendon with which this chapter opened. Addressing a large number of themes raised in this chapter, the Querist asks:

> 183. *Qu.* Whether our Peers and Gentlemen are born Legislators? Or whether that Faculty be acquired by Study and Reflection?
> 184. *Qu.* Whether, to comprehend the real Interest of a People, and the Means to procure it, doth not imply some Fund of

---

83. Fénelon, 'De l'éducation des filles' (1696 text), in *Œuvres*, I.155.
84. Fénelon, *Telemachus*, pp. 18, 110.
85. *The Querist*, I.21, §180.

Knowledge historical, moral, and political, with a Faculty of Reason improved by Learning?

185. *Qu.* Whether every Enemy to Learning be not a *Goth*? And whether every such *Goth* among us be not an Enemy to the Country?

186. *Qu.* Whether therefore it would not be an Omen of ill presage, a dreadful Phænomenon in the Land, if our great Men should take it in their Heads to deride Learning and Education?

187. *Qu.* Whether on the contrary, it should not seem worth while to erect a Mart of Literature in this Kingdom, under wiser Regulations and better Discipline than in any other Part of *Europe*? And whether this would not be an infallible Means of drawing Men and Money into the Kingdom?

188. *Qu.* Whether the governed be not too numerous for the governing Part of our College? And whether it might not be expedient to convert Thirty Natives Places into Twenty Fellowships?

189. *Qu.* Whether, if we had Two Colleges, there might not spring an useful Emulation between them? And whether it might not be contrived, so to divide the Fellows, Scholars, and Revenues between both, as that no Member should be a Loser thereby?

190. *Qu.* Whether Ten thousand Pounds well laid out might not build a decent College, fit to contain Two hundred Persons; and whether the Purchase-money of the Chambers would not go a good way towards defraying the Expence?

191. *Qu.* Where this College should be situated?

The 1750 text here inserts the additional query:

[Whether in Imitation of the Jesuits at Paris, who admit Protestants to study in their Colleges, it may not be right for us also to admit Roman-Catholics into our College, without obliging them to attend Chapel-Duties, or Catechisms, or Divinity-Lectures? And whether this might not keep Money in the Kingdom and prevent the Prejudices of a foreign Education?]

192. *Qu.* Whether it is possible a State should not thrive, whereof the lower Part were industrious, and the upper wise?

193. *Qu.* Whether the collected Wisdom of Ages and Nations be not found in Books, improved and applied by Study?

The 1750 text here has five additional queries:

[Whether Themistocles his Art of making a little City, or a little
People become a great one, be learned any where so well as in
the Writings of the Ancients?

Whether a wise State hath any Interest nearer Heart than the Education of Youth?

Whether the Mind like Soil doth not by Disuse grow stiff; and
whether Reasoning and Study be not like stirring and dividing
the Glebe?

Whether an early Habit of Reflexion, though obtained by speculative Sciences, may not have its use in practical Affairs?

Whether even those Parts of Academical Learning which are
quite forgotten may not have improved and enriched the Soil,
like those Vegetables which are raised, not for themselves, but
plowed in for a Dressing of Land?]

194. *Qu.* Whether it was not an *Irish* Professor who first opened the
public Schools at *Oxford*? Whether this Island hath not been
anciently famous for Learning? And whether at this Day it hath
any better Chance for being considerable?

195. *Qu.* Whether we may not with better Grace sit down and com-
plain, when we have done all that lies in our Power to help
ourselves?

196. *Qu.* Whether the Gentleman of Estate hath a Right to be idle;
and whether he ought not to be the great Promoter and Director
of Industry, among his Tenants and Neighbours?

The 1750 text here has two further queries:

[Whether in the Cantons of Switzerland all under thirty Years of
Age are not excluded from their great Councils?

Whether Homer's Compendium of Education

μύθων τε ῥητῆρ᾽ ἔμεναι πρηκτῆρά τε ἔργων,

would not be a good Rule for modern Educators of Youth? *Iliad* ix][86]

Berkeley's philosophy of education is adumbrated here. The political system is to be reproduced through the education of a paternalistic elite in the study of ancient models of political organisation

86. *The Querist*, I.21–23, §§182–96, and *The Querist* (1750 text), pp. 22–24, §§182–203.
The citation is of Homer, *Iliad*, 9.443, translated on p. 427: 'to be both a speaker of words
and a doer of deeds'.

and defended by the protection of the status of educators and punishment of those who demean that role or any other function of
the state. A division of society into lower and upper parts that is
largely if not entirely based on ethnic-religious difference is to be
naturalised. Different ethnic-religious groups are to be admitted
to educational institutions, not with a secular future in view, but
as part of a plan for coercion into political conformity and inducement towards full religious conversion. The educational institution
is a means of keeping local money in and drawing external investment into the local economy, at the same time as eliminating the
'Prejudices of a foreign Education'. The old and abstract disciplines
of learning (classical languages and history; mathematics, especially geometry, and logic) are to be preserved because they provide
the best models for civic life and the best training for the mind.
Berkeley's educational philosophy is an integral part of his moral,
social, and political philosophy that makes bold interventions into
the economy of individual and collective life, better to regulate the
spirit of the people and to draw them towards God.

CHAPTER SIX

London and Italy

BERKELEY LEFT DUBLIN for London early in 1713. The terms of the request Berkeley made to the vice provost and fellows of TCD to be absent from college give 'health and necessary business' as their justification.[1] On 16 April 1713, the day that Swift wrote to Stella saying that he had introduced Berkeley to John Arbuthnot, physician to Queen Anne, Berkeley wrote to Percival to say that Arbuthnot had become 'the first proselyte I have made by the Treatise I came over to print'.[2] That treatise is the *Three Dialogues*, and its publication was presumably the necessary business for which Berkeley was granted leave. He was in London from January to October 1713 (with six weeks in Oxford during July and August). His London life was sociable; he lodged with Provost Pratt and Samuel Molyneux, met many well-known literary and cultural figures, and some social encounters followed from the publication of his philosophical works. Percival congratulated Berkeley on having heard that Addison was won over to Berkeley's views and that many others found immaterialism acceptable. Richard Steele, the journalist, sought out Berkeley's acquaintance after having read

---

1. TCD MUN V/5/2, minute book 1640–1740, f. 226r (p. 449), 9 March 1713. Given the frequency with which travelling to England for one's health is given as grounds for absence, it must have been understood to be very medically efficacious, or have been a colourable way of justifying a more diverse set of reasons for absence. Berkeley is not, as he would at various points in later life, making much complaint of ill health in his letters at this point.

2. Swift, *Journal to Stella*, letter 63, p. 530; letter 43, p. 88.

Principles of Human Knowledge.[3] Berkeley was in London to publish and propagate his views, but he was also open to opportunities
to engage in further writing and publication projects of a variety of
kinds, all of which served a social and religious purpose.

The Guardian

One such project, and an immediate consequence of meeting Steele,
was Berkeley's employment in periodical journalism. He wrote several essays for *The Guardian*—David Berman's most recent estimate suggests fifteen or so—in the spring and summer of 1713.[4] The
essays echo those parts of Berkeley's previous writings in which he
had hinted at how his view of God's presence in the world, and of
human knowledge as participation in God, extended outwards into
a moral, social, and political programme. By the same token, the
essays also serve as a prospectus for Berkeley's writings of the 1720s
and 1730s on social and moral themes. Just as *Passive Obedience*
had done, Berkeley's essays in *The Guardian* developed the idea of
seeing more and seeing better as moral capacities. The focus of *Passive Obedience* was on moral obligations of a political character—
allegiance to a sovereign and the interdiction against rebellion.
The *Guardian* essays concentrated on obligations to other classes
of people, such as children and fellow subjects. Berkeley did not
challenge a narrowly political threat in the essays, as he challenged
Jacobitism in *Passive Obedience*, but a broader social threat identified as freethinking.

In the *New Theory of Vision*, Berkeley had argued that the visual
world is the language of God, both beautiful and instructive in that
it instructs people how to live—showing them what to seek and
what to shun. Seeing more and seeing better is understanding more
of God, understanding more of those laws of nature—physical, psychological, and moral—that give the human world its character and
guide human actions. Just as some people acquire new sensory
experiences (if born blind, for example, by gaining sight later in

---

3. Letter 38, Berkeley to Percival, 26 January 1713, pp. 78–79; letter 47, 14 May 1713,
p. 94; letter 39, Berkeley to Percival, 23 February 1713, pp. 81–82.

4. Berman, *George Berkeley*, pp. 70–77.

life), so there may be further sensory experiences still more beautiful and instructive than those provided by merely human sensory apparatus. Such are the 'ways of Perception of a more refined and extensive Nature [. . .] which will one Day be adapted to perceive those things which *Eye hath not seen, nor Ear heard, neither hath it entered into the Heart of Man to conceive*'. Such angelic or heavenly views have a corollary in human life: people's cultivation of long, wide, enlarged, or extensive views of things. Understanding that the orderliness of the physical world has a proper analogy in the spiritual world is one such expansion of views.[5] The enlarged views of the higher senses are partly available to people in this life through education, that process of rising 'from the Gratifications of Sense to relish those of the Mind', to 'more enlarged Views and gay Portraitures of a lively Imagination', and finally 'to the sublimer Pleasures of Reason'.[6]

Education into an expanded Christian view of the universe in the *Guardian* essays is part of a concerted attack on the movement Berkeley identifies as freethinking. Freethinking is a set of beliefs antagonistic to Anglican Christianity: 'That there is no such thing as a wise and just Providence; That the Mind of Man is Corporeal; That Religion is a State-trick, contrived to make Men honest and virtuous, and to produce a Subsistence to others for teaching and exhorting them to be so; That the good Tidings of Life and Immortality, brought to Light by the Gospel, are Fables and Impostures'. The freethinker is narrow or minute in focus (the term 'minute philosophers' is used interchangeably) and, whilst claiming to develop large, open views, in fact encourages their opposite:

> The Thoughts of a *Free-Thinker* are employed on certain minute Particularities of Religion, the Difficulty of a single Text, or the Unaccountableness of some Step of Providence or Point of Doctrine to his narrow Faculties, without comprehending the Scope and Design of Christianity[.] [. . .] There is not any Instance of Weakness in the *Free-Thinkers* that raises my Indignation more, than their pretending to ridicule Christians, as Men of narrow Understandings, and to pass themselves upon the World for Persons of Superior Sense, and more

5. *Guardian*, I.156–62, no. 27, Saturday, 11 April [1713], citation from I.161.
6. Ibid., I.387, no. 62, Friday, 22 May [1713]; see also chapter 5.

enlarged Views. But I leave it to any Impartial Man to judge which hath
the nobler Sentiments, which the greater Views; he whose Notions are
stinted to a few miserable Inlets of Sense, or he whose Sentiments are
raised above the common Taste by the Anticipation of those Delights
which will satiate the Soul, when the whole Capacity of her Nature is
branched out into new Faculties? He who looks for nothing beyond
this short Span of Duration, or he whose Aims are co-extended with
the endless length of Eternity? He who derives his Spirit from the Elements, or he who thinks it was inspired by the Almighty?[7]

Berkeley had already been arguing against these philosophers in
Principles of Human Knowledge, which closes with its encouragement to take extensive views and to refuse the minute and misleading focus on matter. His arguments in the *Guardian* essays focus
more closely on the nature of Christian practice in social life.

A central freethinking tenet is that reason must be applied in
the domain of religious belief and practice just as it is in any other
domain. Reason is both a natural and characteristic human faculty,
and far from being impeded, its free use should be encouraged in
all circumstances, including assessment of the truths of revealed
religion. John Toland, a canonical freethinker, explains:

> *Reason* is the only Foundation of all Certitude; [. . .] nothing reveal'd,
> whether as to its *Manner* or *Existence*, is more exempted from its Dis-
> quisitions, than the ordinary Phenomena of Nature. [. . .] Everyone
> experiences in himself a Power or Faculty of forming various Ideas or
> Perceptions of Things: Of affirming or denying, according as he sees
> them to agree or disagree: And so of loving and desiring what seems
> good unto him; and of hating and avoiding what he thinks evil. The
> right Use of all these Faculties is what we call Common Sense, or *Rea-
> son* in general.

People cannot be asked to comply with a law that they do not com-
prehend, so both God's laws and human laws must be reasonable:
'*[A]ll Dominion as well as Religion is founded in Reason*. [. . .]
What Dominion is not founded in Reason, must be doubtless

---

7. Ibid., II.4, no. 83, Tuesday, 16 June [1713]; and I.434, 438, no. 70, Monday, 1 June
[1713].

unreasonable, and consequently Tyrannical'.[8] Thus freethinking has a clear political component. This politics has a heritage in Locke's *Essay*, where, at the end of book I, Locke notes that the existence of some undoubted propositions has led to them being styled innate. Locke criticises 'those who affected to be Masters and Teachers' and who insisted that 'Principles must not be questioned'. This was a way of getting others passively to receive doctrine upon trust, without using reason or judgement, '[i]n which posture of blind Credulity, they might be more easily governed by, and made useful to some sort of Men[.] [. . .] Nor is it a small power it gives one Man over another, to have the Authority to be the Dictator of Principles, and Teacher of unquestionable Truths'.[9]

Peter Miller, in an essay that cites the same passage from Locke, notes that European statesmen, after the revolutions of the sixteenth century, sought social stability.[10] This was certainly the case in England and Ireland after the civil wars. It may have been more pointedly the case in Ireland, and with the living memory of conflict persisting longer into the eighteenth century given the effect of the War of the Two Kings. Michael Brown has said that the death toll, 'which amounted to around 25,000 men in combat, many more in disease-ridden camps, and as a consequence of food shortages and the economic dislocation of the population, raised a philosophical spectre that haunted the ensuing Protestant hegemony'.[11] Miller notes a paradox in responses to such spectres: 'While the spectre of the wars of religion was used to provide a mandate for intellectual uniformity, the discoverers of outer and inner space were, nevertheless, lauded as heroes and exemplars of human possibility precisely because they dared to challenge these conventional certainties'.[12] That is, those thinkers—Newton and Locke in particular—who challenged conventional assumptions were lauded across the spectrum of British thought, including by those, like George Berkeley,

8. *Christianity Not Mysterious*, pp, 7, 21–22, 80, and (in the same volume) "An Apology for Mr Toland", p. 116 (emphasis in original).

9. *Essay*, I.iv.24, pp. 101–2.

10. Miller, ' "Freethinking" and "Freedom of Thought" in Eighteenth-Century Britain', p. 607.

11. Brown, *The Irish Enlightenment*, p. 62.

12. Miller, ' "Freethinking" and "Freedom of Thought" in Eighteenth-Century Britain', p. 600.

who were keen to defend institutions of church and state from the freethinking challenge. I suggested in chapter 3 that Berkeley himself embodied this paradox in his new doctrine: he was both the scientific iconoclast willing to challenge received opinions, and a defender of established religious views seeking to combat atheism and scepticism. That chapter also drew a parallel between Berkeley's assertions that his immaterialism combatted atheism, infidelity, scepticism, and impiety and that it should be approved by friends to knowledge, peace and religion, on the one hand, and William King's assertion that his chief philosophical work was a response to the prevalence of 'Epicurism, Deism, and the denial of revealed religion', on the other.[13] Here I make comparisons to the work of Swift, another Irish Protestant keen to preserve the social order. Berkeley was writing in a context that identified philosophical and religious activism as a means of countering the threat to the social fabric represented by freethinking.

John Toland and Anthony Collins were two of the freethinkers Berkeley had in view. Samuel Johnson would later recall Berkeley saying that he had 'heard Collens declare that he had found a demonstration against the being of a God', a fact at which Berkeley himself hints in the 'Advertisement' to his 1732 text *Alciphron*. The declaration is likely to have been heard in one of Berkeley's visits to coffeehouses, 'in quality of a learner', not long after he arrived in London.[14] Collins's *Discourse on Free-thinking* (1713), which Berkeley knew of by 26 January 1713—when he told Percival it was pernicious—begins like Toland, first formulating an unarguable definition of freethinking as *'[t]he Use of the Understanding, in endeavouring to find out the Meaning of any Proposition whatsoever, in considering the nature of the Evidence for or against it, and in judging of it according to the seeming Force or Weakness of the Evidence'.*[15] The main rhetorical strategy of the *Discourse* is to point to the large number of unresolved disputes in the history of theology as evidence that some religious questions require debate

13. TCD MS 750/2/2/56, 2 February 1700, cited in Greenberg, 'Leibniz on King', p. 206.

14. Johnson, 'Autobiography' in Schneider and Schneider, eds., *Samuel Johnson, President of King's College*, I.26; *Alciphron*, advertisement, I, sigs. A2r–v; see also Berman, *George Berkeley*, p. 78. My thanks to Manuel Fasko for pointing me to these references.

15. Letter 38, p. 79; Collins, *A Discourse of Free-thinking*, p. 5.

and judgement. And yet '[t]he Subjects of which Men are deny'd the Right to think by the Enemys of *Free-Thinking*, are of all others those of which Men have not only *a Right to think*, but of which they are oblig'd in duty to think', that is, '*Religious Questions*'. Collins makes ironic reference to the Society for the Propagation of the Gospel as a freethinking institution when he notes that the SPG must presume that people in other parts of the world practising other forms of religion have an interest in being confronted by Anglican Christianity and being presented with rational arguments to adopt it. Collins suggests that there must be an unspoken corollary, given this commitment to the principle that rational argument in matters of religion will lead to the best outcomes for citizens: that Anglicans should also sponsor the presence of Siamese missionaries in Britain. (The heavy use Collins makes of travel narratives about other parts of the world is a striking contrast to Berkeley.) The right to think freely should be as obvious as the right to see freely, says Collins. People should not be asked to conform to the visual testimony of others, nor should they be prosecuted for stating what they see if it is not what others see. The analogy with vision is aimed at the practice of state insistence on religious conformity, as in the Sacramental Test. To give credence to events or facts, people should be allowed to inspect them visually, and it is absurd when, as with certain Catholic miracles such as the liquefaction of St Januarius's blood, belief is required without visual evidence.[16] Berkeley's dispute with the freethinkers is partly about the role of visual evidence and analogy in producing knowledge of the world and its creator.

Freethinking in matters of religion was deeply and obviously political for Collins. The attack on free thought, he says, dates from the Sacheverell trial and the upsurge in popular support for high Tory positions on church and state matters. Collins fantasises about sending high Tory churchmen such as Atterbury, Milbourne, Higgins, and Swift on SPG missions overseas. The politico-religious argument is connected to a fundamental intuition about the social order: 'MERE Diversity of Opinions has no tendency in nature to

---

16. Collins, *A Discourse of Free-thinking*, pp. 32, 42–45, 15–18, 23–24. Berkeley's response to similar miracles is noted in chapter 7.

Confusion in Society'.[17] Freethinkers advocate the use of reason in religious matters, oppose the predetermination of religious disputes by established authorities, and imagine a social order that is not threatened by diversity of belief and opinion. In opposing them, Berkeley was opposing the radical or modernising tendency of the Enlightenment.[18] Berkeley and his fellow-travellers tended to present the freethinkers as conspirators against Anglican Protestantism who were acting on behalf of some other sect. And Swift presented the freethinking enterprise more broadly as a conspiracy of Catholics to undermine the basis of religious faith in order to unsettle people and drive them towards the institutions of Catholicism.[19] The notion that freethinkers were crypto-Catholics is one that Anne Berkeley presented with reference to Collins. It is one that Berkeley would entertain in *Alciphron*. Toland, it has been argued, presented a rationalistic account of faith in order to undermine the validity of penal laws against Catholics.[20] The rational religion of the freethinkers was taken as an attack on Anglican establishment privileges.

Swift attacked freethinkers in his *Examiner* essays—the same essays Berkeley sent to Percival with seeming approval of their political attitudes. Citing Tindal, Toland, Coward, Collins, and Clendon as freethinkers, Swift claims, with irony directed at his Whig opponent Mainwaring, that the Whigs well understand Saint Paul's assertion that only through heresy is the truth known, as they hired Tindal as a party writer to spread as many heresies as possible.[21] Siding with Swift in a controversy that was partly political, Berkeley was attacking Whigs for their views on the revolution, rights of resistance, and constitutional change because he, like Swift, saw those views, in weakening the claim of the Anglican church to its

17. Ibid., pp. 30, 43, 101.

18. Airaksinen and Gylling, 'A Threat Like No Other Threat', passim and esp. p. 600, note that Berkeley is a deeply reactionary social, political, religious, and scientific thinker, and that the freethinkers might be associated with a Kantian view of Enlightenment as human freedom from self-incurred immaturity in the free, public use of judgement.

19. Swift, *An Argument to Prove that the Abolishing of Christianity*, p. 225.

20. [Anne Berkeley et al.], *The Contrast*, I.126; Berman, *Berkeley and Irish Philosophy*, pp. 118, 122.

21. Ellis, ed., *Swift vs. Mainwaring*, E 23, 4 January 1711, pp. 146–49. Berkeley's opposition to Tindal's views on universal moral law has already been discussed in chapter 4.

legislative, political, and economic privileges, as antagonistic to the Church. The abolition of episcopacy, the establishment of the Presbyterian church in Scotland, and associated events such as 'Rabblings' (mob trials to which episcopal ministers were subjected) strongly marked Swift's imagination and his presentation of both Scotland and dissent in his early texts such as *A Tale of a Tub* (published 1704, written 1696–1697 onwards).[22] Swift's reaction to the establishment of Presbyterianism and the emphasis he placed on the rights of the established Church have been taken to place him amongst 'High Church Tory extremists'.[23]

Swift sets out in an unsettlingly ironic work of 1708 those privileges of the established church that freethinking wishes to undermine: '[T]he Atheists, Deists, Socinians, Anti-Trinitarians, and other subdivisions of free-thinkers, are persons of little zeal for the present ecclesiastical establishment. Their declared opinion is for repealing the Sacramental Test; they are very indifferent with regard to ceremonies; nor do they hold the *jus divinum* of Episcopacy'.[24] The general tendency of this text is to suggest that the goods proposed by varying degrees of disestablishment are actually dangers to Christianity and the social fabric in general, and that any move to greater toleration or disestablishment is very likely to harm both. The ironic thrust at this particular moment is that atheists (and so on) have only *little* zeal for the establishment—they oppose the Tests, they are indifferent about ceremonies, and they do not believe that the existence of bishops is of divine origin. One would expect them to be more thoroughly against the existence of these privileges. Swift's speaker here is using a form of disingenuous understatement. That understatement at the same time permits Swift to suggest that these radical atheists and dissenters share many views with avowedly low-church Anglicans. (One such, Duke Tyrrell, to be introduced in chapter 8, would specifically associate Swift and Berkeley with high-church Toryism). Those who consider abolishing the Tests and so on are thereby aligned with atheists and the heterodox, and freethinkers take the part of nonconformist

22. Swift, *A Tale of a Tub and Other Works*, introduction, p. lxiii.
23. Higgins, 'Jonathan Swift's Political Confession', pp. 11, 13–14.
24. Swift, *An Argument to Prove that the Abolishing of Christianity*, p. 225.

Protestants in opposing the Test Act and other assertions of Anglican privilege because they want to reduce the church to nothing
more than a set of social functions. Freethinkers might be thought
of as entryists into Protestant dissent whose ultimate aim is the end
of Anglican privilege and the colonisation and secularisation of the
British public sphere.[25]

The *Guardian* essays also demonstrate a strong antagonism
towards Shaftesbury, whom Berkeley associated strongly with freethinking at this point and into the 1730s, when Shaftesbury appears
as a talisman for the freethinkers participating in the dialogue *Alciphron*. In number 81, the view of an 'old Friend' view is contrasted
to the supposed dying anguish of a recently deceased wit of the last
age. This wit is likely to be Anthony Ashley Cooper, Third Earl of
Shaftesbury. Eliza Frinsham/Berkeley records an anecdote about
Shaftesbury that Berkeley was fond of telling:

> Bishop Berkeley has frequently told his son, 'that so lamentably ill-
> tempered was he in the latter stages of his life, that his poor lady used,
> when any company arrived, to post out of the room, and conjure them,
> for *her* sake, to assent to *every* thing her Lord asserted or said, or it
> would put him into such a passion as might kill him'. Happy philosophy
> for one on the brink of the grave!!![26]

Shaftesbury fails to practise equanimity in the face of death or to
exhibit any of that railing, dialogical spirit that characterises his
philosophical project. Free thought is presented as a hypocritical
philosophy, one that does not cultivate in practice the dispositions
it claims to value.

The *Guardian* essays, then, are a counterblast to freethinking.
They develop an account of human goods, and the strong association of human goods with pleasures, that challenges unrestrained

25. Jaffro, 'Abolition ou réformation du Christianisme?', passim and esp. pp. 32–33.

26. *Guardian*, I.506, no. 81, Saturday, 13 June [1713]; Eliza Berkeley, preface to Berkeley, *Poems*, p. cccxxxvii (n). The correspondence between the criticism of Shaftesbury in
this *Guardian* essay and the anecdote further strengthens Berman's claim for Berkeley's
authorship of number 81 (made on the grounds that it relates to number 69). Anne Forster/
Berkeley, in her contributions to *The Contrast*, I.115, also hints at Berkeley's view of Shaftesbury, mentioning the latter's 'pride and conceit, peevishness, passion, narrow mindedness,
and violent prejudice against those who opposed him' as 'an echo of one of the best judges,
perhaps, this or any former age has produced'. See Storrie, 'Anne Berkeley's *Contrast*', p. 13.

forms of egoism and impossibly idealistic portrayals of the beauty of virtue (with which Shaftesbury was strongly associated). People should always be thinking of more expansive views and of higher pleasures. The world is naturally pleasing: 'The various Objects that compose the World were by Nature formed to delight our Senses'. When people correctly choose virtue and the promise of everlasting life, they do so from a desire for pleasure. This view is contrasted with that of freethinkers, who insist that virtue be loved and vice abhorred for their own sakes, rather than on account of associated rewards and punishments. Such a view, says Berkeley, is psychologically implausible, as people need more than the idea of disinterested moral beauty to make them act: 'Surely *they* must be destitute of Passion themselves, and unacquainted with the Force it hath on the Minds of others, who can imagine that the mere Beauty of Fortitude, Temperance, and Justice is sufficient to sustain the Mind of Man in a severe Course of Self-denial against all the Temptations of present Profit and Sensuality'. People need the inducement of pleasure to arrive at good choices, and pleasure is interested. The choice of immortality is calculating: 'I can easily overlook any present momentary Sorrow, when I reflect that it is in my Power to be happy a thousand Years hence'.[27] Extensive views do not transcend self-interest, but make the most rational use of it.

Pleasure is not exclusively private, but social pleasures are no less interested. Again beginning from the principle of providential design in creation, Berkeley argues that when promoting 'the common Good, every one doth at the same time promote his own private Interest'. This mutual subservience of human ends results from our being 'linked by an imperceptible Chain to every Individual of the Human Race': it is a fact of providential design, an organisational principle in the universe comparable to the attraction of matter, presented in Newtonian terms.[28] '[A]s the attractive Power

27. *Guardian*, I.298, no. 49, Thursday, 7 May [1713]; I.341, no. 55, Thursday, 14 May [1713]; no. 89, Tuesday, 23 June [1713]; see also Berkeley's first sermon, discussed in chapter 2.

28. *Guardian*, II.220–25, no. 126, Wednesday, 5 August [1713]. The providential purpose of self-interest has been presented as a feature of latitudinarian Newtonianism of the early eighteenth century; see Jacob, *The Newtonians and the English Revolution*, pp. 62–63: 'The latitudinarians proposed that because the atoms render matter into shapes and sizes, not by chance but by an inherent tendency for cooperation and coherence, men

in Bodies is the most universal Principle which produceth innumerable Effects, and is a Key to explain the various *Phænomena* of Nature; so the corresponding Social Appetite in Human Souls is the great Spring and Source of Moral Actions'. Berkeley does seem to be willing to point to social appetite as a determination of our nature (to use a Hutchesonian phrase) that is neither always self-interested nor judgemental. He gives the example of affection for children, which 'is neither founded on the Merit of the Object, nor yet on Self-interest'. It is simply that God has made us animals who feel affection for children, despite their unworthiness, and in the absence of calculated interest. So there are social pleasures that do not necessarily promote self-interest. But on the whole, Berkeley is proposing a view in which common goods are also real individual goods, and that is the reason they are naturally desired.[29]

The *Guardian* essays, then, are committed to the natural sociability of humankind, one recourse of philosophers seeking to domesticate self-interest. Commerce is one mechanism by which self-interest is tempered. One reason philosophers should be admired before men of action such as generals, Berkeley suggests, is that their speculative discoveries (such as Pythagoras's contribution to trigonometry) lead to increased human sociability— in this specific case to 'Navigation, upon which the Commerce of *Great Britain* depends'.[30] Speculative enquiry leads to the solution of practical-technological problems that had stood in the way of increased human sociability and commerce. Another social function of philosophy is seen in the encouragement of large views that relate to higher goods, such as those of the eye and ear, which, as Berkeley remarks in the *Notebooks*, 'surfeit not, nor bring those evils after them as others'.[31] That is, as well as increasing the practical-technological opportunities for greater sociability and commerce,

should likewise exist in relative social harmony'. Throughout this book, however, I raise doubts about the extent of Berkeley's latitudinarianism or ecumenism, and also about his commitment to a unitary principle of physical organisation such as attraction.

29. *Guardian*, II.220–25, no. 126, Wednesday, 5 August [1713].

30. Ibid., II.243, no. 130, Monday, 10 August [1713]. This is one of the additional essays David Berman attributes to Berkeley on the basis of an echo of *Principles of Human Knowledge*, §27, and a reference to the same passage from William Temple that Berkeley cites in 'De ludo algebraico'.

31. *Notebooks*, §787.

philosophy trains our appetites through reasoning to select the best and most enduring pleasures for their satisfaction. Pleasures of the eye and ear are not to be prised away from the whole scene in which objects (commodities) are produced and consumed. Rather, we should regulate them in the same way we regulate our entire economy, animal, domestic, and national:

> As I cannot go to the Price of History-painting, I have purchased at easie Rates several beautifully designed Pieces of Landschape and Perspective, which are much more pleasing to a natural Taste than unknown Faces or *Dutch* Gambols, tho' done by the best Masters. My Couches, Beds, and Window-Curtains are of *Irish* Stuff, which those of that Nation work very fine and with a delightful mixture of Colours. There is not a Piece of China in my House; but I have Glasses of all sorts, and some tinged with the finest Colours, which are not the less pleasing because they are Domestick and cheaper than foreign Toys. Every thing is neat, intire, and clean, and fitted to the Taste of one who had rather be *happy* than *be thought rich*.[32]

There are higher sensory pleasures in well-managed consumption, pleasures inseparable from appetite and self-interest. Managing these appetites well (and that means fulfilling them rather than denying them) is best for us individually and collectively. Having an enlarged view helps one to cultivate and satisfy the best appetites in the best ways.

An enlarged view of this kind might also be called faith, which is, like interest, a supplement to reason in these *Guardian* essays. Faith ought to make us better practitioners of the human: 'In vain is Reason fortified by Faith, if it produces in our Practice no greater Effects than what Reason wrought in meer Man', as Berkeley has 'an old Friend' put it.[33] Faith and interest both push people to make practice accord with reason. Berkeley is proposing an alternative social vision to that which he thinks goes along with being a radical freethinker. He proposes that enlarged, rational self-interest produces good moral and religious choices and actions; that such enlarged self-interest recognises the mutual subservience of

---

32. *Guardian*, I.299–300, no. 49, Thursday, 7 May [1713].
33. Ibid., I.506, no. 81, Saturday, 13 June 1713.

individuals' desires, and so is sociable; and that education and commerce are the means of enlarging views and furthering one's own interest at the same time as others'. Anglicanism is the main instrument of the moral, educational, and even commercial elements of this social project, as parts of this chapter and others of this book will show.

The Ladies Library

Contempt for religion was perceived to be a critical social threat. Berkeley addressed this contempt not only by attacking freethinkers in the *Guardian* but by addressing women. One opportunity Berkeley had to address women also came about through meeting Richard Steele. Essays in the *Tatler* and *Spectator* had called for an anthology of improving writings targeted at women, and one number of the *Spectator* rebuked Steele for not yet having produced the book.[34] The anthology was eventually published with the title *The Ladies Library*, under Steele's name, in 1713. Steele in his preface preserves the notion that 'the Compiler' was a woman who wanted to offer the advantages of her research in the 'several Writings of our greatest Divines' to others of her sex who had not the time. The papers are then said to have been perused by 'a Reverend Gentleman' whom Steele thinks less open to the charge of levity that he himself would be likely to meet. The reverend gentleman, on the other hand, thinks that those who want entertainment from books will be more likely to seek it in one published by Steele.[35] This reverend gentleman was Berkeley. The contract between Steele and Jacob Tonson for the delivery of the preface to the 'Collection or Common place', signed on 15 October 1713, was found in the late 1970s.[36] The contract specifies that Tonson will pay Steele 32 pounds, 5 shillings, for the preface, but states only that 'the sd Jacob Tonson hath paid & Satisfyed the said George Berkley' for producing the anthology.[37] *The Ladies Library* is further evidence

---

34. Kendrick, 'Berkeley's Bermuda Project and *The Ladies Library*', pp. 244–45, referring to *Tatler*, no. 248, *Spectator*, no. 37, and *Spectator*, no. 528.

35. *Ladies Library*, I, sigs. A6r–A8r.

36. Furlong and Berman, 'George Berkeley and *The Ladies Library*'.

37. Parks, 'George Berkeley, Sir Richard Steele, and *The Ladies Library*', p. 2.

of Berkeley's socially oriented educational programme and his willingness to engage in the practices of popular publication in order to further these aims. In what has been identified as an editorial insertion into the anthologised material, it is reported sternly that 'The *Contempt* of *Religion* is grown to such a highth, that hardly the Appearance of Morality and Decency remains: *Ladies* of *Quality* looking upon it as a part of their very liberal Breeding, to shew that their Behaviour in all things depends entirely on their *Humour*, and that they are incapable of all Restraint'.[38] The text had success, notably in America, where it was the 'women's conduct book most widely circulated during the first half of the eighteenth century'.[39]

Berkeley's involvement in the anthology itself poses questions about the nature of authority. *The Ladies Library* was the subject of a copyright dispute: when the borrowings from Jeremy Taylor were quickly spotted, the copyright holder for those works published his grievance. The anthology was published not long into the era of modern copyright law initiated by the Copyright Act of 1710, which was designed to promote intellectual labour by protecting profits for authors. The rights holder for Taylor's works identified several other sources for the anthology and criticised Steele (taken to be the anthologist as well as the publisher) for his hypocrisy, both because he had invaded another's property when his political views were for liberty and property and because *The Tatler* had railed against the infringement of literary copyright.[40] Berkeley and Steele's behaviour flouted the new legal concept of copyright.

By 1713, then, Berkeley either already was or had made himself familiar enough with recent instructional literature, some of it directed to women, to be able to produce the anthology. The texts identified as making up *The Ladies Library* are Richard Allestree, *The Government of the Tongue* and *The Ladies Calling*; Mary Astell, *A Serious Proposal to the Ladies*; Isaac Barrow, *A Brief Exposition of the Lord's Prayer and the Decalogue*; François de Fénelon,

---

38. *Ladies Library*, III.50. See Aitken, 'Steele's Ladies' Library', p. 16, for the attribution of this passage to the anthologist who produced the book and for the sources of three-quarters of the material presented in the anthology. The passage cited is an editorial intervention in material taken from Allestree, *The Ladies Calling*.

39. Hayes, *A Colonial Woman's Bookshelf*, p. 65.

40. [Meredith], *Mr. Steele Detected*, pp. 5–6, 18–19.

Education of a Daughter; William Fleetwood, *Relative Duties of Parents and Children*; John Kettlewell, *The Measures of Christian Obedience*; John Locke, *Some Thoughts Concerning Education*; Richard Lucas, *Practical Christianity* and *Enquiry after Happiness*; Damaris Masham, *Occasional Thoughts in Reference to a Vertuous or Christian Life*; Pierre Nicole, *Moral Essays*; Samuel Pufendorf, *The Whole Duty of Man*; George Saville, Lord Halifax, *Advice to a Daughter*; John Scott, *The Christian Life*; Jeremy Taylor, *Holy Living*; and John Tillotson, 'An Advice and Direction Concerning Receiving the Holy Sacrament', in *The Devout Christian's Companion*, and *Sermons*.[41] An anthology need not represent the views of the anthologist, and there are passages in *The Ladies Library* that would not sort perfectly with the views Berkeley had already published. But it seems reasonable to suggest that he was not working only or cynically for reward, and that he believed the passages he chose to reproduce had at least the potential to improve their readers. I treat the text in this light, particularly where passages touch on the moral and social concerns in which Berkeley continued to take an interest over the rest of his life. The following discussion cites views drawn from a range of the texts included in the anthology.

The explicit aim of the anthology was to offer improving texts for women readers. A chief means of improvement was in the matter of education—either of oneself or one's family. Women should be educated to the degree that they can manage the education of their own children to around the age of ten in English, Latin, arithmetic, geography, and history.[42] A lady of quality may work towards correctness in a first language, basic arithmetic, and comprehension of legal distinctions around rent and property. Reading classical historians in the best translations will provide her with examples of 'great Contempt of [. . .] *private* Advantage when the *publick* Good was in question'. History, poetry, eloquence, and moral

---

41. See Aitken, 'Steele's *Ladies' Library*'; Furlong and Berman, 'George Berkeley and *The Ladies Library*'; and Hollingshead, 'Sources for the Ladies' Library', pp. 1–2. The presence of the texts by Barrow and Masham is my own discovery, which was made much simpler by my ability to use searchable text databases such as JISC Historical Texts.

42. *Ladies Library*, II.216–17, excerpting Masham, *Occasional Thoughts*, pp. 176–77, a source identified here for the first time.

philosophy are all available to her. Reading in French and Italian is recommended, with particular praise for Pascal. The merely sensual delights of poetry, eloquence, music, and painting are warned against, though it is noted that if they serve their true end, 'they may be very usefully employ'd to excite in the Soul lively and sublime Notions of God and Religion'.[43] As well as excerpting texts that delimited a female intellectual world, Berkeley also selected from texts proposing that women could be, if properly habituated, the intellectual equals of men. Women were said to have excelled in all the sciences when appropriately educated, with their current weakness the result of men refusing to admit women to education.[44]

The anthology is clear, however, that wives ought to obey their husbands. Women are more fitted by nature to comply with than to give laws. Marital obedience is a divine command (and so disobedience a sin punishable by eternal death).[45] The obedience to God's law in the moral and political spheres insisted on in *Passive Obedience* is here just as strongly deemed necessary in the domestic sphere. Cases in which a husband may be disobeyed exist, but the wife should invoke an impartial spectator to make that determination: 'The *Wives* must take good Care, that the Commands which they comply not with, may be such as will justifie them to any wise impartial People; that, whoever will be Judges, they may reasonably excuse their Non-complyance, and condemn the Men that gave such Orders'.[46]

Obedience is not just for wives, but is raised to a general moral and religious principle in the anthology, as it is in Berkeley's social thought more generally. Proper deference to authority, known as meekness of the will, is an archetypal social virtue:

> A Will duly submissive to lawful Superiors, is not only an amiable thing in the Eyes of others, but exceedingly happy to ones self. 'Tis the Parent of Peace and Order, both publick and private. A Blessing so considerable, as is very cheaply bought by a little receding from ones own Will

43. Ibid., I.17–23, 25–26, excerpting Fénelon, *Education of a Daughter*.
44. Ibid., I.438, excerpting Astell, *A Serious Proposal to the Ladies*.
45. Ibid., II.112, excerpting Halifax, *Advice to a Daughter*; and I.145–46, in a passage presumably of Berkeley's own writing inserted into an excerpt from Fleetwood, *Relative Duties of Parents and Children* (p. 273 in the 1705 edition).
46. Ibid., II.64–65, excerpting Fleetwood, *Relative Duties of Parents and Children*.

or Humour; Whereas the contrary Temper is the Spring and Original of infinite Confusions; the grand Incendiary, which puts Kingdoms, Churches and Families in Combustion; a Contradiction, not only to the Word, but to the Works of God; a kind of anticreative Power, which reduces things to the Chaos from whence God drew them.

Submission is compliance with a natural order against which it would be a sin to go. Obedience to the will of God is that which enables one to practise all of the virtues, or possess grace: 'Thus is Men's Growth in *saving Grace* not only in some one or in some few Vertues, but in an universal and entire Obedience; and they grow in it when they come to perform the same with more Ease and Pleasure, Constancy and Evenness'.[47]

Christianity promotes the most benevolent system of civic life because its 'Rules and Principles' render '[t]he State of *Subjects* under their *Princes*, the Subjection of *Wives* to their *Husbands*, of *Servants* to their *Masters*, [. . .] abundantly more easie'. It is the best legal dispensation because it puts all people under an obligation to treat everyone as well as possible with respect to others' condition and to their own benefit.[48] This attitude is paradigmatic for Berkeley's Christian moralism: the limiting factors upon our obligation to love others as ourselves are their condition (rank, social position) and our own benefit. Rank is as much a part of the natural order as self-interest (the obligation to preserve our own lives). These constraints do not limit the commitment to natural sociability expressed elsewhere: '*Man*, of all sublunary Creatures, is most adapted to *Society*' because endowed with speech; '*social Virtue*' is 'such a mutual Behaviour as most conduces to our common Benefit and Happiness, as we are in Society with one another'. Yet, still excerpting from the same text, Berkeley selects passages that might be thought to produce a significant tension between egalitarian principles and recognition of superiority that in effect is permission to distribute goods unevenly:

[E]very Man has a Right to be aided and assisted by every one with whom he has any Dealing or Intercourse, to have some Share of the

47. Ibid., I.249, excerpting Allestree, *The Ladies Calling*; and III.494, excerpting Kettlewell, *Measures of Christian Obedience*.
48. Ibid., II.409–10, excerpting Fleetwood, *Relative Duties of Parents and Children*.

Benefit of all that exchange, Traffick, and Commerce, which passes between him and others; and therefore for any Man in his Dealings with others, to take Advantage from their Necessity or Ignorance, to oppress or over-reach them, or to deal so hardly by them, as either not to allow them any Share of the Profit which accrues from their Dealings, or not a sufficient Share for them to subsist and live by, is an injurious Perversion of that natural Right, which the very End and Design of Society gives them[.]

But:

As we are *rational Creatures* related to one another, we are oblig'd modestly to submit to our *Superiors*, and chearfully to condescend to our *Inferiors*, in those respective *Societies* of which we are *Members*. It being necessary to the Order and End of all *Societies*, that their Members shou'd be distinguished into *superior* and *inferior* Ranks and Stations[.][49]

Here, as in so many other locations in seventeenth- and eighteenth-century social thought, the possibility that rank produces, or is otherwise complicit in, the adumbration of natural rights to justice and equity is mysteriously invisible.

The naturalisation and preservation of hierarchy in the texts from which Berkeley excerpts stem from a foundational theological commitment. Religion is a form of hierarchical social obligation, recognising the natural superiority of God. Readers of *The Ladies Library* are pointed to the etymology of 'religion', 'which from its Derivation signifies a *binding*, or *obliging* us to *God*, wherefore *true Religion in the General, is the Obligation of reasonable Creatures, to render such Acts of Worship to God, as are suitable to the Excellency of his Nature, and their Dependence on him*.'[50] Patriarchal submission to God is rational because God's excellence and our dependence are deducible from observation.

Christianity more generally is presented as fundamentally reasonable and prudential, managing and limiting irrational passions and affections. The understanding should play a part in religious practice if we wish it to be enduring: 'what's the Reason that we

---

49. Ibid., III.187–89, 197–98, 211, excerpting Scott, *The Christian Life*.
50. Ibid., III.2–3, excerpting Scott, *The Christian Life* (emphasis in original).

sometimes see Persons unhappily falling off from their Piety, but because 'twas their Affections, not their Judgment, that inclin'd them to be religious?' Living according to Christian prudence is to live according to reason:

> To live *prudently* is to live in the constant Exercise of our Reason, and to be continually persuing such *Ends*, as *right Reason* proposes, by such Means as *right* Reason directs us to, which is the proper Business of all the Vertues of *Religion*; which is therefore so frequently call'd in Scripture, *Wisdom*, or *Prudence*. [. . .] By living in the continual Practice of *religious Prudence*, we shall by degrees habituate our selves to a Life of Reason, and shake off that drowsy Charm of Sense and Passion, which hangs upon our Minds, and renders our *Faculties* so dull and unactive. [. . .] The Health of a reasonable Soul consists in being perfectly reasonable, in having all its Affections perfectly subdu'd, and cloathed in the Livery of its Reason. [. . .] [T]he Soul being cur'd of all irregular Affections, and remov'd from all corporeal Passion, will live in perfect Health and Vigor, and for ever enjoy within it self a Heaven of Content and Peace.[51]

Managing our behaviour in such a way as to recognise the authority of God in the ways of the world, adapting our desires so that they aim at the higher goods, is practical Christian life. This anthology aimed at a female audience reveals many of the textual and argumentative resources Berkeley was using in his programme for social, moral, and political education, centred in an expanded, Anglican view of the world.

Italy

Berkeley went to London to publish *Three Dialogues* and quickly became involved in two other publishing ventures, in journalism and anthology-making. He met many people and worked on them as philosophical converts and social contacts. The cultivation of political moderation and sociability across at least some of

---

51. Ibid., I.446, excerpting Astell, *A Serious Proposal to the Ladies*; and III.129, 132, 147–48, excerpting Scott, *The Christian Life*, which itself seems at points to be excerpting John Howe, *The Blessedness of the Righteous*.

the political spectrum is another outcome of Berkeley's first visit to London, perhaps even a goal. Soon after his arrival in London, Berkeley reported with amusement that some Irish clergymen believed Percival to be a Whig. Berkeley sent him some *Examiners* and referred to the pair of them as belonging to the 'moderate sort of men'.[52] This moderateness allowed Berkeley to socialise with people antagonistic to one another—Addison and Steele, on the one hand, and Swift, on the other. Berkeley reported that both Addison and Steele and 'Jacobite Tories' expected an imminent Jacobite project. As the perceived threat seemed to subside, goodwill between Swift and Addison was read as a sign of the reconciliation of Whig and Tory.[53] Berkeley was present at the premiere of Addison's play *Cato*, which was undoubtedly written to celebrate a Whiggish love of liberty in the face of absolutism, but which, like so many other documents of its time, could be claimed for either side of the debate. Writing to Percival, Berkeley notes, 'Though some Tories imagine his play to have an ill design, yet I am persuaded you are not so violent as to be displeased at the good success of an author (whose aim is to reform the stage) because his hero was thought to be a Roman Whig'. Whigs and Tories famously attempted to out-applaud one another at the play as a way of appropriating its sentiments to their own political ends.[54]

A few weeks after this premiere, Berkeley asked Percival to tell his wife that Berkeley had dined with Whigs at Garth's (a Whig coffeehouse) and drunk the Duke of Marlborough's health—presumably as this news would please or surprise Lady Percival, who was either Whiggishly inclined or took Berkeley for a more committed Tory, or both. A few weeks later, Berkeley met Smalridge and Atterbury,

52. Letter 38, 26 January 1713, p. 80.

53. Letter 39, Berkeley to Percival, 23 February 1713, p. 81; letter 42, Berkeley to Percival, 27 March 1713, p. 85.

54. Letter 43, Berkeley to Percival, 16 April 1713, p. 87. Alexander Pope to John Caryll, 30 April 1713, in Sherburn, ed., *The Correspondence of Alexander Pope*, I.174–75, reports that 'all the foolish industry possible has been used to make it a party play[.] [. . .] The numerous and violent claps of the Whig party on the one side the theatre, were echoed back by the Tories on the other, while the author sweated behind the scenes with concern to find their applause proceeded more [from] the hand than the head. This was the case too of the prologue-writer [Pope himself], who was clapped into a stanch Whig sore against his will, at almost every two lines'.

two of the editors of Clarendon's *History of the Rebellion*, who were accused of tampering with the text to make it more Tory; Atterbury would go on to be exiled for his involvement in a Jacobite plot in 1722.[55] This was a promiscuously sociable period in which Berkeley developed relationships with Whigs close enough to attend the premiere of *Cato*, and with Tories to be thick with Swift and introduced to his associates.

Perhaps the most significant product of the latter form of socialising in London was Berkeley's invitation to serve as chaplain to Charles Mordaunt, Earl of Peterborough, on his mission as ambassador extraordinary to the coronation of the new king of Sicily in 1713–1714.[56] The negotiations to end the War of the Spanish Succession that issued in the Treaty of Utrecht included a provision for taking Sicily from the Spanish and giving it to Victor Amadeus II, Duke of Savoy, a British ally against France.[57] That he was a party to this mission and had a desire to see the coronation suggest Berkeley's faith in the Tory-negotiated peace. It also marks a distinction between Percival's and Berkeley's politics. In addition to the peace treaty, the ministry was negotiating a treaty of commerce with France. The proposed terms were initially widely supported, as they were considered likely to improve overseas trade and general economic conditions at home. But over the summer of 1713 opposition to the treaty mounted, with claims that it would be detrimental to the woollen and silk trades, and in the summer of 1713 the ministry was defeated on the progress of the bill by a combination of Whigs and dissenting Tories. Following an election, and with renewed support from Anne, a treaty of commerce was again a matter of debate. Percival's response to the 'treaty of commerce' was negative: 'I own I don't like it & believe I never shall'. Berkeley responded with a view more loyal to the Tory ministry: 'I have good hopes that the public welfare will be better provided for by our treaty of peace and commerce than you seem to apprehend'.[58]

55. Letter 46, 7 May 1713, p. 93; letter 48, Berkeley to Percival, 2 June 1713, pp. 95–96. See Jones, 'Pope and the Ends of History', for a discussion of the issues.

56. Letter 56, Berkeley to Percival, 15 October 1713, p. 105.

57. Storrs, *War, Diplomacy, and the Rise of Savoy*, pp. 4–5.

58. Letter 54, 10 September 1713, p. 103; letter 55, 2 October 1713, p. 104.

One might associate Berkeley's first trip to the continent with the commercially inflected Toryism he expresses here.

J.G.A. Pocock finds no clear confrontation between political tendencies in early eighteenth-century Britain on the question of trade: both court and country tendencies were happy that trade was essential to national prosperity and the cultivation of the virtues, as, indeed, was land.[59] Yet the Treaty of Utrecht, he suggests, was the origin of a Europe as 'a republic or confederation of states held together by treaties to which wars were merely auxiliary, and by a common system of civilised manners communicated everywhere by commerce'.[60] More recently, however, it has been said that the 1713 treaty was a mark of the increasing importance of trade in political debate and the beginnings of the formulation of coherent party positions on the matter.[61] A Tory view of empire in which land seizure in South America was a means of increasing holdings of bullion and limiting French influence, and in which colonial lands were thoroughly subjected to the metropolis, is contrasted to a Whig view of an integrated commercial empire in which lower labour costs overseas could be exploited to stimulate new technologies and new markets into existence at home. The party-political lines were distinct:

> Early-18th-century whigs wanted an empire of commerce and labour, not an empire that sought to monopolise raw materials. [. . .] Tories had exchanged, in the whig view, the possibility of penetrating Spanish American markets for the chimera of territorial possession.[62]

The Whig view does not demand that the colony be subordinated to the metropolis.

Steve Pincus, in setting out this party-political distinction, notes the case of Jonathan Swift, who complained in 1712 that the Whigs had not enlarged British dominions, but who also seems in the 1720s to have been an opponent of colonialism.[63] Pincus here iden-

59. Pocock, *The Machiavellian Moment*, pp. 447–48, esp. p. 448: 'The Augustan debate did not oppose agrarian to entrepreneurial interests, the manor to the market, and cannot be said to have arisen from a crude awareness of collisions going on between them'.

60. Pocock, 'What Do We Mean by Europe?', p. 23, cited in Ahn, 'The Anglo-French Treaty of Utrecht of 1713 Revisited', p. 128.

61. See Gauci, *The Politics of Trade*, pp. 234–270, esp. pp. 237, 245, 270.

62. Pincus, 'Addison's Empire', pp. 109, 113.

63. Ibid., pp. 107, 105.

tifies a tension but not its source. Nonmetropolitan Tories, significantly the Irish, were likely to modify at least some of the Tory attitude to empire on the basis of their experience as a subject nation (perhaps especially after the declaratory act of 1720). In later parts of this chapter, I suggest that Berkeley too had a qualified Tory attitude to empire: qualified by a greater emphasis on commerce than one might expect from Pincus's scheme, and adjusted by his experience as a nonmetropolitan British subject. This experience is vital, I think, to understanding Berkeley's interest in and relation to the non-British and Irish world.

Berkeley crossed the channel in Peterborough's advance party, arriving in France on 29 October 1713.[64] Once he got to Paris on 17 November, one of Berkeley's first social calls was on Matthew Prior, who 'is a man of good sense and learning, and lives magnificently as becomes the Queen's Plenipotentiary'.[65] Prior had been a Whig, but turned to the Tories around the start of the eighteenth century, and he had a large hand in negotiating the terms of the Treaty of Utrecht. He was at that time in Paris at the will of Henry St John, Viscount Bolingbroke, to attempt greater integration with the French through trade and diplomacy, including the provisions of the treaty of commerce.[66] In order to join this party, Berkeley had to apply again for permission to be absent from TCD and to travel. His request to the Queen to 'give him leave to Travell & remain abroad during yᵉ Space of two years for yᵉ Recovery of his health & his Improvement in Learning' was granted on 6 November 1713; the letter is signed on Anne's behalf by Bolingbroke, as home secretary.[67] By joining Peterborough's mission with Bolingbroke's approval and meeting with Prior, Berkeley was actively favouring the Tory view of the conclusion of the war and the treaty of commerce: he was participating in the formal politics of the Tory peace settlement, albeit at one remove.

After a month at Paris, Berkeley travelled to Lyon in December, then through Savoy, crossing the Alps at Mount Cenis and

64. Rumours that Peterborough's later arrival in Paris had concealed a visit to the Pretender at Bar-le-Duc seem to be unfounded, given James's later assertion to Bolingbroke that 'I never saw Ld Peterborow'. See Cameron, *This Master Firebrand*, pp. 350–51.

65. Letter 57, Berkeley to Percival, 24 November 1713, p. 106.

66. Rippy, 'Prior, Matthew'.

67. TCD MUN V/5/2, minute book 1640–1740, f. 228r–v (pp. 453–54).

arriving in Turin on New Year's Day. He had eleven days in Turin and three weeks in Genoa, where Peterborough joined the party. They then sailed to Leghorn (Livorno), from whence they should have departed for Sicily, but Peterborough went on alone with a small company. The rest of the party remained at Leghorn, where Berkeley said he would 'probably stay a considerable time'.[68] The list of the places he had lodged at since leaving England summarises his route: 'Calais, Boulogne, Montreuil, Abbeville, Poix, Beauvais, Paris, Moret, Ville Neufe le Roi, Vermonton, Saulieu, Chany, Maçon, Lyons, Chambery, St. Jean de Moridune, Lanebourg, Susa, Turin, Alexandria, Campo Maro, Genoa, Lestri di Levante, Lerici, Leghorne'. On 1 May 1714, Berkeley told Percival that he had also seen 'Pisa, Lucca, Pistoia, Florence etc', but still nothing that would make him want to leave England and Ireland for Italy.[69] (One might think here of the slightly younger Berkeley who wrote, when broaching his new doctrine, that his 'speculations have the same effect as visiting forein countries, in the end I return where I was before, set my head at ease and enjoy my self with more satisfaction'.[70]) He was back in Paris in July 1714, having made the return trip by the route he recommended to Tom Prior (via Genoa and Toulon), and this time travelling with Peterborough's full party as far as Genoa. From Paris he booked a place in the Brussels coach, along with 'an Irish gentleman' of his acquaintance, to travel through Flanders and Holland on the way back to London.[71] His next letter was from London a year later.

Though it was a relatively short trip to the continent, this first voyage shows Berkeley's interest in many of the attractions of the grand tour and the lasting impact that travel and tourism would have on his life and work. Berkeley may have thought of the voyage as a means of polishing away any remaining dust from his time as a monkish recluse in a college. He remarks to Percival that the others on the coach from Calais to Paris 'were all perfect strangers to me'; of his interactions with the various people of various nations that made up Peterborough's retinue, he claims that their civility

68. Letter 62, Berkeley to Percival, 19 February 1713/14, p. 113.

69. Letter 63, Berkeley to Prior, 26 February 1713/14, pp. 114–15; letter 66, p. 117.

70. BL Add MS 39304, f. 4r.

71. Letter 67, Berkeley to Percival, 13 July 1714, p. 119.

FIGURE 6.1. G. Keate, 'A Manner of Passing Mount Cenis', 1755,
© The Trustees of the British Museum

made him 'as easy as I hope to be in any company besides those who used to rejoice my heart in Dublin'. The coach trip from London to Dover with Peterborough's Francophone staff had also given him the opportunity to improve his French and Italian.[72]

An ethnographic curiosity may also have been piqued early on. Berkeley shared the longer coach trip from Calais to Paris with other travellers, one of whom was Martin Martin, the Scottish author of a celebrated account of St Kilda, the most remote of the Hebridean islands off the northwest coast of Scotland. There was good cheer on the road, 'and the inhabitants of St. Kilda did not a little contribute to our diversion'.[73] Perhaps Martin's tales of the people who 'feel

72. Letter 57, 24 November 1713, pp. 105–6; letter 62, Berkeley to Percival, 19 February 1713/14, p. 113.
73. Letter 57, p. 106.

the sweetness of true Liberty' in their 'Innocency and Simplicity, Purity, Mutual Love and Cordial Friendship; free from solicitous Cares, and anxious Covetousness; from Envy, Deceit, and Dissimulation; from Ambition and Pride, and the Consequences that attend them [. . .] ignorant of the Vices of Foreigners, and governed by the Dictates of Reason and Christianity', encouraged Berkeley to think of the religious and social value of ethnographic observation, and of the study of marginal native populations, such as he himself would engage in through his later Italian journals and his writing on the native Irish.[74] Martin's utopian account of island life is echoed in Berkeley's proposals of the mid-1720s to found a university in Bermuda: seeking 'a place [. . .] noted for innocence and simplicity of manners' he notes that Bermudians are thought to be 'a contented, plain, innocent sort of people, free from avarice and luxury, as well as the other corruptions that attend those Vices'.[75]

Developing an already existing taste for art and architecture was probably another goal of the trip. Berkeley was a draughtsman at least as early as 1709, when he perhaps self-mockingly referred to one of his drawings being moved from a duchess's closet to her duke's house at St James's 'with the rest of the most precious moveables'.[76] The magnificence of Matthew Prior's style of living included the possession of a notable collection of paintings. Prior had collected during earlier periods on the continent, and he acquired a number of the paintings in his collection during his period in Paris from 1711 to 1715. Paintings he is likely to have acquired at this time include works by Gerard Dou, Artemisia Gentileschi, Carlo Maratta, Bartolomé Esteban Murillo, Rembrandt, Guido Reni, and David Teniers, citing only those artists still well known now.[77] This may have been the first time Berkeley saw a personal collection such as that which later came to adorn the walls of the bishop's palace at Cloyne.[78]

---

74. Martin, *A Late Voyage to St. Kilda*, p. 131.

75. *Proposal*, pp. 8, 12; LJ, VII.349, 352.

76. Letter 7, Berkeley to Molyneux, 26 November 1709, p. 26.

77. Wright and Montgomery, 'The Art Collection of a Virtuoso', pp. 197–204.

78. Smith, *The Antient and Present State of the County and City of Cork*, I.147, notes that Berkeley decorated the palace with 'a Magdalen of Sir Peter Paul Rubens, some heads by Van Dyke and Kneller'.

Berkeley's itinerary of architectural visits in Paris notably includes church and college buildings:

[T]he magnificence of their churches and convents surpasses my expectation. The day before yesterday I visited the place de Vendome, le place de Victoire, and le place Regale, and the Louvre, le convent des Capucins, le Feuillant, l'Eglise des Minims, l'Eglise des Celestins, where are the tombs of the ancient kings. Yesterday we saw the monastery of St. Genevieve, with its library and cabinet of rarities; the English college where the body of King James and that of his daughter are still to be seen exposed in their coffins. The people who take the King for a saint have broke off several pieces of the coffin etc., for relics. We saw likewise the Irish college, and the Sorbonne, where we were present at their Divinity disputations. All is wonderfully fine and curious, but the finest of all is the Chapel in the Church of the Invalides, which the Abbé d'Aubigne assured me was not to be surpassed in Italy.[79]

Berkeley was studying how a different nation provided for its civil administration, its church, and its colleges. He was guided, both physically and in his taste, by his new acquaintance, the Abbé d'Aubigne, who also said that he would introduce Berkeley to Malebranche.[80] As for Italy, whose churches and colleges in Turin were likewise said to be 'magnificent', Berkeley says that it was his business 'to visit the colleges, libraries, and booksellers' shops, both at Turin and here [Genoa]'.[81]

Though he does not mention doing so in his letters, Berkeley preached whilst at Leghorn.[82] Preaching there, perhaps more by accident than design, was a contribution to missionary Anglicanism

79. Letter 57, pp. 106–7.

80. As it is not even known for certain that the scheduled visit took place, I do not speculate about the meeting.

81. Letter 60, Berkeley to Prior, 6 January 1713/14, p. 110; letter 61, Berkeley to Percival, 4 February 1714, p. 111.

82. A copy of the register of the chapel at Leghorn made in 1810 can be consulted at London Metropolitan Archives, CLC/035/MS23782. The register records births, deaths, and marriages. Only sometimes, from the 1730s on, does it record the name of the minister who conducted the ceremony. There is a hint, however, from the following record, that Berkeley might have had family at Livorno: 'Rose Dain daughter of Robert and Jane born January the 7:th 1714 Babtized [sic] the 9:th Godfather Capn.n Barkly; Godmother Mrs Cummings and Mrs Jones' (f. 16r [p. 29]). Berkeley probably did not arrive in Livorno until early February. Could 'Barkly' be the Captain Berkeley whose will is mentioned in letter 347, Berkeley to

that predated Berkeley's much more widely discussed Bermuda project. It was also a moment when Berkeley was thinking through the relationship between Christian practice and an emerging commercial world order from within one of its more telling locations. Livorno had been established as a *de facto* free port by the Medici family in the seventeenth century, became a free port by law in 1675, and was the dominant trading location for British merchants in Italy, who often landed goods there which were sold and distributed in other Italian regions.[83] There was an English factory at Leghorn—an expatriate community established and tolerated for purposes of trade. A Protestant chaplaincy had been established at the factory in 1706, following calls from the SPG and the surge in campaigning Anglicanism of the late seventeenth and early eighteenth centuries. The grand duke of Tuscany was informed that Queen Anne was sending a Protestant clergyman to Leghorn. This clergyman was Basil Kennett—historian of Roman antiquities and translator of Pascal. Kennett arrived in December 1706 and was acknowledged as the consul's private chaplain, though he lodged at the factory. The grand duke soon expressed his dissatisfaction at Kennett's presence, noting that religious matters were beyond his control and policed by Rome and the Inquisition. Anne's letter in defence of the chaplaincy suggested that expatriate communities had the right fully to practise their religion, simultaneously invoking two attitudes in considerable tension with one another: first, that the state must be in control of religious matters and cannot cede authority to a supernational organisation; and second, that confessional states will concede the right of expatriate religious minorities to practise their religion for the sake of improved commercial relations. The Anglican church, that is, recognised (even demanded) state sovereignty over religious matters, but also expected states to act expediently and with a view to commercial gain when it came to religious tolerance. This particular episode in missionary Anglicanism required a secularisation of the geopolitical field that ultimately might not have been in the church's interests.[84]

Prior, 6 February 1747, p. 524? Or the Captain Berkeley, George's brother, who was fighting Jacobite rebels in Arbroath in June 1745? See Roberts, *The Jacobite Wars*, p. 187.

83. De Divitiis, *English Merchants in Seventeenth-Century Italy*, pp. 114–25.

84. This paragraph draws largely on Sirota, 'The Church of England, the Law of Nations'.

When Berkeley preached at Leghorn, then, he was preaching in a missionary Anglican context that pressed the religious rights of British Protestants overseas, even beyond the bounds of the sovereign or colonial state. Later in life at least, Berkeley seemed to be conscious of the missionary nature of the Leghorn enterprise. When writing to John James on the subject of Catholicism, he presented Protestant figures to rival the Catholic saints and martyrs. After a list of good, learned, and pious Protestants containing Cranmer, Ridley, Latimer, Jewel, Hooker, Ussher, Dodwell, Fell, and Hammond came 'Basil Kennet, chaplain to the factory at Leghorne in Queen Anne's reign [who] was esteemed and called a Saint by the papists themselves as the English merchants there assured me'.[85] Kennett's ministry probably did involve considerable personal courage, as there were reports that he had to be guarded by British merchants with drawn swords in order to prevent his seizure by the religious authorities.[86] His brother, White Kennett, suggested that Basil's ongoing ill health was partly caused by a poison administered by the Inquisition.[87] Kennett left Leghorn in February 1712, arriving back in England in July 1713. (Nathaniel Taubman had received a commission for the chaplaincy in October 1711.)[88] When Berkeley preached at Leghorn, then, he did not preach 'for' Kennett, in any traditional sense, as the chaplaincy had passed on to another incumbent.[89] But Berkeley was participating in a tradition of preaching that was missionary in nature, aggressively marking Britain's expansion as a commercial empire able to protect the rights of its subjects overseas and continuing the work of someone he regarded as comparable to saints and martyrs.

The missionary context of preaching in Leghorn was clear to Berkeley; so perhaps was the commercial context, to which Berkeley may well have been sensitised by his inclusion in Peterborough's delegation and his discussion of the treaty of commerce with Percival and others. Simply standing in front of a congregation of merchants would also have been a factor in his choice of approach to

85. Letter 282, Berkeley to James, 7 June 1741, p. 429.
86. 'The Life of Basil Kennet', p. 411.
87. Cheesman, 'Kennett, Basil'.
88. Sirota, 'The Church of England, the Law of Nations', p. 298.
89. As described by Luce, p. 72.

the subjects of his sermons, given his tendency (already remarked upon) to harmonise with his audience. The first of the two sermons from Berkeley's time in Leghorn was on charity—the primary element of any Christian practice. Charity, he explains, is 'an inward, sincere disinterested affection that takes root in the heart and shews itself in acts of kindness and benevolence'. Practising charity becomes a matter of self-interest, as it is the path to eternal life: 'interest and duty go together so that we cannot practise the one without promoting the other'. This is true self-interest rather than any narrow sense of immediate or material good, which is to be avoided: 'We must by all means mortify and subdue that base principle of Self-love whose views are always turned inwards [. . .] we must learn to wean ourselves from self-interest, or rather learn wherein our true interest consists'. Charity expresses itself in universal benevolence, he tells the congregation, as well as in refusing to speak ill of others and loving even those of different sects or those whose interests compete with our own ('his prosperity it interferes with mine').[90]

Charity, it turns out, is realising the mutual interest and subservience of individual and collective goods through commerce— the mutual supply of wants: 'the great advantages of an amicable correspondence between different nations are pl<ainly> to be seen in traffick and commerce, whereby the product of each particular soil is communicated to distant countries, useful inventions are made common and flourish, and men mutually supply the wants of each other'.[91] War—the use of violent means to prevent others from attaining their wants and needs—is the opposite of charity: 'when the spirit of ambition or Revenge begins to operate, when jealousy of each other's wealth and power divides nations and breaks the bonds of Charity, then all those advantages are interrupted, and men, instead of promoting each others benefit are imploy'd in

90. LJ, VII.28, 30, 33.

91. LJ, VII.34. A rare mention of this sermon is made by Kelly, 'Berkeley's *Querist*', p. 202: 'In his 1714 sermon "On Charity" Berkeley claimed that God's plan for providing for man's material needs was to be effected through harmonious cooperation in the mutual exchange of goods and services, both locally and between countries'. Livesey, 'Berkeley, Ireland, and Eighteenth-Century Intellectual History', p. 459, refers to this sermon and notes that charity was '[t]he cornerstone of Berkeley's thinking about the moral integrity of the community'.

destroying one another'. Berkeley recognises that though only a very restricted class of person (the statesman or general—and presumably he has figures such as Matthew Prior and Peterborough in mind) can remedy the ills of war, 'it is in the power of every one of us to avoid those infinite disorders and mischiefs which arise in private life from defect of charity'. The various distributions of personal traits and talents encourage people to cooperate, to join together in useful societies, and to realise the mutual subservience of their desires: '<Hence> it is that men find it necessary <to> unite in friendships and societies, <to> do mutual good offices, and carry on the same design in harmony and concert. [. . .] [E]very one finds his own in<terest> in advancing that of his n<eighbour>'.[92]

Lack of charity in this specific commercial, interested (but not merely self-interested) sense has led to the great problem of early eighteenth-century British political life: 'It is for want of this [charity] that when we have made peace abroad we worry and destroy <each> other at home'.[93] Perhaps Berkeley is thinking specifically of the faction-ridden political scene in London at the time of the negotiation of the end of the war of Spanish succession. Berkeley is preaching a charity that is most practically realised in commerce; he knows that private charity through commerce is available to all of his merchant audience, even if the love of other people expressed through diplomacy or statesmanship is available only to those in positions of responsibility. Berkeley's sermon gives expression in a different form to the views of Mr Spectator, that 'Factors in the Trading World are what Ambassadors are in the Politick World; they negotiate Affairs, conclude Treaties, and maintain a good Correspondence between those wealthy Societies of Men that are divided from one another by Seas and Oceans, or live on the different Extremities of a Continent'.[94] Even if Berkeley was travelling as part of a Tory diplomatic mission, his view of commerce was considerably closer to the Whig than the Tory imperial vision as Pincus defines them. He was one of those Anglican clergymen who sermonised and projected on behalf of commercial

92. LJ, VII.34–35.
93. LJ, VII.36.
94. [Addison et al.], *The Spectator*, I.293, no. 69, Saturday, 19 May 1711.

empire, for the sake of British Protestants overseas and for the sake of Anglican expansion.[95] He was preaching as part of a Tory delegation, but with a sense of the position and expectations of the nonmetropolitan imperial subject.

This sermon is notable for two other features. First, developing remarks in earlier sermons and notebooks on the interpretation of bodily gesture and the inaccessibility of spirit, Berkeley notes that charity is most visible in its effects. 'That most excellent & divine grace that animates and as I may say inspires a true Christian, that foundation of bliss and that source of all vertuous perfection, that most excellent & divine grace of charity is in itself not so easily comprehended as it is defined by its effects'. Pointing forward to the discussion of force and grace in *Alciphron* as terms that refer to no clear and distinct idea but attribute qualities to the spirit behind the ideas, this is a description of what it is like to see or feel the influence of another spirit, and of what it is like to participate in another spirit. Second, Berkeley seems to develop a concept of second-order pleasures that do not come from fulfilling our desires but from knowing that some behaviours are the right thing to do: 'there is a certain peculiar pleasure and [. . .] that is the natural res<ult of a> kind and generous <beha>vior'. And on the other side, Berkeley asks, 'How can you think on the baseness of an uncharitable envious spirit and not despise it?'[96] These are examples of behaviours, attitudes, and emotional states themselves becoming the objects of our feelings—as Shaftesbury thinks the virtues themselves, rather than simply their effects, become the objects of our admiration.[97] It may be that in this sermon Berkeley was not so far

95. See Sirota, 'The Church: Anglicanism and the Nationalization of Maritime Space', p. 208: '[T]he religious writers and activists of the era seemed to have internalized the basic nostrums of English political economy current throughout the broader society. Their projects, sermons, and devotional writings endlessly reaffirm the overwhelming public interest in promoting trade and navigation'.

96. LJ, VII.30, 37–38.

97. Cooper, *Characteristics of Men, Manners, Opinions, Times*, p. 172: 'In a creature capable of forming general notions of things, not only the outward beings which offer themselves to the sense are the objects of the affection, but the very actions themselves and the affections of pity, kindness, gratitude and their contraries, being brought into the mind by reflection, become objects. So that, by means of this reflected sense, there arises another kind of affection towards those very affections themselves, which have been already felt and have now become the subject of a new liking or dislike'.

from Shaftesbury and other writers on moral sense—writers whom he had attacked under only the thinnest of veils—as he was at other times.

The second Leghorn sermon, on the mission of Christ, is self-evidently a missionary sermon. It maintains an interest in the affective response to events or behaviour (this time the life of Christ) as a guide to our own actions: 'Can we think on these things [the sufferings of Christ] which are all the effects of our sins, and at the same time be untouched with any sorrow or compunction for them?' Emotions can be a reliable guide to what is good or right in these circumstances. This sermon also perhaps bears a mark of its place and time of delivery. In describing the exemplary position of Christ, Berkeley touches on Judaism. The Mosaic Law was intended 'by moral laws less severe and figures of things to come to prepare their minds for the more perfect and spiritual doctrine of the Gospel'.[98] Berkeley may have been thinking of the established Jewish community in Livorno, which was, like the English, a merchant community.[99] The presence of this community and the interaction one might presume between the English and Jewish merchants might have made Berkeley's comparison vivid, for both himself and his audience. There was another community lodged in Leghorn of which Berkeley may have taken notice. Maximilian Misson's tourist guide notes of Leghorn that '[t]here is a House built on purpose for the Slaves, or a kind of Hospital, in which they lye, contrary to the Custom of all other places'.[100] Presumably slaves elsewhere lodged with private families, whereas in Leghorn they lodged communally, and they might consequently have been more visible as a social fraction. Berkeley's view of the interaction of

98. LJ, VII.48, 44.

99. Bregoli, *Mediterranean Enlightenment*, p. 2: 'Eighteenth-century Livorno was not only home to the densest and most privileged Jewish community in Italy, but the nazione ebrea ("Jewish nation"), as it was referred to, was also the second largest Jewish enclave in western Europe after Amsterdam at mid-century. Livornese Jewry partook of both Mediterranean-Sephardi and Tuscan-characteristics. An early example of Jewish merchants invited by European rulers to boost the commercial potential of the state, the bulk of its original settlers were former conversos and Levantine Jews of Iberian origin, attracted by a generous charter granted by the Medici at the end of the sixteenth century (the Livornina)'.

100. Misson, *A New Voyage to Italy*, II.161.

different classes of person in the production of the goods of a commercial society might have included the segregation of a group of people engaging in forced labour. Forced labour returns in Berkeley's later thinking as a means of promoting social good.

In travelling to Europe, Berkeley was engaging with the political, diplomatic, and commercial consequences of peace with France and extending his acquaintance with statesmen and diplomats begun in London. He had gone to London to publish a book and propagate his philosophy, but he also became involved there in two publication projects in popular media—journalism and the anthology of conduct literature. These new projects gave expression more fully to the social orientation of the psychological, metaphysical, and occasionally theological writing for which he was becoming known. That social orientation is seen in an emphasis on education and commerce as the means of achieving and realising a vision of human interconnectedness. Berkeley's first, brief practical experience of the organisation of French and Italian society informed his vision of social interdependence, to which he gave a specifically commercial inflection in his Livorno sermon on charity. Interconnectedness for Berkeley, however, continued to mean a proper subordination of the various kinds and ranks of humans. Whilst we can see Berkeley taking some anthropological interest in different kinds of people, we can also see that there were forms of human life to which he was most likely exposed and which other commentators had remarked upon, but which nonetheless remained hidden to him. Berkeley's relationships with other kinds of people are the subject of the following chapter.

CHAPTER SEVEN

Others

IN USING ALGEBRAIC GAMES to persuade students to develop their reasoning and thereby be more capable of knowing God, in ceding to opponents a vocabulary of the wager, or of passive obedience with the hope of making a greater gain—in these and like cases Berkeley was strategising. He was exercising a capacity for which he thought he had 'an unaccountable turn of thought' from his childhood: 'He that wou'd win another over to his opinion must seem to harmonize with him at first and humour him in his own way of talking'.[1] This turn of thought requires that we understand that other people have different points of view before we try to talk them out of those views. It requires a sufficiently deep or plausible understanding of those different points of view that we can imitate and pass off our own way of talking as another person's, or kind of person's, way of talking. Berkeley's interest in strategic talking has been traced through his writing career and presented as a talent for dissimulation and deceit.[2] In this chapter, I present Berkeley's turn of thought as the (limited) capacity for recognising difference that is a necessary preliminary to effecting change (primarily religious and moral conversion) in another person. If the failure of Berkeley's new doctrine of immaterialism and his political discourses in *Passive Obedience* to achieve their objectives reveals shortcomings in Berkeley's imagination or an inability to anticipate how his writings

---

1. BL Add MS 39304, f. 4r.
2. Berman, *George Berkeley*, passim; Berman, 'Berkeley's Life and Works', p. 24.

would strike and be interpreted by their first audiences, this chapter discloses a limitation in Berkeley's capacity for role reversal in imagining the rational, cultural, and spiritual lives of other agents.

It would be misrepresentative to think of Berkeley as a perpetual harmoniser and strategist. He does not seem to have been afraid of confrontation, if his daughter-in-law's anecdotes are accurate. Eliza Frinsham/Berkeley reports that Berkeley and Martin Benson were approached in Pall Mall, London, by two freethinkers who teased Berkeley by asking him what he thought of David—presumably thinking that the uxoriousness of the king of the Israelites would be morally and theologically embarrassing to Berkeley. But Berkeley replied by saying that David was a sinner, and so was he, and so were they, but that David had the sense to repent. In another incident, she reports, when a former bishop of Cloyne visited Berkeley at the palace and declared at dinner that all mankind were either fools or knaves, Berkeley asked his predecessor to which class he belonged—winning the concession that he must be both.[3] These are rhetorical strategies of a very different kind from harmonising, and fit better with the young man who, crossing the Alps, was 'mortified' that a wolf that had approached his party withdrew at the firing of a pistol: 'he did not attack us and give us an opportunity of killing him'.[4] Wolves, atheists, those who counted themselves apart from humankind—they all needed to be confronted, and Berkeley had the desire and the capacity for that confrontation.

It may be that towards the end of his life Berkeley came to think of harmonising less as a strategy for the conversion of other people holding erroneous beliefs and more as a way of producing a social good—the good of harmony itself. Encountering and harmonising with various other people in America, as he did when at Newport—waiting for the funds for his projected Bermuda college—was explicitly part of a programme of conversion that would also secure an institutional future for Anglican Protestantism in America. In his early years in Cloyne, Berkeley was still writing of the urgency of converting the Catholic population of Ireland, in the name of national good. As the Querist in the mid-1730s, he asked whether it

3. Eliza Berkeley, preface to Berkeley, *Poems*, pp. lxxv-vi, ccclix.
4. Letter 82, Berkeley to Percival, 24 November 1716, p. 140.

did not 'greatly concern the State, that our *Irish* Natives should be converted, and the whole Nation united in the same Religion, the same Allegiance, and the same Interest?' Given that merely hearing is not a religious act, might not hearing Protestant sermons be demanded of Catholics in return for their toleration, and even promoted by 'paying their Hearth-Money for them?'[5] These queries are omitted in the 1750 publication of the text, suggesting that Berkeley might have reconsidered even such relatively gentle coercion.

Berkeley's late text *A Word to the Wise* (1749) is more ecumenical than most of his other writing. This pamphlet, like *The Querist*, is aimed at the promotion of industry as the means of personal and national improvement and suggests that Roman Catholic clergy have a responsibility to encourage their congregations to labour.[6] He dismisses the view of '[m]any' that Catholicism is 'the Cause of that notorious Idleness, which prevails so generally among the Natives of this Island, as if the *Roman Catholic* Faith was inconsistent with an honest Diligence in a Man's Calling', giving Italian industry as a counterexample. Calling on people to provide for their own is 'a sound Catholic Doctrine, not limited to *Protestants*, but extending to all, and admitted by all, whether *Protestants* or *Roman Catholics, Christians* or *Mahometans, Jews* or *Gentiles*'.[7] (It is not necessarily to Berkeley's credit that he proposes the Scythian ethnic origins of the native Irish as a more plausible explanation of their sloth, and that he asks, as the Querist, 'Whether the Wisdom of the State should not wrestle with this hereditary Disposition of our *Tartars* [towards nomadic herding], and with a high Hand introduce Agriculture?'[8]) Sloth is 'worse than even Infidelity', as it violates laws of nature as well as those of revealed religions. Berkeley's call to the Catholic clergy was to 'Countrymen and Neighbours', rather than to people from whom he was separated by religious difference.[9] It was for this late attitude, perhaps, that Charles O'Conor, a

---

5. *The Querist*, I.34–35, §§289, 295–96.

6. Berkeley saw individual resistance to or lack of appetite for labour, rather than any structural matter such as landownership or rates of pay, as the chief determinant of earning capacity within a class of people.

7. *Word to the Wise*, pp. 33–35 (LJ, VI.245–47).

8. *Word to the Wise*, p. 4 (LJ, VI.235–36); *The Querist*, III.28–29, §229; see also Breuninger, *Recovering Bishop Berkeley*, p. 155.

9. *Word to the Wise*, pp. 34, 3 (LJ, VI.246, 235).

Catholic antiquarian who worked to integrate the two communities and who was invited to join the Dublin Society, praised Berkeley: 'A FEW *Berkleys*, in every Communion, would soon restore us to that Spirit, and that *Identity*, of *true Christianity*, which *one* hath labored, so apostolically, to revive'.[10] This more ecumenical attitude followed Berkeley's travels to England, France, Italy, and America, but not instantly. He did not return from these travels an anthropological respecter of cultural difference. Rather, letting such differences stand came to seem the best way to further a parallel project of moral and national improvement that would stabilise and confirm the existing social hierarchy.

Human diversity was a subject of philosophical debate in the early modern period and early Enlightenment, particularly with respect to moral and religious practice. Some asked if the perception that people in different parts of the world converged on a set of practices with a recognisable family likeness could be taken as evidence of the divine institution of those practices, or of their derivation from a single (Mosaic) source. To others, the perceived absence of such family likeness was grounds for the view that moral and religious practice were matters of custom only, not of a universal dispensation, and so no uniformity was to be hoped or expected, let alone promoted by coercion. These differing positions had prominent adherents. Michel de Montaigne, the French essayist of the later sixteenth century, relates a wide variety of cultural practices in order to argue that reason is completely bound up with custom and cannot be separated from it, leaving us nothing but faith as the means of knowing what God intends for us.[11] Montaigne does not deny or refuse universal moral standards, but recognises that the supposedly savage cannibal merely violates them in a different way from the Western European torturer of heretics.[12] Locke, on the other hand, recognises moral diversity but argues that as reason

10. O'Conor, *Seasonal Thoughts*, p. 40. See also McBride, *Eighteenth-Century Ireland*, p. 92.

11. Montaigne, 'Of Custom', in Cotton, trans., *Essays of Michel Seigneur de Montaigne*, I.136: 'Humane Reason is a Tincture equally infus'd into all our Opinions and Customs, of what form soever they are; infinite in Matter, infinite in Diversity'. See Carey, *Locke, Shaftesbury, and Hutcheson*, p. 215, for Todorov's critique of Montaigne's scepticism as leading to conservatism.

12. Muthu, *Enlightenment against Empire*, p. 21.

allows people to know God's will, use of reason can produce conformity in moral and religious practice.[13] Both of these positions might be contrasted with Shaftesbury, for whom religious difference is produced by history, meaning that, 'in the context of religion, no agreement should be expected or enforced. Freethought was essential in this arena'.[14] Alciphron, the freethinker who is attacked in the series of dialogues that bears his name, presents this Shaftesburian view. He takes the 'wonderful variety of Customs and Rites, of Institutions Religious and Civil, of Notions and Opinions very unlike and even contrary to one another', as 'a certain Sign they cannot all be true' and argues that they merely 'bottom on one and the same Foundation, the Strength of Prejudice'.[15] One could understand *Alciphron* as a counter to this argument for atheism from diversity of custom. Berkeley's opposition to Shaftesbury's social and religious thought features in other chapters of this book, but it is already clear that whatever diversity Berkeley might have recognised in religious practice, religious tolerance was not to extend as far as allowing others to persist in their ignorance, atheism, infidelity, or, for most of his career, Catholicism.

The desire to win others over to a position to which one has strong, rationally defensible commitments may then involve the strategies of harmonisation or confrontation, or probably some mixture of the two. It will often require one to engage to at least some degree with the ways in which other people arrive at the beliefs out of which one wants to persuade them. Berkeley's encounters with, and writing about, the Catholic Irish and Italians and his practice in relation to enslaved people and Native Americans demonstrate a minimal engagement with these groups that had no radical effect on his attitude to conversion and coercion. Instead, I suggest, these encounters provided him with living evidence that people with different religious and moral beliefs and practices were capable of sustaining social organisation of a form that was evidently no less successful than many Protestant communities. Whether he understood it to be so or not, Berkeley's

13. Carey, *Locke, Shaftesbury, and Hutcheson*, pp. 67–68.
14. Ibid., p. 10.
15. *Alciphron*, I.5.

writing on these subjects—his compilation of what might qualify as an 'integrated account of human customs with a description of the natural environment' (particularly in his Italian journals)—makes him a participant in the early modern debate on diversity.[16] His tourism in Italy engaged him in the business of observing the historical development of a distinct religious group in a way that his domestic experience of Ireland could not, and one fruit of this experience (fed and watered in America), I suggest, was his more pronounced later ecumenism under the broader project of social improvement.

The Native Irish

In some of the latest entries in notebook B, Berkeley raises an eyebrow at ideas of 'insensible extensions', 'insensible lines', and a point that is 'not altogether nothing nor is it downright somthing'. He responds with a national self-identification: 'We Irish men cannot attain to these truths. [. . .] We Irish men can conceive no such lines[.] [. . .] [W]e Irish men are apt to think something & nothing are next neighbours'. This incipient critique of abstract ideas, which lead people into the errors of infinite divisibility and belief in things that are neither something nor nothing, is presented as commonsensical. But both the way in which Irishness is being invoked and the role it is being made to play are complex.[17] The plainness of the Irishman is near vulgarity, and Berkeley puts himself on the side of the vulgar and of the mob at other points in the notebooks. Berkeley also places himself with the vulgar, or represents his philosophy as more in tune with common sense, in both *Principles of Human Knowledge* and *Three Dialogues*. In those texts, he is suggesting that the vulgar identification of the perceived world with the real world is defensible and indeed needs to be defended from the incursions that materialism is making against it in the learned world.[18] But these

---

16. Carey, *Locke, Shaftesbury, and Hutcheson*, pp. 19–20.

17. *Notebooks*, §§392–94. Breuninger, 'Berkeley and Ireland', p. 109, claims the young Berkeley here 'unreflectively identified himself as ' "Irish" '.

18. For example, *Notebooks*, §405; *Principles of Human Knowledge*, introduction, §1, and main text, §52; and *Three Dialogues*, p. 135 (LJ, II.246). For what constitutes common sense, or the opinion of the vulgar, and how Berkeley defends it, see Stoneham, *Berkeley's*

instances lack the identification of common sense with Irishness found in the *Notebooks*. In the valorisation of a commonsense view that refuses to believe the same thing is something and nothing, or that a particular line could be infinitely divided, there is, as well as an assertion of sound sense, the possibility that sound sense is only a step away from being obtuse. Might there be, in the background to Berkeley's claim to Irishness, a hinted devaluation of the perspective of Irishmen, in other things if not in this matter, if they are so close to the vulgar and the mob? Might being Irish mean lacking imagination or ingenuity as much as having plain common sense? Berkeley is adopting a persona at this point, playing the Irishman for rhetorical purposes, and as such his identification is only partial or transient. Often when we make the rhetorical move of insisting that we are just simple folk, we mean to cast doubt on the overrefinement of our antagonist's ideas, and we do so by suggesting that we are not simple really—just that we have seen through this particular illusion. One might also hear in the assertion that something and nothing are close neighbours that, whilst by no means the same thing, they are not so very distant from one another either—just as the Irish might not be so very different from their close neighbours the English. The simple and the complex, something and nothing, the English and the Irish, are not always very easy to distinguish.

Whatever the rhetorical import of Berkeley's identification with the Irish, he is almost certainly identifying with the Protestant Irish. Irish Protestant elites distinguished themselves from the native Irish and also from the 'Old English' (Catholic) settlers of the twelfth century.[19] The Querist distinguishes the two populations in terms that at once call for Irish unity and maintain sharp divisions, asking:

> 96. *Qu.* Whether it be not the true Interest of both Nations [England and Ireland], to become one People? And whether either be sufficiently apprized of this?

World, pp. 15–16, and Bordner, 'Berkeley's "Defense" of "Commonsense"', pp. 324–25, 327–28. I thank one of the anonymous readers at the Press for pointing me to these discussions.

19. See Connolly, 'Old English, New English, and the Ancient Irish', p. 261: 'In the Ireland in which Swift came to adulthood, then, the tripartite division of Old English, New English and native Irish had largely given way to a simpler distinction between Catholic and Protestant'.

97. *Qu.* Whether the upper Part of this People are not truly *English*, by Blood, Language, Religion, Manners, Inclination, and Interest?

98. *Qu.* Whether we are not as much *Englishmen*, as the Children of old *Romans*, born in *Britain*, were still *Romans*?

99. *Qu.* Whether it be not our true Interest, not to interfere with them? And, in every other Case, whether it be not their true Interest to befriend us?[20]

There is no real division between the people of England and the upper part of the Irish population, and bickering with the English over import duties on wool is destructive of the close relationship that should flow from this kinship.[21] But here, from one query to the next, 'we' goes from being 'Englishmen' to the Irish who are to be distinguished from them. Whilst it might sometimes be in the interests of a Protestant governing elite to suggest that Ireland was conquered by the English and, as in Grotius's thinking, had the right only to that degree of autonomy left it by its conqueror, there was nonetheless an Irish Protestant tendency to hold on to and extend the institutional and political autonomy of Ireland.[22] It has been remarked that the Irish brand of the British patriotic movement of the second quarter of the eighteenth century was peculiarly ahistorical, as the standard invocation of an earlier historical moment that enshrined native rights would have regrettable associations, for Ireland, with a Catholic history. The Anglo-Irish patriots had to be English to claim their ancient (pre-Norman) liberty, and yet at the same time they were compelled to assert the independence of an Irish parliament that would

20. *The Querist*, I.12, §§96–99.

21. McBride, *Eighteenth-Century Ireland*, pp. 67–69, presents Molyneux as a strident opponent of English duties on Irish wool and a claimant of the privileges of the English Protestant ruling elite.

22. Livesey, 'The Dublin Society in Eighteenth-Century Irish Political Thought', pp. 618–24, notes the importance of Davenant in presenting Ireland as a dependency; in 'Berkeley, Ireland, and Eighteenth-Century Intellectual History', p. 457, he notes the importance of Grotius to Irish Protestants (and mentions that Berkeley donated Grotius to Yale). See Grotius, *On the Law of War and Peace*, pp. 374–75, III.8, 'On the Right to Rule Over the Conquered', for the degree of liberty conquerors may allow to the conquered.

decentralise power and render it more local and more representative.[23] Whether one regards the relationship between the Protestant elite and the Catholic masses as colonial or as an instance of the confessional statehoods characteristic of the anciens régimes, the separation between Berkeley's 'upper part' of the people and the lower is clear.[24]

The native Irish appear very low in *The Querist* and other texts of Berkeley's Cloyne period.[25] Although Berkeley had travelled to London and other English towns, as well as to France, Italy, and America, his appointment at Cloyne was the first time he was to spend a long time as an adult in Ireland outside the Protestant-majority city of Dublin.[26] Berkeley had barely been a year in Cloyne when *The Querist* was published. He had quickly formed a very strong view of the nonpropertied Irish. They were dirty and lazy:

19. *Qu.* Whether the bulk of our *Irish* Natives are not kept from thriving, by that cynical Content in Dirt and Beggary, which they possess to a Degree beyond any other People in Christendom?

20. *Qu.* Whether the creating of Wants be not the likeliest way to produce Industry in a People? And whether if our Peasants were accustomed to eat Beef and wear Shoes, they would not be more Industrious? [. . .]

138. *Qu.* Whether there be upon Earth any Christian or civilized People so beggarly, wretched and destitute as the common *Irish*? [. . .]

196. *Qu.* Whether a Tax upon Dirt would not be one way of encouraging Industry?[27]

23. Leersen, 'Anglo-Irish Patriotism and Its European Context', pp. 21–22.

24. McBride, *Eighteenth-Century Ireland*, pp. 194–95.

25. Breuninger, 'Berkeley and Ireland', p. 120, notes that Berkeley's plan for the economic improvement of Ireland is bifurcated along racial and sectarian lines, with different models for the natives and the Protestants.

26. Twomey, *Dublin in 1707*, pp. 10–11: 'In the early 18th century, Dublin was a Protestant city. Over 70% of the population was Protestant and in turn over three-quarters of Dublin's Protestants were adherents of the Church of Ireland—the established state church. A significant proportion of the citizens of the city in this period were English by birth or they were the sons or daughters of English parents who had arrived in Dublin in the later 17th century'.

27. *The Querist*, I.3, 17, §§19–20, 138, and II.21, §196.

If these were views arrived at quickly, they persisted until at least 1749 and *A Word to the Wise*, where they are expanded upon at length:

Indolence in Dirt is a terrible Symptom, which shews itself in our lower *Irish* more, perhaps, than in any People on this Side the *Cape of Good Hope*. I will venture to add, that look throughout the Kingdom, and you shall not find a clean House inhabited by clean People, and yet wanting Necessaries; the same Spirit of Industry that keeps Folk clean, being sufficient to keep them also in Food and Rayment.

But alas! our poor *Irish* are wedded to Dirt upon Principle. It is with some of them a Maxim, that the Way to make Children thrive is to keep them dirty. And I do verily believe, that the Familiarity with Dirt, contracted and nourished from their Infancy, is one great Cause of that Sloth which attends them in every Stage of Life. Were Children but brought up in an Abhorrence of Dirt, and obliged to keep themselves clean, they would have something to do, whereas now they do nothing.

It is past all Doubt, that those who are educated in a supine Neglect of all Things, either profitable, or decent, must needs contract a Sleepiness and Indolence, which doth necessarily lead to Poverty, and every other Distress that attends it. [. . .]

In *Holland* a Child of five Years old is maintained by its own Labour; in *Ireland* many Children of twice that Age do nothing but steal, or encumber the Hearth and Dunghill. This shameful Neglect of Education shews itself through the whole Course of their Lives, in a matchless Sloth bred in the very Bone, and not to be accounted for by any outward Hardship, or Discouragement whatever. It is the native Colour, if we may so speak, and Complexion of the People. [. . .]

It is a shameful Thing and peculiar to this Nation, to see lusty Vagabonds strolling about the Country, and begging without any Pretence to beg. [. . .]

A sore Leg is an Estate to such a Fellow[.] [. . .] Such is their Laziness, that rather than work they will cherish a Distemper. This I know to be true, having seen more than one Instance, wherein the second Nature so far prevailed over the first, that Sloth was preferred to Health. [. . .]

It is indeed a difficult Task to reclaim such Fellows from their slothful and brutal Manner of Life, to which they seem wedded with an Attachment that no temporal Motives can conquer; nor is there, humanly speaking, any Hopes they will mend, except their Respect for your Lessons, and Fear of Something beyond the Grave be able to work a Change in them.[28]

The sloth of the native Irish is presented as so native to them that it is not possible to dissuade them from it with any temporal inducement. Instead, religion must be used. There may be strategy here. The near-contradiction that the unsalvageable Irish can only be saved by religion gives their priests great agency and responsibility. But it also carries the risk of being so offensive that it will outrage the Catholic clergy rather than encourage them to share in Berkeley's project.

These attitudes about the engrained traits of the Irish are expressed during a great period of social activism aimed at improving the conditions of life for people Berkeley portrays as beyond improvement (for more on this period, see chapters 13 and 15). Efforts on behalf of the native Irish were not made with a view to the preservation of what Berkeley took to be intrinsic to their culture, but, on the contrary, with a view to transforming their culture into one of industry, health, cleanliness, and Protestantism. Berkeley's views are an early example of an enduring discourse that blames peasants for their own impoverishment, presenting them as backward, unmotivated by consumption, inefficient, resistant to improvement, and politically threatening.[29] (Of course, much of *The Querist* attempts to encourage industry, health, sobriety, and responsibility in the Anglo-Irish elite too; the curse is on both houses.)

Ethnic diversity in Ireland was linguistically marked. When Berkeley took an interest in the Irish language, it was with a view to conversion. In the period just before Berkeley had entered TCD, instruction in Irish for the purposes of conversion had been instituted.[30] As well as this tradition at TCD, Henry Maule, one of Berkeley's precursors at the palace of Cloyne, had considered the

28. *Word to the Wise*, pp. 23–24, 26–29 (LJ, VI.242–44).

29. See Handy, '"Almost Idiotic Wretchedness"', passim, and p. 138, for the persistence of similar views of peasants into the late twentieth century.

30. See O'Connor, 'Marsh's Library and the Catholic Tradition', p. 235, and Hunter, 'Robert Boyle, Narcissus Marsh, and the Anglo-Irish Intellectual Scene', pp. 61, 66–68.

benefits of preaching in Irish around Cloyne, in the context of the inculcation of English manners and the English language through a charter school.[31] The Querist pursues a similar train of thought, with attention to the social background and training of the people tasked with this work:

> 307. *Qu.* Whether there be any Instance of a People's being converted in a Christian Sense, otherwise than by preaching to them and instructing them in their own Language?
>
> 308. *Qu.* Whether Catechists in the *Irish* Tongue may not easily be procured and subsisted? And whether this would not be the most practicable Means for converting the Natives? [. . .]
>
> 311. *Qu.* Whether in Defect of able Missionaries, Persons conversant in low Life, and speaking the *Irish* Tongue, if well instructed in the first Principles of Religion, and in the Popish Controversy, though for the rest on a Level with the Parish Clerks, or the Schoolmasters of Charity-Schools, may not be fit to mix with and bring over our poor illiterate Natives, to the established Church? Whether it is not to be wished that some Parts of our Liturgy and Homilies were publickly read in the *Irish* Language? And whether, in these Views, it may not be right to breed up some of the better Sort of Children in the Charity Schools, and qualify them for Missionaries, Catechists and Readers?[32]

There is here no sense of the intrinsic value of the Irish language, nor of the cultural practices of those with whom it is to be used as the means of engagement. This engagement with a distinctively different culture was not in the service of ethnographic study but of conversion.

The Italians

When Berkeley engaged with the cultures of continental Europe, the sectarian divide was again close to the surface. Travelling through rural France, Berkeley noted the depopulation and immiseration

---

31. Barnard, *Irish Protestant Ascents and Descents*, p. 199.

32. *The Querist*, I.36–37, §§307–8, 311. See also letter 254, Gibson to Berkeley, 9 July 1735, pp. 385–86, for discussion of a scheme to preach in Irish in order to bring Catholics into the Protestant church.

caused by the recent wars, the splendour of the various churches and palaces he visited, and the fact that the clergy gambled at cards. On his first tour of Italy, he noted the poor state of learning in the example of a clergyman who showed him a Hebrew book, 'taking it to be an English one'.[33] His second, more prolonged stay in Italy involved a tour of the south. His journals during that tour thematise the ignorance of different classes of Italian: the common 'fellow reading a book yt / he knew not one word of out of devotion' at Canosa; at Castelnata, 'one of the most knowing fathers asked whether Ireland were a large town'. That same father had, however, heard of Whigs and Tories.[34] Ignorance and poverty were salient features for Berkeley. He remarked on dirtiness and superstition as he travelled through Italy, features that he also took to characterise the native Irish.

Berkeley frequently mentioned saints' lives and relics as objects of superstitious belief. He recorded several of the unusual powers claimed for saints' relics, as when the people of Ascoli 'boast of a saint's finger kept in a church of a convent on a hill overlooking the towne wch so far as the church is visible prevents the bite of the Tarantula', or a phial of the blood of Saint Vitus at Tarentum which, 'being hard miraculously liquefies on the Saint's day'.[35] This last claim was not unique to Saint Vitus's blood at Tarentum; Berkeley held the general attitude of British tourists to such claims, as described by Colin Haydon:

> Visitors to the Continent were unlikely to witness atrocities, but what they saw of Popery could arouse anger, disgust, or, on occasions, amusement. [. . .] Some travellers were deeply offended when they observed "Popish superstitions" at first hand. [. . .] Many tourists scoffed at the belief in "false miracles" such as the liquefaction of St. Januarius' blood at Naples: in their eyes, it typified the irrationality encouraged by Catholicism. Other criticisms concerned the church's wealth, and the ways by which it acquired it. [. . .] Some churches were gorgeously decorated, it was noted, whilst the poor of the community suffered

33. Letter 62, Berkeley to Percival, 19 February 1713/14, p. 112; letter 59, Berkeley to Percival, 28 December 1713, p. 108; letter 61, Berkeley to Percival, 4 February 1714, p. 111.

34. LJ, VII.272–73, 291.

35. LJ, VII.297 (5 June 1717), 288.

immense privations. [. . .] Travellers appeared to be convinced of what English pamphleteers maintained: that Popery gave rise to injustice, poverty, and misery. For young men, taking the Grand Tour, these impressions might remain with them for the rest of their lives.[36]

Berkeley made no specific accusation that Catholicism in Italy was responsible for injustice. Indeed, he rarely remarked on the lowest social orders whilst in Italy, an exception being his dislike of his reception at Venosa on 4 June 1717: 'the men of this town in crouds gaping & following us about the towne, the idlest canaille & most beggarly I have any where seen'.[37] But superstition clearly repelled him, particularly the positive embrace of the physically abject in reports of saints' lives.

In notes that are not recorded in the standard edition of the Italian journals, Berkeley seems particularly interested in the self-imposed physical mortification of Santa Maria Magdalene de'Pazzi. Maria appears today in clinical literature on self-mutilation.[38] Berkeley notes with disgust the valorisation of her abjection: 'S Maria Magdalena de Pazzis or Pazzi commended for wearing rags in y.e consistory. for licking ulcers'. This and suchlike reports made Catholicism reprehensible:

> Confirmed as authentic that Magdalena de Pazzis had heal'd the sick, given sight to the blind thrown out devils. &c. &c.
>
> Nastiness, ill manners, stupidity, madness &c sanctified in the church of Rome.
>
> I heard a priest preach in Rome y.t a certain saint made her usual drink of the water with which she had washed ulcers in an hospital.[39]

When God's organisation of the universe is understood as a system of signs that becomes legible to us through practice, a practice reliant upon an inborn tendency towards what is pleasurable and away from what is painful, such wilful reversal of those polarities is

---

36. Haydon, *Anti-Catholicism in Eighteenth-Century England*, pp. 26–27. See also Sweet, *Cities and the Grand Tour*, p. 147.

37. LJ, VII.296.

38. Favazza, *Bodies under Siege*, p. 37, is very close to Berkeley's notes: 'She reportedly was able to cure diseases; one procedure she followed was to lick the skin lesions of afflicted nuns, including one who was a leper, and to suck the maggots out of skin ulcers'.

39. BL Add MS 39310, ff. 89v, 92.

seen as perverse. The authenticated miracles on the basis of which saints were canonised appear implausible and irrational, but even worse is their appeal to dirtiness and slovenliness as themselves signs of sanctity. Love of dirt is perceived as what unites the Italian Catholic saints and the Irish Catholic poor. The social practices inculcated by Roman Catholicism achieved precisely the opposite of what Berkeley would come to think, in *Word to the Wise*, was the duty of a religious institution: they encouraged the individuals for whom the institution was responsible into sloth, dirtiness, and beggary by promulgating implausible and impossible narratives as objects of belief.

Americans and Enslaved People

The energy Berkeley expended in his social work at Cloyne won him the approval of one Catholic activist at least, and his late address to Catholic priests engaged them as colleagues rather than competitors. But for most of his career he militated against the Catholic church—minimally by being an active member of exclusively Protestant institutions, but also in more aggressive ways. In 1725, he was nominated a member of the Society for the Promotion of Christian Knowledge, which, it has been said, 'could fairly claim to be the national spearhead against Popery, since, soon after its inception in 1699, it had assumed a watching brief on "the practices of the priests to pervert His Majesty's subjects"'.[40] Henry Newman, the Society's secretary, exchanged letters with Berkeley whilst the latter was in America, offering assistance and advice on the possibility of alternative locations for St Paul's College. When Berkeley returned, Newman passed on the Society's wish to welcome him back and angled for the returned funds for the Bermuda project to be used for the 'Protestant mission to East India'.[41] Newman understood that Berkeley's plan for Bermuda was a plan for religious conversion, for the propagation of the institutional structures of

40. Luce, 'Berkeley's Bermuda Project and His Benefactions to American Universities', p. 115, citing a letter from Henry Newman to Percival, 8 January 1725, in Egmont Papers, LXVI.251; Haydon, *Anti-Catholicism in Eighteenth-Century England*, p. 58.

41. Letter 182, Newman to Berkeley, 29 April 1729, p. 275; letter 191, Newman to Berkeley, 17 September 1729, p. 295; letter 214, Newman to Berkeley, 20 January 1731/32, p. 343.

Anglicanism overseas, and concomitantly for personal liberty and social improvement.

The other kinds of people with whom Berkeley engaged during his American expedition were primarily from Christian sects other than Anglicanism. What was striking to Berkeley was seeing different Christian confessions operating alongside one another, to a far greater degree than in Ireland, and without any evident hierarchy, and his letters from Newport concentrate on this coexistence of confessional groups. He reports to Percival:

> The town is prettily built, contains about five thousand souls, and hath a very fine harbour. The people industrious, and though less orthodox, I cannot say they have less virtue (I am sure they have more regularity) than those I left in Europe. They are indeed a strange medley of different persuasions, which nevertheless do all agree in one point, viz. that the Church of England is the second best.

Like many good jokes, this bore telling more than once. In a letter to Benson of 11 April the same year, Berkeley specifies that there are 'four sorts of Anabaptists besides Independents, Quakers and many of no profession at all', who all think Anglicanism second best. He adds in a letter to Prior of 24 April 1729 that in America there are 'fewer quarrels about religion than elsewhere', despite these differences.[42] The earliest colonial history of Rhode Island was concerned with religious dissent and tolerance: Roger Williams, the founder of Providence, had been expelled from Massachusetts for his heterodoxy and was a proponent of liberty of conscience and the separation of church and state. An attempt by James Honeyman, with whom Berkeley became friendly, to encourage an American bishop in the 1710s may have led the General Assembly of Rhode Island to pass a law forbidding state support of any religious denomination.[43] A century of history, with which Berkeley showed no particular sign of familiarity, lay behind the harmonious diversity he was observing.

---

42. Letter 177, 28 March 1729, p. 269; letter 179, p. 269; letter 180, p. 271.

43. James, *Colonial Rhode Island*, pp. 8–9, 15–16, 190. For more on the conception of the state underlying these attitudes, see James, 'Colonial Rhode Island and the Beginnings of the Liberal Rationalized State'.

Berkeley's ecumenism, such as it was, most likely began in this moment, as his response to this social harmony was not to foment disharmony by promoting his own sect, but to preach on 'only those general points agreed by all Christians' and obtain a diverse audience. His strategy was not immediately perfect: he preached against enthusiasm on Whitsunday and reports that some Quakers took against him for doing so.[44] Anne Berkeley says of Berkeley's religious activism during their time in Newport that

> the missionaries for 70 miles around agreed amongst themselves to meet at his house twice a year & receive his instructions—which they did for the two years he resided in that Island—part of those instructions I have heard—and they were, that by all offices of kindness they should conciliate them of different sects unto themselves: and never begin to argue upon controverted points, but preach upon those in wch all must agree, [?]viz the Love of God & Man—and not provoke by trifles of No Moment—such as walking about in Pudding sleeve Gowns—wch they detested—but dress in black or grey except when they went into Church—to hear them all patiently—and answer them from Scripture—[45]

But with a strong, antagonistic reaction to European Catholic culture behind him, Berkeley sensed from this new experience in Newport that social goods (such as industry) might emerge in faith communities other than the Anglican church, and indeed in the interaction between faith communities. His strategy became promoting harmony and unity at the same time as presenting his sect as the most reasonable and organising for its institutional establishment.

A strategy for achieving one part of what Berkeley proposed in establishing his Bermuda college emerged, then, in practice: an ecumenical approach to preaching and gently persuading members of other communions to join the most reasonable community by living as an exemplary Anglican amongst them. This strategy relied on understanding what these different Christian communities

44. Letter 189, Berkeley to Percival, 30 August 1729, p. 286.

45. TCD MS 5936, Stock, *An Account of the Life of George Berkeley*, opposite p. 21. Berman, 'Mrs Berkeley's Annotations in *An Account of the Life of Berkeley* (1776)', p. 192, has 'for' for 'viz'.

believed, building relationships with them based on that common ground, and allowing them what was uncommon. Such strategies of partial identification and gentle persuasion are entirely absent in Berkeley's work with the two other groups identified as requiring the attentions of the Anglican colonist in the *Proposal* for the college in Bermuda: Native Americans and enslaved people. Encounters with people of different ethnicity had led some Christians to reflect on the merely superficial character of human difference and to remark that that all kinds of humans, of whatever ethnicity, gender, or class, would one day be united in God:

> [T]he tawney Moore, blacke Negro, duskie Libyan, ash-coloured Indian, olive-coloured American, should with the whiter European become *one sheep-fold*, under *one great Sheepheard*, till *this mortalitie being swallowed up of Life*, wee may all *be one, as he and the father are one* [. . .] without any more distinction of Colour, Nation, Language, Sexe, Condition, all may bee *One* in him that is One, *and onely blessed for ever.*[46]

This is a vision of assumption into God in the next life that eradicates all the human differences perceptible in this life. Berkeley may or may not have held a view of the equality of humans when reassumed into God. His conduct when encountering ethnically different people certainly demonstrates a concern to preserve social order in more or less its current form in this world.[47]

There is no mention of contact with Native American people in Berkeley's letters from America. He is said to have visited the Narragansett county with Daniel Updike and John Smibert in order to study the 'conditions and character' of the Native Americans.[48] But there is no specific evidence of his study. A rare mention of 'Savage Nations' who 'scalp, roast, torture, and destroy each

46. Samuel Purchas, writing in 1614, cited by Jordan, 'Initial English Attitudes toward Africans', p. 104.

47. Uzgalis, 'Berkeley and the Westward Course of Empire', passim and p. 124, considers many of the issues addressed in this section and adopts the comparable view that Berkeley's attitudes to cultural diversity are best understood in relation to his participation in the formal hierarchy of an established church.

48. Luce, pp. 121–22, citing Updike, *A History of the Episcopal Church in Narragansett*, pp. 176, 523. The claim appears in the 1907 edition of this text published in Boston by D. B. Updike at the Merrymount Press, p. 211. Rousseau, 'Praxis 1', p. 146, takes the visits to the

other, as they are known to do', in *Alciphron*, the work Berkeley was composing in America, presumably refers to supposed practices of Native Americans, but it is not a firsthand report.[49] One clerical colleague wrote to the bishop of London, who was responsible for the church in the plantations, towards the end of Berkeley's time in America in the summer of 1731 that Berkeley 'seems tired of this Country, tho He has seen Nothing of it'.[50]

The earlier stages of Berkeley's preparation for Bermuda do not seem to have included research into Native American life and culture. The *Proposal* states that the Americans 'continue in much the same ignorance and barbarism, in which we found them above a hundred years ago'. Converting Americans is difficult, 'if we consider the difference of language, their wild way of living, and above all, the great Jealousy and prejudice which savage nations have towards foreigners, or innovations introduced by them'. Berkeley presents the natural barbarism of the Native Americans as if it were the absence of all culture:

> [T]he savage Americans, if they are in a state purely natural, and unimproved by education, they are also unincumbered with all that rubbish of superstition and prejudice, which is the effect of a wrong one. As they are less instructed, they are withal less conceited, and more teachable. And not being violently attached to any false system of their own, are so much the fitter to receive that which is true.[51]

Looking back on his American experience in a sermon he was invited to preach before the SPG, Berkeley notes that the religion of enslaved people in Rhode Island, 'as is natural to suppose, takes after that of their Masters'. He has even less sense that enslaved black people might have either cult or culture that predates and endures beyond their arrival in the colonies.[52] The particular difficulty with the 'wild and roving life' of the Americans is that '[h]e

---

Narragansett county and the brief comments in the SPG sermon as a sign of Berkeley's close study of Native Americans.

49. *Alciphron*, V.17.

50. Lambeth Palace, Fulham Papers, vol. V, ff. 40–43, Thomas Harward to Gibson, 19 July 1731 (f. 40r).

51. *Proposal*, pp. 3, 5, 16 (LJ, VII.345–46, 356).

52. *Anniversary Sermon*, p. 19 (LJ, VII.121).

who is obliged to hunt for his daily food, will have little curiosity or leisure to receive instruction'. Agriculture and the trades would therefore be taught to any who could not master more academic disciplines. 'This will assist the spreading of the gospel among them; this will dispose them to social vertues, and enable them to see and to feel the advantages of a religious and civil education'. The urgency of the mission is that 'no part of the Gentile world are so inhumane and barbarous as the savage Americans, whose chief employment and delight consisting in cruelty and revenge, their lives must of all others be most opposite as well to the light of nature, as to the spirit of the Gospel'.[53]

These views take no account of readily available texts that describe the life and culture of Native American people. The very first European account of the people of Rhode Island notes the biodynamic principles of local agriculture as a feature shared with classical cultures: 'They live on the same food as the other people—pulse (which they produce with more systematic cultivation than the other tribes, and when sowing they observe the influence of the moon, the rising of the Pleiades, and many other customs derived from the ancients), and otherwise on game and fish'.[54] Eighty years before Berkeley's arrival, Roger Williams, in one of the most important colonial texts on the indigenous history of the area, noted similarities in customs between Native Americans and the biblical Israelites: people anointed themselves; women kept a separate house during menstruation; dowries were offered. He also noted that women were responsible for pounding corn and all other aspects of its culture.[55] Although Williams's writing on the Americans also planned for their conversion, he conceived of them as a people with a cult (one derived from the Mosaic Law) and with agriculture. Another religiously motivated visitor to America who noted the vestigial presence of religion in everything Native

---

53. *Proposal*, pp. 17–18, 20 (LJ, VII.357, 359).

54. Wroth, *The Voyages of Giovanni da Verrazzano*, p. 139. The text was translated and published in Hakluyt's *Divers Voyages* in 1582 (see pp. 87–88).

55. Williams, *A Key to the Language of America*, 'To the Reader', sigs. A4v–A5r, pp. 31–32, 37. For an account of similar views of the cultural and religious practices of Native Americans from within the Anglican missionary community of the early eighteenth century see Glasson, *Mastering Christianity*, pp. 62–63.

Americans did was the Jesuit Joseph-François Lafitau, whose comparison of the manners of the Americans with those of the ancient peoples was published in the same year as Berkeley's *Proposal*. Though he was writing about people from further north, the Iroquois, he too noted that the women were responsible for the cultivation of maize.[56]

Berkeley shows no obvious interest in the historical and cultural puzzles that Native American culture represented to other visitors— its relation to Mosaic and classical cultures, in terms of both social organisation and belief system. In fact, Berkeley shows no obvious sign of understanding Native Americans as cultural at all, an attitude that has been said more generally to contribute to the ease of enacting colonial and imperial schemes that subject indigenous peoples.[57] As Nancy Kendrick puts it, 'In failing to recognize the cultural life of the "savage" Americans, Berkeley's *Proposal* never considered that their social practices and political structures may have already evinced "public spirited principles and inclinations"' that it was the aim of the college to instill'.[58] Berkeley also presents Bermuda itself as a place lacking any distinctive kind of human cultural practice. It is a place of 'plenty [. . .] great abundance of fruits, and garden-stuff of all kinds in perfection'. He makes only a passing reference to the practice of matting palmetto.[59] Berkeley's presentation of Bermuda either masks the skills and practices of indigenous (and enslaved) people or appropriates them as effects of nature or colonial industry.[60] Native Americans are still more strikingly absent from Berkeley's writings of his time in Rhode Island. The people who gleaned, hunted, and fished, but were ever more dependent on corn; whose women were increasingly isolated by that dependence because they bore responsibility for its cultivation; whose men fashioned wampum and fishing nets and traps; who practised metalwork and incorporated arriving technologies and

---

56. Lafitau, *Moeurs des sauvages amériquains*, I.17, II.63.

57. Muthu, *Enlightenment against Empire*, p. 30: 'understandings of New World peoples as cultural beings were more likely to yield a robust affirmation of their status as human beings' and make colonial repression harder.

58. Kendrick, 'Berkeley's Bermuda Project in Context', p. 38.

59. *Proposal*, p. 11 (LJ, VII.351).

60. For this tendency in colonial accounts of Bermuda, see Kopelson, '"One Indian and a Negroe, the first thes Ilands ever had"', p. 298.

materials into their production; whose religion revolved around the various and contrasting manifestations of Manitou, or spirit; who oriented the bodies of their dead to the southwest, where the home of the ancestors was to be found; whose coercive hospitality and begging practices might have caught the attention of the traveller— these people are not present in any surviving record Berkeley made of his visit to America.[61] As William Uzgalis notes, Berkeley exhibits no particular sense that Native Americans 'have their own religion or religions that are sufficient for their purposes'.[62] Nor does Berkeley leave any evidence of having considered the political or diplomatic agency of Native people such as Charles Augustus Ninigret, the sachem who as a local leader granted ten to twenty acres of land to the General Assembly of Rhode Island in 1727 'for the erecting thereon a house for worship, according to the form of the church of England, or for erecting of a meeting house thereon (he desiring it), for the use of any other society or societies'.[63] The presence of an Anglican church in Narragansett was the result of this agency.

It may be that only someone who conceives of another group of people as not cultural can happily state that the recruits for his proposed seminary will 'be procured, either by peaceable methods from those savage nations, which border on our colonies, and are in friendship with us, or by taking captive the children of our enemies'. The extent of the violence that would be required to carry out Berkeley's 'visionary scheme' was well understood by William Byrd, the Virginia colonist, who asked of Percival,

> where will the Dean find Indians to be converted? There are no Indians at Bermudas, nor within two hundred leagues of it upon the continent, and it will need the gift of miracles to persuade them to leave their country and venture themselves upon the great ocean, on the temptation of being converted. I know but one way in the world to procure Indians for this purpose: the Dean must have the command of half a

61. See Main, *Peoples of a Spacious Land*, pp. 5–17; and Rubertone, *Grave Undertakings*, pp. 117–87.

62. Uzgalis, 'Berkeley and the Westward Course of Empire', p. 114.

63. *Records of the Colony of Rhode Island*, p. 397; see also Fisher, *The Indian Great Awakening*, p. 45.

dozen regiments, with which he or one of his professors in the quality of Lieutenant General must make a descent upon the coast of Florida, and take as many prisoners as he can. This will be altogether as wise, and as meritorious, as the Holy War used to be of old, and then if those Gentiles will not be converted by fair means, he may take the French way, and dragoon them into Christianity. Nor will your Lordship think this extravagant, considering that a wild scheme in order to be consistent with itself, should have wild measures to carry it on.[64]

Byrd was one of those who thought the entire Bermuda project visionary—in the pejorative sense.

Whilst Berkeley had a strong sense, then, of the differences between Christian communions, and that sense enabled him to think at least partly from the position of people of those other communions and identify common ground with them, there is no evidence that he developed this sense with respect to Native Americans. Indeed, though there is no evidence of Berkeley having spent time in proximity to Muslim communities, and his only exposure to Judaism was likely to have been to the Jewish merchant community at Livorno in 1714, he did at least consider those faiths in their relation to Christianity in sermons: Judaism is an imperfect precursor of Christianity, in his telling, and Islam is a rival faith that exploited the weaknesses of the early church.[65] Two years' residence near the Narragansett people provoked no such comparative or sociological thinking about Native American religion.

The Bermuda scheme was, then, a project to bring a people into religion and culture.[66] The *Proposal* also offers a political reason for

64. *Proposal*, p. 6 (LJ, VII.347); *Berkeley and Percival*, Byrd to Percival, 10 June 1729, pp. 244–45.

65. LJ, VII.44, 64, 113, 119; for this sociological view, see p. 126: 'As anciently most unchristian Schisms and Disputes, joined with great Corruption of Manners, made way for the Mahometan in the East, and the Papal Dominion in the West; even so here at home in the last Century, a weak Reliance upon human Politics and Power on the one hand, and enthusiastic Rage on the other, together with Carnal-mindedness on both, gave occasion to introduce Atheism and Infidelity'.

66. Kendrick, 'Berkeley's Bermuda Project in Context', p. 24, suggests that Berkeley wished to initiate Native Americans into an intellectual life distinct from or in addition to converting them to Christianity. This biography portrays Berkeley as someone for whom fulfilment of human potential was necessarily a religious matter. The *Proposal* orients all its discussion of education for Native Americans towards making them missionaries.

wanting to convert Americans to Protestantism: Catholic missionaries (Spanish in the south, French in the north) had been active
amongst the indigenous population, more willing to bear the hard-
ships of living in their midst. Their success, Berkeley says, might
ultimately extirpate the Protestant colonies and significantly reduce
'so considerable a branch of his majesty's revenue'. Berkeley noted
in the Anniversary Sermon he preached for the SPG on returning to
London in 1732 that the missionary success of the Catholic church
had been due to intermarriage with Native Americans and a care 'to
instruct both them and their Negroes, in the *Popish* Religion'.[67] The
efforts of people in Berkeley's American circle were strenuous but
not necessarily successful. James MacSparran 'aggressively sought
out Indians and black slaves in his own parish and made preaching forays onto the Narragansett reservation [. . .]. Over the thirty-
seven years of his ministry, he managed to convert only fourteen
souls of full or mixed Indian ancestry'.[68]

To Berkeley, the social positions of Catholics, Native Americans,
and enslaved black people were comparable, whether the Catholics
were the missionary French and Spanish, willing to endure hard-
ships and submit to hierarchy in a way their Protestant competitors
were not, or the native Irish. *A Word to the Wise* notes of the native
Irish that

> these proud People are more destitute than *Savages*, and more abject
> than *Negros*. The *Negros* in our Plantations have a Saying, *If Negro
> was not Negro, Irishman would be Negro*. And it may be affirmed with
> Truth, that the very *Savages* of *America* are better clad and better
> lodged than the *Irish Cottagers* throughout the fine fertile Counties of
> *Limerick* and *Tipperary*.[69]

Whilst Berkeley's *Proposal* and *Word to the Wise* proposed measures to civilise their targets, the Native Americans and native Irish,
he made no suggestion at any point in his career that baptism would
change or improve the temporal condition of the enslaved people
to whom it was offered. In the Anniversary Sermon, he identified

---

67. *Proposal*, p. 15 (LJ, VII.354); *Anniversary Sermon*, p. 20 (LJ, VII.122).
68. Main, *Peoples of a Spacious Land*, pp. 199–200.
69. *Word to the Wise*, p. 8 (LJ, VI.237).

an 'ancient Antipathy to the Indians' and 'an irrational Contempt of the Blacks, as Creatures of another Species, who had no Right to be instructed or admitted to the Sacraments', as the reasons for what was said to 'have proved a main Obstacle to the Conversion of these poor People'.[70] But far from seeing slavery as a social status from which people should be liberated, Berkeley actually saw it as an occasional social good—or at least as an institution that was preferable to the ingrained sloth and beggary of the native Irish.

The conversion of enslaved people had become a concern before Berkeley left for America, but it was not a concern of the first published edition of the *Proposal* in 1724. The references to baptising enslaved black people were added to the second edition of 1725. This addition may have been made in order to seek further funds for the college. Berkeley wrote to Percival on 10 February 1726 noting that 'Lord Palmerston is desirous that nine hundred and odd pounds in his hands should be disposed of to this our college for breeding up young negroes agreeable to Mr. Delon's will'. Abel Tassin, Sieur D'Allone, had left this money for the conversion of black people on British plantations. Despite the efforts of Daniel Dering and Percival, it was not possible to turn the money to Bermuda, and it ended up being assigned to James Oglethorpe's project, the new colony of Georgia.[71] But beyond this expedient interest in converting and baptising enslaved black people, Berkeley may well have made decisive interventions in the legal discourse on slavery that later served to shore it up against abolition.

Berkeley practised slavery in a slaving plantation. Twenty years before Berkeley's arrival, the governor, Samuel Cranston, had asserted that, excepting a shipment of black people from Africa in 1696, the colony took in only around twenty or thirty slaves a year, from Barbados. Though he claimed that Rhode Island people preferred white servants, there were 220 black servants in Newport, around 10 percent of the town's total population. During Berkeley's time, the General Assembly, 'alleging that "great charge, trouble and inconveniencies" had arisen from people manumitting slaves, ruled that none might be freed unless the erstwhile owner posted

70. *Anniversary Sermon*, pp. 19–20 (LJ VII.122).
71. Letter 143, p. 219; Gaustad, *George Berkeley in America*, pp. 98–103.

bond of at least £100 to indemnify his town in case the freed person became unable to live without charitable aid'.[72] Although Rhode Island, in 'both relative and absolute terms', was 'the most important American carrier of African slaves', there were fewer than ten slaving voyages per year during Berkeley's residence in Newport, as opposed to around fifty at the peak of the trade at the turn of the nineteenth century, and only three slaving ships left from Rhode Island during Berkeley's stay.[73] Berkeley received a letter from Benson on 23 June 1729 that referred to Sir John's project 'for propagating the race of blacks in Europe'.[74] One presumes that propagation was to be under conditions of slavery. Berkeley bought and baptised three slaves whilst in Rhode Island. On 7 October 1730, he bought 'Edward aged Twenty Years or thereabouts' for £86. 'Philip aged Fourteen Years or thereabout' cost £80.[75] That three people named Philip, Anthony, and Agnes Berkeley were baptised in Trinity Church, Newport, on 11 June 1731 suggests that there were more purchases of people and/or changes of name.[76] Berkeley was resident in a slaving colony, practised slavery, and may have entertained a project for extending slavery in Europe.

Berkeley was at pains to point out, both in the *Proposal* and in sermons, that baptism and slavery were compatible. 'Gospel Liberty consists with temporal Servitude', the *Proposal* states, and 'slaves would only become better slaves by being Christian'.[77] When preaching in Newport in October 1729, Berkeley argued that

---

72. James, *Colonial Rhode Island*, pp. 162–64.

73. Coughtry, *The Notorious Triangle*, pp. 25, 28, 241.

74. Letter 186, p. 282.

75. BL Add MS 39316, ff. 31r, 32r. Compare the informal transaction with the founder of Newport's historic Redwood Library reported in a letter from Walter Nugent in Antigua to Abraham Redwood, 11 April 1731, in Adams et al., *Commerce of Rhode Island 1726–1800*, I (1914).15–16: 'I send you two Negroes; if you like them keep them and give my Account credit for what you think they are worth. the Negroe man is a Peice of a Saylor and a fine Papa Slave—cost thirty pounds Sterling out of the Ship. the Negroe woman is a fine Slave. I had another which is a better wather, but suspected somthing I entended against her, on which shee's given us the Slip this morning, but hope to have her againe before Pope sailes. note, this woman I now send I bought her from one John Wilson, and paid him forty-five pounds Cash. I now understand his title is not good, and am advised to ship her off. if you like her I will warrant her to you'.

76. Gaustad, *Berkeley in America*, p. 94, citing Mason, *Annals of Trinity Church*, p. 51.

77. *Proposal*, p. 5 (LJ, VII.346).

'Christianity maketh no alteration in civil rights, servants in the new testament signifying slaves, v.g. Onesimus. hence objection [to baptising slaves] from loss of property answered'. (In Philemon 1:10, Saint Paul refers to Onesimus as a son and servant whom 'I have begotten in my bonds'.) And again this idea is accompanied by the suggestion that baptism improves the slave: 'ob: that baptism makes slaves worse. Resp: This proceeds from an infidel mind. contrary shewn. what they charge on Baptism to be charged on their own unchristian life & neglect of instruction'. The SPG sermon of 1732, after noting that contempt for other ethnic groups has led to indifference to their conversion, remarks that '[t]o this may be added, an erroneous Notion, that the being baptized, is inconsistent with a State of Slavery'.[78]

Berkeley's views were consistent with those of Morgan Godwyn, the Church of England minister who had worked in Virginia and Barbados and who, on his return to England, argued for the baptism of enslaved people. Far from being a threat to the social order, Godwyn argued, Christianity obliged its communicants to submission. It was 'diametrically opposite' to rebellion:

> For first, It presseth *absolute* and entire *Obedience* to *Rulers* and *Superiours*[.] [. . .] It establisheth the *Authority of Masters*, over their Servants and Slaves, in as high a measure, as even themselves [slave owners] could have prescribed [. . .] so far is this *Religion* from a tendencie to *Anarchy*, or any *Levelling Tenets* (as being *founded not in a Parity, but a Superiority*, not in a *Domocracy* [*sic*], but in an *Aristocracie*) that a conformity to that *Axiom*, *Æqualitate nihil iniquius*; *Nothing is more dangerous than Equality*; has been her most professed and *constant Practice* from her first appearance *untill this very day*.[79]

Christianity curbed thoughts as well as actions. Godwyn argued that the instructions to love one's neighbour as oneself and that servants obey their masters were perfectly compatible, and that a more lenient treatment of slaves would be more Christian and would also make the institution more sustainable. Godwyn's texts were

78. LJ, VII.69; *Anniversary Sermon*, p. 20 (LJ, VII.122).
79. Godwyn, *The Negroe's and Indian's Advocate*, pp. 128[misnumbered 112]–29, 140, 160.

influential in the establishment of the SPG.[80] He presented baptism of slaves as a means of reinforcing the institution itself and of social hierarchy and subordination more generally. Berkeley's views, as I shall go on to suggest, were comparable.

Berkeley may have taken active steps to persuade the planters out of the view that slavery and baptism were incompatible. 'To undeceive them in this Particular, which had too much Weight, it seemed a proper Step, if the Opinion of his Majesty's Attorney and Sollicitor-General could be procured. This Opinion they charitably sent over, signed with their own Hands; which was accordingly printed in *Rhode-Island*, and dispersed throughout the Plantations'.[81] This opinion came to be known as the Yorke-Talbot opinion, after the two men who were then attorney and solicitor general. It has recently been argued by Travis Glasson that Berkeley's language here, though in the passive voice, refers to actions taken by himself or members of his circle. Berkeley is reporting that he elicited the Yorke-Talbot opinion. The evidence is good: Berkeley noted the support of both men in drafting the patents for the Bermuda scheme; he had close personal connections with the Talbot family that would only become closer once he sent his son to Oxford; and though republished in two English newspapers, the opinion was first printed in the *Boston Gazette* on 7 September 1730. Glasson summarises the significance of the opinion:

> Without citing any authorities or explaining their reasoning, Yorke and Talbot stated that enslaved people could be held in the same condition and treated the same way everywhere in the British Empire, and in this sense their view has been considered as 'profoundly new "imperial" law'. The opinion ignored the long-standing diversity of colonial slavery laws and their possible divergence from English law to uphold the rights of masters everywhere throughout the empire. [. . .] In the interest of promoting the baptism of enslaved people, Berkeley's circle appears to have solicited and publicized a legal opinion that came to operate as a bulwark for slavery around the British Empire.[82]

80. Wood, 'Godwyn [Godwin], Morgan'.
81. *Anniversary Sermon*, p. 20 (LJ, VII.122).
82. Glasson, ' "Baptism Doth Not Bestow Freedom" ', passim, and pp. 283 and 304.

If Glasson is right, the spiritual gain for enslaved people that Berkeley imagined he was procuring came at a very high temporal cost. The effort to reassure planters that baptism was no threat to their 'property' most likely had the effect of reinforcing the institution of slavery.

Slavery is not merely to be left unchallenged in Berkeley's thinking. It is an institution that he writes of in *The Querist* as a social good, perhaps after having seen the enslaved black people and Native Americans of Rhode Island turned into a source of public and private labour. The Querist asks:

214. *Qu.* Whether other Nations have not found great Benefit from the Use of Slaves in repairing High Roads, making Rivers navigable, draining Bogs, erecting public Buildings, Bridges, and Manufactures?

215. *Qu.* Whether temporary Servitude would not be the best Cure for Idleness and Beggary?

216. *Qu.* Whether the Public hath not a Right to employ those who cannot, or who will not, find Imployment for themselves?

217. *Qu.* Whether all sturdy Beggars should not be seized and made Slaves to the Public for a certain Term of Years?

218. *Qu.* Whether he who is chained in a Jail or Dungeon hath not, for the Time, lost his Liberty? And if so, whether temporary Slavery be not already admitted among us?

219. *Qu.* Whether a State of Servitude, wherein he should be well worked, fed and cloathed, would not be a Preferment to such a Fellow?

220. *Qu.* Whether Criminals in the freest Country may not forfeit their Liberty, and repair the Damage they have done the Public by hard Labour?

221. *Qu.* What the Word *Servant* signifies in the *New Testament*?

222. *Qu.* Whether the View of Criminals chained in Pairs, and kept at hard Labour, would not be very edifying to the Multitude?[83]

Slavery could function as a means of improving public infrastructure, as a means of improving the physical and moral economy of

83. *The Querist*, II.23–24, §§214–22.

the enslaved, and as an example to the rest of society.[84] Berkeley's account of slavery here is penal and temporary. But the last query cited here reduces the distance between servitude and slavery, blurring a more common distinction between relationships governed by contract and those governed by conquest.[85] Samuel Pufendorf distinguishes between temporary and perpetual servitude, both of which are voluntary, and slavery, which is only the result of conquest (and also confers rights to masters over the progeny of enslaved people).[86] Locke echoes this distinction between servitude which 'gives the Master but a Temporary Power over him, and no greater, than what is contained in the *Contract* between 'em' and slavery, which is the exclusion from civil society and property rights that is enforced on 'Captives taken in a just War'.[87] The reality of slavery as Berkeley participated in and enforced it was without judicial or moral 'justification', and it was intergenerational. (Several Rhode Island towns compelled the children of slaves and Native Americans to serve long trade apprenticeships or work on occasional civil projects.[88]) It was an institution that commanded an individual's labour but also, in some towns in Narragansett county at least, forbade association with other slaves. And it allowed slave owners, including Berkeley's reputed associate MacSparran, who recorded many such incidents in his diary, to assault, confine, and torture black people for their perceived affronts and transgressions.[89] The

84. See Caffentzis, *Exciting the Industry of Mankind*, p. 143.

85. *Ladies Library*, II.406, excerpting Fleetwood's *Relative Duties of Parents and Children*, hints at limits given to servitude by natural justice: 'A Servant is not to be so consum'd with Toil, as to be made unfit for other or for farther Services; he is not presum'd to consent to such a Bargain, tho' all his Time and Labour still belong to his Master'.

86. Pufendorf, *The Whole Duty of Man* and *Two Discourses and a Commentary*, pp. 184–87.

87. Locke, *Two Treatises of Government*, II.85, p. 323.

88. James, 'Colonial Rhode Island and the Beginnings of the Liberal Rationalized State', p. 150.

89. Fitts, *Inventing New England's Slave Paradise*, pp. 106–8, 110–11. See MacSparran, *A Letter Book and Abstract*, p. 52: 'Thursday, Aug^st 29th. 1751. I got up this morning early, and finding Hannibal had been out [. . .] I stript and gave him a few Lashes till he begged. As Harry was untying him, my poor passionate dear, saying I had not given him eno', gave him a lash or two, upon wch he ran, and Harry after him as far as William Brown's. As y^y were returning he slipt from Harry naked as he was above ye waist. Peter and Harry found [him] toward night at Block Island Henry Gardiner's, bro't him Home, and then carried

incorporation of slavery into the social and moral vision of *The Querist* requires that its violence and injustice as an institution Berkeley knew intimately be hidden in plain sight.

In presenting slavery as conceptually indistinct from servitude, Berkeley becomes an apologist for slavery. In addition to the historical crimes in which this makes him complicit, his apology does not fit well with his moral philosophy. Like many other writers, Berkeley held that only in voluntary actions can there be moral obligations and duties.[90] Human identity lies in knowing that one is the source of one's actions and is therefore responsible for them: 'I know I act, and what I act I am accountable for', as Euphranor puts it.[91] But Berkeley's apology for slavery reduces the responsibility of agents by depriving them of spheres of voluntary action in which they can act, respect their moral obligations, and be accountable, such as with whom they associate. Berkeley and others were denying enslaved people some of their responsibilities. This aspect of the institution of slavery had been noticed by an earlier writer, in a text on the fruits and produce of the West Indies that Berkeley might have consulted in planning for his Bermuda project. An enslaved person, in a dialogue with his master, asks, as part of a series of questions, 'Have we not the same Faculties, Understanding, Memory and Will? Are we not endued with a reflex Power, whereby to condemn or approve our own Actions as they are either good or evil?'[92] The institution of slavery denies the enslaved the opportunity to bring into practice the moral knowledge they have through reflection, thereby reducing the stock of morally responsible decisions humans can take. Slavery, that is, reduces participation of the divinity.

These arguments were deployed later in the century as the abolitionist movement was growing. A group of enslaved people in Boston petitioned for their freedom in 1774, arguing that slavery

---

him to Duglasse's where he had w^t is called Pothooks put about his Neck. So y^t it has been a very uneasy Day with us o y^t God would give my Servants—the Gift of chastity'.

90. *Passive Obedience*, §33; see Astell, *A Serious Proposal to the Ladies*, p. 128, for one example of the view that irrational creatures act according to the will of their maker, but rational creatures act freely and can therefore be held responsible for their actions.

91. *Alciphron*, VII.22.

92. Tryon, *Friendly Advice to the Gentlemen-Planters of the East and West Indies*, p. 116. Tryon was at first an Anabaptist, but broke from that sect to maintain an idiosyncratic religious practice that included vegetarianism; see White, 'Tryon, Thomas'.

prevented them fulfilling their obligations to their families, as set out in scriptural commandments:

> By our deplorable situation we are rendered incapable of showing our obedience to almighty God. How can a slave perform the duties of a husband or a wife or parent to his child? How can a husband leave master and work and cleave to his wife? How can the wife submit themselves to their husbands in all things. How can the child obey their parents in all things?[93]

In a more general sense, Thomas Jefferson, in notes of 1782 that were published in 1785, recognised that the institution of slavery reduces human worth by altering the relative moral position of the enslaved person:

> That a change in the relations in which a man is placed should change his ideas of moral right and wrong, is neither new, nor peculiar to the colour of the blacks. Homer tells us it was so 2,600 years ago.
>
> > Jove fix'd it certain that whatever day
> > Makes man a slave, takes half his worth away.[94]

Slavery makes people less than fully morally responsible; it forces them to participate less in the divinity. Both practically and discursively, Berkeley placed enslaved people beyond the sphere of persuasion and in the sphere of compulsion, removing any need to enter into the ways of thinking of that class of people for the purpose of talking them into better action.

How, then, could Berkeley have thought slavery as it was practised and as he practised it compatible with Christianity?[95] The question had, after all, been posed. Quakers, one of the sects Berkeley identifies as being strongly represented in Rhode Island, and the only group he reports offending, had raised the issue in the previous decades. Brycchan Carey reports that

> John Farmer, a Quaker from Nantucket Island, Massachusetts, took the slavery question to the Meeting of Newport, Rhode Island, in 1717.

---

93. Cited in Thorn, 'Phillis Wheatley's Ghosts', p. 75.

94. Jefferson, *Notes on the State of Virginia*, p. 142.

95. Airaksinen and Gylling, 'A Threat Like No Other Threat', p. 603, note Berkeley's insensitivity to the problem of slavery.

Since Rhode Island was at the center of the American slave trade, it is perhaps no surprise that he was censured and his pamphlet prevented from being published. Nevertheless, no doubt in part due to his influence, the New England Yearly Meeting did register in that year "A Weighty concern being on this meeting concerning the Importing and keeping Slaves," and asked that "Merchants do write their Correspondents in the Islands and elsewhere to discourage their sending any more in order to be sold by any friends here."

In 1727, the annual meeting of the Friends in London sent a handwritten note to the Rhode Island community on the topic of slavery, and in 1733 Elihu Coleman, having presented a discourse to the Newport meeting, published *A Testimony Against that Antichristian Practice of Making Slaves of Men*, 'the first officially sanctioned antislavery text in the Quaker tradition'.[96] Berkeley's writing in *The Querist*, and his practice as a slave owner, must be taken as direct antagonism to the various forms of uneasiness with and opposition to slavery that were becoming available discursive and practical positions even before his arrival in America, and which were developing in the town he inhabited, at the time he inhabited it, amongst a religious group with which he had extended and significant contact. Berkeley is far closer to the missionaries of a few years later in colonial Georgia who, as Philipa Koch puts it, 'used religion—meaning particularly the hope of slave conversion and future salvation—to "rationalize" the brutality of an institution that they made little real effort to reform or change'. He may, if his writing on the self-evident value of social order in *Passive Obedience* is recalled, be like the Halle Pietists of Georgia, who 'insisted that God worked through temporal authorities and had a plan for slavery that would, eventually, become clear in retrospect'.[97] Importing and enslaving 10 percent of the population of a town is acceptable as a partial evil that produces greater social goods—through enforced industry or simple submission to temporal authority. It is a sign of the extremity of the doctrine of *Passive Obedience*, and of Berkeley's reverence for subordination more generally, that it is so largely compatible with

96. Carey, *From Peace to Freedom*, pp. 142, 146, 163.
97. Koch, 'Slavery, Mission, and the Perils of Providence', pp. 381–82.

Berkeley's slave-owning and his protection and prolongation of the institution of slavery.

No one knows what happened to the people Berkeley bought— Agnes, Edward or Anthony, and Philip. They may have been taken to England and Ireland with the Berkeleys. One reason for thinking so is the set of reading cards for children held in the Elisabeth Ball collection of children's material in the University of Indiana's Lilly Library in Bloomington, exhibited in the Fitzwilliam Museum, Cambridge, in 1995 and remarked upon by Patrick Kelly.[98] The cards name Patrick Norway as Berkeley's servant and Enoch Martyr as his footman at Cloyne. Kelly asks if these people could have been slaves brought back from Rhode Island. That does not seem impossible. An article in the *Freeman's Journal* of 23–25 October 1777 chastises a crowd for gathering and inconveniencing a black mother and child on St Stephen's Green in Dublin, not least because the sight of black people was too common to warrant such attention. A survey of Irish newspapers in the second half of the century notes that black people in Ireland were mostly in domestic service, that slavery shaded into indenture and servitude, and that there was little sign of racial prejudice towards black people. One can imagine that Berkeley and his family of music enthusiasts at Cloyne would have noticed the debut of Rachel Baptist, a black singer, in Dublin in 1750—the start of her twenty-year performing career.[99] Maybe an unremarked and unremarkable life, if it has to be led after two deportations—one of great violence, the other perhaps of less—is no bad thing, and the unremarked existence of Agnes, Edward or Anthony, and Philip is the sign of a less oppressed life than that led by MacSparran's man Hannibal and other brutalised enslaved people. But the fate of Berkeley's slaves is another silence, another omission in his writing about kinds of people other than white Christians. Such silences are disconcerting as one attempts to reconstruct the social, moral, and spiritual motives of Berkeley the tourist, colonist, and bishop.

98. Kelly, 'Berkeley's Servants'.
99. Hart, 'Africans in Eighteenth-Century Ireland', pp. 19, 26–27, 30.

The amount of coercion required by projects for conversion will be considered again in chapters on Berkeley's time in Cloyne. His career as a whole shows relatively little direct engagement with human diversity. Berkeley was relatively incurious about the differences between kinds of human life. He had a greater interest in defending the Anglican colonial project from attacks built upon the diversity of human cultural and religious practice. His tendency not to see human diversity was likely in a relationship of circular reinforcement with his defence of Anglican religious privileges.

CHAPTER EIGHT

London and Italy Again

THERE IS A GAP in Berkeley's correspondence between July 1714 and July 1715 as he travels from Brussels through Flanders and Holland on his way back to London after his first visit to Italy. When the thread of Berkeley's correspondence with Percival picks up in July 1715, the Jacobite rebellion excludes almost every other subject.

The Rebellion

Political instability had gradually become, in different parts of Great Britain and Ireland at different times, open rebellion, and eventually, in Scotland, a military conflict lasting from September 1715 to April 1716.[1] The subject highlights the political differences between Percival and Berkeley that have already been identified. Writing of the riots engaged in by both dissenters and Tories/Jacobites, Berkeley notes that, 'to do the Tories justice (with whom I principally converse here) they express an honest detestation of these proceedings, as I hope I need not tell you I do myself'.[2] Percival chides Berkeley somewhat for the colour of his Toryism, and for entertaining the idea that the Whigs have strategically fomented the riots. He blames the clergy for not preaching strongly enough against rebellion and senior Tories for equivocating about

---

1. Szechi, *1715: The Great Jacobite Rebellion*, p. 104.
2. Letter 70, 28 July 1715, pp. 121–22, p. 122.

the possible return of the pretender, the next in line in the Stuart dynasty, who would have been James III. He draws agreement from Berkeley on the duty of the clergy: 'I think it my duty to disclaim perjury and rebellion on all occasions'. Berkeley becomes more worried about the imminence of a plot, noting the 'general bent of the people towards Jacobitism', and suspecting Tories of 'as barefaced perjury and dishonesty as ever could be imputed to any set of men'. The worst thing about the plotters, says Berkeley, 'is the great dishonour they have done to the Church and religion by public perjury and rebellion'.[3] Though Berkeley is chidden for his Toryism, and for not doing enough to denounce the plot, he is, at least in writing to Percival, openly opposed to Jacobitism on the grounds of the absolute moral obligation to observe negative duties (such as not rebelling) he argued for in *Passive Obedience*. Perjury and rebellion are great moral crimes.

These are themes Berkeley picks up in the anonymously published pamphlet *Advice to the Tories Who Have Taken the Oaths*. Failure to keep an oath would lead to a diminished perception of both the truth and the usefulness of Christianity, especially from the Tories, who had declared themselves to be the great supporters of the Church's privileges:

> [T]he publick and avowed Breach of your Oaths would prove the greatest Injury to the Church, inasmuch as it would be destructive of all Religion. [. . .] Common mutual Faith is the great Support of Society; and an Oath, as it is the highest Obligation to keep our Faith inviolate, becomes the great Instrument of Justice and Intercourse between Men. Whatever, therefore, lessens the Sacredness or Authority of an Oath must be acknowledged at the same time to be highly detrimental both to the Church and the Commonwealth.[4]

3. Letter 71, Percival to Berkeley, 2 August 1715, pp. 122–24; letter 72, Berkeley to Percival, 9 August 1715, p. 126; letter 73, Berkeley to Percival, 18 August 1715, p. 128; letter 75, Berkeley to Percival 22 September 1715, p. 131; letter 76, Berkeley to Percival, 26 September 1715, p. 133.

4. *Advice to the Tories*, pp. 8–9 (LJ, VI.54). Whilst other social theorists note the role of oaths in maintaining contracts, as, for example, Pufendorf, *The Whole Duty of Man* and *Two Discourses and a Commentary*, pp. 123–25, Berkeley's connection of oaths, common faith, public religion, and social compact is distinctive.

Berkeley explicitly distinguishes between the Glorious Revolution and the current rebellion in this pamphlet, something he had failed to do in *Passive Obedience*, and which made it easier to see that earlier text as an equivocation in favour of the Stuarts. One swears allegiance to a sovereign, not a person: 'When therefore the Person ceaseth to be Sovereign, the Allegiance ceaseth to be due to him, and the Oath of course to bind. In the Judgment of most Men this was the Case at the Revolution. But nothing like this can be pretended now'.[5] At the time of a later controversy over Berkeley's loyalty and promotion in the church, Percival would demonstrate his knowledge that this text was by Berkeley and note that only a person with good intentions towards the government would publish such a pamphlet: it was unequivocally a loyalist text that cleared Berkeley, as far as Percival was concerned, of the charge of being 'disaffected'.[6]

The rebellion had a significant impact on university politics in both Ireland and England. Berkeley was worried that TCD was being severely punished for some of its students' support for the Stuarts. The provost and fellows had received a letter from George I on 13 June 1715 suspending the election of fellows until further notice, as a result of 'Tumults & Disputes' in the college. Berkeley had heard that Oxford and Cambridge were worried about similar interference in the terms of their charters as retribution for the behaviour of their students.[7] The college response was the submission of a petition, on 12 July 1715, asking permission to elect fellows and scholars, the normal examinations having taken place with no disruption of studies, as a greater number of candidates for the fellowship than usual demonstrated.[8]

In order to quell the allegation of disloyalty to the nascent Hanoverian regime, the provost and fellows of TCD took the decision to elect the prince of Wales the chancellor of the college.[9]

---

5. *Advice to the Tories*, p. 14 (LJ, VI.57).

6. *Berkeley and Percival*, pp. 283, 286, journal entries for 14 and 15 March 1731/32.

7. Letter 68, 6 July 1715, pp. 119–20; see also chapter 4, for more on the Jacobitish tendencies of students at TCD.

8. TCD MUN V/5/2, minute book 1640–1740, f. 235r (p. 467), f. 235v (p. 468).

9. TCD MUN V/5/2, minute book 1640–1740, f. 237v (p. 472). In the meantime, Berkeley had been granted a further two-year period of absence, 19 November 1715, f. 236v (p. 470), signed by James Stanhope, and with no specific reason given for the absence.

Berkeley cannot have been taken by his colleagues and superiors at TCD as dangerously associated with the Jacobite cause, because he formed part of the delegation to ask this royal favour, as the *London Gazette* reported:

> St James's, April 11. The University of Dublin having on the 16th Day of February last past unanimously elected His Royal Highness the Prince of Wales to be Chancellor of the said University, did on the same Day nominate and appoint the Reverend Dr. Benjamin Pratt, Provost of Trinity-College in Dublin, and the Reverend Dr. Robert Howard, Fellow of the same College, to wait on His Royal Highness in London, in order to present to Him the Diploma of Election, and also to admit His Royal Highness into the due and full Possession of that Office. Accordingly the said Deputies from the University being arrived in London, with the Reverend Mr. George Berkeley, also a Fellow of the same College, did Yesterday attend in their Habits at St. James's, together with all the Persons of Quality and Distinction of Ireland, at this time in London.

The archbishop of Canterbury and then the provost spoke, emphasising the dutiful and loyal nature of the choice of chancellor whose '*undoubted Title is most justly founded*'. Then

> [t]he Provost and Fellows, and other Members of the said University present, had the Honour to kiss his Royal Highness's Hand, and then withdrew: They did afterwards attend on her Highness the Princess, who received them very graciously[.][10]

Stock reports that Molyneux had to dispel rumours that *Passive Obedience* was a Jacobite text at the time of this meeting, but those rumours clearly did not prevent it taking place.[11] Berkeley himself related to Percival that the prince of Wales had recommended him for the living of St Paul's in Dublin.[12] The election of the prince of Wales seems to have been successful for the fellowship of TCD, as on 28 April the lords justices wrote to the college to permit them to proceed with fellowship elections.[13]

10. *London Gazette*, 5425, Saturday, 14 April, to Tuesday, 17 April 1716, pp. 1–2.
11. Stock, *An Account of the Life of George Berkeley*, p. 4.
12. Letter 80, May 1716, p. 137.
13. TCD MUN V/5/2, minute book 1640–1740, f. 238r (p. 473).

Being admitted to the prince of Wales's presence and privately and publicly condemning the rebellion were not, however, enough to prevent Berkeley from paying for his supposed disaffection. His path to the job at St Paul's was blocked. He wrote to Percival on 26 May 1716 to

> beg the favour of you to write a letter next post to the Duke of Grafton, imparting your acquaintance with me, and your confidence of my being well affected to his Majesty's government. Were it necessary I might produce several instances of this, as well as from my endeavours to serve the present establishment by writing, which are more than I care to mention, as from the offer I refused in the times of the late ministry. I make you this request because I believe I have some reason to think my competitors have wronged my character on the other side of the water. [...] I cannot but be solicitous to have my character cleared to the Lords Justices and others there, who are probably misled by the calumny of interested persons who are strangers to me.[14]

Berkeley's suspicions were correct, as David Berman has shown.[15] Duke Tyrrell, who received the living, wrote to Robert Molesworth on 14 May saying that John Forster, the MP and lawyer (and, as it happens, the father of Anne, who was later to become Berkeley's wife) had 'Labourd to fix me in this City because he as well as the Lords justices judge it to be very much for his majestys service to have the parishes in this City filled with Clergymen who have always appeard, nay suffered in the cause of the Hannover succession & the Libertys of their country'. He was writing to Molesworth because

> a patron of publick liberty, who has defended it so learnedly & successfull with his pen will I am persuaded obstruct the promotion of a person who has appeared publickly nay printed a book in defence of the slavish doctrine of passive obedience & carryed it to as great a height as any that went before him. this treatise came out at a time when a dangerous attacque was made not only on the libertys of the kingdom in general but of this City in particular by the Late Ministry

---

14. Letter 81, p. 138. I am not sure what offer Berkeley refused in the time of the late ministry.

15. Berman, *George Berkeley*, pp. 83–85.

for which piece of service he has been ever since highly esteemd by all the Jacobites in this kingdom. the book may be bought in London but in case you have not seen it & cannot meet with it there I shall send you one whenever you will please to command me. he travelled with the Lord Peterburrow in the late times has been & is still a creature of Dean Swift & is reckond here as much in the Tory interest as the highest church man of them all. his preferment will be very unpopular, create much uneasiness & give a general discontent. he has been absent from his duty & business for several years & continued in the measures & esteem of the late ministry as long as they continued in power. if such men by fishing for preferments in London & by neglecting their business here may be able to lay aside those who have been preaching, writing & speaking for the Hannover Succession when it was dangerous to appear in defence of that cause, who have made a sacrifice of their ease of their interest of their character & would of their lives too had things gone in the same channel much longer [. . .]

then things were in a bad way. Berkeley's appointment, Tyrell suggests, would be a betrayal of the loyal Protestants who defended the Hanoverian succession through the populist Tory high points of the Sacheverell trial and after. Tyrell imagines that Molesworth's 'representation of Mr. Barklys character as a tory will have influence enough with the prince' to have the recommendation withdrawn.

The same letter shows how church-state relations and the politics of the various forms of Protestantism contributed to the competition for places. Tyrell wonders whether

perhaps I suffer by being thought too low a Churchman even by some who would willingly pass under that character themselves. I have always declared my self against the independency of the church on the civil powers, I never was for making the clergy a different corporation from the Layety nor for erecting church grandeur on the ruins of publick liberty and the common interests of mankind. I thought that every man ought to judge for himself in matters of religion & that no synods of Ecclesiasticks have any authority to make creeds or articles of faith for their brethren. It has been my constant perswasion that every thing necessary to salvation is plainly reveald in the bible & that every honest man can make as good a collection for himself of articles necessary to be believed out of his bible as any made for him by general councils. I never was ∧ ᶠᵒʳ a sanction on any account nor for making the sacrament which is a token or symbol of our common Christianity the test of a particular church or party.[16]

Tyrell, that is, explicitly identifies himself with those rational low-church attitudes Berkeley had presented as freethinking: the Anglican church has no privilege to regulate forms of worship, nor to politicise communion through the imposition of the Sacramental Test; all that Christianity requires can be deduced by reason from the scripture; and to grant the established Church a legal privilege and quasi-magisterial authority is a threat to public and private liberty. The letter has been described as offering 'a systematic rejection of the entire high church position'.[17] Tyrell made this case to Molesworth, who was an acquaintance of Shaftesbury and would later patronise Francis Hutcheson.[18] It is an appeal to a philosophically, politically, and theologically like-minded patron to block a Tory churchman.

It is perhaps odd, then, that on his return from Genoa to Paris in the Peterborough mission, which Tyrrell took as evidence of Jacobite associations, Berkeley had travelled with 'Mr. Molesworth the late envoy at Florence, and the Colonel his brother', Robert Molesworth's sons.[19] Berkeley would associate closely with the Molesworths in the 1720s, discussing architectural and other matters.[20] It was not, however, necessary that Berkeley be seriously suspected of real support for the restoration of the Stuarts by political or military means for Tyrell to point to Berkeley's activities and associations in such a way as to block his appointment. Indeed, the extent to which even high Tory contact with the Stuarts overseas may be understood as an indication of serious intention to restore the Stuarts has been doubted.[21] The accusation of Toryism worked as a means to manoeuvre Berkeley out of a position of favour; it is one means by which a group of more Whiggish Dublin churchmen and politicians could isolate him, without having really to believe him

16. State Papers Online, SP 63/374, f. 187.
17. Connolly, 'Reformers and Highflyers', p. 161.
18. See Hayton, 'Molesworth, Robert'.
19. Letter 67, Berkeley to Percival, 13 July 1714, p. 119.
20. Chaney, *The Evolution of the Grand Tour*, p. 331.
21. Szechi, *Jacobitism and Tory Politics*, p. 191.

to be a committed Jacobite. Nonetheless, one sees that participants on both sides of the debate about the appropriate political and social privileges of the established Church suggested that the social order was at stake.

This was Berkeley's first known candidature for a post in the Church. The paths taken to a career in the Church of Ireland in the early eighteenth century were various, as were clergymen's attitudes and strategies for pursuing preferment. In an environment where, in the Anglican church more broadly, there were more clergymen than posts and a bishop might refuse to ordain qualified candidates because of the unlikelihood of them achieving employment, it is unsurprising that people developed strategies for preferment.[22] Berkeley's pursuit of preferment throughout his life might be compared to choices made by significant near-contemporaries. Jonathan Swift managed his entrance into the church in an idiosyncratic fashion. Working as secretary to William Temple in the 1690s, thereby engaging closely with his writing and gaining an apprenticeship in the book trade, he extracted the promise of a small sinecure. Swift declined it to seek preferment in the Church, which began, inauspiciously, in 1694 with the embattled parish of Kilroot and soon led to a return to Temple at Moor Park in 1696.[23] William King, on the other hand, was ordained and then promoted by John Parker, bishop of Tuam, who brought King with him to Dublin when he was advanced to that see. King attained positions in the city into the late 1680s and was well placed, following the upheaval of the War of the Two Kings, to be rewarded for his commitment to the Church of Ireland and providential and political justification of William and Mary's regime. In 1692, he was made bishop of Derry. The publication of his treatise *De Origine Mali/ On the Origin of Evil* in 1702 was, in addition to its religious and philosophical merits, a further argument for his preferment, and he became archbishop of Dublin in 1703.[24] Francis Hutchinson,

22. See Gibson, '"Unreasonable and Unbecoming"', p. 44; Connolly, 'King, William', notes that King refused to ordain those who were unlikely to be employed.

23. Ehrenpreis, *Swift*, pp. 91–93, 147, 169; Treadwell, 'Swift's Relations with the London Book Trade to 1714', pp. 6–7.

24. Richardson, 'Archbishop William King (1650–1729)', p. 55; O'Regan, *Archbishop William King of Dublin*, p. 131.

whom King refused to consecrate as bishop of Down when he was promoted to that post in 1720, had sought out patrons to influence Whig statesmen in his favour, and he wrote to the archbishop of Canterbury recommending himself for a bishopric on account of his seniority and Whig loyalty.[25] Berkeley shared some strategies with these colleagues, such as using his connections with Molyneux, Percival, and others to gain patronage, preaching and writing with a view to being recognised for social and religious loyalty and commitment, and writing or having others write on their behalf to assure them of loyalty. He also, particularly later in life, made career decisions that might seem idiosyncratic: refusing a more rewarding bishopric and proposing to resign his bishopric for a canonry. But throughout Berkeley's career it would be his alleged political disloyalty to the Hanoverian settlement and his questionable personal choices in being absent from his university or church commitments that would most often be mentioned by others in the context of his pursuit of preferment.

Italy

It was from Turin that Berkeley next wrote to Percival, this time on a tour with St George Ashe Jr, to whom he was acting as tutor. He had crossed the Alps at Mount Cenis in winter for a second time. He and the young man planned to travel on to 'Milan, Parma, Modena, Bologna, Florence, Siena, Rome etc'.[26] The extensions of his permission to be absent from his fellowship granted by the secretaries of state on 17 August 1717 (Joseph Addison) and 6 May 1719 (Joseph Craggs) gave 'the establishment of his health and his improvement in learning' as his grounds.[27] This was to be 'the most extensive English tour [of Italy] of this period'—or it would have been if the tourists had been English rather than Irish.[28] The organisation of this long tour met the criteria that Bruce Redford lays out for qualification as 'grand tourism': 'first, a young British patrician (that is, a member of the aristocracy or gentry); second, a

25. Sneddon, *Witchcraft and Whigs*, pp. 132–35.
26. Letter 82, 24 November 1716, pp. 139–40.
27. TCD MUN V/5/2, minute book 1640–1740, ff. 244v (p. 486) and 251r (p. 499).
28. Ingamells, *A Dictionary of British and Irish Travellers in Italy*, p. 81.

tutor who accompanies his charge throughout the journey; third, a fixed itinerary that makes Rome its principal destination; fourth, a lengthy period of absence, averaging two or three years'.[29]

Some volumes of Berkeley's journals of this tour survive. From them, his letters, and other sources the following itinerary can be derived: he was in Rome in January 1717 and either returned or was still there on 1 March, when he wrote to Percival.[30] He arrived (with St George Ashe Jr, Compton Domville, and Tyrwhitt) in Naples in the week of 19 March, whence on 6 April he wrote to Percival.[31] On 7 June, he 'returned from a voyage through Apulia', which he called on 18 June 'a tour through the most remote and unknown parts of Italy'. That tour is recorded in two manuscript volumes.[32] On 1 September, he wrote to Percival from Inarime (Ischia), having been unwell. He said that he had been there three months but must have been approximating. On 22 October, he wrote to Alexander Pope from Naples, and on 25 February 1718 he wrote to Tomasso Campailla from Messina, indicating that he had already travelled to Sicily and met this poet and philosopher there.[33] Another manuscript volume in part records the stages of a journey from Naples to Rome, 11–13 April 1718; Berkeley wrote to Percival from Rome on 26 April.[34] The only evidence of Berkeley's location at any point in 1719 is his signature in the visitors' book of Padua University on 15 January, leading one scholar to speculate that he spent the calendar year in the Veneto.[35] In 1720, Berkeley was back in Tuscany, writing to Percival from Florence 9–20 July. It is not certain

---

29. Sweet, *Cities and the Grand Tour*, p. 2n3, citing Redford, *Venice and the Grand Tour*, p. 14.

30. Account in BL MS Add 39307; LJ, VII.231; letter 84, p. 142.

31. State Papers Online, SP 93/32, f. 40v, Consul Fleetwood to P. Methuen, Principal Secretary of State, from Naples, 19 March 1717: 'Just now I have the honour of y.ʳˢ of the 10.ᵗʰ Oct. last past deliver'd me by M.ʳ Ashe son to the Bishop of Clogher who arrived here this week in pretty good health. I shall in obedience to yr Commands do all that lies in my power for him here & hope he will find Naples not only agreable but likewise beneficial to his health w.ᶜʰ seems to be but tender. with him are come Mess.ʳˢ Berkley, Terret & Dumvill'. Letter 85, p. 143.

32. Letter 89, Berkeley to Arbuthnot, October 1717, p. 150; letter 86, Berkeley to Percival, p. 145; LJ, VII.231; BL Add MSS 39308–39309.

33. Letter 88, p. 147; letter 90, pp. 153–54; letter 91, pp. 155–56.

34. BL Add MS 39310; LJ, VII.231; letter 93, pp. 157–58.

35. Chaney, *The Evolution of the Grand Tour*, pp. 322–23, 371.

when Berkeley returned to London, but Secretary Carteret's grant to Berkeley on 6 May 1721 of a further licence 'to continue here for two years longer upon account of some business which requires his attendance', 'here' must have referred to London. He returned to Ireland in September 1721.[36]

The activities Berkeley engaged in and the records he kept over this period of four years reflect his earlier scholarly and scientific interests in natural history and the relationship between landscape and classical literary texts. They also indicate a range of personal and social concerns that figure prominently in his work of the 1720s onwards: a consideration of the visual arts and their place in social life; an interest in systems of government and justice; and agriculture and local economy. The journals and other materials relating to the tour show Berkeley's interests coming together in the study of city- or nation-states with sophisticated legal codes evolving over time in tandem with the built environment and requiring responsible behaviour from a civic elite with respect to public health and prosperity. Before returning to these civic themes, I discuss some of the more evidently touristic aspects of Berkeley's time in Italy.

Addison's *Remarks on Several Parts of Italy* is the text habitually referred to when indicating the tendency of British tourists in Italy to access their environment, both natural and built, through classical literature: 'a Man who is in *Rome* can scarce see an Object that does not call to Mind a Piece of a *Latin* Poet or Historian', Addison says.[37] Berkeley, who was acquainted with Addison, was a tourist in this mode. He mediated his encounter with Brundusium/Brindisi, for example, through Caesar's *Civil Wars*, Lucan, and Strabo, from whom he took a description of 'the town & ports as a stags head & antlers'.[38] The journals suggest little to no separation between the disciplines of natural history and classical literature: Berkeley's description of Vesuvius is interlaced with quotations from Valerius

36. Letter 96, pp. 161–63; TCD MUN V-5-2, f. 256v. (p. 510); letter 98, Berkeley to Percival, 12 October 1721, p. 164.

37. Addison, *Remarks on Several Parts of Italy*, p. 231. See also Sweet, *Cities and the Grand Tour*, p. 5, who describes classical nostalgia as the dominant mode of published and unpublished writing on Italy: 'It reflected the civic humanist education and the dominance of the classical ideal amongst the social elite who comprised the majority of travellers'.

38. LJ, VII.281, 26 May 1717.

Flaccus's *Argonautica*, Statius's *Sylvae*, Aulus Gellius, Diodorus Siculus, Pliny, and Strabo.[39] The standard edition of the journals omits some of Berkeley's transcriptions and comments, such as a long citation from Aulus Gellius's *Attic Nights*. Luce notes that Berkeley quotes from XVII.10, and he prints Berkeley's 'N:B: Virgil's description of Aetna justified by wt I saw of Vesuvius'. The depth of detail in which Berkeley is engaging with classical authors is demonstrated in the full manuscript account. The passage from Gellius in question relates a judgement by the philosopher Favorinus preferring Pindar's description of a volcano erupting to Virgil's description of Aetna. Virgil comes up short because he suggests that black smoke can be seen at the same time as glowing ash (*favilla* in Latin), and because he elaborates incomprehensibly on his Greek model to suggest that matter extruded from the volcano licks the stars.[40] Berkeley defends the poetic description of Aetna on the basis of his experience of Vesuvius: 'he [Gellius/Favorinus] blames Virgil also for mixing smoke & favilla together (w.ch is fact nevertheless) and for licking the stars w.ch appearing to be so justifies the poet, whose description is as just & natural as it is noble'.[41] Close observation of the phenomena is used to defend the poet's metaphor and his use of seemingly incompatible elements in his description. Berkeley's observation of the scene incorporates the history of earlier observation and judgements of the aptness of (poetic) language to observable phenomena.

The defence of Virgil occurs in the course of a critical report on Giovanni Borelli, probably on his text *Historia et meteorologia incendii Ætnæi anni 1669*, in which Berkeley proposes that the activity of volcanoes is effected by a system of deep caverns and passages supplying the volcano with seawater.[42] Berkeley took an interest in volcanology. He reported his observations on Vesuvius, its height and circumference, the appearance of the activity in the crater, the height achieved by projectiles from the crater, the sounds and smells accompanying volcanic activity, and the behaviour of a stream of lava in letters to John Arbuthnot and printed in

39. LJ, VII.326–27.
40. Gellius, *The Attic Nights of Aulus Gellius*, III.247.
41. BL Add MS 39310, f. 55v.
42. LJ, VII.326.

the *Philosophical Transactions of the Royal Society of London*. The letters are more an exercise in vivid description than in scientific analysis:

> You cannot form a juster idea of this noise in the most violent fits of it, than by imagining a mixed sound made up of the raging of a tempest, the murmur of a troubled sea, and the roaring of thunder and artillery, confused all together. [. . .] Imagine a vast torrent of liquid fire rolling from the top down the side of the mountain, and with irresistible fury bearing down and consuming vines, olives, fig-trees, houses; in a word, every thing that stood in its way.

There is only one point in the letters at which Berkeley, in abbreviated form, controverts Borelli: 'I saw the fluid matter rise out of the centre of the bottom of the crater, out of the very middle of the mountain, contrary to what Borellus imagines, whose method of explaining the eruption of a volcano by an inflexed syphon and the rules of hydrostaticks, is likewise inconsistent with the torrent's flowing down from the very vertex of the mountain'.[43] He is otherwise focused on the duty of the natural historian on tour to report with exacting vivacity the impressions made by the phenomena. As we have seen, that exactitude does not exclude a study of the history of observation and its language.

An equally daunting challenge for the observer and describer of phenomena was to be found in the ancient and modern artistic heritage of Italy, and Rome in particular, but by no means exclusively. Berkeley did not behave like Leibniz in Rome, focusing on a scholarly mission and refusing the diversions of the visual environment.[44] He was evidently stimulated by the visual environment, and in a way that influenced his future activities. He educated his taste in the fine and the useful arts and reflected on their connection to the broader social life of a people at different historical moments. It is likely that Berkeley always had some attraction to and facility in design and drawing. We have already seen that in

43. Letter 89, October 1717, pp. 151–52.

44. Robinet, *G. W. Leibniz Iter Italicum*, p. 2: 'en fait de tourisme, Leibniz n'a rien vu'. Leibniz's voyage had a purpose different from Berkeley's: historical research into the connection between the houses of Brunswick and d'Este (p. 5). My thanks to Richard Checketts for referring me to this source.

FIGURE 8.1. John Smibert, *George Berkeley*, 1720,
courtesy of Sean Berkeley

1709 he joked about the prize status of one of his drawings.[45] But this second Italian tour greatly heightened his involvement in the visual arts. He met John Smibert, the portraitist, and later a colleague on the Bermuda project, in Rome in 1720.[46] A portrait of Berkeley by Smibert dates from this moment.

On his return to London, Berkeley was introduced by Pope to Lord Burlington, 'who conceived a high esteem for him on account of his great taste and skill in architecture, an art of which his Lordship was an excellent judge and patron, and which Mr. Berkeley

45. Letter 7, Berkeley to Samuel Molyneux, 26 November 1709, p. 26.
46. Saunders, *John Smibert*, p. 27.

had made his particular study while in Italy'.[47] He was enlisted by Con[n]olly, the speaker of the Irish parliament, to contribute to the design of his great house, Castletown: 'The plan is chiefly of Mr. Connolly's invention, however, in some points they are pleased to consult me. I hope it will be an ornament to the country'.[48] Allesandro Galilei, an architect who travelled from Italy to England and then to Ireland, with John Molesworth, was the chief architect of the house.[49] The house has been understood as a demonstration of economic or colonial patriotism: the choice to build in Ireland, rather than England, using local materials, was a means to stimulate the local economy and counteract the credit crisis, a less oppositional form of economic patriotism than Swift's.[50] The visit to Italy was part of Berkeley's legitimation as a critic and practitioner of the arts. It was also a period that informed his later writing on artworks as a kind of commodity and the possible role of their possession and circulation in the production of human goods such as health and higher or more extensive views.

The lodging of Berkeley's party in Rome was between the Piazza d'Espagna and the Monte Pincio, perhaps in one of the areas to the north or south of the Spanish Steps. Berkeley spent time appreciating this and other views of Rome, particularly that from San Pietro in Montorio in Trastevere, which was said to present Rome 'to the greatest advantage, the Façades of the houses meeting the eye as they fall down the seven hills towards the Tiber on the adverse side. This prospect is truly noble and I believe the noblest of any city in the world'. His party took in the specific architectural and artistic features of each of the locations they visited. Berkeley noted the 'small round Chapel of the Doric order' at San Pietro (that is, the Tempietto by Bramante of c. 1502) and Raphael's *Transfiguration of Christ*, which was then hanging in the church. (Commissioned 1517 and displayed 1520, it is now in the Vatican Museum.)[51] Peregrinations around Rome, with eyes wide open, provided a means of locating and imaginatively entering into the history of the classical

47. Stock, *An Account of the Life of George Berkeley*, p. 12.
48. Letter 110, Berkeley to Percival, 29 July 1722, p. 177.
49. Chaney, *The Evolution of the Grand Tour*, p. 331.
50. Walsh, *The Making of the Irish Protestant Ascendancy*, pp. 184–87, 197.
51. LJ, VII.249–50, 254; see also LJ, VII.265.

world and an opportunity to evaluate and appreciate its material legacy and compare it to current and recent work in the fine arts.[52]

The journals record many of Berkeley's aesthetic responses. He finds ancient sculpture, for example, remarkably lifelike. Of works at the Palazzo Farnese, Berkeley remarks, 'The easiness, the strength the beauty and the muscles of the Hercules cannot be too much admired [. . .] the Bust of Antoninus Caracalla is flesh & blood'. The Barberini Palace contained ancient statues of 'a country-man asleep' ('Nothing can be more soft & natural') and 'a slave eating the hand of a man, in which extream hunger is expressed with great art. Upon the stair-case there is the noblest antique Lion in stone that I have any where seen'. But statues of Brutus and Diogenes, which 'shew the ancients had indifferent statuarys as well as the moderns', were disappointing. Berkeley remarks on the excellent antique statuary at the Villa Borghese, but also on 'three statues of Bernini in these apartments, that raise my idea of that modern statuary almost to an equality with the famous ancients Apollo & Daphne. Æneas with Anchises on his shoulders. David going to fling the stone at Goliah. The grace, the softness, and expression of these statues is admirable'. Back at the Barberini Palace, Berkeley saw a Diana and an Adonis by Mazzuoli, 'a statuary now alive in Rome [. . .] both very fine and I think equal to Bernini'. A second visit to St Peter's, however, made after greater exposure to Roman sculpture, enabled him to say that the modern work was not as great as the ancient: 'They have sometimes a fine expression in the face. But on a near inspection you perceive nothing so finished, none of those delicate contours, those softnesses, that life and breath that you discover in the fine Antiques'.[53] Producing softness and animation from the hard, inanimate stone was the great skill of the statuary, and one in which there were modern contenders.

In painting, too, Berkeley sees connections between the ancient and modern. At the Barberini Palace, he notes an 'an incomparable Madeleine of Guido Reni, reckoned the best piece that ever he did'. He also sees ancient frescoes at the palace, particularly noting one

52. Sweet, *Cities and the Grand Tour*, p. 111: 'The antiquities of Rome were valued for the imaginative associations to which they gave rise (and the consequent opportunity they offered to display one's erudition) and as objects of aesthetic beauty'.

53. LJ, VII.249, 255, 240, 255, 251.

of 'Venus and two cupids incomparably fresh and beautiful. It hath some resemblance to the manner of Guido Reni'. He admired these artworks in large part for their exhibition of the passionate and soft human qualities, rather than the rational and the resistant. In his immediate reactions to art objects, Berkeley made no effort to exclude feminised characteristics. Whilst his responses to art may ultimately have aimed at 'the inculcation of virtue and the promotion of the public good', this was not done, as Rosemary Sweet also suggests, in entirely masculine terms: qualities perceived as feminine were admitted as objects of artistic admiration, even if they were not explicitly identified as prompts to virtue.[54]

It is likely that, in addition to following the itineraries available in earlier travel literature, Berkeley's party followed the practice of hiring a *cicerone*, or antiquarian, to guide them around Rome, and that many of the details Berkeley relates were provided to him by the *cicerone*.[55] He visited St John Lateran twice, regarding it as 'the noblest in Rome [. . .] for the inside'. On the second visit, he was struck by

> 4 noble fluted pillars of bronze gilt in an altar of the church in one end of the same which was built by Constantine there is a much mosaic & gilding on the roof very ancient, probably from Constantine's time. The cloisters of this Church are of that Emperors building. And well worth seeing. One may see a great tendency in that age to the Gothic. the pillars being small and many of them wreathed oddly and adorned with inlaid stones in a very mean manner.[56]

The four smaller green columns that make up the north altar of the church are currently attributed to Constantine's time, but not the larger bronze-fluted columns to which Berkeley refers. The cloister dates from the thirteenth century.

Berkeley says that the most valuable things in the church are

> the sacred antiquities brought from Jerusalem. as the Column—this, I think, was of porphiry—on which the Cock stood when he crow'd and Peter deny'd X.ᵗ. Another pillar of white marble that was rent in two

54. LJ, VII.254–55; and Sweet, *Cities and the Grand Tour*, p. 51.
55. See Sweet, *Cities and the Grand Tour*, pp. 101–3.
56. LJ, VII.262.

on the suffering of our Blessed Saviour. Here is likewise a flat porphiry
stone set in the wall, on wch, they tell you, the soldiers threw lots for
our Saviour's garment. I must not forget the Famous Porphiry Chair,
which some will have to have been introduced upon the Discovery of
Pope Joan, & from that time used at the Coronations.[57]

Who 'they' and 'some' are is not clear, but such third personal pres-
ences are frequently the source of information in Berkeley's journals. They may have been guides at the church, or authors of tourist literature like Maximilian Misson, who notes the same sacred
antiquities, in the same order, in many of the same words, in an
aside where another column (the one on which it is claimed Saint
Paul was beheaded) brings St John Lateran back to his mind.[58]
Misson himself, of course, may have been repeating the traditions
of a local guide. Just as in the case of Berkeley's account of the caves
at Dunmore and those of the near-contemporary visitors, both
written accounts may derive from a local, oral account. Dependence
on locally provided testimony and tradition is a largely unacknowledged challenge to the philosophical tourist.

An appreciation of Roman architectural history and recent practice was very clearly registered in Berkeley's later schemes. Edward
Chaney has suggested that the plans he laid out for the grounds of
St Paul's College Bermuda were based on the layout of the Piazza
del Popolo, with its 'trident of streets laid out by Latino Manetti,
both Fontanas and Bernini'.[59] Berkeley remarks on the location:

> The Piazza de Popolo is contrived to give a traveller a magnificent
> impression of Rome upon his first entrance. The Guglio in the middle,
> the two beautiful Churches of the same architecture that front the

57. LJ, VII.262–63.

58. Misson, *A New Voyage to Italy*, II.73–74: 'This Column puts me in mind of another,
which we saw some days ago in the Cloyster of St. John de Lateran: 'Tis that on which
St. Peter's Cock crew. In the same place there is another, which was cleft asunder from
top to bottom on the day of the Passion. [. . .] And here they also keep the Stone on which
Pilat's Soldiers cast lots for Christ's Garments; [. . .] I cannot forbear telling you that I have
seen the bor'd Chair, about which you desire to be inform'd, that was formerly made use
of in the Ceremony instituted to prevent doubts concerning the Pope's Sex. 'Tis a kind of
arm'd Chair of one single Piece of Porphyry'.

59. Chaney, *The Evolution of the Grand Tour*, pp. 340–42, also notes echoes of Inigo
Jones's Covent Garden.

entrance standing on either side of the end of the Corso, or great street directly opposite to the gate carrying the eye in a strait line through the middle of the city almost to the Capitol while on the sides there strike off two other straight streets, inclined in equal angles to the Corso, the one leading to Piazza d'Espagna, the other towards the Piazza Navona. From the Guglio your prospect shoots through these three streets. All this I say is contrived to produce a good effect on the eye of a new comer.[60]

The plan for Bermuda shows two side streets coming off the central street at much more oblique angles than is the case with the arrangement Berkeley describes at the Piazza del Popolo, before straightening to run parallel to the main street. The planned buildings included the church, markets for different types of produce, parks, baths, a theatre, an academy of the arts, and a cemetery. The college was to be a quarter-mile away, 'in a peninsula'. Berkeley's plan incorporated a degree of specificity in the civic function of the buildings. When, a few years later, on his only trip to Derry, he admired the Italianate look of the town, he may well have been thinking of a comparable arrangement of the streets in relation to the church and square.[61]

The lack of regularity in the streets leading from the Piazza del Popolo disappointed Berkeley. The disposition of the piazza 'wou'd make a very noble prospect', he says, 'if the ordinary houses that make up the greatest part of the streets were more agreeable and regular'. Though he most often remarked upon the great public and imperial feats of design and architecture, Berkeley was also interested in the general taste expressed in ordinary housing. It was not in Rome, however, but in Lecce that he found the highest expression in domestic architecture. He remarks on the 'gusto in the meanest houses, no where so common ornamented doors & windows, balconies, pillars, balustrades all of stone / the stone easily wrought'.[62] The pliability of the stone facilitates this general expression of taste in domestic as well as church and civic architecture. Writing to Percival, Berkeley makes the contrast with Rome explicit: 'You know

60. LJ, VII.250.
61. Letter 125, Berkeley to Percival, 8 June 1724, pp. 196–97.
62. LJ, VII.250, 283.

FIGURE 8.2. Gommarus Wouters, 'View of the Piazza del Popolo in Rome', 1692,
by permission of the Rijksmuseum

that in most cities of Italy the palaces indeed are fine, but the ordinary houses of an indifferent gusto. 'Tis so even in Rome, whereas in Lecce there is a general good *gout*, which descends down to the poorest houses'.[63] Through domestic architecture the people in general, and not just an elite, 'shew some remains of the spirit & elegant genius of the Greeks formerly inhabited these parts', he notes in his journals.[64] The arts, both those that are more fine or the object of dedicated aesthetic attention and those that are useful, constructing spaces or facilitating activities, have their place in an understanding of the total cultural history of a people. They can indicate the transmission of values, or manners of being, from the venerated classical cultures. They make passions and emotions comprehensible and communicable, and they help to delineate an environment into zones associated with specific social and civic functions. In these ways, the practice of the arts is an indicator of social health that remained in Berkeley's mind as he continued to

63. Letter 86, 18 June 1717, p. 145.
64. LJ, VII.285.

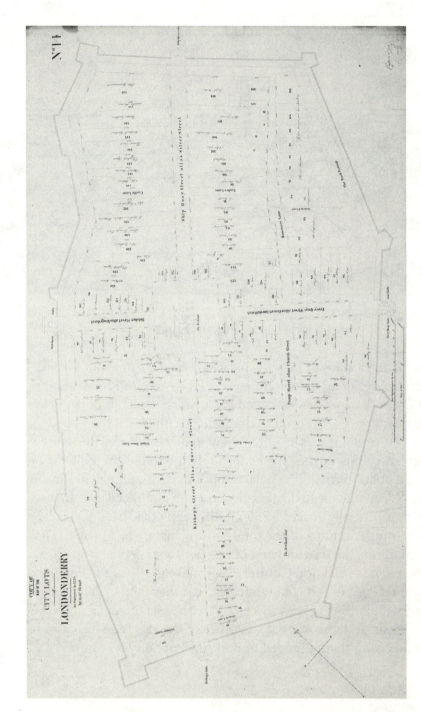

FIGURE 8.3. Stewart Gordon, 'Plan of the city lots of Londonderry as surveyed in 1738 [by Archibald Stewart]', 1857, courtesy of Corporation of London record office

think about the causes of good and ill social health and the remedies that a philosopher could offer for the latter.

It was outside Rome also that Berkeley began to remark more on the state of the soil and crops. This is one branch of the broad project of comparative politics and sociology that, according to Rosemary Sweet, tourism represents: 'remarks relating to the fertility of the soil, the state of agriculture, the condition of the labouring population or the existence of manufactures all comprised an important element of travellers' observations and represented a crucial means of evaluating the prosperity and governance of the state'.[65] Berkeley noted of a southern plain he was passing through on 19 May 1717 that it was 'parched, poor, hardly any corn or houses to be seen', but that he was assured it 'produces much corn every year tho' not alwaies in the same place [. . .] corn throughout Apulia burnt up this year'.[66] Improvement of agricultural practice is of course a major branch of civic management, and one that Berkeley's friends and associates in the (Royal) Dublin Society actively considered in the 1730s.

Berkeley does not make explicit connection between agriculture and other aspects of political and civic management, but he does dedicate pages of his journals to description of the judicial and political systems of some of the places though which he passed. He often acknowledges these as derivative; for example, the remarks on the judicial system of Naples come from Giulio Cesare Capaccio's early seventeenth-century history and Giovanni Batista Pacicchelli's early eighteenth-century book on the town, and those on the political system of Ischia come from 'Signior Giam. Battista'. This was probably also Pacicchelli, though it is tempting to think that Berkeley derived his knowledge of Ischian politics from Vico, who was professor of rhetoric at Naples from 1699. There is no evidence, however, that Berkeley read Vico or met him during his time there.[67]

Berkeley took an interest in how city-states selected their magistrates and civic functionaries, an aspect of the formation of elites.

65. Sweet, *Cities and the Grand Tour*, p. 3.

66. LJ, VII.272.

67. LJ, VII.308, 315; Hollingshead, 'George Berkeley and English Literature of the Eighteenth Century', pp. 157–58.

He notes in Naples, from Capaccio, the relative position and powers of the king, the vice regent, magistrates, and counsellors, particularly in appointing judges to decide issues. From Pacicchelli, Berkeley notes the system of electing popular representatives and the powers and responsibilities held by those elected, such as promoting public health and inspecting imported goods.[68] The evolution of a modern system of legal impartiality from earlier modes of informal, semipublic assembly is noted:

> The Nobility of the several parts or districts of the city of Naples were used anciently to assemble in certain public places or piazzas in each district where they conversed together. these places being much frequented they came to build certain open porticos; sustain'd by arches and railed round, thought in the reign of Carlo Imo who was an Angevino, i.e. in the 13th century see Capaccio. where they met together wch in process were improv'd and beautified in imitation of the Portici of the ancient Greeks and Romans and separated or appropriated to those families that used to assemble in them, and from being places of meer chat or conversation grew to be so many courts in wch they consider'd and debated on choosing magistrates and providing for the health and plenty of the city.[69]

The elite emerged informally, through semipublic deliberation, in an identified space which contributed to the formalisation of the procedures of civic life. The architecture itself drew on ideas about the nature of ancient public association and deliberative practice. Public health and public prosperity were the goals of this elite gathering and deliberation. Such ideas of the emergence of a philosophical elite with a specific public responsibility for health and prosperity were fundamental to Berkeley's writings and actions in the 1730s and 1740s.

When remarking on local political and judicial arrangements, then, Berkeley may be demonstrating his political preferences, as Addison does in his *Remarks*. Addison celebrates republican city-states, but often only equivocally. A number of his views hint at his

---

68. Berkeley may have used other sources, such as Parrino, *Nuova guida de'forastieri*, particularly pp. 28–34, 'De'tribunali, che amministrano la giustizia al la città, ed al regno'.

69. LJ, VII.309–11, 310–11.

politics. The ultimate loyalty of politicians in Venice to their republic legitimises repugnant practices such as the encouragement of public faction and the corruption of the institutions of the church. The unalloyed authority of the pope, which should be an aid to effective government, is counterbalanced by reducing the working population through such large numbers taking vows of chastity and living on the charity of others, and by poor decisions about the taxation of produce rather than land. The happiness of the people of the republic of Lucca is partly self-created: they are happy because they believe themselves to be happy.[70] Addison is aware that different kinds of social goods might be produced by different kinds of political regime: 'tho' the Bulk of the *Roman* People was more rich and happy in the times of the Common-Wealth, the City of *Rome* receiv'd all its Beauties and Embellishments under the Emperors'.[71] Concentration and distribution of wealth produce different kinds of good. Berkeley's notes are not as focused as Addison's text, and his letters record judgements rather than analysis: papal government has turned the Italians into 'the greatest fools and slaves from the wisest and bravest men in the world'.[72] But he goes on in his later work, particularly *The Querist*, to consider some of these questions of state management, population, labour, and happiness in greater detail.

Venice

Venice provides a link to some of the concerns and character of Berkeley's social and economic writings of the 1720s and 1730s. There is no evidence that definitively places him there, but it seems unlikely that he would have been in Padua without visiting Venice. It was a town known for its luxuriousness, particularly at certain times of year. Addison says that carnival and masks are the greatest pastime at Venice and give rise to many love affairs.[73] When he returned to London, Berkeley published two books, *De Motu* (on which more shortly) and a response to the crisis of public and

70. Addison, *Remarks on Several Parts of Italy*, pp. 70, 137–41, 312.
71. Ibid., p. 140.
72. Letter 93 Berkeley to Percival, 26 April 1718, p. 158.
73. Addison, *Remarks on Several Parts of Italy*, p. 73.

private finances—and indeed, of the working of the British state—
caused by the South Sea Bubble of 1720, one of the earliest stock
market crashes. In the *Essay towards Preventing the Ruine of Great
Britain* (1721), the decline of republics is on Berkeley's mind. He
cites gambling, opera, and masquerade as reasons for the decline of
the Venetian republic, calling masquerade 'a most skilful Abridgement, the very Quintessence, the Abstract of all those senseless
Vanities, that have ever been the ruine of Fools and detestation
of Wise Men'.[74] It may be that his detestation of the event came
from firsthand experience as well as accounts such as Addison's.
The *Essay* recapitulates some of Berkeley's ideas on commerce and
freethinking, but also points forward to his Bermuda project and
The Querist.

The commercial train of thought seen in Berkeley's sermon on
charity of 1714 continues in the *Essay*: 'As Industry dependeth upon
Trade, and this, as well as the public Security, upon our Navigation, it concerneth the Legislature to provide that the number of
our Sailors do not decrease'.[75] The *Essay* demonstrates a greater
interest, however, in the intervention of the state and established
religion in economic life in order to curb excess. Berkeley makes
connections between his target for moral criticism from the
1710s—freethinking—and the state of the economy after the South
Sea Bubble. Freethinking legitimises libertinism and unrestrained
self-indulgence. It represents a tendency away from public interest.
Religion is necessary to promote the public good: no other arguments, and no other institution, can be as effective as the Church
in instilling public-spiritedness. On this point, Berkeley mocks the
freethinking claim to enlightenment:

> PUBLIC SPIRIT, that Glorious Principle of all that is great and good, is
> so far from being cherished or encouraged, that it is become ridiculous
> in this enlightened Age, which is taught to laugh at every thing that
> is serious as well as sacred. The same Atheistical narrow Spirit, cen-
> tring all our Cares upon private Interest, and contracting all our Hopes
> within the Enjoyment of this present Life, equally produceth a neglect
> of what we owe to God and our Country.

74. *Essay*, pp. 15–16 (LJ, VI.77–78).
75. Ibid., p. 9 (LJ, VI.74).

(The punishments Berkeley hints at for those offending public spirit by blaspheming or dressing luxuriously are biblical—death and pestilence).[76] Berkeley is inclined to blame the preceding prosperity as much as the South Sea crisis itself for current problems: luxury and faction have followed on from freethinking, and the crash is just one symptom of a wider problem.[77] (Faction was one expression of a lack of charity in the Livorno sermon.) The *Essay* previews Berkeley's more sustained economic thinking of the following decade, in which he will identify industry as the only true way to wealth and declare that money changing hands without any active human industry (which is exactly what made the increase in South Sea stock merely a bubble) is simply gaming.[78] Berkeley in this way illustrates J.G.A. Pocock's thesis that Old Whigs and Tories identified public credit—the commoditisation of relationships between individuals and the state—rather than commerce as a threat to the political and moral order.[79]

Berkeley closes the *Essay* gloomily: 'it is to be feared the final Period of our State approaches'. This millennial sentiment is also present in the verses he wrote five years later, in February 1726, on the prospect of his founding St Paul's College Bermuda. Here is the final stanza:

> Westward the course of Empire takes its way,
> The four first acts already past,
> A fifth shall close the drama with the day,
> The world's great effort is the last.[80]

Berkeley goes to America in a quasi-millennial spirit. Whilst this spirit expresses itself in poetry in this instance, and the mode of expression brings with it real differences of expectation about the function of the utterance, Berkeley later in life claimed for the philosopher a comparable prophetic insight to that of the poet here.

76. Ibid., pp. 17–18 (LJ, VI.79); see also pp. 12–13 (LJ, VI.75–76).

77. Berkeley's critique of the South Sea Bubble did not prevent him investing money in the company. See letter 172, Berkeley to Percival, 3 September 1728, p. 260.

78. *Essay*, p. 5 (LJ, VI.71); see also chapter 15.

79. Pocock, *Virtue, Commerce, History*, p. 69.

80. *Essay*, p. 26 (LJ, VI.84–85); letter 143, Berkeley to Percival, 10 February 1725/26, p. 220.

In *Siris*, Berkeley says that 'analogy, constancy, and uniformity' in phenomena allow us to form general rules and therefore to foresee the future. This 'art of presaging is in some sort the reading of natural letters' that can be called 'vaticination', formed from *vates*, or prophet-poet.[81] Berkeley's poetic millenarianism may be the result of empirical study of the tendency of civilisations to corruption, which can be deduced from phenomena as a general law of nature enabling reasonable certainty in predicting the future. The poetical prophecy of the verses is also a natural and social science.

Bermuda was chosen as a location for the college because it was and at the same time was not commercial. It had no commodities such as sugar or tobacco and so had become a trading post and carrier for other colonies, with a particularly good shipbuilding industry. Though the Bermudans were commercial in the sense of being communicative, they did not exploit raw materials (palmetto being the only real exception). So the Bermudans were poor, but this made them better people: '[I]f they have less wealth, they have withal less vice and expensive folly than their neighbours. They are represented as a contented, plain, innocent sort of people, free from avarice and luxury, as well as the other corruptions that attend those vices'.[82] The missionary project of Bermuda was partly conceived in contrast to an exclusively commercial picture of human good that had taken hold in the American colonies and in which the British presence in America, Berkeley felt, was a corrupting rather than a civilising influence. The prevalence in American utopian and apocalyptic thought of a view in which the balance between virtue and commerce could be maintained only by the westward expansion of frontiers and the creation of new, independent frontiersmen and husbandmen has been noted by J.G.A. Pocock, who remarks that this final stanza of Berkeley's poem is an indication of the necessary geographical and temporal limits to such a balance.[83]

Berkeley in the *Essay* sounds much more like a nostalgic thinker of an uncorrupted and pre-commercial past where simplicity of manners such as the ancients practised—and specifically

81. *Siris*, §252.
82. *Proposal*, pp. 9–10, 12 (LJ VII.350–52).
83. Pocock, *The Machiavellian Moment*, pp. 511, 539–42.

as opposed to luxury—makes a culture more competitive, more successful:

> So just is that Remark of *Machiavel's*, that there is no truth in the common Saying, *Mony is the Nerves of War*. And tho' we may subsist tolerably for a time among corrupt Neighbours, yet if ever we have to do with a hardy, temperate, religious sort of Men, we shall find, to our cost, that all our Riches are but a poor exchange for that Simplicity of Manners which we despise in our Ancestors.[84]

The missionary Catholics in America had turned out to be just this kind of people. Berkeley would remark in the *Proposal* that 'the great number of poor regulars, inured to hard living, and brought up in an implicit obedience to their superiors, hath hitherto given the church of Rome, in regard to her missions, great advantage over the reformed churches'.[85] Missionary activity requires a pre-commercial simplicity. In the *Essay*, there is little sense of charity or Christian love as the mutual subservience of one another's needs achieved through commerce. This is, rather, a nostalgic view of a pre-commercial society as incorrupt on account of the pious public spirit of its citizens. Commerce, when it shades into gaming, is not the most effective private expression of charity, or Christian love, but a high road to corruption. The rhetorical purpose of the *Essay*—to chastise—requires a different attitude to commerce than Berkeley's sermon to the English factory in Livorno.

Sicily, De Motu

Being in the Veneto, then, may have fuelled Berkeley's reflections on corruption and the decline of republics in the *Essay*. It has been suggested that the other work he published on his return to London bears some impression of his time in Sicily. There are two surviving letters from Berkeley to Tomasso Campailla, a Cartesian writer based in Sicily who was most widely known for his cosmological poem *Adamo*. That Berkeley included Sicily in his itinerary is known from Thomas Blackwell, the student of ancient myth,

---

84. *Essay*, p. 11 (LJ, VI.75).
85. *Proposal*, p. 15 (LJ, VII.355).

poetry, and history based in Aberdeen, whom Berkeley would later try to persuade to go with him to Bermuda. Blackwell notes that Berkeley was vitally interested in practical knowledge: 'He travell'd thro' a great part of Sicily *on foot*; clambered over the Mountains and crept into the Caverns to investigate into its natural History, and discover the Causes of its *Volcanoes*'.[86] The degree to which Campailla and Berkeley might have influenced one another has been debated, with the most recent assessment determining that the Cartesian aspects of the essay on movement Berkeley would write for a French Academy essay competition, *De Motu*, was one possible outcome of the conversation with Campailla. The essay's acceptance of the dualistic notion that spirit moves body has been identified as the chief Cartesian influence.[87] There is no record of the essay's reception at the Academy. The competition was won by Crousaz, a professor at Lausanne who would later write a critical commentary on Pope's *Essay on Man*.[88]

De Motu applies to physics and mechanics the basic assumptions of Berkeley's earlier philosophical writings: we can have ideas of what we experience only through the senses. Our idea of motion must be of something in particular, or some things, moving. It may be useful to conjecture about or measure the force or power or speed of that movement. But we do not perceive the force, power, or speed: they are scientific abstractions. When physicists suggest that the cause of motion resides in a body, they are duping themselves with their own abstraction. Motion can only ever be caused by a spirit. This view is supported by philosophical authorities from Aristotle to Newton, but Berkeley's warning is necessary to prevent modern physics becoming a new scholasticism—a philosophy that manipulates meaningless terms.[89]

---

86. Blackwell, *Memoirs of the Court of Augustus*, II.277.

87. Charles, 'Berkeley et Campailla'. See esp. p. 38: 'Si Berkeley choisit le camp de Descartes et de Campailla et non celui de l'occasionnalisme radical, c'est parce que la liberté et la volonté humaines lui paraissent choses trop précieuses pour les sacrifier sur l'autel de la toute-puissance divine'. (If Berkeley chooses the camp of Descartes and Campailla rather than that of radical occasionalism, it is because freedom and human liberty appear to him to be too precious to sacrifice on the altar of divine omnipotence.)

88. See *Pieces qui ont remporté les deux prix de l'academie royale des sciences*. There was also a prize for the design of a mechanism to allow a pendulum to work at sea.

89. *De Motu*, §§22, 32.

Physics may be able to predict phenomena, but it must relinquish the role of assigning causes to them to the higher sciences of metaphysics and theology. To think that physics describes ultimate realities, forces that exist behind and beyond any instantiation of them, is a scientific mysticism that forgets the universe is actually concrete and particular. Such forgetting leads to the construction of misleading thought experiments in which the universe is imagined void of all contents, and yet still possessing qualities (space) or demonstrating the existence of forces (motion).[90] Berkeley says that if one takes everything away, there is simply nothing—no space, no force, nothing. Imagining just one sphere in an otherwise void universe often misleads physicists into faulty thought experiments because they neglect to remove their idea of themselves as observers from that imagined world. Such a sphere in an otherwise empty universe could never have motion or speed, as it would not be moving in relation to anything. Berkeley argues, that is, against absolute space or motion, suggesting that all motion is relative, and that it is all relative in a much fuller and more complex sense than is usually allowed: motion is 'wonderfully compounded' of local movements, such as that of a stone in a sling, and the greater movements, such as that of the planet on which the person swinging the stone in a sling is standing.[91] The movement of the stone is the compound of all these relative movements.

In its Cartesian language, however, *De Motu* might appear to recant on some of Berkeley's most distinctive and philosophically central views. The most striking of the apparent changes of view is Berkeley's proposal of a mind-body dualism.[92] But the apparent abandonment may be an example of Berkeley's harmonising with his audience, or adapting his mode of expression to a different genre and format—here the treatise on mechanics. Berkeley's earlier attitude was that bodies exist only as ideas of minds or spirits. He may do something to preserve that view alongside his use of dualistic language, which might itself be a concession to an audience less

90. Ibid., §§37, 42, 7, 53, 55, 58.
91. Ibid., §§58, 62.
92. Ibid., §21.

converted to his immaterialism even than the British and Irish.[93] When explaining what he means by 'principia' in experimental philosophy, he says it 'signifies the grounds on which it rests, or the sources from which is derived (I do not say the existence, but) the knowledge of material beings, these grounds being sensation and experience'.[94] Sensation and experience are the grounds of knowledge of material beings; Berkeley stops short of saying existence because there is no existence without or apart from knowledge, whether that is our knowledge or God's. That view is consistent with his immaterialism, even though it may be given a Cartesian dress for its anticipated audience.

This text may also appear to extend Berkeley's notion of human will into a power that directly and independently affects the world. It is the distinction of mind from body that mind has 'a power of changing its own state, as well as that of other beings'. Berkeley's earlier view seemed to be that God's will had to be concurrent for human will to produce any bodily movements intended. This view is, however, compatible with the agnosticism of *De Motu*, which says only that 'our mind can at pleasure excite and stop the movements of our limbs, however it is effected. [. . .] [O]ur bodies are moved at the will of our minds, which consequently may not improperly be styled the origin of motion; a particular and subordinate one, indeed, and which itself depends on the first universal origin'.[95] We do not know how our minds produce the regular motions of our bodies, but they do, and Berkeley's previous best guess was that God's establishment and maintenance of the laws of nature is the responsible mechanism.

Tarantulas and Spirits

The question of whether and how human minds control the movements of human bodies was one that must have been behind Berkeley's great interest in the tarantula and its bite, a striking

---

93. Downing, 'Berkeley's Case against Realism about Dynamics', pp. 198, 213, notes that some key statements in this text sound blandly Cartesian and that Berkeley's argument against dynamic realism may have been an attempt to prevent his immaterialism raising objections from Cartesians.

94. *De Motu*, §36. I use the translation from LJ.

95. Ibid., §§33, 25.

feature of his journals as he travelled through the south of Italy. The bite of the tarantula was thought to cause fits of involuntary dancing and a strong attraction to specific music and colours. Historically, there have been outbreaks of tarantism, leading to the conjecture that the behaviour of sufferers is culturally determined, relating to local religious and other beliefs. The personality of the spider, the effects of its bite, and the practices (or treatments) associated with tarantism were issues to which Berkeley's attention was strongly drawn. When he arrived in Taranto, he noted that 'among variety of spiders some also show'd me scorpions for Tarantulas'. He met one P. Vicario who claimed to have a cure for tarantism and suggested that the disease could be caught by eating fruit bitten by a tarantula and that it would cease when the spider that caused it died. People suffering from the disease apparently 'affect different coloured hangings'. When in Canosa, Berkeley discussed the spider with peasants. One claimed to be able to catch the spiders, and of a pair of peasants Berkeley met, one feared the spider and the other 'said he had taken them without harm in his hands'. In Bari, Berkeley spent an evening walking out of town '& searched for tarantulas they shewd us certain spiders with red bodies for 'em, or certain reddish spiders'. Pursuing his interest in the spider during this visit, he reports: 'We employ'd peasants at Canosa, & c to find us tarantulas in vain, because ye hottest season not then come. returning we met a french officer who invited us to dine, and called on us next day, wch we spent hearing of Tarantati dance'. Whilst sitting by a well at Matera, Berkeley discovered he was surrounded by tarantulas.[96]

Berkeley noted connections between tarantism and the practices and beliefs of contemporary Italian Catholicism that in general he found superstitious. Franciscans at Casalnuovo (except Capucins) were neither bitten by nor afraid of tarantulas, as they were 'cursed by St. Francis'. Apparently 'the habit worn 24 hours cures the Tarantato'. At Ascoli, 'they boast of a saint's finger kept in a church of a convent on a hill overlooking the towne wch so far as the church is visible prevents the bite of the Tarantula'.[97] Ignorance, particularly amongst the peasantry, and the tendency of Italian religious orders

96. LJ, VII.272–74, 293.
97. LJ, VII.286, 297.

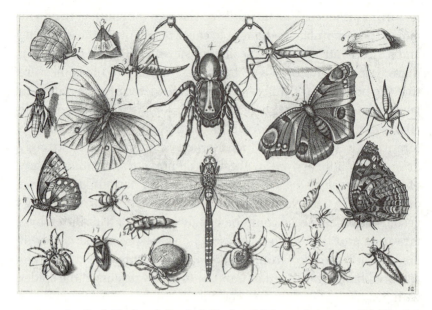

FIGURE 8.4. Jacob Hoefnagel after Joris Hoefnagel, 'Diversae Insectarum Volatilium', 1630, © The Trustees of the British Museum

to indulge in irrational belief in the power of their founders and relics may suggest a degree of scepticism about the disease and its causes, symptoms, and treatments on Berkeley's part.

Yet Berkeley was very attentive to the behaviour exhibited by victims of the bite, as well as to the broader set of social practices that accompanied tarantism. He records a discussion about the disease and the dancing that was its most visible symptom or cure at Bari in his entry for 23 May. One of the most focused entries in the journals, it is quoted here at length:

> The French officer with the Abbate Fanelli & another Abbate all concur in the belief of the Tarantula & that peremptorily / ladies of quality as well as mean folks bitten, v.g. a cousin of the Abbate Fanelli and the wife to the Ricevitore di Malta / nothing given to the Tarantati, they paying the music themselves / The number of the daies of dancing not limited to three / different instruments of music for different patients / they see the Tarantula in the looking-glass which directs their motions / The officer saw 30 Tarantati dance together at Foggi / Tarantula likewise found, say they, in the campagna di Roma. Don Alessio Dolone told me the Tarantati affected those colours that were in

the Tarantula, that he knew an old woman turned of 60 servant in a
nunnery that danced &c He wou'd not believe it at first, but was then
convinced. / as to the time of dancing he & another gentleman said it
was not to a day the anniversary of their being bitten, but it may be
some daies sooner or later / no bite discoverable in the patient / The
Tarantato that we saw dancing in a circle paced round the room. &
sometimes in a right line to & from the glass. staring now and then in
the glass, taking a naked sword sometimes by the hilt and dancing in
a circle ye point to the spectators, & often very near parly to my self
who sate near the glass / sometimes by the point, sometimes with the
point stuck in his side but not hurting him / sometimes dancing before
the musicians & making odd flourishes with the sword all wch seemed
too regularly & discreetly managed for a madman / his cheeks hollow
& eyes somewhat ghastly, the look of a feverish person / took notice of
us strangers / red & blue silks hung on cords round the room / looking
glass on a table at one end of the room drawn sword lay by it (wch he
regularly lay'd down after using it / pots of greens adorned with ribbons of various colours / danced about half an hour the time or bout
we saw him had danced before 4 hours and between whiles was to continue dancing till night / croud of spectators who danced many of 'em
& probably paid the music / we gave money to the music / the man's
bow to us as he came in / my danger from the sword / he did not seem
to regard the colours. Tarantata likewise seen daughter to a man of note
& substance in the city / chamber or large hall adorned as the other
bating the sword & looking glass / danced or paced round in a circle
a man bearing a green bough decked with ribbons of gay colours / she
seemed not to mind the bough colours or company / looked fixed and
melancholy / relations & friends sate round the hall / none danced but
the Tarantata / Her father certainly persuaded that she had her disorder from the Tarantula / his account that she had been ill 4 years, pined
away, and no medicines cou'd do good till one night upon her hearing
the tune of the Tarantula play'd in the street, she jump'd out of bed and
danced, from that time, he told us, he knew her disorder / He assured
us that for 3 months before we saw her she had taken no nourishment
except some small trifle wch she almost constantly threw up again. &
that the next day he expected (according to wt he had found before)
that she wou'd be able to eat & digest well wch was he thought owing
to her dancing at that time of the year. / That this very morning she

looked like death / no mark of a bite on her / no knowledge when or how she came to be bitten / Girl seem'd about 15 or 16, & ruddy look while we saw her.[98]

A week later in Taranto itself, Berkeley was again making detailed notes on the beliefs and practices around tarantism:

Tarantato yt we saw dance here, no looking-glass or sword, stamped screeched seemed to smile sometimes, danced in a circle like the others / The Consul &c inform us that all spiders except the long-legged ones bite causing the usual symptomes tho not so violent as the large ones in the country / he tells me the Tarantula causes pain and blackness to a great space round the bite / thinks there can be no deceit. the dancing is so laborious / tells me they are feverish mad & sometimes after dancing throw themselves into the sea and wou'd drown if not prevented / that in case the Tarantula be killed on biting, the patient dances but one year, otherwise to the death of the Tarantula[.][99]

Berkeley's sustained and detailed observations throughout the southern part of the tour suggest that he was doing something more than cataloguing a further Catholic superstition. This acute interest in tarantism has already been linked to Berkeley's therapeutic interests later in his career, with the regulation of the national economy in *The Querist* seen as one outcome of this earlier interest in regulating the individual animal economy.[100] The therapeutic interest has echoes in all periods and corners of Berkeley's thinking, from his interest in harmonising with others and the distinctive nature of the pleasures of the eye and ear, through to his late interest in the communication of divine fire to animals through universal medicines such as tar-water. There may even be a connection with the metaphysics of spiritual substance of his immaterialist philosophy.

To start with the most speculative hypothesis: there is but one substance, and that is spiritual. The world is the infinite spirit's (God's) means of engaging in dialogue with other, finite spirits. The world is a set of signs instituted and used with a purpose, that of showing us how to behave well, to accord and harmonise with the

98. LJ, VII.277–78.
99. LJ, VII.288–89.
100. Caffentzis, *Exciting the Industry of Mankind*, pp. 331–32.

infinite spirit. Berkeley says that spirits are not directly known to us, but read through signs: in God's case, the world; for other human spirits, facial expressions and other bodily gestures or specific natural languages. Like most Christians, Berkeley also believed in angelic spirits, with Euphranor in *Alciphron* asserting that it is common sense to believe in 'innumerable Orders of intelligent Beings more happy and more perfect than Man', whom he goes on to call angels. There is no reason to doubt that he believed in diabolic spirits too, as Crito, another right thinker in *Alciphron*, makes reference to 'the Nature and Operations of Dæmons' as a determinant of events in world history.[101] Certainly freethinking and 'blasting' (the practice of making blasphemous oaths that Berkeley would add to his list of social ills in the late 1730s) are forms of diabolism, behaviours that show a greater accord with diabolic spirits than with God. Berkeley may be thinking of the tarantula as the means of communication of a peculiar form of spiritual influence. The spider is, or is the medium of, another spirit—say an ambivalent or a demonic spirit. Its bite communicates something of that spirit to its victim. Being bitten is (being forced) to participate in another spirit, in the same way that seeing God's will in the world and following it is to participate in God (in a fuller or better way than merely being in the world).

This view of the spider relates to recent discussions of the problem of volition in Berkeley, and whether or not a person can be said to cause the movements of their own limbs. One commentator has suggested that finite human spirits may be capable of causing things in their own imaginations by their own acts of will, but that any act of will that causes a change in the sensible world also requires God's will, at least to the extent that God permits the usual course of nature to continue. That is, I can summon up the idea of my arm moving in my imagination all by myself, but when I will the moving of my arm and I see and feel my arm moving, then God is causing in me sensible ideas of touch and sight that depend upon his will, active at least in the sense that this experientially dependable relationship of volition to perception is sustained by the laws of nature.[102] God could decide to substitute the sprouting

---

101. *Alciphron*, IV.23, VI.30.
102. Lee, 'Berkeley on the Activity of Spirits'.

of flowers from my shoulder joint for the movement of my arm as the corresponding sensible occurrence for the volition that had formerly resulted in my perceiving the movement of my arm, but God is not usually so capricious. The spider, too, seems to control some bodily movements: the victim sees the spider in a looking glass and is directed to move or dance in a certain way. The will of tarantati is codependent upon that of the spirit of which the spider is the medium.

There seems no clear line between the symptoms of the disease and its cure. Both the expression of the disease and the means of driving it out, the victim's attraction to music, dancing, and certain colours might express the influence of either the ambivalent spirit of the spider or the benevolent spirit of God. The pleasures of the eye and ear, as we have already seen, were what the young Berkeley in his notebooks was determined to encourage others towards.[103] Aesthetic pleasures do not have negative consequences. Berkeley's tour of Italy was amongst other things the time when he substantiated his notions of right taste in the visual arts and architecture. Further, his transition from being a man with 'eyes but no ears', one who falls asleep at concerts, to a man who claimed he and his family were 'musically mad' probably began in Italy.[104] His party ended a day 'with music at S: Agnes in the Piazza Navona' in Rome, and he found the organ of the Franciscans at Bari to be 'fine'.[105] It may, however, have been his observation of the therapeutic, purgative effects of music on tarantati that drew Berkeley to music, as much as attending concerts. Berkeley was not alone in observing the peculiar importance of harmony to the patient and the niceness of patients with respect to the harmonies offered up to them. A historical study of accounts of tarantism notes that music had to be adapted to individual temperaments, and that the disease was accompanied by hypersensitivity to discord:

103. *Notebooks*, §787.

104. Letter 84, Berkeley to Percival, 1 March 1717, p. 142; letter 302, Berkeley to Gervais, 6 September 1743, p. 454.

105. LJ, VII.261, 272. [Addison et al.], *The Spectator*, no. 405, Saturday, 14 June 1712, wishes that religious vocal music, being a rational means of extending and reinforcing the passions appropriate to acts of worship, were better cultivated; see Bond, ed., *The Spectator*, III.513–16. I thank Marta Szymańska-Lewoszewska for bringing this article to my attention.

[T]aranti could not be persuaded to dance to any type of music, for the pace had to be regulated according to the condition of the patients. As the music affected people differently, the tunes had to be selected to suit the temperaments, and both music and the instruments had to be tuned to the individuals before they could reach a crisis. [. . .] If the instruments were out of tune, the victims would sigh and groan until they were repaired, and it is interesting to note that children who had no education could instantly detect a discord, and many showed a great deal of grace and elegance when dancing to these tunes.[106]

Tarantism, one might say, was a queer kind of taste.

The tarantati were often observed by their friends and family, particularly in dancing, and the onlookers sometimes joined in the dancing. The disease and its symptoms and cure were a social phenomenon. What the tarantati might have been doing in their dancing was harmonising with others, bringing their movements into line with the rhythm of the music as well as the rhythm of other people's bodies moving in their environment. This kind of coming to beat time with other people as a means of socialising oneself, of interiorising a set of social rhythms and regulations determined in the collective anticipation by group members of how everyone else in the group will react, is seen in later eighteenth-century texts on the foundations of moral life, notably Adam Smith's *Theory of Moral Sentiments*.[107] Berkeley's remark that '[h]e that wou'd win another over to his opinion must seem to harmonize with him at first and humour him in his own way of talking' has already been noted.[108] Berkeley was highly aware of the need to harmonise with people in order to change their behaviour, to give in to some of their ways of seeing and doing in order to persuade them out of those ways and into new ways. Perhaps this is what the families and friends of the tarantati were doing? Perhaps the whole phenomenon of attraction to music, dancing, and colour in the tarantati was a matter of harmonising with other spirits in the environment?

106. Russell, 'Tarantism', p. 413.

107. Adam Smith has frequent recourse to the image of sympathy as a 'keeping time with', as at Raphael and Macfie, eds., *The Theory of Moral Sentiments*, p. 16 (I.i.3.i): 'The man whose sympathy keeps time to my grief'.

108. BL Add MS 39304, f. 4r.

The difference between the dance as a symptom and as a cure was between the dance that did not harmonise with others and the dance that did.

To the end of his philosophical career, Berkeley continued to think of spirit as mediated by signs or instruments. But his *Siris* (1744) represents a new way of conceiving of the mediation of spirit. It is one of the axioms of *Siris* that the infinite spirit or presiding mind of the universe (God) uses fire to animate the world. This fire, diffused in various forms through the physical elements of the world, is the medium of God's spirit in the world. We have no direct access to God's spirit, just as we have none to any other spirit, but must read it through the various actions of fire:

> The order and course of things, and the experiments we daily make, shew there is a mind that governs and actuates this mundane system, as the proper real agent and cause. And that the inferior instrumental cause is pure æther, fire, or the substance of light which is applied and determined by an infinite mind in the macrocosm or universe, with unlimited power, and according to stated rules; as it is in the microcosm with limited power and skill by the humane mind. We have no proof, either from experiment or reason, of any other agent or efficient cause than mind or spirit. [. . .] No eye could ever hitherto discern, and no sense perceive, the animal spirit in a human body, otherwise than from it's effects. The same may be said of pure fire, or the spirit of the universe, which is perceived only by means of some other bodies, on which it operates or with which it is joined. [. . .] In the humane body the mind orders and moves the limbs: but the animal spirit is supposed the immediate physical cause of their Motion. So likewise in the mundane system, a mind presides, but the immediate, mechanical, or instrumental cause, that moves or animates all it's parts, is the pure elementary fire or spirit of the world. The more fine and subtile part or spirit is supposed to receive the impressions of the first mover, and to communicate them to the grosser sensible parts of this world.

God permeates 'the elementary fire or light, which serves as an animal spirit to enliven and actuate the whole mass, and all the members of this visible world'.[109] All physical causes (improperly so called,

---

109. *Siris*, §§154, 159, 161, 291.

as spirit is the only cause) are operating through this fire in one of its various dispositions or diffusions so as to produce effects in the world.

Our imperfect, finite spirits are patients in these operations of divine fire. We are more or less imbued with or permeated by this medium of another spirit. It does not seem impossible to me that such a conception of the divine presence in the corporeal world is nascent in Berkeley's thinking about the tarantula. Tarantism was particularly associated with the violent heat of the southern Italian summer, and it has sometimes been thought of as a symptom of heat stroke affecting agricultural labourers in particular (hence the surprise that people of higher rank or religious seclusion were also taken by it). Berkeley himself made the connection between the dance and the time of year, the heat and the spider, and he was in the south as the summer heat would have begun to sharpen. That tarantism has more recently been thought of as 'a hysterical phenomenon in which folklore, prejudice, superstition, and local cultural influences play a big part' perhaps only increases the need for an explanation of how spiritual states and conditions can be transmitted from one agent to another, should we think that a Berkeleian explanation by means of divine fire is improbable.[110]

110. Russell, 'Tarantism', p. 424.

CHAPTER NINE

Love and Marriage

WHEN DRAWING TOGETHER texts for *The Ladies Library*, Berkeley chose several relating to marriage that present views Berkeley could be said to sympathise with, at least to the extent he chose to reproduce them in print. 'God by his *After-Prohibition*' has made '*Lusts of the Flesh*' sinful, but 'from that Natural Necessity which he had laid upon us before, we cannot live entirely free from them'. Marriage is the institution, then, for managing sexual desire: 'the Remedy which God has provided [. . .] has a natural Efficacy, besides a Virtue by divine Blessing, to cure the Inconveniences which otherwise might afflict Persons temperate and sober'. Christian marriage is of a distinct kind, contrasted with other ways of living that allow an easier dissolution of the bond:

> The Cases of *Christians* is quite different. They have no Liberty allow'd of any kind. *Christ* has oblig'd them to *Love* each other, and no other even *till Death*. [. . .] This makes it to be infinitely more the Concern of *Christians*, to look they Marry none but whom they *Love*, and fully intend to *Love*, than of other People whose *Laws* and *Customs* allow'd them greater Liberties[.][1]

It is interesting to note here that Christian moral obligations are not universal, although they are absolutely binding on a Christian:

1. *Ladies Library*, III.419, excerpting Kettlewell, *Measures of Christian Obedience*; I.176–77, excerpting Taylor, *Holy Living*; II.25, excerpting Fleetwood, *Relative Duties of Parents and Children*.

non-Christian people are under a lesser obligation to their spouses. Fleetwood, whom Berkeley is excerpting, may be responding to Locke, who, in his *Two Treatises of Government*, remarks that 'natural right' or a contract formed either in the state of nature or in a political society allows married couples to separate and for wives to retain control of their property.[2] Marriage meets a natural need, and its Christian form meets it in specific ways. It involves a form of subordination that is necessary for any social life. 'It is impossible for any Company of People to subsist any while together, without a Subordination of one to the other', says Fleetwood, 'and this should help to convince the *Wives*, who are now going to make up a Family, that there is an absolute necessity of Government, which supposes *Subjection* some-where or other'. Each unit of society, including the family, 'must have its proper Superior, whom all the rest must needs obey'.[3] Fleetwood identifies the husband and father as the superior. Marriage is like other social institutions in which Berkeley participated—schools, colleges, the Church—where subordination was considered requisite to purposeful operation.

Berkeley's Wives

Preparation for the foundation of St Paul's College Bermuda included Berkeley's plan to marry. In 1723, Berkeley was the subject of a satirical address in poetic form, delivered to him by 'a little nymph about five or six years old, dressed all up in flowers and myrtle', who was the pretended author of the verses. The poem, said in Philip Percival's transcription to be by Anne de la Terre (a comic opposition, presumably, to Berkeley's more airy temperament), is a proposal of marriage.[4] The child has supposedly been attracted to Berkeley by his 'Fame' and now lays claim to his 'Person and Virtue'.

2. Locke, *Two Treatises of Government*, II.82, p. 321. I thank one of the anonymous readers at the Press for pointing me to this passage.

3. *Ladies Library* II.59–60, excerpting Fleetwood, *Relative Duties of Parents and Children*.

4. For the petition, see Philip Percival to John Percival, 9 November 1723, in *Berkeley and Percival*, pp. 213–25. The poem and some lines from Berkeley's supposed reply are reproduced by Gaustad, *George Berkeley in America*, pp. 29–30. The petition has more recently been printed in Carpenter, *Verse in English from Eighteenth-Century Ireland*, p. 115.

Berkeley's great interest in virtue—perhaps drawing on the Spartanism of the *Essay towards Preventing the Ruine of Great Britain*, or the emphasis on virtue in Berkeley's informal promotion of his Bermuda scheme in his London and Dublin circles—is the subject of play. So too is the quite explicit sexualization of the child. 'I am Young, I am Soft, I am Blooming and Tender, / Of all that I have I make you a Surrender', the poem declares. It continues by asserting that 'you'r as like Adam as I am like Eve', seeing in Berkeley the founder of a 'new Race'. Adam, after the fall, flew from the sun to the shade, but Berkeley is reversing this process by asking his friends to 'Fly from the Shade to the Sun [. . .] to be wise in [his] Eden'. 'Sure you that have Virtue so much in your mind, / Can't think to leave me who am Virtue behind', the poem asks, projecting a future in which the petitioner will be 'famous for Breeding, you Famous for knowledge, / I'll found a whole nation, you'll found a whole college'. The poem was answered in verse at least twice, once supposedly by Berkeley and once by S. Owens. The former poem declines the offer, the latter is outraged by a child presenting this poem, with its references to marriage, surrender of the body, and childbearing. Owens thinks the girl 'too young to be Marry'd and Sainted [. . .] too forward and free to surrender [. . .] not being at Age'. Owens imagines the girl was sent 'from Shr—n that Youth [. . .] for diversion to Compose a Song / To be carry'd and Cry'd by News Boys along'. It may be that Owens is attributing the poem to Thomas Sheridan, Swift's friend and master at a Dublin school. Owens presents the obscenity and public overexposure of the petition as morally reprehensible.[5] This episode connects Berkeley's Bermuda project with marriage, whether or not it was Berkeley's considered, even public, desire to have a wife with whom to travel to Bermuda.

5. S. Owens's answer, 'Remarks on the Young Ladies PETITION, To the Revnd. Dr B-rk-y', survives as a broadside, NLS Crawford.EB.3821. The petition is not included in Hogan, ed., *The Poems of Thomas Sheridan*, and it displays none of the qualities of Sheridan's verse of the period, such as the carefully managed variety of enjambment and line-medial punctuation in, for example, ll. 20–24 of 'A Poem on Tom Pun—bi On Occasion of his late Death, and in Vindication of Some Verses Written, Entitled "Sheridan's Resurrection"', or the double and triple rhymes and improvised comic imagery (a rivulet is said, teasing its modest size, to steal 'Like rain along a blade of leek', l. 28) of 'A Description of Doctor Delany's Villa'; ibid., pp. 125, 130–31.

Berkeley's marital status in the 1720s was a sufficiently salient topic for him to reply to what must have been a hint from Tom Prior, 'As to what you say of matrimony, I can only answer, that as I have been often married by others, so I assure you I have never married myself'.[6] Marriage was a sensitive topic for the Berkeley siblings in 1726. Knightley Chetwood wrote to John Ussher on 20 August that he had heard a brother of George Berkeley, of the Bermuda scheme, 'married two wives, one of them (the first) a cousin to Whitshed, who condemned him at Kilkenny to die'.[7] Berkeley wrote to Prior on 3 September, asking him to

> pay out of the money in your hands the charges you tell me Dr. Helsham hath been at in my brother's trial. Give my service to him and tell him I am obliged to him as he intended a service to me in advancing that money, without my knowledge, but that if I had been aware of it I would not have disbursed half the sum to have saved that villain from the gallows.[8]

Berkeley was speaking of his youngest brother, Thomas. Thomas had attended the school in Dublin at which Thomas Sheridan, possibly the author of the petition from Anne de la Terre, was master.[9] Berkeley's response was unforgiving, but Thomas had committed an offense against a Christian institution, breaking a law that made possible a life expressing natural appetites and yet free from sin. The oath that one swore in marrying was the kind of oath that made social life possible, a pledge to live according to certain natural and revealed laws and thereby avoid anarchy, the kind of oath Berkeley had repeatedly described as necessary to orderly social life.

---

6. Letter 156, 13 September 1726, p. 238.

7. The letter appears in Lady Mahon's transcriptions in 'The Chetwood Letters, 1726', vol. 10 of the *Journal of the Kildare Archaeological Society*, pp. 105–6, 106. It was cited in Hone and Rossi, *Bishop Berkeley*, p. 139. They offer a source for this citation in the Chetwood-Ussher correspondence in the possession of Lady Mahon, published in the *Irish Archaeological Journal* for 1924 (p. 9n). Some transcriptions from April and May 1726 are presented in 'The Chetwood Letters, 1726', vol. 9 of the *Journal of the Kildare Archaeological Society*.

8. Letter 155, p. 236.

9. Luce, p. 27, notes that Thomas entered TCD on 4 March 1721; see TCD MUN V 23/1, p. 361.

It is likely that by the time Berkeley dispelled rumours of his marriage to Prior, he had proposed marriage at least once, to Anne Donnellan. A letter written just after Berkeley's death by Elizabeth Montagu, one of Anne Donnellan's intimate acquaintances, to Gilbert West, Montagu's cousin and the author of, amongst other works, *Observations on the History and Evidences of the Resurrection of Jesus Christ* (recommended by Berkeley to Percival in a letter of 3 December 1747), states that

> Dr Berkely had formerly made his addresses to Mrs Donnellan, what were her reasons for refusing him I know not; friends were consenting, circumstances equal, her opinion captivated, but perhaps an aversion to the cares of a married life, & apprehensions from some Particularities in his temper, hinder'd the match, however their friendship always continued, & I have always heard her give him for virtue & talents the preference to all Mankind, still his admirers say he excelled every one in the arts of conversation, as to his writings they are some of them too subtile to be even the object of most peoples consideration.[10]

Anne was a member of the Percival circle: 'In 1712/13 Anne's mother married a younger man, Philip Perceval, her second cousin once removed, a civil lawyer and brother of John Perceval, Ist earl of Egmont', and the transcriber, as just noted, of the petition of Anne de la Terre for his brother.[11] Anne appeared in Berkeley's correspondence in 1712 when she received a letter from Mary Parker on the safe arrival of Percival.[12] It seems fair to presume that Berkeley knew Donnellan from the time when her mother married into the Percival family.

From her correspondence with Montagu and other sources, one can gain an insight into Anne Donnellan, at least as to her thoughts and interests twenty-five or thirty years after Berkeley's proposal. There are also hints in the correspondence as to what Berkeley

10. Letter 360, 3 December 1747, p. 538; Huntington Library, Elizabeth Robinson Montagu Papers, MSS MO 1–6923, MO 6697, ff. 2v–3r, Montagu to Gilbert West, 28 January 1753. For a published version, see Climenson, ed., *Elizabeth Montagu, the Queen of the Bluestockings*, II.26. At I.112–14, there is an interesting letter from Anne Donnellan offering advice on behaviour during courtship to Montagu, which probably reflects on her attachment to Berkeley.

11. March, 'Anne Donnellan'.

12. Letter 34, Berkeley to Percival, 17 May 1712, p. 71.

FIGURE 9.1. Rupert Barber, *Anne Donnellan*, 1752,
National Museums of Northern Ireland

was like. Anne was a talented singer, a friend of Swift, and later of
Handel and Richardson. She shared with Montagu her thoughts
on the early education of children.[13] Regarding herself as 'a little of
a Doctress', Anne also advised her friend on her lungs and nervous
health.[14] She guided the reading of Montagu, whose *Essay on the
Genius and Writings of Shakespeare* (1769) is a work of historic
importance in Shakespeare studies. They discussed Conyers Middleton's *History of the Life of Marcus Tullius Cicero*, Pliny's letters,

13. Montagu Papers, MO 834, Montagu to Donnellan, 20 November 1742; MO 767,
Donnellan to Montagu, 21 October 1743.

14. Montagu Papers, MO 778, Donnellan to Montagu, 11 July 1745, f. 1r.

and Montagu's reading (in the French translation by the Daciers) of Horace, to whom she referred in a letter to Anne as Anne's friend.[15] They discussed William Wollaston and John Hutchinson.[16] Donnellan lent Montagu sermons.[17] She shared her views on Shakespeare:

> I went with M:rs Southwell on Saturday to King Lear, to see him Garrick & M.rs Cibber, & both performed extremely well. I think he looks the part of the Old Testy Madman better than the Hero, & M:rs Cibber is the soft tender Cordelia in perfection, I am only provoked that they have altered Shakespears plain sincere artless creature into a whining love sick Maid who only speaks honestly because she is in love, I would have an act of Parliament or at least of Councel, that no body shoud add a word to Shakespear for it makes sad patchwork.[18]

Anne was a person of wide intellectual interests, artistic, literary, social, and physiological, and conscious of her intellectualism. She praised the conversational abilities of the clergyman and poet Edward Young, particularly 'for you & I who love to talk on a subject & sometimes to dispute'.[19] She said of a proposed meeting with Montagu in the countryside that 'I think we could talk & Philosophize (if a woman may be allowed that expression) very well together'.[20] When considering this personal attribute she shared with Montagu, she reflected on a friend of hers, who was likely to be Berkeley. They had been talking about their own nervous dispositions, and Montagu had suggested a form of therapy that was in the individual's hands: 'to cultivate chearfullness by all objects and things in our power, & call every innocent amusement to our aid, to converse with those we love, read such books as we like,

15. Montagu Papers, MO 751, Anne Donnellan to Elizabeth Robinson, 15 April 1741; MO 816, Robinson to Donnellan, 20 April 1741; MO 783, Donnellan to Montagu, 17 November 1747, f. 2r; MO 825, Robinson to Donnellan, 13 September 1741.

16. Montagu Papers, MO 810, Montagu to Donnellan, 23 November 1740, f. 4r; MO 749, Donnellan to Montagu, 1 December 1740, ff. 1v–2r; MO 788, Donnellan to Montagu, 14 August 1750, f. 2r.

17. Montagu Papers, MO 844, Montagu to Donnellan, 22 June 1744.

18. Montagu Papers, MO 783, 17 November 1747, f. 1v.

19. Montagu Papers, MO 767, 21 October 1743, f. 1v.

20. Montagu Papers, MO 778, Donnellan to Montagu, 11 July 1745, f. 1v.

& take such pleasures as are proper'.[21] This advice echoed with Anne:

> [W]hat you say about chearfulness is a Topic I am well read in, a sensible man of my acquaintance ∧ᵃ ᶜˡᵉʳᵍʸᵐᵃⁿ ᵗᵒᵒ in Ireland who loved new notions & disputations was of your opinion that chearfulness is the foundation of all Social virtue, & as he always declared he loved me, because I never balked him in ∧ᵃⁿ argument & I always opposed him in that & every thing else, & spending much time in the same house gave us great opportunity of disagreeing, I wish I coud show him your letter it woud delight him & shew him I am a generous antagonist.[22]

Berkeley certainly loved new notions (immaterialism) and enjoyed disputation; his social virtues are attested to in various places. The declaration of love, owned quite openly, suggests that he might be the man who proposed to her. Donnellan and Berkeley would have spent 'much time in the same house', the Percival house. Berkeley appears here as a lively conversationalist, justifying the vivacity of his social life by, or bending it towards, something like a theory of sociability (which Donnellan thinks is shared with Montagu).

Anne had a high opinion of the married state: 'there cannot be any friendship where the interests of every kind are so united as in the married State ∧ᵗʰᵉʳᵉ is must be the strongest & most lasting, & this I think is a fair concession from a Spinster'.[23] The taste in men she expresses includes a sense of their eligibility. She states that Jeremy Taylor 'must have been a charming husband, a wedding Ring woud feel easy with such a one'. This remark follows on from another, more explicit, remark about Berkeley, responding to something Montagu has said about an American hero: 'you know I have had a disappointment in the matter of geniuses, for I coud never have imagined Doc:ʳ Barkley had such variety of extraordinary talents ∧ᵍⁱᵛᵉⁿ ʰⁱᵐ to live at Cloyne & write upon tar water'.[24] Berkeley was, perhaps in more sense than one, a disappointment

---

21. Montagu Papers, MO 855, Montagu to Donnellan, 14 March 1747/48, f. 1r. Donnellan excused herself for not having written because she was 'bewitched this week with low spirits or histericks or blue devils'; MO 752, 27 April 1740, f. 1r.

22. Montagu Papers, MO 785, Donnellan to Montagu, 16 July 1748, f. 1v.

23. Montagu Papers, MO 773, Donnellan to Montagu, 11 June 1744, f. 1r-v.

24. Montagu Papers, MO 803, Donnellan to Montagu, 15 October 1757, ff. 2r, 1v.

to Donnellan. This disappointment is echoed through Montagu in her letter to West cited earlier:

> I have heard that his understanding was rather hurt by the absolute retirement in which he lived & indeed he had an imagination too lively to be trusted to itself, the treasures of it were inexhaustible, but for want of commerce with mankind he made that rich oar into bright but useless medals which wd otherwise have been stamp'd into current coin, fit for the use & service of mankind. He had a noble benevolence of heart, but like most retired persons spoke with some bitterness against the vanities & follies of Mankind.[25]

It was precisely the lack of sociability that made Berkeley a restrictively destructive philosopher.

The proposal seems not to have hindered the friendship between Berkeley and Donnellan during Berkeley's married years. There is a suggestion that Donnellan intended to join the educational mission to Bermuda, along with her brother and mother.[26] Donnellan stayed with the Berkeleys at Cloyne for a week in 1736. Anne's brother Christopher was known to Swift. He became a member of the chapter at Cloyne on 8 September 1737, as prebendary of Iniscarra.[27] Apparently Berkeley offered him this post, an act that Christopher Donnellan described to Swift as 'unasked and unexpected, and without any regard to kindred or application'.[28] Eliza Berkeley, in the preface to her son's poems, also makes the connection, referring to Anne Donnellan as 'The late Mrs. Donalon, of Chelsea, an old friend, once a FLAME of Bishop Berkeley's'.[29] The association continued after George Berkeley's death: Catherine Talbot wrote in a letter to Anne Berkeley begun 9 August 1756 from St Paul's Deanery that she spent an hour at Parson's Green with Samuel Richardson, the novelist, and was joined by 'Mrs Donnelland'.[30] At her death in

25. Montagu Papers, MO 6697, f. 3r.

26. See Elias, ed., *The Memoirs of Laetitia Pilkington*, II.620–21 (I.228, n), citing BL Add MS 47030 (Egmont Papers), ff. 82v, 136.

27. Representative Church Body of the Church of Ireland Library MS C.12.2.1, p. 92, no. 93.

28. Kelly, 'Anne Donnellan', p. 46.

29. Eliza Berkeley, preface to Berkeley, *Poems*, p. dcviii.

30. Kelly, 'Anne Donnellan', p. 47, with reference to Lady Llanover, ed., *Autobiography and Correspondence of Mary Granville, Mrs. Delany*, I.580, Mrs Pendarves to Mrs Ann

1762, Donnellan left £1,243 to TCD 'for the encouragement of religion, learning, and good manners', which was used, thirty years later, to establish the Donnellan lectures. These lectures 'took the form of six sermons delivered in the College Chapel', and they continue to the present day, with Luce delivering the 1920 series (apparently the first on a secular subject). This gift has been said to show 'the importance which Anne Donnellan placed on intellectual life and its role in polite society'.[31] Donnellan was a musically gifted, widely read, intellectually capable person, closely connected to both Berkeley's emerging circle of friends and his existing circle, and committed (in later life at least) to educational projects of religious improvement.

If the wives Berkeley did not take all shared his interest in educational projects, what about the wife he did take? Anne Forster was born 21 March 1702.[32] She was the daughter of John Forster, a lawyer and Whig politician who was 'successively Counsel to the Revenue, Solicitor and Attorney General[.] [. . .] Following the death of the queen on 30 July 1714, Forster was appointed Chief Justice Common Pleas on 14 October 1714'. John Forster possessed an estate worth £2,000 per annum, but would not have been the one to conduct marriage negotiations with Berkeley, since he died in 1720. Anne's mother Rebecca was of the Monck family.[33] It may be that the Mr Forster with whom Berkeley conversed at Percival's residence in London on 24 May 1725 was a relative of Anne's, and a means of Berkeley's becoming acquainted with her.[34]

Granville, 27 November 1736: 'I had a short letter last night from Donn; she has been at the Bishop of Cloyne's'; BL Add MS 39311, f. 83v.

31. McDowell and Webb, *Trinity College Dublin 1592–1952*, p. 551n38; Kelly, 'Anne Donnellan', p. 57. Kelly's assessment is that, '[w]hile Donnellan was not a learned lady, such as Elizabeth Carter or Elizabeth Elstob [. . .] she was firmly committed to the values of learning, virtue and friendship which Sylvia Myers has identified as the distinguishing feature of the Bluestocking circle' (pp. 56–57).

32. See *Parish Register: Baptisms*, p. 169, record DU-CI-BA-90353, http://churchrecords.irishgenealogy.ie/churchrecords/details/3a71f80090352 (accessed 28 April 2020), for the record of the baptism. The parish was St John's, Dublin, and Anne's parents' address was Fishamble Street.

33. Johnston-Liik, *History of the Irish Parliament*, IV.208–9. It was noted in chapter 8 that Forster supported Duke Tyrrell, a low-church competitor of Berkeley's, for the deanery of St Paul's in Dublin in 1716.

34. See Luce, 'More Unpublished Berkeley Letters and New Berkeleiana', p. 28, citing a loose sheet from BL Add MS 47031.

From April 1727, Berkeley was asking Prior to find him a house just outside of Dublin, earnestly protesting that 'for several reasons' he was 'determined to keep myself as secret and concealed as possible all the time I am in Ireland' and would assume the name 'Mr Brown'. A year later he was still planning this journey, and still insisting on absolute secrecy from Prior. Only one letter from Berkeley survives between this and his next letter to Percival, dated 3 September 1728 and written from Greenwich, in which he announced his imminent departure for America, together with Mr James, Mr Dalton, and

> my wife, a daughter of the late Chief Justice Forster, whom I married since I last saw your Lordship. I chose her for the qualities of her mind and her unaffected inclination to books. She goes with great cheerfulness to live a plain farmer's life, and wear stuff of her own spinning. I have presented her with a spinning wheel, and for her encouragement have assured her that from henceforward there shall never be one yard of silk bought for the use of myself, herself, or any of our family. Her fortune was two thousand pounds originally, but travelling and exchange have reduced it to less than fifteen hundred English money.[35]

Qualities of mind, love of reading, and a commitment to industrious economic self-sufficiency were the characteristics of Anne Forster/Berkeley that George presented to Percival as her great attractions.

Later in life, if not before or when she met Berkeley, Anne held a view very similar to Berkeley's views on participation in the divinity. She said in a letter to one of their surviving sons in 1767 that 'the very quintessence of Religion' is that 'we should be <u>one with him</u> [Christ]', and that the promise of religion is 'that we should be partakers of the divine Nature one Spirit with God'.[36] Writing to William Samuel Johnson, son of Samuel Johnson, she said that crucifying oneself to the world is the best way to purify the spirit. 'No other method can be found out for to make Us partakers of the Divine Nature, one Spirit with God but our escaping the corruption

---

35. Letter 162, Berkeley to Prior, 11 April 1727, pp. 249–50; letter 170, Berkeley to Prior, 6 April 1728, p. 257; letter 172, p. 260. The figure Berkeley puts on Anne's fortunes suggests that she inherited the Forows estate.

36. BL Add MS 39311, f. 200v, Anne Berkeley to George Berkeley Jr, 6 July 1767.

that is in the World through lust'.[37] In another undated letter to
the same recipient, she recommended a text that says 'true Religion is an Union of the Soul with God, a real participation of the
Divine Nature, the very Image of God drawn upon the Soul, or in
the Apostle's phrase, *it is Christ formed within us*'.[38]

Anne Berkeley's tendencies of mind seem to have been educational and corrective, even bordering on the satirical. (Recall that
Berkeley made a note to himself 'to rein in y^r Satyrical nature'.[39])
There are two character sketches of Irish deans written in Anne
Berkeley's hand, the British Library catalogue identifying them as
John Trench, dean of Raphoe (died in 1725), and Richard Daniel,
dean successively of Armagh and Down (died in 1739). The sketches
relate the lives of clergymen more interested in accumulating estates
for their children than in serving God. The personalities of wives,
children, and in-laws are recorded, together with the misery of their
lives or their early deaths. Anne was practising a form of Christian-
Horatian satire in which moral duty is neglected, property that can
never be secured is pursued, and death ends all expectations. Anne's
writing is evocative and pointed. Dean Trench

> lived in a long Mud Cottage thatched [. . .] the owner was intent
> upon making a great fortune [. . .] his Wife was a mild good Natured
> Woman, an Excellent houswife, & joyned with her Husband in the
> greatest cares & scaping [for 'scraping'?] in order to leave a great for-
> tune behind them—I never heard of any good he did Unless the beau-
> tifying his own seats in Church which his Coach Man & he painted
> between them: out of the Church reserves The Dean left upwards of
> L2000 a year to his son & gave large fortunes to his Daughters—one of
> whom married an Old Rake—the other a Rich Alderman who left his
> whole Estate to an only Daughter, who despises her Mother because
> her Husband did so[.]

Anne does not spare her judgement: 'This Dean was commanded
as well as every other Christian is to follow the Example of our Lord
& his Apostles—did he do it? if he did not, he has a whole Eternity

37. Yale University, Beinecke Rare Book and Manuscript Library, GEN MSS 1571, box 1,
file 7, Anne Berkeley to William Samuel Johnson, undated, f. 1v.

38. Ibid., box 1, file 13, f. 1v. The text is Scougal, *The Life of God in the Soul of Man*, p. 5.

39. *Notebooks*, §634.

to mourn that he did not ∧ ^{do so} & to ask himself what shall a man give in Exchange for his Soul'. The Dean marries his eldest son to the daughter of a businessman,

> a comely orderly Man, who never laughed on Sundays, & walked to Church with all his family at his heels—the rest of the week he oppressed the poor which fell into his Net: & concluded the business of the Day at a Tavern from whence he never stirred till four O'Clock in the Morning—& thence returned with no visible Alteration except a degree of tediousness—& perplexity ^{superadded to a} ∧ conversation wch before was Unintelligible. [. . .] [T]he Daughter above mentioned turned fine Lady the Husband being left alone, grew a Sot, the father in Law tricked him out of a large separate maintenance then took away his Daughter & her children = left the poor forsaken Husband to do what he pleased—whilst she enjoyed the fashionable pleasures of Cards visiting &c. her Daughters Educated under such a Mother married all, & are Miserable; & this day I hear of their poor Mothers Death—Vanity of Vanity all is Vanity.

The trajectory of Dean Daniel admits of more nuance and is perhaps of greater personal significance. If the British Library identification is correct, Daniel was preferred to the deanery of Down ahead of Berkeley following the submission of a disparaging letter about Berkeley (see chapter 13). Daniel 'gave honestly the bulk of his fortune to the Poor—& was a good humoured, easy Obliging companion', but he lived far from his parish '& shewed no other zeal for the Glory of God than that of spoyling the Psalms by his Paraphrases— we are told by truth himself that we can not serve two Masters'. (This last phrase, from Matthew 6:24, is a home key for Anne Berkeley, as we shall see.) Dean Daniel's generosity is superficial:

> [T]he Dean gave the Sop of tythes to quiet the Cerberus Conscience— he reflected that he was better then Numbers—for he loved his Wife & Children tenderly & lived peaceably with all Men—And never threw Away one shilling, the care of his Family was the Cloak which covered from himself his Covetousness, Pride, Vanity, & lukewarmness for Gods ^{Glory} it is true that he gave no Offence, & threw no Money away so far he was right—but in his Ideas of Duty, & pursuit of happiness he Agreed with the great Vulgar—who it is tautology to say are in the broad way.

One of three beautiful daughters is married to an earl, but she dies of a fit in early pregnancy, and a year later the earl marries a woman who resembles his first wife and 'whose children are to inherit Dean D—ls fortune [. . .] the Deans second Daughter dyed young & the third married a Gamester who was hanged for Murder [. . .] Vanity of Vanity all is Vanity they are all now dead Lord & Ladies & Dean'.[40] It may be that Anne Berkeley, if she composed these sketches during or not long after the many years Berkeley spent as a dean, had reason to contrast Berkeley's behaviour, open to question though it had been, with that of more grasping churchmen. Her narrative style combines the selection of telling detail with severity of judgement. On at least one occasion, however, she openly disdained any tendency to satire. When George Jr was sent a pamphlet that ridiculed the dean of Christ Church Oxford, Anne advised him to suppress the publication and speak out against it. She noted that she 'ever hated' the 'satyrical' tendency 'yr Uncle liked in his children & allowed in himself', and that 'yr father never was guilty of either'.[41] Anne may not have fully seen or recalled her own satirical tendency, or that tendency of his own which Berkeley had to remind himself to rein in when he was younger.

The sketches may not be Anne's only literary efforts. She is possibly the author of several translations of Fénelon published in Dublin in 1758–1759, and she definitely wrote large parts of *The Contrast* (1791). Stefan Gordon Storrie has demonstrated Anne's authorship of the letters to Adam Gordon that make up the majority of this latter work in two volumes. Gordon hints at Anne's identity in his preface and notes her talent for introducing serious Christian topics in 'a pleasing manner, blended with such variety of entertaining and valuable anecdote' that company allowed her to lead the conversation and make 'her friendly admonitions'. Storrie has also shown how strongly Anne opposed Shaftesbury's suggestion that the test of ridicule might have been applied to Christianity in its infancy and posed a great threat to it, particularly its reliance upon miracles.[42] Her contributions continue both the themes of

<hr>

40. BL Add MS 39316, ff. 34–35.

41. BL Add MS 39312, f. 230v, Anne Berkeley to George Berkeley Jr, 3 July [no year].

42. Storrie, 'Anne Berkeley's *Contrast*', citing the preface to [Anne Berkeley et al.], *The Contrast*, I.5–7.

her character sketches and their language as she insists to Gordon that 'you must come out of the world, and not be conformed to it, for you cannot serve two masters; the attempt to serve God and mammon ends in the final ruin of thousands'.[43] The book testifies to Anne's having spent time in France when younger, and to her reading, which included Fénelon and Pascal as well as Locke on the scriptures, *The Serious Call*, *The Religion of Reason*, *Deism Refuted*, and *The Life of God in the Soul of Man*, the text she recommended to William Samuel Johnson which discussed participation of the divinity.[44] Berkeley himself noted that, 'when she was in France', 'she liked some things' in 'the Church of Rome'.[45]

One of the writers Anne most frequently mentions is Fénelon, whose educational writings were discussed in chapter 5. For Anne, however, more pertinent than Fénelon's educational and sociological work are his writings relating to the love of God and expression of Christian love and piety.[46] Anne also frequently mentions Fénelon in her correspondence with George Jr, encouraging her son to read and translate Fénelon, reporting his views that 'the best Amends for past Vanity [. . .] is present <u>Humility</u>' and that 'the severest of all Penances is to do the Will of God every Day every hour in <u>preference</u> to our own in Spite of all the <u>disgust</u>, <u>dryness</u> & <u>weariness</u> that <u>attends it</u>', and remarking that 'just as I was writing to you an old translation from Fenelon fell into my way'.[47] Fénelon, whom Berkeley excerpted for *The Ladies Library*, was a spiritual and moral resource for Anne.

It is possible that the old translation of Fénelon Anne mentions is by Anne herself. Number 228 in T. E. Jessop's bibliography of Berkeley, listed under *spuria*, is a book comprising five translations from Fénelon 'supposed to be translated by Bishop Barclay, and taken from a work published by his relict, when in Dublin', as the title page reports. Jessop rejects the possibility of either George or

43. [Anne Berkeley et al.], *The Contrast*, I.244.
44. Ibid., I.84, 46, 65, 112, 171, 259–60.
45. Letter 282, Berkeley to James, 7 June 1741, p. 433.
46. [Anne Berkeley et al.], *The Contrast*, I.45 (the *Oeuvres Spirituelles* are recommended), 79, 125, 253.
47. BL Add MS 39311, ff. 200–201, 203.

Anne as the translator.[48] Other writers on Berkeley have taken his excerpting from Fénelon and his possible authorship of one of the *Guardian* essays (number 69) that offers a free translation of the prayer which concludes a work by Fénelon as suggestive of Berkeley's being the translator.[49] But I wish to make a case for Anne as translator. Anne is known to have sent translated passages from Fénelon accompanying letters to William Samuel Johnson.[50] Some of these she identifies as by 'Mr Hooke'.[51] Some of them may be her own translations. In 1758–1759, the Dublin bookseller William Watson published a series of five short works by (or at least then thought to be by) Fénelon—*A Letter upon the Truth of Religion and Its Practice* (1758), *An Extract from a Discourse on Humility* (1758), *Letters to the Duke of Burgundy* (1758), *An Extract from a Discourse on Prayer* (1759), and *A Discourse on Christian Perfection* (1759).[52] The backmatter of the *Letters* includes an advertisement for *Alciphron* in both duodecimo and octavo, in an edition that Jessop says was the first to carry Berkeley's name on the title page. It is also the edition of which a copy survives in the Keynes Collection of Cambridge University Library with 'GIFT OF M.RS BERKELY' embossed around an ornament on the front and back leather covers.[53] The collection of writings in *Five Pieces* is not an exact reprint of the five pamphlets published by Watson. It includes the (extracts from)

---

48. Jessop, *A Bibliography of George Berkeley*, pp. 47–48.

49. Hollingshead, 'Sources for The Ladies' Library', p. 2; Berman, *George Berkeley*, p. 74.

50. Pratt, 'Berkeley-Johnson Correspondence', p. 30.

51. Yale University, Beinecke Rare Book and Manuscript Library, GEN MSS 1571, box 1, file 3, Anne Berkeley to William Samuel Johnson, 21 June 1770, f. 1r.

52. For Watson, see Kennedy, *French Books in Eighteenth-Century Ireland*, p. 122: 'There is little evidence to show that William Watson (fl. 1757–1805), bookseller and printer at the "Poet's Head" in Capel Street, had a particular specialisation in imported foreign literature. Like many other Dublin booksellers he reprinted translations of French works. For example in 1758 he published Letters to the duke of Burgundy from Mr de Fenelon in its English translation'. These texts do not seem to be the same as the typed page listing documents that Anne sent to William Samuel Johnson, which records 'A letter [. . .] on the good use of Crosses', 'Of aridity distractions & coldness in prayer', 'the conversion of St. Paul', 'The mystery of the passion', 'An abridgement of the principles and way of inward Christianity', and 'What is the inward life'; see Yale University, Beinecke Rare Book and Manuscript Library, GEN MSS 1571, box 1, file 1. There are also imprints under the name of William Watson at the Poet's Head in Caple Street, which I will treat as emanating from the same house.

53. *Alciphron* (1755 edition), Cambridge University Library, Keynes.K.4.8.

discourses on humility and Christian perfection, as well as letters to the duke of Burgundy (though not the same selection). It includes pieces called 'The Difference between a Philosopher and Christian' and 'Some Advice to Governesses and Teachers' rather than the letter upon the truth of religion and the discourse on prayer. The *Public Gazetteer* for 17 October 1758 noted that the letters to the duke of Burgundy were 'chiefly for Dispersion', suggesting that they were published not for profit but to be given away, as part of a project of general public spiritual improvement.[54]

One strong reason for connecting the texts to Anne is the presence of what is perhaps her favourite biblical phrase: 'The Generality of those who would give themselves to God, are like the young Gentleman in the Gospel; they have some Reserve, and that Reserve prevents their Perfection, and prevents their being accepted of by God; they would both fain serve God and Mammon, but they cannot serve two Masters. [. . .] [W]e can never serve two Masters'.[55] Seeing life as a choice between serving Mammon or entirely negating the self in the service of God through constant subjection of the self to his will was a persistent way of characterising the dilemma of how to live for Anne. We have already seen Anne using this biblical phrase in letters to Adam Gordon. She writes to George Jr expressing her hope that both she and her son will conduct their lives in a way that registers the force of this characterisation: 'May we remember that we can not serve two masters & therefore may we <u>honestly</u>, <u>openly</u>, <u>avowedly</u>, & <u>Universaly</u> cleave to him whose gift is Eternal life even for his own Merit tho' we were not to be so gloriously rewarded for it'.[56] She also used the phrase when relating the narrative of a man who was converted to active Christianity and gave up his annual income, 'convinced that he could not serve two masters God <u>& Mammon</u>'.[57] This shared language, and the use of Watson as publisher, suggest Anne's authorship of the translations.

54. Pollard, *A Dictionary of Members of the Dublin Book Trade*, p. 595. Watson's 1755 edition of *Alciphron* ends with a list of works 'just publish'd', which, beneath Beveridge's *Private Thoughts*, Leslie's *Deism Refuted* and *The Case of the Jews*, and Addison's *The Evidence of Christianity*, notes that 'Good Allowance will be made to those who take a Number to disperse'.

55. Fénelon, *A Discourse on Christian Perfection*, pp. 11, 15.

56. BL Add MS 39311, f. 204v.

57. Yale University, Beinecke Rare Book and Manuscript Library, GEN MSS 1571, box 1, file 9, undated letter, f. 2v.

Though one might conjecture that Anne was translating Fénelon partly as a means of coping with Berkeley's death, it is by no means impossible that she engaged in translation during Berkeley's life and discussed her work with him. The translations published by Watson sometimes touch on subjects that one imagines would have interested Berkeley. For instance, prayer is a motion of the heart: 'one may pray without any distinct Thought'. Or, in more Berkeleian terms, prayer is a motion of the spirit, not an idea.[58] Also, humility is an important virtue to impart to the young whose education is in our care; young people are to be encouraged to follow illustrious examples.[59] Some aspects of these translations, however, do not sort well with the broader outlines of Berkeley's thinking. Self-love, for example, is presented as an entirely deceptive emotion, whereas for Berkeley it is a more neutral psychological law of nature.[60] Fénelon recommends that we despise even our own virtues in order to be humble and love God.[61] These are thoughts more in line with Anne's spiritual severity than with George's construction of a moral (indeed, total) system of the world from pleasure and pain.

One might note a tension with Berkeley's religious politics at a slightly higher level also. Anne's recommendation that George Jr translate Fénelon is extended to Madame Guyon: 'they were friends God tried in the furnaces of Adversity & came out bright as <u>Gold</u> for their masters finest purposes, ^{viz} to lead Men on to the perfection of <u>Love</u>, & <u>Humility</u>'.[62] She also sent a translation of Madame de Guyon, very probably by herself, to William Samuel Johnson.[63] Madame Guyon was a laywoman whose mystical, self-annihilating experience of God deeply impressed Fénelon. Through Fénelon, who was instructor to the king's children, Guyon may have had an indirect means by which to influence the religious education of the sovereign, a danger that may have led Madame Maintenon, the

---

58. Fénelon, *An Extract from a Discourse on Prayer*, pp. 7–8.

59. Ibid., pp. 9–10; Fénelon, *Letters to the Duke of Burgundy*, pp. 11–12.

60. Fénelon, *Letters to the Duke of Burgundy*, p. 16.

61. Fénelon, *An Extract from a Discourse on Humility*, pp. 13, 15.

62. BL Add MS 39311, f. 200r, 6 July 1767.

63. Yale University, Beinecke Rare Book and Manuscript Library, GEN MSS 1571, box 1, file 12, Anne Berkeley to William Samuel Johnson, undated, f. 1r, hints that the translation is by 'your [. . .]' but the full identification is obscured by a deformity in the MS.

king's clandestine second wife and advisor, and Bossuet, a theologian and sometime tutor to the royal family, to campaign against her and Fénelon, who acted as her institutional champion.[64] The fires that tested Fénelon and Guyon were those of the discipline of the established religion. Although it is not possible to parallel the situations of the Catholic and Anglican churches, Anne was recommending writers who tested authority. Berkeley himself did not wish to encourage tests of the legitimacy of the established church.

We see indications of Anne's character in her long-standing interest in Fénelon, her sharing with him a sense of spiritual self-negation in the service of God, and the echoes of themes such as the importance of morally and spiritually educating the young between these translations and her other writings, which also show her sharing social and religious concerns with her husband.

The Berkeleys' Views of Marriage

Some testimony to Anne's character and her marriage to George survives. Gordon in *The Contrast* refers to her 'brilliant, and general accomplishments'. William Samuel Johnson describes her in old age as 'sensible, lively, facetious and benevolent'.[65] Eliza Berkeley did not share this view. She describes Anne as 'violent spirited fretful' and says that before her marriage to George Jr a relation of hers, Judge Hayes, had told her that Anne beat maids. Eliza regards Anne's perceived failings very gravely. She reports that an 'Irish Nobelman of High Rank once told' her that Anne was 'esteemed the most violent Spirit throughout Ireland May the Mercy of God thro' Christ have pardoned her the unutterable injuries she did to me and to mine'. Eliza claims that Anne beat George Jr: 'I have seen her beat my dear Husband when his Son was old enough to rejoyce "that any Body dared beat his Papa" and not old enough as afterward to be shocked beyond Measure to think that he was descended from such a Spirit'.[66]

64. Bayley, 'What Was Quietism Subversive Of?'.

65. [Anne Berkeley et al.], *The Contrast*, I.5; Pratt, 'Berkeley-Johnson Correspondence', p. 30.

66. TCD MS 3530, ff. 40–41 (pp. 36–37).

Anne's letters to Eliza are revealing about the relationship between the two women and Anne's view of marriage, and also about how both of them viewed Anne's marriage to Berkeley. Anne had written to Eliza in the week before her marriage to George Jr, extolling the marriage in which both partners know all happiness is derived from God. Anne reiterated this view four years later when she expressed the wish that the 'pure and bright flame' of their married love 'be so intermixed with Superior love to God, that at length both may become partakers of the Divine Nature!'[67] Anne rather imposingly reassured Eliza that all would be well after the wedding. Eliza interlineates at this point in the letter, noting how she disliked the quarrelling between Anne and George Jr, and also Anne's way of speaking to her: 'She told me incessantly of real & supposed faults. I cannot say I liked her <u>way</u> & have often told her she made me weep more in a month than my own mother did in my whole life'.[68] Eliza did not accept Anne's view of her marriage with George Sr. Anne wrote on 19 February 1765 that 'the Bishop of Cloyne was the most tender & amiable of Husbands—I remember a misanthropic friend of ours once, railing against matrimony in our presence—looked with an air of spite, & said you two are not included in this general hate, for you are lovers'. Eliza has interlineated: 'After My Marriage she has twice told me how the B[p] & his Xantippe used to squable that she in turn has often told him that he <u>hated</u>, He kept her in great [?] pride made her [?]'.[69] Xantippe was the wife Socrates is reported, in an anecdote from *The Ladies Library*, to have married in order to 'discipline himself to perfect Patience'.[70] Though Eliza's view was hardly detached and neutral, it may be a reason not to assent unquestioningly to Anne's account of her marriage to Berkeley.

People seem to have formed views on all sides of the question of the happiness of the Berkeley marriage. Elizabeth Montagu reported that Anne adored Berkeley,

67. Anne Berkeley to Eliza Frinsham/Berkeley, 19 February 1765, BL Add MS 39311, f. 168v.

68. BL Add MS 39311, ff. 106v–107r.

69. BL Add MS 39311, f. 168r.

70. *Ladies Library*, I.256, excerpting Allestree, *The Ladies Calling*.

to whose humours she had a submission that offended some of the Ladies, who thought her intire obedience a bad precedent. Mrs Berkely said such a Man as Dr Berkely deserved uncommon attentions, & she thought it wd be strange presumption to oppose the designs & inclinations of one so much superior to her, thus she dignified her choice, recommended her obedience or preserved unprejudiced the rights & privileges of other Ladies whose Husbands had not the like plea for their submission.[71]

As has been shown already, Berkeley seems to have regarded disobedience in marriage as a sin incurring eternal punishment. If Anne was obedient, that nonetheless did not prevent her forming a judgement of Berkeley's intellectual contribution that has echoes of the disappointment expressed by Anne Donnellan and echoed by Montagu: '∧^{he has} taken from them the ground they stand on, & had he <u>built</u> as he has <u>pulled down</u> he had been then a <u>Master builder</u> ∧^{indeed} but Unto every Man his Work some must remove rubbish, & others lay Foundations whilst a very few have time to go on to <u>perfection</u>'.[72] Berkeley's wife thought him more destructive than productive as a philosopher.

Berkeley himself attested to the joys of marriage. Three letters touching on marriage (to a member of the Wolfe family, to John James, and to Richard Dalton) can all be dated to 1741. Two letters encourage bachelors to marry, using Dalton as an example, and the third congratulates Dalton on his third marriage. Berkeley calls Dalton 'a prudent man as well as a laudable patriot' whose 'example is indeed a public benefit, when the nation is drained by war and hard times, and when our gentlmen conspire to put marriage out of countenance'. Marriage is said to be a public as well as a personal good. Health and affluence may protect him for a while, 'but when age and infirmities come on [. . .] you will feel and bewail the want of a family of your own, and the comforts of domestic life'. Berkeley seems to attribute refusal to marry in this case to fear of the wife—particularly of her possible faults: 'Fear is unmanly, I will not therefore suppose you are afraid of a woman of your own

71. Huntington Library, Elizabeth Robinson Montagu Papers, MSS MO 1–6923, MO 6697, f. 2v.

72. BL MS Add 39312, f. 227v.

choosing. But how shall you choose? Choose her by reputation. The quicksightedness and malice of the world will not keep the faults of a woman concealed from those eyes that are not already blinded by love. Therefore choose first and love after'. Avoiding faults in a spouse is possible if one takes advantage of the malicious scrutiny of women's characters and remains detached. Berkeley closes the letter by reminding Wolfe that Plato 'sacrificed to nature as an atonement for his not having children' and stating his own preference for children over wealth. The letter to James notes that 'great devastations are made by bloody fluxes, fevers, and want, which carry off more than a civil war'. He wishes James would follow Dalton's example, as otherwise he 'will lose the comforts of domestic life, that natural refuge from solitude and years which is to be found in wife and children. Mine are to me a great joy [the chief of the good things of this world], and alone capable of making a life tolerable so much embittered by sickness as mine has been for several years'. (Berkeley mentions stone, cholic, and scurvy.) The letter to Dalton makes a joke in earnest about those who, like Dalton, 'so magnanimously endeavour to repair the late breaches made upon the public by famine, sickness, and wars'.[73]

The years 1740 and 1741 saw terrible famine indeed in Ireland. Between 310,000 and 480,000 of a total population of 2.5 million died over what was the coldest winter in the history of modern Europe.[74] For most of the previous decade, Berkeley had been considering the obligation of the individual to take steps that would allow the population to be replenished. Having a 'numerous Stock' of people 'well fed, cloathed, and lodged' constitutes a 'flourishing Nation' in *The Querist*, where Berkeley also asks '[w]hether it be not a sure Sign or Effect of a Country's thriving, to see it well cultivated, and full of Inhabitants?' He suggests there that 'the true Strength of the Crown', may be 'the Number and Welfare of the Subjects'.[75] The 1750 revision of *The Querist* integrates the consideration of love in marriage with eugenics and redistribution as a public good (rather than as a necessary corollary of a natural right). There it is asked:

73. Letters 284–86, pp. 435–48.
74. McBride, *Eighteenth-Century Ireland*, p. 106.
75. *Querist*, I.8, 11–12, 16, §§67, 93, 136.

206. Whether the Public is more concerned in any Thing than in the Procreation of able Citizens?

207. Whether to the Multiplying of Human Kind, it would not much conduce, if Marriages were made with good-liking? [...]

214. Whether as Seed equally scattered produceth a goodly Harvest, even so an equal Distribution of Wealth doth not cause a Nation to flourish?

215. Whence it is that Barbs and Arabs are so good Horses? And whether in those Countries they are not exactly nice in admitting none but Males of a good Kind to their Mares?

216. What Effects would the same Care produce in Families?

217. Whether the real Foundation for Wealth must not be laid in the Numbers, the Frugality, and the Industry of the People? And whether all Attempts to enrich a Nation by other Means, as raising the Coin, Stock-Jobbing and such Arts are not vain?[76]

Letters to friends in a famine year pointing them to the private benefits and joys of family life show Berkeley pursuing personally the same objectives that were present in the more public project of *The Querist*. Sexual contact and reproduction, like horse breeding (or, in an instance explored by Tom Prior and his colleagues at the Dublin Society, the sowing of flax seed), require close management in order to produce social goods.[77] Mixture is good for population health, but only good males are to be admitted.

The Berkeleys themselves produced a family. Of seven children, three died in early infancy: Lucia, born and died 1731 in Newport; John, born and died in Cloyne in 1735; and Sarah, born and died in Cloyne in 1739–1740. Henry, George Jr, and Julia all figure in the later part of this book. There were two miscarriages between Lucia and George, one of which left Anne very ill.[78] William, who was baptised at Cloyne on 10 December 1736 and buried there on 3 March 1751, is the subject of a moving letter by Berkeley. He had written to Percival on 24 June 1726 expressing his hope that

---

76. *Querist* (1750 text), pp. 25–26, §§206–7, 214–17.

77. Royal Dublin Society, MS RDS/MAN, register and minute book, vol. 1, f. 26r, 9 December 1731, notes of a practice in Riga and Königsburg to prevent flax seed from degenerating—seed from the uplands was sown in the lowlands and vice versa.

78. Letter 218, Berkeley to Prior, 13 March 1732/3, p. 347.

the Percivals would be able to deal with the death of a son with Christian resignation. His reflections on the death of his own son register the weight of his grief and the seriousness with which he took Christian rejection of all things of this world. It is a letter that shows the tension between the rational preferences for personal and social goods that are the (human psychological) laws of nature established and maintained by God, and a more severe form of religious law:

> I was a man retired from the amusement of politics, visits, and what the world calls pleasure. I had a little friend, educated always under mine own eye, whose painting delighted me, whose music ravished me, and whose lively, gay spirit was a continual feast. It has pleased God to take him hence. God, I say, in mercy, hath deprived me of this pretty, gay plaything. His parts and person, his innocence and piety, his particularly uncommon affection for me, had gained too much upon me. Not content to be fond of him, I was *vain* of him. I had set my heart too much upon him, more perhaps than I ought to have done upon anything in this world.[79]

Love here is seen, as with the choice of a spouse, under restraint, but this restraint is spiritually rather than socially oriented. Love of God is submission to God's will, and that love disciplines excessive love of family.

79. Letter 151, p. 229; letter 375, Berkeley to Benson, 8 March 1751, p. 564.

CHAPTER TEN

Bermuda and Rhode Island

WRITING TO PERCIVAL in March 1723, Berkeley revealed that it was in May 1722 that he decided 'to spend the residue of my days in the island of Bermuda, where I trust in Providence I may be the mean instrument of doing good to mankind'. Berkeley set out his motivations and his reasoning at length:

> Your Lordship is not to be told that the reformation of manners among the English in our western plantations, and the propagation of the Gospel among the American savages, are two points of high moment. The natural way of doing this is by founding a college or seminary in some convenient part of the West Indies, where the English youth of our plantations may be educated in such sort as to supply the churches with pastors of good morals and good learning, a thing (God knows!) much wanted. In the same seminary a number of young American savages may also be educated till they have taken their degree of Master of Arts. And being by that time well instructed in Christian religion, practical mathematics, and other liberal arts and sciences, and early endued with public spirited principles and inclinations, they may become the fittest missionaries for spreading religion, morality, and civil life, among their countrymen, who can entertain no suspicion or jealousy of men of their own blood and language, as they might do of English missionaries, who can never be so well qualified for that work. Some attempts have been made towards a college in the West, but to little

purpose, chiefly I conceive for want of a proper situation wherein to place such college or seminary, as also for want of a sufficient number of able men well qualified with divine and human learning, as well as with zeal to prosecute such an undertaking. As to the first, I do think the small group of Bermuda islands the fittest spot for a college on the following accounts. 1. It is the most equidistant part of our plantations from all the rest, whether in the continent, or the isles. 2. It is the only Plantation that holds a general commerce and correspondence with all the rest, there being sixty cedar ships belonging to the Bermudians, which they employ as carriers to all parts of the English West Indies, in like manner as the Dutch are carriers in Europe. 3. The climate is by far the healthiest and most serene, and consequently the most fit for study. 4. There is the greatest abundance of all the necessary provisions for life, which is much to be considered in a place of education. 5. It is the securest spot in the universe, being environed round with rocks all but one narrow entrance, guarded by seven forts, which render it inaccessible not only to pirates but to the united force of France and Spain. 6. The inhabitants have the greatest simplicity of manners, more innocence, honesty, and good nature, than any of our other planters, who are many of them descended from whores, vagabonds, and transported criminals, none of which ever settled in Bermudas. 7. The islands of Bermuda produce no one enriching commodity, neither sugar, tobacco, indigo, or the like, which may tempt men from their studies to turn traders, as the parsons do too often elsewhere.

It would take up too much of your Lordship's time minutely to describe the beauties of Bermuda, the summers refreshed with constant cool breezes, the winters mild as our May, the sky as light and blue as a sapphire, the ever green pastures, the earth eternally crowned with fruits and flowers. The woods of cedars, palmettos, myrtles, oranges etc., always fresh and blooming. The beautiful situations and prospects of hills, vales, promontories, rocks, lakes and sinuses of the sea. The great variety, plenty, and perfection of fish, fowl, vegetables of all kinds, and (which is in no other of our Western Islands) the most excellent butter, beef, veal, pork and mutton. But above all, that uninterrupted health and alacrity of spirit, which is the result of the finest weather and gentlest climate in the world, and which of all others is the most effectual cure for the cholic, as I am most certainly assured by the information of many very credible persons of all ranks who have been there.

In case I carry [the] Deanery (as I have good hopes I shall) I design
to erect a charity school in Dromore, and to maintain ten savages and
ten whites in the Bermudan University. But whatever happens, go I
am resolved if I live. Half a dozen of the most agreeable and ingenious
men of our college are with me in this project. And since I came hither I
have got together about a dozen English men of quality, and gentlemen,
who intend to retire to these islands, to build villas and plant gardens,
and to enjoy health of body and peace of mind, where they have a soft
freestone like that at Bath, and a soil which produces everything that
grows in America, Europe, or the East, and where a man may live with
more pleasure and dignity for £500 p. annum than for £10,000 here: in
short where men may find, in fact, whatsoever the most poetical imagination can figure to itself in the golden age, or the Elysian fields.

I have been proposing every day this month past to trouble you with
this narrative, and have at last ventured to do it, though I run the risk
of being thought mad and chimerical. [. . .] If I can make a convert of
your Lordship to Bermuda, I doubt not my Lady will be pleased to pass
a few years there for the perfect recovery of her health[.][1]

The university will reform the manners of the colonists and convert
the indigenous population, and Bermuda has been chosen for its
situation and climate and human and physical geography. Berkeley
was already campaigning to make Percival a convert to his scheme,
and he spent the next five years planning and campaigning for this
venture.

The Bermuda project, as it has commonly been known, may
seem like a radical change of direction for Berkeley. But he had
been a member of Protestant educational institutions with the creation and preservation of social order at the centre of their charters
since his early youth. Kilkenny and Trinity Colleges were both cen-
tres of Protestant learning, both located in a country whose majority population was of a different faith and was regarded as providing legitimate subjects for conversion—the native Catholic Irish. As
ordination was required for fellowship, the vocations of the Church
and of education were inseparably intertwined. And Berkeley had
recently returned from a tour of Italy as a personal tutor during
which he had experience both of guiding the education of a young

1. Letter 117, Berkeley to Percival, 4 March 1723, pp. 185–87.

member of the Protestant elite and of observing with some admiration the educational work of the Catholic church—the seminaries for education in logic, philosophy, and theology, as well as, for example, the tradition of sending young preachers out into public squares to practise their art.[2] The failure of the Protestant church to match the missionary efforts of the Catholic church was a recurrent feature of Berkeley's thinking about his Bermuda project, which he saw as continuous with the work of a Protestant educationalist who identified as a member of the nonmetropolitan elite: by choosing to work in the American plantations, Berkeley was choosing to work in a context commensurate with his Irish experience. The choice of Bermuda, however, requires some explanation.

Is it excessively charitable to say of the selection of Bermuda as the location for a college that Berkeley's 'geography, not his judgment, was at fault', and that '[g]ood maps were rare then, and it was very hard to get reliable geographical information about distant places'?[3] What Berkeley says of Bermuda to Percival in this first exposition of the project must derive from sources Berkeley had at his disposal. The prescribed text in geography at Trinity when Berkeley studied there records that Bermuda 'is about 15 or 1600 Leagues from *England*, 400 from *Hispaniola*, and only 300 from the nearest Coast of *Virginia* and *Florida*'.[4] A league is around three nautical miles, over three land miles. Another text Berkeley might have consulted has the islands 'scituate directly east from *Virginia* from which they are distant five hundred *English* Miles and three Thousand three hundred Miles from the City of *London*'.[5] Having sailed for his European tours, Berkeley would have had some reasonable knowledge of nautical speeds on different seas. There were, additionally, several maps of Bermuda in existence by the time Berkeley wrote to Percival.[6] The lavishly illustrated *New General Atlas* placed the islands at 'Lat.32. 35. Long.58. 60 over-against the Coast of *Carolina*, about five hundred and seventy Miles

2. See LJ, VII.288, 265; see also chapter 5.
3. Luce, p. 99.
4. Varenius, *Cosmography and Geography in Two Parts*, p. 439.
5. [R.B.], *The English Empire in America*, pp. 153–54.
6. See Palmer, *The Printed Maps of Bermuda*.

East from Cape *Carteret* in that Country'.[7] The maps themselves leave no doubt about the location of the islands. In any case, it is not reasonable to suppose that Berkeley could not or would not have enquired of someone who had sailed from the mainland to the islands. He asked Prior, for example, about the whereabouts of a Bermuda Jones.[8] It is perhaps more insulting to Berkeley, rather than less, to suggest that he was unaware of the geographical isolation of the islands. After all, there was an established colony on the island, and it did communicate with other plantations, the American mainland, and London, the metropolitan centre.

Much of what Berkeley said of Bermuda to Percival could have been drawn from the geographical literature. Varenius reports that the 'Air is almost always serene [. . .] very healthful [. . .] the Earth is exceeding fertil, yielding two Crops a year; their *Mayz* they gather in *July* and *December*: They have excellent Fruits, as *Oranges, Dates, Mulberries, &c.* [. . .] the *Hogs* which the *Spaniards* formerly carried thither are excellent, and much increased; they have many *Sea-birds*, and other Fowl'. Berkeley does not mention that tortoises are the 'ordinary food', nor that 'they have no fresh Water but that of Wells and Pits, there being neither Fountain nor Stream in these Islands'. Moreover, Varenius contradicts Berkeley's assertion that there was no tobacco or indigo, saying that these commodities, as well as pearls and amber, 'are their principal Riches, for which they have a good trade'.[9] The author of *The English Empire in America* echoes Varenius on the abundance of fish, fowl, hogs, tortoises, and maize, also noting the 'Mulberries, Silkworms, Palmetto's, Cedars, Pearls and Ambergreice'.[10]

The description offered by the *New General Atlas* contains many of Berkeley's observations, but the atlas seems less inclined to think the difficulty of landing on the islands a positive thing, and it also

7. *A New General Atlas*, p. 243. This is generally known as John Senex's atlas, a copy of which was bought from the auction of the Berkeley family library by Charles(?) Burney for 7 shillings, 6 pence; see *A Catalogue of the Valuable Library of the late Right Rev. Dr. Berkeley*, p. 46, no. 1546, 'Senex's Modern Geography of all the known Countries in the World, maps coloured'.

8. Letter 127, Berkeley to Prior, 8 December 1724, pp. 198–99.

9. Varenius, *Cosmography and Geography in Two Parts*, p. 439.

10. [R.B.], *The English Empire in America*, pp. 153–55.

gives an indication of an existing colonial church and educational establishment that Berkeley never mentions:

The Climate is healthful, and the Soil fruitful. It was reckon'd one of the most healthful Places in the World for about eighty Years after the Discovery; so that sick People us'd to come hither from our Suger-Islands to recover their Health; But within these twenty Years, Hurricanes have much alter'd the Air; yet in general 'tis clear, temperate, and calm. [. . .] [H]ere seems to be a perpetual Spring[.] [. . .] All [water] that they have here is brackish, except the Rain-Water they keep in Cisterns for Use. Maiz is their chief Grain, which they sow and reap twice a Year. Their Harvest-time is *July* and *December*. Here's Tobacco, but not very good, with most other Plants found in *America*[.] [. . .] Their Trees are Palmetto's, Piemento's, and wild Palms[.] [. . .] Here's store of odoriferous Trees which produce styptick Berries, that cure Fluxes. Their Cedars are reckon'd the best, and as good as Oaks for building Ships, which is one of the best Parts of their Trade. Here are fine Plantations of Oranges, reckon'd the largest and best in the World, Mulberries &c. which give the Country a beautiful prospect.

NO venomous Creature can live here. [. . .] The Inhabitants are generally healthful: Many live to a hundred Years, but few above, and seem rather to die of Age and Weakness than of Sickness. [. . .] The main Island is fortified by Rocks, which extend themselves round it a great way into the Sea; and this natural Strength is improv'd by Forts, &c. so planted with Cannon, as to command the Channels and Inlets. There are only two Places where Ships can safely put in, but not without a Pilot, because of the hidden Rocks. [. . .] So many Ships were formerly wreck'd here, that the *Spaniards* call'd them the *Devil's Islands*. [. . .] Here's a fair Church, with a good Library, and the Minister has 50 *l. per Ann.* and some Glebe Lands. [. . .] There are two other Ministers who officiate in the Country, and have 40 *l. per Ann.* each, besides their Glebes; and they have parochial Libraries.[11]

The islands that Berkeley set out to inhabit were regarded as peculiarly fruitful and health-giving, but were not without their

11. *A New General Atlas*, pp. 243–44.

connection to the world of commodity trading, and the structures of Anglican religious life were already present.

Berkeley's insistence on Bermuda's detachment from the ills of modern commercial life (the Bermudians are 'carriers' rather than 'traders') and the correlated innocence of its inhabitants are also at odds with other accounts of the economic and social function of the islands. Berkeley had some reason to depict Bermuda as more socially stable, less prone to the ills of the profiteering plantation economy, and populated by self-sufficient sea carriers, but his account of Bermuda glosses over the earlier history of the colony. Initially run by the Virginia Company, and then by the Somers Islands Company, it was the first of the British colonies to import slaves, as well as a greater producer of tobacco than Virginia in the years leading up to the collapse of tobacco prices in the late 1620s. The early history of Bermuda was that of a monopolistic trading colony, albeit one that avoided the extremes of the plantation system.[12] Isaac Richier, a governor of the islands in the late seventeenth century, once the Crown had taken them back, joins the throng celebrating Bermuda's 'good & fresh provision, besides Beef, pork, Turkies, fowles, &c Cabages, Onions in great plenty'. But he notes that the inhabitants are interested only in making their own fortunes by going to sea, rather than by labouring to produce tobacco or sugar: 'y.ᵉ people are generally so sloathfull & Careless y.ᵗ they will not apply y.ᵐselves to labor only going to sea, but will not upon any termes be brought to serve on board y.ᵉ Kings shipps in warr or Peace'. Of the island in general he notes that 'it is in it's present Condition of noe acc.ᵗ to y.ᵉ King & only Occasions Charge to maintaine y.ᵉ Governmᵗ'. He sees its use as a fortified breadbasket for the more southerly Caribbean islands and the mainland.[13] These are not the simple and innocent people of Berkeley's letter, and later his *Proposal*, but a group of truculent planters who go to sea out of sloth and claim no civic identification with the metropolitan government.

12. Jarvis, *In the Eye of All Trade*, pp. 11–118.

13. Huntington Library, Egerton Family Papers, MS EL 9608, ff. 1–2, 'The State & Condition of Bermuda by M.ʳ Richier late Govern.ʳ'.

'The Greatest Hurry of Business'

Campaigning for the Bermuda project led to a period in which Berkeley experienced 'the greatest hurry of business I ever knew in my life'.[14] In giving an account here of this personal activity, I try to comprehend it within a set of broader contexts: the existing programmes for colonial and indigenous education in America and the West Indies; the activities of the Society for the Propagation of the Gospel in Foreign Parts; and the land donations and bequests made in the wills of private individuals or managed by the government that funded Berkeley's and other comparable schemes. Berkeley's utopian educational project, which set itself in opposition to the forces of commercial modernity, nonetheless drew on and contributed to the transformation of the Caribbean into a monocultural, sugar-producing slave society in unintended ways. These unintended consequences of Berkeley's scheme should be placed next to those that have already been acknowledged and discussed in both this book and previous accounts of the scheme, most particularly the contribution Berkeley indirectly made to the American university system.

The settlement of Berkeley's personal finances was one part of his campaign for Bermuda. His letter to Percival mentions the deanery of Dromore as a source of income for a charity school. On Berkeley's return to Ireland in 1721, he sought preferment to this post from the duke of Grafton, specifically as it was a sinecure. Grafton was holding on to the deanery 'in order to create a dependence', which Berkeley thought would only disappoint people. Though Berkeley was granted a patent in February 1722, the bishop of Dromore presented an alternative candidate, and a legal challenge from Berkeley followed on the basis that the Crown held the right to dispose of the deanery rather than the bishop. Berkeley was given £50 to help fund the lawsuit, which would come nowhere near covering expenses, so he toyed with asking the duke of Grafton for another position, the chantership of Christ Church, to fund the suit and 'recover the right of the Crown'.[15] Though the case seems

---

14. Letter 145, Berkeley to Prior, 19 April 1726, p. 222.

15. Letter 98, Berkeley to Percival, 12 October 1721, p. 164; letter 107, Berkeley to Percival, 15 March 1722, p. 174.

never to have been heard, it is worth noting here that Berkeley defended the right of the Crown against the right of the bishop in the matter of ecclesiastical appointments. He was on other occasions a supporter of ecclesiastical authority against commercialised government.

In October, Berkeley mentioned the deanery of Derry as a possible compensation from the duke of Grafton, if the current incumbent died of his palsy and if the rival for the deanery of Dromore was not promoted to a bishopric. There was competition for the deanery that required attendance in the piazza at Dublin Castle. Berkeley felt the appointment was given him in part because Trinity College gave two livings in its gift to Grafton to dispose of, and he appointed Berkeley to them.[16] It must have been decisive, given that only twelve days after recording Berkeley's presentation to Artrea and Arboe he was known to be presented to Derry, and two other clerics (one of whom, John Shadwell, was a rival for the deanery in Derry) were nominated as clerks for Artrea and Arboe. Berkeley resigned his senior fellowship at the college on 18 May 1724.[17] The deanery would contribute to forwarding Bermuda, by its prestige if not financially:

> This Deanery is said to be worth £1,500 per annum, but then there are four curates to be paid, and great charges upon entering, for a large house and offices, first fruits, patent, etc. which will consume the first year's profits, and part of the second. But as I do not consider it with an eye to enriching myself, so I shall be perfectly contented if it facilitates and recommends my scheme of Bermuda, which I am in hopes will meet with a better reception when it comes from one possessed of so great a deanery.[18]

Berkeley appears to have sublet the tithe lands associated with the deanery on his first and only trip to Derry. He might not have achieved the highest rate possible, but preferred 'to have men of substantial fortunes engaged for the punctual payment of the foregoing sum [£1,250], than by keeping them in my own hands to

16. Letter 113, Berkeley to Percival, October 1722, p. 181; Luce, p. 87, citing *Berkeley and Percival*, p. 216; letter 123, Berkeley to Percival, 5 May 1724, p. 194.

17. TCD MS MUN V-5-2, ff. 266v (p. 530), 267v (p. 532).

18. Letter 123, Berkeley to Percival, 5 May 1724, p. 195.

subject myself to all that trouble, and all those cheats which dissenters (whereof we have many about Derry) are inclined to practice towards the clergy of our Church'. Berkeley defended his management of the expenses and profits associated with the deanery to Prior two years later. The people of Derry had made a 'clamour', which Berkeley believed to be 'groundless', as he was spending £76 per annum more than his predecessors, paying curates, in part to preach for absentees such as himself, and increasing the number of charity children.[19]

There was at this juncture an addition to Berkeley's private income as well as preferment in the church. Esther Van Homrigh, perhaps best known as the intimate acquaintance of Jonathan Swift, sometimes under the name Vanessa, named Berkeley in her will. It stated:

> I give and devise all my Worldly substance whether in lands Tenements hereditaments or trusts and all by real and personal estate of what nature or kind soever unto the Revd Doctor George Berkly one of the Fellows of Trinity College in Dublin and Robert Marshall of Clonmell Esqr their heirs Exe°rs and Advis°rs Chargeable nevertheless ∧^with and subject and liable to the payment of all such debts of my own contracting as I shall owe at the time of my death as also unto the payment of the several Legacies herein after bequeathed[.][20]

Berkeley and Marshall were also executors of the estate. Berkeley was surprised, 'having never in the whole course of my life, to my knowledge, exchanged one single word with her'. Stock says that Swift took Berkeley 'often to dine at her house', but Anne Berkeley remarks that 'he never dined with Mrs Vanhomrig, or saw her but once'. Berkeley estimated the legacy's value at £3,000 and noted that he thought ever more of Bermuda, 'this providential event having made many things easy in my private affairs which were otherwise before'. The surprise with which Berkeley greeted this event has led to the suggestion that Swift had been named as the

19. Letter 125, Berkeley to Percival, 8 June 1724, pp. 196–97; letter 156, Berkeley to Prior, 13 September 1726, pp. 237–38.

20. Huntington Library, Jonathan Swift Collection, MS HM 14348, f. 2r, Esther Van Homrigh, last will and testament, registered 1 May 1723 and probate granted 7 June 1723, the executors 'being first sworn personally'.

legatee, only to be removed when Van Homrigh was angered by a combination of a lack of attention from Swift and the rumour of his marriage to another intimate female acquaintance, Esther Johnson (known as Stella). Berkeley was chosen as a respectable person in the same social group whose Bermuda project was probably already being discussed.[21]

The letters between Van Homrigh and Swift seem to have come into Berkeley's hands as executor. When Stock suggests that Berkeley burnt Swift's letters to Van Homrigh, Anne Berkeley notes, 'I have heard the Bp of Cloyne say—that all Swifts letters which came into his hands did the highest honor to the Dean—as they all tended to <u>damp</u>—not to encrease the flame ^{of Vanessa} the poem of Cadenus and Vanessa he never would have published—; its consequences justified his delicacy on that subject, for that Poem caused the death of <u>Stella</u>—as Dr Delany informed me—but Mr Marshal published it Unknown to him'.[22] Clive Probyn, however, claims that Marshall and Berkeley initiated the publication of the letters before it was halted at the intervention of Swift's friend Thomas Sheridan (to whom the petition of Anne de la Terre to Berkeley was attributed, probably wrongly).[23] Sheridan's son, in his biography of Swift, indeed states that in her last illness Van Homrigh 'had laid a strong injunction on her executors, that immediately after her decease, they should publish all the letters that passed between Swift and her, together with the Poem of Cadenus and Vanessa', and he confirms that the publication was initiated.[24] But an editor of the Swift–Van Homrigh correspondence thinks it most likely that Marshall alone initiated the publication of the letters and was responsible for the publication of *Cadenus and Vanessa*, as Swift noted that publishing the poem was not the act of a friend.[25] In any case, it seems the Van Homrigh legacy required Berkeley to adjudicate between the reported wishes of a legatrix, a personal

---

21. Letter 118, Berkeley to Percival, 4 June 1723, p. 188; TCD MS 5936, Stock, *An Account of the Life of George Berkeley*, p. 14 and opposite; letter 118, Berkeley to Percival, 4 June 1723, p. 188; Luce, p. 89.

22. TCD MS 5936, Stock, *An Account of the Life of George Berkeley*, p. 14 and opposite.

23. Probyn, 'Homrigh, Esther Van [known as Vanessa]'.

24. Sheridan, *The Life of the Rev. Dr. Jonathan Swift*, p. 332.

25. Freeman, *Vanessa and Her Correspondence with Jonathan Swift*, pp. 39–41. For Luce's account, see pp. 66–67, 87–90.

friendship with Swift, literary curiosity, and the ethics of unauthorised publication.

The legacy involved Berkeley in several years of negotiation. Peter Partinton, executor to Esther's father and one of her
brothers, had a reversionary interest in part of the brother's estate
and so refused to divide a portion of the father's estate between
the children. Esther had a suit at law against him, but it was not
resolved at the time of her death.[26] Berkeley, then, had to settle this
suit. He engaged his old friend Tom Prior to act as his agent in the
matter, with a premium on Berkeley's share of the legacy, increased
if Prior could bring the Partinton suit to a conclusion by Christmas
1725.[27] Marshall seems to have taken an attitude similar to Partinton's, wearing down claimants on the legacy so as to increase
his own share. Berkeley's frustration with the situation showed
when on 20 January 1726 he wrote to Prior, noting a lack of progress and saying, 'I do not doubt your skill; I only wish you were
as active to serve an old friend as I should be in any affair of yours
that lay in my power'. On 13 March 1733, he could still write to Prior
expressing hopes that 'our affair with Partinton will be finished this
term'.[28] Berkeley had quickly learnt that the estate was indebted
and so would be worth only £2,000. And given that the paintings
in the estate were auctioned, with the help of John Smibert, the
value must have been quite uncertain. They raised £45 'at an auction which was held last week in Covent Garden, at the house of
one Mr. Russel, a painter'.[29] Even though his decanal income and
this new private source of wealth were variable, turned out to be
less than expected, and involved Berkeley in prolonged legal contestation, they provided him with the degree of material security he
felt he needed to commit to the Bermuda project.

Bermuda was a campaign, and Berkeley managed it with significant charisma and persistence. Many of his letters to Percival
in the period between announcing his intentions and departing for
America make an argument for the Percivals to come to Bermuda,

26. Freeman, *Vanessa and Her Correspondence with Jonathan Swift*, p. 89n.

27. Letter 127, Berkeley to Prior, 8 December 1724, pp. 198–99.

28. Letter 140, p. 214; letter 218, p. 347.

29. Letter 121, Berkeley to Percival, 19 September 1723, p. 192; letter 160, Berkeley to
Prior, 1 December 1726, pp. 244–45; letter 161, Berkeley to Prior, 27 February 1727, p. 248.

usually on the grounds of improving Mrs Percival's health. Percival's brother Philip and his extended family, also recipients of Berkeley's persuasives, seem to have been seriously considering the scheme. Berkeley had made 'Proselites' of the sickly in Philip Percival's family: Philip, saying they are 'almost determined that way', imagines himself assisting with 'his Buildings or Academy of Musick'.[30] The conversion efforts might have been aimed as much at turning the Percivals into advocates for the scheme as participants in it. Percival immediately offered Berkeley strategic advice on the prosecution of the scheme:

> [W]ithout the protection and encouragement of the government you will meet with difficulties of sundry sorts from governors abroad, and from persons in office at home, as the Commissioners of the Plantation, the Society de propaganda Fide, and even the Bishop of London, under whom the care of the Plantations in religious matters lies as you know. Not that any of them can oppose the design you go upon, in general, but they may perplex you in the manner of carrying it on, unless you first settle every thing with them in part, and procure an assured protection from the supreme power.

Whether or not Berkeley was fully conscious of the opposition that came from these quarters, he certainly followed Percival's advice and pursued the government for a charter.[31]

Late in 1724, Berkeley worked on two closely associated texts promoting the scheme, a *Proposal for the better Supplying of Churches in our Foreign Plantations* and a petition to the king, eventually scrutinised by the solicitor and attorney general. The *Proposal* was published in 1724 and again, with a revision (as noted later), in 1725. Percival's mention of Berkeley's Bermuda pamphlet in a letter to his brother of 6 February 1725 (a letter in which he gives strong support to the scheme and says of himself and his wife that 'it is not impossible but we may try that air' for her health) places its publication at least ten days before the petition was submitted

---

30. BL Add MS 47030 (Egmont Papers), f. 82v, Philip to John Percival, 15 August 1724, and f. 136r, 24 February 1724/25.

31. Letter 119, Percival to Berkeley, 30 June 1723, p. 189. Percival reiterated his advice a year later; letter 124, Percival to Berkeley, 26 May 1724, p. 196.

on 16 February.[32] This could have been the 1724 *Proposal*, if the imprint reflected 'old style' dates, as they are often called, in which the year started on 25 March. In what follows I cite the 1725 text.

The 1725 *Proposal* has an initial ornament that depicts building construction, a figure fishing, the sun rising over hills, and another figure reading on the steps of a classical building, thus displaying enterprise, natural copiousness, good climate, and retired scholarship. The same ornament was first used by the publisher in 1722, so it was not designed for the *Proposal*, but it may have been chosen, either by the author or printer, for its resonance with the contents of the text.[33] The text opens with an acknowledgement of the work of the Society for the Promotion of Christian Knowledge (SPCK) and the Society for the Propagation of the Gospel in Foreign Parts (SPG), perhaps seeing after Percival's advice the expediency of smoothing relations with these organisations. Not even the 'vigilance and wisdom' of the bishop of London, another interested party mentioned by Percival, could properly supply churches in the plantations 'so long as the aforesaid churches are supplied from England'. The *Proposal* closes by naming the trustees of the scheme: the archbishop of Canterbury, the high chancellor, the principal secretary of state for the plantations in America, and the bishop of London, again suggesting that Berkeley had acted on Percival's advice to anticipate objections from these quarters.[34]

The *Proposal* is focused on the training of indigenous Americans to act as missionaries to their own people, instructing them in a zealous, missionary Christianity and in the great historical examples 'of publick spirit and virtue, to rescue their countrymen from their savage manners, to a life of civility and religion'. To achieve these aims Berkeley asks for a charter for the college, so that it can be built and endowed by private contributions.[35] The reasons given for selecting Bermuda remain largely the same as those set out to Percival: it is fruitful, mild, equidistant from the other colonies,

32. *Berkeley and Percival*, pp. 223–25.

33. *A Proposal for the Better Supplying of Churches in Our Foreign Plantations*. The ornament was also used for the twentieth book of Broome, trans., *The Iliad of Homer*, p. 175. See Goulden, *The Ornament Stock of Henry Woodfall*, pp. 9, 56, ornament number 35.

34. *Proposal*, pp. 5, 25 (LJ, VII.345–47, 361).

35. *Proposal*, p. 7 (LJ, VII.348).

A PROPOSAL *for the better Supplying of Churches in our foreign Plantations, &c.*

ALTHOUGH there are several excellent persons of the church of England, whose good intentions and endeavours have not been wanting to propagate the gospel in foreign parts, who have even combined into societies for that very purpose, and given great encouragement, not only for English missionaries in the West-Indies, but also, for the reformed of other nations, led by their example, to propagate christianity in the East: It is nevertheless acknowledged, that there is at this day, but little sense of religion, and a most notorious corruption of manners, in the English colonies settled on the continent of America, and the islands. It is also acknowledged, that the gospel hath hitherto made but a very inconsiderable progress among the neighbouring Americans, who still continue in much-what the same ignorance and barbarism, in which we found them above a hundred years ago.

FIGURE 10.1. George Berkeley, *A Proposal for the Better Supplying of Churches in our Foreign Plantations* (London: Henry Woodfall and sold by J. Roberts, 1725), p. 3, British Library, © British Library Board

communicative, and uncorrupted. (For a discussion of the *Proposal's* presentation of Native American and enslaved people, see chapter 7.)

The *Proposal* is less explicit on another function the college seems to have been designed for: the promotion of taste. Berkeley returned from his Italian tour with a critical and theoretical skill in architecture and a developed taste for the visual arts more generally. The existence of a plan of St Paul's College Bermuda, developed by Berkeley and modelled on the Piazza del Popolo, has already been noted. Anne Berkeley was the first to note the existence of this plan. She also talked of the college as a place in which people could retire 'in an Elegant & Learned and a <u>Religious Society</u> where the fine Arts were to have flourished'. Anne was clear that a lack of luxury did not mean an absence of taste:

> It may be thought that the great & rich who retired to Bermuda would have brought their Luxury with them but they retired from Luxury to have taste—it likewise may be supposed that fine Arts could not thrive where luxury by reason & fashion & religion was excluded—but in proof of the Contrary An eminent Painter of the first rank went to America with the Bp & one of the first composers and performers in Music of that time had engaged to come there so soon as he was settled—this place was therefore to be the retreat for Men of fine taste & Learning who had seen much of the World & therefore were tired of it and yet intended to carry every thing laudable & lovely with them & do as much good as they could both to themselves & others—[36]

The painter was John Smibert, whom Berkeley had met in Italy in 1720 and with whom he lodged occasionally in Covent Garden. Smibert had settled in Boston in May 1729 to make a living as a painter of portraits and become 'the first London artist, with a background of study and work in Italy, to settle in New England'.[37] The role of the instructors at the college is not detailed in surviving plans, but if it was intended that Smibert lecture alongside the

36. TCD MS 5936, Stock, *An Account of the Life of George Berkeley*, opposite pp. 18–20; see also David Berman's transcription in Berman, *Berkeley and Irish Philosophy*, pp. 191–92, which proposes some different readings from my transcription.

37. Saunders, *John Smibert*, p. 27; Evans, 'The Provenance of the Notebook', p. 3, citing an unacknowledged source.

FIGURE 10.2. John Smibert, *The Bermuda Group*, 1728–1739,
Yale University Art Gallery, gift of Isaac Lothrop

practical work of an academician, his role would have been inno-
vative.[38] The fine arts were to make their contribution to the philosophical and religious retirement and independence of the Bermuda settlement.

A tension already observed in Berkeley's disclosure of the project to Percival persists in the *Proposal*. It is between 'the commerce
of Bermuda'—'they are the only people of all the British plantations, who hold a general correspondence with the rest'—and the
perception of Bermuda as a place 'where there is no great trade,
which might tempt the readers or fellows of the college to become
merchants, to the neglect of their proper business; where there are
neither riches nor luxury to divert, or lessen their application, or
to make them uneasy and dissatisfied with a homely frugal subsistence: lastly, where the inhabitants, if such a Place may be found,

38. Saunders, *John Smibert*, p. 59: 'That Smibert would give lectures on painting and
architecture to inculcate the virtues of Christian and European civilization borders on the
revolutionary'. For a reading of (some of) Smibert's practice as an expression of Berkeleian
philosophy, see O'Donnell, 'Depicting Berkeleyan Idealism'.

FIGURE 10.3. John Smibert, *George Berkeley*, 1730,
© National Portrait Gallery, London

are noted for innocence and simplicity of manners'.[39] The reason Berkeley gives for the insufficiency of 'the college long since projected in Barbadoes' (Codrington College, of which more shortly) is overexposure to trade, wealth, and luxury and the dissolution of morals. The absence of 'avarice and luxury' from Bermuda is the tonic key of the *Proposal*. The fellows of the college will 'dedicate the remainder of their lives to the instructing the youth of America, and prosecuting their own studies upon a very moderate subsistence in a retirement, so sweet, and so secure [. . .] as Bermuda'; Berkeley himself 'values no preferment upon earth, so much as that of being employed in the execution of this design'.[40] The retired life of the missionary academic is conceived in opposition to the preferment system at home (from which Berkeley had just profited considerably) and the world of transatlantic commodity trading.

The petition is a different kind of text. Besides providing a summary rationale for the college and its location, it outlines a skeleton constitution: Berkeley was to be president, with William Thompson, Jonathan Rogers, and James King serving as the first three fellows of nine; only the king could select from the named fellows a new president, in case of vacancy; the fellows and president might elect new fellows by majority; the college would operate as a company under a common seal, in order to be able to manage property and endowments; the president and fellows could make statutes; the bishop of London would act as visitor, resolving differences between the president and fellows and approving or abolishing statutes; the principal secretary of state would be the chancellor; the president and fellows would make rules for and govern the college; a vice president (senior fellow) could stand in for the president; and the college was to send a yearly account of its scholars, statutes, and any remarkable incidents to the chancellor and visitor. The petition also asks that His Majesty's government be obliged to assist and protect the college, that the college have a monopoly to 'teach the Liberal Arts in the Islands of Bermuda', and that 'the said President and Fellows hold their Preferments for a year & a half after their arrival in Bermudas'.[41]

The law officers, Charles Wearg and Philip Yorke (for Yorke's connection to Berkeley and the Yorke-Talbot opinion, see chapter 7),

39. *Proposal*, pp. 10, 8 (LJ, VII.351, 349).
40. Ibid., pp. 8, 12, 14 (LJ, VII.349, 352–53, 354).
41. LJ, VII.364–65.

approved the petition, with some exceptions. They thought it illegal to grant an educational monopoly. Nor was it possible to stipulate a period for which fellows could hold preferments, as some clerical positions required residency. The law officers took this clause as a method of obliging fellows to resign their church positions within a certain period, and thought that this could be done with a different form of words. They also suggested that the king ought to approve fellowship elections, and that statutes ought to be laid before the visitor.[42] The law officers also noted that charters of this kind were normally supported by endowments, but that the nature of the enterprise made it likely that funding would be forthcoming.

Berkeley submitted along with his petition an extract from the will of Nathaniel Rich, dated 2 December 1635, which left 'five Shares of Land in Bermuda Islands for the Maintenance of a free School there, for the Education of Indian Children to be brought from Virginia or New England or some other Continent of America to be Instructed in the Knowledge of true Religion'. Berkeley believed that these lands had not been appropriated, and he supplied an affidavit from Benjamin Bennet, a recent governor, saying that the lands existed and had been used by particular schoolmasters.[43] Rich's will placed responsibility for the school with 'my executor and ye noble Lady', that is, Edward Montagu, Lord Mandeville, and his wife.[44] Rich had held shares of land in Bermuda, and those lands were responsible for a large proportion of the island's tobacco production. He was also on the boards of the Somers Islands, Virginia, and Providence Island companies.[45] Seeking to benefit from Rich's will was one way in which Berkeley's Bermuda project remained connected to the world of trade and commerce it publicly sought to reject.

At their 24 February 1725 meeting, the commissioners for trade and plantations (Mr Dominique, Mr Bladen, Mr Ashe, and Mr Plummer) heard Berkeley's petition and 'ordered that he be acquainted that the Board desire to speak with him on Friday morning next', together with the bishop of London. At the 26 February meeting, with the earl of Westmorland, Mr Chetwynd, and Mr Pelham also present, 'their Lordships took again into consideration

---

42. LJ, VII.365–66.
43. LJ, VII.365.
44. National Archives, PRO Prob 11/172, ff. 253v' and Yerby and Sgroi, 'Rich, Nathaniel'.
45. Swales, 'Rich, Sir Nathaniel'.

the reference from the Duke of Newcastle' for the college, 'and, after some discourse with the Doctor, ordered that the draught of a representation should be prepared thereupon'. It was agreed and signed on 2 March.[46] As I am not aware that this representation has ever been noticed in accounts of Berkeley's Bermuda scheme, I reproduce it here in full:

To the King's most Excellent Majesty.

May it please your Majesty;

In Obedience to your Majesty's Commands signify'd to us by a Reference from his Grace the Duke of Newcastle, One of your Majesty's Principal Secr~ys of State, Dated the 6.th of the last month; We have considered the Petition of George Berkeley, Doctor in Divinity, and Dean of Derry, W.[m] Thompson, Jonathan Rogers and James King, Masters of Arts, and Fellows of Trinity Colledge in Dublin; Praying that your Majesty will be gra: ciously pleasd to grant them your Royal Letters Patents for the erecting a Colledge in the Bermuda Islands, for the better Propagating of the Gospel among the Savage Americans, and for the better supplying of Churches in the Plantations with able and learn'd Ministers, and thereupon take leave to represent to your Majesty:

That we have been attended by the said Doctor Berkeley, and discours'd with him upon the Subject Matter of his said Petition, as well as upon the Scheme thereunto annex'd, According to which the Doctor has propos'd to establish and regulate the aforementioned Colledge.

We have no Objection to so laudable an Undertaking, Provided the said Colledge be not Impowered to purchase or receive above one thousand Acres of Land in the said Bermuda Islds, And that their Revenue in any other Part of your Majesty's Dominions do not exceed two thousands [*sic*] pounds a year.

Which is most humbly submitted.

---

46. [Commissioners for Trade and Plantations], *Journal of the Commissioners for Trade and Plantations*, pp. 151–52. It is interesting to note that on 2 March 1725 the commissioners were also considering proposals for St Christopher's from a Mr Smith. I would like to thank Björn Lambrenos, who during an undergraduate research internship at St Andrews in 2017, assisted me with research on Berkeley's Bermuda project and independently identified this source.

T: Chetwynd.

P: Dominique.

T: Pelham.

M: Bladen.

J: Hobart.[47]

The Board of Trade, like the solicitor and attorney general, strongly approved of the scheme, but not without seeking to impose some limits upon it—in this case, on the landowning and income-generating powers of the college.

In April 1725, Berkeley relayed that he had 'obtained reports from the Bishop of London, the Board of Trade and Plantations, and the Attorney and Solicitor General, in favour of the Bermuda scheme, and hope to have the warrant signed by his Majesty this week'. On 2 June, the charter passed the Privy Seal. On 12 June, Berkeley reported to Prior: 'The charter hath passed all the seals, and is now in my custody. It hath cost me 130 pounds dry fees, besides expedition-money to men in office'.[48] Berkeley now switched his attention to funding, and one of his first targets was the land in St Christopher's ceded by the French as part of the Treaty of Utrecht in 1713 and not yet disposed of. He wrote to Wake, the archbishop of Canterbury and a trustee of the Bermuda scheme, to ask him to use his influence to have those lands used to promote the college.[49] The Abbé Gualteri, or Altieri, is said by Stock to have taken the request for St Christopher's lands to the king.[50] By 15 March 1726, Berkeley told Prior that this idea was most likely 'abortive', given parliamentary delays.[51]

Berkeley's other avenue was the pursuit of private subscriptions. By 28 December 1725, he was able to inform Percival he had raised £3,400, 'though the town hath been very thin ever since I obtained the charter'. By 10 February, that sum had increased to £4,000.[52] Two lists of subscriptions, the shorter of which

47. National Archives, CO 38/8, pp. 27–28.

48. Letter 128, Berkeley to Prior, 20 April 1725, p. 200; letter 129, Berkeley to Prior, 3 June 1725, p. 200; letter 130, Berkeley to Prior, p. 201.

49. Letter 132, 10 August 1725, pp. 203–4.

50. Stock, *An Account of the Life of George Berkeley*, p. 18.

51. Letter 144, p. 221.

52. Letter 137, p. 209; letter 143, Berkeley to Percival, p. 210.

amounted to £2,000, the longer to £3,065, survive amongst the Berkeley papers. Eliza Berkeley calls the longer, in an annotation of 1788, the 'Original List of Subscribers to Bp Berkeley Bermuda Scheme which had it succeeded w^d have introduced Episcopacy and of course prevented [?independence]'.[53] The lists may date from before May 1724, as they contain both the Earl of Oxford (£200) and Edward Harley Esq (£100). Robert Harley, Earl of Oxford, died in that month, when his son Edward became the second earl. The lists hint at the appeal of the scheme to certain groups of people. Friends, patrons, and employers figure prominently: Pembroke (the dedicatee of *Principles of Human Knowledge*, £300), Percival (£200), and Peterborough (£105) are there. Berkeley's connection to the grandees of the Tory ministry of the early 1710s is evident in the presence of this group. Privately wealthy patrons of the arts and speculators also figure. The Harleys were collectors of books and manuscripts. Dr Pelling (£100), rector of St Anne's, Soho, and in 1715 a canon at Windsor, had a notable library.[54] Mrs Drilincourt (now more commonly spelt Drelincourt, £100) was the widow of the dean of Armagh, a lucrative post, who would in 1747 found a charity school in Armagh. James Brydges, the duke of Chandos (£200), was a patron of architects and musicians as well as a speculator in trading and property ventures at home and in the plantations. Matthew Decker (£100) was a merchant who had financial dealings with both Robert Harley and Brydges and was a major funder of the South Sea Company. Lady Betty Hastings, a pious but ecumenical high Anglican whose father was identified as a Jacobite, gave £500. Archibald Hutcheson (£200), a lawyer whom Berkeley called 'my very good friend', was a moderate Tory at the time of the Harley ministry but was suspected of Jacobitism because of his (mostly financial) relationship with the duke of Ormond.[55] He also, through two marriages, had property and business connections in

53. BL Add MS 39311, f. 63.

54. Nichols, *Literary Anecdotes of the Eighteenth Century*, p. 461. Unless otherwise noted, information on subscribers is derived from the following articles in the *Oxford Dictionary of National Biography*: Speck, 'Harley, Robert'; Taylor, 'Harley, Edward'; Whelan, 'Drelincourt, Peter [Pierre]'; Johnson, 'Brydges, James'; Gauci, 'Decker, Sir Matthew'; Guerrini, 'Hastings, Lady Elizabeth [Betty]'; Hanham, 'Hutcheson, Archibald'; Hutchings, 'Hoare, Henry'; and Acheson, 'Rundle, Thomas'.

55. Letter 160, Berkeley to Prior, 1 December 1726, p. 245.

the West Indies, including in St Christopher's. Benjamin Hoare the banker gave £100, and Robert Walpole, whom Anne Berkeley held partly responsible for the ultimate failure to release funds to the scheme, gave £200.[56] Dr Rundle, whose proposal as a candidate for the diocese of Gloucester would later cause problems for the alliance between Walpole and the bishops, and who features alongside Berkeley in Alexander Pope's distribution of the virtues to Anglican bishops, gave £100. (This is not an exhaustive account of the names in the lists.) The lists combine old Tory grandees with those who had been tainted by the accusation of Jacobitism; with those, including Walpole himself, who were much more closely aligned to the developing ministerial ideology of the 1720s and '30s and its more tolerant attitude to trade and speculation; and with those patrons of the arts and education who, through either strict financial management or improvidence, felt able to give large sums to the promotion of taste and Christian knowledge.

One further possible source of funds came to Berkeley's attention. In telling Percival that the subscriptions have reached £4,000, Berkeley also engages his interest as trustee to a bequest: 'Lord Palmerston is desirous that nine hundred and odd pounds in his hands should be disposed of to this our college for breeding up young negroes agreeable to Mr. Delon's will. The trustees for directing the disposal thereof are your Lordship, Dr. Bray, Mr. Hales, his brother, and Mr. Belitha'.[57] Abel Tassin, Sieur D'Allone, died in 1723. Thomas Bray, the driving force behind the foundation of the SPCK (1699) and SPG (1701), a high churchman and a campaigner for institutions of religious education such as parish libraries and for episcopacy in the American plantations, was a foil to Berkeley in their respective campaigns. Bray had already worked closely with D'Allone and regarded the bequest as his to manage. He fended off interest from the SPG and did the same to Berkeley. As has been noted, Berkeley quickly reissued his *Proposal* in 1725 with an additional paragraph on the African population of the colonies. The Bermuda project would now also include an effort

56. TCD MS 5936, Stock, *An Account of the Life of George Berkeley*, p. 19 and opposite. John Wolfe Esq (£100) appears on the list, which may make him a strong candidate for the addressee of letter 284, dated 1741, one of the letters on marriage discussed in chapter 9.

57. Letter 143, p. 219. This legacy is also discussed in chapter 7.

to convert the negroes of our plantations, who, to the infamy of England, and scandal of the world, continue Heathen under Christian masters, and in Christian countries. Which cou'd never be, if our planters were rightly instructed and made sensible [. . .] That gospel liberty consists with temporal servitude; and that their slaves would only become better slaves by being Christian.[58]

Dan Dering, Percival's cousin, also attempted to interest him in the matter, and although Percival sought to maintain his distance, hearing that 'there is a disposition in the other Associates to give the money to Dean Berkeley's Colledge I will on that Condition Act[.] [. . .] But I think it would be proper D.ʳ Bray should be informed of our Design and his approbation given it in writing'.[59] It seems that Bray did prevent the money coming to Bermuda. By the time of his death, the number of people managing the bequest had grown to twenty-nine and included James Oglethorpe, who would later correspond with Berkeley on the possibility of working together on American improvement. In 1730, Percival expounded to Oglethorpe the idea of assisting 'Dean Berkeley's Bermuda scheme, by erecting a Fellowship in his college for instructing negroes', but Oglethorpe had other ideas.[60] His greatest colonial ambition, which would become the state of Georgia, is mentioned later in the chapter.

Berkeley was wrong when he thought the idea of using St Christopher's lands as a means of funding Bermuda was abortive. The Commons debated the issue on 11 May 1726, and Berkeley prepared thoroughly. He gave an impression of the work involved, the nature of the debate, and his sense of the motivations of the opposition:

After six weeks' struggle against an earnest opposition from different interests and motives, I have yesterday carried my point just as I desired in the House of Commons, by an extraordinary majority, none having the confidence to speak against it, and not above two giving their negative; which was done in so low a voice as if they themselves

58. *Proposal*, pp. 4–5 (LJ, VII.346; see also textual notes).
59. BL Add MS 47031, Percival to Daniel Dering, 12 February 1726, cited in Gaustad, *George Berkeley in America*, p. 99. I am heavily indebted to Gaustad's account of the D'Allone legacy and its afterlife, pp. 97–104.
60. Percival, *Manuscripts of the Earl of Egmont*, I.44–45, cited in Gaustad, *George Berkeley in America*, p. 101.

were ashamed of it. They were both considerable men in stocks, in trade and in the city: and in truth I have had more opposition from that sort of men, and from the governors and traders to America, than from any others. But, God be praised, there is an end of all their narrow and mercantile views and endeavours, as well as of the jealousies and suspicions of others (some whereof were very great men), who apprehended this College may produce an independency in America, or at least lessen its dependency upon England.[61]

Establishing a college might lessen the dependent status of a colony.[62] He said to Percival five days later that 'the like step had never been taken in any reign for any college before'.[63] Berkeley's campaign against the mercantile class and those patrician, metropolitan members of the governing elite who feared the power and independence of the nonmetropolitan areas of the empire had been successful. His expansive, Christian educational view had triumphed over narrow and mercantile views that regarded the peripheral territories of the empire only as sources of income.

Once Parliament had approved support for the college, it was left to the king to decide what form that support should take. Berkeley again petitioned the king, noting that the Commons did 'in the last Sessions of Parliament humbly Address Your Majesty That Your Majesty would be graciously pleased to make [such] Provision for the Maintenance of the said President and Fellows as your Majesty shou'd think proper out of the Lands in the Island of Saint Christophers yielded by France to Great Britain by the Treaty of Utrecht, to which Address Your Majesty was pleased to return [a most] Gracious Answer'.[64] The petition concludes by asking the king to give a warrant directing the means of support. That means of support was clarified before the end of the year: it was 'by a rent-charge on the whole Crown lands, redeemable

61. Letter 146, Berkeley to Prior, 12 May 1726, p. 222.

62. For Ireland's dependent status as a factor motivating the patriotic movement for improvement in the 1730s, see Livesey, 'The Dublin Society in Eighteenth-Century Irish Political Thought'.

63. Letter 147, Berkeley to Prior, 17 May 1726, p. 223.

64. The petition appears in Berman, 'Some New Bermuda Berkeleiana', p. 25. Berman dates the petition between 16 May 1726 and 12 June 1727 (the death of George I). The letter to Prior detailing the form of support might, however, suggest that the petition was submitted before that letter was written.

upon the Crown's paying twenty thousand pounds, for the use of the president and fellows of St. Paul's, and their successors'. One further challenge to the grant presented itself when the king died on 12 June, 'our grant being defeated by the King's dying before the broad seal was annexed to it, in order to which it was passing through the offices. I have *la mer à boire* again'. But, on 6 July, Berkeley was able to report to Prior that 'I have obtained a new warrant for a grant, signed by his present Majesty, contrary to the expectations of my friends'.[65] At this point, Berkeley had every reasonable expectation of receiving the significant funding promised for his college.

Having been to Dublin and concluded his marriage to Anne Forster, Berkeley posted fifty-five boxes of books and three boxes of books, papers, and mathematical instruments from Dublin to London.[66] He departed for Rhode Island ('a place abounding in provisions where I design to purchase a piece of land with my own money in order to supply our college with such necessities as are not the product of Bermuda') on 6 September 1728. Berkeley gave his rationale for departure to a correspondent who is thought to have been Edmund Gibson, bishop of London:

> I propose to continue at Rhode Island till such time as Dr. Clayton hath received that money and is come to Bermuda with the rest of my associates where I intend to join them. Going to Bermuda without either money or associates I could not think of. I should have made a bad figure and done no good. Staying here would have been no less disagreeable and to as little purpose, since all I could do here was finished except receiving the money which may be done by others. It should seem therefore that the intermediate time may be passed with more advantage in America where I can see things with my own eyes and prepare matters for the rendering our college more useful.[67]

From Rhode Island, he supplemented that rationale:

> Before I left England I was reduced to a difficult situation. Had I continued there, the report would have obtained (which I found beginning

65. Letter 160, Berkeley to Prior, 1 December 1726, p. 245; letter 165, Berkeley to Prior, 15 June 1727, p. 252; letter 167, p. 253.

66. Letter 171, Berkeley to Fairfax, 7 June 1728, p. 259.

67. Letter 173, Berkeley to Gibson(?), 5 September 1728, p. 261.

to spread) that I had dropped the design after it had cost me and my friends so much trouble and expense. On the other hand, if I had taken leave of my friends, even those who assisted and approved my undertaking would have condemned my coming abroad before the King's bounty was received. This obliged me to come away in the private manner that I did, and to run the risk of a tedious winter voyage. Nothing less would have convinced the world that I was in earnest, after the report I knew was growing to the contrary.[68]

Forced to land at Virginia before continuing to Rhode Island, Henry Newman of the Society for the Promotion of Christian Knowledge had read of Berkeley's arrival in New England in the *Daily Journal* for 12 October 1728.

In Berkeley's first surviving letter from America, he was already considering transferring the location of the college from Bermuda to Newport, but would not have these thoughts publicised until the money from the St Christopher's lands had been paid to Dr Clayton. Four months later, Berkeley's friends were beginning to express doubts about the grant being paid. Benson says that he is glad Berkeley finds Rhode Island pleasing, 'as I find so little likelihood of the £20,000 being paid in order to remove you thence to Bermuda'.[69] This possibility increased into a likelihood in the correspondence, so that Newman thought the transfer would be objected to because the case against Bermuda as a location could be used as an excuse not to pay the grant at all. He suggests that Berkeley 'think of returning to secure your deanery before it can be liable to forfeiture'. On 29 March 1730, Berkeley wrote to Percival that 'I wait here with all the anxiety that attends suspense till I know what I can depend upon or what course I am to take. On the one hand I have no notion that the Court would put what men call a bite upon poor clergymen, who depended upon charters, grants, votes, and the like encouragements. On the other hand, I see nothing done towards payment of the money'. Almost a year later, the project was finished, without ever having been begun: 'I have received such accounts on all hands both from England and Ireland

68. Letter 187, Berkeley to Percival, 27 June 1729, p. 283.
69. Letter 176, Berkeley to Percival, 7 February 1729, p. 264; letter 186, 23 June 1729, p. 280.

that I now give up all hopes of executing the design which brought me into these parts. I am fairly given to understand that the money will never be paid'.[70] The underlying reason Berkeley identified for the money not being paid—the tendency of the times towards free-thinking and his continuing struggle against free thought in this period of his life—occupies a later part of this chapter.

Rivals to Bermuda

When first revealing his scheme to Percival, Berkeley had feared that he might appear mad and chimerical. Indeed, many later commentators thought so. Perhaps its madness was in planning to transport Native Americans from the mainland to be educated, a plan William Byrd thought foolhardy and necessarily involv-ing kidnap?[71] The will of Nathaniel Rich offered a precedent for Berkeley, but Rich had not, as Luce thinks he had, lived in Ber-muda.[72] The location was criticised, often by other clergymen involved in American projects, and often with the suggestion of an alternative. One 'G.G.' wrote to Gibson on 23 September 1725 having read Berkeley's *Proposal* and accurately noted that 'what this Author Chiefly Aimes at, is Communication, Retirement, Plenty & health'. G.G. states that much food has to be imported to Bermuda, however, and suggests that Albany would be far better suited, as it would enable retirement at the same time as being within communicable distance of three hundred towns. 'Also it is in the Center between Boston in New England, New York, Phila-delphia in Penselvania'.[73] Similarly, Simon Smith wrote to Gibson, from St John's, Antigua, on 5 May 1727, questioning the choice of Bermuda:

> I think it (with submission to your Lordships, and the rest of the Hon-
> ourable Societies better judgment) to be the unfittest place in America
> to answer the least intention of such a design, for there are few or no

70. Letter 196, 27 January 1729/30, p. 308; letter 200, p. 321; letter 209, Berkeley to Percival, 2 March 1731, p. 335.

71. See his letter to Percival cited in chapter 7, *Berkeley and Percival*, Byrd to Percival, 10 June 1729, pp. 244–45.

72. See Luce, p. 104, and Swales, 'Rich, Sir Nathaniel'.

73. Lambeth Palace, Fulham Papers, vol. XVII, ff. 9–10.

infidels, the few Negros they have, their Masters take care to instruct in the Christian Religion [. . .] Bermuda is a poore and barren Island [. . .] with humble submission to your Lordship &c I think South Carolina, the best place in America, to build a Colledge in, for the conversion of Indians, they being there very numerous, the climate temperate, the Countrey fertill, and the air wholesome[.]

Smith even offered to design the college buildings.[74]

Newman twice wrote to Berkeley in 1729 suggesting one Mr Winthrop might donate land for a college, either on Fisher's Island in New York or in Connecticut. Very soon after landing in Rhode Island, Berkeley himself thought of founding the college there rather than in Bermuda, as he was convinced 'there is a more probable prospect of doing good here than in any other part of the world'.[75] Considerations of how to manage the translation of the college from Bermuda to Rhode Island constantly entered into his thinking about the payment of the grant. Timothy Cutler, the sometime rector at Yale who had converted from Congregationalism to Anglicanism, and who had called an Episcopal convention at Newport in order to press the SPG and the bishop of London for a colonial bishop, wanted an Episcopal college in New England and tried to persuade Berkeley 'to locate his proposed college in Boston'.[76] Berkeley's purchase of land in Rhode Island to furnish Bermuda with provisions may have been understood by some as

74. Lambeth Palace, Fulham Papers, vol. XIX, ff. 148–49.

75. Letter 182, 9 April 1729, p. 275; letter 191, 17 September 1729, p. 295; letter 176, Berkeley to Percival, 7 February, p. 264. See Fisher, *The Indian Great Awakening*, p. 9, for a summary of missionary work in this area at the time: 'In the 1720s and 1730s, Native communities in southern New England welcomed schoolteachers onto their lands, sent their children to English schools, and generally took part in whatever material benefits missionaries offered, such as food, blankets, and clothing. Such educational attempts, however, were considerably complicated by the simultaneous and contentious controversies over land and an internal struggle for leadership and control within Native communities'.

76. Bridenbaugh, *Mitre and Sceptre*, pp. 68, 72, 73n28. Bridenbaugh bases his evidence on Nichols, *Illustrations of the Literary History of the Eighteenth Century*. The collection contains two letters from Cutler to Zachary Grey that mention Berkeley: IV.289, 20 July 1729: 'Dean Berkeley is at Rhode Island, highly honoured by the whole Church, and Dissenters of all denominations. He will pass the next Winter there, and we promise ourselves he will use his interest to place his College in these parts'; IV.292, 20 April 1731: 'Dean Berkeley is coming home, to leave us lamenting the loss of him'.

FIGURE 10.4. Whitehall, the Berkeleys' home in Rhode Island. 'Whitehall Portrait', used by permission of jjburgess/Whitehall Museum

an indication of his settling the college there.[77] It was the choice of location rather than the method of obtaining students that caused Berkeley doubts.

Berkeley's 'madness' was certainly not in an unusual degree of missionary zeal. His plan for educating and converting Native Americans, baptising enslaved people, and reforming the religious morality of the planters was entirely of a piece with the missionary activities of several hundred other Anglicans of his moment, from both the clerical and lay populations, mostly working through the Society for the Propagation of the Gospel in Foreign Parts but also through other institutions, such as the early American universities and the colonies themselves. Indeed, opposition to Berkeley's scheme likely came from a reasonable apprehension that it would detract from existing missionary efforts. The SPG, granted a royal

77. Letter 185, Percival to Berkeley, 12 June 1729, p. 278, where others at court had disclosed the purchase. The farmhouse Berkeley built on this land was called Whitehall. Gaustad, *George Berkeley in America*, pp. 14–15, suggests that Berkeley likely took the name from the Chapel Royal, Whitehall, at which Gibson would have presided. There is also a small settlement to the east of Kilkenny called Paulstown that since the nineteenth century has also sometimes been called Whitehall. It is not impossible that a farmstead in this settlement was called Whitehall in Berkeley's lifetime, later giving its name to the village.

charter in 1701, was the heart of Anglican missionary activity. Missionary Anglicans in the early eighteenth century regarded close cooperation between church and state, and episcopacy, as necessary for the production of orderly civic life and perceived Catholic and dissenting populations as competitors in a circum-Atlantic arena. They targeted several distinct populations: the nominal Christians of the planter communities who required moral reform, indigenous Americans, and enslaved people. The cooperation they believed necessary between church and state was not always realised, and it was not without its tensions.[78] Berkeley's Bermuda project—in its motivations, in his characterisation of it to his friends and associates, in its planning, failure, and unpredicted consequences, and in almost every other respect—an entirely typical missionary Anglican enterprise. Berkeley might be considered atypical in being a prominent cleric proposing to undertake missionary activity himself. Swift says as much in a letter to John Carteret of 14 September 1724, in which he calls Berkeley an 'absolute Philosopher with Respect to Money Titles or Power' such that 'His Heart will break if his Deanry be not soon taken from Him'.[79] Still, his zeal was not obviously a match for that of others working in the same domain, such as Elias Neau, the charismatic New York missionary working with the enslaved community at the time of the 1712 slave uprising.[80] What is striking is the lack of coordination between Berkeley and those already engaged in missionary Anglican activity in North America, particularly that with a specifically educational focus. Berkeley was not a member of the SPG, though he corresponded with its secretary, Henry Newman, and delivered its anniversary sermon on his return to London from Rhode Island. There is no record of him attending its monthly meetings in London during his time there campaigning for Bermuda. Berkeley's project would have its own charter and its own source of funding.

The lack of coordination between the Bermuda scheme and existing American college- or university-level educational institutions is particularly remarkable. Harvard was one (not particularly

78. Glasson, *Mastering Christianity*, pp. 4, 9, 20, 26–7, 33.
79. Wooley, ed., *The Correspondence of Jonathan Swift*, II.518–19, letter 622.
80. Glasson, *Mastering Christianity*, p. 84.

encouraging) precedent for a theological college attempting to train Native Americans. The New England Company, the chartered body responsible for propagating the gospel since the restoration,

persisted in the idea that Harvard College would train Indians as missionaries. As late as 1685 it noted that it heard of only one Indian at College and asked the Commissioners 'to make up the nomber Tenn in all to be educated mainteyned & brought up there'. But the education of the Indians to university level was hopeless and the Indian College a failure: it was pulled down in 1698[.][81]

Harvard was not the only example. One aim of the 1693 charter of the College of William and Mary was 'that the Christian Faith may be propagated amongst the Western Indians, to the Glory of Almighty God'.[82] Money left by Robert Boyle was used to buy and educate 'half a Dozen captive Indian children'. Though there was doubt about what happened to the Native alumni after graduation, and the Indian College was in decline from the 1710s through to the early 1720s, there was a school system on 'reservations', and the bequest of a farm in Yorkshire raised funds for a new building for the college named for the farm, Brafferton, which was completed in 1723.[83] The reinvigoration of the 'Indian School' at William and Mary, then, was under way when Berkeley was formulating his Bermuda scheme.

Though the 'Indian School' predates the Bermuda project, the latter clearly became its competitor, and people associated with William and Mary may have reacted to Berkeley's proposals. An address of the council and burgesses of Virginia to the king published in September 1726 noted the 'distressed State' of the college and reported the imposition of a duty on all liquors other than those imported from Britain to support it. The council and burgesses hope that not only would the king find this acceptable, 'but that, after the Example of their late Majesties King *William* and Queen *Mary*, and Queen *Anne*, of blessed Memory, you will be graciously pleased, of your Royal Bounty, to contribute your further Assistance towards perfecting this good Work'.[84] Stephen Fouace and James

81. Kellaway, *The New England Company*, p. 113.

82. Hofstadter and Smith, *American Higher Education*, I.33.

83. Morpurgo, *Their Majesties' Royall Colledge*, pp. 66, 68–69, 75.

84. *British Journal*, 209, 17 September 1726.

FIGURE 10.5. Brafferton College, used by permission of the Office of Historic Campus, College of William & Mary

Blair, trustees of the college, were in London in 1727 drafting revised statutes for the college, including provisions for the 'Indian School', which shared a family likeness with Berkeley's *Proposal*:

There are three things which the founders of this college proposed to themselves, to which all its statutes should be directed. The first is, that the youth of Virginia should be well educated to learning and good morals. The second is, that the churches of America, especially Virginia, should be supplied with good ministers after the doctrine and government of the Church of England; and that the college should be a consistent seminary for this purpose. The third is, that the Indians of America should be instructed in the Christian religion, and that some of the Indian youth that are well-behaved and well-inclined, being first well prepared in the divinity school, may be sent out to preach the gospel to their countrymen in their own tongue, after they have duly been put in orders of deacons and priests.[85]

85. Hofstadter and Smith, *American Higher Education*, I,43. The statue at I.44–45 makes provision for the Indian School: 'There is but one master in this school who is to

James Blair, in addition to his role at William and Mary, was a commissary of the bishop of London, who had taken on responsibility for the plantations. He and Berkeley would therefore have been moving in similar circles of patronage—and competing for it—to accomplish their two projects.

The evaluation of a recent historian of the early years of William and Mary does not seem unreasonable:

> [N]ot once in a decade of activity did Berkeley so much as mention that he knew that there was in Williamsburg a college whose proclaimed intentions were exactly consistent with those he was intending to institute—ostensibly for the first time—for the benefit of the American Colonies. [. . .] It is beyond reason to assume that a Fellow of Trinity and a Dean of the Established Church had never heard of the College of William and Mary and it is inconceivable that there was no voice raised in Britain to bring home to him that he was proposing a duplication of effort and, in all probability, a division of funds.[86]

It may of course be misleading to found a judgement on what is missing from a correspondence that is incompletely preserved. But Berkeley had put in at Williamsburg, 'for want of Provisions', as William Gooch, the governor of the colony and president of the College of William and Mary, put it in a letter to Gibson. Gooch reports that he met Berkeley and gave him a 'short view of our Country and Circumstances', which presumably included some account of the college and its mission.[87] Gooch had written two recent letters to Gibson partly concerned with a clergyman who had returned from Bermuda, 'where all sorts of Provisions are very scarce, and consequently dear, and the allowance of ministers but small'. The clergyman 'gives a sad description of the Island, and of the straits to which he was reduced in it'.[88] It is perhaps not surprising, then,

teach the Indian boys to read, and write, and vulgar arithmetick. And especially he is to teach them thoroughly the catechism and the principles of the Christian religion. For a yearly salary, let him have forty or fifty pounds sterling, according to the ability of that school, appointed by the honorable Robert Boyle, or to be further appointed by other benefactors. And in the same school the master may be permitted to teach other scholars from the town, for which he is to take the usual wages of twenty shillings a year'.

86. Morpurgo, *Their Majesties' Royall Colledge*, p. 92.

87. Lambeth Palace, Fulham Papers, vol. XII, f. 136v, Gooch to Gibson, 29 June 1729.

88. Ibid., vol. XII, ff. 124r, 126r, Gooch to Gibson, 26 May and 8 June 1728.

that when Gooch says how sad he was to see Berkeley leave, he passes directly on to the unsuitability of Bermuda as a location for the college:

> Bermuda my Lord is a very poor Island but I can't give your Lordship a juster Idea of it, than by saying 'tis as if fifty Islands were jumbled together, the largest of which is indeed about twenty miles long & half a mile broad, but the rest very small as your Lordship will think when in the whole 'tis not thirty miles long, and taking all in not above five miles over. Rivers or great runs of Water divide every one of these, over which the Inhabitants pass in Boats, and there is not in all the Place a Levell of above a mile. As the Dean's Charter for this Island is not irrevocable, I am in great hopes his further information of Things will turn to our advantage; for the Continent in my Opinion is by much the properest Place for his Purpose, and Virginia my Lord above all the Provinces on the Main seems to be best situated for it.[89]

Presumably Gooch wished Berkeley to settle his project and its funding in his state. Berkeley, however, appears indifferent to this existing institution with a college for the religious education of Native Americans. He told Percival that he received 'many unexpected as well as undeserved honours from the Governour and principal inhabitants' of Williamsburg.[90] But he made no mention of the College of William and Mary. It is, then, easy to be sympathetic with James Blair, who, when asked by Gibson to add Bermuda to the list of territories for which he acted as commissary, suggested that Berkeley, 'a man of some eminence', take on the role instead.[91]

The one rival educational institution Berkeley mentions in his *Proposal*, and even then not by name, is 'the college long since projected in *Barbadoes*', Codrington College.[92] Christopher Codrington (1668–1710), a scholar, governor general, and military commander who had led the campaign that allowed the English to take the French lands on St Christopher's, left his estates and the

---

89. Ibid., vol. XII, ff. 136–37, Gooch to Gibson, 29 June 1729; see also Harrison and Brydon, 'The Virginia Clergy'.

90. Letter 176, Berkeley to Percival, 7 February 1729, p. 263.

91. Lambeth Palace, Fulham Papers, vol. XII, ff. 142–43, 8 September 1729.

92. *Proposal*, p. 8 (LJ, VII.349).

enslaved people on them to found 'a Seminary of Missionaries to be dispersed throughout the Plantations'.[93] The SPG took possession of the plantations in 1712 and from that point became more implicated in slavery as it made Christian reform of the institution more prominent than any more radical critique.[94] Though the SPG anniversary sermon of 1711 suggested that enslaved people on the plantations would be comparatively well treated, in fact, they were branded with the word 'SOCIETY', little other than baptism distinguished their treatment by their agents, and a significant death rate on the plantations saw the enslaved population frequently restocked with newly imported people. Though a building for the college had been very nearly completed by 1725, the institution was to be funded by sugar and rum production, and low profits prevented any serious commencement of the mission. For most of the eighteenth century, the college functioned instead as a grammar school for planters' children.[95]

One of the strongest critiques of the Bermuda scheme was published by Thomas Bray. Insulted by Berkeley's suggestion that missionary activity amongst planters, indigenous Americans, and enslaved people had failed, or not been energetically pursued, Bray broadly condemns the plan. Bermuda is not the fertile place Berkeley depicts ('the Soil being so wash'd away by Hurricanes'), it is populous, land is expensive, and it is very distant from the continent. There will be problems recruiting indigenous people, as there have been for the existing colleges for Native American students, about which Berkeley should have been informed:

> [W]e cannot think it Possible to induce the Indians to send their Youth over the Seas, the Element they so much dread, and this at so great a Distance, to this College, which Experience shews must be mere Imagination. The Reverend Dean, besides that before he had cast his Reproaches so plentifully against the Clergy in *America*, for being so much wanting in their Endeavours to Convert the Indians, ought

93. Craton, 'The Planter's World in the British West Indies', p. 330; Bennet, *Bondsmen and Bishops*, pp. 2–5.

94. Glasson, *Mastering Christianity*, pp. 5, 75–76.

95. Bennet, *Bondsmen and Bishops*, pp. 45, 10, 27, 46–47; Craton, 'The Planter's World in the British West Indies', p. 330.

to have better inform'd himself about several Steps some Time since taken. He might, with the greatest Ease in the World have Known, that besides the College of *New-Cambridge*, in *New-England*, and another lately raised in *Connecticut*, there has been founded by those most Excellent Princes, King *William* and Queen *Mary*, a Noble one at *Williamsburg* in *Virginia*; and which would have been greatly to his Purpose to know; [. . .] it is not without Expensive Gifts to the Parents, that the President and Governors of the said *William* and *Mary's* College can induce them to send their Youth to the College, where some of those Indians Parents, not distant above Forty or Fifty Miles, may come and see their Children, and be satisfy'd by their own Eyes how kindly they are us'd.

Bray has more questions about the plan for conversion. Once the students have tasted the goods of a European life, why would they return to their first culture? If they do, will they not return to the 'former Wild and Savage Ways of the Indians'? Bray has heard of 'humaniz'd' Indians who were murdered by their people on returning to them because

they are infinitely Tenacious of their own Customs; [. . .] they are Jealous of the growing Power of the *English*; and this the more, as finding their Indian Nations to be much wore out with respect to their Numbers, which were formerly much greater than at present, occasion'd by their mutual Wars; but especially by the Small-Pox, which 'till of late Years they were Strangers to; but wherever it Seizes a Clan of them is very Fatal to them.

Bray proposes a system of reservation schools on the mainland, which are much more appropriate than a university and have a much more proximate indigenous population. Bray is galled that his work through a chartered organisation might be losing funds to a fashionable new scheme. He notes that 'very large Grants of Revenues, and moreover of voluntary Contributions are made towards' Bermuda. 'It is really become too Invidious a Thing, and perhaps too dangerous to one's Peace and Quiet to dissent from it, and not most readily to give into it'.[96] Bray's critique, though not perhaps

---

96. Bray, *Missionalia*, sig. B1r–v, pp. 69–72, 75–77, 81–90, 97, 100, 68.

perfectly internally consistent, is sharp, and it calls out Berkeley's apparent lack of concert with existing missionary work.

Bermuda, Trade, Corruption

Berkeley had reasons for seeking the relative isolation and inaccessibility of Bermuda that others sometimes identified as an obstacle. He did not want a location for the college that would enable or encourage its fellows to engage in trade. The isolation of Bermuda was central to Berkeley's project of a retired Christian academic and aesthetic life that would operate as a counterblast to a corrupt modern world of freethinking, commodity trading, and public immorality.[97] Tobacco and sugar might get the better of his fellows if the college were located on the mainland or on sugar islands. Connection to the currents of world history, however, was hard to sever. St Paul's College would not rely on the immediate profit of sugar and rum produced on site, as was the plan for Codrington, nor was its building to be funded by tobacco crops, as at William and Mary.[98] But Bermuda was to be funded by the sale of Crown lands on St Christopher's ceded by the French in the Treaty of Utrecht. Berkeley's proposal for the use of these lands was one of several circulating in the late 1710s and early 1720s. One of these, published in 1722, proposed the sale of plots by lottery at a moderate price to smallholders committed to the intensive production of sugar cane, for the cultivation of which the author of the proposal believed the French lands were particularly well suited.[99] This interest in modest-sized plots was in tune with public concern that a tendency towards larger plantations was driving poorer white people off the island, and that these tenants were needed to constitute an occasional militia and to produce livestock and provision crops that otherwise needed to be imported.[100]

97. Kendrick, 'Berkeley's Bermuda Project in Context', pp. 32–34.

98. Hofstadter and Smith, *American Higher Education*, I.38.

99. [R.M.] *S.B., A General Survey of that Part of the Island of St. Christophers*, pp. 31–48. For another scheme, see [Commissioners for Trade and Plantations], *Journal of the Commissioners for Trade and Plantations*, p. 153.

100. Sheridan, *Sugar and Slavery*, pp. 155–57.

The history of St Christopher's from the 1720s on was determined by such proposals on the use of the Crown lands. St Christopher's was surveyed in 1726 by commissioners who cancelled the provisional land grants that had been made since 1713. The sale of land in plots no larger than two hundred acres was completed in 1728, with no evidence of white settlers having been attracted by smaller plots. Indeed, one 'knowledgeable individual said that the poor whites had left the island because of the "late Sale of the French Lands which has put them into Fewer hands"'.[101] And so the transformation of St Christopher's into a slave-run plantation island was accelerated.[102] Richard Sheridan notes that 'features of the period were land enclosure, emigration of smallholders and white servants, influx of negro slaves, formation of sugar plantations, and the movement toward monoculture'. With the white population holding at approximately 2,000, the enslaved population increased from about 7,500 in 1720 to about 20,000 in 1745. Average sugar production increased tenfold from the final years of the 1720s to the first years of the 1730s. The peculiar fertility of the St Christopher's lands exaggerated the social ills of a plantation economy. In the last quarter of the eighteenth century, the Rev James Ramsay noted:

> It enables the greatest part of its proprietors to live in England; where, insensable of the sufferings of their slaves, they think and dream of nothing but sugar, sugar; to which, in consequence, every spot of land is condemned. Hence [. . .] slaves are more scantily fed, than in the other islands; and the managers are obliged to keep them up to their utmost possible exertion to preserve their employment.[103]

Berkeley's grant, then, despite it never being paid, was part of the history of the transformation of the Caribbean into slave societies forced into monocultural commodity production to satisfy the luxurious and corrupted tastes of the British and the wider European consumer-subject. The narrow views of governors, traders, and people in the city (see letter 146 cited earlier), from which

---

101. Ibid., p. 158.
102. Niddrie, 'An Attempt at Planned Settlement in St. Kitts', pp. 6–11.
103. Sheridan, *Sugar and Slavery*, pp. 150, 159, 160.

Berkeley distinguished his wider view and more expansive prospect for education, were not so easy to shed. Berkeley had objected to this model of global economy in the *Essay towards Preventing the Ruine of Great Britain* and would do so in a more sustained way in *The Querist* on his return from America. But his Bermuda project was obliquely complicit in the modern, import-oriented economy he despised and in the full range of human cruelties it required— bondage, enforced movement of populations, and eradication of indigenous peoples and their ways of life and habitats. Land in St Christopher's was valuable for sugar cultivation, and the value of the land was greater the more efficiently it and the people who worked it were exploited. It is not just that Berkeley's utopian project had served as a distraction from his involvement in 'the brutal *dis*topia of Old World social and religious conflicts', but that this utopia would obliquely but ultimately require the dystopia of plantation colonialism and slavery.[104]

The profits from the land sale did not come to Berkeley, however. For whatever reason, payment was delayed. Bermuda fell out of favour. (For an account of Berkeley's use of the assets accumulated for the Bermuda scheme after its collapse in furthering American higher education, see chapter 5.) Whilst he was in Rhode Island awaiting payment, Percival and James Oglethorpe began to sell him the virtues of another American project, the foundation of Georgia.[105] From the £90,000 realised from the sale of land in St Christopher's, £10,000 was given to the Georgia project by the 'Grand Committee'. As at the passing of the Bermuda grant, 'Nobody spoke against it, not one or two Noes were heard'.[106] Oglethorpe led a group of trustees who would oversee the foundation of a colony in the southern part of Carolina, between the Altamaha and Savannah Rivers. The settlement was to serve many purposes. It would resettle the British poor unable to sustain themselves in a competitive labour market; welcome persecuted Protestants from around Europe; secure Carolina against possible Spanish incursions from Florida; and consist only of white, free settlers in order to do all

104. Fabricant, 'George Berkeley the Islander', p. 263.

105. Letter 206, Percival to Berkeley, 23 December 1730, p. 331; letter 211, Oglethorpe to Berkeley, May 1731, pp. 338–40.

106. Gaustad, *George Berkeley in America*, p. 104, citing Egmont diaries, 16 May 1733.

this. Bringing in enslaved black people was opposed because their presence would drive down the value of labour, reduce the independent spirit of the colonists, and create an imbalance in the population, such as that in Carolina, which had left the colony vulnerable (enslaved people could not serve in a militia). There was to be 'No Appearance of Slavery, not even in *Negroes*; by which means, the People being oblig'd to labour themselves for their Support, will be, like the old *Romans*, more active and useful for Defence of their Government'.[107] Oglethorpe clearly had a view of the noble simplicity of the ancient manners informing his colonial project, just as Berkeley had.

When Oglethorpe published an account of the colony's terrain that doubled as a justification of the project, he made reference to a positive example from England's colonial history. Why should Georgia not be another Londonderry? Derry was founded by the corporation of the City of London, and Oglethorpe was impressed by the profits the corporation had extracted from it, and by its effect on the indigenous population:

> The *Londoners* have drawn above a Hundred Thousand Pounds from that Colony within Ten Years last past, and 'tis not probable that the first Settlement ever cost them Eight Thousand Pounds, which made Four Hundred Families of their poor Freemen happy, at the same Time that it purchased so good an Estate and strengthened the *English* Interest in that Kingdom. No other Part of *Ireland* is now so perfectly free from the native *Irish* as are those two Towns and their Districts[.][108]

A colony of English planters in Ireland displacing the indigenous population was a model for Oglethorpe. It is an extractive model. Georgia's production of articles such as silk and wine would reduce English trade deficits with other countries. The colony was in part an exercise in political arithmetic, built on a qualification of the association of population and wealth: only the productive

107. See Oglethorpe, *A New and Accurate Account of the Provinces of South-Carolina and Georgia*, passim and pp. 16–17, citing Martyn, *Reasons for Establishing the Colony of Georgia*, p. 30. Revulsion at the institution of slavery itself was evident only retrospectively in the early history of the colony. See Wood, *Slavery in Colonial Georgia*, pp. 3–8.

108. Oglethorpe, *A New and Accurate Account of the Provinces of South-Carolina and Georgia*, vi.

population were to be counted as an asset. As there was a cost to the state in making up the difference between average earnings in menial occupations and the cost of living, it was better value to apportion land in a colony to such workers and establish them for life at only twice the annual cost of the subsidy they otherwise required.[109] The relationship between colony and metropolitan centre, the management of population so that it would become industrious, independent, and civic—these are all problems to which Berkeley proposes his own solutions in *The Querist*, where his emphasis is more therapeutic than surgical. The *Querist* might even be taken as an alternative proposal for the renovation of the colonial system in Ireland, the refoundation of a colony of planters closer to home.

Bermuda and Independence

Missionary Anglicanism was treated with suspicion or opposed by planters because the baptism of enslaved people was thought to lead to emancipation or to insubordination. Despite the close cooperation with the state characteristic of the movement, it was not always regarded favourably by all elements of the political elite. This was the case with Berkeley's project. Some thought it would contribute to the economic and institutional independence of the colonies and therefore weaken their bonds to the metropolis. Berkeley identified this fear as a reason for parliamentary opposition to funding Bermuda. He believed, however, that his seminary (particularly if settled in Rhode Island) would make governing the colonies easier: it would 'lessen that party which at present gives uneasiness in New England'. In reply, Benson wrote that Berkeley was thought to have acted in concert with those not wanting to settle a salary on the governor of New England, and that Anne's production of her own cloth was taken as rivalry to English imports.[110] Percival, in the

---

109. Ibid., pp. 36, 40–41, 48, 72; see also Martyn, *Some Account of the Designs of the Trustees*, p. 1, and Martyn, *Reasons for Establishing the Colony of Georgia*, p. 1.

110. Letter 146, Berkeley to Prior, 12 May 1726; letter 179, Berkeley to Benson, 11 April 1729, p. 271; letter 186, 23 June 1729, p. 281. A permanent salary for the governor was one of the points of contestation between the Crown and the House of Representatives

letter in which he explains that the Bermuda project was too good for its era, reports one political objection to the scheme:

> A very good Lord asked me whether I thought the Indians would not be saved as well as we? and if I considered that learning tended to make the plantations independent of their Mother Country?, adding that the ignorance of the Indians and the variety of sects in our plantations was England's security. He was even sorry we had an university in Dublin. And yet the Lord is the ornament of the nobility for learning and sobriety, but he reduced all to policy[.][111]

This good lord drew parallels between Dublin and Bermuda/America and thought that educational institutions tend to produce independence. As a nonmetropolitan member of the governing Protestant elite, Berkeley did not share the fears of these politic people that his project would lead to the economic and institutional independence of the colonies; he envisaged nothing other than their continuing subordination. Consolidating the institutions of the colonies, in Ireland as much as in America, would lead to better, not lesser, political subordination, just as baptising enslaved people would only make them better slaves.

Berkeley's American experience contributed to his thinking on the economic independence of nations and provinces, connecting the *Essay towards Preventing the Ruine of Great Britain* and *The Querist*. Whilst in America, Berkeley's correspondence with Prior on the question of absentee landlords included a discussion of placing a 20 percent tax on all income taken out of Ireland.[112] Berkeley shared his views on free trade: 'That it would be the interest of England to allow a free trade to Ireland, I have been thoroughly convinced ever since my being in Italy'.[113] Nothing in Berkeley's journals says why he developed this view. Perhaps he saw the free port at Leghorn/Livorno, where he preached in 1714, as an

---

in Massachusetts in the late 1720s: the Crown required that one be settled, but the House refused. See Bushman, *King and People in Provincial Massachusetts*, pp. 115, 119–20.

111. Letter 206, Percival to Berkeley, 23 December 1730, p. 331.

112. The absentee landlord, who stripped wealth from the local economy and spent it luxuriously in London, was an issue in the Caribbean islands as in Ireland. See Sheridan, *Sugar and Slavery*, pp. 59, 160.

113. Letter 202, Berkeley to Prior, 7 May 1730, p. 323.

economic benefit to the duchy of which it was a part and imagined that England might experience the same benefits if it abolished imports on Irish goods? Or perhaps free trade between city-states self-evidently produced prosperity? Berkeley was in any case suggesting that it was in England's interest not to impose duties on Ireland.

A more complex circumstance that might relate to Berkeley's thinking on the economic independence of colonies, and the currency questions so central to *The Querist*, is the Rhode Island currency crisis of the late 1720s. From the mid-1710s, there had been demands in Newport for a paper currency to stimulate trade. The currency was printed and secured by mortgages on land worth at least twice as much as the currency issued. The paper currency lost value, and the silver currency in use also lost value. The General Assembly of Rhode Island continued to issue new bills, leading to a crisis in 1731 in which an issue of £60,000 was made without the consent of the governor, who then appealed to the Crown to reject the act of the Assembly. The issue of a paper currency, then, became a question of the right of the chartered colonies to legislate on economic and other matters. Yorke and Talbot were asked for an opinion and found that the Crown had no discretionary powers to repeal laws in the colony, by the terms of the charter.[114] With no mention of this episode in Berkeley's published or unpublished writing, it is not simple to speculate on his knowledge of or views on the crisis. But *The Querist* would come out in favour of provincial banks and the conception of currency as tokens for encouraging industry, deeming their material incidental. Berkeley's views on the economic and institutional life of dependent provinces also suggest that institutional autonomy can better entrench subordination.

The Church Disillusioned with the State

A range of Berkeley's friends and acquaintances attributed the failure of the scheme to the avarice and irreligion of the times. Laetitia Pilkington said that the scheme was 'frustrated' 'by the Avarice of

---

114. James, *Colonial Rhode Island*, pp. 171–76; *Records of the Colony of Rhode Island*, pp. 456–61.

some in Power'.[115] Percival thought the Bermuda scheme was not of a piece with its corrupt times: 'the design seems too great and good to be accomplished in an age where men love darkness better than the light, and nothing is considered but with a political view'. Oglethorpe also noted, with irony, that he was not surprised that Parliament failed to make good on the grant: 'Mankind it is true was to be benefitted, and learning and revealed religion extended, but these were not ministerial points, and consequently might be opposed without danger of losing other pensions or employments'.[116] Berkeley didn't want to believe that an ingenuous clergyman could be bitten by scheming politicians who exploited his faith in charters, votes, and grants. But he responded to Percival in more pointed terms: 'What they foolishly call free thinking seems to me the principal root or source not only of opposition to our College but of most other evils in this age, and as long as that frenzy subsists and spreads, it is in vain to hope for any good either to the mother country or colonies'.[117]

In a letter that opens with discussion of the improbability of the grant being paid, Henry Newman says that he is not sure the gospel is moving, as some were saying, from the east to the west, as the American planters seem just as wicked as Europeans, even if 'there are in America no masquerades, nor robbing on the highway'. (It will be recalled that Berkeley thought the same spirit that encouraged masquerades led to the downfall of the Venetian republic.) Berkeley, he says, 'would be surprised to see what progress infidelity has made here in a short time'. Newman's conclusion is apocalyptic: 'I rather think we are hastening to that period which our Saviour has predicted, when the Son of man comes shall he find faith upon earth'.[118] Berkeley's response to Newman is again pointed towards the freethinkers:

What you observe of the growth of atheism and irreligion hath a fatal aspect upon England but it is no more than hath been carrying on for

115. Elias, ed., *The Memoirs of Laetitia Pilkington*, I.228.

116. Letter 206, Percival to Berkeley, 23 December 1730, p. 331; letter 211, Oglethorpe to Berkeley, May 1731, p. 338.

117. Letter 200, p. 321; letter 209, 2 March 1731, p. 335.

118. Letter 191, Newman to Berkeley, 17 September 1729, p. 296.

many years past by a set of men who under the notion of liberty are for introducing licence and a general contempt of all laws divine or humane. Political societies have their diseases as well as natural bodies and this seems that which will be the death of Great Britain.[119]

The same impulse that had diverted funds from Bermuda to more interested and political schemes was that which had promoted atheism, disloyalty, and immorality more generally. Berkeley's *Alciphron*, composed in Rhode Island, is a sustained attack on free thought as he understood it. I will turn to *Alciphron* in the following chapter. I close this chapter with a consideration of the more personal and direct intellectual influence Berkeley had in America.

The effects of Berkeley's time in Rhode Island are perceptible beyond the system of higher education strictly conceived. His influence was institutional, physical, and personal. Berkeley was said to have been a patron of the 'Society for the promotion of Knowledge and Virtue, by free conversation' established by Henry Collins, Edward Scott, James Searing, Nathan Townsend, and Daniel Updike in Newport in 1730.[120] The Redwood Library in Newport traces its origins to that society.[121] An organ was donated to Trinity Church in Newport, with Newman taking care of the shipping.[122] And as has been noted already, Berkeley preached in Newport, including to the local clergy. One such discourse, delivered in June 1731, was said by Thomas Harward to have 'kept them two Hours, & an Half, wch to Me is somewhat strange for such an Hypochondraical Disposition'.[123] The surviving notes for the Newport sermons give a sense of the distinctive contribution Berkeley might have made to local life from the pulpit. Perhaps unsurprisingly for a preacher who conceived of his presence in that particular location as an urgent Christian mission, the notes return to

---

119. Letter 201, 29 March 1730, pp. 322–23.

120. Gaustad, *George Berkeley in America*, p. 17.

121. Berkeley also lent from his own library, at least in the extreme case of the renegade clergyman embezzling the public library at Providence, leaving others wanting books from which to construct sermons. See Lambeth Palace, Fulham Papers, vol. VIII, f. 266, Arthur Browne to Gibson, 31 August 1730.

122. Letter 227, Newman to Berkeley, 28 August 1733, p. 356.

123. Lambeth Palace, Fulham Papers, vol. V, ff. 40–43, Thomas Harward to Gibson, 19 July 1731, f. 40r.

the notion of human life as participation in God—the better the life, the fuller the participation. There is 'Some sort of union with the Godhead in prophets, apostles, all true Christians, all men. but with men, Xtians, inspired persons, Xt in different degrees'.[124] Acting more in accordance with God's will, that is, being in union with God, is an expression of love: 'We shew love to superiors & benefactors by consulting their honour i.e. by performing their will, & endeavouring that others perform it [. . .] Will of God known 1. by considering his Attributes. 2. by conscience & instinct. 3 by the preaching of Xt & apostles'.[125] Though we might be able to deduce God's will by rule, grace has a pivotal role in enabling us to act in accordance with that will. God 'worketh in us to will & to do' (citing Philippians 2:13), and we have to accept that there is a shift of aspect between understanding our actions as the product of our own free will and understanding them as the action of God's grace. The activity of grace, or God working in and through us, is a subject the sermons ponder:

> Whether to all, whether constantly. whether & in wt sense efficacious. how consists with free will. Questions about nature & degrees thereof. These curious points, more useful to know 1 the marks of it. Galat. 5. 22. 23 no dividing grace from good morals & vertue 2. the means to obtain it. 3. how to behave with respect to it. i.e to pray as if Grace alone did all: to endeavor as if our own free will did all.[126]

The effect of grace and the effect of good free choice are the same: Berkeley's theology, like his metaphysics, finds that the concurrence of God's will is required for humans to act freely.

Establishing a friendship with Samuel Johnson was another important aspect of Berkeley's American residency. Johnson was working in Connecticut, having travelled to England to be ordained in the Anglican church. He would publish widely in philosophy later in his career, including books designed for use in an educational context, and he was involved in the design and administration of American colleges and universities, acting as the first

---

124. LJ, VII.61, sermon 4.
125. LJ, VII.71, sermon 8, first Sunday in August 1730.
126. LJ, VII.83, sermon 14, 28 October 1729.

president of King's College in New York, which became Columbia University. It is not clear how his friendship with Berkeley began, but the first surviving letter between them is Johnson's response to his reading *Principles of Human Knowledge* and *Three Dialogues*. The correspondence began in September 1729 with a consideration of whether God is the cause of all ideas in the mind, or whether some might not have their cause in changes in the environment. Making God the cause of all ideas suggests that God, rather than some weakness of the body not properly regulated by the mind, is the cause of bad human habits:

> [I]f in an habitual sinner, every object and motion be but an idea, and every wicked appetite the effect of such a set of ideas, and these ideas, the immediate effect of the Almighty upon his mind; it seems to follow, that the immediate cause of such ideas must be the cause of those immoral appetites and actions; because he is born down before them seemingly, even in spite of himself.

Even though Johnson granted that ideas are inert, Berkeley responds to him by saying, 'Difficulties about the principle of moral actions will cease, if we consider that all guilt is in the will, and that our ideas, from whatever cause they are produced, are alike inert'.[127] We might feel as though the ideas cause us to act in certain ways, but ideas cannot be causes.

Johnson wonders if Berkeley might not be saved from some of the undesirable apparent consequences of his immaterialism by allowing the archetypes of all ideas to exist in God's mind. He develops this thought so that the ectypes in human minds of God's archetypal ideas are resemblances, and 'there is exterior to us, in the divine mind, a system of universal nature'.[128] Berkeley is happy with Johnson's description of these archetypes. 'But I object against those archetypes by philosophers supposed to be real things, and to have an absolute rational existence distinct from their being perceived by any mind whatsoever, it being the opinion of all materialists that an ideal existence in the divine mind is one thing, and the

---

127. Letter 190, Samuel Johnson to Berkeley, 10 September 1729, pp. 288–89; letter 194, 25 November 1729, p. 304.
128. Letter 190, pp. 290–91; letter 197, 5 February 1730, p. 310.

real existence of material things another'. One should never forget that the existence of things independent of our minds is itself dependent upon God's mind.[129]

Johnson treats ideas and spirits to some of the questioning Berkeley applied to matter.

> These ideas of ours, what are they? Is the substance of the mind the substratum to its ideas? Is it proper to call them modifications of our minds? Or impressions upon them? Or what? Truly I can't tell what to make of them, any more than of matter itself. What is the *esse* of spirits?—you seem to think it impossible to abstract their existence from their thinking. Princ. p. 143. sec. 98. Is then the *esse* of minds nothing else but *percipere*, as the *esse* of ideas is *percipi*?[130]

The idea of an idea is a fugitive thing. Johnson clearly also has some difficulty with Berkeley's account of spirit, the existence of which depends, as he takes it, entirely on the activity of thinking:

> [T]o place the very being of spirits in the mere act of thinking, seems to me very much like making abstract ideas of them. [. . .] Has a child no soul till it actually perceives? And is there not such a thing as sleeping without dreaming, or being in a *deliquium* without a thought? If there be, and yet at the same time the *esse* of a spirit be nothing else but its actual thinking, the soul must be dead during those intervals; and if ceasing or intermitting to think be the ceasing to be, or death of the soul, it is many times and easily put to death.[131]

These views are not directly answered, other than by Berkeley saying he has 'no doubt' that 'the soul of man is passive as well as active', and so presumably existent when not active though perceived by God, a view that is not an obvious inference from his

129. Letter 199, 24 March 1730, p. 318. Winkler, *Berkeley: An Interpretation*, p. 228, suggests that Berkeley could adopt this view of archetypes in God's mind because God has knowledge of the ideas he causes in people: 'to say that divine ideas are archetypes is just to say that God has ideas of the ideas he causes in us, or (taking into account Berkeley's relaxed attitude to sameness) that he has the same ideas he causes in us'. Hight, *Idea and Ontology*, pp. 177–207, provides a different account of divine ideas as numerically the same as the ideas perceived by finite minds, in which 'God created an ideal order external to himself and during sensation we directly perceive these very ideas' (p. 192).

130. Letter 190, p. 293.

131. Letter 197, pp. 313–14.

earlier writings. (*The Principles of Human Knowledge* distinguishes between active spirit and inert ideas, for example.) He is happy to agree on the general points that 'there is nothing within [*sic*; without?] your mind but God and other spirits, with the attributes or properties belonging to them, and the ideas contained in them. This is a principle or main point from which, and from what I had laid down about abstract ideas, much may be deduced'.[132] But that relationship between the finite mind and the infinite mind, if both are to be active, remains mysterious in the correspondence. It is in Berkeley's sermonising and pondering the ways in which finite spirits join, follow, or participate in the divine spirit that an elaboration of this central element of his thinking is to be found. That is a topic to which *Alciphron* also makes its contribution.

132. *Principles of Human Knowledge*, §89; letter 199, p. 319.

CHAPTER ELEVEN

Alciphron

BERKELEY BLAMED THE COLLAPSE of the Bermuda scheme, as we saw, on what he considered the great social and moral problem of his time, freethinking. *Alciphron* is his sustained dramatic portrayal of freethinking attitudes and his fullest presentation of arguments and practical proposals to stem their tide. The text is a series of seven philosophical dialogues between two opposing groups: Crito and Euphranor (let's call them right-thinkers) are the friends of the narrator Dion, who is relating the whole encounter to Theages; Lysicles and Alciphron, houseguests of Crito's, are professed free-thinkers. The structure of the text is for Euphranor to draw views from Lysicles and Alciphron and engage them in Socratic dialogue that undermines the bases of their freethinking. On occasion, Crito and Euphranor offer longer and more expository contributions to the dialogue, setting out positions that either are characteristically Berkeleian, such as the argument for the existence of God from conceiving of the visual world as a language (dialogue IV), or reasonably qualify as orthodox Anglicanism. The book was published in both London and Dublin in 1732, with a second London edition in the same year, which made some revisions to the text. All three of these editions were in two volumes and reprinted the *Essay towards a New Theory of Vision* after the seventh dialogue. A third edition was published in London in 1752 making some further revisions to the text, notably the removal of sections 5 through 7 of the seventh dialogue. This edition did not include the *New Theory of Vision*.[1]

Whilst there is a great deal of continuity between Berkeley's presentation of freethinking in his *Guardian* essays and *Alciphron*, the latter is the more sustained treatment and therefore reveals more of Berkeley's conception of free thought. How are the freethinkers of *Alciphron* presented? In the opening exchanges of the first dialogue, the freethinkers declare themselves committed to a theoretical and practical extirpation of all prejudices of education and custom. This procedure leaves them finally, according to Alciphron, 'at something solid and real, in which all Mankind agree, to wit, the Appetites, Passions, and Senses: These are founded in Nature, are real, have real Objects, and are attended with real and substantial Pleasures; Food, Drink, Sleep, and the like animal Enjoyments being what all Men like and love'. The enunciation of this project leads Crito and Euphranor to agree in their identification of freethinkers with a group of thinkers Cicero (in *De Senectute* and *De Divinatione*) called minute philosophers, 'a sort of Sect which diminish all the most valuable things, the Thoughts, Views, and Hopes of Men; all the Knowledge, Notions, and Theories of the Mind they reduce to Sense; Humane Nature they contract and degrade to the narrow low Standard of Animal Life, and assign us only a small Pittance of Time instead of Immortality'.[2] The confrontation between the two parties is, then, over the nature and status of humans, and over the nature of truly human pleasures, ends, and expectations. It is over rival conceptions of the human, as corporeal or spiritual, as a passive body or an active mind. The challenge remains exactly the same as it was for Berkeley twenty years earlier in his *Guardian* essays on freethinking: to dispute the claims of freethinkers to enlarged and comprehensive views of human nature in their materialist, sceptical, and deistic or atheistic attitudes, and to propose a specifically Anglican faith as the truly superior perspective.

---

1. See Jessop, *A Bibliography of George Berkeley*, pp. 18–19; Brykman, Jaffro and Schwartz, eds., *Berkeley's Alciphron*, p. 13, 'A Note on the Text'.

2. *Alciphron*, I.9–10.

Freethinking, then, is a set of beliefs and practices. But those beliefs and practices are presented as in some sense clandestine. It is recurrently alleged throughout the text that the freethinkers are unwilling to reveal their projects or might be disguising their real intentions. Lysicles says that their work of 'extirpating the Prejudices of particular Persons' has been 'carried on [. . .] for many Years with much Art and Industry, and at first with Secrecy, working like Moles under Ground, concealing our Progress from the Public, and our ultimate Views from many, even of our own Proselytes'. Berkeley suspects, as Swift had a quarter-century earlier (see chapter 6), that free thought is a Catholic conspiracy, whereby people who have lost their prejudices about the immortality of the soul, providence, and so on, will be susceptible to the persuasions of the 'Emissaries of the Church of *Rome* disguised in *England*' whom Euphranor says are in wait. Crito says that these 'Emissaries of *Rome* are known to have personated several other Sects'.[3] In a text first published posthumously, in the same year as *Alciphron*, Anthony Collins presents an argument for the equivalence of any authority over matters of faith on the part of priests or civil magistrates and Roman Catholicism, in rhetorical questions or queries, such as Berkeley would go on to use in *The Querist*. If there could be authority over matters of faith that rightly determines the practices of individuals or groups, the tendency of the queries goes, then the Reformation was illegitimate. The case is stated most extremely—and in a form that might give some credence to the notion that, in destroying prejudices and assumptions, the freethinker attempts to drive people to Catholicism—in query 17: it is said to follow from the preceding queries 'either, that there can be *no Authority at all* among Men *in Matters of Faith*; Or that *all Authority in Matters of Faith* rests in some Person or Persons in the *Roman* Church'.[4] For those unwilling to accept that there is no authority at all in matters of faith, it seems the Roman church is their natural home. At least one later writer took this to be the purpose of the passage.[5] The right-thinkers present the view that freethinking is a conspiratorial,

3. Ibid., II.23, II.26.

4. Trenchard, Gordon, and Collins, *The Independent Whig*, I.144–48 (p. 147).

5. Berman, 'Anthony Collins' Essays', p. 467, notes that Philip Skelton's *Ophiomaches* presents this view.

clandestine Catholic programme for conversion. Combatting it is comparable to combatting Catholic conversion efforts in America through, for example, founding an Anglican university, as Berkeley was attempting at the time of writing *Alciphron*.

Anne Berkeley also made the association between freethinking and Catholicism in a text published long after the death of her husband, *The Contrast*. Before setting out in earnest on an account of *Alciphron*, I will suggest that it registers Anne's presence.[6] The period of the text's composition was one of retirement in which Anne would have been, for the first time, Berkeley's main society.[7] It may be that the 'Woman of Sense' whom Crito says was able to 'reduce two Minute Philosophers, who had long been a Nusance to the Neighbourhood, by taking her Cue from their predominant Affectations', was modelled on Anne. Of these two freethinkers,

> [t]he one set up for the most incredulous Man upon earth, the other for the most unbounded Freedom. She observed to the first, that he who had Credulity sufficient to trust the most valuable Things, his Life and Fortune, to his Apothecary and Lawyer, ridiculously affected the Character of Incredulous, by refusing to trust his Soul, a Thing in his own Account but a mere Trifle, to his Parish-Priest. The other, being what you call a Beau, she made sensible how absolute a Slave he was in point of Dress, to him the most important thing in the World, while he was earnestly contending for a Liberty of Thinking, with which he never troubled his Head: and how much more it concerned and became him to assert an Independency on Fashion, and obtain Scope for his Genius, where it was best qualified to exert itself.[8]

This is quite plausibly the person who composed moral-satirical character sketches of contemporary clergymen and took her role as a moral educator within her family so seriously. And although the elliptical, moralistic character sketches in *Alciphron* hardly want for literary precedents, Anne's satirical portraiture may be behind the portraits of Cleon, amongst others:

6. Livesey, 'Berkeley, Ireland, and Eighteenth-Century Intellectual History', p. 461, suggests that it would be interesting to study Anne's contribution to *Alciphron*, focusing on its politics.

7. See letter 200, Berkeley to Percival, 29 March 1730, p. 321.

8. *Alciphron*, VII.33.

Cleon dressed well, could cheat at Cards, had a nice Palate, understood the Mystery of the Die, was a mighty Man in the Minute Philosophy. And having shined a few Years in these Accomplishments, he died before thirty, childless and rotten, expressing the utmost Indignation that he could not outlive that old Dog his Father; who, having a great Notion of polite Manners, and Knowledge of the World, had purchased them to his favourite Son, with much Expence[.][9]

There is little precedent for this kind of abbreviated sketch in Berkeley's previous writing, and its telescopic moralism echoes Anne's other writings.

Freethinkers, then, are semi-clandestine, conspiratorial, crypto-Catholic materialists seeking to eradicate the prejudices of Christian education, such as a belief in providence, and to reduce the human sphere to the satisfaction of corporeal appetites. Against this tendency, Crito and Euphranor—and Berkeley through his management of the dialogues—will argue for the truth and usefulness of Christianity and also sketch the responsibilities of a Christian subject. This subject will be educated and will take an interest in educating others; he will also exercise mature taste for the most enduring goods, thereby stimulating others to honest industry. This chapter suggests that *Alciphron* presents these kinds of characters with these kinds of attributes in the persons of the right-thinkers, in opposition to the type of human character represented by the freethinkers. *Alciphron* is, then, a further exploration of philosophical persona, an exploration of what type of person, with what type of education, acting in and through what kinds of institutions, constitutes a philosopher. This seems an apt way to consider the text in a biographical study.

Apology

The text announces itself on its title page as containing an apology for the Christian religion, and it does contribute to the main themes of apology. It defends scripture—both the textual reliability of scripture and the plausibility of the events it represents—and it defends the exceptional, providential status of Christianity amongst world religions. (I return to the usefulness of Christianity as an

9. Ibid., II.20.

element of apology later in the chapter.) New forms of scholarship that considered scripture as a historical, textual artefact had a tendency, intentional or otherwise, to undermine its authority by pointing to its corruption.[10] Euphranor argues that the methods for resolving textual difficulties, as well as those for identifying them, should be imported from the new criticism.[11] He gets Alciphron to admit that 'Difficulties must be supposed to rise from different Idioms, old Customs, Hints, and Allusions, clear in one Time or Place, and obscure in another'. Reading scripture with a sensitivity to such old customs and allowing obscurities to refer possibly to some unknown custom, or to draw on a misunderstood idiom, resolves or at least brackets some difficulties. The authenticity of miracles is defended by an account of the reliability of written testimony, particularly when supported by additional evidence in the form of rites, institutions, and monuments.[12] Thus does *Alciphron* address the obscurity and implausibility of scripture.

Alciphron also defends the providential and exceptional nature of Christianity when compared to other religious cults. It has been noted earlier that freethinkers such as Anthony Collins made much use of travel literature in order to demonstrate the diversity of religious belief and practice around the world, and thereby to question the universality of the Christian (or any other) revelation. Alciphron believes that there is no reason other than local custom and education for adherence to a particular faith, and that if the faiths of the world do not have any one thing in common, none of their tenets can be universal; nor, consequently, can they be true. Atheism is therefore the rational position. Such arguments for atheism from 'the Variety of Opinions about Religion' are, however, according to Crito, 'a resting Stone to a lazy and superficial Mind'.[13] Alciphron contests the accuracy of biblical chronology, pointing to Chinese, Egyptian, and Chaldean traditions that stretch back much

10. For the tendency of the new grammatical criticism to distance classical texts while adding to knowledge of them, see Levine, 'Ancients and Moderns Reconsidered', pp. 82–83.

11. *Alciphron*, VI.5; see also Charles, 'Foi, croyance, et raison selon Berkeley', p. 140.

12. *Alciphron*, VI.7, VI.3.

13. Ibid., I.6, I.8, VII.32.

further than the biblical six thousand years.[14] With a textual note to Francesco Bianchini's *La Istoria universale* (1697), Euphranor casts doubt on the accuracy of the claims of these peoples to have observed the stars for millennia. He also notes more generally a 'vain humour of extending the antiquity of nations beyond the truth' amongst people subject to their neighbours: 'Fellow-Subjects [. . .] in proportion as they are below their Neighbours in Wealth and Power, lay claim to a more remote Antiquity; are not the Pretensions of *Irishmen* in this Way known to be very great?' Roderic O'Flaherty's *Ogygia* (1685) is cited, as well as mythical histories of Sicily. The relative lack of attention paid to the emergence of Christianity by Josephus is justified by its not reflecting well on the history of the Jewish people. Referring to Trigaltius's study of China, Euphranor demeans the Chinese: 'they are Men of a trifling and credulous Curiosity, addicted to search after the Philosophers Stone, and a Medicine to make Men immortal, to Astrology, Fortune-telling, and Presages of all Kinds'.[15] By casting doubt on the historical claims of non-Christian peoples, and by minimising their cultural history, Berkeley defends Christianity. The apologetic strain of *Alciphron*, then, is a defence of scripture and an attack on arguments from diversity of religious opinion and practice and in favour of recognising the providential marks of Christianity as the true religion—its miraculous dispersal, its sublimity, and so on.[16]

Natural Humans

The confrontation between freethinkers and right-thinkers is, then, a debate about the nature and status of the human, how humans are or should be shaped, what a noble or flourishing human looks like, and what sorts of views such a human has. The characters in the dialogue embody and perform this debate. My reading

14. For Berkeley's family connection to James Ussher, known for dating the creation to 4004 BCE, see chapter 2.

15. *Alciphron*, VI.21, VI.22, VI.26, VI.21; Trigaltius's text is Nicolas Trigault, *De Christiana expeditione apud Sinas suscepta ab Societate Jesu, ex P. Matthaei Ricci* (1615).

16. *Alciphron*, VII.32. See Harrison, *'Religion' and the Religions in the English Enlightenment*, pp. 99–172, for the role of diversity in the emergence of the concepts of religion and the religions and the modes of studying them, such as comparative religion, that were developing in the eighteenth century.

concentrates on the style or manner of this embodiment, rather than assessing the arguments of the text in a more strictly philosophical manner. The freethinkers are attacking the foundations of the social order by attempting to extirpate the notions, customs, and prejudices of the nation. Education is therefore crucial strategic territory for them. Indeed, the debate between freethinkers and right-thinkers is an acknowledgement of the truth of Cicero's derivation of social bonds from natural reason and education. The fundamental human social bond is 'reason and speech, which by the processes of teaching and learning, of communicating, discussing, and reasoning associate men together and unite them in a sort of natural fraternity'.[17] Understandably, then, different visions of teaching, learning, communicating, discussing, and reasoning lead to different social orders. The freethinkers engage in a kind of reverse education, stripping away all notions that 'have no Foundation in Nature, and are only the Effects of Education'.[18] They are looking 'to get the better of Education'. This (pretended?) freethinking commitment to natural dispositions is contrasted to a therapeutic philosophical regime that engages people in one another's education. Discussing a virtuous disposition, Euphranor asks:

> [M]ay we not suppose an healthy Constitution of Soul, when the Notions are right, the Judgments true, the Will regular, the Passions and Appetites directed to their proper Objects, and confined within due Bounds? This, in regard to the Soul, seems what Health is to the Body. And the Man whose Mind is so constituted, is he not properly called virtuous? And to produce this healthy Disposition in the Minds of his Countrymen, should not every good Man employ his Endeavours?[19]

The right-thinkers hold to this view of philosophy as 'Medicine for the Soul of Man', while Crito contends that being 'inured to Thought and Reflection' would make the young live better. 'Their Minds [. . .] should be formed and accustomed to receive Pleasure

---

17. Cicero, *On Duties*, 53–55 (I.xvi). I thank Marta Szymańska-Lewoszewska for pointing me to Cicero on education.

18. *Alciphron*, II.15 (Lysicles); see also Taranto, 'Le Personage de Diagoras', p. 365, for the freethinkers practising anti-education.

19. *Alciphron*, I.13 (Alciphron), II.12.

and Pain from proper Objects, or, which is the same thing, to have their Inclinations and Aversions rightly placed'.[20]

Though no argument for the necessarily social nature of goods is made in *Alciphron* (as it was in Berkeley's early sermon on charity), there is a paternalistic obligation to educate the appetites of those whose wills are not well directed, evident in the acceptance of the parental metaphor for God's superior wisdom: Alciphron grants to Euphranor that 'the Conduct of a Parent' must 'seem very unaccountable to a Child, when its Inclinations are thwarted [. . .] when it is obliged to swallow bitter Physic, [. . .] to suffer, and do, and see many things done contrary to its own Judgment, however reasonable or agreeable to that of others'. It follows, then, that people will make 'very erroneous Judgments' of 'Parental Providence'.[21] Good people endeavour to educate their less mature compatriots into the correct disposition of their appetites. It may be that in this picture of cultivated, virtuous people striving to guide the conduct of others as an act of patriotism we see the working out of Berkeley's difference from William King's account of free will as proceeding by the election of goods. As Berkeley was writing *Alciphron* in Rhode Island, Edmund Law was preparing his translation of King's *On the Origin of Evil*, with the aim of challenging the *a priori* method of arriving at the necessity of the being and attributes of God, as seen in Samuel Clarke and his followers.[22]

Discipline, therefore, not untutored sense, is the way to right views and right actions. We can be sure of this because Alciphron presents the opposing view. He declares that 'touching this Beauty of Morality in the high Sense, a Man's first Thoughts are best; [. . .] if we pretend to examine, and inspect, and reason, we are in danger to lose Sight of it'. The 1752 edition of the text cites the *Characteristics*: 'Men's first thoughts on moral Matters are generally better than their second: their natural Notions better than those refined by Study'.[23] In the text cited, Shaftesbury is contrasting speculation

20. Ibid., III.16 (Euphranor), VII.34 (Crito).

21. Ibid., VI.17.

22. Stephens, 'Edmund Law and His Circle at Cambridge'. See chapter 2 for the comparison of King and Berkeley.

23. *Alciphron*, III.11; Cooper, *Characteristics of Men, Manners, Opinions, Times*, p. 61 (Sensus Communis).

and common sense as sources of reliable moral guidance. It is one of the main argumentative strategies of Berkeley's text to adapt the terms of this discussion so that moral sense, taste, or intuition are not contrasted with (barren) speculation, but rather with rational evaluation, comparison, and judgement, all of which are nothing but the elaboration of inherent and therefore equally natural human capacities. The right-thinkers, that is, will redefine the terms in which the freethinkers present their case and challenge their view of what is natural, what constitutes a comprehensive or expansive view, and what is noble, aristocratic, or well-bred: they challenge the freethinking view of what an educated person looks like. Berkeley probably has Shaftesbury's presentation of the noble or aristocratic character in mind.[24]

An educated person is a cultivated person, and cultivation is indeed an organising metaphor in the text.[25] It is no coincidence that Euphranor is a farmer as well as a philosopher. The conversation between the two philosophical parties is initiated by a comparison of 'late Improvements which had been made in the adjacent Country by new Methods of Agriculture' and what it means to 'improve the Mind'. Alciphron too thinks 'the Mind of Man may be fitly compared to a piece of Land'.[26] This comparison is sustained by both sides throughout the dialogues, with Lysicles claiming that freethinkers 'have stubbed, and weeded, and cleared Humane Nature to that degree, that in a little time, leaving it alone without any Labouring or Teaching, you shall see natural and just Ideas sprout forth of themselves'. Crito, on the other hand, thinks the minute philosophy itself is an 'unwholesom Weed'.[27] He comes back to the metaphor very near the end of the seventh dialogue, citing

24. See, for example, Carey, *Locke, Shaftesbury, and Hutcheson*, p. 124, on Shaftesbury's aristocratic ethos: '[H]is relative indifference to full empirical confirmation of uniformity emerges in his restriction of common consent, on the whole, to the world of the civil. He provided a hierarchical account in which the lower social orders and, just as importantly, a vast array of non-British or non-European peoples existed outside the circle of consensus'.

25. Taranto, '*Alciphron* ou la théorie du complot', p. 229, notes the prevalence of the agricultural metaphor and that Berkeley's chief objection to freethinking is to its claim to supplant Christian education, which merely sows prejudices.

26. *Alciphron*, I.1, I.2.

27. Ibid., II.23; Taranto, 'Le Personage de Diagoras', p. 365, notes that the freethinkers are amateur, garden farmers, not like the serious agriculturalists, the right-thinkers.

Aristotle's Nicomachean ethics: 'Arguments have not an Effect on all Men, but only on them whose Minds are prepared by Education and Custom, as Land is for Seed'.[28]

It is, however, Alciphron and Euphranor in the first dialogue who engage most completely on the subject of cultivation and its relationship to the natural. Euphranor notes that Alciphron argues from the beauty of nature as a chief motive, and he questions what Alciphron regards as natural. Alciphron responds, 'For a thing to be natural, for instance, to the Mind of Man, it must appear originally therein, it must be universally in all Men, it must be invariably the same in all Nations and Ages'. Human nature is then 'the Senses, and such Passions and Appetites as are discovered upon the first application of their respective Objects'. Euphranor develops the horticultural and agricultural metaphors to suggest that human development be considered natural, as 'after a certain Season, the Appetite of Lust, or the Faculty of Reason shall shoot forth, open, and display themselves, as Leaves and Blossoms do in a tree'. Types and degrees of flourishing depend on factors such as location, climate, and cultivation: an orange tree will not thrive in Scotland, 'but in *Portugal*, or *Naples*, it will produce much better, with little or no pains'. So 'why may we not conclude, by a parity of Reason, that things may be natural to Humane Kind, and yet neither found in all Men, nor invariably the same where they are found?' Languages are natural and yet demonstrate variety; so, Euphranor contends, 'religious Worship and civil Government may be natural to Man, notwithstanding they admit of sundry Forms and different Degrees of Perfection'. The truest expression of human nature is, then, not the universally dispersed state of the appetites before the intervention of any educational practice, but rather the greatest intellectual culture:

> [A]s those Fruits, which grow from the most generous and mature Stock, in the choicest Soil, and with the best Culture, are most esteemed; even so ought we not to think, those sublime Truths, which are the Fruits of mature Thought, and have been rationally deduced by Men of the best and most improved Understandings, to be the choicest Productions of the rational Nature of Man?[29]

28. *Alciphron*, VII.29.
29. *Alciphron*, I.14.

The dialogue redefines what Alciphron, perhaps in Berkeley's mind voicing Shaftesbury, presents as the barren speculation of academics and churchmen as moral, religious, and intellectual culture, the natural form of flourishing humans.

Although the freethinkers seem to favour the natural over cultivation, they nonetheless believe, as do the right-thinkers, that the improved understanding is one that provides clear and extensive views. We recognise the educated person because such an individual has, holds, and communicates these views. This means, for the freethinkers, those whose recognition of human diversity frees them from the prejudices of their own locality, who combine the philosophical detachment of Lucretius (see the opening of the second book of *De Rerum Natura*) with the relish for human diversity of Collins:

> [T]hat Man may thank his Stars to whom Nature has given a sublime Soul, who can raise himself above popular Opinions, and, looking down on the Herd of Mankind, behold them scattered over the Surface of the whole Earth, divided and subdivided into numberless Nations and Tribes, differing in Notions and Tenets, as in Language Manners and Dress. The Man who takes a general View of the World and its Inhabitants, from this lofty Stand, above the Reach of Prejudice, seems to breathe a purer Air, and to see by a clearer Light: But how to impart this clear and extensive View to those who are wandering beneath in the narrow dark Paths of Error![30]

Freethinkers claim their practice elevates the practitioner and seem to delight in the belittlement of the rest of the species.

To the right-thinkers, freethinking is precisely a lack of perspective. Crito accuses the freethinkers of being mired in minute details (of irresolvable textual difficulties in scripture primarily): 'a Point by being controverted, singled out, examined, and nearly inspected, groweth considerable to the same Eye, that, perhaps, would have overlooked it in a large and comprehensive View'.[31] The freethinkers entertain the fantasy that clear and expansive views take one beyond prejudice; the right-thinkers suggest that an extensive

30. Ibid., VI.2 (Alciphron).
31. Ibid., V.20.

view allows one to recognise large and persuasive truths (scripture is dependable testimony) despite smaller difficulties (scripture is occasionally obscure).[32]

The right-thinkers contest the freethinking claim to elevation, which is also a claim to nobility of rank. For Crito, nobility and elevation are fundamentally connected to the will, mastery of the appetites, of 'Man [. . .] ordering and improving his Mind, of being transformed into the Similitude of Angels. Man alone of all Animals hath Understanding to know his God. What availeth this Knowledge unless it be to ennoble Man, and raise him to an Imitation and Participation of the Divinity? Or what could such Ennoblement avail if to end with this Life?'[33] Being raised up from mere appetite to be able to direct the will on the basis of rational comparison is nobility and leads to participation in God. *Alciphron* is, amongst other things, Berkeley's fullest working out of how one participates in the infinite spirit and what kinds of faculties one needs to develop to do so.

The freethinkers want to claim nobility: for them, it is the capacity to recognise the moral beauty of nature. Crito mockingly makes reference to Shaftesbury's sketch of the noble character: 'whoever has any Impression of Gentility (as he calls it) or Politeness, is so acquainted with the Decorum and Grace of Things, as to be readily transported with the Contemplation thereof'.[34] The freethinkers are shown uncritically to associate nobility as rank with nobility as elevation of soul. Alciphron holds that the characters of a nobleman and a noble writer 'are coincident', as Euphranor criticises Shaftesbury's ridicule of academic writing. Crito subjects the aristocratic principle of honour operating amongst freethinking gentlemen to scathing and dramatic critique. In a nested dialogue between Nicander and Menecles, it is revealed that 'to ruin Tradesmen, break Faith to one's own Wife, corrupt another Man's, take Bribes, cheat the Public, cut a Man's Throat for a Word, are all Points consistent

---

32. See Nurock, 'La Conscience morale selon Berkeley', p. 323, for education as the training of vision.

33. *Alciphron*, V.28.

34. Ibid., III.13 (text incorporated from the errata in vol. 1, sig. A4v), with references to Cooper, *Characteristics of Men, Manners, Opinions, Times*, 'Miscellanies' 5.3 (pp. 464–83), and 3.2 (pp. 408–18).

with your Principle of Honour', which respects nothing more than paying gambling debts and responding to provocations to duelling. Lysicles suggests that it is 'manifestly absurd' that the son of God should lead such a low existence on earth, one that would not even be 'decent for an Earthly Prince or Ambassador'.[35] Freethinkers, that is, too readily and unquestioningly accept an association between nobility of rank and nobility of soul, and in doing so they demonstrate their incomprehension of the ethical basis of Christianity.

The freethinkers, as in so many places in the book, are self-satirising. But on the subject of nobility, their unwitting revelation of their prejudices draws out similar prejudices about ranks and classes of people from the right-thinkers. Crito, teasing, says how remarkable it is that 'a young Lady, or a *Petit Maitre*', may 'nonplus a Divine or an old-fashioned Gentleman, who hath read many a *Greek* and *Latin* Author, and spent much Time in hard methodical Study'.[36] It is supposed also to be self-evident that these types of people (the young or the female) are unlikely truly to be able to outwit an educated older man. That is, the right-thinkers sustain established prejudices about gender and age.

The right-thinkers also exploit class prejudice.[37] Lysicles insists that the freethinkers are not made up of fine gentlemen only, but also 'some contemplative Spirits of a coarser Education; who, from observing the Behaviour and Proceedings of Apprentices, Watermen, Porters, and the Assemblies of Rabble in the Streets, have arrived at a profound Knowledge of Humane Nature[.] [. . .] These have demolished the received Systems, and done a world of good in the City'. Alciphron confirms that 'we have Men of all Sorts and Professions, plodding Citizens, thriving Stockjobbers, skilful Men in Business, polite Courtiers, gallant Men of the Army; but our chief Strength and Flower of the Flock are those promising young

---

35. *Alciphron*, V.21, III.2, VI.15.

36. Ibid., I.11.

37. One remark of Eliza Frinsham/Berkeley suggests that Berkeley took some pride in rank. He is said to have responded to a friend who said becoming a bishop would mean that his servants could not wear purple, 'No, sir. My becoming a bishop will not make me give up what the domestics of my ancestors have worn for centuries'. Eliza Berkeley, preface to Berkeley, *Poems*, p. clxxix.

Men who have the Advantage of a modern Education'.[38] It is inherently implausible (in the world of the text, and according to the current of its ironies) that these classes of people could produce philosophers of clear and extensive views, as the right-thinkers understand them.

At times the appeal to class might be explained as a strategic appeal to the aristocratic prejudices of the freethinkers themselves, as when Crito tries to persuade Alciphron that cards are not a noble diversion because 'every Footman [. . .] is as well qualified to receive Pleasure from Cards as a Peer'. There are nonetheless clear right-thinking prejudices against one particular class of person, the office worker, particularly when the work is conducted within the relatively young financial services sector. Crito asks, '[W]ho would choose for his Guide in the Search of Truth, a Man [. . .] whose Education hath been behind a Counter, or in an Office? Or whose Speculations have been employed on the Forms of Business, who is only well read in the ways and Commerce of Mankind, in Stock-jobbing, Purloining, Supplanting, Bribing?' In the choice of what kind of human character we wish to be led by, what kind of mind looks improved, what sort of person we take to have clear and extensive views, Crito is set against anyone working in business and finance. This prejudice seems as unfounded as the freethinking prejudice for nobility of rank; what is more, it occurs in the midst of an argument in which 'Forecast and Computation' or reckoning are listed as the first requirements in being able to proceed to rational determination between possible courses of action. 'Rakes cannot reckon', as Euphranor says of Plato's *Protagoras*.[39] The office worker is a travesty of appropriate human calculation of desirable ends. Right-thinkers despise the financial office worker in particular because that person is a computer, or calculator, but has fundamentally disregarded the rank ordering of pleasures that is the most significant element of moral calculus. The art of the dialogues is to present the philosophical farmer and the studious cleric as the types of person one might depend upon as guides, the models for what an improved mind looks like, and to suggest that

38. *Alciphron*, I.11.
39. Ibid., II.17–19.

the calculations of modern urbanised professions are dangerously narrow.

How might one adjudicate between the freethinking and the right-thinking positions? How does one know which performance of human cultivation is best? Berkeley, through the right-thinkers, will introduce a criterion of use, giving human utility a more than incidental role it has in identifying goods in *Passive Obedience*. I will end this chapter by considering how uses and ends contribute to the text's apology for Christianity by looking at their role in knowing God. Alciphron defends the existence of a distinct faculty of moral sense by drawing an analogy with the perception of visible beauty: they both take pleasure in symmetry and proportion. Euphranor is then able to refer all this work of perception in identifying symmetry and proportion to reason: 'the comparing Parts one with another, the considering them as belonging to one Whole, and the referring this Whole to its Use or End, should seem the Work of Reason: Should it not?' Not only is it the work of reason to weigh and compare various parts, but reason should also refer the whole to its 'Use or End'. Beauty is the pleasure deriving from a rational deduction of how well a particular end is met. Euphranor calls this the 'subordinate relative nature of beauty'. The pleasure that is taken in a visible appearance is drawn from a rational estimation of how well it suits the end for which it was designed. Greek and Roman dress is better than the Gothic because 'the Ancients, considering the Use and End of Dress, made it subservient to the Freedom, Ease, and Convenience of the Body, and having no Notion of mending or changing the natural Shape, they aimed only at showing it with Decency and Advantage'.[40] The principle of subordination to an end is no less applicable to the moral than the aesthetic domain. Moral truths, 'all such Truths as direct or influence the moral Actions of Men', have as their 'Rule or Measure' 'the general Good of Mankind': this is the use to which morality (and indeed beauty) is subordinate.[41]

Use is of course a central element of apologetic: the truth and *usefulness* of the Christian religion are to be demonstrated. But use

40. Ibid., III.8–9.
41. Ibid., I.16 (Euphranor).

has a still more important function in *Alciphron* that I will hint at
here and discuss at greater length in the following chapter.[42] Uses
are things that minds or spirits have uniquely. Knowing something
and judging its goodness requires us to know the end for which it
was made, and that applies as much to the moral world as the natural or phenomenal, as Crito makes clear:

> It is an allowed Point that no Man can judge of this or that part of a
> Machine taken by it self, without knowing the whole, the mutual Rela-
> tion or Dependence of its Parts, and the End for which it was made.
> And, as this is a Point acknowledged in corporeal and natural Things,
> ought we not by a Parity of Reason to suspend our Judgment concern-
> ing the moral Fitness of a single unaccountable Part of the Divine
> Oeconomy, till we are more fully acquainted with the moral System,
> or World of Spirits, and are let into the Designs of God's Providence,
> and have an extensive View of his Dispensations past, present, and
> future?[43]

The freethinkers here are being urged to moral caution by means of
analogy to the curious manufactures of human art.

But one might ask how easy it is to fulfil Crito's criteria for the
legitimate exercise of moral judgement. Knowing the divine economy, the world of other agents (spirits), and the historical unfolding of providence is not the work of a day. And that may be Crito's
point: such knowledge is only likely acquired by those sober older
men who have studied hard and methodically in Greek and Latin
texts and weighed the various dry speculations of previous authors
on biblical history, on the justice of the contemporary distribution
of goods amongst the world's population, and on the likely future
course of individual and collective human life. It is hard to acquire
this extensive view, but we should trust those who have acquired
it (a philosophical and educational elite to which Berkeley himself belonged), as they best know the use for which God made the
world. The world itself is the means of communicating God's ends

---

42. Taranto, '*Alciphron* ou la théorie du complot', pp. 234–35, suggests that the faith
or belief in providence sketched in *Alciphron* is that which allows us to see a connection
between utility and truth. He notes that the visual and emotive language arguments are
well adapted to this end.

43. *Alciphron*, VI.16.

to us. The end is, if we trust the right-thinkers, to ennoble ourselves and participate of divinity. That is, the use God intends the world to indicate to us, the use subordinate to which we ought to judge the natural and moral world, is that it makes us more like God and enables us to reconcile our wills with God's will and see our endeavours as God's grace.

The phenomenal world (the only world) is a language, a set of signs. (For a discussion of language in the *New Theory of Vision*, see chapter 2.) That language is 'operative', a key word in *Alciphron* to which I return in the following chapter. It is operative in as much as it is expressing the will of another agent, a spirit, in this case the infinite spirit God. The world is identifiable as a language on account of the 'Articulation, Combination, Variety, Copiousness, extensive and general Use and easy Application of Signs'.[44] That quality of the signs of the visual world reveals the will of another agent. Although Euphranor, countering Alciphron's contention that scripture contains absurdities, talks of the possibility of 'the Humane Mind' being moved and stimulated 'by a supernatural Power' and of 'the Humane Nature' being 'united to the Divine, in a manner ineffable and incomprehensible by Reason', the text points to demonstrable and comprehensible ways in which God encourages human agents to unite themselves with the divine nature, through the conscious reform of their own behaviour along those lines that the physical and moral economy of the universe, understood as the operative use of signs, communicates to them.[45]

The real presence of another, more perfect spirit, communicating to us through copious signs expressing a conceived good, intending the reform of our conduct: that is the God known to the right-thinkers of *Alciphron*. This knowledge of God is no more acquired by analogy than our knowledge of many things human is acquired by analogy. That is, the right-thinkers do not see any unusual impediment to knowing God. Berkeley remains true to the position he contrasted to William King's in a letter to Percival of 1 March 1709/10: that God is known as 'an understanding, wise, and benevolent Being, in the strict, literal, and proper meaning of

44. Ibid. (1752 text), IV.12.
45. Ibid., VI.9, VI.11.

those words'.[46] Lysicles mocks talk of 'an unknown Subject of Attributes absolutely unknown' or arguing 'from unknown Attributes, or [. . .] from Attributes in an unknown Sense'.[47] Although Crito in response gives an abbreviated intellectual history of the concept of divine analogy, ranging from Dionysius the Areopagite through Pico della Mirandola, Thomas Aquinas, Suarez, and Cajetan, the weight of his argument is carried by a very plain statement: 'Analogy is a *Greek* Word used by Mathematicians, to signify a Similitude of Proportions'. When we talk about attributes that are compatible with perfection, such as knowledge, then they are analogously applied to God only in the sense that God has them in an infinitely greater degree than any finite spirit.[48] The analogy implies nothing unknown of the attribute other than what it would be to possess any attribute infinitely.[49] Other ways of talking about God that have been considered examples of analogy are not cases of proportion, but of metaphors, and metaphors of a kind that are perfectly common in our talk of human agents: 'We believe that God executes Vengeance without Revenge, and is jealous without Weakness, just as the Mind of Man sees without Eyes, and apprehends without Hands'.[50] We have no trouble with fundamental metaphors (or mappings of cognitive domains), such as that between vision and knowledge, when applied to humans; why should they bother us when applied to God, the right-thinkers ask?

Berkeley left Rhode Island for Boston in September 1731 and then sailed for London. He arrived back on either Saturday, 23 October 1731, or the following Saturday, 30 October.[51] In January 1732,

46. Letter 12, p. 36; see also chapter 2.

47. *Alciphron*, IV.17–18.

48. Ibid., IV.21; see also Daniel, 'Berkeley's Rejection of Divine Analogy', p. 150: 'For Berkeley, minds cannot be known apart from their effects, so to say that divine or human minds are wise is to refer to nothing other than their effects. In this sense, predications about God are justified, in that the divine mind is known literally in the same way as human minds are known'.

49. Fasko, 'A Scotist Nonetheless?', p. 43, argues that Berkeley is more like Duns Scotus than Cajetan in claiming that the imperfections must be removed from human attributes in order for them to be properly predicated of the divine, as in OED 'imperfect' A.I.1, 'deficient in quantity'. I take Berkeley's use of 'imperfect' here to mean 'incomplete' or finite, and so to constitute a form of proportion.

50. *Alciphron*, IV.24 (Crito).

51. *Berkeley and Percival*, p. 279, Percival's journal for 1 November 1731.

he was receiving correspondence and callers in Greenwich and St James's in London. On 18 February that year, he gave the Anniversary Sermon for the SPG. His reflections there on the Native American and enslaved populations of the colony have already been discussed. He also noted, however, that projects for conversion abroad required that one address infidelity at home.[52] The desire to convert others is charity, an expression of Christian love. Charity is a matter of self-interest, as it is the best way of attaining immortality. Putting others 'in the Way that leads to Eternal Life' is the best service that can be done them: 'every one of us, who hath any Claim to that Title [sincere Christian], is indispensably obliged in Duty to God, and in Charity to his Neighbour, to desire and promote, so far as there is Opportunity, the Conversion of Heathen and Infidels, that so they may become Partakers of Life and Immortality'. Carrying out this self-interested as well as socially interested charitable work of conversion is the expression of practical Christianity. Practical Christianity is a certain knowledge of God, not 'barren Speculation [. . .] but, on the contrary, an holy practical Knowledge, which is the Source, the Root, or Principle of Peace and Union, of Faith, Hope, Charity, and universal Obedience'.[53]

These are the principles with which Berkeley returns from his American experience, and they are as strongly expressed in *Alciphron* as in the Bermuda project. They also present Berkeley's social and educational obligations to take an interest in the spiritual welfare of all people, in order to produce consent to moral, religious, and political laws. Berkeley is presenting his socially committed educational work, amongst heathens and infidels, as a means of ennoblement and participation of the divinity, a way to know and follow God. That is what all knowledge is for Berkeley: 'an holy practical Knowledge'. For the remainder of his career, his character or persona as a philosopher would also take the form of a practice.

52. *Anniversary Sermon*, p. 30 (LJ, VII.126).
53. Ibid., pp. 5–6, 8 (LJ, VII.115–17).

CHAPTER TWELVE

The True End of Speech

IN *ALCIPHRON*, BERKELEY has the right-thinker Euphranor say that 'the Doctrine of Signs [is] a Point of great Importance, and general Extent, which, if duly considered, would cast no small Light upon Things, and afford a just and genuine Solution of many Difficulties'.[1] In attempting to show why Euphranor holds this view, this chapter briefly reviews Berkeley's writing about language, showing how it is amplified and extended in *Alciphron*. The developments in Berkeley's thinking about language point to his interest in practice in his years at Cloyne (1734–1752) and to his return to the topic of the phenomenal world as a language in *Siris* (1744). As in my discussion of spirits in the introduction, I aim at neither a consistent, technical, philosophical interpretation of Berkeley's philosophy of language nor a full account of the commentary that has grown up around the topic, but intend to broach characteristic Berkeleian themes that are relevant to other parts of this book. I concentrate on two features of Euphranor's view: that words need not signify ideas to be meaningful, and that language is used to an end. Euphranor asserts that signs

> have other Uses besides barely standing for and exhibiting Ideas, such as raising proper Emotions, producing certain Dispositions or Habits of Mind, and directing our Actions in pursuit of that Happiness, which is the ultimate End and Design, the primary Spring and Motive, that

1. *Alciphron*, VII.16.

sets rational Agents at work: [. . .] the true End of Speech, Reason, Science, Faith, Assent, in all its different Degrees, is not merely, or principally, or always the imparting or acquiring of Ideas, but rather something of an active, operative Nature, tending to a conceived Good[.]

Thinking about language requires us to have a view of what it is to be a rational agent. Being a rational agent is to be set at work in the business of attaining happiness, a business of both the understanding and the will, identifying and pursuing proper objects. Euphranor says that 'the Humane Mind [. . .] [is] design'd, not for the bare Intuition of Ideas, but for Action or Operation about them, and pursuing her own Happiness therein'.[2] Speech, reason, science, faith, assent—all aim at happiness: they are not the expressions of an indolent or indifferent judgement, but the activities of motivated agents. Berkeley's doctrine of signs gives definition to a variety of ways in which language is meaningful without signifying ideas. Further, it provides a criterion for distinguishing between speech used towards its true end and speech used to a false end: speech should actively tend to a conceived good. I take these two features in turn.

Signifying Ideas

It was unorthodox in the first half of the eighteenth century to assert, and especially to defend in such detail and with the types of arguments Berkeley employs, the view that words need not signify ideas in order to be meaningful. John Locke expresses the view that the 'use [. . .] of Words, is to be sensible Marks of *Ideas*; and the *Ideas* they stand for, are their proper and immediate Signification'. Locke's purpose in the third book of the *Essay* was ultimately the discipline of speech, such that all its modes could be regulated by the model of scientific or philosophical discourse. The 'using of Words, without clear and distinct *Ideas*', is an abuse of language, seen frequently when people deploy words such as '*Wisdom, Glory, Grace*, etc.' [. . .] with 'no determined *Ideas* laid up in their Minds, which are to be expressed to others by them'.[3] The

2. Ibid., VII.17, VII.14.
3. *Essay*, III.ii.1, p. 405; III.x.2–3, pp. 490–91.

terms used without corresponding ideas in Locke's example come from the domains of moral and religious discourse. The abuse of language is the failure to apply to all its scenes of use the rigours of philosophical and scientific speech. One motivation for Berkeley's thinking about language is to contest the priority of scientific over moral or religious types of language use.

John Toland, a freethinker and an interlocutor of Locke's in the 1690s, applies Locke's thinking to religious language: 'Syllables, though never so well put together, if they have not Ideas fix'd to them, are but *Words spoken in the Air*; and cannot be the Ground of a *reasonable Service*, or Worship'.[4] It would not be reasonable to organise Christian service to God around a term such as 'grace' if that term did not signify a clear and distinct idea. No term in religious language, Toland is saying, ought to be in the least mysterious, and no religious practice ought to be built on mysteries. (Worship and service, it is perhaps worth emphasising, both require loyal subordination: Toland is talking about the appropriate conditions for submission to another will.) The argumentative purpose of Toland's book may, of course, be to undermine the reasonableness of Christianity and its fundamental concepts by hinting that they are in this sense mysterious and so cannot be the basis of an obligation on a rational agent seeking her own happiness. Toland engages in a satirical exposure of people who attempt to derive self-worth and social elevation from the discursive deployment of terms for which they have no corresponding idea. 'Could that Person justly value himself upon being wiser than his Neighbours, who having infallible Assurance that something call'd *Blictri* had a Being in Nature, in the mean time knew not what this *Blictri* was?'[5] There can be no wisdom, nor, importantly, any social distinction derived from that wisdom, in asserting the existence of things of which one has no idea, in talking about a mystery.

Berkeley began his philosophical career as a Lockean on language, stating in his notebooks the axiom 'No word to be used without an idea'.[6] But he lost the conviction that words must signify

---

4. *Christianity Not Mysterious*, p. 34, citing 1 Corinthians 14:9 and Romans 12:1.
5. Ibid., pp. 81–82.
6. *Notebooks*, §356.

ideas in order to be meaningful over the course of composing the *Notebooks*. As noted earlier, colour words used generally and particles or conjunctions that signify relations or acts of mind were two kinds of language that prompted this change of view. Terms that signify other minds and their actions signify notions rather than ideas. Euphranor notes that words may well signify active spirits that are not ideas. Notions are not ideas but are nonetheless properly present to the mind, according to *Siris*: 'there are properly no ideas or passive objects in the mind, but what were derived from sense: but [...] there are also besides these her own acts or operations: such are notions'.[7] Signifying notions is a major function of language that does not require signification of ideas.

Passions, Actions, Rules for Conduct

As well as coming to see that there are classes of words that do not signify ideas, by the time he composed the *Principles of Human Knowledge*, Berkeley also came to see some occasions on which words sometimes signifying ideas need not always do so.[8] These are occasions when the persuasive function of language dominates the referential:

> [T]he communicating of Ideas marked by Words is not the chief and only end of Language, as is commonly suppos'd. There are other Ends, as the raising of some Passion, the exciting to, or deterring from an Action, the putting the Mind in some particular Disposition; to which the former is in many Cases barely subservient, and sometimes intirely omitted, when these can be obtain'd without it, as I think does not infrequently happen in the familiar use of Language.[9]

7. *Alciphron*, VII.8; *Siris*, §308. Winkler, 'Berkeley and the Doctrine of Signs', p. 149, notes that Berkeley's texts, the second edition of the *Principles of Human Knowledge* in particular, seem to follow a distinction in the philosophical terminology of his time: 'notions were regarded as objects more of intellect than of sense, and as objects whose conception requires active intellectual effort, as opposed to passive reception'.

8. Beal, 'Berkeley's Linguistic Criterion', 3.381, offers a summary of the uses of language that have now been noted in Berkeley: signs are meaningful if they mark an idea, mark any one or more of a range of ideas, affect conduct (by establishing rules or raising emotions), or mark something we are aware of that is not an idea (a notion).

9. *Principles of Human Knowledge*, introduction, §20.

Euphranor's view, cited earlier, is, then, a development of the position of *Principles of Human Knowledge* containing a nontrivial addition. It adds to raising passions, exciting a particular action, or encouraging a disposition the requirement that these active states of the spirit tend to a conceived good in order to serve the true end of speech. This is a change in aspect. Berkeley is not merely defending the view that there are some exceptional situations in which words do not signify ideas and yet still perform a function. Rather, he is arguing that language needs to be reconceived not primarily as a matter of signifying, but as a matter of action tending to a conceived good. Though Berkeley frequently invokes custom and daily practice as criteria for philosophical understanding of language, this is an evaluative view, a prescription, not a description.[10] The *true* end of language is active, operative, and tending to a conceived good. Words may signify ideas, but if the discourses containing them are not active, operative, and tending to a conceived good, then they are less than full uses of language—one might even say they are abuses, to adopt Locke's terminology. Nor is this the case for language alone, or for language in any simple sense: all 'speech, reason, science, faith, assent' falls under the same rubric. Language (speech) is not to be separated from the operations of mind that might be said to underlie it, nor from the different acts of mind or mental attitudes that embody degrees or types of certainty, nor from the practices of observation and the manipulation of specialist symbolic systems characteristic of the new science. These are all, like language, actions performed by spirits, and their true end is to tend towards conceived goods. The doctrine of signs that Euphranor thinks will be of such general use specifies not just that language may excite passions, encourage dispositions, or alter conduct, but also that, if it is to pursue its true end, the activities or dispositions the language encourages must tend towards a conceived good. Berkeley has moved from a Lockean paradigm of description (using words to signify ideas) to a paradigm of instruction (using language to get people to do good or be better).

In considering the character of Berkeley's contribution to thinking about language, it may be helpful to take a step back

---

10. *Alciphron*, VII.8, for example.

and consider the genesis of Euphranor's summative statement in the broader context of the seventh dialogue of *Alciphron*, which, in effect, stages the dispute between Locke/Toland and Berkeley sketched here. The arguments Berkeley deploys in this account of language have a twentieth-century feel: his introduction of rules of conduct and changes of behaviour as tests of whether a term is meaningful are revolutionary. He has been thought a precursor of Wittgenstein, Grice, and Austin.[11] The question of whether his arguments propose alternative types of meaning, 'cognitive' and 'emotional', appropriate to different types of human practice (scientific reasoning and theology), and with different criteria (signification of ideas, effects in behaviour) is the subject of continuing controversy.[12] The dialogue discusses two types of language use that do not require signification of ideas: occasions on which a word is not cashed out into the idea which on other occasions it signifies; and occasions on which a sign and the circumstances of its use constitute a rule for conduct. In arguing against Alciphron, who presents the Lockean view, Euphranor develops the notion that we might not always need to cash out the words that we use into the ideas associated with them, just as counters can be used at a card table to stand in for money, without the idea of the money always being raised in the mind of the players: 'Words may not be insignificant, although they should not, every time they are used, excite the Ideas

11. Stewart, 'Berkeley's Introduction Draft', p. 16; Flew, 'Was Berkeley a Precursor of Wittgenstein?', pp. 214–26; Williford, 'Berkeley's Theory of Operative Language in the Manuscript Introduction', p. 286n27, citing Brykman, *Berkeley: Philosophie et apologétique*, I.299–300 and II.109, and *Berkeley et le voile des mots*, pp. 209ff.; Roberts, *A Metaphysics for the Mob*, p. 68; *Pearce, Language and the Structure of Berkeley's World*, pp. 5, 28, 53.

12. See Belfrage, 'Editor's Commentary', pp. 46–50; Berman, 'Cognitive Theology and Emotive Mysteries in Berkeley's Alciphron'; Jakapi, 'Emotive Meaning and Christian Mysteries in Berkeley's Alciphron'. Williford and Jakapi, 'Berkeley's Theory of Meaning in Alciphron VII', provide a full bibliographical footnote (3) on the history of the debate. Woozly, 'Berkeley's Doctrine of Notions and Theory of Meaning', p. 401, notes some symmetries and asymmetries between the ways in which terms in religious and scientific discourse acquire meaning in the formation of rules for conduct. Berkeley's emotive theory of meaning, though striking for its modern feel, is not absolutely original. Stewart, 'Berkeley's Introduction Draft', p. 16, identifies Cicero and Hobbes as precedents; Hans Aarsleff, 'Philosophy of Language', pp. 455–56, identifies the *Port-Royal Logic* and Bernard Lamy's *Art of Speaking* as precedents.

they signify in our Minds, it being sufficient, that we have it in our Power to substitute Things or Ideas for their Signs when there is Occasion'.[13]

This meaningful use without signification of ideas at least partly overlaps with another class of uses: those that are involved in forming rules for conduct. Use of the counter (without signifying the money) enables the card game to be played, or played in a certain way. The counter exists amongst a number of rules that form our conduct, and their forming our conduct does not always require an intermediary idea. As Euphranor says:

> [T]here may be another Use of Words, besides that of marking and suggesting distinct Ideas, to wit, the influencing our Conduct and Actions; which may be done either by forming Rules for us to act by, or by raising certain Passions, Dispositions, and Emotions in our Minds. A Discourse, therefore, that directs how to act or excites to the Doing or Forbearance of an Action may, it seems, be useful and significant, although the Words whereof it is composed should not bring each a distinct Idea into our Minds.[14]

Not every word need signify a distinct idea provided the discourse of which they form a part directs action in some way, either by establishing rules or by encouraging dispositions. There being an observable feature of somebody's conduct that is the result of or that has been influenced by the discourse in which such terms occur becomes, then, a test of the term having a meaning: terms must 'serve to regulate and influence our Wills, Passions, or Conduct'; if the doctrine containing these terms 'becomes a lively operative Principle influencing [a person's] Life and Actions', those terms have meaning.[15]

Some scenarios the right-thinkers describe are cases in which a person does not understand the idea or notion which a word signifies, but in which the word may be said to be meaningful because of the behaviour of that person: 'There is, if I mistake not, a Practical Faith, or Assent, which sheweth it self in the Will and Actions

13. *Alciphron*, VII.8.
14. Ibid., VII.8.
15. Ibid., VII.11.

of a Man, although his Understanding may not be furnished with those abstract, precise, distinct Ideas, which, whatever a Philosopher may pretend, are acknowledged to be above the Talents of common Men'.[16] Commentators sympathetic to Toland's brand of rationalism have taken this and similar statements to mean that, for Berkeley, 'human beings are put in the position that they can be moved by the language of revelation without fully understanding it, or indeed understanding it at all'.[17] But this is to miss Euphranor's irony: the kinds of terms he is describing do not signify ideas at all. They may be, like 'force', meaningful terms that do not signify ideas, but derive their meaning from being a useful 'principle' in 'directing Men how to act'.[18] A philosopher, in the pejorative sense, might claim to have an idea corresponding to 'force', but she cannot have, as force is known by no ideas other than those of its effects: it is a quality of spirits, not ideas. In some cases, such as this of force, or the card game, one might say that the person who has understood the uses of the term demonstrates her understanding by displaying an ability: an ability to play whist, or to calculate the weight that could be withstood by a bridge.[19]

The requirement that in order to serve its true end language must tend to a conceived good is an aspect of Berkeley's account of operative language that has to date received little attention in commentary. It has been noted that the intentions of speakers are important in establishing meanings when ideas are not attached to every term, or when the ideas attached are not brought to mind.[20]

16. Ibid., VII.12.

17. Duddy, 'Toland, Berkeley, and the Irrational Hypothesis', p. 60.

18. *Alciphron*, VII.10. Winkler, 'Berkeley and the Doctrine of Signs', pp. 153–54, has noted the rather devastating potential that acknowledgement of this procedure has for Berkeley's immaterialism, as 'material substance' might be a useful term parallel to 'force'. Kupfer, 'A Note on "Berkeley's Linguistic Criterion"', p. 392, suggests that scientific terms form rules for conduct: 'there is good reason to construe scientific knowledge, in Berkeley, as knowledge of how to perform certain mental acts'.

19. Roberts, 'Berkeley on the Philosophy of Language', p. 432, presents a version of this view of Berkeley's theory of language: 'It suggests that we see concept possession not in terms of the perception of ideas before the mind but rather as the possession of certain abilities. So, I may be said to understand signs because I have mastered their correct usage'.

20. Williford, 'Berkeley's Theory of Operative Language in the Manuscript Introduction', p. 285: 'it is crucial to note that it is certain contextual factors central to language learning, primarily factors involving the intentions of speakers and our capacity to

But it has not been noted that these intentions relate to a global sense of what is good and are focused on getting other participants in the speech situation to do good. One of Berkeley's preferred examples in discussions of speech that does not signify ideas is the promise of a good thing, the Pauline promise of reward in the afterlife. When a person hears Saint Paul's words and grasps his intention, that person is grasping, sharing, and aspiring to a certain conception of the good, and not in any merely incidental or episodic sense. The production of rules for conduct serves as a criterion for the meaningfulness of a term. They have their meaning in a human practice, a practice that should tend towards a conceived good. This additional test can be applied to Toland's vain hypocrite who prides himself on asserting the existence of 'blictri' whilst having no idea of 'blictri'. In Berkeley's account, there would be no shame in having no idea corresponding to 'blictri' if it were a notional term, or if the idea or notion associated with it were not in the person's mind, provided that he could give an account of the behaviours that go along with 'blictri' or embody or perform them himself even without being able to give such an account. But those things all require that the person have a good in mind and is tending in his account of 'blictri', or in his embodiment of it, to a certain conceived good. 'Blictri' in Toland's example is not speech used to its true end because the person he portrays does not have such a good in mind and in fact seeks to exploit the credulity of his neighbours and to exercise his vanity. These are false, not true, ends of speech. The 'blictri' example is not an example that properly parallels the function of terms relating to the Christian mysteries because the speaker of 'blictri' is not using speech to tend to a conceived good.

There is then a test of goodness (at least conceived goodness) to be applied to the meaningfulness of notional terms and of terms that establish rules for conduct. One way in which we might understand the critical procedure of the right-thinkers in *Alciphron* is as the application of the test of a conceived good to the use of terms that the freethinkers introduce into the dialogue. For example, the

recognize them, that allow certain pieces of language that include idea-less terms to be significant'.

freethinkers talk of moral beauty.[21] This phrase could be meaningful if it tended towards a conceived good, but the conversation between the freethinkers and the right-thinkers demonstrates that in the freethinking discursive practice it does not. It is more like 'blictri' than 'faith'. We are not truly reasoning, or speaking, or doing science, or assenting, or having faith, unless there is an identifiable good governing our discursive practice. *Alciphron* is the progressive revelation of the absence of such goods in the practice of freethinking through a dramatic representation of freethinking speech performance.

The demand that there be a conceived good in order for speech, reason, science, faith, and assent to serve their true end extends beyond those linguistic cases in which terms are used that don't signify ideas because they signify notions or promote rules of conduct. All reasoning, discoursing, and assenting, even that about clear and distinct ideas, should have a good in view. This qualification relates closely to Berkeley's lifelong reluctance to separate the faculties of understanding and willing. Spirit is as much a willing as an understanding substance, its understanding a type of activity: 'Understanding is in some sort an Action. [. . .] Substance of a Spirit is that it acts, causes, wills, operates'. A spirit has two aspects, but it 'is one Simple, Undivided, active Being: as it perceives Ideas, it is called the *Understanding*, and as it produces or otherwise operates about them, it is called the *Will*.[22] It is with some reluctance that Berkeley accepts in his last major publication that the faculties can be distinguished: '[I]t must be owned that, as faculties are multiplied by philosophers according to their operations, the will may be distinguished from the intellect. But it will not therefore follow that the Will which operates in the course of nature is not conducted and applied by intellect, although it be granted that neither will understands, nor intellect wills'. This marginal distinction is applied to the phenomenal world understood as a discourse produced by God that tends towards a conceived good:

> Therefore, the phænomena of nature, which strike on the senses and are understood by the mind, do form not only a magnificent spectacle,

21. *Alciphron*, III.3.
22. *Notebooks*, §§821, 829; *Principles of Human Knowledge*, §27.

but also a most coherent, entertaining, and instructive discourse; and to effect this, they are conducted, adjusted, and ranged by the greatest wisdom. This language or discourse is studied with different attention, and interpreted with different degrees of skill. But so far as men have studied and remarked it's rules, and can interpret right, so far they may be said to be knowing in nature, A beast is like a man who hears a strange tongue but understands nothing.[23]

Science is following the discourse of phenomena not only, as it were, for the pleasure of the free play of the understanding, but in order to be instructed in the good; not just to understand, but to know better what to do. As John Russell Roberts puts it:

> Science, at its best, is nothing more (and nothing less!) than a well-managed body of activities that helps us to learn to vaticinate more and more effectively. And in doing so, it does not reveal to us a body of knowledge the contemplation of which is valuable in-itself. [. . .] God's discourse is not cognitive. It is *expressive* discourse, ultimately aimed at a practical end. Its end is [. . .] to teach us how to regulate our own behaviour. The content of the divine language is expressive of his divine love for us.[24]

Those phenomena that humans recognise as the discourse of God aim at a good, the general good of well-regulated human behaviour.

It was noted earlier that Berkeley's introduction of change in conduct as a criterion for meaningfulness has a modern feel. But it has also been noted that Berkeley's employment of this highly progressive criterion for meaningfulness is at the service of an argument that connects use and utility with truth, specifically the truth of Christian providence, in the apologetic project of *Alciphron*.[25] Further, the language used when presenting this criterion is regulatory—disciplinary even: it is about rules, laws, and the direction and evaluation of actions in the light of those laws. That is, it is a moral matter. And whilst morality is a matter of human

---

23. *Siris*, §254.

24. Roberts, *A Metaphysics for the Mob*, p. 66. Roberts contrasts Berkeley to Descartes, for whom knowledge of external reality is of real essences known to the intellect, not a practical knowledge terminating in human pleasures and pains (p. 67).

25. Taranto, 'Alciphron ou la théorie du complot', pp. 234–35.

flourishing, here, as uniformly across his career, Berkeley suggests that moral flourishing requires obedience and the following of rules. He is interested in language that gives rules and laws and that organises behaviour in predetermined ways—language that makes its users better Christians, in effect. There is a strong correlation between this language that gives rules of conduct and the universal laws of morality described in *Passive Obedience*, laws that we should follow because they are God's will, rather than because they produce the best outcomes for people (which in any case they do).[26]

The doctrine of signs has already been shown (in both this chapter and earlier chapters of this book) to be of great extent, inasmuch as Berkeley gives it a role in everything from the theology of mysteries to causation in the physical sciences, optics and the psychology of vision, and understanding the laws of nature and how they operate. Euphranor says that the doctrine will provide a just resolution to many difficulties. What are the difficulties that Berkeley (if Berkeley is speaking through Euphranor) thought would be resolved? The central difficulty solved in *Alciphron* VII is to show that employing the language of religious mystery, given that it does not signify clear and distinct ideas, can still be meaningful. Berkeley might also have solved the problem, posed by Mandeville and others, of the demoralisation of social life. In order for speech, reason, science, faith, or assent to serve their true end, they must have a conceived good in view. Without such a good in view, the rules generated with the help of signs and the actions that follow from those rules will not be organised to serve their true end. Given that not just linguistic exchanges, narrowly understood, but other kinds of exchanges, such as those practised in the economy, can be understood as forms of rational and communicative action, they too share this criterion of being undertaken with a conceived good in view in order to be serving their true end. The following chapters on Berkeley's time in Cloyne will focus on the forms of active, operative, or practical life he engaged in there, and the goods he had in view.

26. *Passive Obedience*, §31, and see the discussion in chapter 4. Pearce, *Language and the Structure of Berkeley's World*, p. 77, notes the importance of convergence around the same rules if language is to work; the same is true of moral laws as described in *Passive Obedience*.

CHAPTER THIRTEEN

Cloyne

DISCIPLINE

THE PERIOD BETWEEN Berkeley's return from America in 1731 and his taking up the bishopric of Cloyne in 1734 was one of considerable professional uncertainty, during which he and his supporters struggled to dispel accusations of whimsicality relating to the Bermuda scheme and of political disaffection. Towards the end of this period, Berkeley produced his major contribution to the philosophy of mathematics, *The Analyst*, a critique of the Newtonian doctrine of fluxions. The book was aimed at his long-standing enemies, the freethinkers, and more generally at the misuse of the language and methods of mathematical science to claim priority over theology. After detailing this period, the chapter then moves to its main focus, a tendency of Berkeley's years at Cloyne that I call disciplinary. Three manifestations of this disciplinary tendency are discussed, beginning with Berkeley's insistence that spiritual and temporal authority are connected, and that civil governments should maintain an interest in the religious practice of their subjects. Next, the chapter covers Berkeley's practice as a bishop, looking at his management of personnel and finances and his guidance to his clergy on how to engage in the project of bringing Catholic inhabitants of Cloyne into the established church. The chapter closes with a consideration of Berkeley's involvement in planning the civil and military defence of Ireland from Jacobite forces in 1745 and the maxims on patriotism he wrote towards the end of his life.

Preferment

Besides tying up the loose ends of the Bermuda project and maintaining his relationships with colleagues with an interest in colonial Christianity, Berkeley was engaged in controversial searches after preferment immediately on his return to England. In December 1731, John Baron Wainwright wrote to Caroline Clayton, Viscountess Sundon (and Daniel Clayton's sister), asking her to '[f]orget Bermuda' and consider Berkeley 'for any good offices and kind impressions that you see time and place for. They will not be lost upon a man unworthy, indiscreet, or ungrateful'.[1] In January 1732, Berkeley was soliciting for the deanery of Down, a post that would have linked his interests to Edward Southwell, as Marmaduke Coghill, previously a Tory ally of Speaker Conolly and now first commissioner of the revenue, said in a letter to Southwell:

> We are told Dean Berkley presses hard to succeed Dean Gore [at Down], he is now att London, and doubtlesse if he gets the deanery of down, he will be fixd to your Interest. I presume you know the deanerys are reservd out of my Ld Leiuts. Commission, and the crown has the sole disposeall of them, tho I Suppose my Ld. Leiuts. recomendation will have its due weight, but if Dr Berkleys Interest be good, it is probable he may gett the deanery of Down, haveing his own deanery to give up, which is worth a 1000l. a year, and the other deanery last year was settt for 1450l.[2]

In February, Berkeley was passed over for the post on account of a letter written by the duke of Dorset, the lord lieutenant of Ireland, at (so Berkeley believed) the request of the archbishop of Dublin, John Hoadly, and the primate Hugh Boulter. In Percival's report, the letter said that Berkeley 'was a madman, and highly disagreeable to all the King's best friends in Ireland'.[3] (It has been noted that Boulter would generally propose English candidates for posts, against the Irish candidates supported by Conolly and his party,

---

1. Clayton, *Memoirs of [Charlotte Clayton,] the Countess of Sundon*, II.165, 31 December 1731; BL Add MS 20105, f. 63r.

2. Hayton, ed., *The Letters of Marmaduke Coghill*, p. 116, no. 90, to Edward Southwell Jr, 28 January 1731/32; BL Add MS 28218, ff. 43–44. See also Hayton, '"Paltry Underlings of State"?', p. 235.

3. *Berkeley and Percival*, p. 282.

emphasising the need for loyalty to England in case of breakdowns in the Anglo-Irish relationship such as that caused by Wood's half-pence and Swift's reaction to it.[4]) Percival remonstrated with the archbishop's brother, Benjamin Hoadly, the bishop of Salisbury, during the lesson at the King's Chapel. Percival reports that Berkeley was 'sat over against us', presumably on the other side of the chapel, and refers to him as 'one of the worthiest, most learned, and most unexceptionable men in the three kingdoms, who has met with the wretchedest usage'. Hoadly suggested that Berkeley had done himself no favours 'by undertaking that ridiculous project of converting the Indians, and leaving his Deanery, where there was business enough for him to convert the Papists, and that his Bishop had writ to him and laid it on his conscience to return home, which he did not comply with'.[5] Dorset had indeed written a letter about the deanery, the contents of which included the view that Berkeley 'was looked upon as a madman'. Lord Wilmington passed the letter to Walpole, who agreed with the assessment and remarked that he 'had always said it where it was proper'. Wilmington also approached the queen, who had already engaged with the king on Berkeley's behalf, and so could not now be brought to support a rival. Still, he asked her to put Dorset's letter before the king, emphasising the part that said Berkeley *'is very particularly disliked by all the King's friends* in Ireland'. Wilmington saw the king personally too, and made the same points. He regarded his efforts as inconclusive, yet likely to result in Berkeley being passed over.[6] (Richard Daniel, of whom Anne Berkeley wrote a satirical portrait at some point after his death in 1739, received the preferment.)

Percival twice recorded Berkeley suggesting that he would be provided for in England, and Edmund Gibson, the bishop of London, whom Percival engaged in conversation on Berkeley's behalf, thought that Berkeley was 'fixt upon not going to Ireland'. Gibson noted the difficulty of obtaining a suitable preferment, and Percival set out Berkeley's reasons for having wanted Down: 'that he might have gone over with a mark of his Majesty's good countenance to

4. See Hayton, '"Paltry Underlings of State"?', p. 241.

5. *Berkeley and Percival*, pp. 281–82, journal entries for 25 and 27 February 1731/32.

6. Historical Manuscripts Commission, *Report on the Manuscripts of Mrs. Stopford-Sackville*, I(1904).148, Lord Wilmington to the Duke of Dorset, 15 February 1731/32.

him, and in a reasonable time repair his private fortune', which had suffered by the Bermuda project. Gibson conjectured that a comment of Lord Wilmington to Queen Caroline, that Berkeley 'was very great with Dean Swift', might have been the source of talk of Berkeley's disaffection for the government. His friends thought they had their own evidence of his loyalty. Percival pointed to Berkeley's *Advice to the Tories*, and Wainwright to his being chosen to represent TCD at the confirmation of the Prince of Wales as chancellor of the university.[7] Percival suggested that 'assurances from hence of making Dean Berkeley a Bishop were absolutely necessary of his going over, that his reputation might be retrieved'; Gibson responded by recommending that Berkeley return to Derry and await a bishopric in Ireland.[8]

It may be that Percival's conversation with Gibson was effective, albeit temporarily. Wainwright notes to Sundon that '[t]he first warmth of the Bishop of London & his present steddy coolness in the Deans behalf makes me begin to suspect whether He w^d. have his interest, if an opportunity sh^d. offer'.[9] Wainwright was keeping an eye out for other opportunities for Berkeley. He noted:

> The last packet brought us the news that the Dean of Christchurch is dead. The way is now open to fix and warm that College in duty and affection to their Majesties and the Royal family. [. . .] I do not write this from an opinion that I can suggest any thoughts which do not occur to you, where you can serve your Sovereigns. A proper Dean to receive Royal guests, a visit, a sight of their persons, and the Duke's continuance any time among them, would make their hearts as the heart of one man.[10]

Berkeley was later known to have a scheme to retire to a life of learning in Oxford. Perhaps this thought of an association with Christchurch began in 1732? Wainwright, keen as he was to solicit for a post for Berkeley, again acknowledged the Bermuda scheme

7. Clayton, *Memoirs of [Charlotte Clayton,] the Countess of Sundon*, II.178; BL Add MS 20105, ff. 65r–66r.

8. *Berkeley and Percival*, pp. 285–87, journal entry for 17 March 1732.

9. 10 February 1732 [i.e., 1733], BL Add MS 20105, Sundon correspondence 1714–1736, vol 4, f. 102v.

10. Clayton, *Memoirs of [Charlotte Clayton,] the Countess of Sundon*, II.181, Wainwright to Clayton, 26 December 1732; BL Add MS 20105, f. 83r.

as an embarrassment. Writing to Clayton on 28 June 1733 to let her know of a visit he would be making to her brother in Killala, Wainwright suggested that on account of their association with Bermuda, they might 'blush but still say something for the scheme'.[11] In the first year of his return to England, then, Berkeley was considering a variety of church positions while he struggled to evade accusations of political disloyalty and whimsicality.

In 1733, Berkeley appears to have been preparing for a return to Ireland. Prior rented a house for him in Arbor Hill, Dublin, from at least March 1733, but Berkeley would not be able to take it up until the summer, as Anne was expecting a child, after two miscarriages. The farmland associated with Berkeley's deanery in Derry had been let out, following Prior's suggestion. Berkeley also enlisted Prior's help in dispelling the notion that 'in certain parts of the kingdom of Ireland, justice is much obstructed for the want of justices of the peace, which is only to be remedied by taking in dissenters'. He suspected that this was an invention, presumably to weaken the Sacramental Test, and asked for a census of Catholics, dissenters, and churchmen from Prior, assuring him that he would be exerting himself 'on a public account', and that 'dispatch [. . .] will be doing the best service to your country'. Berkeley sought to counter the manufactured alarmism of those in London who would suggest that the ratio of Protestants to Catholics was one-to-seven, but he confirmed Prior's thought that no act of toleration was proposed, adding, 'I hope they will be able to do nothing anywhere'.[12] Berkeley's interest in the religious and social demographics of Ireland was oriented by his commitment to the established religion and its role in the magistracy. His tolerance did not extend to equality of civic status, for Catholics or dissenters. He wanted the society of the Protestant church to retain its social and political privileges.

Prior's practical and financial assistance was also required with respect to church preferment. Proposing that he be granted a sinecure in the north, Berkeley asked Prior to value a deanery and chancellorship; he denied that he had been spending his time in London

11. BL Add MS 20105, f. 113r.
12. Letter 218, Berkeley to Prior, 13 March 1733, p. 347; letter 219, Berkeley to Prior, 27 March 1733, p. 348; letter 222, Berkeley to Prior, 1 May 1733, p. 351.

campaigning for preferment and asked for an account of 'the country, the situation, the house, the circumstances of the bishopric of Cloyne; and let me know the charges of coming into a bishopric i.e. the amount of the fees and first-fruits'. In his next letter, Berkeley reported that he had 'kissed their Majestys' hands for the Bishopric of Cloyne, having first received an account from the Duke of Newcastle's office, setting forth that his Grace had laid before the King the Duke of Dorset's recommendation, which was readily complied with by his Majesty'.[13] Berkeley's campaigning was clearly to some effect, given that Dorset had written against him two years previously for the deanery of Down. But the support that Berkeley received was not unqualified. Before Berkeley had even left London to take up his bishopric, Wainwright remarked to Clayton how lucky Berkeley was 'to be made known to those who could abundantly supply his defects. I hope his behaviour in his station, will justify the favour conferr'd on him & He as well as those who value him will know what is due from him & where & how much opposition the Duke got over'.[14] The implication may be that Berkeley himself was not good at overcoming opposition at court.

A further letter from Wainwright to Clayton lends weight to that reading and also indicates that Berkeley was considering taking on an additional role that could have changed radically the character of his tenure of his bishopric. Berkeley met Wainwright in Dublin in May 1734, bringing with him a letter from Clayton. Wainwright's reply to Clayton suggests a new role for Berkeley:

> The education & morals of the University of Dublin is in a very bad way. The Prince is Chancellor, the Bishop of Clogher a worthy ancient Prelate Vice Chancellor, He intends to resign, the Provost & Fellows have their eyes upon the Bishop of Cloyne. He defers the acceptance of the offer & the decent application to His Royal Highness till He may have an approbation, for which He has the greatest regard a Letter in general terms by the Post will be understood. The Station is of dignity & credit, but more expence than profit. It may give many opportunities of shewing the duty & loyalty which He bears to their Majesties, which

13. Letter 231, Berkeley to Prior, 7 January 1734, p. 359; letter 232, 15 January 1734, pp. 360–61; letter 233, Berkeley to Prior, 19 January 1733/34, p. 361.
14. BL Add MS 20105, f. 127r, 21 March 1733/34.

He earnestly desires, & may employ him in promoting the Protestant Religion & virtue. for He is much more fit for a College than a Court, as I perceive by his own account which fully explains your hint.[15]

Here was a role like that of dean of Christchurch, where Berkeley could exercise his religious and educational zeal while expressing his loyalty to the Hanoverian regime. TCD had clearly remained in Berkeley's thoughts, as he met with Percival and Dr King to discuss the possibility of reforming some of the college's statutes to better preserve the library in 1733.[16] It is not known what came of this plan to bring Berkeley back to TCD, but when some gentlemen of the college were considering him for the same role in 1741, he declined, as his 'ill health and distance from the university would not permit me to serve it as I could wish'.[17]

Berkeley continued to enlist Prior's help in ascertaining the value of Cloyne—asking whether the eighty acres attached to the bishop's palace were additional to the estimated £1,200 income, and whether the wardenship of Tuam was in the patent of the diocese—and in buying his predecessor's furniture and cattle.[18] In a letter from the early stages of the process, Berkeley referred to chronic headaches, which he was treating by rising very early and thinking about mathematics.[19] These thoughts would eventually be published as *The Analyst*, to which I shall presently turn. This text, and the controversy that surrounded it, featured in Wainwright's letters to Clayton, which also returned to their theme of seeking preferment for Berkeley despite his own apparent talent for sabotaging his career:

> Residence w^d. now be the Bishop of Cloynes fault, if He was not confin'd to his Diocese by many symptoms of an Ulcer in his kidneys. He has had very ill health, & been in great danger & I much fear He will never see the end of the controversy He has engag'd in soe deep, ag^st. my opinion, as I frequently told him, I don't mean my opinion upon

15. BL Add MS 20105, ff. 128v–129r, 25 May 1734.
16. *Berkeley and Percival*, p. 289, journal entry for 22 May 1733.
17. Letter 280, Berkeley to Henry Clarke, 16 April 1741, p. 420.
18. Letter 235, 28 January 1734, p. 363; letter 238, 7 February 1734, p. 365; letter 240, 23 February 1734, pp. 366–67; letter 248, 30 April 1734, p. 378.
19. Letter 231, Berkeley to Prior, 7 January 1734, p. 359–60.

the controversy, for I have noe knowledge to form one, but in setting himself against the current of all the Mathematicians. To which He answerd, That as Orthodox as I am, if a Person usd an argument in matter of fact or science, in divinity I sh^d. be asham'd only to say, the Clergy are of another opinion. Soe that by what I perceive, He will dispute the point as long as He lives, indeed it is now his amusement, in the remote corner where He lives upon the edge of a bog. & tho' many of his Adversaries now despise his skill, & use him contemptuously, & will scarce allow some words to be his own, I have lately seen authentic proofs, that some of the first rank & foremost in the battle agst. him, have other sentiments of his abilities Your Ladyship will pardon me in making every excuse I can for a friend, in whose favour I was once an instrument of engaging your esteem. & the rather because I think his life will hardly last long enough to give you any farther trouble in his behalf. & indeed I fear if ever it sh^d. be mature & decent to apply for a removal, this controversy will be a dead weight upon his interest. tho' it outliv'd the Bermudan project, by the assistance of your Ladyship.[20]

Wainwright contrasts residence at Cloyne with absenteeism from Derry; remarks on Berkeley's zeal and self-belief, even when it was harming him; and notes Berkeley's ill health and marginalisation. Wainwright seemed to be losing patience with his client, though he still defended his intellectual ability. The same tone of disappointment in Berkeley's career trajectory is found in the assessments of others in his intimate acquaintance, such as Anne Donnellan and Anne Forster/Berkeley.

Berkeley's return from America was a moment of great professional uncertainty, and one showing that the strategic abilities he demonstrated in the rhetoric of his texts and in support of Bermuda were not effective in the pursuit of professional advancement—though his lack of success clearly did concern him, despite his occasional claims to the contrary. He turned down a bishopric, probably Clogher, in 1745, with 'an income at least double that of Cloyne', citing '[q]uiet and content' as his reasons, but also 'an indisposition that ill consists with moving from place to place'. The following year Berkeley was meeting the rumour of preferment with equanimity: 'It is true, the Primacy or Archbishopric of Dublin, if offered, might

20. BL Add MS 20105, ff. 148–49, Wainwright to Clayton, 9 October 1735.

have tempted me by a greater opportunity of doing good', but he did not wish to be removed from Cloyne, or to set aside his Oxford scheme.[21] Though Cloyne was Berkeley's final preferment, he was not entirely without thoughts or indeed opportunities to think of what it would mean to hold one of the two most prestigious appointments in the Church of Ireland.[22] There may have been fine grains to the reasons for particular patrons supporting particular candidates for the range of posts for which Berkeley presented himself throughout his career, relating to the particular political or other interests of clients, patrons, and those gifting the positions. Still, the reasons cited in correspondence from, to, or about Berkeley consistently relate to his supposed political disaffection, demonstrated by closeness to Swift and his circle and the publication of *Passive Obedience*, and to the whimsicality of his personality, demonstrated by his absence on continental tours and utopian schemes in America. If he was not the type of English Whig churchman presented to Irish bishoprics by English politicians seeking to contain the Irish House of Lords, he had been no more in favour with William King, who sought out diligent Irish-born clergymen to maintain the interests of the Church of Ireland and convert the Catholic population.[23] These seem to have been the obstructions to a faster or higher progress in the church hierarchy for Berkeley.

The Analyst

The Analyst is in part a further episode in Berkeley's lifelong campaign against mathematical abstraction, particularly infinitesimals. In 'Of Infinites' (1707), he notes that although it is possible to imagine dividing any line, it is not possible to imagine a line that has been

---

21. Letter 322, Berkeley to Wilmot, 28 June 1745, p. 482; letter 339, Berkeley to Prior, 12 September 1746, p. 508. See also letter 349, Berkeley to Prior, 10 February 1747, p. 526. For the Oxford scheme, see chapter 5.

22. Financial security did not prevent Berkeley from pursuing his financial interest, again through Prior, when he heard that a Captain George Berkeley had died 'worth about eighteen thousand pounds' (letter 348, 9 February 1747, pp. 524–25. See also letter 347, 6 February 1747, p. 524; letter 349, 10 February 1747, p. 525; letter 354, 22 March 1747, p. 531). Berkeley and his brothers entered bills to test the legitimacy of the will on 19 October 1747 and 27 January 1748. See National Archives, C 11/1091/9 and C 11/1093/9.

23. McNally, 'William King, Patriotism, and the "National Question"', p. 59.

infinitely divided. In the queries appended to *The Analyst*, Berkeley directly points his readers to *De Motu* (1720), reiterating its rejection of absolute space.[24] These forms of abstraction, like the habit of 'considering Geometrical Diagrams absolutely or in themselves, rather than as Representatives of all assignable Magnitudes or Figures of the same kind', lead to error and confusion.[25] *The Analyst* also frames its attack on abstraction in the terms of Berkeley's more recent work on the relative claims of scientific and theological language and reasoning. As in *Alciphron*, Berkeley points to overconfidence in the signifying function of scientific (here mathematical) terms as a cause of freethinking: the erroneous belief that these terms signify in a more certain way than theological terms has led to the devaluation of revealed religion. Berkeley argues in *The Analyst* that infidel mathematicians do not have a good in mind as they set out the principles of their language, and so, for the reasons I explored in the previous chapter, they are using language to a false end.

Alciphron had set out Berkeley's thinking on the nature of mathematical symbolism. Algebra has the greatest extent of any language because of the aptitude of its symbolic system to represent particular ideas. Not all algebraic notation, however, represents a particular idea, nor even any particular idea indifferently from the relevant set. The notation must, like other types of language that do not refer to ideas, be regarded as an instrument:

> [E]ven the Mathematical Sciences themselves, which above all others are reckoned the most clear and certain, if they are considered, not as Instruments to direct our Practice, but as Speculations to employ our Curiosity, will be found to fall short in many Instances of those clear and distinct Ideas, which, it seems, the Minute Philosophers of this Age, whether knowingly or ignorantly, expect and insist upon in the Mysteries of Religion.[26]

That is, if we pretend to have precise ideas of mathematical abstractions such as negative numbers we are being empty and jejune, as we would be if we claimed to have a clear and distinct idea of

24. LJ, IV.235; *Analyst*, queries 8–9; see also chapter 8. The *Analyst* consists in a series of numbered paragraphs followed by a series of numbered queries.

25. *Analyst*, query 17.

26. *Alciphron*, VII.14–15, and citation from VII.17.

goodness. If we recognise, however, that such terms are part of extensive sign systems designed to be used in certain ways and to produce certain effects, guided by particular goods, then they are perfectly meaningful.

The Analyst is written as a letter to an infidel mathematician, with Berkeley stating in one of the subsequent works in the controversy it occasioned that he had been informed by Addison 'that the Infidelity of a certain noted Mathematician, still living, was one principal reason assigned by a witty man of those times for his being an Infidel'.[27] Since Stock's biography of 1776, the mathematician has been identified as Edmund Halley, and the wit as Samuel Garth.[28] In *The Analyst*, Berkeley turns the tables on those freethinkers who doubt the meaningfulness of religious language: 'I shall claim the privilege of a Free-Thinker; and take the Liberty to inquire into the Object, Principles, and Method of Demonstration admitted by the Mathematicians of the present Age, with the same freedom that you presume to treat the Principles and Mysteries of Religion'. Fluxions will not meet the criteria demanded of meaningful terms in Berkeley's view of language, let alone correspond to a clear and distinct idea. '[W]ith what appearance of Reason', Berkeley asks, 'shall any Man presume to say, that Mysteries may not be Objects of Faith, at the same time that he himself admits such obscure Mysteries to be the Object of Science?'[29]

The Newtonian theory of fluxions, Berkeley recognises, is very similar to the differential calculus of Leibniz.[30] Both are attempts to calculate the area enclosed by a curve, and to do so in a less laborious way than the ancient geometrical method of exhaustion. The problem as it was formulated in ancient mathematics was to find the rectilinear figure that had the same area as any given circle. The solution was to propose a regular polygon inscribed in the circle and double the number of its sides so that the difference between its area and the area of the inscribing circle is reduced. If this process is repeated, the area of the polygon approaches that of the

---

27. *Defence of Free-thinking in Mathematics*, §7.

28. See LJ, IV.56–57.

29. *Analyst*, §§2, 7.

30. My thanks to Abram Kaplan for helping me with the concepts in this section; any failures or limitations are of course my own.

circle. Without resorting to polygons with infinite numbers of sides, the exercise could be concluded with a double *reductio ad absurdum*. This form of demonstration shows that a particular instance of the polygon has neither a lesser nor a greater area than the circle, and that therefore it must have the same area. Newton and Leibniz were both attempting to resolve this problem more economically.

Leibniz's method required the use of infinitesimals. He worked on areas enclosed by subtangents, taking a point on a curve and forming a triangle from that point to the points at which a subtangent of the curve joined it. Reducing the proportions of this triangle, or reducing the increments of the curve considered, infinitely, one is left with a triangle which is also perfectly coincident with the point on the curve. This infinitely small triangle is then rejected in order to give the differential, or rate of change of the curve. Berkeley rejects this method on straightforward, logical, and commonsense grounds: '*Leibnitz* and his Followers in their *calculus differentialis* [make] no manner of scruple, first to suppose, and secondly to reject Quantities infinitely small'.[31] First the infinitely small triangle is there, then it is not.

Newton recognised that Leibniz's calculus required the use of infinitesimals and sought to present his own solution to the problem that avoided them. The method he presented became known as the method of first and last ratios. For Newton, the problem was one of motion rather than statics, about the generation (or degeneration) of curves. The distance along any given curve from A to B is greater than the straight line joining A and B. The ratio between the curved and straight lines changes the closer B is to A. This ratio diminishes until A and B coincide. If the same ratio is calculated for a point C more distant from A than B, and the ratio of the two ratios is compared, then it is possible to calculate the velocity of the as-yet-unproduced curve when B coincides with A. A fluxion is expressed as a ratio between a velocity in the very moment of its commencement and a velocity that has already generated a curve. By this method, Newton captures the evanescent increment of a curve, the value by which it differs from a right line, or its fluxion.

Berkeley gives a fair summary of Newton's aims:

---

31. *Analyst*, §18.

[W]hereas Quantities generated in equal times are greater or lesser, according to the greater or lesser Velocity, wherewith they increase and are generated, a Method hath been found to determine Quantities from the Velocities of their generating Motions. And such Velocities are called Fluxions: and the Quantities generated are called flowing Quantities. These Fluxions are said to be nearly as the Increments of the flowing Quantities, generated in the least equal Particles of time; and to be accurately in the first Proportion of the nascent, or in the last of the evanescent, Increments. Sometimes, instead of Velocities, the momentaneous Increments or Decrements of undetermined flowing Quantities are considered, under the Appellation of Moments. [. . .] Fluxions are Celerities, not proportional to the finite Increments though ever so small; but only to the Moments or nascent Increments, whereof the Proportion alone, and not the Magnitude, is considered.[32]

Berkeley's response to Newton is to reject the possibility of the increment sought: 'For ought I see, you can admit no Quantity as a Medium between a finite Quantity and nothing, without admitting Infinitesimals. An Increment generated in a finite Particle of Time, is it self a finite Particle; and cannot therefore be a Momentum'. Newton is therefore just as guilty of shifting the hypothesis as the continental mathematicians:

> [W]hen it is said, let the Increments vanish, *i.e.* let the Increments be nothing, or let there be no Increments, the former Supposition that the Increments were something, or that there were Increments, is destroyed, and yet a Consequence of that Supposition, *i.e.* an Expression got by virtue thereof, is retained. [. . .] Certainly when we suppose the Increments to vanish, we must suppose their Proportions, their Expressions, and every thing else derived from the Supposition of their Existence to vanish with them.[33]

Berkeley is arguing from common sense: in order for there to be an increment, something that can provide a value for a ratio, there

32. Ibid., §§3–4.
33. Ibid., §§11, 13.

must be a magnitude, and no magnitude can be discounted for its insignificance in respect to other values.[34]

Newton anticipates the criticism that an increment cannot vanish by presenting it as a limit concept, at the end of *Principia* I.i:

> [U]nderstand the ultimate velocity as that with which a body is moving, neither before it arrives at its ultimate place and the motion ceases, nor after it has arrived there, but at the very instant when it arrives, that is, the very velocity with which the body arrives at its ultimate place and with which the motion ceases. And similarly the ultimate ratio of vanishing quantities is to be understood not as the ratio of quantities before they vanish or after they have vanished, but the ratio with which they vanish.[35]

Yet the concept of limit that Newton is invoking does not figure mathematically in his demonstrations, and most commentators seem to agree that, in terms of late seventeenth- and early eighteenth-century mathematical language, Berkeley's critique is accurate and just. Developments in mathematics over the last two centuries, however, have vindicated the intuitions of Leibniz and Newton: 'Nobody today doubts that the calculus has been made rigorous; the theory of limits and Robinson's nonstandard analysis have vindicated the procedures of eighteenth century [*sic*] calculus, and these versions of the calculus can overcome Berkeley's logical objections'.[36]

Nonetheless, in the terms of eighteenth-century mathematics, Berkeley's criticisms are trenchant and serve a larger philosophical purpose. He presents two possibilities for meaningful talk about mathematical abstractions such as velocity: it can be discussed in terms of specific magnitudes of time and space or by means of a sign. For it is not

---

34. Jesseph, 'Faith and Fluxions', pp. 253, 255–56, has described Berkeley's opposition to both Newtonian and Leibnizian methods of performing the calculus on the grounds that they use a term that is taken as more than and equal to zero at different points in the calculation; he also notes that Berkeley's critique fails to account for the success of both methods despite their inconsistency.

35. Newton, *The Principia*, p. 442, I.i, Scholium.

36. Jesseph, *Berkeley's Philosophy of Mathematics*, p. 198. For an indication of the consensus on this point, see, for example, Sageng, 'Colin MacLaurin and the Foundations of the Method of Fluxions', p. 229; and Mazur, *Enlightening Symbols*, pp. 172–73.

an easy point, to form a clear and distinct Idea of any Velocity at all, exclusive of and prescinding from all length of time and space; as also from all Notes, Signs or Symbols whatsoever. This, if I may be allowed to judge of others by my self, is impossible. To me it seems evident, that Measures and Signs are absolutely necessary, in order to conceive or reason about Velocities; and that, consequently, when we think to conceive the Velocities, simply and in themselves, we are deluded by vain Abstractions.[37]

Without signifying ideas (of actual space and time), and without being considered as an element of a sign system directed towards a conceived good, there is no idea of velocity. Berkeley had been pursuing this argument for specific social reasons: the infidel mathematicians had attempted to challenge theological reasoning by importing their habits of reasoning, challenging the church and attempting to usurp its authority. But Berkeley tells the infidel mathematicians, '[Y]ou have no right, in Virtue of such Habits, to dictate out of your proper Sphere, beyond which your Judgment is to pass for no more than that of other Men'.[38] Berkeley's turning of the tables on the analysts is a defence of the authority of the church, and of a Christian philosophy as the master discourse.[39] Churchmen, not mathematicians, should be giving society its standards of truth.

The Analyst was a controversial text and produced many direct responses, two of which themselves drew responses from Berkeley. James Jurin's response to Berkeley makes no particular ground against the logical critique of Newton, but Jurin does invoke Berkeley's previous writings in the course of his argument. Berkeley has suggested that Newton's use of a variety of methods for calculating fluxions might be a sign of uncertainty. Jurin responds by asking if

37. *Analyst*, §37.

38. Ibid., §49.

39. For the suggestion that Berkeley's argument in the body of *The Analyst* is ad hominem and slightly inconsistent with the full stretch of his mathematical thought, including in the queries to *The Analyst*, see Moriarty, 'The Ad Hominem Argument of Berkeley's *Analyst*'. Moriarty's suggestion that the arguments of the body of the text are intended as a reconstruction of the position of the infidel mathematician do not quite account for the rhetorical strength of Berkeley's attack when he speaks of fluxions as 'the Ghosts of departed Quantities' (§35) and explicitly objects to the logic of the infidel mathematician's use of infinitesimals (§25).

[w]hen you, after all the demonstrations that had been given of the being of a God, by the learned Fathers of the Church, and by the wisest of the Philosophers of all ages, thought fit to introduce that new and singular one of a *Visual Language*, would it be fair in me to suppose that you were suspicious of all the former proofs of the existence of a Deity, and left that great and important truth to depend upon a metaphorical argument?[40]

He also recognises the anti-abstractionist tendency of Berkeley's text and argues, with some exaggeration, that an attitude such as Berkeley's would make botany, or indeed any act of classification of various kinds within a higher kind, impossible, whilst trying to save Locke from saying, as he clearly does, that abstract ideas must unite inconsistent elements of the particular items they place in a class.[41]

Other responses to *The Analyst* point out that fluxions are really not such counterintuitive ideas. John Walton says that Berkeley's criticism is tantamount to saying it is 'illegitimate to suppose that mathematical Quantities can be generated and destroyed by Motion'. Motions can of course be generated, and they can degenerate:

> While a generating Quantity moves back thro' the same Space it before described in moving forward, the Quantity generated, or its Augment, continually lessens; and by persevering in a State of decreasing, it must in some finite Time vanish and become nothing; and therefore mathematical Quantities, by a constant Diminution, may be reduc'd to nothing: And such as are thus generated or destroy'd in equal Times by Motion, or which arise and vanish together, will arise or vanish under certain Ratios, which are their first or last Ratios; or the Ratios with which they begin or cease to be.[42]

This seems so much common sense, and hardly the inconceivable velocity prescinded from all time and space of which Berkeley talks.

Berkeley had also said that the fluxions of fluxions were inconceivable, and that the term seemed to refer to nothing but 'the

40. *Analyst*, §17; Jurin, *Geometry no Friend to Infidelity*, pp. 60–61.
41. Jurin, *Geometry no Friend to Infidelity*, pp. 74–75, 82–83.
42. Walton, *A Vindication of Sir Isaac Newton's Principles of Fluxions*, pp. 26, 18.

Ghosts of departed Quantities'.[43] But Berkeley's enlisting on the side of common sense does not prevent his opponents from doing the same. A further response of 1735 presents fluxions of fluxions as arising from commonly accepted phenomena, already long studied:

> A stone, for instance, in its direct fall towards the earth has its velocity perpetually augmented; and in Galileo's Theory of falling Bodies, when the whole descent is performed near the surface of the earth, it is supposed to receive equal augmentations of velocity in equal times. In this case therefore the velocity augments uniformly, and the second fluxion of the line described by the falling body will in all parts of that line be the same; so that third fluxions cannot take place in this instance; since the variation of the velocity suffers no change, but is every where uniform.
>
> But if the stone be supposed to have its gravity at the beginning of its fall less than at the surface of the earth, the variation of its velocity at first will then be less than the variation at the end of its motion; or in other words, the second fluxions in the beginning and end of its fall would be unequal; consequently, third fluxions would here take place, since the variation would be swifter, as the body in its fall approached the earth.
>
> The stone in this last instance then not only moves with a velocity perpetually varying, as in the preceeding example, but this variation continually changes. In the true theory of falling bodies, neither this last variation nor any subsequent one can ever be uniform; so that fluxions of every order do here actually exist.

Having a physics (and a mathematical language adequate to it) that deals with changes in velocity is necessary if we want to deal with the empirically observed world, as 'an uniform unchangeable velocity is not to be met with in any of those bodies, that fall under our cognisance; for in order to continue such a motion as this, it is necessary, that they should not be disturbed by any force whatever, either of impulse or resistance; but we know of no spaces, in which at least one of these causes of variation does not operate'.[44]

43. *Analyst*, §§4, 39.
44. Robins, *A Discourse Concerning the Nature and Certainty of Sir Isaac Newton's Methods of Fluxions*, p. 31.

This criticism, that a fluxion is really no more inconceivable than a velocity, and in any case commonly observable, was echoed by others, who also noted that Berkeley's exclusion of abstractions and absurdities from mathematical language would require the exclusion of established features of that language, such as negative numbers.[45]

Why didn't Berkeley share the commonsense view that changes in velocity exist and could be the subject of quantification? One reason is that although his philosophy of mathematics allowed for the manipulation of purely conventional symbols in arithmetic (such as negative numbers), he regarded geometry as the science of perceptible form: form that must be perceived in order to exist as the object of geometric science. The first and last ratios, the vanishing increments, are not perceptible, in the sense that they cannot be made to appear in the diagrams of geometric demonstration, which themselves stand for all possible instances of the same type. Douglas Jesseph, from whom I take this distinction in Berkeley's mathematical philosophy, remarks that Berkeley took the proper object of geometry as the tangible object: 'Berkeley regards visible objects as *signs* of tangible objects. Thus, the visible diagrams used in a geometric proof would, on Berkeley's account, be regarded as signs of tangible objects'.[46] So, Berkeley asks, in the queries that follow the main text of *The Analyst*, '[w]hether the considering Geometrical Diagrams absolutely or in themselves, rather than as Representatives of all assignable Magnitudes or Figures of the same kind, be not a principal Cause of the supposing finite Extension infinitely divisible; and of all the Difficulties and Absurdities consequent thereupon?'[47] He is thinking of the lines in diagrams as representing all possible real lines, which must be made of certain numbers of tangible minima.

The argumentative method of *The Analyst* is, like that of *Alciphron* VII, a danger to Berkeley, in that it may end up admitting terms into meaningfulness that it had seemed the entire purpose of the texts to exclude. In the previous chapter, Kenneth Winkler's

---

45. [Bayes], *An Introduction to the Doctrine of Fluxions*, pp. 18–19, 34, 46–48.
46. Jesseph, *Berkeley's Philosophy of Mathematics*, pp. 159, 79.
47. *Analyst*, query 17.

point that parity of reasoning might be applied to the term 'material substance' was noted: it might be found that in specific human practices directed at conceived goods, this term produces rules of behaviour to which people can conform in the pursuit and achievement of the good.[48] Likewise, Berkeley says that behind the term 'fluxion of a fluxion', 'we shall discover much Emptiness, Darkness, and Confusion; nay, if I mistake not, direct Impossibilities and Contradictions'.[49] But Robins presents a simple way of conceiving a fluxion of a fluxion through its effects, and Newton's intuitions have been borne out by later work in differential methods. So should not fluxions be accorded just as much meaning as 'the trinity'? On the face of it, there is nothing more (if not indeed a great deal less) contradictory about the rate of change of a rate of change than there is about God being three people and one person. Either, then, fluxions are admissible by Berkeley's expanded standards of meaningfulness, or the trinity is rightly exposed to the withering critique of its conceivability. *The Analyst* might be taken, in this roundabout way, to legitimise the demystifying criticism of the trinity it sets out to challenge.[50]

The issue might be stated in another way, however. Berkeley is clear that languages may include meaningful terms that don't refer to ideas if they aim at producing a conceived good in human conduct. 'Fluxion' could be one such term, like 'force' or 'grace', but Berkeley holds that it is meaningless. It is not meaningless because it does not refer to an idea, but because it is not part of a language used to produce conceived goods. Somehow this particular term does not contribute to the kinds of good that geometry and mathematics make possible. If this is Berkeley's position, one might look back from the twenty-first century and think that he is being shortsighted about the value of calculus and its associated terms. But he has two reasons, both of which he feels are strong, for rejecting 'fluxions'. First, the notion contains something contradictory in itself: that an element has and does not have a value. This is

---

48. Winkler, 'Berkeley and the Doctrine of Signs', pp. 1535-54.

49. *Analyst*, §8.

50. Schwartz, 'Berkeley et la norme mathématique', p. 430, captures the problem with Berkeley's inconsistent approach, accepting some terms, such as squares of negative numbers, and rejecting others, such as fluxions.

a direct contradiction within the rules of the language it seeks to be adopted into, and so is unlike the assertion, in the language of Christian mysteries, that God is both one and three. Second, and here the polemical nature of the text comes to the fore, the language of mathematics has not always aimed at a conceived good; rather, it is practised by some who openly claim to be infidels, and whose interest in mathematics is not the improvement of human life by ever greater conformity to God's scheme, but rather the erosion of the intellectual, moral, and political authority of the church. Although there is no specific link between a belief in 'fluxions' and infidelity in the text, and it is hard to see what might constitute such a link, Berkeley is saying that those who criticise religious thinkers for inconsistency whilst being willing to entertain 'fluxions' are turning away from God and encouraging others to do so. As when he imagined that the expression of his new doctrine might curb atheism and scepticism, or that his discourses on passive obedience might temper, and be universally accepted as tempering, the fervour of those inclined to Jacobitism, Berkeley here is making assumptions about the ways in which public discourses, both those of the infidel mathematicians and his own, are taken and acted upon. It is not easy to anticipate the kinds of consequence of his and others' discourse that Berkeley thinks are likely. On this reading, he may not be contradictory, but he does demonstrate exaggerated expectations of the efficacy of these discourses.

Church, State, and the Discourse Addressed to Magistrates

This section considers Berkeley's life at Cloyne and his writings of the period as further attempts to address the interrelated social issues in which we have already seen him take an interest—infidelity, Catholicism, indigence, an uneducated gentry, luxury, public ill health, wrongly directed appetites, disorder, and disloyalty. Two attitudes, sometimes very closely intertwined, are adopted towards these issues: the therapeutic and the disciplinary. Sometimes interventions that constitute discipline may be required to produce a healthy set of dispositions in a people; criminals, for example, may have to be put to forced labour to produce individual and collective goods. Sometimes the discipline an established church exerts over those of other denominations is best served by dialogue and a partial extension of privileges (such as education). The therapeutic and disciplinary aspects of Berkeley's work at Cloyne were related. Whichever aspect was uppermost in his writings, Berkeley was addressing the same social concerns.

Berkeley consistently presented the view that the authority and privilege of the established church must be maintained in order to preserve and reestablish morality and public order. He may have had favourable memories of the convocation of the Church of Ireland that in 1703 accorded itself the power of scrutinising government legislation.[51] Whilst his Irish and American experiences complicated his commitment to territorial consolidation, Berkeley expressed the other two elements by which Peter Miller defines a commitment to a Ciceronian conception of the public good— uniform confession and community.[52] The Test Act and a Church interest in Parliament were both necessary to that end. In both the English and the Irish Parliaments, the mid-1730s saw the confrontation of the Church interest with different antagonists. I discuss the situation in the Irish Parliament at the start of chapter 15. In England, the story is one of the collapse of an alliance between Robert Walpole and Edmund Gibson, leader of the bishops in the Lords, an alliance that had limited challenges to the Tests. When the composition of Parliament shifted and Walpole faced more danger in the Commons than the Lords, he modified his strategy, allowing dissenters and radicals to introduce bills challenging the Church interest that the ministry had previously prevented, and yet himself supporting only minor reform rather than repeal of the Tests. This shift has been presented by T.F.J. Kendrick as a change in relations between Church and government:

> By opposing the repeal of the Test and Corporation Acts, Walpole had shrewdly avoided the disaster of turning the whole Church against the administration; yet his support of minor reform had enabled him to be free at last of the querulous Gibson without making enemies of the other bishops. The Church-Whig alliance had collapsed, and the last

51. Connolly, 'Reformers and Highflyers', pp. 154–55.
52. Miller, *Defining the Common Good*, p. 12.

vestige of ecclesiastical independence had been replaced by the complete subservience of the episcopate to partisan politics.[53]

Gibson had a different view of the collapse of the alliance of the Church Whigs and Walpole's government. Church Whigs sought harmony with dissenters, 'we defending them in ye full enjoyment of their Toleration against ye Tories, and they thankful to us, and content with the state of things, as settl'd between ye Church and them at ye Revolution'. He explained his political project in this light:

> My great point was, to bring ye body of ye Clergy and ye two Universities at least to ∧^be easy under a Whig Administration; and it is well known how great progress my self and other Bishops had made in it, and to what degree we succeeded, till ye Whigs began to make open Attempts in Parliament, against y^e ∧ ^Church and Clergy. [. . .] This has been my ∧^uni-form practice, as founded upon ye settl'd Principle of maintaining the Protestant Succession, the Church Establishment and ye Toleration; which, ∧^in my memory, were the distinguishing characters of a Whig for thirty years together. But if it grow into a receiv'd maxim ∧^(as ye notion gains ground apace) that the maintaining ye Protest.^t Succession and ye Toleration will not denominate ∧^one a good Whig, unless he will also sacrifice ye Church and Clergy to ∧^their open and professed Enemies, or at least be passive in ∧^their attempts against them; I and many others must renounce ye name.[54]

The pressure for repeal of the Tests and other such threats to the privileges of the established church had become too much for the clergy to consent to without betraying their institution, so the alliance between church and state was collapsing.

Throughout this process, Berkeley was receiving communications from his episcopal colleagues. Gibson wrote to Berkeley as an ally expressing his fear of the repeal of the Sacramental Test, but saying that he thought it unlikely the government would introduce a bill. He doubted 'the Court will wantonly divest itself at once of the whole Church interest'.[55] Potential repeal of the Tests was

53. Kendrick, 'Sir Robert Walpole, the Old Whigs, and the Bishops', pp. 421–24, 429, 444.

54. St Andrews University Library Special Collections, Gibson Papers, MS 5219, f. 2.

55. Letter 254, Gibson to Berkeley, 9 July 1735, p. 386.

not the only fear that Berkeley and his fellow bishops had from Parliament. Benson gave Berkeley a report on a case decided by the House of Lords that limited the right of the clergy to set values to the monetary equivalent of tithes (moduses).[56] Benson felt that the case was clear, but that it was represented as a threat to 'every man that had an estate'. Only two lords voted with the bishops, and they lost. Benson resented Lord Bathurst for speaking, 'though quite foreign to the purpose, about the clergy having raised their fines'.[57] A year later, Benson reported on a bill that Joseph Jekyll, master of the rolls, had brought that would make it harder for lands to be granted to universities and the Church; a clause in that bill that would repeal university statutes requiring fellows to be ordained; and another bill that would move cases of Quakers not paying their tithes from spiritual courts to justices of the peace. Yorke and Talbot, providers of the opinion on the compatibility of baptism and slavery, were the great opponents to this last bill in the House of Lords, and Bathurst was again agitating against the Church interest. Nearly a year later again, Benson reported that Talbot's death was lamented most strongly by 'the friends of the Established Church': 'he was ready on all occasions so powerfully to have espoused the interests of the Church, and so able to have defended them, that none more than the clergy express their sorrow on this occasion'. Benson also noted that Bathurst was claiming to be a friend to the Church and the universities, despite appearances to the contrary. Benson feared for the Church after Queen Caroline's death, once her influence in its support had become clear.[58]

It was not only Benson writing to Berkeley about fears of the hardening of the laity against the clergy. Thomas Secker, perhaps also with Bathurst in mind, noted, 'Many of those who would

56. Bric, 'The Tithe System in Eighteenth-Century Ireland', p. 272: 'Whether great or small, tithe was traditionally paid in kind. However, during the seventeenth and eighteenth centuries, in an increasing number of tithe transactions, an agreement known as the *modus decimandi* was made between tithe owner and parishioner. This substituted monetary payments for tithe in kind and "established modes of valuing tithe, in some places by the acre, in others by the quantity of produce"'.

57. Letter 251, Benson to Berkeley, 13 May 1735, p. 382.

58. Letter 260, Benson to Berkeley, 20 May 1736, pp. 392–93; letter 262, Benson to Berkeley, 1 March 1736/36, pp. 395–96; letter 268, Benson to Berkeley, 7 February 1738, pp. 406–9.

be thought their [the clergy's] best friends are indeed vehement against us'. Although he was somewhat more sanguine than Benson, Secker judged that, 'considering the increasing disregard to Religion and every thing that deserves the name of principle, together with the strange growth of that wild Spirit which calls it self zeal for Liberty there would be no reason to wonder at any shock how great or sudden soever which might happen either to the Ecclesiastical or the Civil part of our Constitution'.[59] Nicholas Forster, with reference to society in general rather than Parliament in particular, asked, 'When the laity form themselves into a party in opposition to the clergy, how can we expect any good success from our labours among them?'[60] Berkeley's correspondents in London and Ireland perceived him as an ally in the rather pessimistic campaign to maintain the financial privileges and moral authority of the established church.

Berkeley understood the task of maintaining the power of the Church in the face of an increasingly and aggressively secular Parliament and public in an idiosyncratic way: he focused on the power to which subjects were obliged by binding oaths. In *Advice to the Tories Who Have Taken the Oaths*, breaking oaths is said to be extremely detrimental to the Church and the commonwealth, as an oath is a paradigmatic social bond. Berkeley also suggests that his view of language allows terms to be meaningful if they provide rules to which people conform their behaviour—and these rules should probably be thought of not as contingently emerging norms, but as laws that, ultimately, God intends people to follow. Berkeley's part in the campaign on which Benson commented in his letters—arguing against public immorality that partly took the form of, and was partly encouraged by, the swearing of illegitimate and improper oaths—was a continuation of his work against the freethinkers.

Swearing had long troubled Berkeley. He reproduced a passage in *The Ladies Library* saying that 'there is no Noise this side Hell

---

59. Letter 265, Secker to Berkeley, 29 June 1737, p. 404. Secker also thanked Berkeley for his enquiry after Catherine Talbot, the daughter of the recently deceased Charles Talbot. Together with her mother, Catherine lived with Secker, and George Berkeley Jr would form a romantic attachment with her. For more on the political context of this letter and the friendship of Secker and Berkeley, see Jones, 'George Berkeley and Thomas Secker'.

60. Letter 269, 20 February 1737/38, p. 409.

which can be more amazingly odious' than a woman swearing, that being 'so hateful and unnatural a Habit'. He singles out women of quality for appearing to want 'to vindicate their Sex from the Imputation of Timouresness, by daring God Almighty. What shall we say of those Great Ones, who neither the Majesty of Heaven, nor the Presence of their Prince, can keep within the Bounds of Religion and Decency?'[61] The case that troubled him after his appointment to Cloyne was a series of affronts to public morality from a Dublin society called the Blasters, specifically as they challenged the civil authority of the clergy. This society sought to shock Christians by the public use of newly minted oaths. One of its associates was entirely naked when he received the clergyman Samuel Madden (a friend of Berkeley and the initiator of premiums, as noted later) into his home. Blasters harassed Laetitia Pilkington, an acquaintance of Berkeley, in her home, her separation from her husband making her vulnerable. One Blaster, a nephew of Compton Domville, one of Berkeley's travelling companions in Italy, was convicted of the murder of a porter; Domville intervened for his pardon, but then disowned him.[62]

In February 1738, Berkeley spoke to the House of Lords on the subject, and its committee for religion compiled a report that was released in March. This report notes a likely connection between such impiety and declining standards of education and respect for social hierarchy. Probable causes include

> a want of reverence to the laws and magistrates, and of a due subordination in the several ranks and degrees in the community, and an abuse of liberty under our mild and happy constitution; a great neglect in education, and a want of care in parents and masters of families in training up their children in reverence and awe, and keeping their servants in discipline and good order and instructing them in moral and religious duties; a great increase of idleness, luxury and excessive gaming, and an excess in the use of spirituous and intoxicating liquors.[63]

61. *Ladies Library*, I.189, cited from Allestree, *The Ladies Calling*.

62. Ryan, 'The Dublin Hellfire Club', pp. 336, 340, 344, 347–49; see also Elias, ed., *The Memoirs of Laetitia Pilkington*, I.92.

63. LJ, VI.195–98, 198.

Three weeks later, a translation of the thirty-ninth book of Livy's history was published under the title *The Irish Blasters, Or, the Votaries of Bacchus*, with a preface that some have speculated was written by Berkeley.[64] The preface encourages a Christian magistrate to stand up and prosecute the Blasters, as Posthumius did the Bachanalians, 'that Heaven may be saved the Expence of Thunder, which otherwise may come in such a Hurry of Vengeance, as to destroy the Righteous with the Wicked'.[65] The Christian magistrate is pitted against the blasphemer in an attempt to prevent God's collective punishment of the innocent as well as the guilty.

The social consequences of impious oaths are set out fully and in strong terms in Berkeley's *A Discourse Addressed to Magistrates and Men in Authority*, published in Dublin in March 1738. There could not be 'a higher, or more flagrant Symptom of the Madness of our Times, than that execrable Fraternity of Blasphemers, lately set up within this City of *Dublin*'. They engage in 'a calm premeditated Insult upon Religion, Law, and the very Light of Nature' that endangers the social order itself: 'Deliberate, atheistical Blasphemy, is of all Crimes most dangerous to the Public, inasmuch as it opens the Door to all other Crimes, and virtually contains them all. A religious Awe and Fear of GOD being [. . .] the Centre that unites, and the Cement that connects all humane Society'.[66] Berkeley argues in this text that social order cannot be produced if people do not restrain their passions, and that restraint is achieved by opinions and notions: 'Order is necessary, not only to the Well-Being, but to the very Being of a State'.[67] The most effective means of influencing behaviour is reward and punishment, and as religion has the most extreme rewards and punishments to offer, it is the most effective persuasion to civil obedience.[68] 'Therefore it mainly concerns Gov-

64. *The Irish Blasters*; Ryan, 'The Dublin Hellfire Club', p. 345; McGowan, 'Did Berkeley Write *The Irish Blasters?*', p. 1.

65. *The Irish Blasters*, preface, p. 3.

66. *Discourse*, p. 38 (LJ, VI.218–19). Berkeley here may echo Pufendorf, *The Whole Duty of Man*, and *Two Discourses and a Commentary*, p. 67, where religion is called the 'utmost and firmest Bond of Human Society'.

67. *Discourse*, p. 7 (LJ, VI.203). See chapter 4, referring to *Passive Obedience*, §51, on the preferability of any form of social order to none.

68. See Breuninger, *Recovering Bishop Berkeley*, p. 143: 'At the heart of Berkeley's analysis was a belief that the order needed for a state to thrive was best supported by

ernors to keep an attentive Eye on the Religion of their Subjects'.[69]
The bulk of people will never understand the scientific basis of the
notions and opinions to which they assent (which are rightly called
prejudices) and are inculcated by education: a 'proper Education'
is the best way for 'civil and religious Institutions' to 'fashion and
model [man] for Society'. Prejudices are not necessarily, contrary
to what freethinkers might say, erroneous. A religious and political elite is therefore required to instil correct prejudices, to inculcate and discipline the majority, and to regulate the preponderate
physical power of the people with discipline exercised over their
opinions.

> Religious Awe, the Precepts of Parents and Masters, the Wisdom of
> Legislators, and the accumulated Experience of Ages, supply the Place
> of Proofs and Reasonings with the Vulgar of all Ranks: I would say, that
> Discipline, national Constitution, and Laws Humane or Divine, are so
> many plain Land Marks, which guide them into the Paths wherein it is
> presumed they ought to tread.

Christianity is civically the best religion because it commands obedience to the established authorities.[70]

It is in the civil magistrate's interest to encourage reverence for
religion and its teachers because 'Obedience to all civil Power is
rooted in the religious Fear of God: It is propagated, preserved,
and nourished by Religion'; only religious reverence for God 'can
beget and preserve a true Respect for subordinate Majesty in all
the Degrees of Power, the first Link of Authority being fixed at the
Throne of God'. Colbert's *Testament politique* is cited as one of a
number of authorities in favour of Berkeley's argument: 'if once
the Ecclesiastical Character, as such, is vilified, the civil Magistrate, even the Crown itself, will, in Consequence thereof lose all

---

sound morals steeped in religion. By decoupling morality and religion through their attacks
on traditional institutions, freethinkers eroded the security of the state'. For a comparable
reading, see Gylling, 'Berkeley as a Worldly Philosopher', pp. 33–35.

69. *Discourse*, p. 15 (LJ, VI.207). In his discussion of this text, Brown, *The Irish
Enlightenment*, pp. 94–97, notes the importance of religion and prejudice in creating the
social bond but does not discuss Berkeley's suggestion that the state should take an interest
in the religion of its subjects.

70. *Discourse*, pp. 5–15 (LJ, VI.202–8), 5 and 12 (LJ, VI.202, 206); see also Charles,
'Berkeley polémiste, p. 420.

GEORGE BERKELEY D.D.
Fellow 1707, Bishop of Cloyne 1733

FIGURE 13.1. James Latham, *George Berkeley*, 1743, photograph courtesy of the Board of the University of Dublin, Trinity College, Ireland

Authority'. Berkeley is writing to persuade the civil magistrate that his power is derived from the same source as that of the priest and that they therefore share an interest in the preservation of religion. Magistrates should 'discourage that prevailing Prejudice against the Dispensers of God's Word, the Teachers of those Salutary Doctrines, without which the Public cannot thrive or subsist'.[71]

71. *Discourse*, pp. 17–18, 29, 40 (LJ, VI.208–9, 214, 220).

The *Discourse* suggests that certain magistrates might have lost sight of this mutual interest:

> The Magistrate, perhaps, may not be sufficiently aware that those pretended Advocates for private Light, and free Thought, are in reality seditious Men, who set up themselves against national Laws and Constitutions. [. . .] [T]he Freedom pleaded for is not so much Freedom of Thought against the Doctrines of the Gospel, as Freedom of Speech and Action against the Laws of the Land. It is strange, that those who are not blind in other Matters, should yet not see this; or, that seeing it, they should not discern the Consequences thereof. [. . .] [O]ur Government hath been constituted and modelled by Christians; and is still administred and maintained by Men professing Belief in CHRIST.[72]

They profess belief, but is it not strange that some of them don't see the connection between demands for liberty (of conscience, in politics) and denigration of Christianity? Berkeley is implying that certain magistrates, under the guise of liberty of conscience, were conspiring with the freethinkers. Euphranor in *Alciphron* complains of the political effects of such radical freedom of conscience: 'the worst Tyranny this Nation ever felt', he claims, was 'from the overflowing Zeal of an independent Whig', meaning Oliver Cromwell.[73] Thomas Gordon characterised an independent Whig as one who 'scorns all implicite Faith in the State, as well as the Church', and is a Protestant because 'the Principles of that Faith are warranted by the Bible, and consistent with our Civil Liberties'. He thinks a survey of history will reveal that 'abject Slavery in the People is [. . .] and always has been, the certain consequence of Power in the Priests'. The independent Whig is for 'unlimited Toleration of all Dissenters whatsoever'. He believes that 'there are Bounds set to the Power of our Princes by the same Laws which made them Princes'.[74] These attitudes, Berkeley argues, undermine both religion and the state. Perhaps he had in mind seeming friends of the Church who took every opportunity to speak against it in Parliament, as he was told Bathurst did?

---

72. Ibid., pp. 35–36, 39–40 (LJ, VI.217–18, 220).
73. *Alciphron*, V.30.
74. Gordon, *The Character of an Independent Whig*, pp. 3, 4, 6, 12.

It was suggested earlier that Berkeley saw his disappointment with Bermuda as the result of the state failing sufficiently to collaborate with missionary Anglicanism. That disappointment—an instance in which the state had shown that it could not be trusted to maintain its part in preserving the social order in its alliance with the church—became a motivation for his continuing campaign against freethinking. Bermuda was perhaps one reason for the continued stridency in Berkeley's attitude towards religious and civic obligation. Travis Glasson makes a connection between Berkeley blaming the impiety and greed of planters for the persistence of 'heathenism' amongst indigenous Americans and enslaved people and his critique of religiously unconcerned magistrates in the *Discourse*.[75] Berkeley was warning the legislature and the judiciary that they were complicit in the evident collapse of the social order because they were not taking sufficient care to enforce ideological compliance with the notions of Protestant Christianity and reverence for its clergy.

The deterioration in personal alliances that this view marks is evident in Berkeley's correspondence over the publication of the *Discourse*. There was confusion over the London printer for the work for its republication in June, with Percival planning to give it to Samuel Richardson (soon to be the author of *Pamela* and friend to Anne Donnellan and Catherine Talbot), only to find that Roberts had already printed it. Martin Benson was particularly unhappy about this,

> because the objections which I sent you word I heard might be made, I heard soon after actually made by the Master of the Rolls whom I saw at my Lord Chancellor's and by others. They acknowledge that there are several very good things in the tract, but they are so angry that the liberty of the press or of private judgment should be invaded that they are upon the whole more inclined to condemn than commend it, as the Reformation and Protestant religion they say are only to be defended upon the principles which are by you exploded. I need not say to you how much farther they stretch your words than your meaning. But whatever is said by a clergyman is immediately suspected, and a wrong interpretation will be very likely to be put upon it.[76]

75. Glasson, '"Baptism Doth Not Bestow Freedom"', pp. 306–7.
76. Letter 270, Benson to Berkeley, 28 April 1738, p. 410.

Joseph Jekyll, the master of the rolls, was active in the SPG, but was regarded as anticlerical and 'in 1736 called the Test Act "a prostitution of the Sacrament [. . .] that deprives [his majesty] of the service of some of his faithfullest subjects"'. Percival called him 'a great patron of the freethinkers'.[77] He introduced the bill making it harder to donate land to which Benson had objected. If it is unsurprising that an opponent of occasional conformity and the Sacramental Test objected to Berkeley's *Discourse*, his work for the SPG and his presence at the apartments of Philip Yorke, the lord chancellor, must be remembered. Yorke had supported Berkeley's Bermuda petition and supplied the Yorke-Talbot opinion on the compatibility of baptism and slavery. But here his circle was critical of an argument for clerical intrusion into the liberty of conscience as, supposedly, the only way to maintain a threatened social order. Berkeley's rebuke to civil magistrates for their unconcern in the face of apocalyptic social decline was not appreciated by these particular magistrates, who claimed that Berkeley's position was a threat to the liberty from overbearing ecclesiastical authority that the Protestant movement itself represented.

Others at the time were more appreciative of Berkeley's commitment to a Christian magistracy regulating public morality and saw that the purpose of the *Discourse Addressed to Magistrates* was to advocate for its role. A gentleman in the army wrote to Berkeley (whether the letter was sent or received is not known) to corroborate the view that much practice was sustained by prejudices rather than fundamental scientific knowledge, such as the work of a military engineer. He was in no doubt of the need for education and discipline to instil virtue in a state:

> Nor is a good Polity to be established or preserved only by Advice, and the Reason of the Thing; it can prevail upon no other Principles but that of a rigorous Execution of Obedience, and early, strict, and constant Discipline, and, if possible, that they should see or know nothing else, 'till this National Education become easy and natural; that all Virtue was suposed to consist therein, and all the Glory, Strength, and Happiness of the Commonwealth, as it was in *Sparta*.[78]

77. Keirn, 'Jekyll, Sir Joseph'.
78. 'A Letter to the Right Reverend the Lord Bishop of Cloyne', pp. 170, 173.

Patrick Riley has said of Fénelon's *Telemachus*, a text that strongly influenced educational thought in the first half of the eighteenth century in Britain and Ireland, that it promotes a 'demilitarized "Spartanism"' as an antidote to the luxury and belligerence of Louis XIV's reign.[79] As will be seen in the next section, Berkeley's programme for instilling the appropriate prejudices and maintaining the privileges of the established church was, at crucial points, not just Spartan but also militarised.

Cloyne and Diocesan Discipline

The practical administration of his diocese was one proper domain for Berkeley's discipline. After almost a decade in post, he was corresponding with Benson on the possibility of appointing rural deans, a post that Benson noted was a regular part of English church government that he had been able to resurrect. 'But in Ireland, perhaps, it may be a thing quite new, and your beginning it may give offence both to the rest of the Bishops and to the Archdeacons, and also to the inferior clergy'.[80] There was a polite exchange of letters with Richard Lloyd, vicar of Rathcormuck—who let the Methodist John Wesley preach at his church, and who had himself in 1749 attended meetings of the society Wesley had initiated—in which Berkeley asserted his confidence that Lloyd would do nothing 'that may offend your brethren of the clergy, or give occasion to mobs and riots'.[81] Berkeley's reply to Lloyd might seem restrained given Lloyd's insistence that he had nothing to feel guilty about. Lloyd noted that Wesley's innovations in preaching had brought converts to the Church at a time when religion was 'at a very low ebb in the world; and we can scarce see the outward form of it remaining'. His illustration was striking:

79. Fénelon, *Telemachus*, introduction, p. xvii.

80. Letter 301, Benson to Berkeley, 23 April 1743, p. 454.

81. Letter 368, Lloyd to Berkeley, 4 July 1750, p. 558, and letter 369, Berkeley to Lloyd, 4 July 1750, p. 559. Hurley, 'Berkeley and Methodism', p. 2, cites Wesley's journal for August 1749 for this letter from Lloyd. Hurley does not have the text of the letter from Lloyd to Berkeley. Abelove, 'George Berkeley's Attitude to John Wesley', pp. 175–76, notes the existence of the letter and summarises it.

To convince your lordship of this you need only take a survey of the parish of Cloyne, and consider how many real Christians (exclusive of your own family) you have there—I mean, of those who know and have a true Christian faith, and practice agreeable to it. Perhaps not one. But as many as you can suppose in that parish may equally be presumed in others of a like extent and number of people.

Lloyd also noted his surprise that his local clerical brethren ridiculed 'all operations of the Holy Ghost in the souls of men'. He was 'surprised to see some zealots of the doctrine of the Trinity so much oppose it'.[82] Perhaps Berkeley could forgive the suggestion that his own parish contained barely a true Christian beyond his own family in one who held the belief that the Holy Ghost operates in the souls of men and who shared Berkeley's concern with the social consequences of declining public religion?

The only expressions of an attitude to Methodism I know of in the Berkeley family come in Anne's letters after Berkeley's death. Writing to William Samuel Johnson, she seemed ambivalent about Methodism in general, but sympathetic to its critique of antinomianism.[83] Anne chastises George Jr for lack of gratitude for what his father provided, which included 'the friendship of good Men at Oxford whom you had learned to love & like—yr not being carried away with their only fault high Church Narrowness—Yr Acquaintance with Methodists & Aprobation of their zeal & Piety & not being enveloped in their Errors'. She specifies one such error in another letter: 'The Methodists dwell upon what Christ has done for <u>you chiefly</u>—& may perhaps lead others for that reason to depend <u>too much on it</u>—exclusive of what he is to do <u>in us</u>'.[84]

---

82. Baker, ed., *The Works of John Wesley*, vol. 26, Richard Lloyd to John Wesley, 30 July 1750, pp. 435–37, enclosing three letters, one of which is the letter of Lloyd to Berkeley cited here. Hight, *The Correspondence of George Berkeley*, p. 558, prints only excerpts from Lloyd's letter to Berkeley.

83. Yale University, Beinecke Rare Book and Manuscript Library, GEN MSS 1571, box 1, file 10, undated letter, ff. 1–2. The works under discussion are likely John Fletcher's series of *Check[s] to Antinomianism*. John Wesley preached a sermon celebrating Fletcher, a Genevan working in London, on his death in 1785.

84. BL Add MS 393912, f. 228r, undated; BL Add MS 39311, f. 200v, 6 July 1767. See Gregory, 'The Long Eighteenth Century', pp. 34–39, for Wesley representing a balance between enthusiasm and reason in the context of the relationship of the established church, dissent, and enlightenment.

It has been noted that 'an intensely personal sense that salvation is "for me" (*Christus pro me*)' was one structuring feature of early Wesleyan conversion narratives.[85] Anne presented the Methodist model of conversion as too personalised. When she talked of the efficacy of religious belief, she more often had recourse to the idea of union with or participation of Christ and God, a language she shared at least in part with her husband.

Wesley wrote to his own mother in 1725, around forty years before the letters from Anne to George Berkeley Jr, offering a detailed account of Berkeley's arguments in *Three Dialogues*, which had been reissued under a new title page that year. The letter from Wesley's mother to which he was replying was itself a reply to three from John, or 'Jacky' as she addressed him. The first of these, from 4 August (now lost), requires no answer, she says, except one passage: 'You say Berkeley has convinced you "that there is no such thing as matter in the world, if by the real existence of matter is meant a subsistence exterior to the mind, and distinct from its being perceived". What does he mean by imperceptible matter?' Wesley begins his letter by begging leave 'to assure you that before I received yours I was fully convinced' of two things, the first being that 'Mr. Berkeley's notion, which at first sight appeared very plausible, as indeed an ingenious disputant will make almost anything appear, was utterly groundless, and that he either advanced a palpable falsehood, or said nothing at all'. He objects most strongly to arguments in the dialogues whose form, he suggests, is that anything conceived is necessarily in a mind and that therefore the existence of things outside minds is inconceivable.[86] Berkeley does not

---

85. Hindmarsh, '"My Chains Fell Off, My Heart Was Free", p. 911. Hindmarsh cites Wesley's account of his experience of 24 May 1738, published in his journal in 1740, in which he felt that Christ 'had taken away my sins, even mine, and saved me from the law of sin and death' (p. 915).

86. Susanna (Annesley) Wesley to John Wesley, 10 November 1725; John to Susanna Wesley, 22 November 1725, in Baker, ed., *The Works of John Wesley*, vol. 25, pp. 186–87. The relevant part of Wesley's letter runs as follows:

> Mr. Berkeley's reasons, on a second reading, I found to be mere fallacy, though very artfully disguised. From one or two you may easily judge of what kind his other arguments are. He introduces Hylas charging Philonous with scepticism for denying the existence of sensible things, to which Philonous replies that if denying the existence of sensible things constitute a sceptic he will prove those to be <sceptics> who assert sensible things to be material: for if all sensible

comment on the central features of Methodism, but Wesley appears to have been briefly an immaterialist, before this change of heart.

Berkeley's correspondence, then, provides some evidence of his work as a church administrator. Further hints of Berkeley's administrative work can be seen in the surviving diocesan records.

---

things are material, then if it be proved that nothing material exists, it will follow that no sensible thing exists; and that nothing material can exist he undertakes to demonstrate.

Matter, says he (by which you must mean something sensible, or else how came you to know of it?) you define a solid, extended substance, the existence of which is exterior to the mind, and does in no ways depend on its being perceived. But if it appear that no sensible thing is exterior to the mind, your supposition of a sensible substance independent on it is a plain inconsistency.

Sensible things are those which are perceived by the senses; everything perceived by the senses is immediately perceived (for the senses make no inferences; that is the province of reason); everything immediately perceived is a sensation; no sensation can exist but in a mind: *ergo*, no sensible thing can exist but in a mind. Which was to be proved.

Another of his arguments to the same purpose is this: nothing can exist in fact the very notion of which implies a contradiction; nothing is impossible to conceive, unless the notion of it imply a contradiction; but 'tis absolutely impossible to conceive anything existing otherwise than in some mind, because whatever any one conceives is at that instant in his mind. Wherefore, as matter is supposed to be a substance exterior to all minds, and as 'tis evident nothing can be even conceived exterior to all minds, 'tis equally evident there can be no such thing in being as matter.

Or thus: everything conceived is a conception; every conception is a thought; and every thought is in some mind. Wherefore to say you can conceive a thing which exists in no mind is to say you can conceive what is not conceived at all.

The flaws in his arguments, which do not appear at a distance <may be> easily seen on a nearer inspection. He says, artfully enough in the Preface, <that in> order to give his proofs their full force it will be necessary to place them in as many different lights as possible. By this means the object grows too big for the eye, whereas had he contracted it into a narrower compass the mind might readily have taken it in at one view, and discerned where the failing lay.

How miserably does he play with the words *idea* and *sensation*! Everything immediately perceived is a sensation. Why? Because a sensation is what is immediately perceived by the senses. That is, in plain English, everything immediately perceived is immediately perceived. A most admirable discovery. The glory of which I dare say no one will envy him.

And again: all sensible qualities are ideas, and no idea exists but in some mind. That is, all sensible qualities are objects of the mind in thinking, and no image of an external object painted on a mind exists otherwise than in some mind. And what then?

Extracts from the chapter books ratify 'the Grant made by George Lord Bishop of Cloyne of the Office of Vicar General and so forth of the Diocese of Cloyne, unto the Rev'd ^Dr Robert Berkeley', making Berkeley's brother, who was the same day sworn in as treasurer and a member of the chapter, his administrative representative.[87] He replaced Walter Atkin, who had died in November.[88] Earlier, in 1736, it is also reported that Isaac Goldsmith replaced James Ward as dean of Cloyne.[89] The same records discuss procedures for having another preach one's turn. On 19 June 1740, it was 'Resolved and Agreed that for the Future, each Dignitary and Prebendary of the Cathedral who shall not attend and preach his respective Turn, shall pay to M.r Richard Bullen 15s. for every Sermon to be preached by him in such Dignitary's or Prebendary's absence'. A year later, it was 'Resolved and agreed that every Dignitary and Prebendary be, and is hereby at liberty to have their respective turns of Preaching in the Cathedral, supplied by any beneficed Clergyman approved of by the Bishop'. In 1746, it was

> Resolved, that for the future, the licensed Preacher of the Cathedral shall not receive any further or greater Stipend or Salary than half a Guinea for any turn he shall preach in the absence of any Member of the said Cathedral; And that hereafter, no Curate, or any beneficed or other Clergyman shall be admitted to Preach the Turn of any such absent Member, but that the said M.r Bullen be the Person who shall preach the same.[90]

The bishop and chapter were attempting to balance the necessity of substitutes preaching from time to time with the imperative for residency and discharge of clerical duties also seen in the attitudes of Berkeley's episcopal colleagues.[91]

87. Representative Church Body of the Church of Ireland Library, MS C.12.2.1, vol. 99, no. 106, 17 June 1742.

88. *Daily Post*, issue 6945, Wednesday, 9 December 1741. For a summary of Robert Berkeley's roles, see Brady, *Clerical and Parochial Records of Cork, Cloyne, and Ross*, II(1863).390–91.

89. *London Gazette*, 7522, 6–10 July 1736. See Berman, *George Berkeley*, p. 205, for the relationship to Oliver Goldsmith and a biographical sketch of Berkeley.

90. RCBCIL, C12.2.1, 97, no. 105, 19 June 1740; 98, no. 105 [repeats 104 and 105], 18 June 1741; 104, no. 119, 19 June 1746.

91. See, for example, Jenkins, ed., *The Correspondence of Bishop Secker*, introduction, p. xvii.

Church finances were also a matter of concern. In May 1735, it was 'Ordered that the several Tenants in arear to the Dean & Chapter be forthwith sued at Law for the Recovery of such arrears, and that the Chapter Clerk do write to each such Tenant to give him notice thereof'. In 1739, it was 'Ordered that M.r Francis Gore present Oeconomus do pay as soon as he can unto the Rt. Rev. George Lord Bishop of Cloyne the Sum of 20l. borrowed from his Lordship for the use of the Cathedral'.[92] The financial exactitude and invocation of legal obligation seen at other points in Berkeley's life are also present here.

Berkeley's diocesan discipline at Cloyne is seen most actively, however, in his relationship to the Catholic population of his diocese. His 'Primary Visitation Charge' (1737?), which deals almost exclusively with this topic, encourages his clergy to be particularly vigilant,

> as we live among men of a different communion, abounding in numbers, obstinate in their prejudices, backward to acknowledge any merits and ready to remark any defects in those who differ from them. And this circumstance should make us not only more cautious how we behave among such neighbours but likewise more diligent and active in their conversion.

Catholicism works on people by 'addressing to the passions of men, we in applying to their reason'.[93] This text shows how willing Berkeley was, when discussing Catholicism, to weed out erroneous prejudices, using just the language the freethinkers of *Alciphron* do when describing religion more generally: 'prejudices early imbibed and sunk deep in the mind are not immediately got ridd of; but it is as true that in every Humane Creature there is a ray of common sense, an original light of reason and nature which the worst and most bigoted education, although it may impair, can never quite extinguish'. Berkeley sees no reason why Catholics should not attend Protestant worship: 'There is nothing in our worship which you cannot assent to, therefore you may conform to us. But there are many things in yours that we can by no means allow; therefore

92. RCBCIL, C12.2.1, 91, no. 90, 29 May 1735; 94, no. 99, 14 June 1739.
93. LJ, VII.161–62.

you must not expect that we can join in your assemblies'. But he seems to set greater store by a discourse tempered by role reversal and by the strategic introduction of apposite topics in common conversation:

> Adopt as much as you conscientiously can of their waies of thinking: suit your selves to their capacities & their characters; put your selves in their places, and then consider how you should like to be dealt with, and what would offend you. If your intention is rather to gain a proselyte than to triumph over him, you must manage his passions, and skilfully touch his prejudices.
>
> Occasional discourse, I say, that imperceptibly glides from one subject to another, may be so conducted by a prudent person to those topics he hath a mind to treat of, as if they naturally rose from what went before, or came by accident in the way.[94]

The limitations of Berkeley's capacity for role reversal—to think himself into the position of other people, to imagine how his words and actions would strike other people—have been noted earlier, as have the limits on whom he would admit into the circle of consensus, to use Daniel Carey's phrase—those people whom he considered within the bounds of reason.[95] Although Berkeley here suggests that the work of conversion ought to be the product of conscience, he closes his charge by noting that 'there is an express canon directing all ministers to confer with the popish Recusants within their parishes, in order to reclaim them from their errours'.[96] And canons, like any law, ought to be obeyed.

The use of strategy in bringing others to one's own way of seeing was a lifelong concern of Berkeley's. He had the opportunity to practise something like the approach he recommended to his clergy when his friend and partner in the Bermuda project, John James, wrote to him admitting that he was considering converting to Catholicism. There are hints of a magnanimous ecumenism in Berkeley's long reply: 'Christ's religion is spiritual and supernatural, and there is an unseen cement of the faithful, who draw

94. LJ, VII.163–65.
95. Carey, *Locke, Shaftesbury, and Hutcheson*, p. 124.
96. LJ, VII.167.

grace from the same source, are enlightened by the same father of lights and sanctified by the same Spirit. And this, although they may be members of different political or visible congregations, may be estranged or suspected or even excommunicate to each other'. Whilst Berkeley thinks it 'a peculiar blessing to have been educated in the Church of England', he hopes 'not that I shall live and die in this church, but in the true church'. But the letter's argument hinges on authority and the grounds for recognising it. Berkeley notes that the early church did not assert the infallibility of the pope, and that popes had recognised the errors of their predecessors. It was the doctrine of the Protestant church 'that no particular church or congregation of Believers is infallible'. '[O]f what use is an infallible guide without an infallible sign to know him by?' Such claims to authority for the pope and clergy had the inverse effect of rendering the congregation insecure: if the efficacy of the Sacraments was dependent upon the priest's intention, no individual Catholic could know if she was truly within the church.[97] Though Berkeley confessed his attraction to some aspects of Catholic life, such as religious retreat, he scorned the traditions of miracles and canonisations.[98]

The language of vision, clear sight, and evidence permeates the letter and suggests a parallel to the defence of Protestantism and the advocacy of freethinking. Berkeley says that 'Men travelling in day-light see by one common light, though each with his own eyes. If one man should say to the rest, "Shut your eyes and follow me who see better than you all." This would not be well taken'. Anthony Collins had used the parallel between seeing for oneself and thinking for oneself to suggest that it was absurd to repress freethinking.[99] Both Berkeley and Collins are probably thinking of Locke, who defends his departure from accepted views such as the existence of innate principles by saying that the authority he follows is truth, and that 'we may as rationally hope to see with

97. Letter 282, 7 June 1741, pp. 422–33, 427, 433, 426, 427.
98. Letter 282, p. 430; see also chapter 5. Letter 282, pp. 428–29, particularly refers to the canonisation of Pietro d'Alcantara and Magdalena de Pazzi, which was mentioned in his Italian journals of a quarter-century earlier; see chapter 8.
99. Letter 282, p. 425; Collins, *A Discourse of Free-thinking*, pp. 15–18.

other Mens Eyes, as to know by other Mens Understandings'.[100] The same Berkeley who has defended the necessity of certain prejudices being inculcated by education says that '[i]t is our duty to strive to divest our selves of all bias whatsoever', again coming into some alignment with the antagonists of prejudice in *Alciphron*, the freethinkers, and those nonfictional freethinkers like Toland, who argues for the rationality of faith. Toland asserts, 'The Author of the Epistle to the *Hebrews* do's not define *Faith* a Prejudice, Opinion or Conjecture, but Conviction or Demonstration'.[101] When confronting Catholicism, Berkeley uses language not unlike that of the defenders of liberty of conscience and free thought. This is the defence of Protestantism that the private critics of the *Discourse Addressed to Magistrates* thought Berkeley had exploded by insisting on the public inculcation of religious prejudices. Is there a way out of this seemingly inconsistent religious practice and rhetoric?

Berkeley's defence of Protestantism is not, despite appearances, based on the authority of individual reason: it is based on the law of God. Though religious magistrates are required, they are not the source of religious authority:

> I grant it is meet the Law of Christ should like other laws have magistrates to explain and apply it. But then as in the civil State a private man may know the law enough to avoid transgressing it, and also to see whether the magistrates deviate from it into tyranny: Even so, in the other case a private Christian may know and ought to know the written law of God and not give himself up blindly to the dictates of the Pope and his assessors. This in effect wou'd be destroying the law and erecting a despotic government instead thereof. It wou'd be deserting Christ and taking the Pope for his master.[102]

Authority does not lie with the magistrate, and the individual subject has a responsibility to know the law, but this is precisely a responsibility and not a source of authority. The authority is God's, and God's written law is accessible to all. It is therefore incumbent on individuals to follow that law no matter what other authorities

---

100. *Essay*, I.iv.23, p. 101. I thank one of the anonymous readers for the Press for pointing me to this passage.

101. Letter 282, p. 426; *Christianity Not Mysterious*, p. 82.

102. Letter 282, pp. 425–26.

might attempt to usurp God's. This is not an assertion that Anglican Protestantism allows a happy admixture of freedom to its practitioners, in a manner parallel to the constitutional settlement following 1689, with other authorities counterbalancing the authority of the monarch. Rather, God's law is absolute, and any temporal authority that attempts to claim it must be recognised as a usurpation. Berkeley does not suggest that one must actively resist the usurping authority, but that one must recognise the ultimate source of law in God. This sketch, then, maintains the approach of *Passive Obedience*, in which God's laws are rationally accessible to subjects and demand an absolute (negative) moral duty. Temporal authority can be recognised as misplaced or usurped, and when it departs from God's law, as no longer commanding the obedience of the subject. Berkeley develops a position with respect to law comparable to Saint Paul's in texts such as Galatians 2:15–16 and 3:10–14, where Christ is a path to salvation contrasted to the law. An understanding of law as legal covenant is being replaced by an understanding of law as derived from God's and Christ's wisdom and the promise of things to come. This new law and these promised goods are available to the faithful, those who have the gospel.[103]

Whilst commending Protestant clergy and martyrs, in comparison to their Catholic counterparts, Berkeley says that he wishes James had read John Jewel's 'little Latin book in defence of the Reformation. I have not seen it these thirty years but remember I liked it very well'. Berkeley and Jewel are, unsurprisingly, close on a variety of issues. For example, they both doubt that Augustine was truly committed to a doctrine of purgatory and that the doctrine was original, and both contrast the Catholic practice of charging for indulgence with the practices of the reformed church.[104] They also both express strong reservations about the challenge to temporal authorities posed by the pope. In the *Discourse Addressed to Magistrates*, Berkeley says that Christianity is the best religion because it obliges submission to existing temporal authorities. Jewel defends Protestantism from the charge that it encourages political rebellion. The Protestant doctrine is that 'we ought so to obey princes

103. See Rosner, *Paul and the Law*, pp. 30, 44, 69–70, 114.
104. Letter 282, pp. 429, 423–24.

as men sent of God, and that whoso withstandeth them, withstandeth God's ordinance'. The pope, on the other hand, demands sovereignty over all Catholics, even those who might have claimed to be sovereign themselves.[105] The question of allegiance to a power above that of the sovereign state, a question to which Berkeley's time in Leghorn/Livorno in the 1710s would have sensitised him, was about to resurface with the 1745 Jacobite uprising.

Writing to Isaac Gervais, Berkeley was happy to have an unspecified opportunity 'to put a little spirit into our drooping Protestants of Cloyne, who have of late conceived no small fears on seeing themselves in such defenceless condition among so great a number of Papists [. . .]. It is indeed terrible to reflect, that we have neither arms nor militia in a province where the Papists are eight to one'.[106] As the prospect of armed invasion became more likely, Berkeley wrote to the clergy of his parish instructing them to stir up their parishioners in the defence of Protestantism and religious liberty. The letter also addresses strong pragmatic arguments to any clergy who might be considering allegiance to the invaders. Berkeley says that the Pretender struck out a clause that would have protected the Church of Ireland together with the Church of England in a manifesto written by his supporters during a plot in the late reign (presumably either the 1715 uprising or the 1722 Atterbury plot). He says this 'not [. . .] as if I suspected your loyalty'—though there could hardly be another reason—and appeals to the 'spiritual and temporal' motives of his clergy.[107]

Similarly, in writing an open letter to the Catholics of his diocese, Berkeley emphasises the economic entanglement of Protestant and Catholic interests in the case of a Jacobite invasion and Catholic seizure of power:

> Would not all those who have debts or money or other effects in the hands of Protestants be fellow sufferers with them? Would not all those who hold under the Acts of Settlement be as liable as Protestants themselves to be dispossessed by the old proprietors? Or can even those

105. [Jewel], *An Apology or Answer in Defence of the Church of England*, pp. 78–79, 108, 102–4, 108.

106. Letter 307, 16 March 1744, p. 466.

107. Letter 323, Berkeley to his clergy, 15–19 October 1745, p. 483.

who are styled proprietors flatter themselves with hopes of possessing the estates which they claim, which, in all likelihood, would be given to favourites (perhaps to foreigners) who are near the person, or who fought the battles, of their master.

Catholics have enjoyed participation in civil life under Protestant governments, Berkeley reminds them. They cannot 'plead conscience against being quiet', he says, as Christians have in all times and places submitted to sovereigns, even heathen sovereigns.[108] Thus, his arguments to interest run alongside those generated by distinctions between spiritual and temporal authority and the forms of obedience owed to both.

The 1745 Jacobite uprising is the occasion on which Berkeley's commitment to obedience was most obviously militarised. Perhaps encouraged by the activities of his brother William, who was a commander of Hanoverian forces in Fife, and who left an account of the campaign,[109] Berkeley prepared his own militia: 'I have bought up all [the muskets] I could get, and provided horses and arms for four-and-twenty of the Protestants of Cloyne, which, with a few more that can furnish themselves, make up a troop of thirty horse. This seemed necessary to keep off rogues in these doubtful times'. It is not perfectly clear how serious a militia this was: when Berkeley notes to Prior, 'There is handed about a lampoon against our troop, which hath caused great indignation in the warriors of Cloyne', he seems to enter into the spirit of the lampoon himself.[110] Still, Berkeley went on to contribute three open letters to the *Dublin Journal* on military topics. He recommends as little ornament as possible in military apparel, for the sake of greater efficiency in combat and other exercises. He addresses the suitability of shorter men for military service, arguing that a minimum height had been imposed on merely aesthetic grounds, as mixed heights look bad in a parade. Berkeley

108. Letter 324, Berkeley to the Roman Catholics of the Diocese of Cloyne, 15–19 October 1745, p. 485.

109. See Luce, p. 177. The account is cited by Roberts, *The Jacobite Wars*, p. 187, in relation to campaigns in Arbroath, in Angus, without bibliographic details. I have not been able to trace the account.

110. Letter 325, Berkeley to Gervais, 24 November 1745, p. 487; letter 326, ? before 17 December 1745, p. 488.

suggests that squat men armed with blunderbuss, shield, and short (Roman-style) sword, would prevail against larger troops. He cites the absence of military exercises and games amongst the general population and reliance on standing, even foreign, armies as reasons for recent losses to Highlanders, and he advocates local militias of labourers and tradespeople. The call to discipline also has its therapeutic aspect, shaping practice to make better people: 'The military art, like all others is attained by practice, strength and courage grow by repeated acts'.[111] Participating in a militia can be part of the love of God that expresses itself through obedience both to God and to civil and religious magistrates. It is a practice of improvement.

The presentation of the native Irish in Berkeley's pamphlet *A Word to the Wise* has already been discussed. The text exhorts the Catholic clergy to do everything they can to lift the Catholic Irish population out of poverty by encouraging them to industry and cleanliness. Much of the discourse tends towards Berkeley's therapeutic mode, insisting on the common interests of Catholic and Protestant communities. But the disciplinary tendency is also evident. The Catholic clergy should cooperate 'with the public spirit of the legislature, and men in power', in part because they 'are obnoxious to the Laws' and should seek 'to reconcile [themselves] to the Favour of the Public'. Their peripheral status lays them under a special kind of public obligation. The Catholic population is itself bred to recognise authority and follow instruction. The Catholic clergy would therefore have an immediate and great effect should they 'shew [their] Authority over the Multitude, by engaging them to the Practice of an honest Industry'. Berkeley seeks to exploit the motivating effects of various overlapping hierarchies, each of them designed to extract obedience from specific populations, for their own and the general good. Common interest and individual material interest (specifically priests' financial interest in the prosperity of their congregations), the dependence of the Catholic clergy on the toleration of the state, and the dependence of Catholic

---

111. Letter 327, Eubulus to *Dublin Journal*, 17–21 December 1745; letter 328, Eubulus to *Dublin Journal*, 4–7 January 1746, pp. 489–90; letter 330, Eubulus to *Dublin Journal*, 4–8 February 1746, pp. 491–92, 492.

congregations on their priests are levers for changing behaviour, and for demanding obedience.[112]

The latest text Berkeley composed for publication, *Maxims Concerning Patriotism*, again brings together his disciplinary and therapeutic tendencies. The short text, published in Dublin in 1750 as 'by a lady', recalling *The Ladies Library* and leading scholars to suggest Anne Berkeley's participation in the composition, was republished in Berkeley's 1752 *Miscellany*.[113] Its political organicism and paternalism promote the traditional identification of the individual and the public good:[114]

> 4. A Native than a Foreigner, a married Man than a Batchelor, a Believer than an Infidel, have a better Chance for being Patriots. [...]
>
> 9. A Man who hath no Sense of God or Conscience: would you make such a one Guardian to your Child? if not, why Guardian to the State? [...]
>
> 21. A patriot is one who heartily wisheth the public Prosperity, and doth not only wish, but also study and endeavour to promote it. [...]
>
> 24. The patriot aimeth at his private Good in the Public. The Knave makes the Public subservient to his private Interest. The former considers himself as Part of a Whole, the latter considers himself as the Whole.

But there is again underlying this organicism an absolute commitment to specific public oaths of allegiance, either to the state or to an established church, whether explicit or implied by accepting the benefits of social life (to which, as we have seen, Berkeley argues religion is necessary). It is a maxim, one of those added for the 1752 publication of the text, that 'No Man perjures himself for the sake of Conscience'.[115] There is no demand of conscience great enough to countervail against an oath—a paradigmatic oath, taken before a magistrate, on the guarantee of an established religion, to tell the truth. The passingly rare circumstances in which one might

112. *A Word to the Wise*, pp. 3–4, 31, 5, 13, 33 (LJ, VI.235, 245, 236, 238–39, 246).
113. See LJ, VI.253.
114. See Charles, 'Introduction', pp. 1–21, 11.
115. *Maxims*, §§4, 9, 21, 24; *Miscellany*, p. 114, §17.

oppose the sovereign cannot supervene on the obligation to truth; such moments would require open and not clandestine opposition. The oath and the obligation to obey that it entails retained a place in Berkeley's social thought throughout his career. Political loyalty was promoted by established religion, and the relative ecumenism of Berkeley's later life should not be confused for a weakening of his belief in the exclusive temporal rights and privileges of established Protestant Christianity.[116]

116. Breuninger, *Recovering Bishop Berkeley*, p. 157, places greater emphasis on the ecumenism of the *Maxims*.

CHAPTER FOURTEEN

'Early Hours as a Regimen'

BERKELEY'S PHILOSOPHY IS PRACTICAL.[1] Its practicality does not derive from a preeminent commitment to reason as the only authoritative guide to behaviour—his sense of the relationship between finite spirits and the infinite spirit is too personal for that, and his sense of the role of prejudice in shaping human action too acute. Nor is it a commitment to a tightly interlocking set of principles to live by—he is too committed to rational deliberation in the various spheres of life. Berkeley is not, then, easily aligned with either of the two ways of conceiving of the ancient philosophical life presented by John Cooper and Pierre Hadot.[2] His philosophy is practical in a compound sense. If one of philosophy's tasks is to make sense of daily practice (the criterion invoked in a discussion of the use of language in *Alciphron*),[3] it should start from or with what people ordinarily do and test its explanations against that practice. Philosophy should also aim to reform daily practice. When composing his early philosophical works Berkeley had an eye to practice, as well as to returning men of science from speculation to a sense of the

1. Charles, 'Introduction', p. 20, says that Berkeley's philosophy must be understood as a form of practical wisdom in which Christianity plays a large part.

2. Cooper, *Pursuits of Wisdom*, p. 6: 'beginning with Socrates [. . .] ancient philosophers made philosophy the, and the only authoritative, foundation and guide for the whole of human life'; Hadot, *Philosophy as a Way of Life*, p. 267.

3. *Alciphron*, VII.8.

presence of God.[4] Many of his later writings are explicitly practical, such as his works on economics and finance and medicine. They contain guidance not just about how to think, but about what to do: what kinds of institutions to establish and how to administer them; how to spend money; how to prepare and administer medicines. Berkeley's philosophy is practical not only inasmuch as it considers daily practice and attempts to reform that practice. It must also (like any philosophy) be practised—it must be part of a particular life, with a place or places in the more or less planned succession of days in that life. Philosophy must fit into daily practice, be a part of it. Daily practices that might not immediately appear philosophical have a place in facilitating (or challenging) philosophy. They may even themselves be a kind of practical philosophy. It is these last two topics that between them comprehend the interweaving of philosophy and daily life for Berkeley that are the focus of this chapter.

Berkeley's days, of course, present different kinds of ordinariness at different stages of his life, from his early days as 'a sort of monk or recluse in a college' to a period of 'the greatest hurry of business I ever knew in my life' in preparing his case for funding for St Paul's College.[5] But there were continuities as well as changes in Berkeley's philosophical regimen. This chapter starts with the beginning of the day and concludes with the end of life, looking at when, where, and how Berkeley thought philosophy should be practised.

Early Rising

The opening exchange between Hylas and Philonous in *Three Dialogues* is a strong proleptic judgement of their argumentative positions:

> *Philonous.* Good Morrow, *Hylas*, I did not expect to find you abroad so early.
>
> *Hylas.* It is indeed something unusual, but my Thoughts were so taken up with a Subject I was discoursing of last Night, that

---

4. See chapter 1; see also BL Add MS 39304, f. 4r.

5. Letter 34, Berkeley to Percival, 17 May 1712, p. 72; letter 145, Berkeley to Prior, 19 April 1726, p. 222.

> finding I could not sleep, I resolved to rise and take a turn in
> the Garden.
> *Philonous.* It happened very well, to let you see what innocent and
> agreeable Pleasures you lose every Morning.

This opening indicates a difference in attitude between the partners
in the dialogue that is sustained throughout. Hylas has to apologise
to Philonous for being late at the recommencement of their conversation the following morning. Intellectual and physical laziness
go together. One reason for Hylas finally being won over to immaterialism is the plain efficiency of its arguments that appeal to his
nature: 'I am by Nature lazy', he says.[6] Philonous (like the young
Berkeley, who saw the value of quietly harmonising with one's
adversaries in argument) emphasises the simplicity and efficiency
of immaterialism, thinking it likely that these aspects will appeal to
Hylas's temperament.

The quotation from *Siris* which gives this chapter its title makes
large claims for early rising. It is to become, in a way I explore further in the next chapter, a means of being closer to God. Berkeley laments the effects of drinking spirits, saying that one need not
look as far as the 'savage natives of America' to see those ill effects.
Drinking spirits is one of the factors that leads to shorter and
grosser life amongst 'our Insulars', that is, the native Irish. Berkeley
recommends 'tar water, temperance, and early hours' as a remedy:

> [T]he last is a sure addition to Life, not only in regard of time, which,
> being taken from sleep, the image of death, is added to the waking
> hours, but also in regard of longevity and duration in the vulgar sense. I
> may say too in regard of spirit and vivacity, which, within the same com-
> pass of duration, may, truly and properly be affirmed to add to man's
> life: it being manifest, that one man, by a brisker motion of his spirits
> and succession of his ideas, shall live more in one hour, than another in
> two: and that the quantity of Life is to be estimated, not merely from
> the duration, but also from the intenseness of living. Which intense liv-
> ing, or, if I may so say, lively life, is not more promoted by early hours
> as a regimen, than by tar water as a cordial[.][7]

6. *Three Dialogues*, pp. 1, 67, 158 (LJ, II.171, 208, 259).
7. *Siris*, §§108–9.

Early rising enables the elevation of the spirits. It is particularly to be recommended to the low people, but for all it brings an intensity to life that is the mark of an increase in spirit, of becoming more spiritual and participating more in the divinity.

Philonous says the pleasures of the early morning are innocent: solitude and tranquillity allow us to meditate upon nature (that is, refer nature to God). Berkeley would present early rising as a good not just in the setting of philosophical dialogue but throughout his life—even for his family after his death—and as a significant part of right living and of living philosophically. Mary Pendarves noted in 1734 that 'Dean Berkley that was (now Bishop of Cloyne), and his lady rise every morning *at four* o' the clock: they are the most primitive couple that ever I heard of'.[8] ('Primitive' is used here to indicate that they replicated the manners and habits of life of our first parents in their simplicity.) Anne, Berkeley's wife, gave an account of Berkeley's habits of early rising to their son George Jr to defend Berkeley from George Jr's slight against his father (probably the complaint that he was not sent to a public school, but educated at home). She explains how Berkeley was able to benefit from his talents:

> [H]is Talents were great, & so are those of many others—but in his own Words: his Industry was greater; he struck a light at twelve to rise & study; & pray, for he was very Pious & his studies were not barren speculations— for he loved God & Man, silenced & confuted atheists disguised as Mathematicians & fine Gentelemen—[9]

Anne connects Berkeley's habits of life with the practical, moral orientation of his philosophical work.

Berkeley himself makes relatively little of his early rising in his correspondence, but he is clear in his endorsement of the practice, and the use of those hours in promoting study. Although not specifying a time at which John Percival should rise, Berkeley tells him that 'there is nothing else wanting to complete [his] happiness' than spending 'regularly and constantly two or three hours of the morning in study and retirement'.[10] This habit should be fixed before

---

8. Lady Llanover, ed., *Autobiography and Correspondence of Mary Granville, Mrs. Delany*, I.432, Mrs Pendarves to Mrs Ann Granville, 2 March 1733/34.

9. BL Add MS 39312, f. 227.

10. Letter 4, Berkeley to Percival, 22 September 1709, p. 20.

marriage, as it will be easier to maintain than to introduce after that moment in life. Berkeley reports on the recovery of his health in a letter to Tom Prior from London on 7 January 1733/34: '[B]y regular living, and rising very early (which I find the best thing in the world), I am very much mended; insomuch, that though I cannot read, yet my thoughts seem as distinct as ever. I do therefore, for amusement, pass my early hours in thinking of certain mathematical matters, which may possibly produce something'.[11] That something was *The Analyst*, discussed in the previous chapter. Fifteen years later, Berkeley wrote to Samuel Johnson, his American friend, philosophical interlocutor, and fellow educational projector, offering some guidance on the aims and institutional organisation of a college to be founded in New York, which became King's College (later Columbia University). Good teaching of the classics is to be the first care pedagogically, '[b]ut the principal care must be good life and morals to which (as well as to study) early hours and temperate meals will much conduce'.[12] Inculcating a habit of early rising is conducive to good life, to study, to morals, to health, and to the production of works of learning and philosophy.

Anne Berkeley's invocation of her late husband's early rising was part of a continuing attempt to inculcate in George Jr a practice of good living. Her letter just cited goes on to make much of the importance of early rising to George Jr, who may have appeared to need the advice: a document entitled 'Memoirs of Dr Berkeley written by a Friend' records that George Jr 'had an unconquerable indolence, and has often confessed to one of his most intimate friends that at no period of his life was he capable of long & intense application'.[13] Anne felt it not just her privilege but her duty to advise her son on the way in which his daily practice of living affected his capacity to do good as a Christian. In a different letter she touches on the subject and suggests that it has been the cause of conflict between them:

I know that God has blessed you with more Nobleness of Mind & Love & Generosity & friendship than Any Man I know he is as ready to give

11. Letter 231, p. 359.
12. Letter 363, Berkeley to Samuel Johnson, 23 August 1749, p. 541.
13. BL Add MS 46889, f. 16v.

you Patience, regularity—& Constancy You must not be wavering—
make good Sermons—you are very correct—but you must read much
in order to be a full Man—& in order to read you must rise early—that
always touches to the quick & whilst it does so shews the need of prob-
ing that wound. What an Infaithful Monster to God & you should I be
were I not to speak truth when I dare—that is to say when My Dear Son
& only friend invites me to it Soon I shall be silent for ever—& will you
say the sooner the better.[14]

The subject is one of such seriousness that Anne sees it as a duty to
speak the truth out loud, even if, as she conjectures, she will have
made George Jr wish for her death.

George Jr himself expressed a concern about early rising in a
journal dating from the period after Berkeley's death. The first day
(Friday, 26 July 1754) records an appropriately early rise, but it is
followed by failures:

up at 6 went to Lat: Prayrs, till breakfast read in Fenelon [. . .] Sunday,
overslept. [. . .] I am very much dispirited to day; partly from reflecting on
the shameful wicked loss of Time y.^{t} my Conscience reproaches me with
(wch I heartily Pray God to forgive & by his Grace to prevent for ye future)[15]

(The other reason George Jr gives for being dispirited is the mental
ill health of his sister Julia, which I discuss in chapter 16.) Early rising and study are what make goodness possible. Failure to rise early
and make the best of time is a cause of moral self-reproach.

The period immediately after Berkeley's death was, then, and
perhaps unsurprisingly, a time when surviving family members
reflected on their daily habits. Anne's plan of life for the days after
Berkeley's death is recorded in some notes that also incorporate
reminders on attitudes to adopt and tasks that require immediate
attention. Early rising is again prominent:

Rise at 4 call Sevts at 7 in Winter & 5 in Summer.
read Pray & dress till 8
See H read to him till 9
Breakfast.

14. BL Add MS 39311, f. 202v.
15. BL Add MS 46889, ff. 1r (26 July 1754), 2r (28 and 29 July 1754).

Walk.

go to Church

take care of my family

read to H—make him read to me

dine at 3

have your house in good Order amuse your self & Children take the
    Air, Visite, receive company from 4 till 9 which is 5 hours[16]

In the ordering of a day ('an exemplary day's time-table', as it has been called),[17] early rising, reading, praying and worshipping, instructing (and providing an example to) servants, and educating and caring for family (H is Henry, the son who, like Julia, seems to have experienced severe mental ill health throughout most of a long life) are the priorities to be observed.

Sociability and Conversation

The tranquillity offered by early rising may be understood as freedom from social interruptions. In an editorial intervention into material presented in *The Ladies Library*, the anthology he made for Richard Steele, Berkeley criticises the social whirl of life:

> It is now a Piece of good Breeding to ramble three or four Days in a Week from House to House, not in doing good, but in doing nothing, and to sit at Home the rest of it, expecting as great Triflers as themselves. *Dress, Meals, Visit, Park, Opera,* and *Play*, take up all the Hours that are not given by them to sleep; in which, if the Morning is not spent, *Dress* consumes it all: the Noon is not long enough for Dinner, the Afternoon is loiter'd away in the *Park*, and the rest of the Day at the *Theatres*: What Part of it can they spare for the Church and the Closet?[18]

The pattern of contemporary social life excludes study and worship. After the great rush of business preparing for St Paul's College in 1726 came a period of retirement in Newport, Rhode Island,

16. TCD MS 453, f. 50v. These remarks are written from the other end of the volume that contains Berkeley's *Manuscript Introduction* to *Principles of Human Knowledge*.

17. Tipton and Furlong, 'Mrs George Berkeley and Her Washing Machine', p. 38.

18. *Ladies Library*, I.42. See Aitken, 'Steele's *Ladies' Library*', 16–17, for this passage as an editorial intervention in material taken from Jeremy Taylor's *Holy Living*.

awaiting the funds. Berkeley wrote to Percival at a moment when the rest of his party, other than Anne, was off in Boston:

> We have passed the winter in a profound solitude on my farm in this island, all my companions having been allured five or six months ago to Boston, the great place of pleasure and resort in these parts, where they still continue. After my long fatigue of business this retirement is very agreeable to me; and my wife loves a country life and books so well as to pass her time contentedly and cheerfully without any other conversation than her husband and the dead.[19]

This moment must have been peculiarly quiet, but *Alciphron* gives the impression that life in the colony was in general less prone to interruption than in London. Again demonstrating the links between early and late rising, right and wrong thinking, Dion notes the circumstances in which the sixth dialogue opens:

> The following Day being Sunday, our Philosophers lay long in Bed, while the rest of us went to Church in the neighbouring Town, where we dined at *Euphranor*'s, and after Evening Service returned to the two Philosophers [. . .] the next Morning assembled at the same Place as the Day before [. . .] being all seated, I observed, that the foregoing Week our Conferences had been carried on for a longer Time, and with less Interruption than I had ever known, or well could be, in Town: where Mens Hours are so broken by Visits, Business, and Amusements, that whoever is content to form his Notions from Conversation only, must needs have them very shattered and imperfect.[20]

A rural, retired life provides far better opportunities for communing with others, and for developing intellectually by that means, than does city life.

Dion's comment here is a response to Lysicles's view, expressed in the fourth dialogue, that 'much is to be got by conversing with ingenious Men, which is a short way to Knowledge, that saves a Man the Drudgery of Reading and Thinking'.[21] Berkeley clearly does not think improvement by conversation the best means, but

---

19. Letter 200, Berkeley to Percival, 29 March 1730, p. 321.
20. *Alciphron*, VI.1.
21. Ibid., IV.18.

such intellectual improvement is clearly a better motivation to socialise and a better use of social time than other possibilities. (Berkeley's first publication, we might remember, was a Latin treatise on mathematics that included instructions on how to play an algebraic game that would improve students' minds much more than the trifling activity of playing chess in which Berkeley saw so many students engaged at TCD in his early years as a fellow.[22]) In the letter to Percival recommending two to three hours a day of study, Berkeley makes a contrast between conversation and private study and indicates his preference:

> I have observed in you that you seem to prefer the improving ones self
> by conversation before private study. This proceeds either from an over
> modest opinion of your own parts (which fault I know is very incident
> to you) or else from a belief that the latter is not so profitable and pleas-
> ant as is pretended. For my part I am of a different opinion[.][23]

If people have an unalterable temperamental inclination to learning by conversation rather than private study, those conversations, like any other form of study, are to be undertaken with as little social interruption as possible.

Pleasure and Temperance

In addition to early rising, Berkeley recommended temperate meals to the future college students of New York. Such temperance was likely to apply to drink as much as food, and to have been the 'habitual temperance' he called fasting.[24] He was, by Anne's account, a very temperate drinker: 'his own Temperance in regard to <u>Wine</u> was a better lesson to you than forbidding it would have been', she would say to George Jr.[25] In his treatise on tar-water, Berkeley condemns the medicinal uses of liquor, 'which render many lives

---

22. Sampson, ed., *The Works of George Berkeley*, I.51.

23. Letter 4, Berkeley to Percival, 22 September 1709, p. 20.

24. LJ, VII.56, sermon 5.2, preached at Newport, RI, 2 March 1728/29; see also *Ladies Library*, III.311, excerpting Taylor, *Holy Living*: '*Fasting* is not to be commended as a Duty, but as an Instrument, and in that Sense no Man can reprove or undervalue it, who knows either spiritual Art or spiritual Necessities'.

25. BL Add MS 39312, f. 227r.

wretched, that would otherwise have been only ridiculous'.[26] Berkeley seems to have drunk according to the norms of privileged sociability of his time. He 'drank healths', a practice that was condemned in 1716 by Peter Browne, the provost when Berkeley enrolled at TCD, as irreligious.[27] In one case, perhaps significantly, Berkeley drank the health of Henry Sacheverell, the high Tory preacher, along with that of Percival. Other sociable drinking took place. At the opening night of Addison's *Cato*, which Berkeley attended with the author and 'two or three more friends', 'two or three flasks of burgundy and champagne' made 'a pleasant refreshment to us all between the acts'.[28] Berkeley at points indulged in the pleasures of the table. Early in life, visiting the Percival estate in Burton, he passed his time without any particular restraint or project: 'My business here has been little else than eating drinking sleeping discoursing & variously sporting to pass away the time. My curiosity has not led me to make any diligent search after the antiquities or other observables that may possibly be here about, though I believe there are not many'.[29]

Dining was of course one of the major social engagements of Berkeley's time, and a means of forming and confirming allegiances and offering (implicitly or explicitly) reward for work or other forms of support. John Nichols, the late eighteenth-century bibliophile and anecdotalist, had it that 'Bp. Berkeley had a guinea and a dinner with STEELE for every Paper he furnished' for Steele's *Guardian*.[30] There is reason to believe that Berkeley enjoyed food. Anne Berkeley suggests in the letter to her son in which she mentions Berkeley's temperance with wine that he not only occasionally relaxed into the gratification of his appetites but recruited his reason into the justification of their indulgence. Eating presented a philosophical challenge to Berkeley, one in which appetites were pitted against reason. It was a challenge he was, at least in the judgement of his wife, unable to meet. Indeed, she suggests that

---

26. *Siris*, §105.

27. See Browne, *A Discourse of Drinking Healths*.

28. Letter 12, Berkeley to Percival, 1 March 1710, p. 36; letter 43, Berkeley to Percival, 16 April 1713, p. 87.

29. Letter 3, Berkeley to Molyneux, 1 August 1709, p. 18.

30. Stephens, ed., *The Guardian*, 'Introduction', p. 27. Letter 43, Berkeley to Percival, 16 April 1713, p. 87, and letter 46, Berkeley to Percival, 7 May 1713, p. 93, also mentioning dining, with Arbuthnot and with Whigs at Garth's.

indulgence hastened Berkeley's death: 'had he denied his <u>Apetites</u> more & used more <u>exercise</u> & had he not bribed his reason to plead for his Apetite he might have blest you & yrs now, have been a mine of Gold & Wisdom to you'.[31] Berkeley did not follow his own recommendation of habitual temperance.

Anne Berkeley thought that George should have exercised more. On this point too he may not have followed his own advice: he had recommended that the general public ought to engage in military exercises to prevent the need for standing armies,[32] but restraining the appetites and actively practising public virtues were not easy achievements. Still, Berkeley did not avoid exercise entirely. A bishop of Cloyne writing in the very early nineteenth century records that the rock shrubbery near the cave in the palace garden was Berkeley's favourite walk, and that what was now a vegetable patch was formerly Berkeley's bowling green. The property facilitated moderate exercise, perhaps suiting a bishop of over fifty years of age.[33]

Berkeley identified the sedentary life of the scholar and preexisting medical conditions as hindrances to physical activity. In *Siris*, he characterises the life of a scholar—or a monkish recluse in a college, as he put it to Percival—as one, like those of ladies and seafarers, that particularly benefits from the drinking of tar-water:

> Studious persons also pent up in narrow holes, breathing bad air, and stooping over their books, are much to be pitied. As they are debarred the free use of air and exercise, this I will venture to recommend as the best succedaneum to both. Though it were to be wished, that modern scholars would, like the ancients, meditate and converse more in walks and gardens and open air, which upon the whole, would perhaps be no hindrance to their learning, and a great advantage to their health. My own sedentary course of life had long since thrown me into an ill habit, attended with many ailments, particularly a nervous colic, which

31. BL Add MS 39312, f. 227v. For the management of the appetites, see *Ladies Library*, II.240, excerpting Tillotson, *Sermons*: 'It is a good Saying, *Magna Pars Virtutis est bene moratus Venter; a well manner'd and well govern'd Appetite*, in Matter of *Meats* and *Drinks*, is a great *Part of Virtue*'.

32. Letter 330, Eubulus (Berkeley) to *Dublin Journal*, 4–8 February 1746, p. 491.

33. Brady, *Clerical and Parochial Records of Cork, Cloyne, and Ross*, III(1864),18n and 27n, 'Bishop Bennet's MSS—History of the Property of the See of Cloyne'.

rendered my life a burthen, and the more so, because my pains were exasperated by exercise.[34]

Berkeley could not take exercise to correct the distempers to which the scholar's life was prone, as it aggravated his colic. This illness had been with him for ten years already. He had a 'cruel periodical cholic', a relapse of which in 1724 made him think of taking the waters at one of the English spa towns. It remained with him for at least a further eight years. He says that he would have travelled to see a friend, '[b]ut for above three years together I have not gone three miles off, being nailed down to Cloyne by a cholic and pain in my side which is irritated by the motion of a horse or a coach'.[35]

Berkeley also experienced gout, which may have been connected, as Anne implies, to his diet. He writes to Prior that he has had a bout of the illness, and that after it passed he had a tenderness in his feet and caught cold whilst taking the air in the park at Cloyne, leading to further confinement.[36] At least for treating his colic, Berkeley reports, tar-water has become 'the greatest of all temporal blessings'.[37] Illness may have followed from an unphilosophical recruitment of reason in the service of the appetites, but it may also have imposed certain forms of retirement and regular or orderly life that were supportive of the philosophical regime to which Berkeley aspired and mostly followed.

Sensual pleasure is by no means excluded from Berkeley's account of the good, or the good life. In the *Notebooks*, he states that 'Sensual Pleasure is the Summum Bonum. This the Great Principle of Morality'. Pleasures can of course be ranked, so the ill effects of enjoying a pleasure can be explained as causes of pain, inasmuch as they prevent taking some greater pleasure. Pleasures of the appetites deny us higher sensual pleasures, such as health. Berkeley notes the importance of pointing people to higher sensual pleasures, such as those of the fine arts: 'Mem. to excite men to the pleasures of the Eye & the Ear wch surfeit not, nor bring those evils after them as others'.[38] At

34. *Siris*, §119.

35. Letter 126, Berkeley to Percival, 9 September 1724, pp. 197–98; letter 298, Berkeley to Percival Jr, 2 July 1742, p. 451.

36. Letter 238, Berkeley to Prior, 7 February 1734, p. 365; letter 241, Berkeley to Prior, 2 March 1734, p. 369.

37. See chapter 9, where Berkeley uses similar terms about having a family.

38. *Notebooks*, §§769, 773, 787.

certain periods the pleasures of the eye and ear figured very large in Berkeley's daily life. The journals of his time in Italy, in Rome in particular, but also throughout the country, indicate days passed almost entirely in the contemplation of works of visual art. At Cloyne, from 1734 onwards, the Berkeley family was very actively engaged in music-making. As Berkeley told his friend Gervais, music 'is at present the reigning passion at Cloyne. To be plain, we are musically mad. If you would know what that is, come and see'. This is a considerable change in Berkeley's relationship with music since 1717, when he wrote to Percival from Italy that he had 'eyes but no ears' for music and fell asleep at concerts. The employment of resident music teachers in the Berkeley household testifies to this passion and the organising effect it would have had on the family's days. One Monsieur DuBois 'lived on a familiar foot in my family for some years', presumably as a music tutor.[39] Eliza Berkeley records that a Pasquilino was employed as a music teacher, and that 'Bishop Berkeley, at one time, for several years paid four hundred pound *per annum* to different masters to instruct his children in Music, Painting, Fencing, Riding and French; the Latin and Greek he entrusted to none but himself'.[40] For all that Berkeley and his family did not lack a passion for the pleasures of the eye and ear that surfeit not, it is unreasonable to think that they always felt an appetite for such innocent diversion, throughout all days and seasons, with equal force. John Locke recognises that these higher pleasures are not always appealing: 'He that loves Reading, Writing, Music, *&c.* finds yet in himself certain Seasons wherein those things have no Relish to him: And if at that time he forces himself to it, he only pothers and wearies himself to no purpose'.[41] The arts may not surfeit, but they are not always what one wants.

Although in the previous chapter it was noted that the *Discourse Addressed to Magistrates* calls for the restraint of the passions for the sake of the public good, strict stoic attitudes to the management of the passions are perhaps unlikely in a philosophy that makes sensual pleasure the chief good. Personal pleasure is a real and valuable element of human life. Berkeley shares some, but not all,

39. Letter 302, Berkeley to Gervais, 6 September 1743, p. 454; letter 84, Berkeley to Percival, 1 March 1717, p. 142; letter 392, Berkeley to DuBois (Annesley), [1752], p. 579.

40. Eliza Berkeley, preface to Berkeley, *Poems*, pp. ccccxii (n), ccxliv.

41. Locke, *Some Thoughts Concerning Education*, p. 135.

of his thinking on the goods of the body and, crucially, the goods of the social body, with Malebranche:

> To destroy Stoic wisdom completely, one need know but one thing, which is sufficiently proved through experience and by what has already been said, that we are tied to our body, to our parents, to our friends, to our prince, to our country, by bonds we cannot break, and would even be ashamed to try to break. Our soul is joined to our body, and through our body to all visible things by a hand so powerful that it is impossible to loosen them by ourselves. [. . .] God, having made us in order to live in a society with other men, gave us an inclination toward everything capable of binding us to them, which inclination we cannot overcome by ourselves. [. . .] We are united to all creatures by God's order, and we depend upon them absolutely because of the disorder of sin.[42]

Such views are close to those Berkeley expresses in his *Guardian* essay entitled 'The Bond of Society':

> [W]e are linked by an imperceptible Chain to every Individual of the Human Race. [. . .] And as the attractive Power in Bodies is the most universal Principle which produceth innumerable Effects, and is a Key to explain the various *Phœnomena* of Nature; so the corresponding Social Appetite in Human Souls is the great Spring and Source of Moral Actions.[43]

The appetites are to be managed only inasmuch as they can be used to produce higher or more public goods for us. They are not to be altogether repressed, and it would be folly to imagine, with the Stoics, that the only real goods are independent of all externals and accidentals.

Berkeley did not write at any length on regulating the passions, but advocated the modified Christian stoicism that sees passions as natural, to be controlled by reason.[44] Christian fasting should be a habitual temperance to be applied also to the passions, 'each whereof inebriates like wine & obfuscates like meat'.[45] The passions should be regulated: 'it is certain that as the miseries incident to

42. Malebranche, *The Search after Truth*, pp. 182–83.
43. *Guardian*, II.222–23, no. 126, Wednesday, 5 August [1713].
44. Harris, 'The Government of the Passions', p. 274.
45. LJ, VII.56, sermon 5.2, Newport, RI, 2 March 1728/29.

mankind, arise from the irregularity of the passions, senses and natural inclinations, so our happiness consists in their subordination to right reason and in governing them by just rules'. In the ill consequences that follow the mismanagement of the passions, Berkeley sees evidence of God's intentions: 'All our appetites and passions are in themselves, so admirably fitted for our preservation and welbeing, and whenever we apply them to wrong objects, or suffer them to exceed their due bounds, we meet with such sore mortifications, as put the intention of the Author of nature beyond all dispute'.[46] The personal mismanagement of the animal economy and its consequences are means by which God discourses humans on the natural limits to natural appetites.

Berkeley's works, his letters, and what records there are of his character do not suggest someone who found the passions a challenge in daily life (no episodes of anger, avarice, jealousy, or remorse seem to have overtaken him, for example). If a negative emotional tone ever emerges from his letters, it is in his letters to Tom Prior on the various matters of law and financial management in which Prior acted as Berkeley's agent in the 1720s and '30s, when Berkeley could be short-tempered about what he perceived to be Prior's inertia: 'I do not doubt your skill; I only wish you were as active to serve an old friend as I should be in any affair of yours that lay in my power'.[47] Berkeley could be exigent. One striking moment at which Berkeley disciplined his emotions was on the death of his and Anne's son William, to whom he was deeply attached. 'I had set my heart too much upon him, more perhaps than I ought to have done upon anything in this world. [. . .] God, I say, in mercy, hath deprived me of this pretty, gay plaything'.[48] Even in a moral world organised around the highest pleasures, the pleasures of familial love must come second to love of God. A family is only to be loved in God. That, at least, was Anne's view as she put it to Eliza Frinsham/ Berkeley in the weeks before the latter married George Jr, saying that the truly happy marriage was one in which both partners realised that all happiness is derived from God.[49]

46. LJ, VII.136, 133, sermon X, Cloyne, Whit Sunday 1751.
47. Letter 140, Berkeley to Prior, 20 January 1726, p. 214.
48. Letter 375, Berkeley to Benson, 8 March 1751, p. 564.
49. BL Add MS 39311, f. 106v.

Death

For Berkeley, daily life is a challenge of regulating the passions and appetites with respect to reason and, more importantly, love of God, understood as participating in God. If Berkeley did not seem to find this regulation a particular challenge, with the exception, perhaps, of the pleasures of the table, one curious anecdote about his life suggests that he may have felt an antagonistic urge—the urge towards death, rather than the preservation of life through heeding the passions and appetites. A biographical article, thought to be by Oliver Goldsmith, relates the incident and mentions Thomas Contarine, Goldsmith's uncle, and probably the source of the anecdote:

> [C]uriosity leading him [Berkeley] one day, in the crowd, to go to see an execution, he returned home pensive and melancholy, and could not forbear reflecting on what he had seen. He desired to know what were the pains and symptoms a malefactor felt upon such an occasion, and communicated to his chum the cause of his strange curiosity; in short, he resolved to tuck himself up for a trial, at the same time desiring his companion to take him down at a signal agreed upon.
>
> The companion (whose name was Contarine) was to try the same experiment himself immediately after. Berkely was, accordingly, tied up to the cieling, and the chair taken from under his feet; but soon losing the use of his senses, his companion, it seems, waited a little too long for the signal agreed upon, and our enquirer had like to have been hanged in good earnest; for as soon as he was taken down, he fell, senseless and motionless, upon the floor. After some trouble, however, he was brought to himself; and observing his band, 'Bless my heart, Contarine', says he, 'you have quite rumpled my band'. When it came to Contarine's turn to go up, he quickly evaded the proposal; the other's danger had quite abated his curiosity.[50]

Several elements of this anecdote are worth remarking. Berkeley is curious about an execution, the ultimate form of social discipline. He is curious about what a malefactor feels—physically, presumably, but perhaps also morally. Berkeley is identified as an enquirer, and his attempt to hang himself as a speculative activity, perhaps

---

50. 'George Berkely', in Mortimer, ed., *The British Plutarch*, p. 161. See Berman, *George Berkeley*, pp. 203–7, for the grounds of the attribution.

one worthy of the attitude of mild ridicule that can be sensed in the application of the term in this sketch.

Berkeley is not the only person to have felt curious in this way (if indeed he did). Francis Bacon remembers

> to have heard of a certaine *Gentleman*; That would needs make Triall, in Curiositie, what men did feele that were hanged; So hee fastened the Cord about his Necke, raising himselfe upon a Stoole, and then letting himselfe fall; Thinking it should bee in his power, to recover the Stoole at his pleasure; which he failed in; But was helped by a Friend, then present. He was asked afterward, what he felt? He said; Hee felt no paine; But first, he thought, he saw before his Eyes, a great Fire, and Burning; Then hee thought, he saw all Black, and Darke: Lastly, it turned to a pale Blew, or Sea-water-Greene; which Colour is also often seene by them which fall into *swoonings*.[51]

It is possible that Berkeley knew this account, and even that he added the safeguard of the signal to be given the friend to avoid the hazard faced by Bacon's curious gentleman. Another reason Berkeley might have known this passage is to be found in that which precedes it. Bacon has just alerted his reader to the

> many Examples of *Men*, in shew, *Dead*; Either laid out upon the *Cold Floare*; Or *carried* forth to *Buriall*; Nay, of some *Buried* in the Earth; which notwithstanding have lived againe; which hath beene found, in those that were buried; (The Earth being afterwards opened,) By the Bruising and Wounding of their Head, through the strugling of the Body, within the Coffin: Whereof the most Recent and Memorable Example, was that of *Ioannes Scotus*, called the *Subtile*, and a *Schooleman*; who being digged up againe by his Servant, unfortunately absent at his Buriall; (And who knew his Masters Manner in such Fits;) Was found in that State. And the like happened in our Dayes, in the Person of a *Player*, buried at *Cambridge*.

Berkeley's will specifies that his 'body, before it is buried, be kept five days above ground, or longer, even till it grow offensive by the cadaverous smell'.[52] A combination of intense curiosity about death

---

51. Bacon, *Historie Naturall and Experimentall*, pp. 367–68.
52. Luce, p. 222.

and the sensations that accompany it with vivid fear of certain kinds of death (burial alive) is not unique. But Berkeley's drive to test death and his need to make a provision in a will against premature burial indicate that death, like life, was a test of his philosophy.

Philosophy was to be practised in the mornings, and by rising early. Retirement, reading, study, and prayer were preferable to the acquisition of knowledge through conversation in the course of days fragmented by socialising in town. The education that was the realisation and transmission of philosophy was facilitated by temperance with respect to the appetites, and yet the pleasures of the table might have been those Berkeley found it least easy to resist. Sensual pleasures being real goods, those that can never be exhausted (the arts) were to be integrated into a daily practice of education as part of the social life of the family, the domestic economy. The management of the passions was to be undertaken for sociable reasons: as an expression of our being made for one another, of human good being a social good. Seeing that our good and the good of others imply one another was an imaginative act, or an act of extended vision.[53] Loving others, including one's family, was a way to love God, or a way to be in God, in Berkeley's philosophical universe. Christian stoic management of the passions might feel extreme when the death of a child is related to loving that child too much, but love should only ever be in and for God.

Seeing death and preparing for it is a traditional aim of philosophy. Berkeley may have confronted death as a natural philosopher, an experimental philosopher, with the example of Bacon's report on the vision of death in his mind. Or he may have had a more personal fear that, in a much more practical sense, death might not be the end unless one's family can smell one's body rotting. Berkeley managed his philosophy as part of his practical daily life in various ways. It is perhaps no particular surprise that a philosopher so often considered in his own time and later as a whimsical visionary might have had more than an ordinary way of relating philosophy and life.

53. See Taranto, 'Le Travail de la sagesse', p. 270.

CHAPTER FIFTEEN

Cloyne

THE WRITINGS AND PRACTICES of Berkeley's years at Cloyne can be understood as attempts to help others bring their wills into conformity with God's will. I have already shown that this effort involved the maintenance of the civil authority of the clergy, the legitimation of state surveillance of religious opinion, and concerted attempts to maintain the privileges of the established church and convert other religious denominations to it. If this suggests a disciplinary character to Berkeley's activities centred on the privileges and powers of the institution of the Church, there is also a more therapeutic side to them. He also acts as a philosophical therapist who helps others better to direct their desires and appetites. That is the ambition of his two major texts of his time in Cloyne, *The Querist* and *Siris*, which this chapter discusses in turn. *Siris* seeks to heal the body and mind, the body by treatment with tar-water, the mind by reflection upon the ordering of causes and the subordination of the phenomenal world to the will of a creator. *The Querist*, on the other hand, analyses human behaviour as a system of supplying demands and seeks to modify it from the conviction that such systems ought always to aim at a conceived good. I begin by establishing some contexts for *The Querist*. It is a text that draws on and extends the tradition of Irish economic patriotism already evident in the 1720s. It is closely connected to the work of the (Royal) Dublin Society and other philanthropic projects of the time. It also constitutes one of the Irish chapters in a narrative of conflict between the Church interest and the modern state. These contexts inform a discussion of the different means chosen for the reform of the appetites of different sections of the Irish population, and of the social institutions and practices that Berkeley believed were necessary to achieve those reforms.

Patriotism and Charity

Irish patriotism might be understood as the commitment on the part of the Protestant elite to the interests of their nonmetropolitan corner of a multiregional, confessional state.[1] Its economic character in the 1720s and 1730s was pronounced. In the mid-1720s, Jonathan Swift took on the character of the drapier to compose his letters opposing the introduction of a halfpence coin, which, he argued, would have been ruinous for the economy, and *Gulliver's Travels* offers a glimpse of Swift's proposed remedy for Irish economic problems in the rational management of agriculture on the estate of Lord Munodi.[2] A 'buy Irish' movement which existed from the 1720s sought to promote Irish linen in both Ireland and England.[3] Berkeley localised still further. In a short biographical sketch commissioned by his son in 1760, Berkeley is said during his time at Cloyne to have contributed to 'promoting Industry by purchasing nothing for himself or Family from any remoter place, which was manufactured however imperfectly in his own little Town'.[4] A series of poor harvests in the late 1720s led many to support agricultural improvement as the great public good.[5] Percival, as a prominent member of an Irish lobby, promoted Irish trade and industry in the English Parliament in the late 1720s and early 1730s.[6] Economic patriotism had a theoretical and discursive character prior to Berkeley's *Querist*. Thomas Prior wrote about Irish

1. Leersen, 'Anglo-Irish Patriotism and Its European Context', p. 20, notes the connection between Irish patriotism and arguments for regionalist heteronomy elsewhere in Europe.

2. Swift, *Gulliver's Travels*, pp. 252–54.

3. Barnard, *Irish Protestant Ascents and Descents*, p. 278, and McBride, *Eighteenth-Century Ireland*, pp. 149–50, both referring to Katherine Connoly.

4. BL Add MS 39311, f. 92, William Price to GB Jr, 17 July 1760.

5. Hayton and Karian, 'Select Document', p. 307.

6. Barnard, *Improving Ireland?*, p. 122.

coinage in the late 1720s (of which more shortly). Arthur Dobbs, in an essay on trade he produced between 1728 and 1730, held that trade 'makes the people of the world as one great family supplying each other's wants' and aimed at improving the standard of living for the poor, small farmers, and artisans through improved infrastructure, longer tenancies, and other proposals.[7]

Thomas Prior helped to give institutional form to Irish economic patriotism by founding the Dublin Society in 1731 (the Royal Dublin Society from the granting of its charter in 1750), which held its first meeting on 25 June of that year.[8] The Society has been described recently as a way of creating civil society in Ireland that strove to promote public happiness despite the island's dependent status.[9] Since the 1710s, Prior had demonstrated a practical interest in agricultural and other improvement, renting a large area in County Wicklow and requiring tenants to drain and fence the land, plant trees, and build cottages.[10] Agricultural improvement was one of the main aims of the Society. The minute books of the Society contain the texts of some papers presented to it, and Prior's first paper concerned draining bogs using a method that caused no loss of land.[11] Prior remained an engine of the Society's activities, writing an estimated thirteen of the fifty-two papers offered at Society meetings in 1737 and 1738.[12] The Society also drew up numbered lists of queries on topics in agriculture to be pursued by the Society or submitted to practitioners in other parts of the world where the cultivation of particular crops was successful.[13] The Society noted successful practices, such as that in Riga and Königsberg of sowing seed from lowland flax in the uplands, and vice versa, in order to prevent the degeneration of the crop.[14]

7. Clarke, *Arthur Dobbs Esquire*, pp. 29–30.

8. Meenan and Clarke, 'The RDS 1731–1981', pp. 3, 9.

9. Livesey, 'The Dublin Society in Eighteenth-Century Irish Political Thought'.

10. Mulligan, *The Founders of the Royal Dublin Society*, p. 28.

11. Royal Dublin Society, RDS/MAN, register and minute book, 1731–1733, 1733–1741, 1741–1746, 1750–1757 [facsimile volume containing vols. 1–3], vol. 1, ff. 5–7, 30 September 1731.

12. Mulligan, *The Founders of the Royal Dublin Society*, p. 29.

13. Royal Dublin Society, MS RDS/MAN, register and minute book, vol. 1, ff. 7r, 30 September 1731; 17r, 10 November 1731; 21r, 25 November 1731.

14. Ibid., vol. 1, f. 26r, 9 December 731.

FIGURE 15.1. Charles Spooner, 'Thomas Prior (1682–1751),
Founding Member and Secretary to the Dublin Society', 1752,
courtesy of the National Gallery of Ireland

Activity was not limited to agriculture. A committee of useful
arts met fortnightly on those weeks the Society did not meet; the
heads of a treatise on the problems caused by the lack of small coin
in Ireland were to be drawn up; and Prior himself was to give an
account of the value of imports into Ireland 'distinguisht into two
Heads Viz: such as may be raised or manufactured in this Kingdom and such as cannot be raised or manufactured here'.[15] From

15. Ibid., vol. 1, ff. 30r, 18 December 1731; vol. 2, f. 19r, 24 April 1735; vol. 2, f. 32r, 23
February 1735/36.

31 January 1740, when Samuel Madden gifted £130 personally and £500 in subscriptions for the foundation of prizes for performance in the applied arts, the Society's minutes become more oriented to the administration of the premia. On 5 June that year, the list of premia to be advertised began with those for wheat, barley, hops, and cider, then continued with various kinds of fertilising and cultivation of different kinds of trees or food crops. There were also awards for spinning, weaving, refining flax, and plough design.[16] In 1745, Kilkenny won the prize 'of ten pounds to the City or large town who should best clear themselves of beggars, by employing the poor at work'.[17]

It is often said that Berkeley was a member of the Dublin Society.[18] There is no record of his attendance at a meeting, and it would be highly surprising if he had attended, given his near-continual residence at Cloyne. One bishop of Cloyne, Edward Maule, did attend; he proposed the composition of catechistical instructions for use in charity schools.[19] Berkeley's own references to the Society do not support the case for his membership. He wrote to Prior asking if Prior could provide hemp seed, 'or does your society distribute any?' The pronoun indicates that it was not Berkeley's society. Berkeley uses the same pronoun again nearly ten years later when he encourages the work of Prior's society on the manufacture of glass and paper. By the same token, however, Berkeley was evidently in sympathy with the Society's projects for improvement. He was requesting hemp seed for his own schemes to occupy the poor of his diocese and increase tillage:

> Our spinning-school is in a thriving way. The children begin to find a pleasure in being paid in hard money; which I understand they will not

16. Ibid., vol. 2, 97, 139–42.

17. Ibid., vol. 3, 127, 30 May 1745. See chapter 7 for Berkeley's interest in civic goods made possible through the forced labour of the indigent.

18. See, for example, Rashid, 'Berkeley's *Querist* and Its Influence', p. 38; Breuninger, *Recovering Bishop Berkeley*, p. 144. Both Rashid and Breuninger are taking Luce's statement that Berkeley's projects for the poor of Cloyne were 'extensions of the work of Prior and Madden and the Dublin societies' as a foundation; see Luce, p. 192. Berkeley does not appear in the *List of Members of the Dublin-Society* under 'Berkeley' or 'Dean of Derry'.

19. Royal Dublin Society, MS RDS/MAN, register and minute book, vol. 1, f. 32r, 6 January 1731/32.

give to their parents, but keep to buy clothes for themselves. Indeed I
found it difficult and tedious to bring them to this; but I believe it will
now do. I am building a workhouse for sturdy vagrants, and design to
raise about two acres of hemp for employing them.[20]

Anne describes Berkeley's involvement in textile manufacture in
her notes on Stock's *Life*:

[H]e took great Pains to settle the linen manufacture in Cloyne supplying the inhabitants with flax and paying for all they spun how bad
so ever he gave an house for this purpose hired a Mistress to teach the
girls to Spin and bought a linen Weaver but all to no purpose—they
chose to spin Wool—and thought he meant to raise a great fortune by
their Work——& during the time of the hard frost he gave ᴸ20 a week
for a [deleted word] considerable time to the poor[.][21]

The commitment to agricultural improvement is entirely in accord
with the work of the Dublin Society. It is combined with Berkeley's
interest in turning the behaviour of the native Irish, here the young
in particular, away from customary sloth and profligacy. It is also
possible that Berkeley's interest in agricultural improvement as a
means of producing virtuous society is another connection to the
work of Fénelon, who, through his *Telemachus* and political campaigning, argued for the centrality of agricultural production.[22]

Berkeley presented this work as charity.[23] (Anne Berkeley said
of her late husband in an undated letter to their son George that
'Charity to Mens Souls & Bodies was the sole end of all his projects & ∧^the business of his life'.[24]) He thought of the local popula-

20. Letter 263, 5 March 1737, p. 398; letter 337, 3 July 1746, p. 506. Similar projects
continued nearby, such as the earl of Grandison's construction of the village of Villierstown
on his Dromana estate, establishing the linen industry there in the 1750s. See McBride,
Eighteenth-Century Ireland, p. 138. Percival also planned a settlement near Lohort that
would have employed women in cultivating and spinning flax. See Barnard, *Improving
Ireland?*, p. 137.

21. TCD MS 5936, Stock, *An Account of the Life of George Berkeley*, opposite p. 80.

22. See Rothkrug, *Opposition to Louis XIV*, pp. 234–86.

23. Livesey, 'Berkeley, Ireland, and Eighteenth-Century Intellectual History', p. 462,
notes that for Berkeley charity was 'an inspiration for the alternative strategy of economic
development, centred on the improvement of agricultural productivity and domestic
industry, promulgated by "economic societies" such as the Dublin Society'.

24. BL Add MS 39312, f. 227v.

FIGURE 15.2. William Hincks, 'Spinning', 1791, © The Trustees of the British Museum

tion of Cloyne as 'objects of charity' both material and spiritual. He presented the duty of the people of condition to provide relief and employment following the famine and epidemics of 1741 as partly a matter of self-interest: ultimately they too would suffer if the poor were not relieved.[25] Berkeley told John James that his wife directed 'above a hundred men every day in agriculture of one kind or other'. It was 'a charity which pays it self'.[26] The Berkeleys also ran a medi-

25. Letter 259, Berkeley to Samuel Johnson, 12 March 1736, p. 392; letter 281, Berkeley to Prior, 19 May 1741.

26. Smith, *The Antient and Present State of the County and City of Cork*, I.147, notes the potential of the soil: 'The soil in this neighbourhood is a loamy, grey earth mixed with sand, affording plenty of wheat, small Barley, and potatoes. The chief manure is seasand and burnt clay'.

cal centre: 'we are used to lodge a few stroling sick with a poor tenant or two in Cloyne, and employ a poor woman or two to tend them, and supply them with a few necessaries from our house'.[27] During Berkeley's tenure of the bishopric of Cloyne, the administration of the charity for the clothing, educating, and apprenticing of boys from the diocese continued, with Robert Berkeley in his role as treasurer of Cloyne signing off on the accounts from 1741 (and continuing after Berkeley's lifetime, to 1785).[28] Increasing production to provide for wants, healing, and educating were all expressions of a Christian love of God with long antecedents in Berkeley's thinking.[29]

The charity of Berkeley's time at Cloyne was a contribution to an established Irish economic patriotism, and *The Querist* was a contribution to its established discourse. The text is also, however, a claim by a churchman to a central role for moral and religious education in bringing about economic goods. Others have presented the text as a production in the Church interest, noting that there had been a revolt against the payment of the tithe of agistment, paid on pasturage for cattle.[30] In 1735, Edward Synge, then bishop of Ferns and Leighlin, brought suits to establish his clergy's right to the tithe which were appealed by farmers. A parliamentary committee investigated and found for the farmers, leading to a bill to recover the tithe. There was an outburst of anticlericalism, with some accusing the clergy of holding the economy back. The tithe may, however, have cooperated with one model of improvement, which sought to turn land away from pasture to cropping. And the project of improvement was also still associated for some with the clergy and the imposition of Protestant culture on the native Irish. The division list for the vote on the bill does not suggest that the lines were drawn on grounds of improvement, but

27. Letter 282, 7 June 1741, p. 433; letter 346, Berkeley to Prior, 24 January 1747, p. 523.

28. Representative Church Body of the Church of Ireland Library, MS 870, Bishop Crowe's Charity [volume reversed and paginated], pp. 31, 50, 112. For the charity school movement as a means of producing a suitably educated workforce, rather than necessarily converting Catholics, see Hayton, 'Did Protestantism Fail in Early Eighteenth-Century Ireland?', pp. 169, 177–78.

29. Barnard, 'Improving Clergymen, 1660–1760', p. 138, notes that the religious impulse to improvement combined and sometimes competed with politeness, secular rationalism, or civic humanism.

30. Caffentzis, *Exciting the Industry of Mankind*, pp. 4–5.

that representatives whose regions were significantly pastoral tended to vote against the tithe, and those identified with the Toryism of the reign of Anne and the early Hanoverian period voted for it. A commitment to the legal privileges of the established church was, then, a factor in attitudes to the tithe.[31] Berkeley thought those privileges rested on philosophical grounds.

The Querist

In his economic thinking, Berkeley refused to separate the moral and religious agent from the economic agent.[32] He might be regarded as premodern, in this respect, as modern economics, some have argued, requires such a separation of moral judgement from the indifferent economic mechanism.[33] Berkeley maintained that the economy (which he sometimes simply called 'the nation', as Patrick Kelly notes) requires individual and collective moral endeavour to manage: it is one of those 'public Institutions' in which there should be 'an End proposed, which is to be the Rule and Limit of the Means'. That end should be 'the Well-being of the Whole'.[34]

The economy is not autonomous; it is governed by people who conceive of themselves as a public, a self-conception that requires the renunciation of private interest—or rather, the recognition that true private interest consists in living in a well-ordered state—as well as the collective coordination of wills aiming at proper objects. Such coordination is the public good. The Querist believes that financial institutions are better managed by the public than private investors and asks '[w]hether [. . .] the Community of a Danger, which lulls private Men asleep, ought not to awaken the Public?' The Querist is opposed to political operators who play on private

31. Hayton and Karian, 'Select Document', pp. 304–12. I am deeply indebted to Hayton and Karian in my account. See also McBride, *Eighteenth-Century Ireland*, p. 141.

32. Rashid, 'The Irish School of Economic Development', pp. 365–66, notes that Christianity is an organising principle of the thought of the school he identifies.

33. Letwin, *The Origins of Scientific Economics*, pp. 147–48; see also Kelly, 'Berkeley's *Querist*', p. 209: 'Berkeley's view of economic activity as a necessary, but definitely subordinate, part of the divine plan for mankind revealed him as fundamentally out of sympathy with the confidence in the beneficial effects of the growth of commercial society so widespread among the thinkers of the Enlightenment'.

34. Kelly, 'Berkeley and the Idea of a National Bank', pp. 167, 171; *Querist*, I.17, §137.

interests to the detriment of public spirit and notes that the public has to think for those who will not.[35] The public can claim the labour of criminals for its works and can declare fine gentlemen and gentlewomen of fashion who consume irresponsibly to be public nuisances.[36] The Querist asks '[w]hether there be not an Art or Skill in governing human Pride, so as to render it subservient to the Public Aim?'[37] Passions such as pride must be governed by an elite group of philosophical legislators to produce public goods, which do not simply follow from the passions, or from consumption, because increased productivity without the right kind of activity in the body of the subjects is not a true good.

The governing class are responsible for ensuring the people produce and consume in the right ways. The three volumes of *The Querist* culminate in Berkeley formulating his own economic indicator. The Querist asks '[w]hether the Sum of the Faculties put into Act, or, in other Words, the united Action of a whole People doth not constitute the *Momentum* of a State?'[38] The term 'momentum' is a provocation to the analysts and infidels with whom Berkeley was controversialising over mathematical terms and procedures in his first years at Cloyne. Berkeley had cast doubt over the existence of the objects the analytical language claimed to name, the 'momentaneous Increments' or 'the Moments or nascent Increments': 'An Increment generated in a finite Particle of Time, is it self a finite Particle; and cannot therefore be a Momentum'.[39] Movement is not an object, but the effect of a will, an effect that can signify that will, if we are good readers of other minds. Thus, to increase momentum is to increase spirit or to inspire. The Querist asks if a national bank would not be 'the ready Means to put Spirit into this State', if it would not be useful, for supplying manufactures and trade with stock, for regulating exchange, for quickening commerce, and for putting spirit into the people?[40] He asks '[w]hether

35. *Querist*, III.6, §30; I.7, §§51, 54.

36. Ibid., I.7–8, §§58–59; I.8, §62; I.18, §147.

37. Ibid., II.18, §161.

38. Ibid., III.38, §308.

39. *Analyst*, §§3, 4, 11. Caffentzis, 'Algebraic Money', offers a full contextual account of the relationship between *The Analyst* and *The Querist*.

40. *Querist*, III.39, §315; II.16, §142.

the immediate Mover, the Blood and Spirits, be not Money, Paper or Metal, and whether the Soul or Will of the Community, which is the prime Mover, that governs and directs the Whole, be not the Legislature?'[41] The state moves the economy by means of money. A more spirited economy, one with more momentum, is not just more active but also more orderly; it participates more of the divinity by doing more to realise God's intentions for humans.

SECTARIANISM

Berkeley's economy is not only moralised but sectarian.[42] When social strata are distinguished, the sectarian divide is often implicit: the Querist asks '[w]hether the upper Part of this People are not truly *English*, by Blood, Language, Religion, Manners, Inclination, and Interest?'[43] On occasion Berkeley's inclusivity is marked. The (Catholic) peasant might aspire to form part of the public: 'Suppose the Bulk of our Inhabitants had Shoes to their Feet, Cloaths to their Backs, and Beef in their Bellies? Might not such a State be eligible for the Publick, even though the 'Squires were condemned to drink Ale and Cyder?'[44] But although the Querist thinks the native Irish should be included in schemes of prosperity, and does not think forced conversion is advisable, many recommendations are directed towards persuading and inducing Catholics to convert: they could be made to hear sermons, or to swear allegiance to the king in temporal matters; lower-ranking clergy, speaking Irish, could be employed in conversion; Catholics could be apprenticed out to Protestant masters.[45] Here the therapeutic (the educated

41. Ibid., III.39, §318.

42. Breuninger, 'Berkeley and Ireland', pp. 114, 116–17, 120, notes that Berkeley's inclusive economic plan was nonetheless differentiated along the sectarian divide, with plans to stimulate the activity of the Catholic peasantry and curb the luxury of the Protestant landowners.

43. *Querist*, I.12, §97; see also I.8, §64, and I.19, §164, for the metaphor of the roots and upper parts of a tree in the same context.

44. Ibid., I.14, §118.

45. Ibid., I.34–37, §§288–311; Breuninger, *Recovering Bishop Berkeley*, pp. 141, 157, notes Berkeley's attention to the Catholic community in various texts of the Cloyne period, but shies away from addressing the consistently missionary aspect of Berkeley's social project.

attempt to help others correct their desires) approximates to the disciplinary (the governors inducing the people towards loyalty and obedience).

The literary form of *The Querist* might have primed readers for its treatment of the relative duties and privileges of different ethnic-religious strata of a population. The format was not new, having been practised at least since the early 1690s.[46] It was used as a means to defend dissenters from accusations of disloyalty and to argue for the repeal of the Tests, as an overreaching expression of the authority of the established church:

> Whether any thing can threaten the *Church* so much, as the Unchari-tableness of any great Number of her own *Clergy*, their unreason-able Jealousies, their Affectation of a Monopoly of Civil Power, their attempting to set up what is call'd the *Spiritual Discipline of the Church* over the Laity, by *Codes* of Ecclesiastical Canons; and to obtain new Laws, and retain old ones, in their Disfavour and Prejudice? All which tend to alienate the Affections of the People from her, and to raise their Passions against her? And some, or all of which, have been the great Sources of all Misfortunes that ever befel Her.[47]

This text may have provoked Swift to write his *Queries Relating to the Sacramental Test* of 1732, in which he suggests that the role of Protestant dissent in the wars of the seventeenth century was just as pernicious as that of the Catholics at any time before or since; he also accuses dissenters of manipulating fear of Jacobite invasion in requesting the repeal of the Tests, notionally so that they might serve in the army. Dissenting desire for 'more than a bare Tolera-tion' is a recent and dangerous innovation, one fanned by 'that great Tenderness towards Sectaries, which now so much prevails', and that owes less to 'Fears of *Popery*' than to 'that Spirit of Atheism, Deism, Scepticism, and universal Immorality, which al good Men

---

46. See McBride, *Eighteenth-Century Ireland*, pp. 298–99: 'The queries format, the list of rhetorical questions sometimes thought to have been invented by Bishop Berkeley, was in fact used as early as 1691 with the short tract *Weighty queries*, a demand for a punitive land settlement'.

47. *Queries Concerning the Reasonableness of Repealing the Corporation and Test Acts*, p. 16, §16; see also pp. 22–23, §26, for the view that dissenters are more loyal to the Hanoverian regime than (Scottish?) Episcopalian ministers.

so much lament'.[48] Berkeley's queries sit within a tradition of questioning and then asserting the privileges and authority of the established church in the face of free thought, dissent, and Catholicism.

The larger project for the conversion of the native Irish in which Berkeley was engaged has its specifically economic component. He may have been responding to earlier considerations of the relationship between religious schism and the economy. William Petty, whose work on 'political arithmetic' in the late seventeenth century was foundational for economic thinking of the eighteenth century, points to personal religious allegiance rather than the form of government as a key correlate of economic activity: 'it is to be observed that Trade doth not (as some think) best flourish under Popular Governments, but rather that Trade is most vigorously carried on, in every State and Government, by the Heterodox part of the same, and such as profess Opinions different from what are publickly established'.[49] Petty does not say explicitly that this is the result of dissenters being excluded from forms of civic participation that might otherwise satisfy ambition (and/or greed), but that would be a reasonable inference. Petty's motives for writing are close to Berkeley's: 'To shew the great effect of *Unity, industry,* and *obedience,* in order to the Common Safety, and each Man's particular happiness'.[50] But Petty is an economic modern for whom politics itself has become a form of arithmetic. His interest in unity, of the four kingdoms of Great Britain and Ireland principally, is on account of the cost of government, with its creation of rivalries and suspicions between different national groups and different orders of law (civil and ecclesiastical). Government, he recognises, is cheaper for concentrated, urbanised populations, living under one disambiguated legal code. Declining to govern the conscience of subjects is therefore a saving. For Petty, government is a cost, not the exercise of a philosophical elite fulfilling their part of a providential scheme. He makes no place for the philosophical education of an elite and

48. Swift, *Queries Relating to the Sacramental Test*, pp. 351–52.

49. Petty, *Political Arithmetick*, p. 25. Berkeley's use of the title suggests his knowledge of the text and hints that there may be more to the matter than Petty acknowledges: 'Whether we are apprized, of all the Uses that may be made of political Arithmetick?' (*Querist*, II.22, §199).

50. Petty, *Political Arithmetick*, p. 117.

suggests that 'study of the *Metaphysicks*, or other such needless *Speculation*', is only to be tolerated insofar as it refreshes the mind for useful labour.[51] Berkeley, as we have seen, has an interest in the government of conscience, and in economy as a domain in which human flourishing might be encouraged, interests more characteristic of the political economist than the political arithmetician, as Mary Poovey makes the distinction.[52]

The case of Ireland was unusual in Europe, in that it saw a large Catholic rather than a small Protestant population brought under the control of a multiregional confessional state.[53] Berkeley certainly wants to unify the interests of the different populations. In queries added to the collected edition of the text in 1750 and extended in the republication in the *Miscellany* of 1752 (and no doubt reflecting on the scare of Jacobite landings in 1745), he notes, both perhaps echoing Petty and complicating the underlying association of Catholicism with the underdeveloped peasantry, that Catholics are predominant traders in port towns, and that it would be best if their interests could be more closely united with those of the government by enabling them to buy land:

> 265. Whether a 'Squire possessed of Land to the Value of a thousand Pounds *per Annum*, or a Merchant worth twenty thousand Pounds in Cash would have most Power to do good or evil upon any Emergency? And whether the suffering Roman Catholics to purchase forfeited Lands, would not be good Policy as tending to unite their Interest with that of the Government?
>
> 266. Whether the Sea-ports of *Galway, Limerick, Cork*, and *Waterford*, are not to be looked on as Keys of this Kingdom? And whether the Merchants are not possessed of these Keys; and who are the most numerous Merchants in those Cities?
>
> 267. Whether a Merchant cannot more speedily raise a Sum, more easily conceal or transfer his Effects, and engage in any desperate Design with more safety, than a landed Man, whose Estate is a Pledge for his Behaviour?
>
> 268. Whether a wealthy Merchant bears not a great Sway among

51. Ibid., pp. 87, 91–92, 23–27, 38.
52. Poovey, 'Between Political Arithmetic and Political Economy', pp. 62–63.
53. McBride, *Eighteenth-Century Ireland*, pp. 205–6.

the Populace of a trading City? And whether Power be not ultimately lodged in the People?[54]

Popular power is a threat (as was recognised in the *Discourse
Addressed to Magistrates*), and it can be controlled by the exaction
of a pledge, here not explicitly an oath of allegiance but a proximate
oath in the form of landownership that implies willing subjection
to the authorities who ensure the preservation of property.[55] It is a
tension in *The Querist* that a philosophy of money that defines it as
power or the entitlement to another's industry, and that identifies
property with transferable power, distinguishes between land and
money in a way so redolent of the political discourse of the land
in the reign of Queen Anne, such as Swift's history of its four last
years.[56]

ENCOURAGING AND RESTRAINING APPETITES

The hints of the Querist are, then, divided along broad, but not
rigid, class and sectarian lines: the Protestant gentry ought to
restrain their appetite for imported luxuries in order to stimulate
the local economy, and the Catholic peasantry ought to strive to
fulfil their appetites through the exercise of industry.[57] The greed
and luxury of landowners constitutes a national evil because they
draw agricultural produce and small coinage out of the country

54. *Miscellany*, p. 149.

55. For the suggestion that the changes made for the 1750 republication of *The Querist*
reflect a loss of faith in the political nation as the willing manager of public finances, with
a concomitant increase in emphasis on civil life and civil structures and less conditional
toleration of Catholics, see Livesey, 'Berkeley, Ireland, and Eighteenth-Century Intellectual
History', pp. 468–72.

56. *Querist*, I.4–5, §33: 'Whether it be not the Opinion or Will of the People, exciting
them to Industry, that truly enricheth a Nation? And whether this doth not principally
depend on the Means for counting, transferring and preserving Power, that is, Property
of all Kinds?' For a discussion of the further additional queries directly preceding these,
treating the conversion of Catholics through preaching and schooling in Irish, and for the
underlying racialisation of Irish poverty, see chapter 7; Swift, *The History of the Four Last
Years of Queen Anne*, pp. 68–70.

57. See Breuninger, *Recovering Bishop Berkeley*, p. 134. See also Kelly, 'Berkeley's
Querist', pp. 202–3: 'For Berkeley the Irish poor were not fully rational, and thus needed to
be incentivized to labour by awakening their appetite to consume (rather than appealing
to their reason, as was the case with the gentry)'.

and stimulate only foreign markets. The native Irish are depicted as little better than beasts. These two tendencies may be illustrated very fully from the first part of the text. The Querist asks:

> 19. *Qu.* Whether the Bulk of our *Irish* Natives are not kept from thriving, by that cynical Content in Dirt and Beggary, which they possess to a Degree beyond any other People in Christendom?
>
> 20. *Qu.* Whether the creating of Wants be not the likeliest way to produce Industry in a People? And whether if our Peasants were accustomed to eat Beef, and wear Shoes, they would not be more Industrious?
>
> 61. *Qu.* Whether he whose Luxury consumeth foreign Products, and whose Industry produceth nothing domestic to exchange for them, is not so far forth injurious to his Country?
>
> 62. *Qu.* Whether, consequently, the fine Gentlemen, whose Employment is only to dress, drink, and play, be not a public Nuisance?
>
> 110. *Qu.* Whether those, who drink foreign Liquors, and deck themselves and their Families with foreign Ornaments, are not so far forth to be reckon'd Absentees?
>
> 172. *Qu.* Whether national Wants ought not to be the Rule of Trade? And whether the most pressing Wants of the Majority ought not to be first consider'd?
>
> 196. *Qu.* Whether the Gentleman of Estate hath a Right to be idle; and whether he ought not to be the great Promoter and Director of Industry, among his Tenants and Neighbours?[58]

Both sectors of the population are to be encouraged to industry, which alone is wealth.[59] Berkeley's programme hinged on a transformation as paradoxical as that of matter into ideas, as Patrick Kelly has noted:

> Berkeley stood on its head the apparently insoluble problem of the Irish economy, namely its inability to provide a living for its starving masses. The very needs of the people now became the motor to transform the economy, and the technical key to bringing this about lay in

---

58. *Querist*, I.3, §§19–20; I.6, 61–62; I.13, §110; I.22, §196.
59. Ibid., I.1, §3; I.5, §40.

the adoption of paper money to transform their real physical needs into economic demand.[60]

More will be said shortly on the scheme of a national bank that was to facilitate the transformation of need into demand.

If Berkeley's insistence on the necessity of a philosophical legislator to govern a nation/economy might be called premodern, there is nothing unsophisticated about the psychological modelling of choice in which he engages. Berkeley does not think human appetites are given in advance, but rather formed through a practice that engages people's beliefs and opinions, individually and collectively, in the forming of wants. It is 'the Opinion or Will of the People, exciting them to Industry, that truly enricheth a Nation'. The industry that constitutes wealth is dependent on opinion—the opinion of what is desirable, which itself therefore becomes a matter of public policy.[61] The Querist asks

> 10. *Qu.* Whether Fashion doth not create Appetites, and whether the prevailing Will of a Nation is not the Fashion?
> 11. *Qu.* Whether the Current of Industry and Commerce be not determin'd by this prevailing Will?
> 12. *Qu.* Whether it be not owing to Custom that most Fashions are agreeable?
> 13. *Qu.* Whether it may not concern the Wisdom of the Legislature to interpose in the making of fashions [. . .] ?[62]

Appetites are subject to change based on custom, change that can be influenced by other people and by the human tendency towards imitation.[63] Our individual and collective wants or appetites can be educated, and so economic problems are ultimately best addressed as questions of thinking, for which the governing elite are responsible. The Querist asks '[w]hether Reflection in the better Sort might not soon remedy our Evils? And whether our real Defect be not a

---

60. Kelly, 'Berkeley and the Idea of a National Bank', p. 169; see also Kelly, 'Berkeley's *Querist*', p. 199.

61. *Querist*, I.4, §33; I.6, §46; see chapter 11 for Berkeley's treatment of human capacities as dependent on cultivation.

62. Ibid., I.5, §§10–13.

63. Ibid., II.2, §14.

wrong way of thinking?'[64] Thinking differently, wanting different things, and living differently to attain them are real solutions to economic ills.

I would like to make two contrasts to Berkeley's thinking on appetite and economy, one with Bernard Mandeville and one with William King. Mandeville suggests that the moral status of individual or collective acts of production or consumption is irrelevant to the economic good they can produce. In *The Querist*, a legislator should be a reflective individual who is able to elicit mutual benefit from the activity of different kinds of people, for 'the general Good of the Whole', or the 'Well-being of the Whole'.[65] Berkeley's position is to be distinguished from Mandeville's, which he satirises through the person of Lysicles in *Alciphron*. Lysicles tells his audience that they will be amazed 'at the wonderfully extended Scene of Benefits which arise from the single Vice of Drunkenness, so much run down and declaimed against by all grave Reformers'.[66] Mandeville had argued that 'Virtue is made Friends with Vice' in activities such as distilling spirits:

> The short-sighted Vulgar in the Chain of Causes seldom see further than one Link; but those who can enlarge their View, and will give themselves the Leisure of gazing on the Prospect of concatenated Events, may, in a hundred Places see *Good* spring up, and pullulate from *Evil*, as naturally as Chickens do from Eggs. The Money that arises from the Duties upon Malt, is a considerable Part of the National Revenue, and should no Spirits be distill'd from it, the *Publick* Treasure would prodigiously suffer on that Head. But, if we would set in a true Light the many Advantages, and large Catalogue of solid Blessings that accrue from, and are owing to the Evil I treat of, we are to consider the Rents that are received, the Ground that is till'd, the Tools that are made, the Cattle that are employ'd, and above all, the Multitude of Poor that are maintain'd, by the Variety of Labour, required in Husbandry, in Malting, in Carriage and

---

64. Ibid., I.7, §50.

65. Ibid., II.19, §170; I.17, §137.

66. *Alciphron*, II.2. For the view that Berkeley perhaps knew Mandeville only at second hand, and that Mandeville was, in fact, a thorough critic of contemporary vice who merely took a more absolute view of the cleavage between secular, commercial society and a religious society, see dos Santos, 'Berkeley face à Mandeville', esp. pp. 173–76.

Distillation, before we can have that Product of Malt, which we call *Low Wines*, and is but the Beginning from which the various Spirits are afterwards to be made.

Mandeville does not discriminate between the luxury of the debauchee and of the person of taste: in his enlarged view, all forms of consumption are equally beneficial to the state. The goods of private individuals and families are not necessarily commensurate with the goods of the state. It is a delusion to believe that individual goods are found in public goods. Though Berkeley and Mandeville may ultimately prescribe a similar course of action (state intervention to maximise productivity, especially by employing the lower orders), their ways of thinking about psycho-social and moral goods are strongly antagonistic.[67]

Berkeley, perhaps spurred by the 1731 publication of Edmund Law's translation of *De Origine Mali*, may also be challenging William King's suggestion that people can make objects good by conferring value upon them in an act of election. I suggested in chapter 2 that King's account left open the possibility of people choosing goods that were intended to be understood by his audience as ills, using his example of an atheist who sees undergoing torture in defence of his beliefs (or lack of them) as a good. Such an example is intended, and would have been taken by someone like Berkeley, as an example of how depraved human will can be. King seems to accept that depravity as part of a universe in which partial ills generate the greatest possible universal good: 'God', he says, 'will procure the Good of the whole by our Folly no less than by our Wisdom'. He has just given an example of the accumulation of an estate through an ill choice, and its being spent on idle luxuries by an heir: this is just the same, from King's point of view, as if the money had been gifted to the poor.[68] From a perspective focusing on the corruption of the human will, then, King comes to a position not unlike Mandeville's, in which social goods may truly

---

67. Mandeville, *The Fable of the Bees*, pp. 117, 123–24, 144, 209 ('it is the Interest of all Rich Nations, that the greatest part of the Poor should almost never be Idle, and yet continually spend what they get'), 211–12. For the best account of these issues, see Tolonen, 'Berkeley and Mandeville'.

68. King, *An Essay on the Origin of Evil*, pp. 204–5, 280–81, 281.

follow from individual choices that are vicious.[69] Berkeley does not imagine that human choices are so detached from the choices of higher spirits. Indeed, it is the purpose of his economic writings to impress upon higher human spirits their responsibility to guide and shape the choices of lower human spirits; Berkeley's sense of this personal responsibility extends upwards to God, whose management of the phenomenal world is guidance and instruction to humans as to how they should choose. For Berkeley, it matters what kinds of choices individuals make in the accomplishment of God's providence: it is not all the same whether an estate is squandered in idle luxury or well managed in procuring the continuous health of all classes of people who depend upon it. While both King and Berkeley recognise that people can choose objects to value, Berkeley is more emphatic about the role of education, cultivation, and guidance in shaping those choices so that they conform with God's will.

MONEY AND BANKS

The Querist strongly hints at the best practical means of improvement. They mostly concern the availability, value, and function of money. Thomas Prior had written on coinage before Berkeley published *The Querist*. In his view, absenteeism contributes to a critical shortage of coin: coin leaves the country to pay absentee landlords when the value of exports drops below the rent to be paid, and the smaller-denomination coins leave the country first. There was far less money in circulation in Ireland than in England; Prior estimated the figures as 'above 40 Shillings for every Head, 13s.4d. in Silver, and the rest in Gold' in the latter, and 'but 4s. 5d. ¼ for each Head, 5d. in Silver, and the rest in Gold' in the former.[70] Ireland had no currency of its own and attributed values other than the face value of the coin to currencies from elsewhere. Prior notes the contribution this situation made to Ireland's currency difficulties, which arose

69. For the possibility of Mandeville holding an Augustinian view of morality, see Maurer, 'Self-interest and Sociability', pp. 294–96, and, more cautiously, Tolonen, *Mandeville and Hume*, pp. 26–27.

70. Prior, *Observations on Coin in General*, pp. 294, 319.

[f]irst, from our Coin's being made up of the Money of several countries, each of them of different Alloys, Weights, and Values. Second, from our reckoning our money by pounds shillings and pence, without having anyone species that answers any of these denominations; third, from our Coin's being divided into such gross and unequal parts, that it is almost impossible to make alterations in their Value, without running into inconvenient fractions[.][71]

Prior considers alterations in the nominal value of coin as a response and recognises that money exhibits some of the same prejudices or customary dispositions as its users: 'tho' the Rates of Commodities may not always immediately rise or fall in the same Degree, that Money is raised or lowered, in Time they will not fail to come to the same nominal Values of the Coins'.[72]

The way to address these currency issues, Berkeley thought, and their dragging effect on the economy, particularly in smaller transactions, was a national bank. Queries treating the subject of a national bank were selected from the three volumes of *The Querist* and republished in 1737 as *Queries Relating to a National Bank*, together with a public letter Berkeley had published in Dublin newspapers through Prior in early April 1737.[73] Berkeley travelled to Dublin at this time, as is known from his presence before the Irish Lords committee on religion in February 1738 in connection with the Blasters. It is very likely that the foundation of a national bank was another campaigning objective of Berkeley's visit to the capital.[74]

Proposals for an Irish bank had been put before Parliament in the 1720–1721 session, and rejected. Hercules Rowley, one of the opponents, argued that either the measure would be repealed

71. Ibid., p. 332; see also Johnston, *Bishop Berkeley's Querist in Historical Perspective*, pp. 55–57: 'We have here the tremendous paradox of Irish money in this period. There was no Irish currency—the standard coins in circulation were English or foreign—but there was an Irish monetary unit and what may be called a purely conceptual Irish monetary system. [. . .] Monetary contracts, leases, etc., continued to be made in terms of a conceptual Irish currency'.

72. Prior, *Observations on Coin in General*, p. 324.

73. Letters 263–64, Berkeley to Prior, 5 March 1736/37, and Berkeley to A.B., 26 March 1737, pp. 397–403.

74. Caffentzis, 'The Failure of Berkeley's Bank', p. 230, imaginatively reconstructs the quotidian form of this campaign, without citing specific evidence, speaking of 'the objections, rejections, retorts, and evasions he encountered in the endless dinner parties, social gatherings, and lobbying in the course of his campaign for the National Bank'.

by the English Parliament or the Irish would be punished by the English through withdrawal of trade. The Irish Parliament wrote to the king after the rejection of the bill, and an interdiction was placed on future proposals for a bank. Following the crashes of 1720, Irish economic patriots remained sceptical of financial innovation.[75] Berkeley's queries therefore constitute a risk not unlike the risk Swift took in writing the *Drapier's Letters*, and he may have modelled his pamphlet series as a form of civil disobedience on Swift's letters. The 'Advertisement on Occasion of Re-publishing the Querist', however, probably has Swift in view when it distinguishes the Querist's hints from a more aggressive form of Irish satire that 'exasperates the Minds of Persons affected thereby, does not always manifest either the Policy or good Nature of the Authors; as this way of treating the Subject is more likely to frustrate than promote the good Ends for which perhaps the Piece was principally written'.[76]

Due consideration was given to existing or proposed models for national banks in *The Querist*. The Bank of England as it was, and the bank of Scotland as John Law had proposed it, put too much power in private hands—those of their shareholders. The problem of political manipulation of the bank could be avoided 'by excluding the Managers of the Bank from a Share in the Legislature'.[77] The prospect of officers of a bank becoming parliamentarians and exerting influence over the constitution was a fear of the author of an anonymous pamphlet Berkeley refers to, *The Vindication and Advancement of our National Constitution and Credit*.[78] Berkeley's reference to this pamphlet concerns the circumstances in which a bank might usurp sovereign power. The argument is based on a parallel between the banks of England and Genoa. Genoa borrowed from its citizens to pay for a war (as did William III). It gave over its monopoly on customs to a bank to repay the people. The government then borrowed more from the bank, mortgaging towns and lands. A bank that is principal lender to a government may

75. Ibid., pp. 233–35.

76. Ibid., I.i–ii.

77. Ibid., I.25, §216; I.26, §222; I.26, §224.

78. Ibid., I.24, §214; *The Vindication and Advancement of our National Constitution and Credit*, p. 45.

subvert it, 'taking the Supreme Power to it self. [. . .] [W]hen this is done, there is a Foundation laid of perpetual Revolutions in the Government; the *Means of Subversion* being constantly transferable from one Sort of Men to another'.[79] (Again, liquidity of assets is linked to political instability.) The author proposes a way out for England: the government should issue notes for its existing debts to individuals, which would then become the object of trade; at the same time, their owners would contract an interest in the preservation of the government. This scheme would make lenders dependent on the government, rather than the reverse.[80] (It should be noted that Swift thought William III's policy was precisely to give individual lenders an interest in preventing the government from defaulting on its debts.[81]) Berkeley is in agreement that the bank must not be allowed to become a risk to the constitution, nor to the concentration of power in the hands of those who have traditionally inherited it.

The Querist associates the steadiness, stability, and discretion of public banks with the same qualities in the states that run them. He asks of the Bank of Venice '[w]hether the great Exactness and Integrity, with which this Bank is managed, be not the chief Support of that Republick?' The banks of Venice and Amsterdam could not be broken other than by the collapse of the states themselves.[82] Appropriate relations between banks and sovereign powers, it is suggested, produce a tendency away from absolutism in a monarch and towards discreet public management in the people. The Querist asks '[w]hether an absolute Monarchy be so apt to gain Credit, and whether the Vivacity of some Humours could so well suit with the slow Steps and discreet Management which a Bank requires?'[83] The dispositions associated with the banking profession (discretion) are preferable to those associated with absolute monarchy (caprice). The Querist is saying that establishing a national bank in an appropriate relationship with sovereign power will help to produce socially useful dispositions such as discretion. (One might

79. *The Vindication and Advancement of our National Constitution and Credit*, p. 6.

80. Ibid., pp. 77–78, 98.

81. Swift, *The History of the Four Last Years of Queen Anne*, pp. 68–69.

82. *Querist*, II.4, §36; II.6, §54.

83. Ibid., II.7, §66.

recall at this point the scorn expressed by the right-thinkers in *Alci-phron* for people who have passed their days in offices casting up accounts.)

John Law and Louis XIV were in Berkeley's mind when the Querist criticised vivacity of disposition. Law's proposal for a land bank for Scotland, first published in 1705 and in a second edition in 1720, was judged by the bookseller who reissued it to have modified the dispositions of the French monarch and stabilised his relation-ship with the people: 'He has made the Increase of the Revenues of an Arbitrary Government depend upon the Subjects free Enjoy-ment of their Property'.[84] Law was an innovator, but doubts about his methods increased after the collapse of his Mississippi scheme, which had combined a paper currency issue with the accumula-tion of monopolistic control over colonial expansion and other state functions. Yet Law's project shared much with Berkeley. He was writing for the benefit of a nation that had all the advantages of geography and natural resources but whose people, like the Irish, were a burden, for 'Laziness and want of Honesty are natural to us'.[85] Law saw that a stock of money, available to all, facilitated prosperity:

> As Money encreas'd, the Disadvantages and Inconveniencies of Barter were remov'd; the Poor and Idle were employ'd, more of the Land was labour'd, the Product encreas'd, Manufactures and Trade improv'd, the Landed-men lived better, and the People with less dependance on them.

So vital is money that ''tis with little Success Laws are made, for employing the Poor or Idle in Countries where Money is scarce'.[86]

Making land the security for the issue of a paper currency is the other significant feature Berkeley's proposals shared with Law. For Law, land had the advantage over silver as a guarantor for a paper currency because its value could be raised by improvement. His scheme proposed the issue of notes on the basis of land sales or valuations conducted by commissioners.[87] The Querist's proposal

84. Law, *Money and Trade Consider'd*, Bookseller to Reader, sig. A1.
85. Ibid., pp. 89–90.
86. Ibid., pp. 10–11.
87. Ibid., pp. 69–70, 81. But note that Law acknowledges demand as a determinant of value, and that silver can be in greater or lesser demand.

is that 'the Notes [. . .] be issued in Lots, to be lent at Interest on mortgaged Lands, the whole Number of Lots to be divided among the four Provinces, rateably to the Number of Hearths in each'.[88] As well as to Law, Berkeley makes reference to the problems of land banks issuing paper money in New England. The problems there have 'sprung from the over-rating their Lands, and issuing Paper without Discretion, and from the Legislators breaking their own Rules in Favour of themselves, thus sacrificing the Public to their private Benefit'.[89] Patrick Kelly has argued that the lack of enforcement of the conditions for note issues had an effect on their value and caused problems for the paper currency of Rhode Island. He has suggested that Berkeley thought paper currencies issued on land values particularly well suited for underdeveloped colonial economies, including Ireland. But he has also pointed to the peculiarity that Berkeley should want land to back a currency when money has been identified as nothing other than the power to excite industry.[90]

According to the Querist, money is 'in Truth, Tickets or Tokens for conveying and recording [. . .] Power' 'to command the Industry of others'. Money is 'a Ticket, which entitles to Power'. '[F]acilitating and quickening the Circulation of Power to supply Wants' is the motive for monetary reform. There should only be enough money to record the surplus power of a population (i.e., the quantity by which their productive power exceeds need or demand in any given period).[91] Understanding money as nothing more than the sign of a power to command others makes it easy for Berkeley to be a committed cartalist.[92] But once a certain form of ticket or token is employed, it becomes a factor in the human interactions

88. *Querist*, I.27–28, §233.

89. Ibid., I.32, §275.

90. Kelly, 'Berkeley and the Idea of a National Bank', pp. 178, 182–83.

91. *Querist*, I.5, §37; III.23, §176; III.24, §186; II.14, §122.

92. Berkeley was not the first to recognise that monetary values are the work of imagination rather than the presence of a certain mass of a certain metal. Law, *Money and Trade Consider'd*, p. 9, noted that silver could gain two additional forms of value when it was used as money—simply by being money (and so useful) or being in particular demand as money. 'If either of these Values are imaginary, then all Value is so; for no Goods have any Value, but from the Uses they are apply'd to, and according to the Demand for them, in proportion to their Quantity'.

of which it is part. Berkeley considers altering the value of coin in addition to or alongside the foundation of the bank and suggests that the total face value should be maintained in any revaluation. These considerations are found in the vicinity of the Querist's recognition that people's prejudices must be taken into account when a bank is founded—it should be introduced slowly.[93] Money is only the mark of a power; once it is integrated into the set of rules by which people might live better lives, however, consideration must be given to its material (phenomenal) form and the history of that form in human transactions. The Querist's attitude to money is, like *Alciphron*, an instance of Berkeley recognising that changes in behaviour are gradual, not the sudden determinations of reasoning given instant effect.[94] Even though ideas are entirely passive, and all causes ultimately reside in spirits, the ways in which certain ideas have historically made it possible for spirits to behave means that they cannot simply be altered at will. They may be arbitrary signs, but once they have played a role in shaping practice towards some conceived good, prejudice associates them with the power of which they are a sign.

LUXURY AND THE ARTS

The campaign for a national bank failed, but Berkeley remained committed to his therapeutic (and disciplinary) vision of the morally improved Irish economy. He wrote to John Percival Jr in the early 1740s encouraging him to pursue an agrarian law, even if the times made its successful passage very unlikely: 'As luxury seems the real original root of those evils under which we groan, avarice, ambition & corruption; must it not seem at the same time that agrarian and sumptuary laws are highly expedient if we would cut out the core of the national evil'.[95]

93. *Querist*, III.21, 22, §§164, 169; III.17, §131.
94. Grzelinski, 'Berkeley's Redefinition of Free-Thinking', p. 186, notes of *Alciphron* V: 'Here [. . .] Berkeley puts much more emphasis, than in his previous works, on the gradual progress and soothing of customs by means of religion. [. . .] These remarks manifest Berkeley's withdrawal from rational and religious rigors typical of his *Passive Obedience* in favour of an affirmation of the necessity of a gradual progress of the whole society'.
95. Letter 291, 24 January 1742, p. 442; letter 296, 26 March 1742, p. 448.

Berkeley's critique of luxury never extends to one class of objects that one might reasonably consider superfluous: the objects of taste and aesthetic pleasure. The Querist thinks that art objects are some of the best examples of the creation of wealth through human industry and presents the Italian villa as a social, economic, and aesthetic model for the gentry.[96] Berkeley's own episcopal palace was not wanting ornament. He is regarded by one topologist as having

> successfully transplanted the polite arts, which heretofore flourished only in a warmer soil, to this northern climate. Painting and musick are no longer strangers to *Ireland*, nor confined to *Italy*. In the episcopal palace of *Cloyne*, the eye is entertained with a great variety of good paintings, as well as the ear with concerts of excellent musick. There are here some pieces of the best masters, as a *Magdalen* of Sir *Peter Paul Rubens*, some heads by *Van Dyke* and *Kneller*, besides several good paintings performed in the house, an example so happy, that it has diffused itself into the adjacent gentlemen's houses, and there is at present a pleasing emulation raised in this country, to vie with each other in these kind of performances. The great usefulness of *Design* in the manufactures of stuffs, silks, diapers, damasks, tapestry, embroidery, earthern ware, sculpture, architecture, cabinet work, and an infinite number of other arts is sufficiently evident.[97]

Though Italy was the example, the art collection centred on Dutch and Flemish masters who spent time in Britain. Paintings by the Berkeleys themselves hung nearby, and had stimulated other artistic activity in the region. Local manufactures in the useful arts also possessed their share of finesse, and the use of design, a principle shared by the fine and useful arts, is present in Smith's description just as it is in *The Querist*.[98]

Smith is also struck by the musical culture of Berkeley's home. Its suffusion in the life of the household was evident in Berkeley's correspondence with Isaac Gervais—who had provided Anne (later said to be 'inferior to no singer in the kingdom') with Italian

---

96. *Querist*, I.10, §76; I.15, §126.
97. Smith, *The Antient and Present State of the County and City of Cork*, I.146–47.
98. *Querist*, I.9–10, §§69–75.

FIGURE 15.3. Bernard Mulrenin, 'View of the Palace of Cloyne from the South or Garden Front', between 1787 and 1829, courtesy of the National Library of Ireland

psalms—asking him to procure a bass violin and an old viol from France. Berkeley also asked Percival for help in finding strings for cellos. He told Gervais that music 'is at present the reigning passion at Cloyne. To be plain, we are musically mad. If you would know what that is, come and see'.[99] Berkeley's musical taste was shaped in part by his tours in Italy, where he observed the role of music and dancing as something between symptom of disease and the therapy that cured it in the behaviour of tarantati in southern Italy. For Berkeley, music is a means of harmonising the passions, of bringing the soul into the state of health described in *Alciphron*, that 'healthy Constitution of Soul, when the Notions are right, the Judgments true, the Will regular, the Passions and Appetites directed to their proper Objects, and confined within due Bounds'.[100] As early as the *Notebooks*, Berkeley had identi-

99. Letter 289, 12 January 1742, p. 441; letter 290, 19 January 1742; letter 292, 2 February 1742; letter 303, 29 October 1742, p. 455; letter 353, Berkeley to Percival, 14 March 1747, p. 530; letter 302, Berkeley to Gervais, 6 September 1743, p. 454.

100. *Alciphron*, II.12 (Euphranor).

fied the pleasures of the eye and ear as those that do not surfeit. Their therapeutic value was evident in the practices of the Berkeley household in Cloyne.

The epidemic of dysentery that followed the famine of 1740–1741 may have been the immediate prompt for Berkeley to begin his amateur medical practice with tar-water (water infused with pine resin). Berkeley wrote to Prior in February 1741 reporting his successes with a resin broth in the treatment of the bloody flux.[101] He later reported that it 'seemed every glass to refresh, and infuse life and spirit into the patient'.[102] But the infusion of spirit through drinking pine resin dissolved in water had applications in another critical public health problem. A regime of tar-water is presented as an alternative to the luxurious lifestyles that the Querist had in view. Switching from rich food and wine to tar-water would have a beneficial effect on the health and disposition of the elite and thereby improve government. Berkeley's medical analysis focuses on psychic health:

> As the body is said to cloath the soul, so the nerves may be said to constitute her inner garment. And as the soul animates the whole, what nearly touches the soul relates to all. Therefore the asperity of tartarous salts, and the fiery acrimony of alcaline salts, irritating and wounding the nerves, produce nascent passions and anxieties in the soul; which both aggravate distempers, and render men's lives restless and wretched, even when they are afflicted with no apparent distemper. This is the latent spring of much woe, spleen, and *tedium vitæ*. Small imperceptible irritations of the minutest fibres or filaments caused by the pungent salts of wines and sauces, do so shake and disturb the microcosms of high livers, as often to raise tempests in courts and senates[.][103]

Addressing public health is a public service; it is part of the charitable obligation upon members of a philosophical elite, who must train the governing elite. Berkeley thinks himself 'indispensably obliged, by the Duty every man owes to mankind': 'charity obligeth

---

101. Letters 276, 8 February 1741, and 277, 15 February 1741, pp. 417–18.
102. *Siris*, §77.
103. Ibid., §86.

me to say, what I know'. Just as Euphranor felt it an obligation to dispense 'Medicine for the Soul of Man', so Berkeley is obliged by charity to dispense his tar-water.[104]

Siris: *Medicine for the Soul*

AIR, AETHER, AND FIRE

There were philosophical motivations for the book on the use of tar-water that Berkeley published in 1744, *Siris*. It is an exploration of how mind can act on body, or spirit on idea, to use Berkeley's terms. Berkeley is far from alone in investigating this question. Even a mechanist like Robert Boyle sees its purchase, recognising that there are 'some faculties and operations of the reasonable soul in man [. . .] of so peculiar and transcendent a kind' that they won't admit of mechanical explanation, which suggests that the spirit of man may 'act by and upon his body', or 'that an incorporeal and intelligent being may work upon matter'.[105] *Siris* represents a way of accounting for this possibility by suggesting that certain phenomena are closest to spirit, the ultimate cause. Those phenomena are air, aether, fire, and light.[106] As Timo Airaksinen has noted, Berkeley suggests that 'Tar is pure because it is created in trees out of pure, invisible fire, or omnipresent aether and light. This fire, or light, is the vehicle of the soul of the world, or the animal, and as such a mediating element between God's reason and will and vulgar sublunar events'.[107] Analysis of diverse phenomena in the physiology and operation of plants, animals, and humans reveals the aether, fire, or light in the air as the first register of the operations of the will of the one spiritual substance.

104. Ibid., introduction, p. 3, §82; *Alciphron*, III.16. Holtzman, 'Berkeley's Two Panaceas', p. 487, has noted this connection and suggested further that *Siris* itself is a form of medicine that should lead the mind on to consideration of higher things.

105. Stewart, ed., *Selected Philosophical Papers of Robert Boyle*, p. 173 ('An Essay Containing a Requisite Digression, Concerning Those That Would Exclude the Deity from Intermeddling with Matter').

106. Moked, *Particles and Ideas*, p. 72, recognises that aether, fire, and light are synonymous in the text.

107. Airaksinen, 'The Chain and the Animal', p. 235.

The ideas presented in *Siris* can seem highly idiosyncratic, but many are commonplaces of ancient philosophy or modern physical science, and sometimes both. Silvia Parigi has noted that Berkeley's association of aether, light, fire, and spirit had a long historical precedent and would have been 'understandable and acceptable' to his contemporaries.[108] Berkeley presents what might seem to a twenty-first-century reader a peculiar view:

> The air or atmosphere that surrounds our earth contains a mixture of all the active volatile parts of the whole habitable world, that is of all vegetables, minerals and animals. Whatever perspires, corrupts, or exhales impregnates the air; which, being acted upon by the solar fire, produceth within it self all sorts of chymical operations, dispensing again those salts and spirits in new generations, which it had received from putrefactions. [. . .] Nothing ferments, vegetates, or putrefies without air, which operates with all the virtues of the bodies included in it[.] [. . .] The air therefore is an active mass of numberless different principles, the general source of corruption and generation; on one hand dividing, abrading, and carrying off the particles of bodies, that is, corrupting or dissolving them; on the other, producing new ones into being; destroying and bestowing forms without intermission. [. . .] [N]umberless instances there are of salts produced by the air, that vast collection or treasury of active principles[.] [. . .] Air, the general menstruum and seminary, seemeth to be only an aggregate of the volatile parts of all natural beings[.][109]

This view is not far from the advanced scientific writing of Berkeley's era. Robert Boyle reports some observations that would make one think 'that the Air is so vast and rich a Rendevouz of innumerable *seminal* Corpuscles and other Analogous particles, that almost any body long expos'd to it may there meet with particles of kin to it, and fit to repair its wrongs and losses, and restore it to its natural Condition'. Noting the 'exotic Effluviums that rove up and down in our Air', he speaks with more scepticism of 'Mysterious Writers about the *Philosophers-stone*' who make claims for 'what they call

---

108. Parigi, '*Siris* and the Renaissance', p. 154. Parigi cites a number of Berkeley's likely sources, including a book sold from the library of the Berkeley family, Henry Power's *Experimental Philosophy* (1664).

109. *Siris*, §§137, 140, 142, 145.

their *Philosophical Magnet*, which, they seem to say, attracts and (in their phrase) corporises the *Universal Spirit*, or (as some speak) the *Spirit of the World*.[110] Berkeley may edge towards the alchemical view of which Boyle is sceptical, but the air is a menstruum or rendezvous for all qualities for them both.

Bernard Nieuwentijt, one of the mathematicians from whom Berkeley distinguished himself in his early talk 'Of Infinites', also regards the air as 'a common Magazine or Warehouse' of volatile particles separated from bodies by heat: 'Fire mingles itself with Air', and even particles of metals 'may be sublimed and mix'd with the Air by the Heat of Fire'.[111] As a more subtle medium than the air, Isaac Newton proposed the existence of aether, which was capable, for example, of transmitting heat through a vacuum. Human sensory experience is attributed to aethereal vibrations being communicated to the organs, mostly through the air. Newton calls the heat that generates such aethereal vibration fermentation and makes it one of the fundamental attractive forces of the universe.[112] Newton's followers, such as Stephen Hales, explain processes of fermentation and putrefaction, the processes of generation and decay of organisms and substances, by reference to the 'amphibious property of the air', its capacity to collect and deposit volatile particles thrown off by substances. Reactions in fermenting mixtures can produce so much heat that sudden flames can be produced.[113] Soul, understood as animation or animal soul rather than the intellectual or agential spirit, is said by Thomas Willis to be bipartite, 'the one of these rooted in the blood we call a Flame, and the other dwelling in the Brain and nervous stock, Light'. Life is 'a certain kind of Flame'.[114] Berkeley, in focusing on air, aether, light, and heat as either the transmitters or the substance of (animal) spirit or soul, was working with the natural philosophy of his time, but the terms

110. Boyle, *Tracts*, pp. 30, 48 ('Suspicions about some Hidden Qualities of the Air; with an Appendix touching Celestial Magnets, and some other Particulars') [*Siris*, §142]. Many of the texts to which I refer in this discussion of *Siris* are mentioned in the text itself. When this is the case, I provide a reference to the paragraph number of *Siris* in which the reference may be found in square brackets following a citation.

111. Nieuwentijt, *The Religious Philosopher*, II.416–17, 421 [*Siris*, §190].

112. Newton, *Opticks*, pp. 349, 353–54, 399–400 [*Siris*, §238].

113. Hales, *Statical Essays*, preface, p. v, and pp. 315–16 [*Siris*, §196].

114. Willis, 'Of the Growing Hot or Inkindling of the Blood', pp. 24, 27, 31 [*Siris*, §205].

of that discourse were transformed when integrated into Berkeley's spiritual universe.

Though he was responding to current scientific thinking about air and the transmission of heat, Berkeley was also engaging wholeheartedly with an ancient philosophical tradition in his writing about air and its connection through light or fire or heat to divinity. He says, in one of his supplementary texts on tar-water, that he 'had, of a long Time, entertained an Opinion, agreeable to the Sentiments of many ancient Philosophers, *That Fire may be regarded as the animal Spirit of this visible World*'.[115] It is indeed an ancient view. Anaximenes is reported to have held that 'air is the first principle of things, since it is the source of everything and everything is dissolved back into it'. Augustine reports that Anaximenes thought the gods emerged from air.[116] Heraclitus says a 'dry soul, a beam of light, is wisest and best'; according to Aristotle, Democritus the atomist says the soul 'is a kind of fire and warm' and that 'breathing is the mark of life'.[117] The Hippocratic writings frequently associate fire and the soul or life, imagining the body as a circuitry of different qualities of fire: 'The hottest and strongest fire, which controls all things, ordering all things according to nature, imperceptible to sight or touch, wherein are soul, mind, thought, growth, motion, decrease, mutation, sleep, waking. This governs all things always, both here and there, and is never at rest'. Elsewhere the intelligence is said to receive its nutriment 'by a pure and luminous bath coming from a distillate of the blood', rather than by the standard means of nourishment.[118] Cicero's *The Nature of the Gods* reports (often critically) various views of the ancient Greek philosophers, such as Zeno the Stoic's identification of the aether with God, or Cleanthes locating 'the supreme godhead in the encircling fire of the upper air, which we call the aether'.[119] The stoic character participating in the dialogue, Lucilius Balbus, suggests that

115. 'A Letter to T.P. Esq; From the Author of *Siris*', in *Siris*, §16.

116. Waterfield, *The First Philosophers*, p. 18, T30, T33 [*Siris*, §168]. See also Cicero, *The Nature of the Gods*, p. 80.

117. Waterfield, *The First Philosophers*, p. 44, F47 [*Siris*, §166]; p. 186, T24.

118. Hippocrates, 'Regimen I', p. 249 [*Siris*, §174]; Hippocrates, 'Heart', p. 67 [*Siris*, §204].

119. Cicero, *The Nature of the Gods*, pp. 84–85.

'there is a fiery power which permeates and preserves the whole universe'. This heat creates a vapour which 'rising from the earth feeds the air and the aether and all the heavenly sphere'. Cotta, the academic, suggests that life 'is in fact a mixture of fire and air'.[120] As will become clearer in the following discussion, Berkeley works to make ancient physiology and cosmology compatible with modern corpuscularian philosophy for his peculiar ends. The argumentative burden of *Siris* is largely that the air or aether (which are not perfectly distinguished) communicates fire or light to effect physical change, thereby demonstrating their intimacy with spirit understood as the active principle of the universe—God.[121]

PLANTS

The air or aether is then a medium for fire or light, and fire or light is the phenomenon by means of which the infinite mind first acts— first at least in the analytical sense that finite minds have of the operation of the ultimate cause, if not truly first in the synthetic act of the infinite mind itself. The divine fire or light elaborates itself in a variety of different ways: it produces plenitude. In *Siris*, Berkeley focuses on the way in which plant life represents this variation and differentiation and produces different forms from the same ambience. Plants, one might say, function analytically: they separate out the qualities that are to be found in the menstruum of the air, and they produce substances with very specific qualities, such as the therapeutic qualities of pine resin. Berkeley compares the functions of plant anatomy to chemical operations, such as saponification: 'They who know the great virtues of common soap, whose coarse lixivial salts are the product of culinary fire, will not think it incredible, that virtues of mighty force and extent should be found in a fine acid soap, the salts and oyl whereof, are a most elaborate product of nature and the solar light'.[122] Pines produce oils and salts with benefits like the soaps manufactured by humans.

120. Ibid., pp. 134 (adopting the alternative reading proposed in the footnote), 157, 207.

121. See Moked, *Particles and Ideas*, passim and, for example, p. 3: 'aether is regarded in *Siris* as the nearly universal "secondary cause", or the main "instrument" of the supreme spiritual Agent'.

122. *Siris*, §73.

A plant is therefore a chemist, isolating elements in the environment and refining them into a higher or purer form. Berkeley says as much himself when summarising the medical reasoning behind his support for tar-water, and how such beneficial properties came to be found in plants: 'I considered, that Nature was the best Chymist and Preparer of Medicines'.[123] One might say that plants, in Berkeley's reading, have a tendency to refinement and purification, towards a particular good. They are not unlike the practitioner of true science, faith, and reason in *Alciphron*, being of an active operative nature and tending to a good—though plants do not conceive the good towards which they tend.

This emphasis on the refinement of substances rather than the laws that govern the interaction of particles might make Berkeley sound more like a chemist, even an alchemist, than a physicist, and so he is. He does not want to integrate all phenomena into an account of nature based on the transfer of motion between particles, and he resists the explanatory tyranny of a single physical principle (such as attraction). He is much more like the chemist for whom Boyle has some scorn, for, Boyle says, 'the chemical ingredient itself, whether sulphur or any other, must owe its nature and other qualities to the union of insensible particles in a convenient size, shape, motion or rest, and contexture, all which are but mechanical affections of convening corpuscles'. Boyle says that presenting the variety of deposits in the chemist's furnace as a reason to doubt the mechanical philosophy is like saying that because there are many tunes they could not possibly all be produced by the few notes of the scale.[124]

Plants elaborate difference from the light and heat in the air. At the same time, they refine substances. Plants work with the same materials, but produce different essences: 'the water, earth, and fixed salt are the same in all plants; that, therefore, which differenceth a plant or makes it what it is, the native spark or form, in the language of the chymists or schools, is none of those things, nor yet the finest oyl, which seemeth only it's receptacle or vehicle'. This

123. 'A Letter to T. P. Esq; From the Author of *Siris*', §15, in *Siris*.

124. Boyle, 'About the Excellency and Grounds of the Mechanical Hypothesis', in *Selected Philosophical Papers*, pp. 138–54 (pp. 146–47, 151).

'distinguishing principle' of vegetables is 'some extremely fine and subtle spirit' or 'vegetable salt' in a fine oil and which can depart from that oil 'without any sensible diminution'. Upon this 'native spirit' depend 'the peculiar flavour and odour, the specific qualities and virtues of the plant'. 'It should seem that the forms, souls, or principles of vegetable life, subsist in the light or solar emanation, which in respect of the macrocosm is what the animal spirit is to the microcosm; the interior tegument, the subtile instrument and vehicle of power'.[125] Light or the solar emanation produces the different oily spirits in plants that are otherwise substantially and environmentally identical. Light or solar emanation is to the whole universe what animation is to the individual organism. Berkeley frequently asserts in the text that this quality 'is in it self imperceptible' and may leave the oil or water 'without any sensible diminution of them'.[126] This may seem strange because, in various ways throughout his career, Berkeley has opposed the inference of imperceptible substances and also questioned the conceptual validity of infinitely small quantities as used, for example, in the differential calculus. Yet here he seems to avail himself of both argumentative resources.[127]

ECLECTIC PHILOSOPHY

The difference that plants produce or are is one aspect of the plenitude of creation, of God's elaboration of many things from her/him/ itself, the one unified, self-existing cause. This association of the plenitude of the universe with fire or aether as the soul of the world has ancient precedent. Timaios of Locri supposed that the different elements were made up of different kinds of triangle that gave them different properties: 'fire, because of its fineness penetrates all of the others, while air penetrates all but fire, and water penetrates earth. All things, therefore, are full, leaving nothing empty'.[128] This is plenitude as the contrary to vacuum rather than as optimal differentiation. But Berkeley refers to Timaios's suggestion that all of

125. *Siris*, §§47, 121, 136, 43.

126. Ibid., §§189, 215.

127. Moked, *Particles and Ideas*, pp. 44–45, suggests that aether is a hypothetical entity which is not available to the senses but introduced to explain the phenomena.

128. Timaios of Locri, *On the Nature of the World and the Soul*, p. 51.

soul but the intellectual or rational part is derived from the celestial bodies (i.e., from solar emanation) through the medium of light, in the context of a discussion of the principles that lead to the elaboration of different natures.[129] Berkeley presents a vision of a full and rich creation organised in a chain, where every nature participates in the nature above it in the series. This is a vision he believes he holds in common with Pythagoreans and Platonists, who teach that 'each nature [is] informed and perfected by the participation of a higher': 'the connection of different natures, each lower nature being, according to those philosophers, as it were a receptacle or subject for the next above it to reside and act in'.[130] Higher natures participate in lower ones by sharing with them the solar emanation or light or fire most commonly communicated by the air. Here, then, is one way in which Berkeley thinks people may (mediately, distantly) participate of the divinity, in structured subordination.

The differentiation of plant life may be related back to the original act of differentiation, as represented in Platonic and Pythagorean philosophy, that by which the original, unified, self-existing being becomes more than one. Berkeley, in *Siris*, joins an enterprise of assimilating this pagan philosophy to the Christian doctrine of the trinity inherited from various seventeenth-century thinkers, not least the Cambridge Platonists, amongst them Ralph Cudworth. The ambition of the Cambridge Platonists to defend classical learning both from Puritans and mechanical scientists by emphasising the continuity of certain ancient philosophical schools with Christianity is partly shared by Berkeley, though he does not make a plausible Latitudinarian, given the rigidity of his commitment to established Anglicanism.[131] Cudworth argued that the Pythagoreans and Platonists had a conception of the trinity from a divine revelation that was made to the ancient Hebrew people and imperfectly communicated. The '*Supermundane, Eternal,* and *Intelligible Gods,* of these *Pythagoreans* and *Platonists,* were first of all and Principally, [. . .] those *Three Divine Hypostases,* that have the Nature of *Principles* in the Universe, *viz. Tagathon* or *Hen, Nous*

---

129. *Siris*, §282.
130. Ibid., §274.
131. See Levine, 'Latitudinarians, Neoplatonists, and the Ancient Wisdom', pp. 92, 100.

and *Psyche*; or *Monad, Mind,* and *Soul*.[132] The project of demonstrating a community of opinion between Pythagoreans, Platonists, and Christians is substantially Berkeley's project in *Siris*, with its additional interest in solar emanation as the medium of God's will. Berkeley suggests that the analogy between the hypostases of the divinity and the trinity is the result of 'a divine tradition from the author of all things'. His view is confirmed by Plotinus's assertion that the 'doctrine of a Trinity, father, mind, and Soul, was no late invention, but an ancient tenet'.[133]

In the very broad tradition with which Cudworth and Berkeley are working, the reason for the creation of a differentiated world is found in an attribute of the creator. Plato has Timaeus say that the creator 'was good, and the good can never have any jealousy of anything. And being free from jealousy, he desired that all things should be as like himself as they could be. This is in the truest sense the origin of creation and of the world'.[134] Alcinous's reading of Plato is that God does not create the soul of the world, but 'according to his own will he filled all things with himself, exciting the Soul of the World, and converting it to himself, for he is cause of that Intellect, which being adorned by the Father, adorneth also the Nature of all this World'. For Alcinous, it 'is manifest, that the World was endued by God, both with a Soul and mind'.[135] Proclus's commentary on Plato's *Parmenides* also presents a trio of derivations from the one: '"the One" can be used in three senses. We have the One that transcends all beings, and that which is present together with all beings, which also, with the One, produces all the orders of beings, and thirdly we have that which is inferior to Being and which is, as it were, "swallowed down" by it'.[136] Plotinus describes

---

132. Cudworth, *The True Intellectual System of the Universe*, p. 546, I.iv.36. That there is a God, that virtues are not arbitrary, and that people are responsible for their actions together make up the true intellectual system that Cudworth wants to show is held in common.

133. *Siris*, §360.

134. Plato, *Timaeus*, pp. 1162–63, 29e–30c [*Siris*, §166].

135. 'The Doctrine of Plato Delivered by Alcinous', in Stanley, *The History of Philosophy*, pp. 186, 188 [*Siris*, §284].

136. Proclus, *Proclus' Commentary on Plato's* Parmenides, p. 381 (V.1035) [*Siris*, §263; see also §179n].

the elaboration of the three hypostases from the One (Cudworth's monad) that is other than being:

> [I]n order that Being may be brought about, the source must be no Being but Being's generator, in what is to be thought of as the primal act of generation. Seeking nothing, possessing nothing, lacking nothing, the One is perfect and, in our metaphor, has overflowed, and its exuberance has produced the new: this produce has turned again to its begetter and been filled and has become its contemplator and so an Intellectual-Principle. [. . .] Soul arises as the idea and act of the motionless Intellectual-Principle—which itself sprang from its own motionless prior—but the Soul's operation is not similarly motionless; its image is generated from its movement.[137]

Here the generative attribute is exuberance: the one naturally becomes more than one. Reflection and action follow from the effervescence of the one. Berkeley is working very closely with these ancient texts, and within the tradition of commentary that seeks to reconcile ancient mysticism and this central Christian mystery.

There is a distinct political edge to Cudworth's insistence on the unity of God. God's singularity is necessary as the basis of God's just monarchic authority.[138] As Berkeley approaches the conclusion of his treatise he tends towards the same language of divine authority in his reconciliation of pagans and Christians:

> 361. Certain it is, that the notion of a Trinity is to be found in the writings of many old heathen philosophers, that is to say, a notion of three divine hypostases. Authority, light, and life did, to the eye of Reason, plainly appear to support, pervade, and animate the mundane system or macrocosm. The same appeared in the microcosm, preserving soul and body, enlightening the mind, and moving the affections. And these were conceived to be necessary universal principles, co-existing, and cooperating in such sort, as never to exist asunder, but on the contrary to constitute one Sovereign of all things. And, indeed, how could power or authority avail or subsist without knowledge? Or either without life and action?

---

137. Plotinus, *The Enneads*, pp. 361–62, V.ii, 1 [*Siris*, §360].
138. Cudworth, *The True Intellectual System of the Universe*, I.iv.11, p. 208.

362. In the administration of all things there is authority to establish, law to direct, and justice to execute. There is first the Source of all perfection, or *fons deitatis*, secondly the supreme Reason, order or λόγος, and lastly the Spirit which quickens and inspires. We are sprung from the father, irradiated or enlightened by the son, and moved by the spirit. Certainly, that there is father, son, and spirit; that these bear analogy to the sun, light, and heat; and are otherwise expressed by the terms principle, mind, and soul; by one or τὸ ἕν, intellect, and life; by good, word, and love; and that generation was not attributed to the second hypostasis, the νοῦς or λόγος, in respect of time, but only in respect of origin and order, as an eternal necessary emanation; these are the express tenets of Platonists, Pythagoreans, Ægyptians, and Chaldeans.[139]

Berkeley's interest in reconciling pagans and Christians is in part a preservation of hierarchy, understood in both its metaphysical and social sense. The implicit politics of the passage may even point to the naturalisation of episcopacy in church government. Some respondents to *Siris* claimed to have identified its political attitude. One critic suggests that the book is a contribution to the Counter-Reformation. The author of *Anti-Siris* suggests that 'the Cure of the *natural Body*, was not the only View of this universal Physician; he had the *Body Politic* likewise in View; and probably that of the *Soul* too: For we find him directly prescribing his *Tar-Water* as a *Panacea* for curing all Evils of State; and indirectly *Tradition*', making the book 'in direct Opposition to the Tenets of the Reform'd Church'.[140] Berkeley's interest in divine tradition and authority gives the text a political character, one that is read as conservative, and that even tends to put the Reformation in question, as some early readers had also suggested was a consequence of Berkeley's arguments in *A Discourse Addressed to Magistrates*.

The concept of enchainment is relevant again here. If the chain allows participation of divinity, in various degrees to the various ranks of being, it also confirms their subordination. Participation is *by* subordination. The analogy between physical and social forces on which Berkeley is drawing in *Siris* takes a different form here

---

139. *Siris*, §§361–62.
140. Anon., *Anti-Siris*, p. 33.

than when, thirty years previously, he had stated that 'we are linked by an imperceptible Chain to every Individual of the Human Race'. In that essay, Berkeley says that as 'the attractive Power in Bodies is the most universal Principle which produceth innumerable Effects, and is a Key to explain the various *Phœnomena* of Nature; so the corresponding Social Appetite in Human Souls is the great Spring and Source of Moral Actions'.[141] Berkeley's approving paraphrase of Ocellus Lucanus in *Siris* suggests a continuity of view: '[A]s life holds together the bodies of animals, the cause whereof is the soul; and as a city is held together by concord, the cause whereof is law; even so the world is held together by harmony, the cause whereof is God. And in this sense, the world or universe may be considered either as one animal or one city'.[142] *Siris* is clear that harmony does not emerge happily and spontaneously from human appetites, but that it is the product of laws instituted by a sovereign God to whom all creatures are subordinated.[143] This God, as I shall go on to show, is not constrained by any single physical principle, or by a rule of reason. The idiosyncratic authority of the divine sovereign is the ultimate source of physical and social harmony. Such a picture of the divinity might have been evident in *Passive Obedience*. It is less so in the *Guardian* essay on the bond of society. But social harmony is intimately connected to sovereign authority here, as it often was in Berkeley's life and work.

The image of the chain as Berkeley inherits it from his ancient sources is about the production of unity as difference. Iamblichus describes the Egyptian doctrine according to which the chain, 'proceeding from on high as far as to the last of things, begins from one principle, and descends to a multitude which is governed by this one; and every where an indefinite nature is under the dominion of a certain definite measure, and of the supreme unical cause

141. *Guardian*, II.222–23, no. 126, Wednesday, 5 August [1713].

142. *Siris*, §279. Lucanus, *Ocellus Lucanus on the Nature of the Universe*, pp. 28–29 ('Ocellus Lucanus on Laws. A Fragment Preserved by Stobaeus, Eclog. Phys. Lin. I. Cap. 16.'): 'Life, connectedly—contains in itself bodies; but of this, soul is the cause. Harmony comprehends, connectedly, the world; but of this, God is the cause. Concord binds together families and cities; and of this, law is the cause. Hence, there is a certain cause and nature which perpetually adapts the parts of the world to each other, and never suffers them to be disorderly and without connection'.

143. See Holtzman, 'Berkeley's Two Panaceas', p. 489, for the soul reconciling itself to the structure of the universe through the study of natural philosophy.

of all things'. For Alcinous, the chain is that which unites the elements. For Proclus, it is 'the truly "golden chain" of beings, amongst which everything derives from the One, but some immediately, others through one intermediary, others through two, and others through more than two, but all alike from the One'. Or, in the view of Balbus the Stoic in Cicero's dialogue, 'this chain is nature itself, which pervades the whole and orders everything to a rational plan, turning and attracting all the outward parts towards the middle'.[144] The chain means unity with the divinity is possible. In Iamblichus, that unity is prior to knowledge, as knowledge implies otherness: '[A]n innate knowledge of the Gods is coexistent with our very essence; and this knowledge is superior to all judgment and deliberate choice, and subsists prior to reason and demonstration. It is also counited from the beginning with its proper cause, and is consubsistent with the essential tendency of the soul to *The Good*'.[145] It is through individual unity, Berkeley says, that participation in the divinity is possible:

> 345. It is the opinion of Plato, and his followers, that in the soul of man, prior and superior to intellect, there is somewhat of a higher nature, by virtue of which we are one; and that by means of our one or unit, we are most closely joined to the Deity. And, as by our intellect we touch the divine intellect, even so by our τὸ ἓν or unite the very flower of our essence, as Proclus expresseth it, we touch the first one.
>
> 346. According to the Platonic Philosophy, *ens* and *unum* are the same. And consequently our minds participate so far of existence as they do of unity. But it should seem that personality is the indivisible center of the soul or mind, which is a monad so far forth as she is a person. Therefore Person is really that which exists, inasmuch as it participates the divine unity.[146]

144. Iamblichus, *On the Mysteries of the Egyptians, Chaldeans, and Assyrians*, p. 138, VIII.III [*Siris*, §269]; 'The Doctrine of Plato Delivered by Alcinous', in Stanley, *The History of Philosophy*, p. 187; Proclus, *Proclus' Commentary on Plato's* Parmenides, p. 446 (VI.1100); Cicero, *The Nature of the Gods*, p. 170.

145. Iamblichus, *On the Mysteries of the Egyptians, Chaldeans, and Assyrians*, p. 23, I.III.

146. *Siris*, §§345–46.

Souls know themselves intuitively as units, but as units intrinsically connected to the divine unity.[147] Berkeley is here making use of an alternative philosophical language and tradition to explicate the evidence of a spirit to itself, remarked on in the *Principles of Human Knowledge*.[148]

There is, however, a question about Berkeley's consistency here. Berkeley had maintained that unity and number were entirely in the mind.[149] In *Siris* itself he states, 'Number is no object of sense: it is an act of the mind'.[150] The sense of unit and therefore number in the passage from *Siris* referring to participation in divine unity just cited is not in the particular finite mind by being a quality projected onto an idea, but is something that the finite mind can know reflexively of itself. Indeed, the unity of the individual mind is the most real thing about it, the thing that links it to God. In what way might these earlier and later views be reconciled? Stuart Brown has suggested that the solution relies on Berkeley's assertions that mind is the only substance and the ultimate cause, and additionally truly unified.[151] Berkeley attempts the reconciliation himself. In 'things sensible and imaginable, as such, there seems to be no unity, nothing that can be called one, prior to all act of the mind'. It is the intellect (according, Berkeley reports, to Themistius's commentary on Aristotle's *De Anima*) that gives unity, not 'sense or fancy'. Berkeley explains, again with reference to Themistius: '[A]s being conferreth essence, the mind by virtue of her simplicity conferreth simplicity upon compounded beings. And, indeed, it seemeth that the mind, so far forth as person, is individual, therein resembling the divine one by participation, and imparting to other

147. For the seeming assumption that unity characterises soul, see Aristotle, *De Anima*, p. 20 (I.5, 411b5–10): '[S]ome say that the soul has parts and that reasoning is by means of one part and desiring by means of another. What, then, holds the soul together, if it naturally has parts? For it is surely not the body; on the contrary, the soul seems rather to hold the body together. At any rate, when the soul has departed, the body disintegrates, and putrefies. If, then, something else makes the soul one, that, more than anything else, would be soul; and then one will again need to inquire whether it is one or many-parted'.

148. *Principles of Human Knowledge*, §89.

149. *Notebooks*, §104; *New Theory of Vision*, §109; *Principles of Human Knowledge*, §§13, 120.

150. *Siris*, §288. I thank one of the anonymous readers for the Press for pointing me to this passage.

151. Brown, 'Leibniz and Berkeley', pp. 249–50.

things what itself participates from above'.[152] Unity is in the divine mind by being one of its properties rather than one of its objects. There could hardly be anything else unified in Berkeley's scheme of the universe, with only one spiritual substance and an infinite mind in which all others participate. Unity is of the mind only, but not in the sense that, for example, solidity is: solidity is a sensible or imagined quality; unity, on the other hand, is a real property of the infinite mind and ultimate cause. Knowledge of unity of this kind is not like unity attributed by the mind to sensible phenomena. It is not even knowledge of an archetypal abstract idea in the mind of God that becomes an ectypal particular idea in any finite mind.[153] It is a reflexive knowledge, implied in the reflexive knowledge we have of ourselves as subjects and agents, and related to the intuition, perhaps prior to knowledge, of the connection of our personal unity to the truly unified cause of all things, God. Whilst the manner in which Berkeley writes about unity in *Siris* can easily be labelled 'mystical', these comments, blending interpretation of Platonic tradition with argument, perhaps offer the fullest gloss of Berkeley's earlier remarks, in *Notebooks* and *Principles of Human Knowledge*, that the mind is known by a reflex act.[154]

Timo Airaksinen has suggested that Berkeley's aim in his eclectic study of ancient philosophical traditions was not so much to describe the chain of beings as to create a chain of hypotheses that lead the reader to God, a chain of philosophical reasonings, as the subtitle to the text calls them.[155] That purpose entailed a reclamation of the traditions of ancient philosophy from Berkeley's longstanding enemies, the freethinkers. Berkeley is demonstrating that the ancient philosophers believed in a god, whether internal or

152. *Siris*, §§355–56.

153. Wenz, 'Berkeley's Christian Neo-Platonism', pp. 544–45, offers this as a means of making Berkeley's opposition to abstract ideas compatible with his Christian neo-Platonism.

154. See Roberts, *A Metaphysics for the Mob*, p. 29, for a summary of the issue, relating to *Principles of Human Knowledge*, §12: 'Berkeley works in sympathy with that aspect of the Platonic tradition that identifies *ens* with *unum*. Keeping this in mind, we can see that *Principles* 12—and, as we shall see, its companion, *Principles* 13—is designed to help elucidate the sense of dependence according to which the very *being* of natural objects (i.e., "sensible things") requires minds in order to provide them with some kind of unity'.

155. Airaksinen, 'The Chain and the Animal', pp. 238–39.

external to the soul of the world, and that therefore they can provide no support to the modern atheists who have attempted to turn
the ancients to their own ends:

> [W]hether the νοῦς be abstracted from the sensible world, and con-
> sidered by it self, as distinct from, and presiding over the created sys-
> tem, or whether the whole universe, including mind together with the
> mundane body, is conceived to be God, and the creatures to be partial
> manifestations of the divine essence, there is no atheism in either case,
> whatever misconceptions there may be; so long as mind or intellect is
> understood to preside over, govern, and conduct the whole frame of
> things. And this was the general prevailing opinion among the phi-
> losophers. [. . .] [N]either Heraclitus nor Parmenides, nor Pythagoras
> nor Plato neither the Ægyptians nor Stoics, with their doctrine, of a
> divine whole or animal, nor Xenophanes with his ἕν καὶ πᾶν, are justly
> to be accounted atheists. Therefore modern atheism, be it of Hobbes,
> Spinosa, Collins, or whom you will, is not to be countenanced by the
> learning and great names of antiquity.[156]

Berkeley had attempted to defend his contemporaries from the
threat of freethinking by popular journalism; a philosophical dialogue; and campaigns for a university, against luxury, swearing
oaths, and public indecency. He now defends the philosophical tradition itself from absorption into the canons of modern atheism by
delegitimising the freethinkers' claim to an ancient heritage.

NATURAL LAWS

Cudworth wants to claim that atomism was the common property
of ancient philosophy, and not exclusively of the materialists such
as Democritus and Epicurus.[157] He, like Boyle and Newton, thinks
an atomism perfectly compatible with Christianity. Boyle thinks
that God not only put matter into motion, but gave its motions
guidance and rule so that they would produce the universe, including the prototypical forms of specific organisms. The mechanical

---

156. *Siris*, §§326, 354.
157. Cudworth, *The True Intellectual System of the Universe*, I.i, pp. 1–2 (the contents).

hypothesis does not seek to intrude on this ground.[158] It 'seems probable' to Newton 'that God in the Beginning form'd Matter in solid, massy, hard impenetrable, movable Particles, of such Sizes and Figures, and with such other Properties, and in such Proportion to Space, as most conduced to the End for which he form'd them'.[159] These natural philosophers make God responsible for creating matter and those principles that govern its formation into different kinds of bodies—in Boyle's case motion, in Newton's the two principles of gravity and fermentation, which are comprehended under the principle of attraction.

Berkeley challenges the idea of a God who merely creates matter and communicates specific types of motion to it. He believes that diverse laws of nature were instituted by God and are not necessarily reducible to a single principle (motion, attraction). Berkeley praises Newton, but points out that 'attraction it self is not to be explained by physical or corporeal causes'. It requires, rather than provides, an explanation. Berkeley suggests that Newton agrees with the ancient philosophers that gravity is the product of an intelligence.[160] Berkeley is an advocate of the diversity, rather than the unity, of natural laws: 'The laws of gravity, magnetism, and electricity are divers. And it is not known, what other different rules or laws of motion might be established, by the author of nature. [. . .] [N]umberless [. . .] effects seem inexplicable on mechanical principles, or otherwise than by recourse to a mind or spiritual agent'. It is important for Berkeley that laws be diverse, as diversity indicates the personality of a creator actively at work in creation. 'Why may we not suppose certain idiosyncrasies [. . .] depending [. . .] merely and altogether on the good pleasure of the Creator, in the original formation of things?' Idiosyncrasy indicates the presence of 'an incorporeal agent, who connects, moves, and disposes all things, according to such rules, and for such purposes as seem good to him'.[161] Berkeley's God is not constrained by anything other

158. Boyle, 'About the Excellency and Grounds of the Mechanical Hypothesis', in *Selected Philosophical Papers*, p. 139.

159. Newton, *Opticks*, p. 400.

160. *Siris*, §§245, 246.

161. *Siris*, §§235, 237, 239, 237.

than what seems good to him.[162] This God has the creativity of an artist who, like nature as Zeno described it according to Balbus in Cicero's dialogue, is a 'creative fire which goes its own way, as an artist does, to bring its works to birth'.[163] Berkeley proposes an idiosyncratic God, one who might present highly dependable laws of nature that 'direct us how to act, and teach us what to expect', but a God who can always exceed our expectations.[164]

Boyle had argued against importing discussion of 'such indeterminate agents as the *soul of the world*, the *universal spirit*, the *plastic power*, and the like' into the explanation of phenomena:

> [T]hough they may in certain cases tell us some things, yet they tell us nothing that will satisfy the curiosity of an inquisitive person, who seeks not so much to know what is the *general* agent that produces a phenomenon, as *by what means*, and *after what manner*, the phenomenon is produced. [. . .] [I]f, besides rational souls, there are any immaterial substances (such as the heavenly intelligences and the substantial forms of the Aristotelians) that regularly are to be numbered among natural agents, their way of working being unknown to us, they can but help to constitute and effect things, but will very little help us to conceive *how* things are effected: so that, by whatever principles natural things be *constituted*, it is by the Mechanical principles that their phenomena must be clearly *explicated*.[165]

Siris is, in this way, as Airaksinen has noted, an attempt to relegate mechanical science beneath religion in the work of explaining phenomena.[166] It is a rearguard attempt to dethrone mechanical philosophy from its preeminence in explaining the sensible world and to place an idiosyncratic spirit, operating through emanation and participation, at the centre of any explication of natural laws.

The agent who understands herself to be a part of the universe of Berkeley's *Siris* is understanding something different from a

162. For a presentation of Berkeley's empiricism as supporting his voluntarism from the earliest development of his philosophy, see Ayers, 'Nature and Laws from Descartes to Hume', pp. 101–4.

163. Cicero, *The Nature of the Gods*, p. 145.

164. *Siris*, §234.

165. Boyle, 'About the Excellency and Grounds of the Mechanical Hypothesis', in *Selected Philosophical Papers*, pp. 144–45, 150.

166. Airaksinen, 'Berkeley's *Siris*', p. 217.

Boylean or Newtonian natural philosopher. Understanding nature is not understanding the local communication of motion. Understanding is an ascent of the mind, following the chain of hypotheses upwards to acquire, in the language of Berkeley's earlier writings, an enlarged view of things; it is to be, like plants, an instrument of refinement, to tend towards a higher good; it is to practice magic or divination; it is to converse with and participate of God. In asserting the legibility of nature, Berkeley emphasises the dependability of God's actions:

> There is a certain analogy, constancy, and uniformity in the phænomena or appearances of nature, which are a foundation for general rules: and these are a grammar for the understanding of nature, or that series of effects in the visible world, whereby we are enabled to foresee what will come to pass, in the natural course of things. Plotinus observes, in his third Ennead, that the art of presaging is in some sort the reading of natural letters denoting order, and that so far forth as analogy obtains in the universe, there may be vaticination. And in reality, he that foretells the motion of the planets, or the effects of medicines, or the results of chymical or mechanical experiments, may be said to do it by natural vaticination. [. . .] [T]he phænomena of nature, which strike on the senses and are understood by the mind, do form not only a magnificent spectacle, but also a most coherent, entertaining, and instructive discourse; and to effect this, they are conducted, adjusted, and ranged by the greatest wisdom. This language or discourse is studied with different attention, and interpreted with different degrees of skill. But so far as men have studied and remarked its rules, and can interpret right, so far they may be said to be knowing in nature, A beast is like a man who hears a strange tongue, but understands nothing.[167]

The person who understands nature can, in a sense, prophecy or augur; she comes to understand the discourse of nature, to

167. *Siris*, §§252, 254. It is not the passage Berkeley has in mind, but Plotinus, II.3, 7, pp. 80–81, says: 'All teems with symbol; the wise man is the man who in any one thing can read another, a process familiar to all of us in not a few examples of everyday experience. // But what is the comprehensive principle of co-ordination? Establish this and we have a reasonable basis for the divination, not only by stars but also by birds and other animals, from which we derive guidance in our varied concerns. // All things must be enchained; and the sympathy and correspondence obtaining in any one closely knit organism must exist, first, and most intensely, in the All'.

distinguish herself from a beast who merely perceives the phenomena without comprehending their arrangement into order and sense. Understanding phenomena in this way is becoming a truly human being by understanding one's place in the chain of beings, but also recognising that the chain has a tendency to draw its parts upwards.[168] The ancients might have shared a concept of the fall, but they also acknowledged the tendency of the soul to refinement: 'Theology and philosophy gently unbind the ligaments, that chain the soul down to the earth, and assist her flight towards the sovereign Good. There is an instinct or tendency of the mind upwards, which sheweth a natural endeavour to recover and raise our selves, from our present sensual and low condition, into a state of light, order, and purity',[169] When reasoning in this way, a person is oriented towards the 'true End of Speech, Reason, Science, Faith, Assent, in all its different Degrees [. . .] something of an active, operative Nature, tending to a conceived Good'.[170] Understanding the laws is understanding the will of a person, God, communicated in language.

Siris was a popular book, and the subject of a great deal of public discussion. Berkeley's treatment was adopted by many people across Europe and in America. He continued to produce materials relating to tar-water almost until the end of his life. These materials frequently connect his medicinal project with other long-standing concerns. Like the construction of *The Ladies Library*, medical practice was a way in which Berkeley expressed his interest in female experience. Tar-water was said to be a good treatment for 'Cancerous and sore Breasts [. . .] such cruel Cases [. . .] that it is a necessary Piece of Humanity, to contribute all we can to the Prevention and Cure thereof'. It was also a good treatment at that 'Age or Time of Life, when the female Sex runs no small Risk from the ceasing of their natural Evacuations'.[171] The theory and practice of tar-water as a medicine was part of a territorial dispute with proponents of mechanical approaches to the physical and mathematical sciences, especially those who felt qualified,

---

168. Alexander Pope also presents a view of humans as occupying a fixed place in the chain of being and yet striving to ever higher and more comprehensive views. See Pope, *An Essay on Man*, IV.327–40, and introduction, pp. lxxxv, cxi.

169. *Siris*, §302.

170. *Alciphron*, VII.17 (Euphranor).

171. 'Farther Thoughts on Tar Water', in *Miscellany*, pp. 9–28 (pp. 15, 17) (LJ, V.211, 213).

mistakenly, to speak about religion. Berkeley had contextualised his contribution to the development of calculus as a counterattack against infidel mathematicians, and now he similarly says, 'If Physicians think they have a right to treat of religious Matters, I think I have an equal Right to treat of medicine'. This territorial dispute was part of Berkeley's long campaign against freethinking, a campaign in which he sometimes strategically adopted the kinds of language used by freethinkers themselves to frame their project. As he speaks, in his 'Primary Visitation Charge', of the weeding out of prejudices, so he disavows authority and asserts that 'Reason is the common Birthright of all'.[172]

Berkeley conceives of his work as a contribution to public health, and public health implies both medical and moral reform. As *The Querist* had attempted to persuade the Irish gentry to reform their manners, live simply, and care for the education of their children, so tar-water is recommended as the best means 'generally and effectually [to] contribute to repair the Constitutions of our Gentry and Nobility, by strengthening the Children, and casting off in their Infancy those Impurities and Taints, which they often bring into the World'.[173] Further, when Berkeley expands on his reasoning for suggesting that tar-water might be a good preventative and remedy for plague, he presents plague as a moral judgement on a people. A 'prognostic may [. . .] be made from the moral and religious disposition of the inhabitants. [. . .] How far we of these islands have reason to expect this messenger of divine vengeance, will best appear if we take a view of the prevailing principles and practices of our times, which many think have long called aloud for punishment or amendment'. Plague is a judgement of God. Even if no outbreak is imminent, Berkeley believes his discussion will have been of use 'if the apprehension of this destroyer shall beget serious thoughts on the frailty of human life, and, in consequence thereof, a reformation of manners'.[174] The freethinking that threatens social stability, weakens the public and private morals of the gentry, and restricts the authority of the church has apocalyptic potential.

172. 'A Letter to T.P. Esq; From the Author of *Siris*', in *Siris*, §§6–7.
173. 'Farther Thoughts on Tar Water', in *Miscellany*, p. 12 (LJ, V.209).
174. *A Letter from the Author of* Siris *to Thomas Prior, Esq*, pp. 4–5, 19–20 (LJ, V.190–91, 199).

Leaving Cloyne

By 1750, Berkeley had clearly recovered enough from his cholic to be able to visit Percival's estate. His stay at Lohort is recorded in a letter from William Cooley, its warden, to Percival. Berkeley's party consisted of 'his Lordship M:rs Berkley his 2 Sons George and William and his Nephew George Berkley, together with M.r Prior a great Patriot on this Side of the Water, M.r Palliser, & M.r Jackson Clergymen, M.r Mitchell a Painter M.r DuBoise a Master of Musick, their Servants and my Lord's Servants'. Palliser had advised Cooley of the visit and told him that Berkeley 'intended to make the Castle his Home to be sole Master and provide every Thing himself at his own Charges'.[175] The Percival estate seems to have incurred some modest charges from the visit: John Foxe and Darby Guinea billed for clearing and preparing the castle, and attending upon the party and their horses.[176] In addition to the seriousness with which the artistic education of the male Berkeley children was still being taken (William drew the castle), Cooley's letter also reported that Prior was continuing to think of the coinage issue in Ireland, and that 'the Bishop & he' entertained strong views on the most useful coins to be struck in a proposed Irish mint.[177]

What finally took Berkeley away from his long residence at Cloyne was his Oxford scheme and the prospect of semi-retirement, either by taking a lower-ranking role in the Church, such as a canonry, or simply by taking the time to oversee the education of George Jr. Also, Cloyne might not have been perfectly congenial. The weather in the later 1740s seems to have been extreme, with the cathedral chapter resolving to pay for a new arch in the cathedral steeple and repairs to windows damaged by 'the late great Thunder' in June 1748. There were also reports of lightning striking the round tower, accompanied by pressurised air causing the stonework to burst and damage nearby properties in January 1749.[178] Berkeley himself reports on this episode:

175. BL MS Add 47006, ff. 76–77, William Cooley to Percival, 4 September 1750. The letter is reprinted by Luce, pp. 212–13.

176. BL MS Add 47006, ff. 92v, 93v.

177. BL MS Add 47006, f. 77r.

178. Representative Church Body of the Church of Ireland Library, MS C.12.2.1, vol. 107, no. 128, 23 June 1748; Smith, *The Antient and Present State of the County and City of Cork*, II.397.

Our round tower stands where it did; but a little stone arched vault on the top was cracked, and must be repaired: the bell also was thrown down, and broke its way through three boarded stories, but remains entire. The door was shivered into many small pieces, and dispersed; and there was a stone forced out of the wall. The whole damage, it is thought, will not amount to twenty pounds. The thunder-clap was by far the greatest that I ever heard in Ireland.[179]

Two years previously, Berkeley and Prior corresponded on the causes of the weather, with Berkeley suggesting that the lack of pattern in wind and rain made it unlikely that they were the result of planetary movement and resultant changes in atmospheric pressure:

> If the bulk, figure, situation, and motion of the earth are given, and the luminaries remain the same, should there not be a certain cycle of the seasons ever returning at certain periods? To me it seems, that the exhalations perpetually sent up from the bowels of the earth have no small share in the weather; that nitrous exhalations produce cold and frost; and that the same causes which produce earthquakes within the earth produce storms above it.[180]

Unusual weather events, Berkeley theorises, are more likely the result of gases and combustion in the interior of the globe than its relationship to other planets.

In his later years, then, Berkeley sustained the interest in atmospheric pressure that was evident in 1706 and in 1717 on his Italian tour.[181] Berkeley picked up the same concerns in an open letter to the *Dublin Journal* in April 1750, where he contests the view that a recent tremor in London was not an earthquake 'because the motion was lateral'. He reports having experienced lateral motion in an earthquake at Messina in 1718 and again asserts 'a correspondence between the subterraneous air and our atmosphere. It is probable that storms or great concussions of the air do often, if not always, owe their origin to vapours of exhalations issuing from below'. Recalling a verbal

179. Letter 362, Berkeley to Prior, 2 February 1749, p. 540.
180. Letter 347, 6 February 1747, p. 523; see also letter 351, Berkeley to Prior, 20 February 1747, p. 527.
181. For more on Berkeley's interest in atmospheric pressure, see letter 2, Berkeley to Sloane, 11 June 1706; LJ, VII.326; and chapter 6.

account of the earthquake in Catania, Sicily, in 1692, and referring to Pliny, Berkeley notes that 'Britain is an island [. . .] and in this island are many mineral and sulphureous waters'. Berkeley then hints at the type of communication from God that an earthquake represents. It is not the regular series of events produced by celestial movements, but something more unpredictable. 'I see nothing in the natural constitution of London, or the parts adjacent, that should render an earthquake impossible or improbable. Whether there be any thing in the moral state thereof that should exempt it from that fear, I leave others to judge'.[182] As he had argued in *Siris*, the laws through which God acts are reasonably dependable, but are ultimately the product of what seems good to God: they may exhibit variety and idiosyncrasy, and they certainly exhibit agency. Weather phenomena are examples of God acting, in ways that people cannot yet predict, through the air and what it communicates. The earthquake is a divine communication, warning and admonishing, as are all such communications. London has greater reason to fear such admonishment than other places, Berkeley implies, given its corruption and irreligion, just as, as he wrote in the letter to Prior on tar-water, the islands generally may have some reason to fear an outbreak of plague.

The lightning that struck Cloyne's round tower, just as much as an earthquake in London, was to be understood as an expression of God's agency. Lightning, as a form of fire, connected Berkeley's interest in meteorological phenomena as an expression of God's will to the presentation of God as fire in *Siris*. Berkeley integrated some of the more eclectic elements of his thinking in *Siris* into his preaching at Cloyne. He preached on the text of the Lord's Prayer, Matthew 6:10, in Cloyne on Whitsunday 1751.[183] A manuscript page survives amongst Berkeley's papers that I take to be an alternative opening to this sermon when it was delivered on a different occasion. (The superscript corrections to the citation below suggest that it might have been used more than once, and for the first time at Pentecost.) It suggests that fire is a fit representation of the third person of the trinity, the Holy Ghost, and offers in various ways a reprise of many elements of Berkeley's thinking, early and late:

182. Letter 367, p. 556–57.
183. LJ, VII.129.

The holy Spirit, as it enlightens the mind and warms the affections, is fitly represented by fire. ~~Light~~ It includes light to enlighten, in other words, to improve and enlarge our views, to brighten up the defaced image of God in our Souls, to give us more distinct notions of our duty and true interest; Heat also to inspire us with an ardent love of our maker, to raise our thoughts from Earth, to animate our hearts in the pursuit of heavenly things. The divine majesty in the holy Scripture is generally described and represented to us, by light and splendour, fire and flames, the purity force and lustre whereof are emblems of the divine glory and energy, and the miraculous effusion of the holy ghost on ye feast of Pentecost, ~~commemorated this day~~, was attended with the ∧visible appearance of cloven tongues of fire.

But the internal workings of the Spirit, how it doth influence and move the Soul, in what manner it inspires zeal, communicates knowledge and purifies the affections; the manner, I say, of these things is neither visible to the eye nor yet comprehended by the mind, so as to make the subject of a popular discourse. Wherefore it may not be amiss, rather than to dwell on the dark side of things, to consider the object and end of the mission and operation of this divine person, w.ch is as plain and clear, as the manner of them is difficult and obscure.

Now the great aim and design of this dispensation is, that the divine doctrines of religion may be notified to men, to the end that the will of God may be done upon earth. The doing of which contains a full though short summary of our true happiness and duty. And as such, our B: Saviour hath enjoyned us to pray for it in the words of my text: Thy will be done in earth as it is in heaven. In treating of w.ch words &c[184]

The Holy Spirit here seems to take on qualities of all other persons of the trinity, as described in *Siris*: 'We are sprung from the father, irradiated or enlightened by the son, and moved by the spirit'.[185] It warms and enlightens as Christ is said to, producing those higher and larger views that are so often the ambition of Berkeley's accounts of spiritual progress. Duty and true interest are one with love of the maker. They are, as was the case in Berkeley's sermon to the English merchants in Leghorn in 1714, charity. Souls are touched by divine fire when they actively show its influence, attend properly to the

184. BL Add MS 39306, f. 215v.
185. *Siris*, §362.

image of God, see in an enlarged way, and have distinct notions, pure affections, ardent love, and a true sense of duty. Fire is a fit representation of these qualities: it has more of the properties of an analogy as it was described in *Alciphron*, a real proportion between qualities shared by finite and the infinite spirits.

It is not possible to see the operations of the Holy Ghost in any simple sense, as Berkeley had acknowledged since the first decade of the century (when he said, in an early set of notes, that immediate powers are not recognised as such and that we do not see power). Neither is it a simple matter to comprehend the operations of the spirit. These operations cannot, in any case, form the subject for a popular discourse, an address to the people from the pulpit, with the practical view of addressing the practice of a congregation, all of whom, how little philosophical they might be, are included in God's dispensation. Everyone may see what the purpose of the operations of the Holy Ghost is: expressing the will of God through the phenomenal world and thereby instructing other spirits in what their duties are, in what their practice should be. The laws of nature, known through vision and its relation to touch, or through the more advanced speculations of the mathematical and physical sciences, or through contemplation of duties necessary to maintain political order, are advertised in the divine administration of the world and available to all who attend to it. Berkeley had been saying so since he began to write and publish in the second half of the first decade of the century. In the 1750s, Berkeley was no less certain that the phenomena of the world could offer a guide to practice, and that they should always be thought of as guides to practice. The practice at which people should aim, he preached, is summarised in the Lord's Prayer, particularly the verse specified as the text for the sermon: 'Thy kingdom come. Thy will be done in earth as it is in heaven'. To bring the kingdom of God to earth is to bring human wills into alignment with God's will, to achieve that participation of the divinity that is perhaps the centre that holds together Berkeley's very diverse actions and writings as a religious philosopher over the half-century of his career.

CHAPTER SIXTEEN

Afterlife

IN THE MONTHS leading up to Berkeley's departure for Oxford, many visitors came to Cloyne to seek relief from a variety of conditions by taking tar-water. Another visitor in 1752 was Cornelius Magrath, who stayed with Berkeley for a month. Just before his sixteenth birthday Magrath was seven feet, nine inches tall, his rheumatic and growing pains having been treated by 'going into Salt Water' at Youghal.[1] Berkeley is said to have taken very good care of him. The medical properties of saline solutions may also connect Berkeley to the doctor by whom he was treated in Oxford. He arrived there in the middle of August 1752 'in pretty good Health considering his Age and Infirmities: His Lordship was brought in a large Bed-Carriage'.[2] The doctor in question was Richard Frewin, a successful and respected practitioner in Bath and Oxford.[3] His medical research and (modest) publication concern the use of sea-water in the treatment of various conditions, particularly stones and general distension of the nerves. (A half-pint is to be drunk in the early morning before a nap, so that one is not affected by the

---

1. *London Evening Post*, 3868, 1–4 August 1752; Luce, p. 187.

2. *London Evening Post*, 3876, 20–22 August 1752. Berkeley arrived 'Thursday last'. From an entry by Anne in TCD MS 453, f. 50r, 4 April 1754, it seems that the Berkeleys lived in Holywell. Tipton and Furlong, 'Mrs George Berkeley and Her Washing Machine', attempt to trace the house on Holywell Street in which the Berkeleys lived, without coming to an incontrovertible conclusion.

3. *London Daily Advertiser*, 666, Saturday, April 28, 1753, p. 2 [or the verso of the broadsheet]: 'We hear from Bath, that Dr. Frewin, a very eminent Physician there, is so ill of a Fever, that it is thought he cannot recover'. Loudon, 'Frewin, Richard'.

thirst that normally follows.[4]) One might say, then, that Frewin, like Berkeley, was a student of the health benefits associated with drinking saline solutions. He succeeded William Freind as lecturer in chemistry at the University of Oxford, where Frewin was also Camden professor of history, but it is not clear whether he engaged in any teaching or publication in either discipline. He was also a reader in rhetoric at Christ Church and, like Freind, a high Tory.[5] Clearly his political views were not so repugnant to Berkeley that he could not be employed as a physician. He was a benefactor to the university, to which he left his library. Philosophy was poorly represented amongst Frewin's books, with no texts by Berkeley present, and Shaftesbury's *Characteristics* the only notable text of modern philosophy.[6] It is unlikely that the two men were close philosophically, then, even if medically and politically they were not distant.

It is known that Frewin attended Berkeley because a question was raised over his conduct by Elizabeth Montagu in a letter to Gilbert West, already cited in chapter 9: '[W]hat can [one] say for Dr Frewins behavior? I suppose he must excuse himself on the accounts representing the Bishop as already dead. I think it was happy for that good man he could not be recall'd'.[7] Perhaps Frewin did not arrive at the scene with sufficient speed? It seems from what Montagu says, however, that Berkeley's death may not have been as 'instantaneous, and gentle as sleep', as Luce says: it may not have been a moment of '[s]erenity and quiet beauty'.[8] Perhaps Montagu can be understood to be saying that Berkeley appeared to have died, Frewin was summoned, and, although in the interval before his arrival it became obvious that Berkeley was not yet dead, once he did arrive Berkeley proved to be in an irrecoverable condition. If the stipulation in Berkeley's will that he not be buried until evidently putrefying expressed a fear that loss of vital signs could lead to live internment, as I suggested earlier, then any such interval of

4. 'Letter I. From Dr. Frewin, to Dr. Russel [from Oxford, 24 February 1748/9]', in Russel, *A Dissertation on the Use of Sea Water*, pp. 103–10.

5. Williams, Chapman, and Rowlinson, *Chemistry at Oxford*, pp. 62–64.

6. Bodleian Library, MS. Radcliffe Records, H.10 Catalogue of Mr Frewin's Books, 1867.

7. Huntington Library, Elizabeth Robinson Montagu Papers, MSS MO 1–6923, MO 6697, f. 3v, Elizabeth (Robinson) Montagu to Gilbert West, 28 January 1753.

8. Luce, pp. 220–21.

lifelessness before his actual death would have shown that such a fear was not baseless.

The care of Berkeley's remains was to be one of Anne's duties in the years after her husband's death. Forty years before his death, Berkeley had made extracts from *The Ladies Calling* for the anthology he prepared for Richard Steele, *The Ladies Library*, that advised widows how to maintain 'Conjugal *Love*, transplanted into the *Grave*', so that it 'improves into *Piety*, and lays a kind of Sacred Obligation upon the *Widow*, to perform all Offices of Respect and Kindness, which his *Remains* are capable of. // Now those *Remains* are of three sorts, his *Body*, his *Memory*, his *Children*'. Honouring the body through internment, the widow should honour the memory by protecting it from calumny: 'she who has been Wife to a Person of Honour, must so remember it, as not to do anything below her self, or which he, could he have foreseen it, should justly have been asham'd of'.[9] Anne Berkeley may, then, have conceived of the death of her husband as a new phase in her commitment to him.

Within days of Berkeley dying, his surviving family received letters of condolence from old friends. Thomas Secker, bishop of Oxford, writing to Anne Berkeley, was 'beyond expression surprised and grieved' at the news of the death of 'that excellently good & very great man'. He attests to a 'large, though [. . .] very unequal <sh>are' of the grief, and having since he began his letter received one from George Berkeley Jr, he thanks God the young man has been able 'to think so immediately in so reasonable' a manner.[10] Edward Synge also received a letter from George Jr and in his reply attests to a friendship of forty-three years with George Sr, saying that his best wish for George Jr 'is that you may inherit the perfections of yor Excellent Father, & emulate his virtues'.[11] As he noted the intransigence of Anne Berkeley's grief, George Jr's letter to Secker of 1 February 1753 hints at the support that Secker's extended family had already provided and would continue to provide to the Berkeleys:

> Notwithstanding the kind Sympathy of y.^{r} Lordship & the good Ladies as well as of all our friends here & the utmost endeavours of my Sister

9. *Ladies Library*, II.347–49.
10. BL Add MS 39311, f. 69.
11. BL Add MS 39311, f. 70, 26 January 1753.

FIGURE 16.1. Berkeley's monument at Christ Church, Oxford

& myself to conceal our grief, I can not say that I perceive my poor Mothers at all abated. What Humane Aid can't do, I trust that Divine, Will do. My Sister is extremely thankful for Miss Talbots very usefull & friendly letter[.][12]

Catherine Talbot was an important figure for the family in the years following George Sr's death. Catherine and her mother had lived with Thomas Secker and his wife Catherine Benson (sister of Martin, Berkeley's friend since his Italian travels) since their marriage in 1725. Charles Talbot, Catherine's father, had died before she was born. Through mostly posthumously published works, such as her *Reflections on the Seven Days of the Week*, various essays, and a substantial body of poetry, Catherine participated in the various traditions of literary, moral, and religious writing of the midcentury.[13] She was friendly with Samuel Richardson and was enlisted by the printer-turned-novelist to edit, indeed contribute to, *Sir Charles Grandison* as it was produced.[14] Samuel Richardson had been on the fringes of the Berkeleys' world since the mid-1730s. Percival records that on 27 May 1736 he 'sent Bishop Berkeley's second part of Queries to Mr. Richardson to be reprinted'.[15] Percival had also intended to give the *Discourse Addressed to Magistrates* to Richardson to print, until discovering it had already been undertaken by Roberts.[16] In a meeting with Richardson at Parson's Green in August 1756, Catherine Talbot reported to Anne Berkeley, they were joined by 'Mrs Donneland', that is, Anne Donnellan, the woman to whom George Berkeley Sr first proposed.[17]

Of Catherine Talbot's many social connections with the Berkeley family, the closest was with George Berkeley Jr. It is likely that they met in Oxford as soon as the Berkeleys arrived from Ireland. In a journal entry dated 29 September 1752, she reported that 'Good

12. BL Add MS 39311, f. 72r.

13. See Staves, 'Church of England Clergy and Women Writers', pp. 85, 90.

14. See Eaves and Kimpel, *Samuel Richardson*, pp. 357–64, which includes a brief sketch of the relationship between Talbot and the Berkeleys, particularly George Jr.

15. Percival, *Manuscripts of the Earl of Egmont*, II.275.

16. Letter 270, Benson to Berkeley, 28 April 1738, p. 411.

17. BL Add MS 39311, f. 83v, letter begun 9 August 1756.

FIGURE 16.2. Charles Heath, 'Catherine Talbot', 1812,
© The Trustees of the British Museum

Mr B: stayd with us till Octr 2^d'.[18] The references to the Berkeley family in Talbot's journals and letters soon came to be dominated by her compassion for their loss of a husband and father. Talbot and George Jr seem to have fallen in love and to have intended to marry. The couple perhaps made some attempt to express their feelings to Anne Berkeley. In a journal entry for Sunday, 29 July 1753, that Talbot exchanged with Jemima Grey, she wrote that 'G: a dit aujourdhui a sa Mere qu'il souhaittoit que je fusse sa sœur. Jai repondü a Mrs B qui me le redisoit que de tout mon Cœur Je l'acceptois pour mon Frere. Voilá donc le bien. Je suis son Ainée, & Julie ma Chere Cadette. Quand vous connoitrez mon Frére vous l'aimerez. En attendant Je l'aime pour vous & pour moi'. [G: said to his mother today that he wished I had been his sister. I responded to Mrs B who retold it to me that with all my heart I accepted him as my brother. And there is the good. I am his older sister, and Julie my dear younger sister. When

18. BL Add MS 46690, Catherine Talbot's journal addressed to Jemima, Marchioness Grey, f. 68r.

you know my brother you will love him. Until then I love him for you and me.]¹⁹ Talbot sent Grey what she called a complete eulogy on the subject of George in the entry for 15 July 1753:

Ce que Sʳ Charles [that is, Sir Charles Grandison, eponymous hero of Richardson's novel, which Talbot had edited] etoit a 18, G: l'est. Il est tout a fait aimable. [four or five words crossed out] Un Esprit droit autant que le Cœur, Une Solidité qui s'accorde avec une Vivacité Charmante. Un Amour pour l'Etude qui ne lui laisse jamais perdre un Moment, avec une disposition gaye & sociable qui lui fait entrer avec la meïlleur humeur du Monde dans tout ce qu'on propose pour l'amuser. Un discernement vif & penetrant, corrigé par une bonté & une Candeur qui ne lui permet jamais de dire du Mal de qui que ce soit. Mais il voit les défauts si clair & si justement que Je suis presque en peine dans la peur de faire ou de dire aucune sottise ou même d'en penser. Je le vois si attentif a sa Sœur, qu'un Pere ne le pourrait être plus. Jai presque Envie de le prier d'être mon Frère aussi, d'observer ma Conduite & mes dispositions, & de me faire aussi des reprimandes quand il les desap-prouve & même sans celá Je sens que ce respect qu'il faut qu'on aye pour lui me ferà Corriger mille petites choses a quoi Je n'aurois pas pensée apres sans celà. Ceci vous paroitra bizarre, mais je vous assure qu'il est absolument son Père, seulement à ce que je Pense—mais Jai trop peu connuë le Pere respectable. Quel Tresor pour Mrs B: qu'un tel Fils! Dans ses maniéres il est poli, attentif a tout ce peut etre obli-geant ou apropos. Il a cette Modestie ce Reserve qui sied si bien a une si grande Jeunesse & ne parle guères dans les compagnies melées ou il [words crossed out] n'y est pas particulièrement apellé. Mais si Eng: le prie de recevoir & entretenir sa Compagnie il le fait avec une Franchise un Agrèment une Politesse dont nous sommes tous Charmés.

Il fait honneur a la Religion. Sans Affectation, sans Parade il est ponctuel en tous ses devoirs, & avec une Reverence une Attention tout à fait edifiante.

Dans toutes les Affaires on se soumet a sa Prudence & son discerne-ment. Cest ce qui fait qu'en riant nous l'appellons le Gouverneur.

Il prend le soin de former lui même les Mœurs des Domestiques. Sa Mere avoit pris un Valet dont l'ignorance dans tout ce qui concerne la

19. BL Add MS 46690, f. 90v. Translations from Talbot's French journals are my own, with kind assistance from Emily Butterworth.

Religion etoit celle d'un Hottentot. Ce bon Jeune Homme l'a priée de lui permettre quand elle l'avoit dechargé de le prendre pour le sien dans la seule vuë de l'instruire & s'il etoit possible d'en faire un Chretien. Dans son College il est exemplaire, & son Example a dejá fait beaucoup de bien.

Avec toutes ces Qualités Essentielles il a beaucoup d'Esprit & de Ton. Il scait rire badiner raillier, faire d'excellentes repartis, & pourtant Je ne lui ai jamais entendû dire le moindre mot leger ou inconsideré.

Voilá Ang: un Eloge Complet, mais Je n'en puis rien retrancher.[20]

[What Sr Charles was at 18, G: is. He is entirely amiable. A Spirit as upright as his Heart, a Solidity which harmonises with a charming vivacity. A love of study that does not let him lose a moment, with a gay and sociable disposition which makes him enter into everything one proposes to amuse him with the best humour in the world. A lively and penetrating judgement, moderated by a goodness and candour that never lets him speak ill of anyone whomsoever. But he sees faults so clearly and justly that I am almost in fear of doing or saying anything stupid or even thinking it. I see him so attentive to his sister that a father could not be more so. I almost want to ask him to be my brother also, to observe my conduct and dispositions, and to reprimand me when he disapproves of them & even without that I feel that the respect one has to have for him leads me to correct a thousand little things that I wouldn't have thought about afterwards without that. This will seem odd to you, but I assure you he is absolutely his father, at least I think so—but I knew the respectable father too little. What a treasure for Mrs B: such a son! In his manners he is polite, attentive to everything that might be obliging or apropos. He has that modesty that reserve that becomes so well at such a young age & hardly speaks in mixed company where he is not particularly called to. But if Eng asks him to receive and entertain the company he does it with a frankness an agreeableness a politeness with which we are all charmed.

He does honour to religion. Without affectation, without show he is punctual in his duties, & with a reverence an attention that is entirely edifying.

In all our affairs we submit to his prudence and discernment. For that reason we laughingly call him the Governor.

20. BL Add MS 46690, ff. 86r–87r.

He takes the responsibility himself of training the manners of the servants. His mother had taken a valet whose ignorance in everything concerning religion was that of a Hottentot. This good young man asked her to permit him when she had discharged him to take him on with the sole view of instructing him and if possible making a Christian of him. In his College he is exemplary, & his example is already doing much good.

With all these essential qualities he has a good deal of spirit and style. He knows how to laugh joke jest, make excellent comebacks, & yet I have never heard him speak the slightest light or ill-considered word.

There you are Ang: a complete eulogy, but I can cut nothing from it.]

Although this is hardly a neutral description, it is perhaps the fullest of George Jr to survive. It demonstrates the interweaving of moral character, moral correction, and sociability in the Berkeley circle just after George Sr's death. It is one testimony, from a unique position, to the character produced by the Berkeleys' care in rearing and educating George Jr.

Talbot and George Jr did not marry. Eliza Frinsham, who married George Jr in 1761, offers an interpretation of his relationship with Talbot. Beneath a transcription of part of one of Talbot's poems ('In vain fond tyrant hast thou tried'), she writes that George Jr did not allow her to meet Talbot before they were married and notes that Talbot 'was obliged by <u>Parental</u> Authority to give him up for herself'.[21] It seems likely, given this private note and Eliza's activity in publishing and providing explanatory material for the literary remains of members of her family, that she is the author of the letter published in the *Gentleman's Magazine* under the title of 'A Singular Tale of Love in High Life'. The piece, which is followed by two of Talbot's poems, including 'In vain fond tyrant hast thou tried', relates anonymously the outlines of the failed romance. The author reports the single lady frequently saying 'when I sacrificed———- to *parental* authority, I never ceased to pray that, as I could not marry him myself, Heaven would send him the woman upon earth the most calculated to make him happy; and,

21. BL Add MS 39316, f. 42r.

I am *sure, if ever any* prayer *was* answered, *that* has been, to my *great* consolation'. Eliza (if it is her) reports:

> Their attachment commenced very soon after the gentleman went to the University; it continued unnoticed, alas! by their cruelly *negligent* parents for more than *six* years; when, on an application being made for permission to unite in the bonds of marriage, a *positive* prohibition was the fatal consequence: fatal I call it; for, it occasioned, although some years after, the death of the lady.[22]

Eliza is not on firm ground: Talbot's death twelve years after this prohibition was more likely to have been caused by cancer.[23] It was cruelly negligent of the parents of these people not to notice they were in love, says Eliza. (We have already seen that she did not hold Anne Berkeley in the highest esteem.) Perhaps, even given the desire for family attachment expressed by both George Jr and Talbot, the fact that Talbot was the older, by twelve years, made the prospect of marriage seem too distant for these families to have considered it a possibility? The refusal of permission to marry evidently did not by any means end the association of Talbot with the Berkeley family. She was made godmother to George and Eliza's son, George Monck Berkeley.[24]

Whether or not she was aware of the attachment to Talbot, Anne Berkeley was not negligent of her son after the death of her husband. She emphasised in a letter already cited the importance Berkeley had placed on educating George Jr. Toby Barnard has noted that women of 'the uppermost stratum of Irish Protestant society', particularly following the deaths of their husbands, necessarily 'attended to concerns which had absorbed their husbands—religion, politics, writing, publishing, farming, manufactures, money and education—but not simply because these matters had been imposed by their spouses'.[25] Anne inherited some of George Sr's educational responsibilities towards George Jr. Part of the Oxford scheme was, after all, overseeing his college education. Letters from Anne to George Jr suggest a relationship that

22. *Gentleman's Magazine*, 66:2.ii (August 1796), 631–32.
23. Zuk, 'Talbot, Catherine'.
24. BL Add MS 39311, f. 143r, Catherine Talbot to George Berkeley Jr, 9 October 1763.
25. Barnard, *Irish Protestant Ascents and Descents*, p. 287.

was sometimes tense, with the mother's expectations not always being met. Whilst one might discern in these letters the traits of an imposing, even violent, character, as sketched by Eliza, there is no reason to presume that a character is fixed or stable, nor that considerations of role might not have influenced Anne's writing to her son. Anne may well have felt that she was required to continue with, and intensify, her contribution to the moral and religious instruction of her son after the death of his father—and given the starkly contrasting views of George Jr's disposition (terminally indolent, according to the obituary by a close friend, but ceaselessly industrious, according to Talbot), she may have had reasons to attempt to impose herself upon him. On 7 July 1767, she set out some moral and spiritual maxims to her son and recommended the mystic writers. In what seems to be a separate undated letter, she recommended Fénelon's attitude to correcting one's past life and encouraged George to add regularity and constancy to his virtues and to read more for the sake of his sermons.[26] Anne was continuing George Berkeley's educational project in the life of their son.

George Jr was not the only educational project Anne was left with. There were two further surviving children, Henry and Julia. Luce says that Julia is 'little more than a name to us', while noting that she, like her brother Henry, was delicate and was not in good health when the family lived in Dublin in 1755–1756.[27] Both Henry and Julia, it seems, experienced prolonged periods of mental illness that probably interrupted Henry's prospects of studying at Oxford as well as Julia's programme of privately acquiring polite accomplishments. Henry is very seldom mentioned in correspondence. Even a letter of George Sr's taken as referring to his long illness

26. BL Add MS 39311, ff. 199r–202v. *Ladies Library*, II.34, excerpting Fleetwood's *Relative Duties*, notes, in support of both Anne's apparent sense of her continuing parental role and George Jr's independence: 'But when the *Mother* is the only *Parent*, then her Authority increases, and she is then solely to be regarded. Indeed the Civil *Laws* do generally free the *Sons* at such an Age, supposing them the Masters of the Family, and by the Advantage of their *Sex* and *Education*, fit to govern and dispose of themselves and their Affairs'. See also II.151, still excerpting Fleetwood: 'The other thing a *Parent* should not be unmindful of, is this, that whatever great *Provision* he intends to make for his *Children*, he do by all Means inure them to Diligence and Industry, to Application and Attention, of Mind'.

27. Luce, pp. 183, 223.

and delicate constitution does not mention him by name.[28] Luce notes that Henry signed himself in the Berkeley papers as a student of Christ Church, Oxford, but that the college records suggest he never matriculated.[29] He was with the family in Oxford in the period after Berkeley's death, as Anne's notes to herself record that she would spend some of each day reading to and being read to by 'H' (Henry). Henry would have been twenty-three when Berkeley died. Anne, Henry, and Julia were in Dublin from October 1754.[30]

Eliza Berkeley's will provides the only further information about Henry. David Berman has already noted that this document states that in 1795 Henry and Julia were both living incarcerated on account of their mental illness.[31] At the very end of 1794, Eliza described them as 'the poor insane Son and Daughter of Bishop Berkeley', and bequeathed various rings, snuff boxes, and so on, to people as an encouragement to them to take a charitable interest in the pair. She was particularly concerned that 'the care of them may never on any Account devolve on the very unworthy George and as he chooses to stile himself George Berkeley Mitchell youngest Son of their I believe worthy present Keeper M.rs Mitchell Widow of Thomas Mitchell under whose care they were placed by their own Mother'.[32] Anne Berkeley died in 1786.[33] Henry and Julia were certainly in Ireland in 1798, as Eliza was worried 'lest in these dreadul Times in Ireland [an armed uprising encouraged by the French was occurring] my poor Brother and Sister in Law Henry Berkeley Esq.r and M.rs Julia Berkeley should suffer'.[34] She suggested that the pair be moved to West Malling in West Kent and placed under Dr Perfect's care if necessary.[35]

28. Letter 321, Berkeley to Gervais, 3 June 1745, p. 481.

29. Luce, p. 183, refers to BL MS Add 39306, f. 218r, but it is at f. 232r that Henry's signature is found.

30. Yale University, Beinecke Rare Book and Manuscript Library, GEN MSS 1571, box 1, file 2, George Berkeley Jr to Samuel Johnson, 7 April 1755, f. 1r.

31. Berman, 'Introduction' to Luce, *The Life of George Berkeley Bishop of Cloyne*, p. ix.

32. TCD MS 3530, f. 23r (p. 20). For a discussion of who these Mitchells might be, see chapter 5.

33. Luce, p. 223.

34. TCD MS 3530, f. 108r (p. 104).

35. Ibid., f. 109r (p. 105).

The funding of care for Henry and Julia was clearly an issue. Eliza thought of a scheme of publication to support the pair: '7.th July 1794 My wish is that after my Death all B.^{p} Berkeleys M.S. Books and Papers be delivered to H. Grimston Esq. to be by him sold to some great Bookseller to be printed for the benefit of H. B. Esqr and his Sister'. On the same date she asked her sister to consider giving them six pence a week, should they need it.[36] Eliza asked, without putting a figure to it, that 'the first attention' be paid to Henry and Julia, as she had 'been informed that their Income is too small to keep them comfortably after the Death of my Dear Sister'.[37] Told that she had power to bequeath the exchequer annuities of Henry and Julia, she had made them over to her executors.[38] An estate in Ballysinode (County Tipperary) was to be charged with £200 to Charles Berkeley Kippax following the deaths of Henry and Julia, presumably meaning that £200 per annum in rent drawn from this estate was supporting the siblings whilst they lived.[39]

Henry and Julia would live long lives in what seem to have been significantly constrained material and financial circumstances and in seriously ill health. Not much can be said of Henry's experiences or activities, but a portrait of Julia in the months immediately following George Berkeley Sr's death can be sketched from the letters and journals of Catherine Talbot and from George Jr's journal. Julia's manners and accomplishments said, and were taken to say, something about her education. George Berkeley Sr had said, in a playful letter to Dalton written when Julia was three, that she was 'so bright a little gem! that to prevent her doing mischief among the illiterate squires, I am resolved to treat her like a boy and make her study eight hours a day'.[40] Julia's education was not, however, like that of her brothers. After Berkeley's death, she became an educational opportunity for Catherine Talbot.

The first attempt at describing Julia's temperament in Talbot's journal to Jemima Grey comes on 26 June 1753 and makes it clear both that Talbot perceived shortcomings in the way Julia had been

36. Ibid., ff. 10r–11r (pp. 6–7).

37. Ibid., f. 13r (p. 9).

38. Ibid., f. 28r (p. 24), probably on 29 December 1794.

39. Ibid., f. 42r (p. 38).

40. Letter 286, Berkeley to Dalton, 1741, p. 438.

brought up and that she considered Julia the object of her own educational programme:

Pour cette pauvre Enfant ∧ ^{aimable en toutes maniéres} elle m'effraye quelque-fois—il y à une vivacité dans son tempèramment, une fermeté de Vouloir—quelque Chose qui pourra la rendre malheureuse—Que Je ressens de Reconnaissance a cette Divine Providence qui m'a donée dès mon Enfance de tels Amis, & a Ces Chers Amis∧^{La Chere Aristie fort particulière-}^{ment} des soins qu'ils ont eûs de corriger de rèprimer des dèfauts & des Vivacités qui m'auroient renduë miserable. Sur tout ils m'ont inspirée un certain Amour de l'Ordre, une dèference, une peur de malfaire d'incommoder ou de desobliger, que Je trouve fort utile. La Chere Julie n'a fait Je crois toute sa Vie que ce qu'elle vouloit. Quel dommage! Elle m'aime infiniment—Comment trouverai Je le moïen de lui être utile! C'est pourtant mon Devoir.[41]

[For this dear child lovable in all ways she sometimes scares me. There is a vivacity in her temperament, a firmness of will—something that could make her unhappy—How grateful I feel to that Divine Providence that gave me since my childhood such friends, and to these friends the dear Aristie most particularly the care that they took to correct to curb my faults and vivacities that would have made me miserable. Above all they inspired me with a certain love of order, a deference, a fear of doing ill inconveniencing or disobliging, that I find very useful. Dear Julie I believe has done nothing other than what she wanted to all her life. What a shame! She loves me infinitely—How will I find the means of being useful to her! It is nonetheless my duty.]

Talbot was in her early years regarded as a prodigy of wit and vivac-ity.[42] She contrasted the powerful, positive, constraining influence of her family and intimates over her disposition with Julia's vivacity and force of will and regretted that Julia seemed not to have expe-rienced such helpful constraint. Berkeley, that is, had not imparted his own respect for subordination (love of order and deference), as a social and metaphysical principle, to his daughter. Thirty-two-year-old Talbot felt that fourteen-year-old Julia showed the signs

41. BL Add MS 46690, ff. 80v–81r.
42. Zuk, 'Talbot, Catherine'.

of having been allowed too much liberty in growing up, and she decided to take the girl in hand.

A later journal entry gives a fuller description:

[M]a Chere Julie elle est plus enfant, elle est la pauvre un peu paresseuse, elle est telle que nous l'aurions èté a son Age dans les mêmes Circonstances, mais avec des Passions plus vives. Elle a quelques petites maniéres dont il faut la Corriger, mais aussi elle a tout ce qu'il faut pour la rendre dans quelques Années une Personne Aimable et accompli. Il faut seulement lui inspirer quelque application quelque Persèvérance, lui enseigner de se moderer[.][43]

[[M]y dear Julie is more a child, she is poor thing a little lazy, she is as we would have been at her age in the same circumstances, but with stronger passions. She has some little habits that need to be corrected, but equally she has everything needed to make her in a few years an agreeable and accomplished person. All that is necessary is to inspire her with some application some perseverance, to teach her to moderate herself.]

Talbot felt that she needed to quell Julia's vivacity and encourage her in greater perseverance and industry. Other entries record Talbot's irritation at Julia's inability to respect Talbot's privacy.[44] For the 29 July 1753 entry, calling the girl 'that madcap Julia', Talbot notes that her role is to look out 'tous ses petits défauts & de les redresser' [all her little faults and to redress them].[45] On 1 August, Talbot takes some pleasure in what she takes to be Julia's improvement: 'Je vois la Chere Julie se guerir insensiblement & presque par habitude de quelques petits défauts qu'elle avoit acquises dans un Tems de Tristesse & de Negligence'.[46] [I see the dear Julie imperceptibly and almost habitually cure herself of certain little failings that she acquired in a time of sadness and negligence.] When Talbot went to London to visit the Berkeleys on 6 August 1753, she was delighted to see Julia 'so fond of following her little Plan of

43. BL Add MS 46690, 15 July 1753, f. 87r.
44. Ibid., 27 June 1753, ff. 82v–83r; 9 July 1753, f. 85r.
45. Ibid., f. 90.
46. Ibid., f. 91r.

Employments'.[47] By 12 August, it had been agreed that the Berkeleys would stay at Cuddesdon, the bishop of Oxford's palace,
'[m]ais ils reviennent sous des Loix bien severes. Julie ne doit rien
retrancher de son Plan, Peinture Musique tous ses Emplois iront
leur train, & nous ne nous verrons qu'aux heures de Repas & de
Promenade'.[48] [But they will return under strict laws. Julie must
not cut anything from her plan, painting music all her employments will have their turn and we will only see each other at meal
times and for walks.] On their departure on 31 August 1753, Talbot
notes having had 'a Serious half hour talk with Julia that I reflect
upon with pleasure'.[49]

Talbot's side of an exchange of journals and letters with Julia
from late October 1753 survives. In this half of the conversation,
Talbot's educational plan is seen in action. There is also evidence
of Julia's illness: 'You have not been well my Julia [. . .] I had first
received your letter. I thank you for it my Julia, but am grieved
to hear you say you want Spirits. I am sure my love when you are
quite well, & drink Tar Water constantly, & use constant Exercise,
& go on diligently & regularly with your employments & your Journal this complaint will cease of it self'.[50] Talbot encourages Julia to
continue with her employments after refreshing breaks of reading,
being in the garden, or playing the harpsichord.[51] She berates Julia
for sending an unsigned entry/letter and for letting an opportunity
of improvement pass:

> I have been half unhappy about You all day. What will become of my
> Julia if she dreams away, & in dull unpleasant dreams too, this golden
> Opportunity of uninterrupted leisure with the benefit of Mrs B: & the
> Governess to assist, regulate, applaud & delight in her daily improve-
> ments. "He that will not Plough in the Winter by reason of the Cold—
> do you remember the rest of that Text my Julia? I do not mean to apply
> it harshly, but this Winter of Retirement & leisure is the time in which
> you should sow & cultivate the seeds of every valuable Quality every

47. Ibid., f. 93r.
48. Ibid., f. 94v.
49. Ibid., f. 99r.
50. BL Add MS 46688, ff. 20r, 21r, entries for 7 and 9 November 1753.
51. Ibid., f. 21v.

amiable Accomplishment. Let me have the delight of seeing them in their promising bloom when Spring restores the days of Cuddesden.[52]

Talbot practised religious exhortation in an attempt to dispel mental illness and its symptoms.

Talbot's letters and journals give details of Julia's probable accomplishments. Her mention of music suggests, unsurprisingly given the musical life at Cloyne, that Julia was musically literate. Talbot asked the girl if she knew arias from Handel's *Acis and Galatea*, or *Solomon*, and offered to copy some pieces for her.[53] Julia's standard in French is also made clear when Talbot writes on 1 December 1753: 'Je ne souhaitte pas que vos Journaux soient en François parce que cette difficulté ajoutée les rendroient trop fatiguants pour vous, & moins exacts'.[54] [I don't want your journals to be in French because this added difficulty would make them too tiring for you, and less precise.] That Julia did not have a mastery of Italian but wanted to acquire it is clear in the last surviving entry, in which Talbot offers a critique of Julia's journal and her mode of life:

And now my Julia I will make some remarks upon Your Journal. On the whole it is the best I have had.

Monday. When You are not allow'd to rise early my Dear, no excuse is needful. I am in the same case. Only the shorter ones Time is, the more one is bound to improve it. And another Admonition for us both, what is a necessary relaxation on account of Health must not grow into Habit when Health cannot be pleaded for it.

Trifling Books are a necessary Medicine sometimes, but I would always defer them till after Dinner if Possible. The Princesse de Cleves is a very bad one, its Principles are Romantick & Abominable. Your Judgment of it is very just.

Well in this day you had some Musick, some Writing, some usefull Reading, & Mrs Hatsell [?].

Tuesday. A very good day. Up at 5. Drew Well. Playd & Painted 3 hours. Read in a variety of Books. Does not the variety sometimes confuse your Ideas? Isahiah is a Writer I never heard of, but I know You mean

52. Ibid., f. 24.
53. Ibid., 17 November 1753, f. 25r; 3 December 1753, f. 30r.
54. Ibid., f. 29v.

Isaiah. I am glad the Arabian Tales amuse You so well. Your sleepy Page is a very pretty one, You talk in your sleep, but You talk like a good girl.

Why do You write ungainly upon a Chair? Have you no Table? And why with a bad Pen? And why sit up till 11? Wednesday. I suppose You did not send for an Italian Master without Mrs B:s approbation, & then I am sorry You could not get one. But my Dear do not undertake too many things at once. When I taught myself Italian I had neither Painting nor Musick to attend to. However my Love I do not mean to check Ingenuity or rob You of any innocent Amusement, I only mean to warn You against flying from Book to Book & from Scheme to Scheme[.][55]

Julia Berkeley at fourteen had some French, but not enough to make composition in that language easy, and she aspired to Italian; she painted, played the harpsichord, and probably had some knowledge of contemporary music such as that of Handel; she read slightly haphazardly and for diversion, but not without moral judgement. Talbot imagined her becoming lazy and distracted in response to the sadness of her father's death and through her own (and perhaps her mother's) negligence at that time; these traits were seen to manifest as a chronic want of spirits amounting to serious illness.

Talbot took an active role in the management of Julia's education. To further the physical, moral, and spiritual health of her young friend, she combined her chivvying with improving reflections based on events from her own life that she shared. Talbot's work on a piece of cross-stitch intended for Anne Berkeley provided such an opportunity: 'Such a piece of Work is very instructive. A Wrong Stitch upon Canvas may be set right, but a faux pas in Life is not so easily retrieved: how much ought one therefore to study the Art of Living while so happy as to be still but at the Sampler!'[56] Another came on a day trip to Eton when a Dr Burton showed her some drawings which impressed her with their mastery and simplicity: 'So it is in Life as in Painting. Let Persons proceed upon a few just & unerring Rules, Observe proper proportions, & avoid doing any thing wrong, & a Life so led will be a Masterpiece &

55. Ibid., early January 1754(?), f. 37.
56. Ibid., 23 November 1753, f. 27.

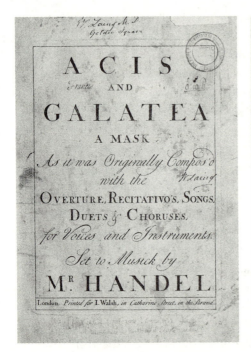

FIGURE 16.3. G. F. Haendel, *Acis and Galatea*, 1743, title page and p. 80
('Heart thou seat of soft delight'), University of Toronto Music Library

command the Admiration that it does not seek'.[57] An interest in the
arts and a desire to develop daily practice, Talbot urged her student,
would facilitate moral improvement.

Julia's illness was confirmed by her brother's journal. On Friday,
26 July 1754, in his first entry, he noted, 'Poor Julia still in a very
dismall way, God relieve her!'[58] Two days later, she was 'in yᵉ same
Melancholy way', and the next day one cause of George Jr's low
spirits was 'the Melancholy Condition of Poor Julia, Good God! to
see so hopeful & accomplished a young Woman suddenly deprived
of Reason'.[59] George Jr's language here suggests a significant aggra-
vation of the symptoms of Julia's illness. Julia was treated by Dr
Battie and others, and debate over her symptoms and the prog-
nosis delayed a planned departure for Dublin, which was delayed

57. Ibid., 24 November 1753, f. 27v.
58. BL Add MS 46689, f. 1r.
59. Ibid., f. 2r.

again when Julia's nurse, Mrs Quarterman, suffered an epileptic fit.[60] Julia and Anne finally left for Dublin on 24 September 1754. On 25 May 1756, George Jr wrote to Samuel Johnson from Christ Church in Oxford saying that Julia 'has been for above a year in a very bad State of Health, & subject to violent fitts wch have reduced her much & made my Mothers life very unpleasant'.[61] If Eliza's will is accurate, Julia, of whom I have found no other mention in the intervening period, not even in Anne's letters to George Jr, may have spent the next forty years and more suffering, along with her brother Henry, the forms of help that were then available to treat mental illness.

60. Ibid., 7 August–24 September 1754, ff. 5v–7v.

61. Pratt, 'Berkeley-Johnson Correspondence', pp. 32–33, citing Yale University, Beinecke Rare Book and Manuscript Library, GEN MSS 1571, box 1, file 2, f. 1r.

CHAPTER SEVENTEEN

Conclusion

BERKELEY WAS BORN into an Anglo-Irish family with a degree of local prominence and a history of modest public service. He was educated in Protestant foundations that conceived of themselves as societies in which subordination and loyalty were necessary for the public good. The regimented life of early rising and study that characterised Berkeley's adulthood had its roots in the organisation of days and weeks of study, worship, and limited recreation at Kilkenny College and Trinity College Dublin. In his later years of college study and first years as a fellow, Berkeley developed the distinctive philosophy of immaterialism. This philosophy was the product of a striving between different philosophical personalities and objectives: the philosopher as an iconoclast, committed to truth above all, and to experimental methods of demonstrating it; the philosopher as a spiritual guide, bringing himself and others closer to God; and the philosopher as a conservative, a preserver of social order and the appearances of things. The form given to Berkeley's immaterialism in the *Notebooks*, the *Manuscript Introduction*, *Principles of Human Knowledge*, and *Three Dialogues* draws on all these conceptions of philosophers and philosophising. It is with the explication of the central tenets of immaterialism in these works that most commentary on Berkeley produced by historians of philosophy has focused. Only two of those early immaterialist works were published in Berkeley's lifetime, and they were not particularly widely read or well received. It was not until the publication of *Alciphron* (1732) that Berkeley would command a larger readership. But since the 1730s, there have always been commentators on Berkeley's thought who emphasise his social, political, moral, theological, and other commitments, sometimes as they related to his immaterialism. This biographical study is conceived as a continuation of the long-standing tradition of commentary that sees immaterialism as one of Berkeley's many philosophical commitments, and with no less a theological and social aspect than those other commitments.

Berkeley's immaterialism was one expression of a central feature, perhaps the central feature, of his thought. Berkeley conceived of God as a person; of the laws of nature as the idiosyncratic expression of that person's will, a 'series of free Actions produced by the best and wisest Agent'; and of all phenomena as part of a discourse God intends for the instruction of other spirits.[1] God's instructive discourse tends towards a conceived good, the good of other spirits participating more fully in divinity, concurring more in the divine will. The phenomenal world, then, understood as the infinite spirit talking to finite spirits, is the standard by which all speech, all reason, science, faith, and assent should be judged. Berkeley's attempted social, educational, political, moral, and medical interventions were attempts to hold himself to the standard of the discourse of God, to engage in discourse himself by following the will of God as expressed through the appearances of nature. Those appearances include the various forms of human conduct, and it remained important for Berkeley to depict in his writings and to aspire to instantiate in his actions the best-regulated form of human existence.

Participating in the divinity, then, demands some commitment to practical, social, and political life. It also confers corresponding privileges in those domains. The commitment, as far as Berkeley was concerned, was to be an Anglican missionary. Close to home, that meant having the conversion of Irish Catholics and the faith of one's family and friends constantly in view. Further afield, it meant sharing the true faith with people all over the world, including the Western colonies with their indigenous, enslaved, and Catholic populations. Commitment brought privilege. Being a member

1. *Passive Obedience*, §14.

of the established religion provided access to legal and civic privileges that were legitimate and not to be shared with those of other denominations: for full entrance into the temporal and eternal society of God, Catholics and dissenters, Jews and Muslims, enslaved African and Native American peoples, would all have to enter the Anglican church. Berkeley did assert in a letter to his friend John James that true religion is not dependent upon denomination, and that he hoped to die in the true church rather than any particular sect. He was nonetheless entirely committed to the established religion. Reverence for sovereignty was fully dependent on reverence for God, and the state had to recognise the value of established religion and its functionaries in producing reverence for, and fear of, its institutions. Given that it was necessary to be of the established church in order to lead an obedient life as a subject, it was rational to insist on the temporal as well as the spiritual privileges of that communion.

The university in Bermuda Berkeley spent much of the 1720s planning was perhaps his grandest missionary project, but it is possible to see his missionary spirit throughout his career. Nor was there any separation between Berkeley's missionary and charitable activities. He believed that one ought to practise charity by sharing with others one's knowledge, transforming their practice so that they would find themselves in better physical, moral, and spiritual health. Charity could be expressed in philosophical and religious education, through the pulpit and the press, or through the administrative work of founding an educational institution, and also through the practical work of creating employment, applying remedies, correcting appetites, or acquiring and diffusing a taste for the fine and useful arts. It could be expressed in private life by marrying, having children, and educating them. It could be expressed publicly by condemning luxury and insisting on being guided by the public good when engaging in economic activity and economic reform (themselves both forms of communicative action). The direction of others' practice was to be both charitable and missionary.

In his philosophical writing, Berkeley would never unequivocally separate the will and the understanding. All forms of understanding are ultimately volitional, as they are the understandings of willing agents. One might say that Berkeley's conception of spirits was not just as willing beings, but as wilful beings. Such a conception draws equally on Berkeley's own temperament and his vision of God. One sees a wilful and idiosyncratic temperament in Berkeley's determined adherence to his immaterialist principles, in the peculiarities of his temper that might have caused Anne Donnellan to reject his proposal of marriage, in his strong commitment to his college in America, and in his belief in the near-universal therapeutic value of tar-water. There was a place for the idiosyncratic and the unpredictable in Berkeley's world. He was captivated by phenomena that are evidently and deeply systematic and yet resistant to prediction, such as the phenomena of weather and climate, of liquids and gases under varying pressures, and of health and illness (illnesses as diverse in their symptoms as tarantism and dysentery). He saw these complex, variable phenomena as expressions of God's creative free choice in organising a world that is best for people and admonishing them when their behaviour has taken insufficient notice of the instructive discourse all around them. That there are various and not necessarily integrated principles of organisation in the physical and moral world permits their expressive deployment by the infinite will, adjusting a discourse to the particular requirements of the historical situation and the need for particular instructions that weaker wills demonstrate in their failures and shortcomings, their disobedience, and their shortsightedness.

There were real enemies to fight in Berkeley's view of the world, principally the freethinkers. They came in many guises: independent Whigs, people who sought to challenge divine authority by attacking the principles of subordination in both social and religious life, people who claimed to have seen through illusions and taken a higher view. They represented a conspiracy, crypto-Catholic or atheist, against the established church. Freethinkers embodied the soul in a state of ill health, agitated by the failure to manage the passions and impose a rank order upon them, and so left at the mercy of fashion, luxury, and appetite. Their encouragement of swearing oaths against God struck at what Berkeley took to be the core of social order, the use of speech to commit oneself to a superior will by an oath of allegiance, just as one committed oneself to God through the rites of the established church. They were sceptics, given heart by the general assertion of a material world existing beyond our ideas and therefore inaccessible. The failure of their creed was illustrated by the failure of individual freethinkers to lead good lives, whether they were the unnamed men of fashion described in *Alciphron* or Anthony Ashley Cooper, third Earl of Shaftesbury, who failed (as Berkeley and his wife told the story) to meet his final illness and death with the temper of a philosopher.

Just as Berkeley was inclined to see the agency of God everywhere, he was also inclined to see the agency of the freethinkers. They were active as philosophers, in clubs and coffeehouses, in the state; they sank the scheme for St Paul's College on Bermuda with their narrow and mercantile views; and they were mathematicians attempting to usurp the authority of religion and religious language as the first and best means of comprehending the world. Fighting free thought was a social, moral, and religious obligation, and it was to be carried out through education. Berkeley was a member of a philosophical and religious elite whose duty was to educate those born to be legislators on account of their social privilege. These educationalists had the lives of other social strata in view also. They would enforce a regime of virtuous living upon the lower orders, partly through charitable inducement and partly through the discipline of forced labour. Prosperity without reference to virtue was not enough: social, economic, and political activity had to be undertaken in the belief that it would tend towards public goods. It was incumbent on consumers as much as lawmakers to hold this belief of their actions, and with reason, or they could not be good actions. Berkeley was engaged in battle with the freethinkers for at least forty years, and the moral education of the polite and noble classes was its terrain.

In various ways, Berkeley was an antagonist of the philosophical and social-scientific attitudes that characterised some versions of Enlightenment. It is clear that he was an opponent of radical enlightenment, as Jonathan Israel defines it, which favoured deistic, atheistic, naturalistic explanation, denied providence, revered mathematical science, and tended away from social hierarchy towards democracy. It is even somewhat doubtful that Berkeley could be characterised as a participant in Israel's moderate or mainstream Enlightenment that 'aspired to conquer ignorance and superstition, establish toleration, and revolutionize ideas, education, and attitudes by means of philosophy but in such a way as to preserve and safeguard what were judged essential elements of the older structures, effecting a viable synthesis of old and new, and of reason and faith'.[2] Berkeley wanted to conquer ignorance and superstition—qualities he associated with the Catholic church and more radical dissenting sects, not with Anglican Protestantism. He did not talk of ending toleration, but he hoped the Tests would be maintained and did not want to see rights for Catholics or dissenters extended other than as part of programmes of targeted conversion or social control. There was something revolutionary about his immaterialism, but it was one of those conservative revolutions that seeks to leave things as they are. And the major changes in education and attitudes he sought to bring about often targeted the restoration of a traditional set of powers and responsibilities, understood on a new philosophical basis, rather than turning to a new set of relationships or conceptions of the interrelation of people or social groups—parents and children, for example, or the Irish Protestant elite and Catholic peasantry. The balance was towards preserving or restoring an older way of life rather than establishing a new one. I have tried to show in various ways that Berkeley's social philosophy made use of a traditional idea of the promotion of virtue as the goal of social organisation, but did so, as perhaps one could have expected of the philosopher who believed that immaterialism brought God closer, as a way of making human social practice converge better with God's will, of increasing the participation of finite spirits in the infinite spirit.

Making a particular life and career the focus of an extended study can have the effect of making that life appear idiosyncratic or anomalous. Holding in mind the finer details of a life and its work makes difficult the reconciliation of that life and work to any larger historical pattern or general description. Indeed, that is one value of such a study for intellectual, cultural, and social history: as an attenuation of the process of assimilation, an attenuation that requires the revision of categories that are always to be revised, reclaimed, qualified, and restored. But at the same time as

2. Israel, *Radical Enlightenment*, pp. 11–12.

a biographical study draws out distinctions between the subject of a biography and that individual's predecessors and contemporaries, considered collectively and individually, it runs the risk of attributing a great or even implausible degree of internal coherence to a particular life. Individual lives and careers are difficult to reconcile with the higher-level descriptive terminology of intellectual history. They may be just as resistant to the attempts of a biographer to find consistencies of thought, attitude, and action across them.

At the start of this study, participation of the divinity was established as a ground for interpreting Berkeley's diverse actions and writings. I have not shied away from the diversity of those actions and writings, though perhaps they have been rendered too neatly as part of a consistent religio-social project (although never articulated as such in its entirety) in which Berkeley was engaged from his early twenties. I have not given much room to contingency in the shaping of Berkeley's actions. I have taken very seriously Berkeley's claim to want to establish the nearness and omnipresence of the divinity in the organisation of the phenomenal world in his early works on vision and metaphysics. Those early writings are also, however, evidently the works of an ambitious young ordained academic seeking patronage from influential aristocratic figures, in the knowledge that a more varied, rewarding, and illustrious career would require such patronage. Producing essays for *The Guardian* and putting together *The Ladies Library* were opportunities to bring a programme for social and spiritual reform, earlier expressed in a philosophical text, to a wider audience. They were also, however, fulfilments of contractual arrangements that conferred payment and the social and cultural prestige of association with people such as Richard Steele. Likewise, touring Italy was probably attractive not only as a break from more rigorously scheduled college duties but as an opportunity for intercultural education. Berkeley may have been collecting information about the tarantula and tarantati for a particular correspondent or the scientific community more broadly, but he was also developing his interest in the relationship between natural signs and divine intentions, and in medicine as an aspect of the rectification of the spirit.[3] St Paul's College was a

---

3. See Stock, *An Account of the Life of George Berkeley*, p. 10; and Fraser, *The Works of George Berkeley, D.D.*, IV.82n. See also Luce, p. 78, who says that Berkeley 'records

very eye-catching scheme that might have provided a springboard to future advancement in the church should Berkeley have been intending ever to return, as well as a missionary project. Accepting and staying in the diocese of Cloyne when there were other, more rewarding places on offer, and, perhaps, requesting the exchange of the bishopric for a canonry at Christ Church, may have been signs of stubbornness and the conspicuous rejection of advancement, as well as opportunities to serve the people of Cloyne and to oversee the education of his son. There may well be such additional, sometimes contradictory motives shaping a career at its various stages and junctures which the organising categories of this book should not be allowed to exclude.

An associated risk of the attempt to find or impose consistency on a life is the diminution of surprise and intrigue at its more idiosyncratic turns. My treatment of immaterialism and tar-water run this risk. I have suggested that immaterialism was a good intrinsic solution to the pressures Berkeley experienced in his early intellectual life—it was a solution that drew simultaneously on the new science and its associated philosophy and on a pious sense of the presence of the deity, creating a picture of the philosopher as iconoclast and as spiritual guide. I noted that it was not necessarily a good extrinsic solution, finding so little purchase in the intellectual culture of the time. Some readers may feel that I understated the idiosyncrasy of the solution, even considered from an intrinsic point of view, implying, as it does, Berkeley's belief that his arguments would be persuasive and would be generally adopted and effect the revolutionary or restorative outcomes of curbing atheism and scepticism. If Berkeley held that belief, it was resting on rather slender grounds, given the modesty of his reach as a teacher, philosopher, and person in intellectual society: his first essays were rejected by Sloane and the *Philosophical Transactions of the Royal Society*, and he had only two modest treatises in mathematics and optics to his name. Berkeley's belief in the power of his arguments, so often since called whimsical, suggests that he was impervious to a range of objections that for others of his time weighed heavily

---

observations and reports of the tarantati, which he was collecting at the request of Dr. Freind'. Luce's evidence seems to be Stock's mention of a letter from Berkeley to Freind that we no longer have, and Fraser's reference to Stock.

against his new doctrine. I have pointed in this study to Berkeley's occasional selection of rhetorical means or forms of communicative action that ill suited his objectives and were unlikely to persuade his audience (of immaterialism, for example, or the true meaning of passive obedience).

Siris could be considered in this view also. Berkeley presents tar-water as a means of ingesting fire, that which the third person of a triune God, the Holy Ghost, uses to activate the animal soul of the world. The practical effects of the drink are a matter of empirical report; the eclectic conjectures of *Siris* answer the need of a remotely situated bishop to harmonise the wisdom of the ancients, the word of God, and recent science. My interpretation of this text was guided by the suggestion that much of Berkeley's activity might be understood as a means of increasing participation of the divinity. It responds to some features of the text that others have long remarked on and addresses more recent research into the plausibility, in contemporary scientific terms, of Berkeley's approach. The central claim of the text as just stated, however, remains an idiosyncratic solution to the issues Berkeley was addressing, even if it can be made to harmonise with other aspects of his philosophical career. The relatively high degree of public response to this text was largely restricted to its practical guidance on making and taking tar-water.[4] It may have been less successful in promoting its metaphysical and spiritual cure.

Even in less striking or more mundane cases than those just cited, the words and actions of other people and the motives for those words and actions will always be open to further question. In the introductory chapter, I noted how accommodating Berkeley's philosophy was to the need to make reasonable conjectures about the existence, volitions, and intentions of other agents, based on the phenomena that present themselves to our senses and our reflex sense of our own existence and agency. We interpret phenomena, including the phenomena that signify the activity of other agents like us. Those interpretations are normative, inasmuch as they require repeated instances of observation and have a predictive function: we see that agents trying to achieve this or that will

4. See LJ, V.5.

do (should do) this or that. The business of bundling instances into groups governed by laws is useful, but might strip the instances of their specificity. It proves useful to generalise from the past conduct of individuals and groups of people in order to ready ourselves for what they might do next, but it may be possible that the information disregarded at the moment of generalising was itself of value. In reading across such a diverse career as Berkeley's, seeking to make sense of his actions by reference to a religio-social mission that was expressed only in fragments and in passing, if telling, asides, it is inevitable that some aspects of the life have been obscured, even if others have been illuminated. As Talia Bettcher notes in her discussion of Berkeley's philosophy of spirit, the subject is elusive, never fully the object of its own perception.[5] Given that, according to Berkeley, our sense of our own subjectivity is that which allows us to infer the existence of others, it should be no surprise that other subjectivities are elusive also.

For all the evocation of lawlike regularity in the phenomenal world, produced by God so that people can better find their way in it and know God's will, Berkeley also insists that God is not constrained by law, that God operates freely and perhaps even idiosyncratically. God need not have organised the creation such that all its operations can be derived from one law (such as the law of attraction): laws may be diverse and need not necessarily impinge on one another. Berkeley was attracted to complex systematic phenomena throughout his life, up to the end of his time in Cloyne, and thought of the weather and of human health as complex, regular, but freely expressive indications of divine will. This characterisation of God as an agent capable of idiosyncratic expression through diverse laws is of relevance to Berkeley's philosophy of spirit and to an understanding of him as a spirit. God and people are spirits, or personal agents, in a perfectly literal sense, according to Berkeley. It should not, perhaps, be surprising if Berkeley believed that the regular behaviour in which humans engage is also idiosyncratic.

In discussing Berkeley's account of language in *Alciphron*, I noted his establishing a criterion for the meaningfulness of terms that do not refer to ideas in their generation of rules or laws for

5. Bettcher, *Berkeley's Philosophy of Spirit*, p. 129.

conduct. Other commentators have already pointed to the alliance of this criterion—so strongly proleptic of twentieth-century pragmatic and use-oriented accounts of meaning, and so open an invitation to think of meaning other than as true correspondence with an ideal or real world—with an argument for the truth of Christian revelation and providence. It is an argument that takes rules and laws to be central to human conduct, and it has been noted at various points throughout this book that laws for Berkeley were often absolute and necessarily implied subordination to higher wills. Must the appeal, for pragmatists, of this Berkeleian account of meaning, taken alongside his account of the phenomenal world as a form of discourse—an appeal that was clearly felt by William James, to cite just one later thinker—be tempered and even altogether undone by our understanding that for Berkeley rules for conduct meant the subordination of wills?[6] The personal idiosyncrasy permitted by the plurality of laws offers a means of preserving some of the progressivism of the pragmatic criterion for meaning. People can express their freedom and responsibility through a number of laws that need not tend always to one unifying centre. There may be regularity in speech and conduct, and it may equally be complex, the idiosyncratic product of a free agent attempting to find the best expressive means to communicate to others what seems to her best to do. There may also, of course, be innumerable forms of speech used to something other than what Berkeley thought was the true end of tending to a conceived good.

Recognising some of the ways in which my interpretive scheme might not have captured all that is important or relevant about Berkeley's life is not then merely a plea for sympathy by anticipating the perception of this book's weaknesses and shortcomings. It is also a recognition that the spirits revealing themselves to us through signs from which we infer agency are always inferences, not phenomena that can be experimentally observed in repeated, controlled circumstances. (And even such phenomena are expressive—of God's will—in Berkeley's view.) Nor are we necessarily

6. James, *Pragmatism* and *The Meaning of Truth*, p. 47: 'Berkeley's criticism of "matter" was [. . .] absolutely pragmatistic'. C. S. Peirce's review of A. C. Fraser's edition of Berkeley's works is regarded as one of the key moments in the emergence of American pragmatism. See Friedman, 'Pragmatism'.

perfectly transparent to ourselves, as observers of our own agency. These issues of perspective and interpretation are part of Berkeley's account of other spirits, as much as the mechanisms he describes for attributing phenomenal signs to another's will. Berkeley's philosophy of spirit provides a rationale for pursuing a biographical approach to his career. It also provides a rationale for never being satisfied with the interpretation at which one has arrived, and for remaining open to new phenomena that might provide grounds for different inferences about this other spirit and his complex, expressive actions.

BIBLIOGRAPHY

Manuscripts

BODLEIAN LIBRARY

MS Radcliffe Records, H.10 Catalogue of Mr Frewin's Books, 1867

BRITISH LIBRARY

BL Add MS 20105, Original letters addressed to Charlotte Dyves, wife of Robert Clayton, Lord Sundon, 1713–1736

BL Add MS 39304–39306, 39310–39312, 39316, Berkeley Papers: autograph commonplace books; correspondence and travel journals of George Berkeley, D.D., Bishop of Cloyne, 1734–1753; correspondence of Berkeley's family; and literary remains of Francis Cherry, the nonjuror, Martin Benson, Bishop of Gloucester, Thomas Secker, Archbishop of Canterbury, and Catherine Talbot

BL Add MS 46688, Berkeley Papers: vol. I, miscellaneous papers, arranged chronologically, 1729–1776

BL Add MS 46889, Berkeley Papers: vol. II, commonplace book of George Berkeley the younger, 1754–1755

BL Add MS 46690, Berkeley Papers: vol. III, journal of Catherine Talbot addressed to 'Angelina' [Jemima, Marchioness Grey; cf. the reference to her daughter, Amabel, at f. 24b], 4 May 1751–10 September 1753

BL Add MS 47006, Egmont Papers: vol. LXXXVII, 1748–1753, diaries and memoranda: W. Cooley, Warden of Lohort Castle, County Cork, 1742–1748

BL Add MS 47030, Egmont Papers: vol. CXI, March 1723–September 1725

BL Add MS 47031, Egmont Papers: vol. CXII, September 1725–1726

HUNTINGTON LIBRARY

Elizabeth Robinson Montagu Papers, MSS MO 1–6923

Egerton Family Papers, MS EL 9608, 'The State & Condition of Bermuda by M.ʳ Richier late Govern.ʳ'

Jonathan Swift Collection, MS HM 14348, Esther Van Homrigh, last will and testament: [copy from the Registry of H.M. Court of Prerogative in Ireland] [. . .] copy made for Sir Walter Scott and presented by him to James Smith

IRISH CHURCH RECORDS

Irish Genealogy, "Church Records," http://churchrecords.irishgenealogy.ie/churchrecords/

LAMBETH PALACE

Fulham Papers, Papers of the Bishops of London, 1–40 Fulham Papers Colonial, vols. V, VIII, XII, XVII, XIX

LONDON METROPOLITAN ARCHIVES

CLC/035/MS23782, 'Chapel Register of the Protestant Society at Leghorn from . . . 1707 to 1783'; transcribed 1810; index compiled c. 1908

NATIONAL ARCHIVES

C 11/1091/9, Court of Chancery, Six Clerks Office: pleadings 1714 to 1758, Bishop of Cloyne v Brome

C 11/1093/9, Court of Chancery, Six Clerks Office: pleadings 1714 to 1758, Bishop of Cloyne v. Young

CO 38/8, Colonial Office: commissions, instructions, Board of Trade correspondence, 4 July 1723–21 December 1748

PRO Prob 11/172, Records of the Prerogative Court of Canterbury: will of Sir Nathaniel Riche of Dalham, Suffolk, 1 December 1636

THE PAPERS OF BENJAMIN FRANKLIN

'Paper on the Academy', minutes of the Common Council, 31 July 1750, vol. 4, https:// franklinpapers.org/framedVolumes.jsp, vol. 4

REPRESENTATIVE CHURCH BODY OF THE CHURCH OF IRELAND LIBRARY

MS C.12.2.1, Records of St Colman's Cathedral, Cloyne, County Cork, 1663–1956: 2. chapter books and other administrative papers; 1. book of abstracts from early chapter books of the dean and chapter of St Colman, referred to as vols. 1 and 2 (no longer extant), outlining orders, resolutions, and other items of business of the chapter, 14 July 1663–26 July 1787

MS 870 Bishop Crowe's Charity

ROYAL DUBLIN SOCIETY

MS RDS/MAN, register and minute book, 1731–1733, 1733–1741, 1741–1746, and 1750–1757 (facsimile volume containing minute books, vol. 1, 25.6.31–1.11.33; vol. 2, 22.11.33–12.11.41; vol. 3, 19.11.41–3.7.46)

ST ANDREWS UNIVERSITY LIBRARY SPECIAL COLLECTIONS

Gibson Papers, MS 5219, draft of Edmund Gibson's case relating to the ministry and the Whigs, 1726 [for 1736?]

STATE PAPERS ONLINE

SP 63/374, State Papers Ireland, 1716

SP 93/32, State Papers Foreign, Sicily and Naples, miscellaneous letters and papers, 1621–1777

TRINITY COLLEGE DUBLIN

TCD MS 453 (listed in inventory as Chapman MS D.5.17), introduction to Berkeley's *Principles of Human Knowledge*

TCD MS 888 (also recorded as Molyneux I.4.17, 19), natural history of Ireland, vols. I and II

TCD MS 2016, Kilkenny College rules

TCD MS 2019, Kilkenny College register

TCD MS 2167/misc. box 17, letters of George Berkeley, Bishop of Cloyne, and notes about him

TCD MS 2215, journal of Matthew French, F.T.C.D., 11 November 1713–15 February 1713/14

TCD MS 2642, Josias Haydocke, a commonplace book

TCD MS 3530, Elizabeth Berkeley's will

TCD MS 5936, Joseph Stock, *An Account of the Life of George Berkeley, D.D. Late Bishop of Cloyne in Ireland. With notes, containing strictures upon his works* (London: J. Murray, 1776): 'FIRST EDITION, 8vo, contemporary half calf, interleaved and supplied with copious manuscript corrections by Berkeley's widow, Anne Berkeley'

TCD MS 7971/misc. aut. 271, John Shadwell, account of TCD curriculum, 1703

TCD MS MUN-P-1-518a, Kilkenny College statutes, 1684/85

TCD MS MUN V-5-2, minute book, 1640–1740

TCD MS MUN V 23/1, admission records, 1637–1725

TCD MS MUN V 23/3, admission records, 1725–1758

TCD MS MUN V 27, Trinity examinations, 1731–1749

YALE UNIVERSITY, BEINECKE RARE BOOK AND MANUSCRIPT LIBRARY

GEN MSS 1571, Anne Forster Berkeley letters to William Samuel Johnson

Works by Berkeley

PRINTED WORKS BY BERKELEY

Advice to the Tories Who have Taken the Oaths (London: printed by R. Baldwin and sold by R. Burleigh, 1715).

Alciphron: Or, The Minute Philosopher, 2nd ed., 2 vols. (London: J. Tonson, 1732).

Alciphron: Or, The Minute Philosopher, 3rd ed. (London: J. and R. Tonson and S. Draper, 1752).

Alciphron: Or, The Minute Philosopher (Dublin: Thomas Watson, 1755).

The Analyst; Or, A Discourse Addressed to an Infidel Mathematician (London: J. Tonson, 1734).

A Defence of Free-Thinking in Mathematics (London: J. Tonson, 1735).

De Motu; Sive, De Motus Principio & Natura, et de Causa Communicationis Motuum (London: Jacob Tonson, 1721)

A Discourse Addressed to Magistrates and Men in Authority, 2nd ed. (Dublin: George Faulkner, 1738).

An Essay towards a New Theory of Vision, 2nd ed. (Dublin: Aaron Rhames for Jeremy Pepyat, 1709).

An Essay towards Preventing the Ruine of Great Britain (London: J. Roberts, 1721).

A Letter from the Author of Siris *to Thomas Prior, Esq; Concerning the Usefulness of Tar-Water in the Plague* (Dublin: George Faulkner, 1747).

George Berkeley's Manuscript Introduction: An Editio Diplomatica, edited and with an introduction by Bertil Belfrage (Oxford: Doxa, 1987).

Maxims Concerning Patriotism (Dublin: [n.p.], 1750).

A Miscellany, Containing Several Tracts on Various Subjects (London: J. and R. Tonson and S. Draper, 1752).

Passive Obedience, Or, The Christian Doctrine of Not Resisting the Supreme Power, Proved and Vindicated upon the Principles of the Law of Nature, 3rd ed. (London: H. Clements, 1713).

Philosophical Commentaries Generally Called the Commonplace Book, edited by A. A. Luce (London: Thomas Nelson and Sons, 1944).

Principles of Human Knowledge: A Treatise Concerning the Principles of Human Knowledge (Dublin: Aaron Rhames for Jeremy Pepyat, 1710).

A Proposal for the better Supplying of Churches in our Foreign Plantations, and for Converting the Savage Americans to Christianity, By a College to be Erected in the Summer Islands, Otherwise Called the Isles of Bermuda (London: printed by H. Woodfall and sold by J. Roberts, 1725).

The Querist, 3 vols. (London: J. Roberts, 1736–1737).

The Querist, 2nd ed. (Dublin: George Faulkner, 1750).

A Sermon Preached before the Incorporated Society for the Propagation of the Gospel in Foreign Parts [. . .] On Friday the 18th of February, 1731. Being the Day of their Anniversary Meeting (London: J. Downing, 1732).

Siris: A Chain of Philosophical Reflexions and Inquiries Concerning the Virtues of TarWater and Divers Other Subjects Connected Together and Arising One from Another, 2nd ed. (Dublin: Margt. Rhames for R. Gunne, 1744).

The Theory of Vision, or Visual Language [. . .] Vindicated and Explained (London: Jacob Tonson, 1733).

Three Dialogues between Hylas and Philonous (London: G. James for Henry Clements, 1713).

A Treatise Concerning the Principles of Human Knowledge [. . .] To Which Are Added Three Dialogues between Hylas and Philonous (London: Jacob Tonson, 1734).

A Word to the Wise: Or, An Exhortation to the Roman Catholic Clergy of Ireland. By a Member of the Established Church (Dublin: George Faulkner, 1749).

The Works of George Berkeley, edited by A. A. Luce and T. E. Jessop, 9 vols. (London: Thomas Nelson, 1948–1957).

The Works of George Berkeley, D.D., edited by Alexander Campbell Fraser, 4 vols. (Oxford: Clarendon Press, 1871).

The Works of George Berkeley, edited by George Sampson, introduction by A. J. Balfour, 3 vols. (London: George Bell and Sons, 1897).

BERKELEY'S CORRESPONDENCE

Berkeley and Percival: The Correspondence of George Berkeley Afterwards Bishop of Cloyne and Sir John Percival Afterwards Earl of Egmont, edited by Benjamin Rand (Cambridge: Cambridge University Press, 1914).

The Correspondence of George Berkeley, edited by Marc A. Hight (Cambridge: Cambridge University Press, 2012).

COLLECTIVE WORKS TO WHICH BERKELEY CONTRIBUTED

[Steele, Richard, et al.], *The Guardian*, 2 vols. (London: J. Tonson, 1714).

——, *The Guardian*, edited by John Calhoun Stephens (Lexington: University Press of Kentucky, 1982).

——, *The Ladies Library, Written by a Lady, Published by Mr Steele*, 3 vols. (London: J.T., 1714).

Printed Works by Others Written before 1800

Abbadie, Jacques, *The Art of Knowing One-Self; or, An Enquiry into the Sources of Morality* (Oxford: Leonard Lichfield for Henry Clements and John Howell, 1695).

Abstract of the Proceedings of the Incorporated Society in Dublin for Promoting English Protestant Schools in Ireland (Dublin: George Grierson, 1737).

Addison, Joseph, *Remarks on Several Parts of Italy, &c In the Years 1701, 1702, 1703*, 2nd ed. (London: Jacob Tonson, 1718).

[Addison, Joseph, et al.], *The Spectator*, edited by Donald F. Bond, 5 vols. (Oxford: Clarendon Press, 1965).

Anon. [From a Foreign Gentleman at London to his Friend Abroad], *Anti-Siris: Or, English Wisdom Exemplify'd by Various Examples, But, Particularly, The Present General Demand for Tar Water, On so Unexceptionable Authority as that of a R—t*

R—d Itinerant Schemist, and Graduate in Divinity and Metaphysicks (London: M. Cooper, 1744).

Aristotle, *De Anima*, translated and with an introduction and commentary by Christopher Shields (Oxford: Clarendon Press, 2016).

Astell, Mary, *A Serious Proposal to the Ladies*, edited by Patricia Springborg (Peterborough, Ontario: Broadview, 2002).

[R.B.], *The English Empire in America* (London: Nath. Crouch, 1685).

Bacon, Francis, *Historie Naturall and Experimentall, of Life and Death*, translated by William Rawley (London: Iohn Haviland for William Lee, and Humphrey Mosley, 1638).

Barrow, Isaac, *A Brief Exposition of the Lord's Prayer and the Decalogue* (London: M. Flesher for Brabazon Aylmer, 1681).

[Bayes, Thomas], *An Introduction to the Doctrine of Fluxions, And Defence of the Mathematicians Against the Objections of the Author of the Analyst, so Far as they are Designed to Affect their General Methods of Reasoning* (London: J. Noon, 1736).

[Berkeley, Anne, et al.], *The Contrast*, 2 vols. (London: John Stockdale, 1791).

Berkeley, Eliza, preface to George Monck Berkeley, *Poems* (London: J. Nichols, 1797).

Blackwell, Thomas, *Memoirs of the Court of Augustus*, 2 vols. (Edinburgh: Hamilton, Balfour and Neill, 1753–1764).

Bolton, Robert, *A Translation of the Charter and Statutes of Trinity-College, Dublin. Together with the Library-Statutes, and the Rules of the University. To which is added a Table of Expences for each Degree* (Dublin: Oli. Nelson for the translator, 1749).

Boyle, Robert, *Selected Philosophical Papers of Robert Boyle*, edited by M. A. Stewart (Manchester: Manchester University Press, 1979).

——, *Tracts* (London: W.G. to be sold by M. Pitt, 1674).

Bray, Thomas, *Missionalia: Or, A Collection of Missionary PIECES Relating to the Conversion of the Heathen; Both the African Negroes and American Indians* (London: W. Roberts, 1727).

Brinsley, John, *The Posing of the Parts, or, A Most Plain and Easie Way of Examining the Accidence and Grammar* (London: [n.p.], 1669).

Browne, Peter, *A Discourse of Drinking Healths Wherein the Great Evil of this Prevailing Custom is Shewn* (Dublin: John Hyde, 1716).

Burthogge, Richard, *An Essay on Reason and the Nature of Spirits* (London: John Dunton, 1694).

Carpenter, Andrew, ed., *Verse in English from Eighteenth-Century Ireland* (Cork: University of Cork Press, 1998).

A Catalogue of the Valuable Library of the late Right Rev. Dr. Berkeley, Lord Bishop of Cloyne. Together with the libraries of his Son and Grandson, the late Rev. GEORGE BERKELEY, D.D. PREBENDARY of CANTERBURY, and the later GEORGE MONK BERKELEY, Esq. To be sold by Leigh and Sotheby, Monday June 6, 1796, and the Five following days (annotated sale copy in the British Library at S.C.S.28).

Charnock, Stephen, *A Treatise of Providence* (London: Thomas Cockerill, 1680).

Cheyne, George, *Philosophical Principles of Natural Religion: Containing the Elements of Natural Philosophy, and the Proofs for Natural Religion, Arising from Them*, 2 vols. (London: George Strahan, 1705).

Cicero, *On Duties*, translated by Walter Miller (Cambridge, MA: Harvard University Press, 1913).

——, *The Nature of the Gods*, translated by Horace C. P. McGregor, introduction by J. M. Ross (Harmondsworth: Penguin, 1972).

Clayton, Charlotte, *Memoirs of [Charlotte Clayton,] the Countess of Sundon, Mistress of the Robes to Queen Caroline*, edited by Katherine Thomson, 2 vols. (London: Henry Coburn, 1847).

Coghill, Marmaduke, *The Letters of Marmaduke Coghill, 1722–1738*, edited by D. W. Hayton (Dublin: Irish Manuscripts Commission, 2005).

Collins, Anthony, *A Discourse of Free-thinking, Occasion'd by the Rise and Growth of a Sect Call'd Free-Thinkers* (London: [n.p.], 1713).

——, *An Essay Concerning the Use of Reason in Propositions, The Evidence Whereof Depends upon Human Testimony* (London: [n.p.], 1707).

[Commissioners for Trade and Plantations], *Journal of the Commissioners for Trade and Plantations*, vol. V, *January 1722–1723 to December 1728* (London: His Majesty's Stationery Office, 1928).

Cooper, Anthony Ashley, Third Earl of Shaftesbury, *Characteristics of Men, Manners, Opinions, Times*, edited by Lawrence E. Klein (Cambridge: Cambridge University Press, 1999).

Cudworth, Ralph, *The True Intellectual System of the Universe* (London: Richard Royston, 1678).

Descartes, René, *The Philosophical Writings of Descartes*, translated by John Cottingham, Robert Stoothoff, and Dugald Murdoch, 2 vols. (Cambridge: Cambridge University Press, 1985).

Dixon, Robert, *A Short Essay of Modern Divinity* (London: S.R. for R. Clavell, 1681).

Fénelon, François de, *A Discourse on Christian Perfection* (Dublin: W. Watson, 1759).

——, *An Extract from a Discourse on Humility* (Dublin: W. Watson, 1758).

——, *An Extract from a Discourse on Prayer* (Dublin: W. Watson, 1759).

——, *Letters to the Duke of Burgundy* (Dublin: W. Watson, 1758).

——, *A Letter Upon the Truth of Religion and its Practice* (Dublin: W. Watson, 1758).

——, *Œuvres*, edited by Jacques le Brun, 2 vols. (Paris: Gallimard, 1983 and 1997).

——, *Telemachus, Son of Ulysses*, translated and edited by Patrick Riley (Cambridge: Cambridge University Press, 1994).

Flamsteed, John, *The Correspondence of John Flamsteed, First Astronomer Royal, III 1703–1719*, edited by Eric G. Forbes, Lesley Murdin, and Frances Willmoth (Bristol: Institute of Physics Publishing, 2002).

Franklin, Benjamin, *Proposals Relating to the Education of Youth in Pensilvania* (Philadelphia: [n.p.], 1749).

Gellius, Aulus, *The Attic Nights of Aulus Gellius*, translated by John C. Rolfe, 3 vols. (Cambridge, MA: Harvard University Press, 1927).

Godwyn, Morgan, *The Negroe's and Indian's Advocate, Suing for their Admission into the Church; Or A Persuasive to the Instructing and Baptizing of the Negro's and Indians in our Plantations* (London: printed by J.D. for the author, 1680).

[?Goldsmith, Oliver], 'George Berkely', in *The British Plutarch*, edited by Thomas Mortimer, vol. 12 (London: Edward Dilly, 1762), pp. 160–71.

Gordon, Thomas, *The Character of an Independent Whig* (London: J. Roberts, 1719).

Granville, Mary, *The Autobiography and Correspondence of Mary Granville, Mrs. Delany: With Interesting Reminiscences of King George the Third and Queen Charlotte*, edited by Lady Llanover, 6 vols. (London: Richard Bentley, 1861–1862).

Grotius, Hugo, *On the Law of War and Peace*, edited by Stephen C. Neff (Cambridge: Cambridge University Press, 2012).

Hales, Stephen, *Statical Essays: Containing Vegetable Staticks; Or, An Account of Some Statical Experiments on the Sap in Vegetables*, 2nd ed. (London: W. Innys, T. Woodward, and J. Peele, 1731).

Higden, William, *A View of the English Constitution, with respect to the Sovereign Authority of the Prince, and the Allegiance of the Subject, in Vindication of the Lawfulness of Taking the Oaths, to Her Majesty, by Law Required*, 2nd ed. (London: Samuel Keble, 1709).

Hippocrates, 'Heart', in *Coan Prenotions, Anatomical and Minor Clinical Writings*, edited and translated by Paul Potter (Cambridge, MA: Harvard University Press, 2010), pp. 51–70.

——, 'Regimen I', in *Nature of Man. Regiment in Health. Humours. Aphorisms. Regimen 1–3. Dreams. Heracleitus: On the Universe*, translated by W.H.S. Jones (Cambridge, MA: Harvard University Press, 1931), pp. 223–96.

Histoire de l'académie royale des sciences depuis son établissement en 1666 jusqu'à 1686, vol. I (Paris, 1733).

Historical Manuscripts Commission, *Report on the Manuscripts of Mrs. Stopford-Sackville of Drayton House, Northamptonshire*, 2 vols. (London: Stationery Office, 1904–1910).

Homer, *The Iliad of Homer, with Notes. By Madam Dacier*, translated by William Broome, vol. 4 (London: printed by H. Woodfall, for Bernard Lintot, 1722).

——, *Iliad, Volume I: Books 1–12*, translated by A. T. Murray, revised by William F. Wyatt (Cambridge, MA: Harvard University Press, 1924).

Hooper, George, 'A Calculation of the Credibility of Human Testimony', *Philosophical Transactions of the Royal Society of London*, 21 (1699), 359–65.

Horace, *Satires, Epistles, Ars Poetica*, translated by H. R. Fairclough (Cambridge, MA: Harvard University Press, 1926; rev. ed., 1929).

Hume, David, *Essays Moral, Political, and Literary*, rev. ed., edited by Eugene F. Miller (Indianapolis: Liberty Fund, 1987).

Hyde, Henry, Earl of Clarendon, *The History of the Rebellion and Civil Wars in England*, 3 vols. (Oxford: At the Theatre, 1707).

Iamblichus, *On the Mysteries of the Egyptians, Chaldeans, and Assyrians and Life of Pythagoras*, translated by Thomas Taylor (Sturminster Newton, Dorset: Prometheus Trust, 1999).

The Irish Blasters, Or, the Votaries of Bacchus (Dublin: [n.p.], 1738).

Jefferson, Thomas, *Notes on the State of Virginia*, edited and with an introduction by William Peden (1954; Chapel Hill: University of North Carolina Press for the Institute of Early American History and Culture at Williamsburg, Virginia, 1995).

[Jewel, John], *An Apology or Answer in Defence of the Church of England*, translated by Anne Bacon, edited by Patricia Demers (Cambridge: Modern Humanities Research Association, 2016).

Johnson, Samuel, *Samuel Johnson, President of King's College, His Career and Writings*, edited by Herbert Schneider and Carol Schneider, 4 vols. (New York: Columbia University Press, 1929).

Jurin, James [Philalethes Cantabrigiensis], *Geometry no Friend to Infidelity: Or, A Defence of Sir Isaac Newton and the British Mathematicians, In a Letter to the Author of the Analyst* (London: T. Cooper, 1734).

King, William, *Divine Predestination and Fore-Knowledge, Consistent with the Freedom of Man's Will* (Dublin and London: J. Baker, 1709).

——, *An Essay on the Origin of Evil [. . .] To which is prefix'd A Dissertation Concerning the Fundamental Principle and Immediate Criterion of Virtue*, translated by Edmund Hall (Cambridge: W. Thurlborn, 1731; New York: Garland, 1978).

——, *A Sermon, Preached at St Patrick's Church Dublin, on the 16th of November 1690* (Dublin: Joseph Ray, 1691).

Lafitau, Joseph-François, *Moeurs des sauvages amériquains comparées aux moeurs des premiers temps*, 2 vols. (Paris: Chez Saugrain and Charles Estienne Hochereau, 1724).

Law, John, *Money and Trade Consider'd; With a Proposal for Supplying the Nation with Money*, 2nd ed. (London: W. Lewis, 1720).

'A Letter to the Right Reverend the Lord Bishop of *Cloyne*. By a Gentleman in the Army, in the Year 1739', in *The Harleian Miscellany* III (London, 1745), pp. 169–77.

'The Life of Basil Kennet', in *British Biography*, vol. 7 (London: R. Baldwin and J. Towers, 1772).

List of Members of the Dublin-Society for the Improvement of Husbandry and other Useful Arts for the Year 1733 (Dublin: A. Rhames, 1734).

Locke, John, *The Correspondence of John Locke*, edited by E. S. de Beer, vol. 4 (Oxford: Clarendon Press, 1979).

——, *An Essay Concerning Human Understanding*, edited by P. H. Nidditch (Oxford: Clarendon Press, 1975).

——, *Some Thoughts Concerning Education*, edited by John W. and Jean S. Yolton (Oxford: Clarendon Press, 1989; reprint, 2003).

——, *Two Treatises of Government*, edited by Peter Laslett, student ed. (Cambridge: Cambridge University Press, 1988).

Lucanus, Ocellus, *Ocellus Lucanus on the Nature of the Universe* [and other texts by Taurus, Julius Firmicus Maternus, and Proclus], translated by Thomas Taylor (London: printed for the translator and sold by John Bohn, Henry Bohn, and Thomas Rodd, 1831).

MacSparran, James, *A Letter Book and Abstract of Out Services Written During the Years 1743–1751*, edited by Daniel Goodwin (Boston: D. B. Updike, Merrymount Press, 1899).

Madden, Samuel, *Reflections and Resolutions Proper for the Gentlemen of Ireland* (Dublin: R. Reilly, 1738).

Malebranche, Nicolas, *The Search after Truth*, translated and edited by Thomas M. Lennon and Paul J. Olscamp (Cambridge: Cambridge University Press, 1997).

Mandeville, Bernard, *The Fable of the Bees*, edited by Philip Harth (Harmondsworth: Penguin, 1970).

Martin, Martin, *A Late Voyage to St. Kilda* (London: D. Brown and T. Goodwin, 1698).

Martyn, Benjamin, *Reasons for Establishing the Colony of Georgia* (London: W. Meadows, 1733).

———, *Some Account of the Designs of the Trustees for Establishing the Colony of Georgia in America* (London: [n.p.], 1732).

Masham, Damaris, *Occasional Thoughts in Reference to a Vertuous or Christian Life* (London: A. and J. Churchill, 1705).

Mead, Richard, *Of the Power and Influence of the Sun and Moon on Humane Bodies; And of the Diseases that Rise from thence* (London: Richard Wellington, 1712).

[Meredith, Royston], *Mr. Steele Detected; Or, The Poor and Oppressed Orphan's Letters to the Great and Arbitrary Mr. Steele; Complaining of the Great Injustice Done, to the Publick in General, and to Himself in Particular, by the Ladies Library* (London: John Morphew, 1714).

Misson, Maximilian, *A New Voyage to Italy*, [translated by anon.], 2 vols. (London: R. Bently et al., 1695).

Molyneux, William, *Dioptrica Nova; A Treatise of Doptrics in Two Parts* (London: Benj. Tooke, 1692).

Montagu, Elizabeth, *Elizabeth Montagu, the Queen of the Bluestockings: Her Correspondence from 1720–1761*, edited by Emily J. Climenson, 2 vols. (London: John Murray, 1906).

Montaigne, Michel de, *Essays of Michel Seigneur de Montaigne*, translated by Charles Cotton, 3 vols. (London: J. Brown et al., 1711).

More, Henry, *The Theological Works* (London: Joseph Downing, 1708).

Newton, Isaac, *Opticks, or A Treatise on the Reflections, Refractions, Inflections & Colours of Light* (based on 4th ed., 1730), foreword by Albert Einstein, introduction by Edmund Whittaker, preface by I. Bernard Cohen, and analytical table of contents by Duane H. D. Roller (New York: Dover, 1979).

———, *The Principia: Mathematical Principles of Natural Philosophy*, translated by I. Bernard Cohen and Anne Whitman, assisted by Julia Budenz (Berkeley: University of California Press, 1999).

Nieuwentijt, Bernard, *The Religious Philosopher*, translated by John Chamberlayne, 3 vols., 4th ed. (London: J. Senex et al., 1730).

Norris, John, *Practical Discourses*, vol. 3 (London: Samuel Manship, 1701).

———, *A Practical Treatise Concerning Humility* (London: S. Manship, 1707).

O'Conor, Charles, *Seasonal Thoughts Relating to Our Civil and Ecclesiastical Consti-tution* (Dublin: [n.p.], 1754).

Oglethorpe, James, *A New and Accurate Account of the Provinces of South-Carolina and Georgia* (London: printed for J. Worrall and sold by J. Roberts, 1732).

Owens, S., 'Remarks on the Young Ladies PETITION, To the Revnd. Dr B-rk-y', NLS Crawford.EB.3821

Parrino, Domenico Antonio, *Nuova guida de'forastieri per osservare e godere la curi-osità più vaghe, e più rare della Real Fedeliss: Gran Napoli* (Naples, 1712).

Pascal, Blaise, *Thoughts on Religion and Other Subjects*, translated by Basil Kennet (London: W.B. for A. and J. Churchill et al., 1704).

Percival, John, *Manuscripts of the Earl of Egmont: Diary of Viscount Percival, after-wards first Earl of Egmont*, 3 vols. (London: HMSO, 1920–1923).

Petty, William, *Political Arithmetick, Or a Discourse Concerning The Extent and Value of Lands, People, Buildings [. . .]* (London: Robert Clavel and Hen. Mortlock, 1691).

Pieces qui ont remporté les deux prix de l'academie royale des sciences, proposés pour l'année mil sept cens vingt (Paris: Claude Jombert, 1721).

Pilkington, Laetitia, *The Memoirs of Laetitia Pilkington*, edited by A. C. Elias Jr, 2 vols. (Athens: University of Georgia Press, 1997).

Plato, *Timaeus*, translated by Benjamin Jowett, in *The Collected Dialogues of Plato*, edited by Edith Hamilton and Huntington Cairns (New York: Bollingen Founda-tion, 1961), pp. 1151–1211.

Plotinus, *The Enneads*, translated by Stephen MacKenna, edited by John Dillon (Harmondsworth: Penguin, 1991).

Pope, Alexander, *The Correspondence of Alexander Pope*, edited by George Sherburn, 5 vols. (Oxford: Clarendon Press, 1954).

——, *An Essay on Man*, edited by Tom Jones (Princeton, NJ: Princeton University Press, 2016).

——, *The Works of Alexander Pope*, edited by William Warburton, 9 vols. (London: A. Millar et al., 1766).

Prior, Thomas, *Observations on Coin in General With Some Proposals for Regulating the Value of Coin in Ireland* [Dublin: A. Rhames for R. Gunne, 1729], in *A Select Collection of Scarce and Valuable Tracts on Money*, edited by J. R. McCulloch (London: Political Economy Club, 1856), pp. 291–338.

Proclus, *Proclus' Commentary on Plato's Parmenides*, translated by Glenn R. Morrow and John M. Dillon, introduction by John M. Dillon (Princeton, NJ: Princeton University Press, 1987).

Pufendorf, Samuel, *The Whole Duty of Man, According to the Law of Nature*, translated by Andrew Tooke and Jean Barbeyrac, and *Two Discourses and a Commentary*, translated by David Saunders, both edited by Ian Hunter and David Saunders (Indianapolis: Liberty Fund, 2003).

Queries Concerning the Reasonableness of Repealing the Corporation and Test Acts (London: printed for J. Wilford and sold by A. Dodd and H. Whitridge, 1732).

[R.M.], *A General Survey of that Part of the Island of St. Christophers [. . .] Together with an Estimate of the Value of those Lands, and a Proposal and Scheme for raising a very considerable Sum of Money, for the Use of the Publick, on the Produce thereof* (London: J. Roberts, 1722).

Records of the Colony of Rhode Island, vol. 4, *1707–1740* (Providence: Knowles, Anthony & Co., 1859).

Robins, Benjamin, *A Discourse Concerning the Nature and Certainty of Sir Isaac Newton's Methods of Fluxions, and of Prime and Ultimate Ratios* (London: W. Innys and R. Manby, 1735).

Russel, Richard, *A Dissertation on the Use of Sea Water in the Diseases of the Glands*, [translated by anon.], 4th ed. (London: W. Owen, 1760).

Scougal, Henry, *The Life of God in the Soul of Man, or, The Nature and Excellency of the Christian Religion* (London: Charles Smith and William Jacob, 1677).

Secker, Thomas, *The Correspondence of Bishop Secker*, edited by A. P. Jenkins (Far Thrupp, Stroud: Alan Sutton for the Oxfordshire Record Society, 1991).

Senex, John, *A New General Atlas, Containing a Geographical and Historical Account of All the Empires, Kingdoms, and Other Dominions of the World: With the Natural History and Trade of Each Country* (London: Daniel Brown et al., 1721).

Sergeant, John, *Solid Philosophy Asserted, Against the Fancies of the Ideists; Or, The Method to Science Farther Illustrated* (London: Roger Clavil, Abel Roper, and Thomas Metcalf, 1697).

Sheridan, Thomas, *The Life of the Rev. Dr. Jonathan Swift*, vol. 1 (London: C. Bathurst et al., 1784).

———, *The Poems of Thomas Sheridan*, edited by Robert Hogan (Newark: University of Delaware Press; London and Toronto: Associated University Presses, 1994).

Śmiglecki, Marcin, *Logica Martini Smiglecii* (Oxford: A. Lichfield et al., 1658).

Smith, Adam, *The Theory of Moral Sentiments*, edited by D. D. Raphael and A. L. Macfie (Indianapolis: Liberty Fund, 1982).

Smith, Charles, *The Antient and Present State of the County and City of Cork*, 2 vols. (Dublin: A. Reilly for the author and sold by J. Exshaw, 1750).

Southerne, Thomas, *The Works of Thomas Southerne*, edited by Robert Jordan and Harold Love, 2 vols. (Oxford: Clarendon Press, 1988).

Spinoza, Benedict de, *Ethics*, edited and translated by G.H.R. Parkinson (Oxford: Oxford University Press, 2000).

Stanley, Thomas, *The History of Philosophy: Containing the Lives, Opinions, Actions, and Discourses of the Philosophers of Every Sect*, 2nd ed. (London: Thomas Bassett et al., 1687).

Stock, Joseph, *An Account of the Life of George Berkeley, D.D. Late Bishop of Cloyne in Ireland* (London: J. Murray, 1776).

Swift, Jonathan, *An Argument to Prove that the Abolishing of Christianity in England, May as Things now Stand, Be Attended with Some Inconveniences, and Perhaps Not Produce those Many Good Effects Proposed thereby*, in *The Major Works*, edited by Angus Ross and David Woolley (Oxford: Oxford University Press, 1984), pp. 217–27.

———, *The Correspondence of Jonathan Swift*, edited by David Wooley, 5 vols. (Frankfurt am Main: Peter Lang, 1999–2014).

———, *Gulliver's Travels*, edited by David Womersley (Cambridge: Cambridge University Press, 2012).

——, *The History of the Four Last Years of Queen Anne*, edited by Herbert Davis, introduction by Harold Williams (Oxford: Basil Blackwell, 1951).

——, *Journal to Stella*, edited by Abigail Williams, (Cambridge: Cambridge University Press, 2013).

——, *Queries Relating to the Sacramental Test*, in *The Works of Jonathan Swift*, vol. 4 (Dublin: G. Faulkner, 1746), pp. 350–58.

——, *Swift vs. Mainwaring: The Examiner and The Medly*, edited by Frank H. Ellis (Oxford: Clarendon Press, 1985).

——, *A Tale of a Tub and Other Works*, edited by Marcus Walsh (Cambridge: Cambridge University Press, 2010).

Timaios of Locri, *On the Nature of the World and the Soul*, edited and translated by Thomas H. Tobin (Chico, CA: Scholars Press, 1985).

Tindal, Matthew, *Four Discourses* (London: [?J. Darby], 1709).

Toland, John, *Christianity Not Mysterious: Text, Associated Works, and Critical Essays*, edited by Philip McGuiness, Alan Harrison, and Richard Kearney (Dublin: Lilliput Press, 1997).

Trenchard, John, Thomas Gordon, and Anthony Collins, *The Independent Whig*, 2 vols. (London: J. Peele for J. Osborn, 1732).

Tryon, Thomas, *Friendly Advice to the Gentlemen-Planters of the East and West Indies* ([?London]: Andrew Sowle, 1684).

Varenius, Bernhardus, *Cosmography and Geography in Two Parts: The First [...] being a Translation from that Eminent and much Esteemed Geographer Varenius [...] The Second Part, Being a Geographical Description of all the World, Taken from the Notes and Works of the Famous Monsieur Sanson*, translated by Richard Blome (London: S. Roycroft and sold by William Abington, 1683).

The Vindication and Advancement of our National Constitution and Credit (London: Jonah Bowyer, 1710).

Wallis, John, 'The Sentiments of the Reverend and Learned Dr. John Wallis, R.S. Soc. upon the Aforesaid Appearance, Communicated in a Letter to the Publisher', *Philosophical Transactions of the Royal Society of London*, 16 (1686–1692), 323–29.

Walton, John, *A Vindication of Sir Isaac Newton's Principles of Fluxions, Against the Objections Contained in the Analyst* (London and Dublin: J. Roberts, 1735).

Ward, John, *The Young Mathematician's Guide* (London: Edw. Midwinter for John Taylor, 1707).

Waterfield, Robin, trans., *The First Philosophers: The Presocratics and the Sophists* (Oxford: Oxford University Press, 2000).

Wesley, John, *The Works of John Wesley*, vol. 25, *Letters I, 1721–1739*, edited by Frank Baker (Oxford: Clarendon Press, 1980).

——, *The Works of John Wesley*, vol. 26, *Letters II, 1740–1755*, edited by Frank Baker (Oxford: Clarendon Press, 1982).

Williams, Roger, *A Key to the Language of America* (London: Gregory Dexter, 1643; Menston: Scolar Press, 1971).

Willis, Thomas, 'Of the Growing Hot or Inkindling of the Blood', in *Five Treatises* (London: T. Dring et al., 1681), pp. 24–33.

PRE-1800 PERIODICALS

British Journal
Daily Post
Gentleman's Magazine
London Daily Advertiser
London Evening Post
London Gazette

Printed Works by Others Written after 1800

Aarsleff, Hans, 'Philosophy of Language', in *The Cambridge History of Eighteenth-Century Philosophy*, edited by Knud Haakonssen, 2 vols. (Cambridge: Cambridge University Press, 2006) I.451–95.

Abelove, Henry, 'George Berkeley's Attitude to John Wesley: The Evidence of a Lost Letter', *Harvard Theological Review*, 70 (1977), 175–76.

Acheson, Alan R., 'Rundle, Thomas', in *Oxford Dictionary of National Biography*, https://www.oxforddnb.com/view/10.1093/ref:odnb/9780198614128.001.0001/odnb-9780198614128-e-24279 (accessed 7 August 2019).

Adams, Charles Francis, et al., eds., *Commerce of Rhode Island 1726–1800*, 2 vols. (Boston: Massachusetts Historical Society, 1914–1915).

Ahn, Doohwan, 'The Anglo-French Treaty of Utrecht of 1713 Revisited: The Politics of Rivalry and Alliance', in *The Politics of Commercial Treaties in the Eighteenth Century: Balance of Power, Balance of Trade*, edited by Antonella Alimento and Koen Stapelbroek (Basingstoke: Palgrave Macmillan, 2017), pp. 125–49.

Airaksinen, Timo, 'Berkeley's *Siris*: An Interpretation', in *The Bloomsbury Companion to Berkeley*, edited by Richard Brooke and Bertil Belfrage (London: Bloomsbury, 2017), pp. 216–44.

——, 'The Chain and the Animal: Idealism in Berkeley's *Siris*', in *Eriugena, Berkeley, and the Idealist Tradition*, edited by Stephen Gersh and Dermot Moran (Notre Dame, IN: University of Notre Dame Press, 2006), pp. 224–43.

Airaksinen, Timo, and Heta Gylling, 'A Threat Like No Other Threat: George Berkeley against the Freethinkers', *History of European Ideas*, 43 (2017), 598–613.

Aitken, George A., 'Steele's *Ladies' Library*', *The Athenaeum: Journal of English and Foreign Literature, Science, the Fine Arts, Music, and the Drama*, 2958 (5 July 1884), 16–17.

Ashworth, E. J., 'Do Words Signify Ideas or Things? The Scholastic Sources of Locke's Theory of Language', *Journal of the History of Philosophy*, 19 (1981), 299–326.

Atherton, Margaret, 'Berkeley without God', in *Debates in Modern Philosophy: Essential Readings and Contemporary Responses*, edited by Stewart Duncan and Antonia Lolordo (New York: Routledge, 2013), pp. 201–15.

——, 'The Coherence of Berkeley's Theory of Mind', *Philosophy and Phenomenological Research*, 43 (1983), 389–99.

Ayers, M. A., 'Nature and Laws from Descartes to Hume', in *The Philosophical Canon in the 17th and 18th Centuries: Essays in Honour of John W. Yolton*, ed. by G.A.J. Rogers and Sylvana Tomaselli (Rochester, NY: University of Rochester Press, 1996), pp. 83–108.

Ayers, Michael, and Daniel Garber, 'Introduction' to *The Cambridge History of Seventeenth-Century Philosophy*, edited by Michael Ayers and Daniel Garber, 2 vols. (Cambridge: Cambridge University Press, 1997), I.1–6.

Bantock, G. H., *Studies in the History of Educational Theory*, 2 vols. (London: George Allen & Unwin, 1980–1984).

Barnard, Toby, 'Improving Clergymen, 1660–1760', in *As by Law Established: The Church of Ireland since the Reformation*, edited by Alan Ford, James McGuire, and Kenneth Milne (Dublin: Lilliput Press, 1995), pp. 136–51.

——, *Improving Ireland? Projectors, Prophets, and Profiteers, 1641–1786* (Dublin: Four Courts Press, 2008).

——, *Irish Protestant Ascents and Descents, 1641–1770* (Dublin: Four Courts Press, 2004).

Bayley, Peter, 'What Was Quietism Subversive Of?', *Seventeenth-Century French Studies*, 21 (1999), 195–204.

Beal, Melvin W., 'Berkeley's Linguistic Criterion', in *George Berkeley: Critical Assessments*, edited by Walter E. Creery, vol. 3 (London: Routledge, 1991), pp. 375–87.

Belfrage, Bertil, 'Dating Berkeley's Notebook B', *Berkeley Newsletter*, 7 (1984), 7–13.

——, 'Notes by Berkeley on Moral Philosophy', *Berkeley Newsletter*, 2 (1978), 4–7.

——, 'Editor's Commentary', in *George Berkeley's Manuscript Introduction: An Editio Diplomatica*, edited and with an introduction by Bertil Belfrage (Oxford: Doxa, 1987).

Bennet, J. Harry, Jr, *Bondsmen and Bishops: Slavery and Apprenticeship on the Codrington Plantations of Barbados, 1710–1838* (Berkeley: University of California Press, 1958).

Berman, David, 'Anthony Collins' Essays in *The Independent Whig*', *Journal of the History of Philosophy*, 13 (1975), 463–69.

——, *Berkeley and Irish Philosophy* (London: Continuum, 2005).

——, 'Berkeley's Life and Works', in *The Cambridge Companion to Berkeley*, edited by Kenneth Winkler (Cambridge: Cambridge University Press 2005), pp. 13–33.

——, 'Cognitive Theology and Emotive Mysteries in Berkeley's *Alciphron*', in *Alciphron in Focus*, edited by David Berman (London: Routledge, 1993), pp. 200–213.

——, *George Berkeley: Idealism and the Man* (Oxford: Clarendon Press, 1994).

——, 'Introduction' to A. A. Luce, *The Life of George Berkeley Bishop of Cloyne* (London: Thomas Nelson, 1949; London: Routledge/Thoemmes Press, 1992).

——, 'Mrs Berkeley's Annotations in *An Account of the Life of Berkeley* (1776)', in *Berkeley and Irish Philosophy* (London: Continuum, 2005), pp. 186–201.

——, 'Some New Bermuda Berkeleiana', *Hermathena*, 110 (1970), 24–31.

Bettcher, Talia Mae, *Berkeley's Philosophy of Spirit: Consciousness, Ontology, and the Elusive Subject* (London: Continuum, 2007).

Bordner, S. Seth, 'Berkeley's "Defense" of "Commonsense"', *Journal of the History of Philosophy*, 49 (2011), 315–38.

Bourne, H. R. Fox, *A Life of John Locke*, 2 vols. (New York: Harper and Brothers, 1876).

Bracken, Harry M., *The Early Reception of Berkeley's Immaterialism*, rev. ed. (The Hague: Martinus Nijhoff, 1965).

——, *George Berkeley* (London: Palgrave Macmillan, 1974).

Brady, William Maziere, *Clerical and Parochial Records of Cork, Cloyne, and Ross*, 3 vols. (Dublin: Alexander Thom, 1863–1864).

Bregoli, Francesca, *Mediterranean Enlightenment: Livornese Jews, Tuscan Culture, and Eighteenth-Century Reform* (Stanford, CA: Stanford University Press, 2014).

Breuninger, Scott C., 'Berkeley and Ireland: Who Are the "We" in 'We Irish Think Otherwise"?', in *Anglo-Irish Identities 1571–1845*, edited by David A. Valone and Jill Marie Bradbury (Lewisburg, PA: Bucknell University Press, 2008), pp. 104–25.

——, *Recovering Bishop Berkeley: Virtue and Society in the Anglo-Irish Context* (Basingstoke: Palgrave Macmillan, 2010).

Bric, Maurice J., 'The Tithe System in Eighteenth-Century Ireland', *Proceedings of the Royal Irish Academy: Archaeology, Culture, History, Literature*, 86C (1986), 271–88.

Bridenbaugh, Carl, *Mitre and Sceptre: Transatlantic Faiths, Ideas, Personalities, and Politics 1689–1775* (New York: Oxford University Press, 1962).

Brook, Richard, 'Berkeley's Theory of Vision: Transparency and Signification', *British Journal for the History of Philosophy*, 11 (2003), 691–99.

Brown, Michael, *The Irish Enlightenment* (New Haven, CT: Yale University Press, 2016).

Brown, Stuart, 'Leibniz and Berkeley: Platonic Metaphysics and "The Mechanical Philosophy"', in *Platonism at the Origins of Modernity: Studies on Platonism and Early Modern Philosophy*, edited by Douglas Hedley and Sarah Hutton (Dordrecht: Springer, 2008), pp. 239–53.

Brykman, Geneviève, *Berkeley: Philosophie et apologétique* (Lille: Atelier national de reproduction des thèses, 1984).

——, *Berkeley et le voile des mots* (Paris: J. Vrin, 1993)

——, 'La Sémantique dans le Dialogue VII', in *Berkeley's Alciphron: English Text and Essays in Interpretation*, edited by Geneviève Brykman, Laurent Jaffro, and Claire Schwartz (Hildesheim, Zürich: Georg Olms, 2010), pp. 407–12.

Brykman, Geneviève, Laurent Jaffro, and Claire Schwartz, eds., *Berkeley's Alciphron: English Text and Essays in Interpretation* (Hildesheim, Zürich: Georg Olms, 2010).

Bushman, Richard L., *King and People in Provincial Massachusetts* (Chapel Hill: University of North Carolina Press, 1992).

Caffentzis, C. George, 'Algebraic Money: Berkeley's Philosophy of Mathematics and Money', *Berkeley Studies*, 18 (2007), 3–23.

——, *Exciting the Industry of Mankind: George Berkeley's Philosophy of Money* (Dordrecht: Kluwer, 2000).

——, 'The Failure of Berkeley's Bank: Money and Libertinism in Eighteenth-Century Ireland', in *The Empire of Credit: The Financial Revolution in the British Atlantic*

World, 1688–1815, edited by Daniel Carey and Christopher J. Finlay (Dublin and Portland, OR: Irish Academic Press, 2011), pp. 229–48.

Cameron, Bridget, *This Master Firebrand: A Life of Charles Mordaunt 3rd Earl of Peterborough, 1658–1735* (Norwich: Michael Russell, 2009).

Campbell, John, and Quassim Cassam, *Berkeley's Puzzle: What Does Experience Teach Us?* (Oxford: Oxford University Press, 2014).

Carey, Brycchan, *From Peace to Freedom: Quaker Rhetoric and the Birth of American Anti-Slavery, 1657–1761* (New Haven, CT: Yale University Press, 2012).

Carey, Daniel, *Locke, Shaftesbury, and Hutcheson: Contesting Diversity in the Enlightenment and Beyond* (Cambridge: Cambridge University Press, 2006).

Chaney, Edward, *The Evolution of the Grand Tour: Anglo-Italian Cultural Relations since the Renaissance* (London: Frank Cass, 1998).

Charles, Sébastien, 'Berkeley et Campailla: Rencontre infructueuse ou influence probable?', *Giornale Critico della Filosofia Italiana*, 88 (2009), 25–40.

——, 'Berkeley polémiste: Des Sermons sur l'obéissance passive (1712) aux Maximes sur le patriotism (1750)', *The European Legacy*, 13 (2008), 413–24.

——, 'Foi, croyance, et raison selon Berkeley', *Science et Esprit*, 63 (2011), 135–47.

——, 'Introduction' to *Berkeley Revisited: Moral, Social, and Political Philosophy*, edited by Sébastien Charles (Oxford: Voltaire Foundation, 2015), pp. 1–21.

Cheesman, C.E.A, 'Kennett, Basil', in *Oxford Dictionary of National Biography*, https://www.oxforddnb.com/view/10.1093/ref:odnb/9780198614128.001.0001/odnb-9780198614128-e-15401 (accessed 5 August 2019).

Clark, Stephen R. L., 'God-Appointed Berkeley and the General Good', in *Essays on Berkeley: A Tercentennial Celebration*, edited by John Foster and Howard Robinson (Oxford: Clarendon Press, 1985), pp. 233–53.

Clarke, Desmond, *Arthur Dobbs Esquire, 1689–1765: Surveyor-General of Ireland, Prospector, and Governor of North Carolina* (London: Bodley Head, 1958).

Condren, Conal, Stephen Gaukroger, and Ian Hunter, 'Introduction' to *The Philosopher in Early Modern Europe: The Nature of a Contested Identity*, edited by Conal Condren, Stephen Gaukroger, and Ian Hunter (Cambridge: Cambridge University Press, 2009), pp. 1–16.

Connolly, Philomena, 'The Royal College at Kilkenny, 1690', *Archivium Hibernicum*, 44 (1989), 110.

Connolly, S. J., 'King, William', in *Oxford Dictionary of National Biography*, http://www.oxforddnb.com/view/article/15605 (accessed 5 June 2015).

——, 'Old English, New English, and the Ancient Irish: Swift and the Irish Past', in *Politics and Literature in the Age of Swift*, edited by Claude Rawson (Cambridge: Cambridge University Press, 2010), pp. 255–69.

——, 'Reformers and Highflyers: The Post-Revolution Church', in *As by Law Established: The Church of Ireland since the Reformation*, edited by Alan Ford, James McGuire, and Kenneth Milne (Dublin: Lilliput Press, 1995), pp. 152–65.

Conroy, Graham P., 'Berkeley and Education in America', *Journal of the History of Ideas*, 21 (1960), 211–21.

Cooper, John M., *Pursuits of Wisdom: Six Ways of Life in Ancient Philosophy from Plato to Plotinus* (Princeton, NJ: Princeton University Press, 2012).

Copenhaver, Rebecca, 'Perception and the Language of Nature', in *The Oxford Handbook of British Philosophy in the Eighteenth Century*, edited by James A. Harris (Oxford: Oxford University Press, 2013), pp. 107–27.

Coughtry, Jay, *The Notorious Triangle: Rhode Island and the African Slave Trade, 1700–1807* (Philadelphia: Temple University Press, 1981).

Craton, Michael, 'The Planter's World in the British West Indies', in *Strangers within the Realm: Cultural Margins of the First British Empire*, edited by Bernard Bailyn and Philip D. Morgan (Chapel Hill: University of North Carolina Press for the Institute of Early American History and Culture, 1991), pp. 314–62.

Cust, L. H., and Anthony R.J.S. Adolph, 'Mitchell, Thomas', in *Oxford Dictionary of National Biography*, https://www.oxforddnb.com/view/10.1093/ref:odnb/9780198614128.001.0001/odnb-9780198614128-e-18850 (accessed 22 July 2019).

Daniel, Stephen H., 'Berkeley's Doctrine of Mind and the "Black List Hypothesis": A Dialogue', *Southern Journal of Philosophy*, 51 (2013), 24–41.

——, 'Berkeley's Rejection of Divine Analogy', *Science et Esprit*, 63 (2011), 149–61.

Darwall, Stephen, 'Berkeley's Moral and Political Philosophy', in *The Cambridge Companion to Berkeley*, edited by Kenneth P. Winkler (Cambridge: Cambridge University Press, 2005), pp. 311–38.

De Divitiis, Gigliola Pagano, *English Merchants in Seventeenth-Century Italy*, translated by Stephen Parkin (Cambridge: Cambridge University Press, 1997).

Dos Santos, Antônio Carlos, 'Berkeley face à Mandeville: de *La Fable des abeilles* à la *Lettre à Dion*', *Science et Esprit*, 63 (2011), 163–77.

Dowd, Marion A., Linda G. Lynch, and Margaret McCarthy, 'Recent Archaeological Discoveries in Dunmore Cave, County Kilkenny: Further Questions Regarding Viking Activity at the Site', *Old Kilkenny Review*, 59 (2007), 7–17.

Downing, Lisa, 'Berkeley's Case against Realism about Dynamics', in *Berkeley's Metaphysics: Structural, Interpretive, and Critical Essays*, edited by Robert G. Muehlmann (University Park: Pennsylvania State University Press, 1995), pp. 197–214.

Duddy, Thomas, 'Toland, Berkeley, and the Irrational Hypothesis', *Eighteenth-Century Ireland/Iris an dá chultúr*, 1999 (14), 49–61.

Eaves, T. C. Duncan, and Ben D. Kimpel, *Samuel Richardson: A Biography* (Oxford: Clarendon Press, 1971).

Eccleshall, Robert, 'Anglican Political Thought in the Century after the Revolution of 1688', in *Political Thought in Ireland since the Seventeenth Century*, edited by D. George Boyce, Robert Eccleshall, and Vincent Geoghehan (London: Routledge, 1993), pp. 36–72.

Ehrenpreis, Irvin, *Swift: The Man, His Works, and the Age*, vol. 1, *Mr Swift and His Contemporaries* (London: Methuen, 1962).

Evans, Sir David, 'The Provenance of the Notebook', in *The Notebook of John Smibert, with Essays by Sir David Evans, John Kerslake, and Andrew Oliver* (Boston: Massachusetts Historical Society 1969), pp. 1–13.

Fabricant, Carole, 'George Berkeley the Islander: Some Reflections on Utopia, Race, and Tar-Water', in *The Global Eighteenth Century*, edited by Felicity A. Nussbaum (Baltimore: Johns Hopkins University Press, 2003), pp. 263–78.

Fasko, Manuel, 'A Scotist Nonetheless? George Berkeley, Cajetan, and the Problem of Divine Attributes', *Ruch Filozoficzny*, 74 (2018), 33–50.

Favazza, Armando, *Bodies under Siege: Self-Mutilation, Nonsuicidal Self-Injury, and Body Modification in Culture and Psychiatry*, 3rd ed. (Baltimore: Johns Hopkins University Press, 2011).

Fisher, Linford D., *The Indian Great Awakening: Religion and the Shaping of Native Cultures in Early America* (Oxford: Oxford University Press, 2012).

Fitts, Robert K., *Inventing New England's Slave Paradise: Master/Slave Relations in Eighteenth-Century Narragansett, Rhode Island* (New York: Garland, 1998).

Flage, Daniel E., *Berkeley's Doctrine of Notions: A Reconstruction Based on His Theory of Meaning* (London and Sydney: Croom Helm, 1987).

——, 'Relative Ideas and Notions', in *Minds, Ideas, and Objects: Essays on the Theory of Representation in Modern Philosophy*, edited by Phillip D. Cummins and Guenter Zoeller (Atascadero, CA: Ridgeview, 1992), pp. 235–53.

Fleetwood, William, *The Relative Duties of Parents and Children, Husbands and Wives, Masters and Servants* (London: Charles Harper, 1705).

Flew, Anthony, 'Was Berkeley a Precursor of Wittgenstein?', in *Alciphron in Focus*, edited by David Berman (London: Routledge, 1993), pp. 214–26.

Ford, Alan, 'Ussher, James', *Oxford Dictionary of National Biography*. http://www.oxforddnb.com/view/article/28034 (accessed 10 March 2015).

Freeman, A. Martin, ed., *Vanessa and Her Correspondence with Jonathan Swift* (London: Selwyn and Blount, 1921).

Friedman, Lesley, 'Pragmatism: The Unformulated Method of Bishop Berkeley', *Journal of the History of Philosophy*, 41 (2003), 81–96.

Furlong, E. J., and David Berman, 'George Berkeley and *The Ladies Library*', *Berkeley Newsletter*, 4 (1980), 4–13.

Gauci, Perry, 'Decker, Sir Matthew, First Baronet', in *Oxford Dictionary of National Biography*, https://www.oxforddnb.com/view/10.1093/ref:odnb/9780198614128.001.0001/odnb-9780198614128-e-7408 (accessed 7 August 2019).

——, *The Politics of Trade: The Overseas Merchant in State and Society, 1660–1720* (Oxford: Oxford University Press, 2001).

Gaustad, Edwin S., *George Berkeley in America* (New Haven, CT: Yale University Press, 1979).

Gay, Peter, 'Locke on the Education of Paupers', in *Philosophers on Education: New Historical Perspectives*, edited by Amélie Oksenberg Rorty (London: Routledge, 1998), pp. 190–91.

Gibson, W. T., '"Unreasonable and Unbecoming": Self-Recommendation and Place-Seeking in the Church of England, 1700–1900', *Albion*, 27 (1995), 43–63.

Girard, Jérémy, 'La Bonne société d'après Berkeley: Entre éducation religieuse et coutume raisonnable', in *Berkeley Revisited: Moral, Social, and Political Philosophy*, edited by Sébastien Charles (Oxford: Voltaire Foundation, 2015), pp. 227–41.

Glasson, Travis, ' "Baptism Doth Not Bestow Freedom": Missionary Anglicanism, Slavery, and the Yorke-Talbot Opinion, 1701–30', *William and Mary Quarterly*, 67 (2010), 279–318.

——, *Mastering Christianity: Missionary Anglicanism and Slavery in the Atlantic World* (Oxford: Oxford University Press, 2011).

Goulden, Richard J., *The Ornament Stock of Henry Woodfall, 1719–47: A Preliminary Inventory* (London: Bibliographical Society, 1988).

Greenberg, Sean, 'Leibniz on King: Freedom and the Project of the *Theodicy*', *Studia Leibnitiana*, 40 (2008), 205–22.

Gregory, Jeremy, 'The Long Eighteenth Century', in *The Cambridge Companion to John Wesley*, edited by Randy L. Maddox and Jason E. Vickers (Cambridge: Cambridge University Press, 2009), pp. 13–39.

Grush, Rick, 'Berkeley and the Spatiality of Vision', *Journal of the History of Philosophy*, 45 (2007), 413–43.

Grzelinski, Adam, '*Alciphron; Or The Minute Philosopher*: Berkeley's Redefinition of Free-Thinking', in *The Bloomsbury Companion to Berkeley*, edited by Richard Brooke and Bertil Belfrage (London: Bloomsbury, 2017), pp. 174–95.

Guerrini, Anita, 'Hastings, Lady Elizabeth [Betty]', in *Oxford Dictionary of National Biography*, https://www.oxforddnb.com/view/10.1093/ref:odnb/9780198614128 .001.0001/odnb-9780198614128-e-12564 (accessed 7 August 2019).

Gylling, Hetta Aleksandra, 'Berkeley as a Worldly Philosopher', in *Berkeley Revisited: Moral, Social, and Political Philosophy*, edited by Sébastien Charles (Oxford: Voltaire Foundation, 2015), pp. 23–35.

Hadot, Pierre, *Philosophy as a Way of Life: Spiritual Exercises from Socrates to Foucault*, edited by Arnold I. Davidson, translated by Michael Chase (Oxford: Blackwell, 1995).

Hamilton, Alastair, 'Huntington, Robert', in *Oxford Dictionary of National Biography*, https://doi.org/10.1093/ref:odnb/14242 (accessed 12 July 2019).

Handy, Jim, ' "Almost Idiotic Wretchedness": A Long History of Blaming Peasants', *Journal of Peasant Studies*, 36 (2009), 325–44.

Hanham, A. A., 'Hutcheson, Archibald', in *Oxford Dictionary of National Biography*, https://www.oxforddnb.com/view/10.1093/ref:odnb/9780198614128.001.0001 /odnb-9780198614128-e-53923 (accessed 7 August 2019).

Hans, Nicholas, *New Trends in Education in the Eighteenth Century* (1951; London: Routledge, 2001).

Harman, Graham, *Immaterialism* (Cambridge: Polity, 2016).

Harris, James A., 'The Government of the Passions', in *The Oxford Handbook of British Philosophy in the Eighteenth Century*, edited by James A. Harris (Oxford: Oxford University Press, 2013), pp. 270–88.

——, 'Introduction' to *The Oxford Handbook of British Philosophy in the Eighteenth Century*, edited by James A. Harris (Oxford: Oxford University Press, 2013), pp. 1–17.

Harrison, Fairfax, and George McLaren Brydon, 'The Virginia Clergy: Governor Gooch's Letters to the Bishop of London 1727–1749', *Virginia Magazine of History and Biography*, 32 (1924), 209–36.

Harrison, Peter, 'The Natural Philosopher and the Virtues', in *The Philosopher in Early Modern Europe: The Nature of a Contested Identity*, edited by Conal Condren, Stephen Gaukroger, and Ian Hunter (Cambridge: Cambridge University Press, 2009), pp. 202–28.

——, *'Religion' and the Religions in the English Enlightenment* (Cambridge: Cambridge University Press, 1990).

Hart, W. A., 'Africans in Eighteenth-Century Ireland', *Irish Historical Studies*, 33 (2002), 19–32.

Haydon, Colin, *Anti-Catholicism in Eighteenth-Century England, c. 1714–80: A Political and Social Study* (Manchester: Manchester University Press, 1993).

Hayes, Kevin J., *A Colonial Woman's Bookshelf* (Knoxville: University of Tennessee Press, 1996).

Häyry, Matti, *'Passive Obedience* and Berkeley's Moral Philosophy', *Berkeley Studies*, 23 (2012), 3–14.

Hayton, David, 'Did Protestantism Fail in Early Eighteenth-Century Ireland? Charity Schools and the Enterprise of Religious and Social Reformation, c. 1690–1730', in *As by Law Established: The Church of Ireland since the Reformation*, edited by Alan Ford, James McGuire, and Kenneth Milne (Dublin: Lilliput Press, 1995), pp. 166–86.

——, 'Irish Tories and Victims of Whig Persecution: Sacheverell Fever by Proxy', (special feature) *Faction Displayed: Reconsidering the Impeachment of Dr Henry Sacheverell, Parliamentary History*, 31 (2012), 80–98.

——, 'Molesworth, Robert, First Viscount Molesworth', in *Oxford Dictionary of National Biography*, https://www.oxforddnb.com/view/10.1093/ref:odnb/9780198614128.001.0001/odnb-9780198614128-e-18901?rskey=BgBH17&result=4 (accessed 13 April 2020).

——, '"Paltry Underlings of State"? The Character and Aspirations of the "Castle" Party, 1715–1732', in *Politics and Literature in the Age of Swift*, edited by Claude Rawson (Cambridge: Cambridge University Press, 2010), pp. 221–54.

Hayton, D. W., and Stephen Karian, 'Select Document: The Division of the Irish House of Commons on the "Tithe of Agistment", 18 Mar. 1736, and Swift's "Character . . . of the Legion Club"', *Irish Historical Studies*, 38 (2012), 304–21.

Herdt, Jennifer A., 'Affective Perfectionism: Community with God without Common Measure', in *New Essays on the History of Autonomy: A Collection Honoring J. B. Schneewind*, edited by Natalie Brender and Larry Krasnoff (Cambridge: Cambridge University Press, 2004), pp. 30–60.

Higgins, Ian, 'Jonathan Swift's Political Confession', in *Politics and Literature in the Age of Swift*, edited by Claude Rawson (Cambridge: Cambridge University Press, 2010), pp. 3–30.

Hight, Marc A., *Idea and Ontology: An Essay in Early Modern Metaphysics of Ideas* (University Park: Pennsylvania State University Press, 2008).

Hill, Christopher, 'Freethinking and Libertinism: The Legacy of the English Revolution', in *The Margins of Orthodoxy: Heterodox Writing and Cultural Response, 1660–1750*, edited by Roger Lund (Cambridge: Cambridge University Press, 1995), pp. 54–70.

Hindmarsh, D. Bruce, '"My Chains Fell Off, My Heart Was Free": Early Methodist Conversion Narrative in England', *Church History*, 68 (1999), 910–29.

Hofstadter, Richard, and Wilson Smith, eds., *American Higher Education: A Documentary History*, 2 vols. (Chicago: University of Chicago Press, 1961).

Hollingshead, Gregory Albert F., 'George Berkeley and English Literature of the Eighteenth Century 1710–1770 with Special Reference to Swift, Pope, Blackwell, and Smart' (PhD dissertation, University of London, 1974).

——, 'Sources for the Ladies' Library', *Berkeley Newsletter*, 11 (1989–1990), 1–9.

Holtzman, Matthew, 'Berkeley's Two Panaceas', *Intellectual History Review*, 21 (2011), 473–95.

Hone, J. M. and M. M. Rossi, *Bishop Berkeley: His Life, Writings, and Philosophy*, introduction by W. B. Yeats (London: Faber & Faber, 1931).

Hoppen, K. Theodore, *The Common Scientist in the Seventeenth Century: A Study of the Dublin Philosophical Society, 1683–1708* (London: Routledge and Kegan Paul, 1970).

——, ed., *Papers of the Dublin Philosophical Society*, 2 vols. (Dublin: Irish Manuscripts Commission, 2008).

——, 'The Papers of the Dublin Philosophical Society: Introductory Material and Index', *Analecta Hibernica*, 30 (1982), 153–248.

Hunter, Ian, 'The History of Philosophy and the Persona of the Philosopher', *Modern Intellectual History*, 4 (2007), 571–600.

Hunter, Michael, 'Robert Boyle, Narcissus Marsh, and the Anglo-Irish Intellectual Scene in the Late Seventeenth Century', in *The Making of Marsh's Library: Learning, Politics, and Religion in Ireland, 1650–1750*, edited by Muriel McCarthy and Ann Simmons (Dublin: Four Courts Press, 2004), pp. 51–75.

Hurley, Michael, 'Berkeley and Methodism: A New Letter', *Berkeley Newsletter*, 2 (1978), 1–2.

Hutchings, Victoria, 'Hoare, Henry', in *Oxford Dictionary of National Biography*, https://www.oxforddnb.com/view/10.1093/ref:odnb/9780198614128.001.0001/odnb-9780198614128-e-47085 (accessed 7 August 2019).

Ingamells, John, *A Dictionary of British and Irish Travellers in Italy 1701–1800, Compiled from the Brinsley Ford Archive* (New Haven, CT, and London: Yale University Press for the Paul Mellon Centre for Studies in British Art, 1997).

Israel, Jonathan, *Radical Enlightenment: Philosophy and the Making of Modernity 1650–1750* (Oxford: Oxford University Press, 2001).

Jacob, Margaret C., *The Newtonians and the English Revolution 1689–1720* (Hassocks, Sussex, and Ithaca, NY: Harvester and Cornell University Press, 1976).

Jaffro, Laurent, 'Abolition ou réformation du christianisme? L'argument de Swift contre les libres penseurs', *La Lettre clandestine: Protestants, protestantisme, et pensée clandestine*, 13 (2003), 15–33.

——, 'Le Cogito de Berkeley', *Archives de Philosophie*, 67 (2004), 85–111.

Jakapi, Roomet, 'Emotive Meaning and Christian Mysteries in Berkeley's Alciphron', *British Journal for the History of Philosophy*, 10 (2002), 401–11.

James, Sydney V., 'Colonial Rhode Island and the Beginnings of the Liberal Rationalized State', in *Essays in Theory and History: An Approach to the Social Sciences*, edited by Melvin Richter (Cambridge, MA: Harvard University Press, 1970), pp. 165–86.

——, *Colonial Rhode Island: A History* (New York: Charles Scribner, 1975).

James, William, *Pragmatism* and *The Meaning of Truth*, edited by Fredson Bowers and Ignas K. Skrupskelis, introduction by A. J. Ayer (Cambridge, MA: Harvard University Press, 1975).

Jarvis, Michael J., *In the Eye of All Trade: Bermuda, Bermudans, and the Maritime Atlantic World, 1680–1783* (Chapel Hill: University of North Carolina Press, 2010).

Jesseph, Douglas, *Berkeley's Philosophy of Mathematics* (Chicago: University of Chicago Press, 1993).

——, 'Berkeley's Philosophy of Mathematics', in *The Cambridge Companion to Berkeley*, edited by Kenneth P. Winkler (Cambridge: Cambridge University Press, 2005), pp. 266–310.

——, 'Faith and Fluxions: Berkeley on Theology and Mathematics', in *New Interpretations of Berkeley's Thought*, edited by Stephen Daniel (Amherst, NY: Humanity Books, 2007), pp. 247–60.

Jessop, T. E., *A Bibliography of George Berkeley*, 2nd ed. (The Hague: Martinus Nijhoff, 1973).

Johnson, Joan, 'Brydges, James, First Duke of Chandos', in *Oxford Dictionary of National Biography*, https://www.oxforddnb.com/view/10.1093/ref:odnb/9780198614128.001.0001/odnb-9780198614128-e-3806 (accessed 7 August 2019).

Johnston, Joseph, *Bishop Berkeley's Querist in Historical Perspective* (Dundalk: Dundalgen Press, 1970).

Johnston-Liik, Edith Mary, *History of the Irish Parliament 1692–1800*, 6 vols. (Belfast: Ulster Historical Foundation, 2002).

Jones, Tom, 'George Berkeley and Thomas Secker: A Note', *Berkeley Newsletter*, 17 (2006), 14–19.

——, 'George Berkeley and the Value of the Arts', *1650–1850: Ideas, Aesthetics, and Inquiries in the Early Modern Era*, 21 (2014), 89–108.

——, 'Pope and the Ends of History: Faction, Atterbury, and Clarendon's *History of the Rebellion*', *Studies in Philology*, 110 (2013), 880–902.

Jordan, Winthrop D., 'Initial English Attitudes toward Africans', in *Race, Prejudice, and the Origins of Slavery in America*, edited by Raymond Starr and Robert Detweiler (Cambridge, MA: Schenkman Publishing, 1975), pp. 97–127.

Keirn, Tim, 'Jekyll, Sir Joseph', in *Oxford Dictionary of National Biography*, https://www.oxforddnb.com/view/10.1093/ref:odnb/9780198614128.001.0001/odnb-9780198614128-e-14709 (accessed 8 August 2019).

Kellaway, William, *The New England Company 1649–1776: Missionary Society to the American Indians* (New York: Barnes and Noble, 1961).

Kelly, Patrick, 'Anne Donnellan: Irish Proto-Bluestocking', *Hermathena*, 154 (1993), 39–68.

——, 'Berkeley and the Idea of a National Bank', in *Money and Political Economy in the Enlightenment*, edited by Daniel Carey (Oxford: Voltaire Foundation, 2014), pp. 163–84.

Kelly, Patrick, 'Berkeley's *Querist*: "Hints . . . What is to be Done in this Critical State of Our Affairs" or Proposals for a Hyperborean Eutopia?', in *The Bloomsbury Companion to Berkeley*, edited by Richard Brooke and Bertil Belfrage (London: Bloomsbury, 2017), pp. 196–215.

——, 'Berkeley's Servants', *Berkeley Newsletter*, 14 (1995–1996), 13–14.

Kendrick, Nancy, 'Berkeley's Bermuda Project and *The Ladies Library*', in *Berkeley Revisited: Moral, Social, and Political Philosophy*, edited by Sébastien Charles (Oxford: Voltaire Foundation, 2015), pp. 243–57.

——, 'Berkeley's Bermuda Project in Context', in *The Bloomsbury Companion to Berkeley*, edited by Richard Brooke and Bertil Belfrage (London: Bloomsbury, 2017), pp. 21–48.

Kendrick, T.F.J., 'Sir Robert Walpole, the Old Whigs, and the Bishops, 1733–1736: A Study in Eighteenth-Century Parliamentary Politics', *Historical Journal*, 11 (1968), 421–45.

Kennedy, Máire, *French Books in Eighteenth-Century Ireland* (Oxford: Voltaire Foundation, 2001).

Keogh, Andrew, 'Bishop Berkeley's Gift of Books in 1733', *Yale University Library Gazette*, 8 (1933), 1–25.

Koch, Philippa, 'Slavery, Mission, and the Perils of Providence in Eighteenth-Century Christianity: The Writings of Whitefield and the Halle Pietists', *Church History*, 84 (2015), 369–93.

Kopelson, Heather Miyano, ' "One Indian and a Negroe, the first thes Ilands ever had": Imagining the Archive in Early Bermuda', *Early American Studies*, 11 (2013), 272–313.

Kupfer, Joseph, 'A Note on "Berkeley's Linguistic Criterion" ', in *George Berkeley: Critical Assessments*, edited by Walter E. Creery, vol. 3 (London: Routledge, 1991), pp. 388–92.

Lee, Richard N., 'What Berkeley's Notions Are', *Idealistic Studies*, 20 (1990), 19–41.

Lee, Sukjae, 'Berkeley on the Activity of Spirits', *British Journal for the History of Philosophy*, 20 (2012), 539–76.

Leersen, Joep Th., 'Anglo-Irish Patriotism and Its European Context: Notes towards a Reassessment', *Eighteenth-Century Ireland/Iris an dá chultúr*, 3 (1988), 7–24.

Leonard, John, 'Kilkenny's Short-Lived University (Feb–July 1690)', *Archivium Hibernicum*, 43 (1988), 65–84.

Letwin, William, *The Origins of Scientific Economics: English Economic Thought 1660-1776* (London: Methuen, 1963).

Levine, Joseph, 'Ancients and Moderns Reconsidered', *Eighteenth-Century Studies*, 15 (1981), 72–89.

——, 'Latitudinarians, Neoplatonists, and the Ancient Wisdom', in *Philosophy, Science, and Religion in England 1640-1700*, edited by Richard Kroll, Richard Ashcraft, and Perez Zagorin (Cambridge: Cambridge University Press, 1992), pp. 85–108.

Lindberg, David C., *Theories of Vision from Al-Kindi to Kepler* (Chicago: University of Chicago Press, 1976).

Livesey, James, 'Berkeley, Ireland, and Eighteenth-Century Intellectual History', *Modern Intellectual History*, 12 (2015), 453–73.

——, 'The Dublin Society in Eighteenth-Century Irish Political Thought', *Historical Journal*, 47 (2004), 615–40.

Losonsky, Michael, 'Locke on Meaning and Signification', in *Locke's Philosophy: Content and Context*, edited by G.A.J. Rogers (Oxford: Clarendon Press, 1994), pp. 123–41.

Loudon, Jean, 'Frewin, Richard', in *Oxford Dictionary of National Biography*, https://www.oxforddnb.com/view/10.1093/ref:odnb/9780198614128.001.0001/odnb -9780198614128-e-10182 (accessed 9 August 2019).

Luce, A. A., 'Berkeley's Bermuda Project and His Benefactions to American Universities, with Unpublished Letters and Extracts from the Egmont Papers', *Proceedings of the Royal Irish Academy*, 42 (1934–1935), 97–120.

——, *Berkeley and Malebranche: A Study in the Origins of Berkeley's Thought* (London: Oxford University Press, 1934).

——, *The Life of George Berkeley Bishop of Cloyne*, introduction by David Berman (London: Thomas Nelson, 1949; London: Routledge/Thoemmes Press, 1992).

——, 'More Unpublished Berkeley Letters and New Berkeleiana', *Hermathena*, 23 (1933), 25–53.

Luce, J. V., *Trinity College Dublin: The First 400 Years* (Dublin: Trinity College Dublin Press, 1992).

Lund, Roger D., *Ridicule, Religion, and the Politics of Wit in Augustan England* (Aldershot: Ashgate, 2012).

Mahon, Lady, 'The Chetwood Letters, 1726', *Journal of the Kildare Archaeological Society*, 9 (1918–1921), 273–76, 381–86, 410–15.

——, 'The Chetwood Letters, 1726', *Journal of the Kildare Archaeological Society*, 10 (1922–1928), 32–36, 100–106, 150–53, 195–96.

Main, Gloria L., *Peoples of a Spacious Land: Families and Cultures in Colonial New England* (Cambridge, MA: Harvard University Press, 2001).

March, Jessica, 'Anne Donnellan', in *Dictionary of Irish Biography*, edited by Aidan Clarke et al., 9 vols. (Cambridge: Cambridge University Press/Royal Irish Academy, 2009).

Mason, George C., *Annals of Trinity Church, 1698–1821* (Newport, RI: G. C. Mason, 1890).

Maurer, Christian, 'Self-interest and Sociability', in *The Oxford Handbook of British Philosophy in the Eighteenth Century*, edited by James A. Harris (Oxford: Oxford University Press, 2013), pp. 291–314.

Mazur, Joseph, *Enlightening Symbols: A Short History of Mathematical Notation and Its Hidden Powers* (Princeton, NJ: Princeton University Press, 2014).

McBride, Ian, *Eighteenth-Century Ireland: The Isle of Slaves*, New Gill History of Ireland (Dublin: Gill & Macmillan, 2009).

McCracken, Charles J., 'Berkeley's Notion of Spirit', *History of European Ideas*, 7 (1986), 597–602.

McCracken, Charles J., 'Stages on a Cartesian Road to Immaterialism', *Journal of the History of Philosophy*, 24 (1986), 19–40.

McCracken, C. J., and I. C. Tipton, eds., *Berkeley's Principles and Dialogues: Background Source Materials* (Cambridge: Cambridge University Press, 2000).

McDowell, R. B., and D. A. Webb, *Trinity College Dublin 1592–1952: An Academic History*, with a foreword by F.S.L. Lyons (Cambridge: Cambridge University Press, 1982).

McGowan, William, 'Did Berkeley Write *The Irish Blasters*?' *Berkeley Newsletter*, 6 (1982–1983), 1–4.

McNally, Patrick, 'William King, Patriotism, and the "National Question"', in *Archbishop William King and the Anglican Irish Context, 1688-1729*, edited by Christopher J. Fauske (Dublin: Four Courts Press, 2004), pp. 47–72.

McNeill, Charles, 'Rawlinson Manuscripts (Class D)', *Analecta Hibernica*, 2 (1931), 44–92.

Meenan, James, and Desmond Clarke, 'The RDS 1731–1981', in *The Royal Dublin Society, 1731-1981*, edited by James Meenan and Desmond Clarke (Dublin: Gill and Macmillan, 1981), pp. 1–55.

Migely, Genevieve, 'Berkeley's Actively Passive Mind', in *Reexamining Berkeley's Philosophy*, edited by Stephen H. Daniel (Toronto: University of Toronto Press, 2007), pp. 153–71.

Miller, Peter N., *Defining the Common Good: Empire, Religion, and Philosophy in Eighteenth-Century Britain* (Cambridge: Cambridge University Press, 1994).

——, '"Freethinking" and "Freedom of Thought" in Eighteenth-Century Britain', *Historical Journal*, 36 (1993), 599–617.

Milne, Kenneth, 'Irish Charter Schools', *Irish Journal of Education*, 8 (1974), 3–29.

Moked, Gabriel, *Particles and Ideas: Bishop Berkeley's Corpuscularian Philosophy* (Oxford: Clarendon Press, 1988).

Monod, Paul, 'Jacobitism and Country Principles in the Reign of William III', *Historical Journal*, 30 (1987), 289–310.

——, 'Voyage out of Staffordshire; Or, Samuel Johnson's Jacobite Journey', in *Samuel Johnson in Historical Context*, edited by Jonathan Clark and Howard Erskine-Hill (Basingstoke: Palgrave, 2002), pp. 11–43.

Moriarty, Clare Marie, 'The Ad Hominem Argument of Berkeley's *Analyst*', *British Journal for the History of Philosophy*, 26 (2018), 429–51.

Morpurgo, J. E., *Their Majesties' Royall Colledge: William and Mary in the Seventeenth and Eighteenth Centuries* (Williamsburg, VA: Endowment Association of the College of William and Mary of Virginia, 1976).

Mulligan, Fergus, *The Founders of the Royal Dublin Society* (Dublin: Royal Dublin Society, 2005).

Murtagh, Ben, and Mark E. Hall, '1989:061—"Dysart", Dysart, Kilkenny', in *Excavations.ie: Database of Irish Excavation Reports*, https://excavations.ie/report/1989/Kilkenny/0000895/ (accessed 27 April 2020).

Muthu, Sankar, *Enlightenment against Empire* (Princeton, NJ: Princeton University Press, 2003).

Nichols, John, *Illustrations of the Literary History of the Eighteenth Century*, 4 vols. (London: John Nichols, 1822).

———, *Literary Anecdotes of the Eighteenth Century*, vol. VIII (London: Nichols, Son and Bentley, 1814).

Niddrie, David L., 'An Attempt at Planned Settlement in St Kitts in the Early Eighteenth Century', *Caribbean Studies*, 5 (1966), 3–11.

Nurock, Vanessa, 'La Conscience morale selon Berkeley', in *Berkeley's* Alciphron: *English Text and Essays in Interpretation*, edited by Geneviève Brykman, Laurent Jaffro, and Claire Schwartz (Hildesheim, Zürich: Georg Olms, 2010), pp. 319–30.

O'Connor, Thomas, 'Marsh's Library and the Catholic Tradition', in *The Making of Marsh's Library: Learning, Politics, and Religion in Ireland, 1650–1750*, edited by Muriel McCarthy and Ann Simmons (Dublin: Four Courts Press, 2004), pp. 235–55.

O'Donnell, C. Oliver, 'Depicting Berkeleyan Idealism: A Study of Two Portraits by John Smibert', *Word and Image*, 33 (2017), 18–34.

Oestreich, Gerhard, *Neostoicism and the Early Modern State*, edited by Brigitta Oestreich and H. G. Koenigsberger, translated by David McLintock (Cambridge: Cambridge University Press, 1982).

O'Regan, Philip, *Archbishop William King of Dublin (1650–1729) and the Constitution in Church and State* (Dublin: Four Courts Press, 2000).

Ott, Walter, 'Descartes and Berkeley on Mind: The Fourth Distinction', *British Journal for the History of Philosophy*, 14 (2006), 437–50.

Overhoff, Jürgen, 'Franklin's Philadelphia Academy and Basedow's Dessau Philanthropine: Two Models of Non-Denominational Schooling in Eighteenth-Century America and Germany', *Pedagogica Historica*, 43 (2007), 801–18.

Palmer, Margaret, *The Printed Maps of Bermuda* (London: Map Collectors' Circle, 1965).

Pappas, George S., *Berkeley's Thought* (Ithaca, NY: Cornell University Press, 2000).

Parigi, Silvia, '*Siris* and the Renaissance: Some Overlooked Berkeleian Sources', *Revue Philosophique de la France et de l'Étranger*, 200 (2010), 151–62.

Parkin, Jon, 'Probability, Punishments, and Property: Richard Cumberland's Sceptical Science of Sovereignty', in *Natural Law and Civil Sovereignty: Moral Right and State Authority in Early Modern Political Thought*, edited by Ian Hunter and David Saunders (Basingstoke: Palgrave Macmillan, 2002), pp. 76–90.

Parks, Stephen, 'George Berkeley, Sir Richard Steele, and *The Ladies Library*', *The Scriblerian*, 13 (1980), 1–2.

Parry, Geraint, 'Education', in *The Cambridge History of Eighteenth-Century Philosophy*, edited by Knud Haakonssen, vol. 1 (Cambridge: Cambridge University Press, 2006), pp. 608–38.

Pearce, Kenneth L., *Language and the Structure of Berkeley's World* (Oxford: Oxford University Press, 2017).

———, 'William King on Free Will', *Philosophers' Imprint*, 19 (2019), 1–15.

Perinetti, Dario, 'Philosophical Reflection on History', in *The Cambridge History of Eighteenth-Century Philosophy*, edited by Knud Haakonssen, vol. 2 (Cambridge: Cambridge University Press, 2006), pp. 1107–40.

Pincus, Steve, 'Addison's Empire: Whig Conceptions of Empire in the Early 18th Century', *Parliamentary History*, 31 (2012), 99–117.

Pocock, J.G.A., *The Machiavellian Moment: Florentine Political Thought and the Republican Tradition, with a New Afterword by the Author* (Princeton, NJ: Princeton University Press, 2003).

——, *Virtue, Commerce, History: Essays on Political Thought and History, Chiefly in the Eighteenth Century* (Cambridge: Cambridge University Press, 1985).

——, 'What Do We Mean by Europe?', *Wilson Quarterly*, 21 (1997), 12–29.

Pollard, M., *A Dictionary of Members of the Dublin Book Trade, 1550–1800: Based on the Records of the Guild of St Luke the Evangelist, Dublin* (London: Bibliographical Society, 2000).

Poovey, Mary, 'Between Political Arithmetic and Political Economy', in *Regimes of Description in the Archive of the Eighteenth Century*, edited by John Bender and Michael Marrinan (Stanford, CA: Stanford University Press, 2005), pp. 61–76.

Pratt, Anne S., 'Berkeley-Johnson Correspondence', *Yale University Library Gazette*, 8 (1934), 29–41.

Probyn, Clive, 'Homrigh, Esther Van [*known as* Vanessa]', in *Oxford Dictionary of National Biography*, https://www.oxforddnb.com/view/10.1093/ref:odnb/9780198614128.001.0001/odnb-9780198614128-e-28090 (accessed 7 August 2019).

Rashid, Salim, 'Berkeley's *Querist* and Its Influence', *Journal of the History of Economic Thought*, 12 (1990), 38–60.

——, 'The Irish School of Economic Development: 1720–1750', *Manchester School of Economic and Social Studies*, 56 (1988), 345–69.

Redford, Bruce, *Venice and the Grand Tour* (New Haven, CT: Yale University Press, 1996).

Richardson, Joseph, 'Archbishop William King (1650–1729): "Church Tory and State Whig"?', *Eighteenth-Century Ireland/Iris an dá chultúr*, 15 (2000), 54–76.

——, 'William King—European Man of Letters', in *Archbishop William King and the Anglican Irish Context, 1688–1729*, edited by Christopher J. Fauske (Dublin: Four Courts Press, 2004), pp. 106–22.

Richey, Rosemary, 'Madden, Samuel Molyneux [called Premium Madden]', in *Oxford Dictionary of National Biography*, https://www.oxforddnb.com/view/10.1093/ref:odnb/9780198614128.001.0001/odnb-9780198614128-e-17754 (accessed 22 July 2019).

Rippy, Frances Mayhew, 'Prior, Matthew', in *Oxford Dictionary of National Biography*, https://www.oxforddnb.com/view/10.1093/ref:odnb/9780198614128.001.0001/odnb-9780198614128-e-22814 (accessed 5 August 2019).

Roberts, John L., *The Jacobite Wars: Scotland and the Military Campaigns of 1715 and 1745* (Edinburgh: Polygon at Edinburgh, 2002).

Roberts, John Russell, 'Berkeley on the Philosophy of Language', in *The Bloomsbury Companion to Berkeley*, edited by Richard Brooke and Bertil Belfrage (London: Bloomsbury, 2017), pp. 421–34.

——, *A Metaphysics for the Mob: The Philosophy of George Berkeley* (Oxford: Oxford University Press, 2007).

Robinet, André, *G. W. Leibniz Iter Italicum (Mars 1689–Mars 1690): La Dynamique de la République des Lettres* (Florence: Leo S. Olschki, 1988).

Rorty, Amélie Oksenberg, 'The Ruling History of Education', in *Philosophers on Education: New Historical Perspectives*, edited by Amélie Oksenberg Rorty (London: Routledge, 1998), pp. 1–13.

Rorty, Richard, 'A World without Substances or Essences', in *Philosophy and Social Hope* (London: Penguin, 1999), pp. 47–71.

Rosner, Brian S., *Paul and the Law: Keeping the Commandments of God* (Downers Grove, IL: Apollos/InterVarsity Press, 2013).

Ross, Ian Campbell, 'Was Berkeley a Jacobite? Passive Obedience Revisited', *Eighteenth-Century Ireland/Iris an dá chultúr*, 20 (2005), 17–30.

Rothkrug, Lionel, *Opposition to Louis XIV: The Political and Social Origins of the French Enlightenment* (Princeton, NJ: Princeton University Press, 1965).

Rousseau, G. S., 'Praxis 1: Bishop Berkeley and Tar-Water', in *Enlightenment Borders: Pre- and Post-Modern Discourses: Medical, Scientific* (Manchester: University of Manchester Press, 1991), pp. 145–75.

Rubertone, Patricia E., *Grave Undertakings: An Archaeology of Roger Williams and the Narragansett Indians* (Washington, DC: Smithsonian Institution Press, 2001).

Russell, Jean Fogo, 'Tarantism', *Medical History*, 23 (1979), 404–25.

Ryan, David, 'The Dublin Hellfire Club', in *Clubs and Societies in Eighteenth-Century Ireland*, edited by James Kelly and Martyn J. Powell (Dublin: Four Courts Press, 2010), pp. 332–52.

Sageng, Erik Lars, 'Colin MacLaurin and the Foundations of the Method of Fluxions' (PhD dissertation, Princeton University, 1989).

Saunders, Richard H., *John Smibert: Colonial America's First Portrait Painter* (New Haven, CT: Yale University Press and Barra Foundation, 1995).

Schneiders, Werner, 'Concepts of Philosophy', in *The Cambridge History of Eighteenth-Century Philosophy*, edited by Knud Haakonssen, vol. 1 (Cambridge: Cambridge University Press, 2006), pp. 26–44.

Schwartz, Claire, 'Berkeley et la norme mathématique: De l'*Alciphron* à l'*Analyste*', in *Berkeley's* Alciphron: *English Text and Essays in Interpretation*, edited by Geneviève Brykman, Laurent Jaffro and Claire Schwartz (Hildesheim, Zürich: Georg Olms, 2010), pp. 423–33.

Serjeantson, Richard, 'Becoming a Philosopher', in *The Oxford Handbook of British Philosophy in the Seventeenth Century*, edited by Peter R. Anstey (Oxford: Oxford University Press, 2013), pp. 9–38.

Sgarbi, Marco, *The Aristotelian Tradition and the Rise of British Empiricism: Logic and Epistemology in the British Isles (1570–1689)* (New York: Springer, 2012).

Sheridan, Richard B., *Sugar and Slavery: An Economic History of the British West Indies 1623–1775* (Lodge Hill, Barbados: Caribbean Universities Press, 1974).

Sirota, Brent, 'The Church: Anglicanism and the Nationalization of Maritime Space', in *Mercantilism Reimagined: Political Economy in Modern Britain and Its Empire*, edited by Philip J. Stern and Carl Wennerlind (Oxford: Oxford University Press, 2013), pp. 196–210.

Sirota, Brent, 'The Church of England, the Law of Nations, and the Leghorn Chaplaincy Affair, 1703–1713', *Eighteenth-Century Studies*, 48 (2015), 283–306.

Sneddon, Andrew, *Witchcraft and Whigs: The Life of Bishop Francis Hutchinson, 1660–1739* (Manchester: Manchester University Press, 2008).

Speck, W. A., 'Harley, Robert, First Earl of Oxford and Mortimer', in *Oxford Dictionary of National Biography*, https://www.oxforddnb.com/view/10.1093/ref:odnb /9780198614128.001.0001/odnb-9780198614128-e-12344 (accessed 7 August 2019).

——, 'Sacheverell, Henry', in *Oxford Dictionary of National Biography*, https:// www.oxforddnb.com/view/10.1093/ref:odnb/9780198614128.001.0001/odnb -9780198614128-e-24440 (accessed 9 August 2019).

Staves, Susan, 'Church of England Clergy and Women Writers', *Huntington Library Quarterly*, 65 (2002), 81–103.

Stephens, John, 'Edmund Law and His Circle at Cambridge: Some Philosophical Activity in the 1730s', in *The Philosophical Canon in the 17ᵗʰ and 18ᵗʰ Centuries: Essays in Honour of John W. Yolton*, edited by G.A.J. Rogers and Sylvana Tomaselli (Rochester, NY: University of Rochester Press, 1996), pp. 163–74.

Stewart, M. A., 'Berkeley's Introduction Draft', *Berkeley Newsletter*, 11 (1989–1990), 10–19.

Stoneham, Tom, *Berkeley's World: An Examination of the Three Dialogues* (Oxford: Oxford University Press, 2002).

——, 'Response to Atherton: No Atheism without Skepticism', in *Debates in Modern Philosophy: Essential Readings and Contemporary Responses*, edited by Stewart Duncan and Antonia Lolordo (New York: Routledge, 2013), pp. 216–26.

Storrie, Stefan Gordon, 'Anne Berkeley's *Contrast*: A Note', *Berkeley Studies*, 22 (2011), 9–14.

Storrs, Christopher, *War, Diplomacy, and the Rise of Savoy, 1690–1720* (Cambridge University Press: 1999).

Swales, Robin J. W., 'Rich, Sir Nathaniel', in *Oxford Dictionary of National Biography*, https://www.oxforddnb.com/view/10.1093/ref:odnb/9780198614128.001 .0001/odnb-9780198614128-e-23488 (accessed 7 August 2019).

Sweet, Rosemary, *Cities and the Grand Tour: The British in Italy, c. 1690–1820* (Cambridge: Cambridge University Press, 2012).

Szechi, Daniel, *1715: The Great Jacobite Rebellion* (New Haven, CT: Yale University Press, 2006).

——, *Jacobitism and Tory Politics 1710–1714* (Edinburgh: John Donald, 1984).

Taranto, Pascal, '*Alciphron* ou la théorie du complot', *Science et Esprit*, 63 (2011), 223–36.

——, 'Le Personage de Diagoras', in *Berkeley's Alciphron: English Text and Essays in Interpretation*, edited by Geneviève Brykman, Laurent Jaffro, and Claire Schwartz (Hildesheim, Zürich: Georg Olms, 2010), pp. 361–70.

——, 'Le Travail de la sagesse: Philosophie et exercice spirituel chez George Berkeley', in *Berkeley Revisited: Moral, Social, and Political Philosophy*, edited by Sébastien Charles (Oxford: Voltaire Foundation, 2015), pp. 259–75.

Taylor, Stephen, 'Harley, Edward, Third Earl of Oxford and Mortimer', in *Oxford Dictionary of National Biography*, https://www.oxforddnb.com/view/10.1093

/ref:odnb/9780198614128.001.0001/odnb-9780198614128-e-57263 (accessed 7 August 2019).

Thorn, Jennifer, 'Phillis Wheatley's Ghosts: The Racial Melancholy of New England Protestants', *The Eighteenth Century*, 50 (2009), 73–99.

Tighe, William, *Statistical Observations Relative to the County of Kilkenny, Made in the Years 1800 & 1801* (Dublin: Graisberry and Campbell, 1802).

Tipton, I. C., and E. J. Furlong, 'Mrs George Berkeley and Her Washing Machine', *Hermathena*, 101 (1965), 38–47.

Tolonen, Mikko, 'Berkeley and Mandeville', in *The Oxford Handbook of George Berkeley*, (Oxford: Oxford University Press, forthcoming).

——, *Mandeville and Hume: Anatomists of Civil Society* (Oxford: Voltaire Foundation, 2013).

Treadwell, Michael, 'Swift's Relations with the London Book Trade to 1714', in *Author/Publisher Relations during the Eighteenth and Nineteenth Centuries*, edited by Robin Myers and Michael Harris (Oxford: Oxford Polytechnic Press, 1983), pp. 1–36.

Twomey, Brendan, *Dublin in 1707: A Year in the Life of a City* (Dublin: Four Courts Press, 2009).

Updike, Wilkins, *A History of the Episcopal Church in Narragansett, Rhode Island* (New York: [n.p.], 1847).

Uzgalis, William, 'Berkeley and the Westward Course of Empire: On Racism and Ethnocentrism', in *Race and Racism in Modern Philosophy*, edited by Andrew Valls (Ithaca, NY: Cornell University Press, 2005), pp. 108–26.

Vermeulen, Ben, 'Berkeley and Nieuwentijt on Infinitesimals', *Berkeley Newsletter*, 8 (1985), 1–5.

Walsh, Patrick, *The Making of the Irish Protestant Ascendancy: The Life of William Conolly, 1662–1729* (Woodbridge: Boydell, 2010).

Welch, H. T., 'Edward Hinton', in *Dictionary of Irish Biography*, edited by Aidan Clarke et al., 9 vols. (Cambridge: Cambridge University Press/Royal Irish Academy, 2009).

——, 'A History of Kilkenny College, 1538–1903: A Study of the Vicissitudes of a Privately Endowed Grammar School in Ireland' (PhD dissertation, Trinity College Dublin, 2001).

Wenz, Peter S., 'Berkeley's Christian Neo-Platonism', *Journal of the History of Ideas*, 37 (1976), 537–46.

Whelan, Ruth, 'Drelincourt, Peter [Pierre]', in *Oxford Dictionary of National Biography*, https://www.oxforddnb.com/view/10.1093/ref:odnb/9780198614128.001.0001/odnb-9780198614128-e-8045 (accessed 7 August 2019).

White, Robert, 'Tryon, Thomas', in *Oxford Dictionary of National Biography*, https://www.oxforddnb.com/view/10.1093/ref:odnb/9780198614128.001.0001/odnb-9780198614128-e-1001302 (accessed 5 August 2019).

Williams, Robert Joseph Paton, Allan Chapman, and John Shipley Rowlinson, eds., *Chemistry at Oxford: A History from 1600–2005* (Cambridge: Royal Society of Chemistry, 2009).

Williford, Kenneth, 'Berkeley's Theory of Operative Language in the Manuscript Introduction', *British Journal for the History of Philosophy*, 11 (2003), 271–301.

Williford, Kenneth, and Roomet Jakapi, 'Berkeley's Theory of Meaning in *Alciphron* VII', *British Journal for the History of Philosophy*, 17 (2009), 99–118.

Winkler, Kenneth, *Berkeley: An Interpretation* (Oxford: Clarendon Press, 1989).

——, 'Berkeley and the Doctrine of Signs', in *The Cambridge Companion to Berkeley*, edited by Kenneth P. Winkler (Cambridge: Cambridge University Press, 2005), pp. 125–65.

Wittgenstein, Ludwig, *Philosophical Investigations*, translated by G.E.M. Anscombe, 3rd ed. (Oxford: Blackwell, 1968).

Wood, Betty, 'Godwyn [Godwin], Morgan', in *Oxford Dictionary of National Biography*, https://www.oxforddnb.com/view/10.1093/ref:odnb/9780198614128.001 .0001/odnb-9780198614128-e-10894 (accessed 5 August 2019).

——, *Slavery in Colonial Georgia 1730–1775* (Athens: University of Georgia Press, 1984).

Woozly, A. D., 'Berkeley's Doctrine of Notions and Theory of Meaning', in *George Berkeley: Critical Assessments*, edited by Walter E. Creery, vol. 3 (London: Routledge, 1991), pp. 393–403.

Wright, H. Bunker, and Henry C. Montgomery, 'The Art Collection of a Virtuoso in Eighteenth-Century England', *Art Bulletin*, 27 (1945), 195–204.

Wroth, Lawrence C., *The Voyages of Giovanni da Verrazzano 1524–1528* (New Haven, CT: Yale University Press for the Pierpoint Morgan Library, 1970).

Yerby, George, and Rosemary Sgroi, 'Rich, Nathaniel', in *The History of Parliament*, http://www.historyofparliamentonline.org/volume/1604-1629/member/rich -nathaniel-1585-1636#footnoteref210_im70p7i (accessed 15 August 2017).

Zuk, Rhoda, 'Talbot, Catherine', in *Oxford Dictionary of National Biography*, https:// www.oxforddnb.com/view/10.1093/ref:odnb/9780198614128.001.0001/odnb -9780198614128-e-26921 (accessed 21 June 2015).

A NOTE ON THE TYPE

THIS BOOK has been composed in Miller, a Scotch Roman typeface designed by Matthew Carter and first released by Font Bureau in 1997. It resembles Monticello, the typeface developed for The Papers of Thomas Jefferson in the 1940s by C. H. Griffith and P. J. Conkwright and reinterpreted in digital form by Carter in 2003.

Pleasant Jefferson ("P. J.") Conkwright (1905–1986) was Typographer at Princeton University Press from 1939 to 1970. He was an acclaimed book designer and AIGA Medalist.

The ornament used throughout this book was designed by Pierre Simon Fournier (1712–1768) and was a favorite of Conkwright's, used in his design of the *Princeton University Library Chronicle*.